International Ha
of
Social Media Laws

International Handbook
of
Social Media Laws

Paul Lambert

Bloomsbury Professional

Bloomsbury Professional Limited, Maxwelton House, 41–43 Boltro Road, Haywards Heath, West Sussex, RH16 1BJ

© Paul Lambert 2014

Bloomsbury Professional is an imprint of Bloomsbury Publishing Plc

A CIP Catalogue record for this book is available from the British Library.

ISBN 978 1 78043 829 0

Typeset by Phoenix Photosetting, Chatham, Kent
Printed and bound in Great Britain by CPI Group (UK) Ltd, Croydon, CR0 4YY

Foreword

When I was asked to write this foreword, my thoughts went something like this: 'Oh well, all right. I suppose this will be something like a catalogue or compendium. Worthy but rather dull'. But then I hadn't seen the text. Paul Lambert emailed it to me. I found myself in Madrid airport lounge waiting for a connecting flight with time to kill. So I started to look at the anticipated worthy text on a tablet. Within a short while, I was simply riveted. The book is in three parts: Section A is a good introduction, and Section C contains detailed country-by-country exposition of the law by local lawyers. Mostly these are of a very high order indeed.

But it is Section B – called 'Developing Issues' – which makes this book so much more than a worthy compendium of SM laws and cases. It simply brings the whole subject alive. Every aspect of law which could be affected by SM is covered: the ordinary citizen or lawyer would be amazed at the huge range of things which are touched. Chapter 1 gives a handy list of some of them. I cannot resist copying it out: specific SM laws; SM criminal and civil cases; online abuse, online bullying and cyberbullying laws; other laws that have been applied to online abuse, online bullying and cyberbullying; laws or rules specific to children and SM; SM and employees/employment, such as employee use of SM; laws or cases involving students in schools and universities in relation to the use of SM; a right or human right of access to the internet and/or SM; bans or restrictions on the use or of access to the internet or SM; identity theft (or equivalent); hacking (or equivalent); privacy by design (PbD); Tweeting from courts; television courtroom broadcasting or television cameras in court; the use of SM in courtrooms, whether by the public, journalists, broadcasters, bloggers, jurors, lawyers, witnesses or judges; the use of SM as evidence in courts; privacy, data protection and SM; SM and family law cases; and sports persons, sports clubs and SM.

In each case, it not merely describes what is going on. It makes you think. That is why this book is so valuable. Any lawyer faced with a problem touched by SM can go to it, see if has been considered in his own country or elsewhere, and give better advice. Any journalist writing about some SM (for example, should or can footballers or employees be sanctioned for inappropriate Tweets?) can see very quickly what, if anything, has been decided about it.

My time in the airport lounge was not wasted.

The Rt. Hon. Professor Sir Robin Jacob
Bentham House,
University College London,
November 2014

Introduction

A number of years ago (in 2001, to be exact), I wrote about the developing issue of electronic evidence. I referred to how sometimes modern litigation, pre-litigation, discovery, disclosure and related strategies increasingly search for elusive electrons, the hidden or less obviously traditional areas of evidence in legal cases, such as metadata.

More recently, litigators, courts, corporations, educational institutions, policy makers and society generally have had to consider non-elusive electrons, the ever-present content, ever obvious, sometimes wanted, sometimes not, sometimes loved, sometimes tolerated, sometimes below the line, sometimes above the line, sometimes viral content of social media (SM).

'Sometimes viral ...', which begs another question: why should something so wonderful, informative and socially valuable ignore the dark sides of SM so much, and adopt negative terms and associations for that which should be positive, such as the terms 'viral', 'fraped' and 'revenge porn'? Are there equivalent positive-focused terms in SM? Should there be? Should we emphasise the positive, but still responsibly deal with the dark side of SM?

Today, SM is used by and impacts upon most individuals, organisations, corporations, universities, schools and governments. This occurs not just in one country or the most advanced industrialised nations, but across all countries east, west, north and south. The success of SM is perhaps that its popularity is quite often unnoticed. One has to stop to take stock of the current and ongoing effects, changes, positives and negatives.

The following chapters seek to take stock of some of the more legally pertinent SM issues and also to compare these across a significant number of jurisdictions.

I must acknowledge the work of the various members of the team at Bloomsbury Professional who have worked diligently and professionally, as always, in helping to bring the project to fruition.

None of this would have been possible without the efforts of the many local experts in jurisdictions around the world who have kindly assisted and contributed their knowledge and expertise.

I do hope that you as readers, from whatever discipline or sphere, will be similarly enthused with the issues presented by technology, and SM in particular, and that the following text does some justice to the variety of issues presented.

Paul Lambert
November 2014

Contents

Contents

Contributor Details

Argentina

J Darío Veltani
AVOA – Attorneys at Law

J Darío Veltani. Lawyer. Expert on Technology Law. Academic Coordinator of the Postgraduate Course on High Technology Law at Universidad Católica Argentina (Argentina Catholic University). Professor of Intellectual Property and Technology at the Master in Intellectual Property of Universidad Austral (Austral University).

Address: Av. Corrientes 1302, Buenos Aires (1425), República Argentina

Web: www.avoa.com.ar

Australia

Dr David Rolph
Faculty of Law, University of Sydney

Dr David Rolph is an Associate Professor at the University of Sydney Faculty of Law, specialising in media law. He is the author of two books, as well as many book chapters and journal articles, on all aspects of media law. From 2007 to 2013, Dr Rolph was the editor of the *Sydney Law Review*, one of Australia's leading law journals. He currently serves on the editorial boards of the *Media and Arts Law Review*, the *Communications Law Bulletin* and the *International Journal of the Semiotics of Law*. Dr Rolph is also a regular columnist for the *Gazette of Law and Journalism* and a frequent media commentator on a range of media law issues.

Address: Faculty of Law, University of Sydney, NSW, 2006, AUSTRALIA

Web: http://sydney.edu.au/law/about/people/profiles/david.rolph.php

Belgium

Brendan Van Alsenoy, Valerie Verdoodt, Dr Eva Lievens, Ruben Roex, Ellen Wauters and Dr Els Kindt
Interdisciplinary Centre for Law and ICT (ICRI), KU Leuven, iMinds

Brendan Van Alsenoy is a legal researcher at the Interdisciplinary Centre for Law and ICT (ICRI), KU Leuven, iMinds. He joined ICRI in March of 2007, where his research has focused on topics of data protection, privacy, security and trust services. Sectors of study have included eHealth, eGovernment, Identity Management and Online Social Networks.

Valerie Verdoodt is a legal researcher at the Interdisciplinary Centre for Law and ICT (ICRI), KU Leuven, iMinds. She joined ICRI in March 2014, where her research has focused on the topics of social media, usere empowerment and data protection.

Dr Eva Lievens has been a member of the Interdisciplinary Centre for Law & ICT (ICRI), KU Leuven, iMinds, since 2003. She is currently a Postdoctoral Research Fellow of the Research Fund Flanders and a Guest Professor at Ghent University. Her research addresses legal challenges posed by new media phenomena, such as the regulation of audio-visual media services, user-generated content, and SNs, with a specific focus on the protection of minors and fundamental rights.

Ruben Roex is a legal researcher and web content manager at the Belgian Cybercrime Centre of Excellence for Training, Research & Education (B-CCENTRE), KU Leuven, iMinds. He joined the B-CCENTRE in 2009, where his research has focused on legal aspects of cybercrime and cyber security.

Ellen Wauters is a legal researcher at the Interdisciplinary Centre for Law and ICT (ICRI), KU Leuven, iMinds. She joined ICRI in February of 2012, where here research has focused on the legal challenges of social media and more in particular if social media can be regulated in a more user-oriented environment.

Dr Els Kindt has been a full member of the Interdisciplinary Centre for Law and ICT (ICRI), KU Leuven, iMinds since December 2003. Her main areas of expertise include data protection and privacy law, the legal aspects of electronic commerce, copyright, contracts, and IT litigation.

Acknowledgments: the responses to this questionnaire have been made possible by funding received from the Flemish Institute of Science and Technology (IWT) in the context of the SBO projects on Security and Privacy for Online Social Networks (SPION) (www.spion.me) and User Empowerment in a Social Media Culture (EMSOC) (www.emsoc.be), as well as the Flanders Research Fund and the Flemish research institute iMinds (www.iminds.be).

Address: Sint-Michielsstraat 6 B-3000 Leuven – Belgium

Web: www.law.kuleuven.be/icri – www.iminds.be

Brazil

Roberto Fragale Filho (PPGSD-UFF, Brazil)
Socio-Legal Researcher

Rua Presidente Pedreira, 62, Ingá, Niterói, RJ, Brazil, Zip Code 24210-470

Email: fragale@alternex.com.br

José Carlos de Araújo Almeida Filho (SPP-UFF, Brazil)
Civil Procedure and Electronic Law Researcher

Rua Nelson Silva, 294, Carangola, Petrópolis, RJ, Zip Code 25715-310

Email: jcaaf@dgaf.com.br

Web: www.profalmeidafilho.com.br

Sonia Barroso (ICM-UFF, Brazil)
Law and Economics Researcher

Av. Treze de Maio, 47 Sala 2707, Centro, Rio de Janeiro, RJ, Brazil, Zip Code 20031-921

Email: sbbsoares2013@gmail.com

Web: www.soniabarroso.pro.edu

Bernardo Menicucci Grossi
Attorney at Law, Intellectual Property and Cyber Law Researcher

Rua Guaicuí, 20, 11° andar, Cidade Jardim, Belo Horizonte, MG, Zip Code 30380-380

Email: bernardo@grossipaiva.com.br

Web: www.grossipaiva.com.br

Marcus Vinícius Brandão Soares (AUDIT-SUSEP, Brazil)
Information Technology and Electronic Procedure Researcher

Av. Presidente Vargas, 730, 13° Andar, Centro, Rio de Janeiro, RJ, Brazil, Zip Code 20071-900

Email: mvbsoares@gmail.com

Web: doutorlinux.com

Bulgaria

Rossitsa Voutcheva, Donika Ilieva and Teodor Milev
BWSP Ilieva, Voutcheva & Co Law Firm

Ms Rossitsa Voutcheva, Attorney-at-law

Education: 1995 – LLM, Law Faculty, Sofia University St. Kliment Ohridski; 2002 – Negotiating, drafting and understanding international commercial agreements London, Hawksmere; 2009 LLM, Specialization Corporate and Securities Law, University of London, Queen Mary College;

Professional Career: 2003-to date: Attorney-at-law, Managing Partner, Ilieva Voutcheva & Co Law Firm; 2000–2003: Attorney-at-law in Legal and Tax practice of PricewaterhouseCoopers Bulgaria; 1999–2000: In-house Legal

Counsel in Central Cooperative Bank AD, Sofia Branch; 1998–1999: Notary-Assistant in a private notary office.

Memberships: 1999 – Member of Sofia Bar Association.

Other activities: 2011: Qualified Mediator, Professional Association of Mediators in Bulgaria; 2010: Industrial Property Representative with the Patent Office of the Republic of Bulgaria.

Ms Donika Ilieva, Attorney-at-law

Education: 2003–2008 LLM Law Faculty, University for National and World Economy; 1997–2003 William Gladstone – School of Western and Eastern Foreign Languages.

Career: 2011 to present: Junior Associate, Ilieva, Voutcheva & Co Law Firm; April 2009–December 2010: Legal Consultant, Ilieva, Voutcheva & Co Law Firm; 2008–March 2009: Legal Assistant, Ilieva Voutcheva & Co Law Firm.

Memberships: January 2013–December 2013: Member of the Membership & Nominating Committee of Globalaw.

Publications: November 2013: Study on the Application of the Cross-Border Mergers Directive; August 2013: Amendments to the Energy Act, Utilities Magazine; June 2012: Activities Licensing in the Energy Sector, Utilities Magazine.

Mr Teodor Milev, Legal trainee

Education: 2011–2016: law student, Law Faculty at Sofia University St Kliment Ohridski; 2007–2011: middle education, National School Complex of Culture and Lyceum of Italian language and Culture Study with the Participation of the Republic of Italy.

Career: January 2014 to date: Legal Trainee at Ilieva, Voutcheva & Co Law Firm; November 2012–December 2013: coordinator with Italian and English language at IBM Procurement centre in Sofia.

BWSP Ilieva Voutcheva & Co Law Firm is a team of reliable and trustworthy professionals – an independent practice combining excellent lawyers and paralegal support staff committed to the provision of client focused and partner led service.

Since 2007, BWSP Ilieva Voutcheva & Co Law Firm has been a member of Globalaw a worldwide network of independent law firms. This gives us access to 5000 lawyers from over 108 member firms covering more than 80 jurisdictions with offices in more than 160 cities. We are also well connected to local, regional and international business communities.

In September 2012 Ilieva Voutcheva & Co Law Firm participated in the establishment of a new structure allying together prominent law firms from 4 Central and Eastern European countries. They operate under the name

BWSP with view to provide unified legal services and be 'a one stop shop' for corporate clients across Central and Eastern Europe.

Specialties: Corporate, M&A, Tax, TMT, Real Estate, Structuring of Foreign Investments, Debt Collection, Energy & Natural Resources, Competition Law & EU Legislation, Bankruptcy Corporate Restructurings, Banking & Finance, Capital Markets, Intellectual Property.

Address: Bulgaria, Sofia, 1000, blvd. "Hristo Botev" No 28

Web: www.ivlawfirm.com

China

Eric Su (Su Jianfei)
HFG CHINA

Eric Su (Su Jianfei) is a Partner and Attorney at Law, and is a recommended lawyer by Legal500, obtained his bachelor degree at North University of China majoring in Chemical Engineering and Technology, and later got his LLM degree at East China University of Politics and Law. Eric joined HFG in 2008 and was promoted to partner in 2011. Eric Su has handling thousands of IP cases, and he is talented in handling with various IPR disputes, relating to trademark infringement, anti-counterfeiting, anti-unfair competition, trademark prosecution, patent disputes, domain names and internet disputes, civil litigation and criminal prosecution. Through in-depth involvement of all IPR related disputes, he has obtained valuable experience in this area, and diversified problem solutions. Furthermore, he is also experienced in handling with food safety and product quality cases.

Founded in 2003 by 10 professionals in the IP sector, HFG counts nowadays 90 professionals distributed in Shanghai, Beijing and Guangzhou and consisting of three entities authorized by Ministry of Justice, recorded with CTMO and licensed under the SIPO for all patent related practice. Since its foundation HFG has focused its practice in litigation, anti-counterfeiting, trademark filing and administrative disputes, patent filing and prosecution, copyright, and media. In 2013 HFG is recommended practice by Legal 500 since 2010 (No.1 in Shanghai) and by MIP, ranked in Chambers and Partners and WTR 1000.

Collectively the firm commands a profound and diversified knowledge base and represents the clients at various levels before all the state-level agencies and administrative and judicial authorities. The firm has a strong experience – and a high success rate – in litigations before courts, arbitration commissions and administrative enforcement committee.

HFG services have a special focus on IT and telecom, petrochemical, wine and liquors, fashion, cosmetics, retail and e-commerce, food and pharma regulatory, licensing and monetization of patented technology. HFG provides both IP and corporate services to several Fortune 500 size public and private multinational companies and Small-Medium Enterprises. HFG professionals consist of attorneys at law, patent attorneys, trademark attorneys and IP consultants

The team can boast an International and multi-jurisdiction background with multi-language command.

Web: www.hfgchina.com/Browsers/about_en.html

Czech Republic

Ronald Given, Partner

Katerina Kulhankova, Associate
Wolf Theiss

Established in 1957, Wolf Theiss is one of the leading European law firms in Central, Eastern and South-Eastern Europe with a focus on international business law. With 340 lawyers in 14 offices located in Albania, Austria, Bosnia and Herzegovina, Bulgaria, Croatia, Czech Republic, Hungary, Poland, Romania, Serbia, Slovakia, Slovenia and Ukraine, Wolf Theiss represents local and international industrial, trade and service companies, as well as banks and insurance companies. Combining law and business, Wolf Theiss develops comprehensive and constructive solutions on the basis of legal, fiscal and business know-how.

Email: ronald.given@wolftheiss.com, katerina.kulhankova@wolftheiss.com

Web: www.wolftheiss.com/index.php/Czech_Republic.html

Denmark

Alexandra Huber / Karina Emmertsen
Lead Advokatpartnerselskab

Partner and advokat Alexandra Huber is a Danish Attorney mainly advising on clients on employment and procurement matters. Originally from Austria and with an extended stay in Washington, D.C., Alexandra is appointed Special Counsel of the Austrian Embassy and primarily advises German and English-speaking clients.

Advokat & Rechtsanwältin Karina Emmertsen is primarily advising clients on disputes and commercial contracts.

LEAD is a young law firm mainly advising foreign business clients investing in Denmark on grounds of a unique background understanding of the respective country of origin. The LEAD team consists of highly skilled Danish lawyers that come with the additional qualification of substantial work experience and cultural in-depth knowledge from at least one other country than Denmark. Three of our attorneys are additionally barred in a second jurisdiction (Germany, France, New York and China).

Address: Frederiksholms Kanal 20, st., 1220 Copenhagen K

Web: www.leaddenmark.com

El Salvador

Morena Zavaleta, Regional Partner, responsible of the Intellectual Property division
Arias & Muñoz

Since 1942, Arias & Muñoz has been at the forefront of the Central American legal market, showcasing excellence in client service, supported by the best legal talent of the region. We are pioneers in expanding our legal services throughout the region and the only Central American firm to operate with 8 fully integrated offices, spanning 6 countries: Guatemala, El Salvador, Honduras, Nicaragua, Costa Rica and Panama.

Our team of over 140 lawyers has the capability of serving in over 30 practice areas. Our leadership goes beyond our borders, offering our clients a world of solutions to their legal matters.

Address: Calle La Mascota No. 533, Colonia San Benito, San Salvador

Web: www.ariaslaw.com

Estonia

Professor Katrin Nyman-Metcalf

Head of the Chair of Law and Technology, Tallinn University of Technology; Tallinn Law School, Tallinn University of Technology; Professor of Law, Head of Chair in Law and Technology; Head of Research, Estonian e-Governance Academy

Address: Akadeemia tee 3, 126 18 Tallinn, Estonia

Email: katrin.nyman-metcalf@ttu.ee

Web: www.ttu.ee (also www.ega.ee)

Finland

Markus Myhrberg
Lexia Attorneys Ltd

Lexia is a Finnish law firm with a simple mission: We help our clients to succeed.

Our mission requires high professional skill, an uncompromising attitude and ambition. We look for the best legal solutions to generate measurable commercial advantage and added value for our clients.

Address: Kalevankatu 20, 00100 Helsinki, Finland

Web: www.lexia.fi

France

Florence Chafiol Chaumont
Partner, August & Debouzy

Address: August & Debouzy, 6-8 Avenue de Messine, 75008 Paris, France

Web: www.august-debouzy.com/

Germany

Dr Ingo Schöttler
GAD eG

Dr Ingo Schöttler, LLM IP law, is in-house counsel at GAD eG (one of Germanys leading companies for financial IT-services) with a focus on IT, intellectual property, outsourcing, compliance and data protection. He has published more than 40 articles in well-respected law journals and is a frequent speaker for a variety of organizations, including the International Association of Privacy Professionals and the German Association of Law and Informatics.

Address: GAD-Straße 2-6, 48163 Münster, Germany

Web: de.linkedin.com/pub/dr-ingo-schöttler/65/67/3b9/en

Greece

Dr Marina Perraki, Partner

Gerry Kounadis, Associate

Maria Chaidou, Elina Kefala, Katerina Kontolati, Ioanna Tapeinou, Trainee Lawyers
Tsibanoulis & Partners Law Firm

Tsibanoulis & Partners was founded in 2002 following the merger of Tsibanoulis & Associates (est 1996) and Bailas & Partners (est 1972). It is a law firm with 27 lawyers advising clients on the legal issues in relation to all aspects of commerce.

The firm has concentrated the development of its capabilities and the growth of its expertise in business law. Tsibanoulis & Partners has one of the most pre-eminent financial and commercial law practices in Greece, having been at the forefront of legal developments in the Greek market for many years. We have represented a variety of clients that includes international and domestic corporations, financial institutions and government agencies. Our experience in cross-border transactions gives our work an international flair.

Our team of creative and dedicated legal practitioners works together to understand and respond effectively to all kind of legal problems our clients face. We have worked with major corporations, large Greek and foreign banks and investment firms, the Greek State and many public authorities providing ground breaking advice, clear legal solutions within a complex environment.

We specialise in the fields of corporate, commercial, finance, dispute resolution, regulatory, competition, intellectual property, EU/internal market, international and unfair trade, employment and data protection issues, public procurement and consumer law.

The firm has a well-established reputation for excellence and innovation and aims to deliver a practical and commercial response to the legal requirements of business throughout Greece but also undertaken in conjunction with international players.

Address: 18 Omirou St, 10672 Athens, Greece

Web: www.tsibanoulis.gr

Hungary

Szabolcs Szentléleky dr

Case Handler at the Hungarian Competition Authority's Decision- Making Support Section and lecturer at the Károli Gáspár University of The Reformed Church in Hungary, Infocommunication Law Department since 2012.

Profile: Competition law, Consumer protection law, media law.

India

Raghunath Ananthapur
Tatva Legal, Bangalore

Raghunath graduated in law from Bangalore University in 2000 and has also obtained a Master's degree in International Business Laws from the University of Hull, U.K. He is a Solicitor, with the Law Society of England and Wales (non-practising), and Barrister, Lincoln's Inn (non-practising).

Raghunath's practice includes general corporate advisory, commercial contracts, foreign investment advice, legal audits, acquisitions, venture capital & private equity investments, software licensing, IP and IT advisory and transactional work.

Raghunath has worked with leading law firms in India and also for a short period was an in-house legal counsel with IT products and Services Company.

Address: Tatva Legal, B-3, 2nd Floor, Embassy Heights , Annex Block, 13 Magrath Road, Bangalore 560025, India

Email: raghunath.ananthapur@tatvalegal.com, raghunath86@hotmail.com

Web: www.tatvalegal.com

Ireland

Patrick Carroll BA Barrister-at-Law

Patrick is a Barrister, practising in the Irish courts, and an Accredited Mediator.

Paul Lambert. Lawyer and Adjunct Lecturer

Email: paul.lambert@merrionlegal.com

Italy

Giovanni Maria Riccio (with the kind assistance of Ms Silvia Surano and Maria Laura Salvati)
Professor of Comparative Law, University of Salerno

Attorney at law, founder and partner at E-Lex – Belisario Scorza Riccio & Partners (Rome, Italy)

Giovanni M Riccio is an academic and a lawyer with a wide experience in internet-related law issues. His area of practice includes copyright law, data protection and intellectual property, providing assistance to national and international clients of the IT sector.

Address: E-Lex – Belisario Scorza Riccio & Partners – Via dei Barbieri 6 – 00186 – Rome (Italy)

Web: www.e-lex.it

Malta

Dr Antonio Ghio
Fenech & Fenech Advocates

Dr Antonio Ghio is a partner at Fenech & Fenech Advocates and heads its ICT Law Department. For the past twelve years his work has solely revolved around ICT law issues, trying to find solutions to the constant struggle existing between law and technology, both inside and outside of the courtrooms. Ghio lectures ICT law and Cyber Crime at the University of Malta and is a regular supervisor and examiner on technology law related matters. He held the position of Chairman of the Malta Communications Authority after having served as a member of the Board of Directors for the last five years. He has an LLM in ICT law from the University of Strathclyde where he specialised on legal aspects of Internet security and online privacy. He is a regular speaker on ICT law issues in local and international conferences and has a regular column on ICT law issues on the Sunday Times of Malta. He is also a founding

Member and current President of the Malta IT Law Association. His personal blog on ICT Law issues can be found at ictlawmalta.blogspot.com. Ghio is also the Malta contributor for *Electronic Signatures in Law* (Cambridge University Press) and author of the Malta chapter of *Data Protection: Laws of the World* (Sweet and Maxwell).

Established in 1891, Fenech & Fenech Advocates is the oldest and one of the largest law firms in Malta. The firm is multi-disciplinary and has a highly specialized ICT Law Department which handles data protection law, e-commerce and internet law, remote gaming law, ICT contracting amongst others. Clients typically range from international blue chip companies, governments as well as start-ups.

Address: Fenech & Fenech Advocates, 198, Old Bakery Street, Valletta, VLT1455, Malta

Web: www.fenechlaw.com

Mexico

Jose Luis Ramos-Zurita, Javier Uhthoff-Rojo, Saul Santoyo, Ignacio Dominguez-Torrado
Uhthoff Gomez Vega & Uhthoff, SC

Saúl Santoyo

Partner of the firm in charge of the Litigation Department, whose main practice focuses on IP litigation and enforcement, anti-piracy and anti-counterfeiting issues, Domain Names disputes and counselling. His experience comprises complex patent and trademark litigation, including legal actions aimed to obtain correction of the life term of pipeline patents and the inclusion of use and formulation of pharmaceutical patents in the Linkage Gazette periodically published by the Mexican Institute of Industrial Property (IMPI), as well as designing and implementing anti-counterfeiting programs.

With over 20 years of experience in IP, he has been involved in handling enforcement actions related to the protection of IP rights before diverse authorities such as the IMPI, the Mexican Copyright Office, the General Prosecutor's Office, and other authorities that collaborate with anti-counterfeiting efforts, ie the Mexican General Customs Administration and the Federal Commission for the Protection from Sanitary Risks. His area of specialization also includes subsequent appeals heard by Judicial Authorities, such as the Federal Court of Fiscal and Administrative Affairs, District and Circuit Courts, among others.

He has a Law Degree from the Universidad La Salle, Faculty of Law, México City, 1997, with postgraduate studies in intellectual property, international commerce and internet Law. He is the author of "The well-known trademarks", Mexico, 1997 and several articles on intellectual property related topics.

He is an active member of Mexican Association for the Protection of the Industrial Property (AMPPI), Mexican Bar Association (Barra Mexicana – Colegio de Abogados) and the International Trademark Association (INTA).

Email: saulso@uhthoff.com.mx

Ignacio Dominguez-Torrado, LLM

Partner of the firm with over 15 years of experience, he has worked for the firm in different areas, among which are Corporate Law, Licensing, Contracts, Trademarks and Copyrights. Currently, he is in charge of Corporate Law Department of the firm. He graduated from the Universidad Panamericana (UP) with a Degree in Law, he also received a Master of Laws from the University of Virginia, USA, and he did postgraduate studies in Business Law at the Universidad Panamericana (UP).

Member of: Mexican Bar Association, Mexican Association for the Protection of Industrial Property (AMPPI), Asociación Nacional de Abogados de Empresa (ANADE), International Bar Association (IBA) y Licensing Executive Society (LES).

Jose Luis Ramos-Zurita and Javier Uhthoff-Rojo

Associates of the firm, whose practice focuses on IP litigation and enforcement, anti-piracy and anti-counterfeiting issues, Domain Names disputes and counselling, as well as designing and implementing anti-counterfeiting programs. Also, their areas of specialization includes subsequent appeals heard by Judicial Authorities, such as the Federal Court of Fiscal and Administrative Affairs, District and Circuit Courts, among others.

Uhthoff, Gómez Vega & Uhthoff is distinguished by its tradition in service; our clients come first and as of today, with more than one century of existence, we confirm our historical priority and project it into the second century of our history.

In this manner, we are prepared and have the necessary experience to provide comprehensive and quality services to our clients. Supported by over a century of experience, this Firm provides continuing legal advice of excellence for the best decision-making for the benefit of our clients, the industry, and commerce of our country.

In addition to our main office in Mexico City, we have an office in Guadalajara, Jalisco (Mexico), where we address the needs of our clients in the central region of Mexico.

Our Firm is structured in different practice areas, comprised by specialists who provide services to domestic and foreign clients, offering high quality advice and case management.

Our areas of expertise are anti-counterfeiting and enforcement; biotech and pharma; copyrights; corporate; domain names; entertainment law; foreign trade and customs; franchises; information technology; licensing; litigation; patents; personal data protection; plant breeder's rights; sports law; trade marks.

Uhthoff, Gómez Vega & Uhthoff, maintains its global presence as a member of multiple organizations and international associations, maintaining close relationships with highly qualified firms around the world and establishing business relationships with the most distinguished companies around the world in order to play a major role in the development of Intellectual Property in Mexico and around the world.

Web: www.uhthoff.com.mx

New Zealand

Judge David Harvey

David Harvey has been a judge of the district court in New Zealand for 25 years. He also teaches law and information technology for the Faculty of Law, Auckland University, and has written a text on Internet and computer technology law titled *internet.law.nz*, now in its 3rd edition. He has written extensively in the field of law and technology and has presented a number of papers both in New Zealand and internationally on law and technology matters.

He graduated with an LLB from Auckland University in 1969, MJur from University of Waikato in 1994, and PhD from Auckland University in 2012. His doctoral dissertation was on the influence of a new technology (the printing press) on law and legal culture in England in the Early Modern period.

Address: Judges Chambers, District Court Private Bag 92069 Auckland 1142, New Zealand

Web: www.theitcountreyjustice.wordpress.com

Norway

Thomas Olsen
Advokatfirmaet Simonsen Vogt Wiig AS

Thomas Olsen PhD is a lawyer at Simonsen Vogt Wiig advising Norwegian and international clients on all aspects of privacy and data protection law. Olsen holds a PhD in data protection law and he is the leader of the Norwegian Bar Association's committee for ICT and privacy.

PhD Thomas Olsen is a lawyer at Simonsen Vogt Wiig's Technology, Media and Telecom (TMT) department. The TMT department offers the largest team of lawyers dedicated to the TMT sector and is widely acknowledged by clients and peers for its leading practice. Simonsen Vogt Wiig was ranked no. 1 in Chambers 2014 within TMT, as the only law firm in Norway.

Olsen holds a PhD in data protection law from Norwegian Research Center for Computers and Law at the University of Oslo and a LLM in European IT Law from the University of Southampton, UK. He regularly advices Norwegian and international clients on data protection aspects related to all aspects of privacy law, including Social Media, international data transfers, Big Data, Cloud Computing, Privacy by Design, and privacy and employment.

Olsen and Simonsen Vogt Wiig's TMT department has made its mark advising on several principal cases. Olsen has eg advised in the first applications to the Norwegian Data Protection Authority for approval of Binding Corporate Rules (BCR) and BCR for Processors (BCRP) regarding intra-corporate transfers of personal data. He also has extensive experience on advising clients on privacy and security issues related to outsourcing of IT services and Cloud Computing. For example he assisted the Municipality of Narvik in a principal case on the lawfulness of Google Apps which has provided significant clarifications on the requirements for using Cloud Computing services in Norway.

Olsen is a frequent lecturer on topics regarding the intersection between IT and the law. He has long time experience as lecturer, external examiner and teaching supervisor at the Faculty of Law in Oslo, and has published several articles in Norwegian and international journals. Olsen has carried out reports and research work for the EU Commission, the Data Protection Authority and the Data Protection Tribunal. Olsen is the leader of the Norwegian Bar Association's committee for ICT and privacy.

Address: Advokatfirmaet Simonsen Vogt Wiig AS, Filipstad Brygge 1, PO Box 2043 Vika, 0125 Oslo, Norway

Web: www.svw.no/

Senegal

Boubacar Borgho DIAKITE
Geni & Kebe Law Firm

Mr Boubacar Diakite attended the Faculty of Law of the University of Dakar Bourgiba, graduating with a LLB in Business Law he also earned a Bachelor's degree in Management of Projects from the Senegalese State School of Economics based in Dakar based in Dakar. In 2008 he worked at the West African Reserve Bank where he was involved in financial markets and bank refinancing. He is actually the Head Office Manager of Geni & Kebe Law Firm.

Address: 47, Bd de la République – Immeuble Sorano – BP: 14392 – Dakar – Senegal

Web: www.gsklaw.sn

Serbia

Bojana N Novaković, Attorney at Law
Law office Baklaja & Igrić

Work Department: Litigation, Dispute Resolution, Administrative and Misdemeanour proceedings, Employment, Intellectual Property, Personal Data Protection, Media Law.

Ms Novakovic possesses the highest level of expertise in matters concerning the protection of personal data. In addition, Ms Novakovic has extensive experienced in the area of intellectual property law, where apart from advising clients on application of local legal provisions regulating this matter and protecting clients' interest before the court, she performs the trade-mark, service-mark and other registration services. She actively advised on the local media market with respect to compliance with the set of media related laws, and in particular regarding the possibility of protecting their (privacy) rights and interests of individuals and journalists.

Bojana is experienced litigator carrying out efficient general civil and commercial litigation and dispute resolution, including developing and executing litigation strategies in front of local courts and foreign arbitration panels in various civil and commercial disputes, enforcement proceedings, recognition and enforcement of foreign judgments and decisions, intellectual property and media disputes, as well as labour related disputes etc.

Languages: Serbian (native), English (fluent), Russian (basic)

Member: Belgrade Bar

Education: Faculty of Law, Belgrade University

Law office Baklaja & Igrić provides a wide range of legal services in various fields, such as: Commercial Law and M&A, Corporate Law, Competition Law, Real Estate Law, Finance and Banking Law, Insolvency Law, Public Procurement, Personal Data Protection, Labour Law, Intellectual Property, Dispute Resolution and other law related services.

Our Clients benefit from our great blend of experience and understanding of the local legal and cultural complexities and issues necessary for conducting business activities in the Republic of Serbia and region.

Our extensive experience in law, full understanding of the market and focus on industry specifics put us in the best position to advise our Clients on the appropriate and most beneficial form of their businesses and to provide them with premium solutions to eliminate any legal obstacle. Members of Baklaja & Igrić team work through a highly professional and qualified team of lawyers who specialize in different fields of law and are able to work in a variety of international and local languages, which allows us to communicate easily with international as well as local clients.

Baklaja & Igrić provides its clients with complex legal assistance in all fields, which affect their rights, interests and business. We can deliver even the most complicated projects, always maintaining the highest standard of services provided. We can cooperate with large multinational companies as well as large and medium-sized local entities in various sectors.

Address: Terazije no. 8, 11000 Belgrade, Republic of Serbia

Tel: +381 63 30 65 21

Email: bojana.novakovic@baklaja-igric.com

Tel: +381 11 3812 147

Email: boris.baklaja@baklaja-igric.com; djordje.igric@baklaja-igric.com

Singapore

Sharmini Sharon Selvaratnam

See profile at www.harryelias.com/people/Sharmini-Sharon-Selvaratnam/

Assisted by Mr Lin Chun Long and Ms Jaclyn Leong.

See Harry Elias Partnership LLP Firm's profile at www.harryelias.com

Address: SGX Centre 2, #17-01, 4 Shenton Way, Singapore 068807

Web: www.harryelias.com

Slovenia

Klara Miletič LLM, Senior Associate

Mojca Ilešič LLM, Associate
Wolf Theiss

Established in 1957, Wolf Theiss is one of the leading European law firms in Central, Eastern and South-Eastern Europe with a focus on international business law. With 340 lawyers in 14 offices located in Albania, Austria, Bosnia and Herzegovina, Bulgaria, Croatia, Czech Republic, Hungary, Poland, Romania, Serbia, Slovakia, Slovenia and Ukraine, Wolf Theiss represents local and international industrial, trade and service companies, as well as banks and insurance companies. Combining law and business, Wolf Theiss develops comprehensive and constructive solutions on the basis of legal, fiscal and business know-how.

Email: klara.miletic@wolftheiss.com, mojca.ilesic@wolftheiss.com

Web: www.wolftheiss.com/index.php/Slovenia.html

South Africa

Rosalind Davey and Rovina Asray, assisted by Sthembile Shamase
Bowman Gilfillan

Rosalind Davey is a Director at Bowman Gilfillan. Ros has obtained a BA (LLB) from the University of Natal, Pietermaritzburg. Ros has extensive experience in various areas of general Employment Law, more especially in the provision of advice and opinions on: the Basic Conditions of Employment Act; retrenchments, performance management, disciplinary hearings and arbitrations.

Ros regularly acts for a number of large corporate clients on matters relating to employment litigation which include urgent applications, interdicts, reviews, dismissal disputes, arbitrations and general litigation. In addition, Ros assists and advises clients on a wide range of non-litigious employment law matters and matters of a commercial nature with employment implications such as strategic planning, restructuring and outsourcing.

Ros is very interested in Social Media Law and advising on aspects of and risks posed by the use of Social Media Websites. Ros's background in Employment law places her in a unique position to deal with legal issues arising out of the use of Social Media Websites by both companies and their employees.

Practice Focus: General employment law; discrimination law; unfair labour practices; alleged unfair dismissals; employment litigation (including appearance work); chairing disciplinary hearings; prosecuting disciplinary hearings; general social media law; drafting social media policies.

Rovina Asray is an Associate at Bowman Gilfillan. Rovina has obtained a BCom (LLB) from the University of Kwazulu Natal. She provides advice and opinions on *inter alia*: the Labour Relations Act and the Basic Conditions of Employment Act; retrenchments, disciplinary hearings and arbitrations. She has experience in general litigation as well as employment litigation which include urgent applications and interdicts.

Sthembile Shamase is a Candidate Attorney at Bowman Gilfillan.

Address: 165 West Street, Sandton, 2146

Web: www.bowman.co.za

Spain

José M Baño Fos
Baño Leon Abogados

José M Baño Fos joined Baño Leon Abogados in 2012 from Cleary Gottlieb where he worked as an associate specialized in European and Competition law. During that time, José María advised Google Spain in the ECJ "Right to be Forgotten" case. Prior to that, José María worked in the firm Perez-Llorca in Madrid in the Corporate and EU law departments. José María Baño Fos graduated with the highest honors from the University of Valencia (LLB) and Fordham University (LLM), where received a full tuition and board scholarship from the Fundación Caja Madrid. He is admitted to the bar in Madrid since 2008 and New York since 2009, and combines his private practice with his academic position as Administrative Law Professor at the IE Law School.

Founded in 1992 by José María Baño León, senior professor of administrative law at the Complutense University in Madrid, José María Baño León Abogados is a firm specialized in public law, planning law, environmental law, data protection and competition law. Throughout its 20 years of existence, the firm has characterized itself by providing rigorous, independent and high quality legal advice.

Address: Calle Sagasta 26, 2, 28004 Madrid

Web: www.jmbleon.com

Sweden

Erica Wiking Häger (partner), Sara Backman (senior associate)
Mannheimer Swartling Advokatbyrå AB

Erica Wiking Häger is a partner with Mannheimer Swartling, working within the law firm's specialist department for IT, telecom, technology and corporate commercial matters. Before working at Mannheimer Swartling, she worked as a legal counsel at a U.S. software company, within the Swedish court system and as a senior university lecturer at the Uppsala University. She holds a Swedish law degree from the Uppsala University and an LL.M. from Harvard Law School. Erica is a member of the Swedish Bar Association and the New York State Bar Association.

Sara Backman is a senior associate with Mannheimer Swartling, specialised in intellectual property, marketing and media law. She holds a Swedish law degree and a Bachelor of Science in Business and Economics from Lund University. She has also studied LL.M. courses in London and in Hong Kong. Sara is a member of the Swedish Bar Association.

Address: Norrlandsgatan 21, PO Box 1711, SE-111 87 Stockholm, Sweden

Web: www.mannheimerswartling.se

Switzerland

Dr Simon Schlauri
Associate Professor, University of Zurich, Switzerland, and Partner at Ronzani Schlauri Attorneys, a Swiss boutique law firm for technology law.

Simon Schlauri (1973) combines rich experience in the IT-/Telecom industry, in-depth technological know-how and an excellent academic background, including an associate professorship at the University of Zurich. His focus is in the regulation of network industries and IT law, particularly in the areas of e-commerce and payment systems, contract, consumer, antitrust, unfair competition, copyright and data protection law.

Address: Technoparkstrasse 1, 8001 Zurich, Switzerland

Web: www.ronzani-schlauri.com

Taiwan

CF Tsai Sr and Lu-Fa Tsai (aka Law Tsai)
Deep & Far Attorneys-at-law

Mr Tsai is the first patent practitioner in the country who has both technological and law backgrounds and is qualified as a local attorney-at-law. Mr Tsai majored in marine engineering at National Chiao Tung University. Since his first involvement in intellectual property in 1982, he has become extensively involved in works related to the mechanical, electric, electronic, civil engineering, chemical, semiconductor and medical fields. During the course of his practice, he finished his law degree at National Taiwan University and then passed the bar examination, which has an average pass rate of about 5%. While majoring in his law subjects, Mr Tsai experienced and handled diversified disputes related to intellectual property laws. While earning his master's degree in comparative law from Soo Chow University, Mr. Tsai had the opportunity to perceive, interlink and integrate the interdependency, interaction and macroscopic strategy in various aspects of law.

Mr Tsai was subsequently admitted to practice before the ROC Supreme Court, Administrative Court, Taiwan High Court, IP Court, and various district courts. He was also admitted to practice before the ROC Intellectual Property Office. He is a member of the ROC, Taipei, Kaoshiung and Hsinchu Bar Associations, the Asian Patent Attorney Association, the American Intellectual Property Law Association, AIPPI and INTA.

Mr Tsai, Jr, earned his LLB degree from National Taiwan University, and his LLM from the same university. Mr Tsai, Jr, also known as Law Tsai, was admitted to practice before the ROC Supreme Court, Administrative Court, Taiwan High Court, and IP Court. He is a member of the ROC and Taipei Bar Associations, and INTA.

Deep & Far attorneys-at-law was founded in 1992 and deals with all phases of law, with a focus on the practice in separate or in combination of all aspects of intellectual property rights (IPRs) including patents, trademarks, copyrights, trade secrets, unfair competition, and/or licensing, counselling, litigation and/or transaction thereof.

It is Deep & Far's philosophy to provide competent legal services that other firms cannot comparably provide. The ensuing challenge then became: how can we provide such services? Deep & Far achieved this goal by selecting, edifying and nurturing people who have the following personality traits: learned in expertise, morally earnest, sincerely behaved in mind and strictly disciplined between give and take. It is widely believed that such traits are key factors for people to properly and competently behave themselves.

The attorneys-at-law, patent attorneys and patent engineers at Deep & Far typically hold outstanding and advanced degrees and generally graduated from the top five universities in the country. Through perseverance that we carefully choose and perform work which enables this firm to be deep and far, Deep & Far can then equate its objectives with its name. More information about the firm can be found on our website.

Address: 13 Fl, 27 Sec. 3, Chung San N Rd, Taipei 104, Taiwan

Web: www.deepnfar.com.tw

United Kingdom

Jonathan McDonald
Travers Smith LLP

Jonathan is a UK qualified commercial lawyer with a focus on technology/ outsourcing, intellectual property and data protection. He frequently advises clients on issues related to social media.

Address: Travers Smith LLP, 10 Snow Hill, London EC1A 2AL

Web: www.traverssmith.com/en/practice-areas/commercial-ip-and-technology

United States

Eric P Robinson, Esq

Eric P. Robinson is an attorney and scholar focused on legal issues involving the media, including the internet and social media. He is currently co-director of the Program in Press, Law and Democracy at Louisiana State University and of counsel to the First Amendment law firm, The Counts Law Group.

He was previously an associate scholar with the Digital Media Law Project at Harvard Law School's Berkman Center for Internet and Society; deputy director of the Donald W. Reynolds National Center for Courts and Media at the University of Nevada, Reno; a staff attorney at the Media Law Resource Center; and a legal fellow at the Reporters Committee for Freedom of the Press. He has taught media law and ethics at the Louisiana State University, City University of New York Graduate School of Journalism, Baruch College, and the University of Nevada, Reno.

Mr Robinson also has an active research agenda on media and internet law issues, with several articles published in professional and academic publications, including the American Journal of Trial Advocacy, the Journal of Internet Law, the Encyclopedia of the First Amendment, and The Labor Lawyer. He has also written frequent blog posts for Harvard Law School's Berkman Center for Internet and Society and continues to maintain his own blog, bloglawonline.com.

He is admitted to the bar in New York, New Jersey and before the United States Supreme Court.

Uruguay

Federico Florin
Guyer & Regules

Federico Florin, lawyer, works mainly in the Litigation Department of Guyer & Regules. Participated in complex administrative, civil and commercial litigation and arbitration. His practice also includes giving advice in civil and commercial matters, agreements and settlements.

Email: fflorin@guyer.com.uy

Web: www.guyer.com.uy

List of Abbreviations

BYOD	bring your own device
CJEU	Court of Justice of the European Union
COPPA	Child Online Privacy Protection Act 2000 (US)
DMCA	Digital Millennium Copyright Act (US)
ESI	electronically stored information
FTC	Federal Trade Commission (US)
ICH	internet content host
ICO	Information Commissioner's Office (UK)
ISP	internet service provider
ITU	International Telecommunication Union
NSP	network service provider
PbD	privacy by design
PII	personally identifiable information
RTBF	right to be forgotten
SM	social media
SN	social networking
SNs	social networks
TSP	telecommunications service provider
URL	uniform resource locator
WIPO	World Intellectual Property Organisation
WP29	Article 29 Working Party (EU)

Table of Cases

Table of Cases

Table of Cases

Table of Legislation

[All references are to paragraph number]

Table of International Materials

[All references are to paragraph number]

Section A
Introduction

Chapter 1

Introduction and Right to be Forgotten

1.1   INTRODUCTION

'JP Morgan Chase reveals massive data breach affecting 76m households.'

'Facebook knows who your friends are. Soon it could know about your health.'

'Gerry McCann calls for example to made of "vile" internet trolls.'

These are just three headlines from the *Guardian* newspaper on one day in October 2014.[1] This signifies the increasing importance of SM legal issues, and which are no longer discrete issues but are front-page stories and issues impacting mainstream public consciousness.

This book, and individual chapters from expert contributors in various jurisdictions throughout the world, examines topics such as:

- specific SM laws;

- SM criminal and civil cases;

- online abuse, online bullying and cyberbullying laws;

- other laws that have been applied to online abuse, online bullying and cyberbullying;

- laws or rules specific to children and SM;

- SM and employees/employment, such as employee use of SM;

- laws or cases involving students in schools and universities in relation to the use of SM;

---

1   D Rushe, 'JP Morgan Chase reveals massive data breach affecting 76m households', Guardian, 3 October 2014, available at www.theguardian.com/business/2014/oct/02/jp-morgan-76m-households-affected-data-breach; 'Facebook knows who your friends are. Soon it could know about your health, Company exploring creation of online "support communities" that would connect users suffering from various ailments', Guardian, 3 October 2014, available at www.theguardian.com/technology/2014/oct/03/facebook-health-market-app; 'Gerry McCann calls for example to made of "vile" internet trolls', Guardian, 3 October 2014, available at www.theguardian.com/technology/2014/oct/03/gerry-mccann-calls-example-made-vile-internet-trolls. All accessed 4 October 2014.

- a right or human right of access to the internet and or SM;

- bans or restrictions on the use or of access to the internet or SM;

- identity theft (or equivalent);

- hacking (or equivalent);

- privacy by design (PbD);

- Tweeting from courts;

- television courtroom broadcasting or television cameras in court;

- the use of SM in courtrooms, whether by the public, journalists, broadcasters, bloggers, jurors, lawyers, witnesses or judges;

- the use of SM as evidence in courts;

- privacy, data protection and SM;

- SM and family law cases;

- sports persons, sports clubs and SM;

- personal relations and relationships;

- SM personal data of deceased persons;

- SM, website, service provider or ISP defences (similar to EU eCommerce Directive or US DMCA eCommerce defences);

- eCommerce defences;

- the importance of laws providing for the protection of personal data or personally identifiable information; and

- data breach laws providing that customers, users and/or regulators be notified if an organisation's data or systems have been hacked or data has otherwise been lost.

Given the diversity of SM, and the fact that technologies, business models, case law and legislation are constantly changing, there are undoubtedly other areas which will be added to this list in future. Indeed, in particular instances (such as music and film copyright), distribution, technology and commercial models sometimes change in reaction to the latest legal cases.

One of the developing themes relates to how individuals (and sometimes companies) can achieve takedown of online abuse, defamation, personal data and other materials which are damaging, threatening or otherwise objectionable. The 'dark side' problem areas of SM include: suicide (teenage and adult) caused and contributed to by online abuse; revenge porn; trolling; online celebrity photographs; online non-celebrity photographs; identity theft and online identity theft; Gamergate; hacking; and blackmail. Errant or ex-employees, whom might post material online, may also cause organisations to be concerned to have such material taken down.

At the time of writing, one of the biggest legal stories relates to a potential legal case against Google by a number of Hollywood celebrities claiming that Google is not taking down and removing hacked nude photographs at all or expeditiously enough. The legal letter to Google threatens a claim of $100 million.[2]

1.2 RIGHT TO BE FORGOTTEN

One of the most significant internet legal and policy-related issues relates to what has become known as the 'right to be forgotten' ('RTBF'). The main reason why this has attracted sometimes heated discussion, in legal, political, media and public circles, is as a result of a recent decision of the Court of Justice of the European Union (CJEU). The case is known as the *Google Spain* case.[3]

The case confirms that, in certain circumstances, individuals are entitled to vindicate their personal data protection rights by requiring of websites (or, in this instance, an internet search engine) that the personal information in question no longer be made available to the general public on account of its inclusion in such a list of search results by that search engine. The original applicant in the case, supported by the Spanish data protection authority, had requested that certain outdated personal information be de-listed or de-indexed from the list of Google search results regarding the individual in question. Google appealed the national Spanish decision, which required de-listing, to the CJEU.

When the CJEU decision was issued, and subsequently, there were equal measures of, sometimes heated, support and criticism of the decision. However, on one view, the decision is not at all surprising and was altogether to be expected.[4] The EU Data Protection Directive[5] already makes clear, for example, that individual data subjects have a right 'to object at any time on compelling legitimate grounds relating to [their] particular situation to the processing of data relating to [them]' (Article 14). It is also unsurprising because of the nature of the changes to information which the internet brings. A further reason why it is unsurprising is the increasing nature of the 'dark

---

2   A Hern and D Rushe, 'Google threatened with $100m lawsuit over nude celebrity photos', Guardian, 2 October 2014, available at www.theguardian.com/technology/2014/oct/02/google-lawsuit-nude-celebrity-photos.

3   *Google Spain SL and Google Inc v Agencia Española de Protección de Datos (AEPD) and Mario Costeja González* CJEU, Case C-131/12, 13 May 2014, available at http://curia.europa.eu/juris/document/document.jsf?docid=152065&doclang=EN.

4   See, for example, P Lambert, *A User's Guide to Data Protection* (Bloomsbury Professional: 2013), in particular at chapters 29 and 27.

5   Directive 95/46/EC of the European Parliament and of the Council of 24 October 1995 on the protection of individuals with regard to the processing of personal data and on the free movement of such data, *Official Journal L 281, 23/11/1995, pp 31–50*.

side' of the internet (comparatively small as it is), involving online abuse such as trolling, abuse threats and related tragic instances of suicide.

1.3 CONTEXT: THE DIRECTIVE

The legal context of the *Google Spain* case is the EU Data Protection Directive.[6] Specifically, the case concerns the interpretation of Articles 2(b) and (d), 4(1) (a) and (c), 12(b) and 14(a) of the Directive, and Article 8 of the Charter of Fundamental Rights of the European Union (the 'EU Charter').[7]

1.4 THE DIRECTIVE: ARTICLE 2(B) AND (D)

This Article provides that:

'For the purposes of this Directive:

(a) "personal data" shall mean any information relating to an identified or identifiable natural person ("data subject"); an identifiable person is one who can be identified, directly or indirectly, in particular by reference to an identification number or to one or more factors specific to his physical, physiological, mental, economic, cultural or social identity;

(b) "processing of personal data" ("processing") shall mean any operation or set of operations which is performed upon personal data, whether or not by automatic means, such as collection, recording, organization, storage, adaptation or alteration, retrieval, consultation, use, disclosure by transmission, dissemination or otherwise making available, alignment or combination, blocking, erasure or destruction;

...

(d) "controller" shall mean the natural or legal person, public authority, agency or any other body which alone or jointly with others determines the purposes and means of the processing of personal data; where the purposes and means of processing are determined by national or Community laws or regulations, the controller or the specific criteria for his nomination may be designated by national or Community law;

(e) "processor" shall mean a natural or legal person, public authority, agency or any other body which processes personal data on behalf of the controller;

...

(h) "the data subject's consent" shall mean any freely given specific and informed indication of their wishes by which the data subject signifies their agreement to personal data relating to their being processed.'

---

6   Ibid.
7   Charter of Fundamental Rights of the European Union, 2000/C 364/01. Available at www. europarl.europa.eu/charter/pdf/text_en.pdf.

1.5   THE DIRECTIVE: ARTICLE 4(1)(A) AND (C)

This Article provides:

'National law applicable

1. Each Member State shall apply the national provisions it adopts pursuant to this Directive to the processing of personal data where:

(a) the processing is carried out in the context of the activities of an establishment of the controller on the territory of the Member State; when the same controller is established on the territory of several Member States, he must take the necessary measures to ensure that each of these establishments complies with the obligations laid down by the national law applicable;

(b) the controller is not established on the Member State's territory, but in a place where its national law applies by virtue of international public law;

(c) the controller is not established on Community territory and, for purposes of processing personal data makes use of equipment, automated or otherwise, situated on the territory of the said Member State, unless such equipment is used only for purposes of transit through the territory of the Community.

2. In the circumstances referred to in paragraph 1 (c), the controller must designate a representative established in the territory of that Member State, without prejudice to legal actions which could be initiated against the controller himself.'

1.6   THE DIRECTIVE: ARTICLE 12(B)

This Article provides:

'Right of access

Member States shall guarantee every data subject the right to obtain from the controller:

(a) without constraint at reasonable intervals and without excessive delay or expense:

– confirmation as to whether or not data relating to him are being processed and information at least as to the purposes of the processing, the categories of data concerned, and the recipients or categories of recipients to whom the data are disclosed,

– communication to him in an intelligible form of the data undergoing processing and of any available information as to their source,

– knowledge of the logic involved in any automatic processing of data

7

concerning him at least in the case of the automated decisions referred to in Article 15 (1);

(b) as appropriate the rectification, erasure or blocking of data the processing of which does not comply with the provisions of this Directive, in particular because of the incomplete or inaccurate nature of the data;

(c) notification to third parties to whom the data have been disclosed of any rectification, erasure or blocking carried out in compliance with (b), unless this proves impossible or involves a disproportionate effort.'

1.7   THE DIRECTIVE: ARTICLE 14(A)

This Article provides:

'The data subject's right to object

Member States shall grant the data subject the right:

(a) at least in the cases referred to in Article 7 (e) and (f), to object at any time on compelling legitimate grounds relating to his particular situation to the processing of data relating to him, save where otherwise provided by national legislation. Where there is a justified objection, the processing instigated by the controller may no longer involve those data;

(b) to object, on request and free of charge, to the processing of personal data relating to him which the controller anticipates being processed for the purposes of direct marketing, or to be informed before personal data are disclosed for the first time to third parties or used on their behalf for the purposes of direct marketing, and to be expressly offered the right to object free of charge to such disclosures or uses.

Member States shall take the necessary measures to ensure that data subjects are aware of the existence of the right referred to in the first subparagraph of (b).'

1.8   EU CHARTER: ARTICLE 8

This EU Charter Article relates to personal data and provides:

'Protection of personal data

1.   Everyone has the right to the protection of personal data concerning him or her.

2.   Such data must be processed fairly for specified purposes and on the basis of the consent of the person concerned or some other legitimate basis laid down by law. Everyone has the right of access to data which has been collected concerning him or her, and the right to have it rectified.

3.   Compliance with these rules shall be subject to control by an independent authority.'

1.9   THE *GOOGLE SPAIN* CASE

The judgment of the Grand Chamber (that is, full court) of the CJEU of 13 May 2014 was in certain quarters unexpected, although the concerns raised were well known and the decision could have been predicted.

The request had been made in proceedings between, on the one hand, Google Spain SL ('Google Spain') and Google Inc and, on the other, the Agencia Española de Protección de Datos (the Spanish Data Protection Agency, the 'AEPD') and Mr González, concerning a decision by the AEPD upholding the complaint lodged by Mr González against those two companies and ordering Google Inc to adopt the measures necessary to withdraw personal data relating to Mr González from its index and to prevent access to the data in the future.

The Court held as follows,

'1.   Article 2(b) and (d) of [the Data Protection] Directive ... are to be interpreted as meaning that, first, the activity of a search engine consisting in finding information published or placed on the internet by third parties, indexing it automatically, storing it temporarily and, finally, making it available to internet users according to a particular order of preference must be classified as "processing of personal data" within the meaning of Article 2(b) when that information contains personal data and, second, the operator of the search engine must be regarded as the "controller" in respect of that processing, within the meaning of Article 2(d).

2.   Article 4(1)(a) of [the Data Protection] Directive ... is to be interpreted as meaning that processing of personal data is carried out in the context of the activities of an establishment of the controller on the territory of a Member State, within the meaning of that provision, when the operator of a search engine sets up in a Member State a branch or subsidiary which is intended to promote and sell advertising space offered by that engine and which orientates its activity towards the inhabitants of that Member State.

3.   Article 12(b) and subparagraph (a) of the first paragraph of Article 14 of [the Data Protection] Directive ... are to be interpreted as meaning that, in order to comply with the rights laid down in those provisions and in so far as the conditions laid down by those provisions are in fact satisfied, the operator of a search engine is obliged to remove from the list of results displayed following a search made on the basis of a person's name links to web pages, published by third parties and containing information relating to that person, also in a case where that name or information is not erased beforehand or simultaneously from

9

those web pages, and even, as the case may be, when its publication in itself on those pages is lawful.

4. Article 12(b) and subparagraph (a) of the first paragraph of Article 14 of [the Data Protection] Directive ... are to be interpreted as meaning that, when appraising the conditions for the application of those provisions, it should inter alia be examined whether the data subject has a right that the information in question relating to him personally should, at this point in time, no longer be linked to his name by a list of results displayed following a search made on the basis of his name, without it being necessary in order to find such a right that the inclusion of the information in question in that list causes prejudice to the data subject. As the data subject may, in the light of his fundamental rights under Articles 7 and 8 of the Charter, request that the information in question no longer be made available to the general public on account of its inclusion in such a list of results, those rights override, as a rule, not only the economic interest of the operator of the search engine but also the interest of the general public in having access to that information upon a search relating to the data subject's name. However, that would not be the case if it appeared, for particular reasons, such as the role played by the data subject in public life, that the interference with his fundamental rights is justified by the preponderant interest of the general public in having, on account of its inclusion in the list of results, access to the information in question.'[8]

The accompanying press release states,

'An internet search engine operator is responsible for the processing that it carries out of personal data which appear on web pages published by third parties.

Thus, if, following a search made on the basis of a person's name, the list of results displays a link to a web page which contains information on the person in question, that data subject may approach the operator directly and, where the operator does not grant his request, bring the matter before the competent authorities in order to obtain, under certain conditions, the removal of that link from the list of results.'[9]

The EU Article 29 Working Party, an official EU data protection body comprised of members of respective EU national data protection authorities, met with representatives of Google, Microsoft and Yahoo! on 25 June 2014 and

---

8   *Google Spain SL and Google Inc v Agencia Española de Protección de Datos (AEPD) and Mario Costeja González* CJEU, Case C-131/12, 13 May 2014, available at http://curia.europa.eu/juris/document/document.jsf?docid=152065&doclang=EN.

9   Court of Justice of the European Union, Press Release No 70/14, Luxembourg, 13 May 2014, available at http://curia.europa.eu/jcms/upload/docs/application/pdf/2014-05/cp140070en.pdf.

further sent a questionnaire to Google in relation to its implementation. Google responded in a letter dated 31 July 2014.

A number of complaints to data protection authorities are arising following index linking takedown requests. The Article 29 Working Party indicates that the European data protection authorities have all agreed on a common 'tool-box' to ensure a coordinated approach to the handling of complaints resulting from search engines' refusals to 'de-list' complainants from their results.[10]

1.10 THE ISSUES ARE UNIVERSAL AND NOT EU LIMITED

Even US commentators have agreed with the EU court and the need for a right to be forgotten.[11] Jeffrey Toobin, in an article in the *New Yorker*, highlights examples of how similar issues of concern arise in the US as in the EU and elsewhere where one would expect that individuals should have a legitimate interest in achieving certain linking takedowns and takedowns generally.[12] When non-public police photographs of the severed head of a traffic accident victim were emailed by police staff and went viral, the family were naturally concerned to have the images taken down. In the US, this presented great difficulty and was not altogether successful.[13] The victim's father is reported as saying that he 'believes that the ruling by the European Court of Justice represents a broader victory. "I cried when I read about that decision," he told me. "What a great thing it would have been for someone in our position. That's all I wanted. I would do anything to be able to go to Google and have it remove those links".'[14] A possible solution, not yet considered in instances like this, may be to license the content in such a manner that the victim-licensee is entitled to request appropriate takedowns. Indeed, such an avenue also potentially works in instances where there may be an argument that personal data rights do not fully assist, to the extent that they might apply to living individuals only.

1.11 EVOLVING RTBF ISSUES

The issues, fallout and, importantly, the legal, political and public lobbying will continue, at least in the short term. Further cases may ensue, particularly

---

10 See Article 29 Working Party Press release dated 18 September 2014.
11 *New Yorker* podcast with Jeffrey Toobin and Tim Wu, [no date] September 2014, available at https://soundcloud.com/newyorker/jeffrey-toobin-and-tim-wu-on-the-right-to-be-forgotten, accessed 28 September 2014.
12 J Toobin, 'The Solace of Oblivion, In Europe the Right to be Forgotten Trumps the Internet', *New Yorker*, 29 September 2014, available at www.newyorker.com/magazine/2014/09/29/solace-oblivion, accessed 29 September 2014.
13 Ibid.
14 Ibid.

where individuals or national data protection authorities feel that legitimate requests for takedown or de-indexing are not being complied with.

The procedures implemented by individual organisations in terms of implementing the RTBF will most likely continue to evolve. As with procedures for dealing with online abuse and online safety issues, some organisations may implement better protocols and procedures than others. Some other organisations may fail to implement procedures, even when they should, for legal, corporate prudence and safety, user rights and safety, publicity and reputation and also shareholder reasons.

It is already widely acknowledged that the proposed update to the EU data protection legal regime has been the most lobbied legal measure ever to occur in the EU. Various industries and industry sectors have engaged in heavy lobbying. Some politicians have even been criticised for adopting a wholesale 'copy and paste' of industry materials in their own submission documentation.

The EU Commission has also issued a myth-busting factsheet in relation to the ruling.[15] It states,

'Myth 3: The judgment contradicts freedom of expression

The Court ruled that the right to personal data protection, of which the right to be forgotten is a part, is not absolute. It will always need to be balanced against other fundamental rights, such as the freedom of expression and of the media – which are not absolute rights either.

That's why the judgment limits the right to be forgotten and recognises that there may be a public interest in all links to content remaining online.

According to the Court, the right to be forgotten applies where the information is inaccurate, inadequate, irrelevant or excessive for the purposes of data processing. This means that the company running the search engine must assess requests on a case by case basis. This assessment must balance the interest of the person making the request and the public interests to have access to the data by retaining it in the list of results.

The ruling does not give the all-clear for people or organisations to have search results removed from the web simply because they find them inconvenient.

Myth 4: The judgment allows for censorship

The right to be forgotten does not allow governments to decide what can and cannot be online or what should or should not be read.

It is a right that citizens will invoke to defend their interests as they see fit. Independent authorities will oversee the assessment carried out by the search engine operators.

---

15 European Commission, 'Myth Busting and the Right to be Forgotten', available at http://ec.europa.eu/justice/data-protection/files/factsheets/factsheet_rtbf_mythbusting_en.pdf.

First, the search engine operators will act under the supervision of national data protection authorities. In Europe, these are legally required to be independent. Second, national courts will have the final say on whether a fair balance between the right to personal data protection and the freedom of expression was struck.

Balancing tests are not unusual in fundamental rights protection cases. For example, a landlord's right to property could be balanced with the right to a home of a long-term tenant. An employer's freedom to conduct business might be balanced with his workers' right to strike.

Over time, the decisions of the national authorities and courts will create an increasingly predictable framework within which search engine operators will handle right to be forgotten requests.

Myth 5: The judgment will change the way the internet works

The internet will remain an important source of information as content will remain in the same location and be accessible through search engines.

The way search engines function will also remain the same, since they already filter out some links from search results.'

Some of the issues which may have to be resolved, and are deserving of research, are issues such as,

- Whether and to what extent lobbying may have influenced (legitimately or illegitimately) the proposal and amendments to the updating of the EU data protection regime;

- The crossover and interplay between the RTBF and online abuse;

- The crossover and interplay between the RTBF and online safety;

- The influence of online safety measures on the RTBF;

- Calls for national RTBF in jurisdictions outside the EU, in particular Canada and the US;

- The internationalisation of RTBF;

- Consideration of *Rights* to be Forgotten;

- Graduated *Rights* to be Forgotten;

- Assessments of the need and enhanced need for *Rights* to be Forgotten in certain topical areas of online activity, specific types of websites, and assessments as between websites A, B and C;

- Tools for comparing the specific need for RTBF as between websites A, B and C;

- Tools for comparing the specific RTBF procedures as between websites A, B and C;

13

A: Introduction

- Methods for comparing statistics for the need for RTBF;

- Methods for comparing statistics for requests for RTBF and across different RTBF takedown categories, information categories, website categories;

- Methods for comparing statistics for RTBF takedown and takedown requests as between (indexing of) press content and non-press content;

- Methods for comparing statistics for RTBF takedown and non-takedown;

- Methods for comparing statistics for the need for RTBF for specific categories of information and personal data;

- Methods for comparing statistics for the need for RTBF for specific categories of personal data,

- Methods for comparing statistics for the need for RTBF for specific gravity of and harm of online abuse and as between, for example, death, suicide, trolling, threats, adults, juveniles, children, public figures, non-public figures;

- Consideration of RTBD and content online relating to an individual who is dead;

- Consideration of attempts to defeat and hamper RTBF;

- Consideration of defamation and RTBF;

- Consideration of hacked content and RTBF;

- Consideration of blackmail and RTBF;

- The role and (greater) responsibility of public broadcasters and broadsheets generally in relation to RTBF, but also in relation to online abuse, etc;

- Critical consideration of the extent to which deliberate attempts to defeat individual RTBF requests may infringe, perhaps in an aggravating manner, the very interests sought to be protected;

- Detailed critical consideration of the extent to which large sections of the media/press may be seduced into being a pawn in the stratagem of separate industry interests;

- Consideration of how tenable, or untenable, the position of Wikipedia and Jimmy Wales with regard to RTBF actually is (ie the 'No RTBF Full Stop' position).

A follow-on consideration, subject to the above, may also be whether Wikipedia and Jimmy Wales are somewhat naive and may have become an unwitting pawn in third party activities with potentially specific agendas regarding RTBF nuances and/or RTBF more generally.

While Wikipedia and Jimmy Wales can generally be lauded, their apparent position that there should be no RTBF per se (ie 'no RTBF full stop') might be fully examined. With respect to Google, while it disagrees with the CJEU decision, its representatives have many times indicated that they feel that the decision got the balance wrong, not that there are no instances of and no legitimate user/individual interests to be protected and content should be take down and which RTBF can assist to protect. It might be suggested that the 'No RTBF Full Stop' position of Jimmy Wales on a balanced analysis would be shown to be extreme and untenable. One might consider whether a 'No RTBF Full Stop' position is reasonable and would prevent links or content being taken down relating to and identifying an individual who is the victim of:

- revenge porn;
- child pornography;
- online abuse trolling;
- threats, including of rape, death or harm;
- hacked images;
- hacked financial data;
- hacked information; or
- defamation.

Is it reasonable that a 'No RTBF Full Stop' position should hinder individuals who wish to have information taken down which indicates that they may have previously self-harmed or attempted suicide? Is the 'No RTBF Full Stop' position reasonable when it prevents or hinders individuals getting into college or obtaining employment (or assists in so preventing)?

Is the 'No RTBF Full Stop' position actually irresponsible if the concern of Wikipedia and Jimmy Wales is really a concern with certain categories of information online – namely, or in particular, media published information and/or information with a clear public interest (eg political comment)? Is a blunt and indiscriminate 'No RTBF Full Stop' position, without sophistication or nuance, untenable? Is a blunt wedge of the 'No RTBF Full Stop' position at odds with Google's position that the balance of the CJEU's RTBF decision might be recalibrated somewhat?

While these are cutting questions, no individual answer is available in any particular jurisdiction; however, the issues are being felt in most, if not all, jurisdictions where the internet and SM apply. In time, there may be RTBF cases which will come to be reported in updates to the chapters below. For present purposes, we can say that the literature, policies, procedures, academic, industry, rights and political discussions relating to RTBF issues will continue – and not least in relation to the individual personal, individual harm and individual rights issues at stake.

Based on the large number of RTBF requests that we are currently aware of as having been made with Google, it would appear that there is a demand for RTBF. This should only increase as more individuals see how it is implemented and as their needs and interests in takedown protection dictate.

One UK expert, Professor Lillian Edwards, indicates that the problem of revenge porn is a perfect example of why there is a need for RTBF.[16] While some US commentary[17] recognises the need for RTBF and that the CJEU decision was largely correct and seeks to meet a legitimate need (but with caveats in relation to its rollout in the US), other notable experts have said that the decision does not go far enough.[18] The dynamic of how RTBF is treated in the US and the EU will be interesting, and important, to consider over the coming year, and particularly as the update to EU data protection law progresses.

Ultimately, the arguably outlier 'No RTBF Full Stop' approach of Jimmy Wales and Wikipedia may come under increasing scrutiny and pressure to change to a more nuanced, balanced and reasonable position. Julia Powles in the *Guardian*, for example, comments that Jimmy Wales is wrong, and that outside of public interest we should be able to have a say in the public memory of who we are, and that '[w]ithout the freedom to be private, we have precious little freedom at all'.[19]

At a legal policy level, SM and enhanced search capabilities bring the (human and legal) need for rebalancing the protection of human interests with a mechanism to delete information online. The needs identified by Viktor Mayer-Schönberger in his 2009 book *Delete: The Virtue of Forgetting in the Digital Age* have now gathered pace, from unfortunate incidents to online abuse and deliberate attacks. The immediate aftermath of the *Google Spain* decision and the level of RTBF requests across many nations might also indicate that the need for forgetting/takedown has only increased with SM. Brazil, for example, is also considering RTBF laws.

---

16 L Edwards, 'Revenge porn: why the right to be forgotten is the right remedy', *Guardian*, 29 July 2014, available at www.theguardian.com/technology/2014/jul/29/revenge-porn-right-to-be-forgotten-house-of-lords.

17 For example, *New Yorker* podcast with Jeffrey Toobin and Tim Wu, [no date] September 2014, available at https://soundcloud.com/newyorker/jeffrey-toobin-and-tim-wu-on-the-right-to-be-forgotten, accessed 28 September 2014.

18 T Brewster, 'CIA security luminary: "Right to be forgotten is not enough"', *Guardian*, 15 August 2014, available at www.theguardian.com/technology/2014/aug/15/cia-security-danger-right-to-be-forgotten.

19 J Powles, 'Jimmy Wales is wrong: we do have a personal right to be forgotten', Guardian, 8 August 2014, available at www.theguardian.com/technology/2014/aug/08/jimmy-wales-right-to-be-forgotten-wikipedia.

Section B
Developing Issues

Developing SM and SN Issues

2.1   INTRODUCTION

There are billions of regular users of SM and SN. In fact, the SM user population of some individual websites is even greater than the population of many nation states. The popularity is without doubt. There are tremendous and wonderful uses and benefits to SM. However, in a small number of instances, there are less than welcome activities going on, most notably certain instances of online abuse. The small but dark side is gaining prominence and undermining the many positives to SM. Left unaddressed, it is almost inevitable that there will be increasing calls for more regulation, and that self-regulation or individual website rules alone may sometimes be insufficient. From a commercial perspective, we might consider how many potential users stay away, leave or are less active online than they might otherwise be if there was a greater perception of a safer internet or safer SM.

As the size, popularity and indeed complexity of SM and SN evolve further, the number of legal, technical, policy, commercial and other issues involved will also increase. Indeed, on occasion these become headline news, and sometimes for the wrong reasons. The imperative for organisations is to try and ensure that they are not on the wrong side of those headlines and legal issues.

Sometimes, these issues may have a continuity with existing legal precedent. Increasingly, however, courts, policy makers, employers, schools and others are faced with entirely new legal issues stemming from SM and SN.

Frequently, the scale, complexity and expedition of the issues are at a level unprecedented in collective memory.

The number of topics below are just one indication of the breadth of issues arising in relation to SM. These issues are highlighted below, including reference to both civil law and common law perspectives, as well as separately in the following individual country chapters.

2.2   SPECIFIC SM AND SN LAWS

The second-generation internet (Web 2.0) and the use of social media (SM), including social networking (SN), create a whole new tapestry of changes in

19

society and in law. The growth of new social media,[1] social networks (SNs)[2] and new service applications (such as new business marketing tools)[3] raise new issues and concerns. There are obvious concerns regarding child safety. This is especially so when we consider that frequently all one needs to register an account is a valid email address, without any further verification[4] of name or age. There are, therefore, frequently no direct age checks. It is possible for almost any age of person to join and, worse still, to pretend to be someone they are not.

While originally developed for students, SM is now being fully embraced by all kinds of individuals, companies and organisations.[5] People judge others according to their online popularity, 'social networking IQ',[6] etc. One can even be accused of being antisocial if not widely connected on SM.[7] Other commentators openly speak of SM and networking tools for the 21st century.[8] There can be a perception that one is not 'normal' without fully engaging in SM, including on occasion the dark side of the internet.

SM has many advantages, such as communications, maintaining contact from a distance, entertainment, rich content, personal development and socialising skills.[9] A website was used by a school in Bolton, Lancashire during a period of heavy snow to assist schoolchildren with online lessons.[10] The students' grades were reported to have increased.[11] Using SM can possibly educate younger people in the use of technology, increase confidence and enhance interpersonal skills.[12]

---

1   See, for example, H Jenkins, *Convergence Culture: Where Old and New Media Collide* (New York University Press, New York, 2006).

2   DC Bechstrom, 'Who's Looking at Your Facebook Profile? The Use of Student Conduct Codes to Censor College Students' Online Speech' (2008) (45) *Williamette Law Review* 261 at 267–270.

3   R Barrett, 'A Story of Social Capital Invested Wisely in LinkedIn' (Jan–Feb 2008) (34) *Law Practice* 43.

4   M Maher, 'You've Got Messages: Modern Technology Recruiting Through Text-Messaging and the Intrusiveness of Facebook' (2007) (8) *Texas Review of Entertainment and Sports Law* 125 at 137.

5   C Barnes, 'Social Networking: Not Just for Youngsters Anymore' (2008–2009) (33) *Bar Technology* 19.

6   MA Behnke, 'What is Your Social Networking IQ' (2008–2009) (33) *Bar Leader* 2.

7   LS Rosen, 'Are You Antisocial?' (2008–2009) (31) *Family Advocate* 6.

8   L Glankler, 'Networking Tools for the Twenty-First Century' (2009) (19) *Trends in Law Library Management and Technology* 29.

9   'Facebook Interactions Can Help Boost Personal Ones, Study Finds', *Irish Times*, 26 November 2010, available at www.irishtimes.com/newspaper/finance/2010/1126/1224284180450.html.

10   I Knight, 'Illiteracy? Try Blogging', *Sunday Times*, 13 February 2011, News Review section, 4.

11   Ibid.

12   'Benefits of Online Social Networking', ParentFurther, available at www.parentfurther.com/technology-media/social-networking/benefits.

The use of SM plays an increasing part in people's daily lives.[13] SM makes changes to 'evolving social norms'.[14] Some of these can be obviously undesirable. An example would be SNs collecting and storing categories of personal data that users were not made aware of and had not consented to. Many can also hold dangers. This is most notable in the case of children and teenagers. The 'new world' has many pitfalls,[15] online abuse of personal data and risks for children being perhaps those most emphasised.

The age profile for SM is much lower than the average age for internet usage.[16] There are obvious concerns, therefore, in terms of children as well as teenagers using SM. Amanda Todd, a victim of online abuse, is just one example. The US, Canada, UK, Ireland and other jurisdictions all have examples of online abuse.

MySpace began in 2003[17] and originally focused on providing personalised webpages for music bands and facilitating communications between bands.[18] Facebook was established on 4 February 2004 by a college student at Harvard University as a means of its students communicating with each other.[19] In 2006, Facebook had over 6.6 billion friend requests on its website.[20] It grew to 750 million active users,[21] and now has over 1 billion regular active users.[22] The scale of SN popularity can mean that, where things do go wrong, the online abuse of personal data that can occur will be on a significant scale. Some might say that traditional bullying ends at the school yard; however, texting, calls, emails and the internet do not.

---

13   S Nelson, J Simek and J Foltin, 'The Legal Implications of Social Networking' (2009–2010) (22) *Regent Law Review* 1 at 2.

14   'Facebook, Facebook Principles', at www.facebook.com/principles.php, as referred to in A Blank, 'On the Precipe of E-Discovery: Can Litigants Obtain Employee Social Networking Web Site Information Through Employers?' (2010) (18) *CommLaw Conspectus* 487 at 490.

15   Ibid.

16   KM Gurney, 'MySpace, Your Reputation: A Call to Change Libel Laws for Juveniles Using Social Networking Sites' (2009) (82) *Temple Law Review* 241 at 246.

17   For a brief history of MySpace see, for example, EP Stedman, 'MySpace, But Whose Responsibility? Liability of Social-Networking Websites When Offline Sexual Assault of Minors Follows Online Interaction' (2007) (14) *Villanova Sports & Entertainment Law Journal* 363 at 363–364.

18   Ibid, 367.

19   RM Groves, 'Facebook 2 Blackberry and Database Trading Systems: Morphing Social Networking to Business Growth in a Global Recession' (2009–2010) (112) *West Virginia Law Review* 153 at 160.

20   Referred to in JJ Ator, 'Got Facebook?' *GPSOLO*, March 2009, 4.

21   Facebook statistics, available at www.facebook.com/press/info.php?statistics.

22   J Kiss, 'Facebook Hits 1 Billion Users a Month', *Guardian*, 4 October 2012, available at www.guardian.co.uk/technology/2012/oct/04/facebook-hits-billion-users-a-month. There are concerns that there are significant numbers of false and non-real accounts, thus distorting this figure.

There are increasing calls for empirical research of the effects of SM and the relationship between law and SM.[23] While many concerns are apparent, the full extent of the issues that SM raises – and how to deal with them – is only just beginning to be seen. One example of this occurred recently with the first data protection audit of Facebook by the Irish Data Protection Commissioner's Office on foot of several complaints.[24] That Data Protection Commissioner's second re-audit report[25] included two requirements: Facebook should be more transparent as to what it wished to do with users' personal data; and certain practices, such as automated facial recognition features for photographs, were not permissible under the EU data protection regime and should be discontinued. More recently, the UK Leveson Inquiry was critical of the trade in illegally obtained personal data.[26] Some argue that more transparency is needed of SM and related websites as regards online abuse, abuse reports and abuse-reporting tools, procedures, protocols and resolutions, as well as preventative measures.

One of the concerns relating to online abuse relates to its nature. Whereas traditional abuse and bullying, not condoning either, were limited to a location and a rather defined number of people, the advent of SM brings a whole new escalation in damage, scale and permanence. It also brings a new set of problems for victims and parents seeking to deal with, prevent and take down online abuse.

Grimmelmann describes how SN users,

'socialize on the [Web]site, why they misunderstand the risks involved, and how their privacy suffers as a result. Facebook offers a socially compelling [website] that also facilitates peer-to-peer privacy violations: users harming each other's privacy interests. These two facts are inextricably linked; people use Facebook with the goal of sharing information about themselves. Policymakers cannot make Facebook completely safe, but they can help people use it safely'.[27]

The imperative for doing more has escalated with the drastic results of some of the online abuse occurring. The UK Prime Minister David Cameron, for

---

23 Highlighted by Zarsky, *op. cit*, 782–783. The author also refers to the lack of empirical research in relation to television cameras and new social networking activities in court, such as Twitter. See P Lambert, *Courting Publicity, Twitter and Television Cameras in Court* (Bloomsbury, West Sussex, 2011).

24 See *Facebook Ireland Limited, Report of Audit*, Data Protection Commissioner, 21 December 2011, available at www.dataprotection.ie.

25 See *Facebook Ireland Limited, Report of Re-Audit*, Data Protection Commissioner, 21 September 2012, available at www.dataprotection.ie.

26 *Leveson Inquiry. An Inquiry into the Culture, Practices and Ethics of the Press: Report*, The Right Honourable Lord Justice Leveson, November 2012. Available at www.official-documents.gov.uk/document/hc1213/hc07/0780/0780.asp. Also see the main inquiry website at www.levesoninquiry.org.uk/.

27 J Grimmelmann, 'Saving Facebook' (2009) (94) *Iowa Law Review* 1137.

instance, has called for a boycott of certain 'vile' websites. He has also been putting pressure on websites to block and deal with child pornography.

SM 'harms' include cyberbullying, threats, abuse, grooming, defamation, privacy and data protection infringements, disclosure, surveillance, instability, disagreements, spillovers and denigration.[28] 'While online SN is nothing new, its legal ramifications are just beginning to come into focus'.[29] Our critical analytical skills in assessing SM and the nuances need to improve. That goes for parents, educators, policy makers, those representing victims, etc. Data protection authorities also need to be properly resourced. The Irish Data Protection Commissioner is on record a number of times highlighting his office's lack of resources. However, the problem is multifaceted, as will be the solutions. This will of course inevitably include legal recourse, as this will sometimes be the only avenue, or only timely avenue, available. However, other practical solutions can equally be looked at.

We 'cannot overstate the pervasive nature and rampant use of social-networking websites'.[30] SM has literally changed how we socialise.[31] The opposite is also true. Many victims of online abuse and SM online abuse become more and more isolated and cannot connect with real friends online or in person. They are prevented from availing of what should be a safe online experience. Today, 'relationships now exist in an alternative online world and communal responsibilities thus have changed forever'.[32] Teenagers and school children now routinely communicate in a way which, up until now, would have been reserved for evenings and weekends.[33] SM 'represent[s] the fastest growing segment of internet usage'.[34] The amount of information gathered and made available is significant. However, this amount and level of detailed information is increasing rapidly. This is due to the popularity of SM. It is also due to the increasing number and variety of 'apps' or applications (services and features) on SM.[35]

---

28 Ibid.
29 EE North, 'Facebook Isn't Your Space Anymore: Discovery of Social Networking Websites' (2010) (58) *University of Kansas Law Review* 1279 at 1286.
30 EP Stedman, 'MySpace, But Whose Responsibility? Liability of Social-Networking Websites When Offline Sexual Assault of Minors Follows Online Interaction' (2007) (14) *Villanova Sports & Entertainment Law Journal* 363 at 366.
31 DC Davis, 'MySpace Isn't Your Space: Expanding the Fair Credit Reporting Act to Ensure Accountability and Fairness in Employer Searches of Online Social Networking Services' (2006–2007) (XVI) *Kansas Journal of Law and Public Policy* 237.
32 Stedman, *op. cit*, 365.
33 KD Williams, 'Public Schools Vs MySpace: The Newest Challenge to Student Rights' (2008) (76) *University of Cincinnati Law Review* 707 at 708.
34 *The Social Media Guide Website*, http://mashable.com/2009/04/20/the-fastest-growing-social-sites/, referred to in AJ Bojorquez and D Shores, 'Open Government and the Net: Bringing Social Media into the Light' (2009–2010) (11) *Texas Tech Administrative Law Journal* 45 at 46.
35 Nelson *et al., op. cit*, 21.

There has been ongoing controversy in relation to the impact of SM and mobile telephones on education and language.[36] Is it having a detrimental effect? While pertinent, this is beyond the scope of the present discussion.[37]

One of the fastest-growing SM involves individuals connecting on video chat (discussion) with completely random strangers.[38] This may create personal safety issues for adults, not just children.

Nelson *et al* state that,

> 'SN and social media websites represent a shift in how people discover, read, and share news, information, and content; they are a fusion of sociology and technology, transforming monologues (one-to-many) into dialogues (many-to-many), and they are "the democratization information, transforming people from content readers into content publishers." The social nature of these websites helps to build online communities of people who share interests, activities, or both, or people interested in exploring the interests and activities of others'.[39]

The pace of change can be frightening and our knowledge catch-up lags behind. There is a generational gap. In addition, policy makers and laws frequently tend to react to problems as they arise, as opposed to being proactive. It also means that issues like online abuse are considered only when they make front-page headlines and there is a political or business imperative. SM and related websites can also be more proactive and more supportive in relation to victims and dealing with online abuse. Where websites do have measures in place, they may not always filter into wider public and user consciousness.

There are many privacy and data protection concerns, in particular those brought about by SM and second-generation internet (Web 2.0). In some instances, we are only beginning to see the problems which are arising. Only time will tell what solutions will follow and which ones will be successful. In other instances, there remains an education deficit in terms of compliance issues.

SN and related websites are used for many legitimate purposes. However, such websites 'contain a virtual treasure trove of personal information'.[40] As

---

36   As just one example, see N Bramhill, 'Exams in Text: CU in 10 Years', *Sunday Times*, 20 February 2011. On a separate but not altogether unrelated note, given advertising, marketing and children on social networks, note G Farrell, 'McDonald's Sued Over Toys With Meals', *Financial Times*, 16 December 2010, 27.

37   There is, however, a lot of literature available on this subject.

38   See ChatRoulette.com. There is also a ChatXRoulette.com.

39   AJ Bojorquez and D Shores, 'Open Government and the Net: Bringing Social Media into the Light' (2009–2010) (11) *Texas Tech Administrative Law Journal* 45 at 47. References omitted.

40   Nelson, *et al.*, *op. cit*, 21.

a result, '[p]erils await on all sides'.[41] The popularity of SM opens the door to misuse and online abuse of personal data, such as,

- online abuse, including cyberbullying;
- blackmail;
- threats of rape, violence, murder;
- trolling;
- revenge porn;[42]
- misuse of personal data of SN users;
- collecting personal data without transparency, knowledge or consent;
- identity theft;
- cyberstalking;[43]
- child solicitation, grooming and predation;[44]
- undesirable employer vetting and monitoring;[45]
- unwanted direct marketing;
- evidence gathering;
- behavioural advertising;[46]
- spamming (unwanted and unsolicited electronic direct marketing);
- malicious software, such as botnets, malware websites and viruses; and
- use of personal photographs for other people's products and services, such as dating websites or pornographic websites.[47] In one instance, a man found a picture of his wife on a singles advert on Facebook after it was copied from her Facebook profile.[48]

---

41 Ibid, 1.
42 Uploading intimate pictures and videos of ex-partners as an act of revenge or to embarrass them.
43 For example, M Baer, 'Cyberstalking and the Internet Landscape We Have Constructed' (2010) *Virginia Journal of Law & Technology* 153.
44 See, for example, Nelson, *et al.*, *op. cit*, 23 *et seq.*
45 DB Garrie, M Duffy-Lewis, R Wong and RL Gillespie, 'Data Protection: The Challenges Facing Social Networking' (2009–2010) (131) *International Law & Management Review* 127 at 128.
46 See M Hilderbrandt and S Gutwirth, *Profiling the European Citizen* (Springer Science, 2007), referred to in Garrie *et al*, above.
47 Nelson, *et al.*, *op. cit*, 2 and references therein.
48 Ibid, above at 2, and footnote 10 at 2.

SM 'makes traditional protection mechanisms and means of controlling privacy outdated in many respects'.[49] While it may seem strange, many users do not avail of the privacy control settings available.[50] Policy makers as well as SM need to appraise users of the need to avail of current privacy settings and of ongoing changes to protection measures. The Irish Data Protection Commissioner has required greater transparency by Facebook in relation to one of the areas examined in the audit report.[51] However, there are many other areas where transparency can be improved across various websites.

Security online is an ever-important issue. Pictures and personal details from closed private SM profiles have been used in attempts to blackmail individuals.[52] The recent Leveson Inquiry Report also highlights the illicit trade in personal data as well as personal data being used for blackmail purposes.[53] A Scottish teenager, Daniel Perry, is also reported to have committed suicide as a result of online blackmail threats.

There is a general lack of awareness and expertise in relation to what can happen to one's personal data once posted online. Many people are still unaware that their SM content can be used against them. In *Cedric D v Stacia W*, for example, a father lost custody of his child after the court viewed his MySpace profile, suggesting that his lifestyle was not in the best interest of the child.[54]

In addition, the use of direct and indirect profiling of personal data and the online activities of individuals for targeted marketing needs careful consideration, and arguably more transparency.[55]

---

49 D Findlay, 'Tag! Now You're "It". What Photographs on Social Networking Sites Mean for the Fourth Amendment' (2008) (10) *North Carolina Journal of Law & Technology* 171 at 175.

50 A Lenhart and M Madded, 'Teens, Privacy & Online Social Networks' (2007) (ii) *Pew Internet & American Life Project*, http://pewinternet.org/pdfs/PIP_Teens_Privacy_SNS_Report_Final.pdf, as referred to in D Findlay, 'Tag! Now You're "It". What Photographs on Social Networking Sites Mean for the Fourth Amendment' (2008) (10) *North Carolina Journal of Law & Technology* 171 at 182.

51 See *Facebook Ireland Limited, Report of Re-Audit*, Data Protection Commissioner, 21 September 2012, available at www.dataprotection.ie.

52 Giving the example of a blackmail attempt on Miss New Jersey 2007, A Jenner, 'NJ Miss in a Fix Over Her Pics', *New York Post*, 6 July 2007, 5, referred to in Nelson *et al.*, *op. cit*, 21.

53 Leveson Inquiry. *An Inquiry into the Culture, Practices and Ethics of the Press: Report, The Right Honourable Lord Justice Leveson*, November 2012. Available at www.official-documents.gov.uk/document/hc1213/hc07/0780/0780.asp. Also see the main inquiry website at www.levesoninquiry.org.uk/.

54 *Cedric D v Stacia W* No 1 CA-JV 07-0056, 2007 WL 5515319, at *4 (Arizona Court Appeal 20 September 2007), referred to in HI Parness, 'Toward 'Social Networking Law?' (March–April 2009) *Landslide* at 13, 16, and Nelson *et al.*, *op. cit*, 22.

55 The Irish Data Protection Commissioner's Facebook audit review and the proposed EU Data Protection Regulation are steps in this direction. Proposed Data Protection Regulation, available at http://ec.europa.eu/justice/data-protection/document/review2012/com_2012_11_en.pdf.

While many laws which exist already may have direct relevance to SM issues, they may not expressly use the term 'SM' and/or 'SN'. A large number of jurisdictions will have experience of SM posts, materials and identifiers being admitted as evidence in legal cases.

However, as particular SM issues and concerns, and related activities, as opposed to SM per se, become more mainstream concerns for the public and policy makers, there will be an increasing justification in considering whether new specific laws (or updated laws) are needed to address these specific issues.

One example of this might be the issue of revenge porn, whereby generally male ex-partners upload onto specific revenge porn websites sexual images of the female from the previous relationship, or to more general pornography, dating or other websites.

A number of other similar activities are also a worry and are sometimes classified as or associated with revenge porn. One example is where a hacker may break into the computers (and also online accounts) of many people in an effort to find sexual images which they will then upload to a specific website and ultimately demand payment from the victims in order to have the personal images taken down.

Lilian Edwards, a Professor of Internet Law, states that the right to be forgotten (RTBF) is one of the appropriate remedies for revenge porn.[56] It does not mean that it will be the only remedy, nor that RTBF and other remedies may not require specific recognition in law where certain jurisdictions do not already afford such recognition.

In assessing these problem issues, one should assess the extent to which existing laws may afford a route to remedy for law enforcement, for individual victims, appropriate organisations and regulators. As an example of the latter, we might consider whether the US FCA, in protecting personally identifiable information (PII), or EU data protection authorities, in protecting personal data, might have sufficient scope to shut down or prosecute a specific revenge porn website. In terms of victims filing complaints with the police, we might consider whether such complaints are adequately categorised and recorded for statistical purposes, and also whether such complaints are acted upon under criminal investigation and prosecution, and how successfully.

In terms of assessing, for example, how adequate existing civil law remedies may be for victims of revenge porn, we might consider how easily, how often and how successfully civil revenge porn actions and/or prosecutions actually are. Given that these involve internet issues, particular consideration is required

---

56   L Edwards, 'Revenge porn: why the right to be forgotten is the right remedy, The 'right to be forgotten' ruling is actually a powerful tool for victims of revenge porn, but a new House of Lords report says no new laws are needed', Guardian, 29 July 2014, www.theguardian.com/technology/2014/jul/29/revenge-porn-right-to-be-forgotten-house-of-lords.

in terms of immediate and injunctive type remedies, identification of persons responsible, etc.

While revenge porn and related activities are a prominent issue of concern, it is worth noting that these issues generally relate to private and personal images. There are, however, separate examples of images being taken in public and uploaded to 'rate' type websites, pornography websites and other payment demand type websites. These include 'upskirt' photographs take in public settings without consent or knowledge but which are nonetheless personal and private. It may also include beach photographs, public transport photographs, etc.

In considering these issues, due consideration should be taken of the harm, demands for money and other profit motives, as well as trolling type motivations.

One view may be that, as the number of internet and SM problem issues exponentially increase and the level/number of new harm issues escalate as the internet and SM exponentially increases, the strength of the argument that there should per se be no (new) internet laws weakens. There may be a rule that, over time, a blanket argument for no (new) internet laws must diminish, as specific problem issues increase on a significant scale.

In terms of considering self-regulation and specific website rules, policies, tools, etc, might there be a need for an exponential increase of the details, implementation and effectiveness of the same (and updating of the same) as the potential harm and exponential volume of the same increases and as new problem issues arise? If the self-regulatory remedies do not increase to match the increase in problem issues, this may in some way diminish the argument for self-regulation and for no (new) internet laws.

The speed and efficacy of solutions can be important, regardless of self-regulatory or legal remedies. As well as intermediary remedies such as injunctions, identification of persons responsible may not always be as timely as victims and law enforcement would wish. There might possibly be a need for graduated responses and graduated identification, some being quicker when the harm is highest. A House of Lords Committee has also said that SM and related websites should establish the identity of people opening accounts to assist in dealing with the harm of revenge porn.[57]

One of the civil means for victims obtaining identification details of those responsible for online abuse, defamation, revenge porn, etc is Norwich Pharmacal orders,[58] whereby websites, telecoms companies, etc are required by court order to furnish identification details. However, while this is one of

---

57 'Sites must end anonymity to tackle "revenge porn", say peers', BBC, 29 July 2014, www. bbc.com/news/uk-politics-28528277.
58 *Norwich Pharmacal Company & Ors v Customs and Excise* [1973] UKHL 6 (26 June 1973) [1973] 2 All ER 943, [1973] 3 WLR 164, [1973] FSR 365, [1973] UKHL 6, [1974] AC 133, [1974] RPC 101.

the main legal tools available to victims of online abuse such as revenge porn, the Norwich Pharmacal tool resulted from a case in 1974. Considering 1974 was well before: internet registration begins for .com, .net, .org, .edu, and .gov (1992); the internet takes off (1993); Netscape, the first successful commercial web browser, is founded (1993); the World Wide Web is developed in CERN in Switzerland (1993); the EU Data Protection Directive becomes law (1995); Google is founded (1999); the EU eCommerce Directive becomes law (2000); Wikipedia is launched (2001); Facebook is founded (2004); YouTube is founded (2005); Twitter is founded (2006); Twitter and Facebook and the Arab Spring(s) (2011); Facebook hits 1 billion (real) users; the year of online abuse (threats, defamation, data protection, etc), the year that the dark side of the internet comes to the fore (2012), etc, one might ask whether we are in need of a more modern Norwich Pharmacal order suitable for dealing with modern internet and SN issues. Possibly we need a Norwich Pharmacal 2.0 order.

2.3 SM CRIMINAL LAW CASES

Eric P Robinson (in chapter C33) indicates that,

> 'In addition to the criminal provisions discussed in the specific sections below, there have been several criminal cases that have involved use of social media.

> In its 2014–15 term the US Supreme Court will hear an appeal from a man who was convicted of communicating threats against his wife in postings to SM. The Third Circuit Court of Appeals upheld the conviction on the grounds that a reasonable person would understand the posts to be threatening; the defendant argues that the conviction should be reversed because he did not intent to actually carry out the threats. *Elonis v United States* No 13-983 (US cert granted June 16, 2014) (appeal of *United States v Elonis* 730 F3d 321 (3d Cir 2013).

> While most "flash mobs" – large groups of people organized via SM which suddenly appear at a specific location, perform some action, then disperse – are benign and even amusing, there have been some instances where flash mobs have resulted in violence and criminal activity. Concerns over such instances led the city of Cleveland, Ohio to amend its anti-rioting ordinance in 2011 to specifically address use of electronic devices to organize violent "flash mobs." Ord No 1393-11 (Cleveland, Ohio 2011) (amending Cleveland City Code § 625.08(a)(6)).

> The same year the Los Angeles County Sheriff's Department did not pursue a threatened prosecution of rapper The Game after he Tweeted a sheriff's department phone number to his followers, saying they should call the number to apply for an internship with him.

> SM material has also been used as evidence. In one such case, an Iowa man pleaded guilty to a federal gun charge after his probation officer saw

a picture of him on MySpace holding a rifle and a handgun. *US v Figueroa* No 1:09-cr-00033-LRR (ND Iowa 2009).'

Jonathan McDonald in the UK indicates that,

'since at least 2011, there have been a very large number of SM criminal law cases each year. A response to a Freedom of Information request (a request for the release of data held by public bodies in the UK) made by Sky News in 2014 revealed that, across 34 police forces, since 2011, 19,279 adults had been investigated for SM-related offences (predominantly abusive behaviour). Of these, 11,292 were subject to police action (either charged with a criminal offence, fined, cautioned or warned verbally) including 1,203 children. The majority of such cases, however, do not reach the higher courts that have power to create precedents (ie the courts whose judgments are binding on lower or equivalent courts) and whose judgments are usually reported in the law reports, but instead take place in the magistrates' courts (the lowest criminal court in England, where all criminal cases start) and are therefore rarely reported in the law reports.

With respect to those SM-related cases that have been reported, in *Paul Chambers v Director of Public Prosecutions* [2012] EWHC 2157 the English High Court confirmed that the offence of "improper use of a public electronic communications network" under section 127(1)(a) of the Communications Act 2003 could apply to a message posted on Twitter. Section 127(1)(a) provides that a person is guilty of an offence if he sends by means of a public electronic communications network a message or other matter that is grossly offensive or of an indecent, obscene or of menacing character. It did not matter that Twitter was a private company as it operated via a public electronic communications network. It equally did not matter that the message was viewed as content on the Internet, it still constituted a message. The court however overturned a criminal conviction ruling that a Tweet saying "Crap! Robin Hood Airport is closed. You've got a week and a bit to get your shit together otherwise I am blowing the airport sky high!!" was not a menacing message as it did not create fear or apprehension in those to whom it was communicated or who might reasonably be expected to see it.

The offence of improper use of a public electronic communications network is the most common criminal offence that directly relates to SM. *Paul Chambers v Director of Public Prosecutions* is the only case to be heard by the English High Court involving SM and the offence of improper use of a public electronic communications network. There have, however, been a number of other cases that have not been reported but have gained notoriety through the press involving this offence or the closely related offence of "sending letters etc with intent to cause distress or anxiety" under section 1 of the Malicious Communications Act 1998.

R v Azhar Ahmed (9 October 2012) – an individual was convicted under section 127 of the Communications Act 2003 of sending a grossly offensive message via Facebook after posting messages following the deaths of six

British soldiers in Afghanistan including the comment "all soldiers should die and go to hell".

R v Duffy (13 September 2011) – an individual was convicted under section 1 of the Malicious Communications Act 1998 of sending grossly offensive messages after writing abusive messages on Facebook tribute pages for teenagers who had died.

There are also numerous examples of criminal cases in which SM played a part, although the offences may have been committed even if SM was unavailable, albeit in a different way (ie naming a rape victim, breaching an injunction etc).'

Belgium, another EU jurisdiction, has such cases, for example,

'*Correctional Court of Leuven, 8 November 2010, Case n° AR nr LE53. L7.4816-09*

This case involved a dispute between two police officers and a private individual. The individual had been handcuffed by the officers after a traffic accident for being recalcitrant. Following this event, the individual repeatedly sent provocative and insulting personal messages via Facebook. The court decided that these messages severely disturbed the peace of mind of the police inspectors and that this constituted 'stalking' within the meaning of Article 442bis of the Criminal Code.[59]

Council Chamber (Raadkamer) of Nijvel, 4 December 2013, Case n° 75/11

This case concerned an animal rights activist who had insinuated through SM that a certain company that sold puppies had broken the Belgian Animal Welfare Law of 14 August 1986. According to the activist, the company sold fake dog passports and illegally ended the lives of unsold puppies. However, the activist did not have any real evidence to back up these statements. The Council Chamber considered that the distribution of these kind of libellous statements on a Facebook discussion forum constituted a press offence (Article 150 of the Belgian Constitution).'[60]

2.4   SM CIVIL LAW CASES

Eric P Robinson (in chapter C33) indicates that,

'*Defamation:* There have now been several trials and verdicts in defamation lawsuits stemming from SM. In two highly publicized cases, singer

---

59   This judgment was annotated by J Ceuleers, 'Belaging via Facebook is Ernstig Misdrijf', *Auteurs & Media* 2011, issue 1, p 115.

60   This judgment was annotated by A Godfroid and A Vandecasteele, 'Kritiek op grootschalige hondenfokkerij zindert na', *Juristenkrant* 2014, afl. 283, p 3. The full text of this judgment is available (in French) at www.kluwer.be/files/communities/legalworld/rechtspraak/RK%20 Nijvel%204%20december%202013.pdf.

Courtney Love settled one case stemming from her Twitter posts, and won a jury verdict in her favour in another. See *Simorangkir v Love* No BC410593 (Cal Super LA County) (settled Feb 2011); *Gordon & Holmes v Love* No BC462438 (Cal Super LA County) (jury verdict Jan 24, 2014). Several federal and state courts have held that SM defendants enjoy the same First Amendment protections in libel suits as traditional journalists, including the same standards of proof for plaintiffs, see eg *Obsidian Finance Group, LLC v Cox* 740 F3d 1284 (9th Cir 2014), cert denied, 134 SCt 2680, 189 L Ed 2d 223 (US May 27, 2014), and protection under state reporters' shield laws from being forced to reveal confidential sources. See *O'Grady v Superior Court* 139 Cal App 4th 1423, 44 Cal Rptr 3d 72 (Cal App, 6th Dist 2006); *Mortgage Specialists, Inc v Implode-Explode Heavy Indus, Inc* 160 NH 227, 999 A2d 184 (NH 2010). But a few courts have reached the contrary conclusion when they have deemed that the SM material was not journalistic in nature. *Obsidian Fin Group, LLC v Cox* No CV-11-57-HZ, 2011 US Dist LEXIS 120542 (D Or Oct 18, 2011), clarified by No CV-11-57-HZ, 2011 US Dist LEXIS 137548, 40 Media L Rep 1084 (D Or Nov 30, 2011), rev'd on other grounds, 740 F3d 1284 (9th Cir 2014), cert denied, 134 SCt 2680, 189 L Ed 2d 223 (US May 27, 2014).

Service of process: Several courts have approved service of process via email in appropriate circumstances, see Comment (Svetlana Gitman), (Dis) service of Process: The Need to Amend Rule 4 to Comply With Modern Usage of Technology, 45 J Marshall L Rev 459 (2012) (collecting cases), and Florida requires service via email in most cases. Florida Rule of Judicial Administration 2.516(a).

A few courts have explicitly allowed service by SM: See *Marriage of Jessica Mpafe v Clarence Mdjounwou Mpafe* Court File No 27-FA-11 (Minn Dist Ct, Fam Div, Hennepin County) (May 10, 2011) (allowing service via email, Facebook, MySpace or other SM sites); *FTC v PCCare* 247 Inc, 2013 US Dist LEXIS 31969, 2013-1 Trade Cas (CCH) P78294 (SDNY Mar 7, 2013) (allowing service via email and Facebook); *FTC v Pecon Software LTD* 2013 US Dist LEXIS 134205 (SDNY Sept 18, 2013) (same). But see *FTC v Pecon Software Ltd* 2013 US Dist LEXIS 111375, 2013-2 Trade Cas P78475 (SDNY Aug 7, 2013) (rejecting proposed service via Facebook when FTC had not conclusively shown court that the named defendants were "highly likely" to be reached by such service) … Other court rulings that have considered such service and have rejected it include *Fortunato v Chase Bank USA*, NA, 2012 WL 2086950 (SDNY June 7, 2012); and *Joe Hand Promotions, Inc v Carrette* 12-2633-CM (D Kan July 9, 2013).'

Jonathan McDonald in the UK indicates that,

'*Chris Lance Cairns v Lalit Modi* [2012] EWHC 756 (QB). In this case the High Court awarded £90,000 in damages to the New Zealand cricketer, Chris Cairns, in a successful libel claim against Lalit Modi, the former chairman and commissioner of the Indian Premier League, following a Tweet by

Modi that accused Cairns of match-fixing. The court found that although the Tweet was only sent to Modi's 65 followers, Modi was considered an expert in his field and he was likely to have a specialist cricket-loving audience, increasing the likelihood that his message would go viral. Since then, the Court of Appeal has upheld the judgment and the size of the award.

Lord McAlpine of West Green v Bercow (21 October 2013) (unreported). This was a common law libel action brought by Lord McAlpine, a former politician, against the defendant (who had 56,000 followers on Twitter and held what could be described as minor celebrity status in the UK). The defendant had issued a Tweet saying "Why is Lord McAlpine trending? *Innocent face*". This was in the wake of a BBC current affairs programme that reported on the abuse of boys at children's homes and included an interview in which two victims said that they suffered sexual abuse at the hands of a "leading Conservative politician from the Thatcher years", a description which could apply to Lord McAlpine. The defendant said in a statement, the making of which was part of a settlement agreed between the parties, that her allegation was completely without foundation. Her allegation caused the claimant great distress and embarrassment and her irresponsible use of Twitter contributed substantially to the claimant's eventual decision to issue a public statement denying the allegations. The defendant also apologised to the claimant and agreed to pay him damages and his costs.'

In Belgium, examples include,

'*Court of Brussels (20th Chamber), 20 June 2011*

As indicated earlier, the publication of libellous remarks on social media can constitute a so-called "press offence" in Belgium. In practice, many cases involving such press offences are brought before civil courts. In the case of 20 June 2011, the Civil Court of Brussels decided that the unnecessary use of hurtful and insulting words can constitute a tort, especially if there is no public interest. According to the Court, it is unlawful to purposely degrade someone's honour or reputation, for merely subjective reasons, by using unacceptably sharp language which is clearly disproportionate and unnecessary to express the opinion. The fact that the victim of the defamatory comments did not try to react directly to the weblog did not prevent a claim for civil liability.'[61]

2.5 CASES WHERE SM-RELATED EVIDENCE USED OR ADMISSIBLE

There are increasing numbers of cases where SM-related evidence has been used or been admissible. This includes criminal, civil and family law cases.

---

61   A Dutch summary of this judgment can be found in *Auteurs & Media* 2012, Issue 5, p 463.

Jonathan McDonald indicates that there are UK examples,

> 'Examples are limited. In *R v Wright (Jackson)*, *R v Cameron (Daniel)*, *R v Martin (Craig)* [2013] EWCA Crim 1217 the Court of Appeal ruled in relation to three convictions of inflicting grievous bodily harm that the first defendant's (Cameron) appeal against a sentence of eight years' detention should be dismissed, noting that "[the defendant] had made entries on the social media site 'Facebook' after the event [at which the attack was committed]. Those entries were a disgrace and showed no appreciation of the seriousness of the attack."'

A Belgian example includes,

> '*Court of Appeal of Antwerp, 22 February 2011, Case n° 2009/AR/1908*
>
> The Antwerp Court of Appeal accepted that the Belgian treasury could rely on information made public by tax payers through social media as a way to help demonstrate tax fraud. In this case a taxpayer had submitted certain costs relating to his Land Rover Defender as deductible expenses. The tax controller, however, decided to take a look at the SM page of the taxpayer, on which he discovered that the car was actually regularly used for the taxpayer's alpinism and diving trips, as well as for foreign travel. Therefore, the tax controller lowered the amount of deductible expenses, a reasoning which was accepted by the Court.'

2.6 SPECIFIC ONLINE ABUSE/ONLINE BULLYING/ CYBERBULLYING LAWS

Across jurisdictions, there any specific online abuse/online bullying/ cyberbullying laws.

Online abuse, bullying, stalking, harassment, bullying and grooming and such issues are important SM and SN matters.

The media and interest groups variously highlight the recognised difficulties of online abuse, bullying, stalking, harassment and, most particularly, sexual grooming of under-age persons for purposes of sexual exploitation.

The issue of bullying and harassment is also frequently referred to in discussion. This can take a number of forms. The primary example perhaps relates to mobile and social networking bullying and harassment of teenagers or schoolchildren by some of their peers. It is not limited to children, however. Bullying and harassment can also arise in the workplace among adults.

Many solutions are being suggested, some better than others, and even some unrealistic. Other issues have not yet been considered in great detail. On occasion, traditional laws and torts have to be reconsidered in relation to new technology-related activities.[62] Some people are also suggesting new laws, updated laws, self-regulation, co-regulation and even that no regulation is needed. There is clearly a complex social, technological, legal and policy discussion at play, as better solutions are sought.

2.6.1 Sexting online abuse

Unsolicited sexual comments via mobile devices and SM is increasingly recognised as a problem. Solicited sexual comment is also perceived as a problem. This is sometimes now known as 'sexting'.[63] One author describes it as the 'digital exchange of sexually explicit images between teenagers using text messaging services on camera-equipped cell phones'.[64] It is also described as the practice of posting or sending text messages or images that are sexually suggestive or even graphic, including nude or semi-nude photographs, whether via mobile phone or internet.[65] This raises issues of potential online abuse, bullying, harassment, revenge porn, blackmail, unauthorised access to accounts, phone numbers, passwords and or personal data, any of which can also be in contravention of the personal data regime in addition to other specific offences. These issues can encompass school, work and home environments.

Teenagers may be more sexually active now than previously. Teenagers in the US have been convicted of child pornography-related offences and have been required to register as sex offenders.[66] The impact of SM and mobile technologies are new relevant factors to be considered.

A Revenue employee, in Ireland, was convicted of sending sexual messages to his female supervisor, some of which indicated that he was threatening to rape and kill women.[67]

A lady was banned by a court in Texas from (1) using the internet; and (2) texting anyone other than a family member.[68] She was convicted in relation to

---

62 N Hoffman, 'Battery 2.0: Upgrading Offensive Contact Battery to the Digital Age' (2010) *Case Western Reserve Journal of Law, Technology & the Internet* 61.
63 S Livingston, L Haddon, A Gorzig and K Olafsson, 'Risks and Safety on the Internet: The Perspective of European Children. Full Findings', in *EU Kids Online* (LSE, London, 2011), 7. See reference at Social Networking, Age and Privacy, referred to in *EU Kids Online*, previously available at www2.lse.ac.uk/media@lse/research/EUKidsOnline/Home.aspx. See also www.eukidsonline.net.
64 EC Eraker, 'Stemming Sexting: Sensible Legal Approaches to Teenagers' Exchange of Self-Produced Pornography' (2010) *Berkeley Technology Law Journal* 555.
65 C Arcabascio, 'Sexting and Teenagers: OMG RU Going 2 Jail???' (2009–2010) *Richmond Journal of Law and Technology*, 1.
66 Ibid, 556. Note also, Arcabascio, *op. cit*, 1.
67 This relates to an Irish case. 'Meath Man to be Sentenced for Text Harassment', Breaking News, available at www.breakingnews.ie/ireland/meath-man-to-be-sentenced-for-text-harassment-503520.html.
68 'Katy Mom Banned from Internet After "Sexting" Son's Friend', *CBS Houston*, 14 November 2011, available at http://houston.cbslocal.com/2011/11/14/texas-housewife-banned-from-internet-over-sexting-sons-friend/; 'Mother Banned from the Internet After Pleading Guilty to "Sexting" 16 Year Old Son's Classmate Naked Pictures of Herself', *Daily Mail*, 14 November 2011.

sending a nude photograph of herself (she was aged 38) to a 16-year-old boy. The recipient was a friend of her son.

A German national was convicted for sending 'chilling, disturbing and ominous' text messages and emails to a psychologist.[69] He received a three-year suspended sentence.

A related concern is where the sexual communications are solicited or reciprocated between non-adults.[70] Can children, and consenting children, be held to the same liability as would an adult? Ethical, social and legal policy issues also arise.

However, one of the problems with many current laws is that they are arguably, to some extent, emotive and reactionary. Child pornography laws, for example, were generally drafted prior to SM as we now know it. As such, current laws generally do not cater for the offenders being children and young persons themselves. Child pornography laws, as well as sexting laws, may require amendment, to reflect this nuance.[71] However, some have called for more restraint on the part of official prosecutors, short of legal changes and self-regulation by websites.

There is also increasing recognition that issues from the child's perspective may affect this discussion, for example, the child's or teenager's rights of free speech, freedom of expression or 'right to sexual privacy'[72] – and potentially express constitutional rights in future. Pavia also makes the novel argument that sexting should be constitutionally protected privacy – but as part of the fundamental rights of parents.[73]

As more and more problem cases come to light, there will be increased discussion of the need for a right, or rights, to be forgotten.

2.6.2 Texting online abuse

A somewhat related issue is texting in vehicles while driving. This is increasingly penalised. It may also amount to an offence of dangerous or unsafe driving. Texting while driving is now often expressly banned in road traffic safety

---

69 This was a case in Ennis Circuit Court in Ireland. See G Deegan, 'Man Sent "Ominous" Texts to Psychologist', *Irish Times*, 24 February 2011, available at www.irishtimes.com/newspaper/ireland/2011/0224/1224290732379.html.

70 See *CC v Ireland*, Supreme Court, 23 May 2006, available at www.courts.ie/judgments.nsf/f69fbd31c73dda2580256cd400020877/877f6b6773b3dcee80257177003c6586?OpenDocument; *MD (a Minor) v Ireland*, Supreme Court, 14 April 2011. D McDonald, 'Businessman in Challenge Over Underage Sex Law', *Irish Times*, 29 November 2011.

71 JL Barry, 'The Child as Victim and Perpetrators: Laws Punishing Juvenile "Sexting"' (2010–2011) *Vandenberg Journal of Entertainment & Technology Law* 129.

72 See ibid, 166–171.

73 CJ Pavia, 'Constitutional Protection of "Sexting" in the Wake of *Lawrence*: The Right of Parents and Privacy' (2011) *Virginia Journal of Law & Technology* 1. Referring to *Lawrence v Texas* 539 US 558 (2003).

legislation. For example, a British MP was sentenced for dangerous driving linked to texting while driving.[74] In another case, in Allen County in Indiana, a man was convicted in a road traffic case where his daughter was killed after his texting caused a car crash.[75]

Possibly, browsing or updating one's SM profile while driving may now be included in texting offences, depending on the specific technical definitions of the offences. In future, there may be calls to create specific offences relating to the use of SM while driving.[76] These will ultimately be debated in superior court cases.

There has also been argument that (certain) bans for texting while driving may be unconstitutional.[77]

2.7 OTHER LAWS APPLIED TO ONLINE ABUSE/ ONLINE BULLYING/CYBERBULLYING

Sometimes, other laws have been applied to online abuse, online bullying and cyberbullying.

The House of Lords Select Committee on Communications Report on Social Media and Criminal Offences (1st Report of Session 2014–15, 29 July 2014) lists social media and criminal offences in Appendix 3, namely,

'Behaviour	Offence
Breach of court orders	Contempt of Court Act 1981
Breach of court orders, eg naming a person	Sexual Offences Amendment Act 1992, s 5 (identification of a victim of sexual offence)
Cyber bullying	Offences Against the Person Act 1861, s 16 (threat to kill)
Cyber bullying	Protection from Harassment Act 1997, s 4 (fear of violence)

---

74 Referred to in 'British MP Sentenced for Driving Dangerously; Was Texting at the Time', *Media Law Prof Blog*, 25 February 2009, available at http://lawprofessors.typepad.com/ media_law_prof_blog/2009/02/british-mp-sent.html.

75 'Man Sentenced in Texting While Driving Case', *HomeTownStations*, 29 March 2011, available at www.hometownstations.com/Global/story.asp?S=14341541.

76 Penalty points can be issued for texting while driving. Note *Survey of Mobile Phone Use by Car Drivers*, Road Safety Authority (RSA), September 2010, available at www.rsa.ie/ Documents/Campaigns/Mobile%20Phone/Mobile%20Phone%20Survey%202009.pdf.

77 A Lazerow, 'Near Impossible to Enforce at Best, Unconstitutional at Worst: the Consequences of Maryland's Text Messaging Ban on Drivers' (2010–2011) *Richmond Journal of Law and Technology* 1.

'Behaviour	Offence
Cyber bullying	Protection from Harassment Act 1997, s 2 (harassment)
Cyber bullying	Protection from Harassment Act 1997, s 2A (stalking)
Revenge pornography	Communications Act 2003, s 127; Malicious Communications Act 1988, s 1
Stalking	Protection from Harassment Act 1997, s 4A (stalking involving fear of violence, serious alarm of distress)
Threats	Malicious Communications Act 1988, s 1
Virtual mobbing	Communications Act 2003, s 127
Racial or religious aggravation	Crime and Disorder Act 1998, s 28
Disability, sexual orientation or transgender identity aggravation	Criminal Justice Act 2003, s 146'

Eric P Robinson (in chapter C33) indicates that,

> 'In two cases with implications for government acquisition and use of SM content in criminal prosecutions, the US Supreme Court has distinguished between government's role as an employer and its police function.

> In *City of Ontario v Quon* 560 US 746 (2010), the court held that a public employer may review the text messages sent from and received to a government-owned pager used by a police sergeant as part of his employment. The review, done because of overage charges, showed that most of the sergeant's messages were not work related, and included several sexually oriented messages. "Because the search was motivated by a legitimate work-related purpose, and because it was not excessive in scope," the court held, the search was reasonable under the Fourth Amendment. Id at 764.

> But in *US v Jones* 132 SCt 945, 181 LEd2d 911 (US 2012), the court unanimously held that the police must obtain a warrant before attaching a GPS tracker to a suspect's car, even though the police would not need a warrant to physically follow the car to determine its location.

> The US Supreme Court recently held that a warrant is required for a police search without consent of the data contained in a cellphone in the possession of someone who has been arrested, except under "exigent circumstances," such as imminent erasure of the data. *Riley v California* ___ US ___, 134 SCt 2473, 189 LEd2d 430 (June 25, 2014). The law

regarding use of cellphones as tracking devices may be affected by the *Riley* decision, but currently remains unclear. Prior to the ruling in *Riley*, the 5th Circuit held that a warrant is not required to access cell phone tower records that can be used to track an individual phone. *In re Application of the United States for Historical Cell Site Data* 724 F 3d 600 (5th Cir Tex 2013). But the 11th Circuit recently reached the opposite conclusion, ruling that a warrant *is* required. *US v Davis* 754 F3d 1205 (11th Cir June 11, 2014) ...

Most courts that have considered police searches of SM have held that a warrant is not required because users should not have a reasonable expectation of privacy in their SM posts. See eg *Guest v Leis* 255 F3d 325 (6th Cir 2001) (internet bulletin board); *US v Meregildo* 883 FSupp2d 523 (SDNY 2012) (Facebook); *US v Lustig* 3 F Supp 3d 808 (SD Cal 2014) (Craigslist).'

See also C33.19 below.

Jonathan McDonald, referring to the UK, indicates that,

'Online abuse/online bullying/cyberbullying can be considered a criminal offence under the Protection from Harassment Act 1997 (which is, on the whole, relevant for incidents that have happened repeatedly), which prohibits behaviour amounting to harassment of another (section 1), provides a criminal offence for such behaviour (section 2), and provides a more serious criminal offence of someone causing another person to fear, on at least two occasions, that violence will be used against them.

Also see C32.3 for details of the offence under section 127 of the Communications Act 2003 ...'

In Belgium,

'The Criminal Code contains a number of provisions that may be applicable to bullying in SM.

First, Article 422bis of the Criminal Code, which punishes persons who menace an individual, while they knew or should have known that through their behaviour they would seriously disturb the peace of that individual (see also C3.3).

Secondly, Articles 443–444 of the Criminal Code criminalise defamation and libel. Cyberbullying through SM may, under certain conditions, be classified as libel or defamation.

Thirdly, Article 448 of the Criminal Code punishes persons who offend or insult someone by means of writings or images. The perpetrator must have a malicious intent and the insult must be public. These Articles could also be applied in the context of SM.

Article 383 of the Criminal Code criminalises the display, sale or distribution of writings or images that are indecent. If this is done in the presence of minors below the age of 16, more severe sentences are imposed according to Article 386. In addition, Article 384 stipulates that the production of indecent writings or images is also a criminal offence. In cases of cyberbullying where sexually explicit images are used ("sexting"), these provisions may be relevant.[78]

If the cyberbullying involves the spreading of images of the victim without his or her consent, it could be covered by Article 10 of the Belgian Copyright Law which protects the right to one's image. Moreover, this type of harassment could qualify as the processing of personal data, for which a person may need the consent of the data subject according to Article 5 of the Belgian Data Protection Law.

All the aforementioned provisions are formulated in a broad and technology-neutral manner, so in theory they could be applied in the SM context. Not all of these provisions have already been applied in case law. However, several instances do exist, which are discussed below. See C3.3 (on criminal law cases), C3.14 (on hacking) and C3.13 (on identity theft).'

2.8 CHILDREN AND SM LAWS OR RULES

There is increasing attention on the need for laws or rules specific to children and SM.

The internet can be a dangerous place for children.[79] Some of the biggest concerns in relation to children are often online abuse (especially cyberbullying), online sexual solicitation and exposure to online sexual or pornographic content.[80] There is undoubtedly an increase in predatory risks with SN, whereby sexual predators seek to make contact with or profile children through SNs.[81] SM is said to 'create an environment'[82] which assists sexual predators in communicating with children. A study compiled for Safer Internet Day found that 73 per cent

---

78 Child pornography is addressed in article 383bis of the Criminal Code. This article criminalises the display, sale, rental, distribution, transmission, delivery, possession or (knowing) obtainment of access of or to images that depict poses or sexual acts with a pornographic character which involve or depict minors.

79 EP Stedman, 'MySpace, But Whose Responsibility? Liability of Social-Networking Websites When Offline Sexual Assault of Minors Follows Online Interaction' (2007) (14) *Villanova Sports & Entertainment Law Journal* 363 at 372.

80 JS Groppe, 'A Child's Playground or a Predator's Hunting Ground? – How to Protect Children on Internet Social Networking Sites' (2007) (16) *CommLaw Conspectus* 215 at 216.

81 Referred to in, for example, S Hetcher, 'User-Generated Content and the Future of Copyright: Part One – Investiture of Ownership' (2008) (10) *Vanderbilt Journal of Entertainment and Technology Law* 863 at 869.

82 Stedman, *op. cit*, 364.

of children surveyed were afraid of being contacted by strangers online.[83] Policy makers have sometimes been criticised for acting slowly to address these problems.[84] The UK National Society for the Prevention of Cruelty to Children (NSPCC) in a 2013 survey found that one in five children have been the victims of cyberbullying, and also note that significant numbers of children under the age of 13 are members of SM and related websites.[85]

2.8.1 Child concerns online and on SNs

Reid refers to the issues of protecting children online,

'The twenty-first century generation are the first to grow up completely immersed in the information technology age. They are growing up in an era of ubiquitous and pervasive, mobile computing and 24/7 online connectivity and communication. Their world is interactive, interconnected and instantaneous. They use information technology to play games, to learn about the world around them and for social interaction and to generally furthering their personal development through defining, refining and expressing their personal preferences. Thus, mobile information technology offers limitless opportunities but also many pitfalls for the unwary user, especially young adopters of the technology. Young people are naturally inquisitive and enthusiastic adopters of new technology, thus the trend of information technology use by children and young persons is likely to exponentially increase.

The dangers that manifest themselves in children's and young people's use of online services are well-documented and can be conveniently grouped into three broad classifications: Content, Contract and Commerce. These dangers include, but are not limited to: sexual grooming and contact with strangers; exposure to pornography and other harmful content, such as hate [web]sites, pro-anorexia and pro-suicide [web]sites, cyber-bullying and harassment; advertising and increased financial pressure and online liability, for example misuse of intellectual property and publishing defamatory statements online, through the use of peer-2-peer services, social network [web]sites and the creation of user-generated content'.[86]

---

83 Referred to in A Healy, '73% of Children Fear Internet Strangers – Survey', *Irish Times*, 8 February 2010, available at http://irishtimes.com/newspaper/ireland/2010/0208/1224263954466.html. Survey total N=860 children in 37 schools aged 9–16. Survey published by the National Centre for Technology in education. EU Safer Internet Day occurs on 9 February each year.
84 Groppe, *op. cit*, 216.
85 'One in Five Children in UK Victim of Cyberbullying: Survey', *Times of India* 12 August 2013. Also note U Schrott, 'High Cybercrime Levels and Worrying Youth Cyber-bullying, Latest Irish Survey Shows' *ESET Ireland* 4 April 2013 available at http://blog.eset.ie/2013/04/04/high-cybercrime-levels-and-worrying-youth-cyber-bullying-latest-irish-survey-shows/.
86 AS Reid, 'Online Protection of the Child Within Europe' (2009) (23) *International Review of Law Computers & Technology* 217.

However, despite the enhanced dangers for children and younger people, there is no additional protection in the 1995 Data Protection Directive.[87] While protecting personal data, the Directive does not explicitly refer to or address children's personal data[88] or the risk of solicitation. In contrast, the US enacted the Child Online Privacy Protection Act 2000 (COPPA)[89] in order to address some of these issues.[90] In one case a company was fined $1 million for breaches when it collected children's personal data[91] in contravention of the Act. However, the effectiveness of the legislation has also been queried.[92] There is increasingly commentary, research and even acknowledgements from service providers that significant numbers of users are under the age of 13.

Further concerns relate to the SNs themselves, and in particular in relation to what responsibility they have or should have. Are they legally responsible for third-party actions and comments? Many would suggest that they need to share at least some of the responsibility for child protection, including some liability. There are many policy reasons, however, for suggesting that they should not. Indeed, the most developed arguments in relation to intermediary and website liability relates to the European eCommerce Directive[93] and the US Digital Millennium Copyright Act.[94] These types of laws recognise that websites and intermediaries should have lesser liability in relation to third-party content transmitted via their services. Despite the copyright jurisprudence and intermediary defences, there have been some attempts to fix liability for child sex predators on SM. For example, MySpace was sued, unsuccessfully, when a rapist was introduced to a child via its social network.[95] However, this area will continue to receive attention, given the controversial nature of the issues.[96]

---

87 Ibid, 218.
88 E Bartoli, 'Children's Data Protection vs Marketing Companies' (March–July 2009) (23) *International Review of Law Computers & Technology* 35 at 36.
89 Children's Online Privacy Protection Act 15 USC S 6501(1) (2000).
90 DH Montes, 'Living Our Lives Online: The Privacy Implications of Online Social Networking' (2010) (5) *I/S: A Journal of Law and Policy* 507 at 509 *et seq*.
91 Press Release, Federal Trade Commission, 'Xanga.com to Pay $1 Million for Violating Children's Online Privacy Protection Rule' (7 September 2006) available at www.ftc.gov/news-events/press-releases/2006/09/xangacom-pay-1-million-violating-childrens-online-privacy.
92 LA Matecki, 'Update: COPPA is Ineffective Legislation! Next Steps for Protecting Youth Privacy Rights in the Social Networking Era' (2010) *Northwestern Journal of Law and Social Policy* 369. Generally, see also D Levine, 'Facebook and Social Networks: the Government's Newest Playground for Information and the Laws that Haven't Quite Kept Pace' (2011) *Hastings Communications & Entertainment Law Journal* 481.
93 Directive 2000/31/EC on Electronic Commerce.
94 Digital Millennium Copyright Act 1998. Note also US Communications Decency Act 1996.
95 *Doe v MySpace Inc* No D-1-GN-06-002209, 1 (District Court of Travis County Texas, filed 19 June 2006), as referred to in Stedman, *op. cit*, 364 and note 8 at 364.
96 On defence issues generally, note, for example, C Marsden, 'Network Neutrality and Internet Service Provider Liability Regulation: Are the Wise Monkeys of Cyberspace Becoming Stupid?' Global Policy (2011) (2(1)) 1–14.

2.8.2   Sexual exploitation

Sexual exploitation facilitated by SM is a grave concern, as is indicated above. Children can be befriended by third-party adults with less than innocent intentions. Sexual predators use SM to make contact with children, to profile children and even to make arrangements to meet children in actuality.

2.8.3   Harmful content

A further issue is harmful content. Adults are concerned that children may access or have sexually related content, both accidentally and otherwise. One problem is that harmful SN content may or may not be illegal.[97] Criminal laws must always be drafted with certainty and specificity in mind. Therefore, new technological problems may not always be covered sufficiently in criminal law. How should we define 'harmful' content? There is significant disagreement as to what constitutes harmful content.[98] Problems also arise in defining 'inappropriate' content and in dealing with it.[99]

Some of those affected can be children who are deliberately targeted. Other material, however, may be aimed generally at adults, or adults and children. In some instances, children or young persons can deliberately or accidentally access particular inappropriate content.

2.8.4   Cyberbullying

Cyberbullying is also a worrying problem.[100] 'Cyberbullying is a form of online harassment that may be accomplished through the posting of cruel or even threatening messages online. Unlike cyber-harassment or cyber-stalking, which involves adults, cyberbullying involves minors on both sides of the harassment'.[101] There is also the associated issue of text bullying, which can often go hand in hand with online bullying.

The Lori Drew case provides a graphic example. In this case an adult pretended to be a younger person and befriended an acquaintance of one of her children. She set up a false profile to contact the 13-year-old. This resulted in a stream of communications. A final message from the adult to the 13-year-old stated

---

97   Reid, *op. cit*, 220.
98   Ibid, 221.
99   Ibid. This also occurs in relation to video and film classification, despite attempts at consensus. See ibid. In *Dynamic Medien*, case C–244/06 [2008] ECR I-505, the ECJ held that Germany was able to restrict the import of games not bearing the German rating system ratings. Referred to ibid, 221. This ultimately led to the Audio Visual Directive, Directive 2007/65. See ibid, 212.
100 U Munukutla-Parker, 'Unsolicited Commercial Email, Privacy Concerns Relating to Social Network Services, Online Protection of Children, and Cyberbullying' (2006) (2) *I/S: A Journal of Law and Policy* 627 at 644–550.
101 Ibid, 628.

that '[t]he world would be a better place without you'.[102] The 13-year-old soon afterwards hanged herself.[103] There is also the much-publicised case of Phoebe Prince, an Irish girl being bullied in school when her family moved to the US. While some activity was physical, much centred on SM, apparently even after she died.[104] There have been a number of convictions. Prime Minister Cameron has also pushed service providers to do more to deal with child pornography and separately commented upon 'vile' cyberbullying websites.

2.8.5   Children and advertising

In addition to harmful-type dangers, there are also what Reid refers to as the 'commercial dangers',[105] such as advertising, marketing, spam, profiling and targeting. Children are particularly vulnerable to advertising, marketing and profiling. In addition, they are deliberately enticed with 'free' games and tokens.[106] Sometimes,

> 'children are ready to give away their personal data in exchange for a present illustrates the fact that children tend to consider their immediate interest rather than their long term interest. Children are not mature enough to have the skills to defend themselves against the dangers that the internet may present for privacy'.[107]

Increased awareness and promotion of child safety issues online is welcome generally,[108] including marketing, advertising and profiling activities.

From a data protection perspective, queries arise in relation to if, and when, children are able to consent to particular online policies and terms and conditions, and then to the further collection of their preferences, activity histories, etc. What should the minimum sign-up age be for children on SM? What responsibilities do SNs have? Should the responsibilities and the level of transparency and consent be higher for children on SM than adults?

Children as well as adults can be the recipients of spam or unsolicited direct marketing communications. Spam or unsolicited commercial communications 'refers to the dissemination of identical email advertisements to thousands or more recipients'.[109] It is unsolicited, often involves and infringes data protection rights, and takes up considerable bandwidth. Children are less informed and less mature than adults. While greater care should be afforded in terms of

---

102 Montes, *op. cit*, 513–519.
103 Ibid.
104 A Drew, 'Bully Writes "Accomplished" on Phoebe Prince's Facebook Page on Day of Death', 2 April 2010, available at www.irishcentral.com/news/Bully-writes-accomplished-on-Phoebe-Princes-Facebook-page-on-day-of-death-89764722.html.
105 Reid, *op. cit*, 224.
106 Bartoli, *op. cit*, 35–36.
107 Ibid, 37.
108 Groppe, *op. cit*, 242–248.
109 Munukutla-Parker, *op. cit*, 627.

advertising and marketing, where should the line be drawn? What should the obligations be?

These are difficult issues to address. US Congress responded to the problem with the CAN-SPAM Act 2003, as have most US states with local legislation of one sort or another. It is enforced on a practical level by the Federal Trade Commission (FTC) and Department of Justice.[110] In Europe, the Data Protection Directive 1995 does not expressly refer to children. The proposed EU Data Protection Regulation does refer to children.[111]

2.8.6 UK

The UK Information Commissioner issued a good practice guide in relation to the taking of photographs in schools.[112] SM is not expressly addressed, but similar considerations could well be expanded or interpreted to encompass the use of SM in, and in relation to, schools.

Some aspects of the above UK guide do appear to be relevant. Consider, for example, how easy it is to take photographs on a mobile phone and post them on SM such as Facebook or Bebo. The guide refers to 'videophones in schools' and states,

'Schools can play a crucial role in setting out precautions for the use of MMS, audio and video recording where personal data referring to third parties are involved, without the data subjects' being aware of it. Schools should warn their students that unrestrained circulation of video recordings, audio recordings and digital pictures can result in serious infringements of the data subjects' right to privacy and personal data protection'.[113]

It also states that the Data Protection Directive 1995 should be interpreted in line with children's rights and international children's law.[114] It concludes with the following statement,

'The role of data protection authorities is four-fold: to educate and inform, especially children and authorities responsible for the well-being of young people; to influence policy makers to make the right decisions as regards children and privacy; to make controllers aware of their duties; and to use their powers against those who disregard legislation or do not adhere to codes of conduct or best practice in this area.

---

110 Ibid, 629.
111 It also remains to be seen if a recent constitutional referendum in Ireland may also affect these considerations, albeit not originally considered at the time of the referendum itself.
112 Information Commissioner, *Data Protection Good Practice Note: Taking Photographs in Schools*, 1 December 2005.
113 *Opinion 2/2009 on the Protection of Children's Personal Data (General Guidelines and the Special Case of Schools)*, Article 29 Data Protection Working Party, 398/09/EN, WP 160, Adopted on 11 February 2009 at 18.
114 Ibid, 18–19.

An effective strategy, in this context, can be the formulation of agreements between DPAs, Ministries of Education and other responsible bodies, defining clear and practical terms of mutual cooperation in this area to foster the notion that data protection is a fundamental right.

Children should be made aware, in particular, that they themselves must be the primary protectors of their personal data. According to this criterion, the gradual participation of children in the protection of their personal data (from consultation to decision) should be made effective. This is an area where the effectiveness of empowerment can be demonstrated'.[115]

Hart discusses the UK Information Commissioner's good practice note on the collection of personal data by websites. He states,

'The Note also deals with Web sites directed at children. It points out that Web sites that collect information from children must have stronger safeguards in place to ensure any processing is fair. Privacy notices must be appropriate to the child's level and should not exploit any lack of understanding. The language used should be clear and appropriate to the age group the Web site is aimed at. It will often be necessary to seek verifiable consent from a parent. A child is generally considered to be a person aged 16 or under, but there is a general requirement not to use information from children under 12 without first obtaining the permission of a parent or guardian. Parental consent must be verified. It will not usually be enough to ask children to confirm that their parents have agreed by using a mouse click. The ICO goes as far as to say that if parental consent is required but verifying the consent would involve a disproportionate effort then the proposed activity should not be carried out'.[116]

The UK Direct Marketing Association[117] also has a Code of Practice for Commercial Communications to Children Online. While the Irish Direct Marketing Association has various separate guidelines, including in relation to data protection, email marketing, etc, there is apparently none yet dedicated to children.[118]

2.8.7   *Ireland*

The Irish Data Protection Commissioner has had to deal with complaints in relation to direct marketing to Irish schoolchildren.[119] He does not appear to

---

115 Ibid, 20.
116 H Hart, 'Collecting Personal Information Using Web Sites', *Society of Computers and Law*, 2 July 2007, available at www.scl.org/site.aspx?i=ed979.
117 At www.dma.org.uk.
118 Irish Direct Marketing Association, see guides at www.idma.ie/guidelines.html.
119 Case Study 10/2004, Bank of Ireland Marketing of 12 and 13 Year Old School Children, available at www.dataprotection.ie/docs/Case_study_10/04_-_Bank_of_Ireland_marketing_of_12_and_13_ye/269.htm.

have any specific guide dealing with data protection and children's SM in relation to schools. He does, however, have a guide in relation to biometrics in educational institutions.[120] There is also a special 'tool' resource for schools.[121]

The Irish Data Protection Commissioner's website states the following,

'The data protection issues relate to consent (particularly if the person is under 14) for the processing of their information and the right of an individual to seek blocking of any personal data in relation to them that is incorrect or that was placed on the [web]site without their consent. This might be a picture of a teacher perhaps taken in a classroom context without their knowledge or factual statements that are false in relation to a person. The powers of the Office do not extend to material that is offensive, pornographic or just simply defamatory. However, such abuses require the same response on the part of the websites in question and that is an effective complaints mechanism that is appropriately staffed with trained personnel who can respond quickly to the issues raised'.[122]

2.8.8   EU Article 29 Working Party Opinion 2/2009

Opinion 2/2009 of the EU Article 29 Working Party (WP29)[123] is one of the few official references to children and data protection. It is limited specifically to the uses of children's personal data in a school and educational setting, which it refers to as 'school data'.[124] One will recall that the Data Protection Directive 1995 does not explicitly refer to or acknowledge children's rights. It refers, however, to a separate EU initiative[125] from the EU Commission, *Towards an EU Strategy on the Rights of the Child.*

Opinion 2/2009 also states, in relation to the children's right to participate,

'Children gradually become capable of contributing to decisions made about them. As they grow, they should participate more regularly about the exercise of their rights, including those relating to data protection.

The first level of this right is the right to be consulted.

This duty of consultation consists of taking into account – though not necessarily submitting to – the child's own opinions.

---

120 *Biometrics in Schools, Colleges and Other Educational Institutions*, available at www.dataprotection.ie/viewdoc.asp?DocID=409&ad=1.

121 Available at www.dataprotection.ie/docs/Training_and_Public_Awareness/805.htm.

122 '1.6 Do Data Protection Requirements Apply to Material Placed on Social Networking Sites?', available at www.dataprotection.ie/viewdoc.asp?DocID=592.

123 *Opinion 2/2009 on the Protection of Children's Personal Data (General Guidelines and the Special Case of Schools)*, Article 29 Data Protection Working Party, 398/09/EN, WP 160, Adopted on 11 February 2009.

124 Ibid, 2.

125 Ibid.

But when children attain adequate capacity, their participation can increase, even resulting in a joint or autonomous decision.

The right to participate can apply to various different matters, such as geolocation, use of children's images or others'.[126]

The EU data protection regime, comprising the Data Protection Directive 1995 and ePrivacy Directive,[127] does not explicitly mention the privacy or data protection rights of the child.[128] While now included for the first time in the proposed EU Data Protection Regulation, it remains to be seen how this will be fully addressed in the final version.

In terms of fulfilling the privacy rights of children, the,

'data protection needs of children must take into account two important aspects. These are, firstly, the varying levels of maturity which determine when children can start dealing with their own data and, secondly, the extent to which representatives have the right to represent minors in cases where the disclosure of personal data would prejudice the best interests of the child. The following will deal with the question of how the existing rules of the Directive could best be applied to ensure that children's privacy is adequately and effectively protected'.[129]

In terms of ensuring transparency and the right of data subjects to be informed (of data collection, data processing and the nature of the data itself), and in particular children and/or their representatives,

'special emphasis should be put on giving layered notices based on the use of simple, concise and educational language that can be easily understood. A shorter notice should contain the basic information to be provided when collecting personal data either directly from the data subject or from a third party (Article 10 and 11). This should be accompanied by a more detailed notice, perhaps via a hyperlink, where all the relevant details are provided'.[130]

These series of notices and 'information must (always) be given to the legal representatives, and, after attaining adequate capacity, also to the child'.[131]

However, one can envisage issues arising in relation to SM and children's internet use. Indeed, it should be recalled that Opinion 2/2009 does not deal with SM generally or SM of children.

---

126 Ibid, 5.
127 Directive 2002/58/EC.
128 *Opinion 2/2009 on the Protection of Children's Personal Data (General Guidelines and the Special Case of Schools)*, Article 29 Data Protection Working Party, 398/09/EN, WP 160, Adopted on 11 February 2009, at 7.
129 Ibid, 5.
130 Ibid, 10.
131 Ibid, 10.

The Opinion acknowledges that '[s]pecial requirements are applicable to information posted online'.[132] It adds,

'As the Working Party has noted in its recommendation about online data processing, it is fundamental for the notices to be posted at the right place and time – ie they should be shown directly on the screen, prior to collecting the information. As well as being a requirement under the Directive, this is especially important as a tool to raise children's awareness of the possible risks and dangers arising out of online activities. Indeed, it might be argued that in the online environment, unlike in the real world, this is the only opportunity for children to be appraised of such dangers'.[133]

It is noted that Opinion 2/2009 is primarily in relation to the use of children's personal data *by* schools. It does not set out to address the concerns of children's SM – whether at school, at home or elsewhere. Only subsequently does it say,

'A special problem concerns the publication of school results on the internet, which is a convenient way of communicating them to the interested persons. The risks inherent in this mode of communication demand that access to the data should only be possible with special safeguards. This might be achieved by using a secure website, or personal passwords assigned to the legal representatives or, when they are already mature, to the children'.[134]

The Article 29 Working Party (WP29) recognises that children have a right to non-surveillance via CCTV in the classroom (possibly from teachers, supervisors or parents online). It notes that,

'in classrooms, … video surveillance can interfere not only with students' freedom of learning and of speech, but also with the freedom of teaching. The same applies to leisure areas, gymnasiums and dressing rooms, where surveillance can interfere with rights to privacy.

These remarks are also based on the right to the development of the personality, which all children have. Indeed, their developing conception of their own freedom can become compromised if they assume from an early age that it is normal to be monitored by CCTV. This is all the more true if webcams or similar devices are used for distance monitoring of children during school time'.[135]

In relation to school websites, it states,

'A growing number of schools create websites targeted at students/pupils and their families, and those websites become the main tool for external communications. Schools should be aware that disseminating personal

---

132 Ibid, 10.
133 Ibid, 10.
134 Ibid, 14.
135 Ibid, 16.

information warrants more stringent observance of fundamental data protection principles, in particular data minimisation and proportionality; additionally, it is recommended that restricted access mechanisms are implemented with a view to safeguarding the personal information in question (eg login via user ID and password)'.[136]

In a related section dealing with children's photographs, it states,

'Schools are often tempted to publish (in the press or on the internet) photos of their pupils. Special attention should be drawn to the publishing by schools of photos of their pupils on the internet. An evaluation should always be made of the kind of photo, the relevance of posting it, and its intended purpose. Children and their legal representatives should be made aware of the publication.

If the school intends to post individual photographs of identified children, prior consent from parents or other legal representatives (or from the child, if already mature) should be obtained.

In the case of collective photos, namely of schools events, and always in accordance with national legislation, schools might not require prior consent from the parents where the photographs do not permit easy identification of pupils. Nevertheless, in such cases schools must inform children, parents and legal representatives that the photograph is going to be taken and how it will be used.

This will give them the opportunity to refuse to be included in the photograph'.[137]

Children's SM, both in the school environment and generally, needs to be considered further, particularly in light of recent tragic events.

2.8.9 Children: Consent and EU Article 29 Working Party Opinion 2/2010

Opinion 2/2010 of the EU Article 29 Working Party refers to consent in relation to children, SM and behavioural advertising. The Opinion states,

'Informed consent: children

In Opinion 2/2009 the EU Article 29 Working Party has addressed the protection of personal data of children. The problems related to obtaining informed consent are further emphasized as far as children are concerned. In addition to the requirements described above (and below) for consent to be valid, in some cases children's consent must be provided by their parents or other legal representatives. In the case in point this means that

---

136 Ibid, 17.
137 Ibid, 17.

ad network providers would need to provide notice to parents about the collection and the use of children's information and obtain their consent before collecting and further using their information for the purposes of engaging in behavioural targeting of children.

In the light of the above and also taking into account the vulnerability of children, the EU Article 29 Working Party is of the view that ad network providers should not offer interest categories intended to serve behavioural advertising or influence children'.[138]

2.8.10   Children: EU Article 29 Working Party Opinion 5/2009

Opinion 5/2009 of the EU Article 29 Working Party on Online SN refers to children, minors and SM. It sets out the environmental context and the options available. It states,

'A large proportion of SNS services [SN services] are utilised by children/ minors. The Working Party's Opinion WP147 focused on the application of data protection principles in the school and educational environment. The Opinion emphasised the need for taking into account the best interest of the child as also set out in the UN Convention on the Rights of the Child. The Working Party wishes to stress the importance of this principle also in the context of SNS.

Some interesting initiatives have been undertaken by Data Protection Authorities world wide which focus mostly on awareness-raising regarding SNS and possible risks. The Working Party encourages further research on how to address the difficulties surrounding adequate age verification and proof of informed consent in order to better address these challenges.

Based on the considerations made so far, the Working Party believes that a multi-pronged strategy would be appropriate to address the protection of children's data in the SNS context. Such a strategy might be based on:

– awareness raising initiatives, which are fundamental to ensure the active involvement of children (via schools, the inclusion of DP-basics in educational curricula, the creation of ad-hoc educational tools, the collaboration of national competent bodies);

– fair and lawful processing with regard to minors such as not asking for sensitive data in the subscription forms, no direct marketing aimed specifically at minors, the prior consent of parents before subscribing, and suitable degrees of logical separation between the communities of children and adults;

---

138 *Opinion 2/2010 on Online Behavioural Advertising*, Article 29 Data Protection Working Party, WP 171, Adopted on 22 June 2010.

- implementation of Privacy Enhancing Technologies (PETs) – eg privacy-friendly settings by default, pop-up warning boxes at appropriate steps, age verification software);

- self-regulation by providers, to encourage the adoption of codes of practice that should be equipped with effective enforcement measures, also disciplinary in nature;

- if necessary, ad-hoc legislative measures to discourage unfair and/or deceptive practices in the SNS context'.[139]

2.8.11   Children: problems with the Data Protection Directive

There is no express reference to children in the Data Protection Directive 1995. It is as if children were not even in contemplation when the main EU data protection measure was being drafted. Commenting in relation to the prior information and consent requirements specified in the Data Protection Directive 1995,[140] it has been queried,

'[How] are children expected to understand the likely implications for them of providing their data? How can they judge whether the data collection process is in their best interests? To this extent the requirement to inform websites' users before collecting any personal data is not relevant as it stands if applied to children's personal data. It should at least be specified that web users are to inform their users in terms understandable by any class of age'.[141]

One of the rights provided in Article 12 of the Data Protection Directive 1995 is a right of access by the data subject to the data held by the data controller (eg websites) in relation to them. This should also apply equally to children. However, is this access right given to the child directly or to their parent?[142] Or indeed a guardian? A further complication is the line and balance between a child's privacy rights in relation to his or her parent.[143] Can children have an overriding interest over and above that of the parents in the details of their online activities, including their personal data held by SNs?

Also, with spyware (filtering/monitoring) software being installed by parents on the computer devices being used by their children, the issue of free speech, children's rights, children's privacy and data protection rights and proportionality will need to be considered. Consider, for example, whether

---

139 *Opinion 5/2009 on Online Social Networking*, Article 29 Data Protection Working Party, 011189/09EN, WP 163. Adopted on 12 June 2009, at 11–12.

140 Directive 95/46/EC of the European Parliament and of the Council of 24 October 1995 on the protection of individuals with regard to the processing of personal data and on the free movement of such data.

141 Bartoli, *op. cit*, 40.

142 Ibid.

143 Ibid, 40–41.

it may be more proportionate for a parent to ensure that a child uses a laptop, for example, only while in the kitchen or living room, as opposed to installing spyware monitoring software if he or she were to be permitted to use the laptop in the bedroom unsupervised. Which is more proportionate? Is installing blocking and filtering software (and availing of device and internet browser settings) a more graduated and proportionate response? Is one to be preferred under the data protection regime? It is also queried how effective the provisions in relation to unsolicited commercial communications are as regards children. '[H]ow can one expect [that] a child [is] mature enough to [understand and] request ... not to have his/her personal data used to receive unsolicited mail?'[144] If children decide to assert or claim rights, there is clearly potential for some difficult court litigation.

2.8.12 EU Commission: no children in data protection

The EU Commission recognises the threats and issues raised by children's SM and has stated that it will 'consider ... introducing specific obligations for data controllers on the type of information to be provided and on the modalities for providing it, including in relation to children'.[145] It will also consider introducing standard data protection notification forms for data controllers and also a framework for breach notifications.[146]

One of the proposals in the Data Protection Regulation is to allow the EU Commission to specify and introduce more specific measures or related acts pursuant to the Regulation, once passed.

There are, however, other measures to consider. The Lisbon Treaty expressly recognises children's rights in Article 2.3. The EU Charter also refers to the protection of children's data.[147] The 1981 Council of Europe Convention Concerning the Processing of Personal Data refers to children's data privacy concerns. The 2001 Council of Europe Convention on Cybercrime incorporates a criminal offence in relation to the production of child pornography.[148] In addition, the 2004 EU Framework Decision on combating the sexual exploitation of children and child pornography creates offences in relation to child pornography.[149] It has been indicated that this decision also attaches

---

144 Ibid, 41.
145 Communication from the Commission to the European Parliament, the Council, the Economic and Social Committee of the Regions, A Comprehensive Approach on Personal Data Protection in the European Union, 4 November 2010, COM (2010) 609 Final, 6.
146 Ibid, 6–7.
147 Article 24 of the EU Charter of Fundamental Rights of the European Union provides that a child's best interests must be a primary consideration and that children shall have the right to such protection and may express their views freely.
148 Referred to in Reid, *op. cit*, 218.
149 Framework Decision 2004/68 on combating the sexual exploitation of children and child pornography [2004] OJ L13/44. Referred to ibid. This may even be updated under proposals made by the Commission, see ibid, 220.

liability to websites 'who directly allow sexually explicit material to be made available to young persons'.[150] Corporate liability can also arise under the 2001 Convention.[151]

2.8.13   US responses to children

One study, which was commissioned in advance of the Children's Online Privacy Protection Act 1998 (COPPA), suggested that, of the 212 websites targeted at children which were examined, 89 per cent gathered children's personal data, 12 per cent notified parents of their data collection activities, and the majority disclosed personal data obtained to third parties.[152] There may be a need for more research, including in the EU and the US.

The first US effort to deal with these concerns was the Communications Decency Act 1996 (CDA).[153] This was held, however, to be an overbroad infringement of free-speech rights in the case *Reno v ACLU*.[154] The balancing of competing constitutional rights is always a difficult exercise.

The second US effort in relation to this area was the COPPA. The Child Pornography Prevention Act 1996 (CPPA) was also enacted, although the Supreme Court held that it too was overly broad.[155]

The US Children's Internet Protection Act 2000 requires schools and libraries to install pornography-filtering software.[156] Liberties groups have raised free-speech concerns in relation to many library restrictions.

The US Adam Walsh Child Protection and Safety Act 2006 provides for a public national register of sex offenders.[157] John McCain also proposed legislation enhancing reporting obligations on websites.[158]

The COPPA, and the rules established by the FTC pursuant to it, make clear that they apply to websites targeting children.[159] The factors that will assist in determining this include,

---

150 Reid, *op. cit*, 218.
151 Article 26. Referred to ibid, 219. We also wait to see how the constitutional referendum dealing with constitutional children's rights in Ireland may also affect these issues.
152 *Privacy: A Report to Congress*, Federal Trade Commission, June 1998, previously available at www.ftc.gov/reports/privacy3/priv-23c.pdf; now available at www.ftc.gov/sites/default/files/documents/reports/implementing-childrens-online-privacy-protection-act-federal-trade-commission-report-congress/07coppa_report_to_congress.pdf. Referred to in Bartoli, *op. cit*, 37.
153 Groppe, *op. cit*, 229.
154 *Reno v ACLU* 521 US 844 (1997), referred to in Groppe, *op. cit*, 229.
155 See *Ashcroft v Free Speech Coalition* 535 US 234, 240 (2002), referred to in Groppe, *op. cit*, 220.
156 Groppe, *op. cit*, 224–225 and 231–233.
157 Ibid, 235–236.
158 The Stop the Online Exploitation of Our Children Act 2006, referred to in Groppe, *op. cit*, 236.
159 Bartoli, *op. cit*, 37–38.

- the website subject matter;
- the audio or visual content on the website;
- the age of models on the website;
- the website language;
- whether there is advertising on the website; and
- other empirical evidence relating to the age of actual or intended users, including the use of animated characters or child-orientated features.[160]

The COPPA rules also set the age threshold for children at 13. However, one commentator questions the plausibility of websites being able to know and verify this in practice.[161] A further difficulty raised is the importance of whether the website must be targeted solely at children under 13.[162] What happens if there is a mixed-age audience? There may also be so-called general websites, which do not target children but which have users who are children.[163] Children may also provide false information, including a false age.[164] This is a difficult practical issue.

One commentator states, in the context of COPPA, that 'research indicates that children are willing to trade away personal information for speculative reasons – for instance in order to win a prize or to enter a contest. This suggests that many young people do not care about privacy'.[165]

The US federal approaches seek to restrict the download of inappropriate content for children as well as the uploading of impermissible material by children.[166] There have been at least two state efforts to establish 'controversial' registers of children's email addresses.[167]

There are also a number of local state laws in the US, apart from federal initiatives. An example is a law in New York, the Electronic Security and Targeting of Online Predators Act (eSTOP Act), which seeks to oblige registered sex offenders to also register all of their email accounts and identifiers, including SM details, with the New York State Division of Criminal Justice.[168] Then these details will be passed to SM websites to screen, block and remove them from these websites.[169] It remains to be seen how these measures may deal with possible constitutional challenges.

---

160 Ibid, 38.
161 Ibid, 38.
162 Ibid, 38.
163 Ibid, 38–39.
164 Ibid, 38.
165 Ibid, 39.
166 Munukutla-Parker, *op. cit*, 641.
167 Referred to ibid, 641.
168 M Morrissey, 'Legislative Update: Banning Sex Offenders from Using Social Networking Websites' (2008) (28) *Children's Legal Rights Journal* 89 at 90.
169 Ibid.

2.8.14   Children and commercial matter

There is other potentially relevant legislation that can affect the commercial matters and transactions that children might engage with. One example is the Unfair Commercial Practices Directive.[170] Commenting on the Directive, Reid states,

> '[i]n the case of vulnerable consumers, the threshold at which a practice becomes unfair is significantly lower than that for the average consumer, thus it is essential that not only is significant information about the products and services offered to the young person but that that information is as clear, accessible and understandable as possible. Information provided to young children must be communicated to them in easy to read, comprehensible language, rather than in small print legalese, to enable these rights to be meaningful and indeed to avoid legal action'.[171]

2.8.15   UN Convention on the Rights of the Child

The UN Convention on the Rights of the Child[172] sets out special protection and entitlements in relation to children. Article 1 of the Convention states that a child is someone under the age of 18, as do 'most relevant international instruments'.[173] The most fundamental interests in relation to children and children's rights include,

- the best interests of the child;
- protection and care necessary for the wellbeing of the child;
- privacy rights and interests;
- representation;
- balancing privacy and best interests of the child;
- adapting to the degree of maturity of the child; and
- the right to participate.[174]

In relation to privacy, it refers to the right of a child as a human being to have privacy; in particular, Article 16 of the Convention provides that no child shall be subject to arbitrary or unlawful interference with his or her privacy,

---

170 See also Reid, *op. cit*, 224.

171 Generally, see comments of Reid, *op. cit*, 225.

172 Convention on the Rights of the Child, United Nations, adopted General Assembly Resolution 44/25 on 20 November 1989. Referred to in Bartoli, *op. cit*, 37.

173 *Opinion 2/2009 on the Protection of Children's Personal Data (General Guidelines and the Special Case of Schools)*, Article 29 Data Protection Working Party, 398/09/EN, WP 160, Adopted on 11 February 2009, at 3, and references therein.

174 Ibid, 4–7.

family, home or correspondence, or to unlawful attacks on his or her honour and reputation.[175]

2.8.16   Hotlines

The solutions to deal with these concerns can be legal, but they can also involve forms of self-regulation and co-regulation. Examples include internet hotlines. The International Association of Internet Hotlines, Inhope, for example, promotes internet hotlines so that people can alert appropriate agencies and complain when they are concerned in relation to particular online material aimed at or relating to children.[176]

Technology solutions also exist, such as forms of filtering and blocking technology. Software keyword filtering systems block or raise alerts for particular content. There is no fail-safe solution, however. Filtering technologies, etc are not without their own issues. They can be subject to errors and false positives. They are sometimes criticised in that they unjustly interfere with normal commercial activities.[177] Legal issues also surround the competing legal rights. Notwithstanding that, the EU Safer Internet programme 2009–2013 calls for the use of more filtering technologies.[178]

Spyware and its compliance with the data protection regime when used in relation to children, as well as any future enumerated children's constitutional rights, have yet to be fully considered.

Self-regulation by industry is reported to have a number of successes, such as the MySpace software reporting application Zephyr[179] and the Sentinel Safe software, which bans sex offenders from the website.[180] The issue of banning convicted sex offenders is gaining popularity in certain quarters in the US. A question arises as to whether SM and related websites can act to ban convicted or (certain) registered sex offenders only once mandated or required to do so by a specific law or court order. Can industry access and act on registered sex offender lists voluntarily? Can they be mandated to? Under what circumstances can they access registered sex offender lists? As the concepts of internet rights and rights of access to the internet increasingly come to the fore, to what extent will defendants' or convicted persons' rights of access to the internet have to be balanced against other competing rights?

---

175 We await how the constitutional referendum developments regarding children in Ireland may be interpreted in the internet arena.
176 See www.inhope.org.
177 Munukutla-Parker, *op. cit*, 221.
178 Referred to ibid.
179 See Groppe, *op. cit*, 237–240.
180 Ibid, 239.

2.8.17 Age verification

One of the proposed solutions refers to chat and discussion board moderation. This involves people actually examining and vetting the content of communications online. Another solution involves developing age-verification software.[181] However, there are issues with proposed suggestions for children's age-verification systems. While adults (and students) can verify their age, it is quite difficult for a child to prove their age.[182] Other alternatives are design related, for example, having children pass a series of knowledge questions online.[183]

There have been unsuccessful attempts to force SNs to implement age-verification systems.[184] However, the Communications Decency Act 1996 in the US affords some protection to these websites by providing defences for third-party materials.

2.8.18 Age and website rules/settings

Both Facebook and MySpace have minimum age restrictions of 13.[185] However, there are significant numbers of under-age users of SM generally.[186]

MySpace is reported as requiring a click agreement from users that they are at least 14 years old.[187] There have also been calls to have stricter default privacy settings for those under 16 years of age.[188] Subsequent protections were introduced whereby an adult must be able to provide details of a person under 16 before being able to contact them and must already be that person's friend on MySpace.[189] That is, there must be some prior context or connection.

2.8.19 Age and technology solutions

Some might suggest that any solution involving technology should be the least expensive.[190] Various website access options can be triggered once a person keys in his or her date of birth. These can include blocking access or guiding the child through a course on safety awareness.[191] Of course, this

---

181 Ibid, 221.
182 Stedman, *op. cit*, 394–395.
183 Ibid, 395.
184 See, for example, MD Martin and CV Popov, '*Doe v MySpace*: Liability for Third Party Content on Social Networking Sites' (Spring 2007) *Communications Law* at 3, referred to in Nelson *et al., op. cit*, 24. See also, F Gilbert, 'Age Verification as a Shield for Minors on the Internet: A Quixotic Search?' (2008) *Shilder Journal of Law Communications & Technology* 6.
185 Nelson, *et al., op. cit*, 24.
186 Ibid.
187 See Stedman, *op. cit*, 369–371, and references therein.
188 Ibid, 369–371, and references therein.
189 Ibid, 371.
190 Ibid, 397.
191 See ibid, 395.

on its own does not deal with people keying in a false age. However, tests and questions can also be added on to help limit under-age applicants for particular services.

2.8.20   Self-regulation/soft law

One avenue to consider is 'soft law' or regulation, which can involve a number of potential avenues.[192] An example is the UK Direct Marketing Association (DMA) Code of Practice for Commercial Communications to Children Online. In Ireland, for example, there is also the Irish Direct Marketing Association.[193]

Another solution relates to attempts to label and categorise children's content centrally, for example under the umbrella of a central generic descriptive .kid domain name.[194]

In 2009, MySpace removed 90,000 registered sex offenders from its website.[195] This is an example of websites banning or restricting access. This is clearly one possible solution. However, a number of legal as well as practical issues arise. For example, there is the increasing prospect of competing rights being litigated, with the arrival of the concept of a human right of access to the internet. Free-speech issues also arise.

The US has a number of (proposed or enacted) laws which seek directly or indirectly to deal with online sexual predators, such as: tort law; the Communications Decency Act 1996; the Children's Online Privacy Protection Act 1998 (COPPA); the Deleting Online Predators Act 2007; and state laws.[196] It has been argued that self-regulation is a better option.[197] Ultimately, it may be that hard law and soft law are needed in conjunction.

2.8.21   Regulation/liability

Can and should SNs be liable for third-party content? How do intermediary defences interact with privacy and data protection? There is insufficient research of this issue.

In *Doe v MySpace*[198] the plaintiff mother failed in claiming that MySpace was negligent in not preventing the communications of sexual predators. The court

---

192 Bartoli, *op. cit*, 35.
193 Irish Direct Marketing Association, see www.idma.ie/.
194 Reid, *op. cit*, 223–224.
195 Montes, *op. cit*, 513.
196 Referred to in van der Heide, 'Social Networking and Sexual Predators: The Case for Self-Regulation' (2008–2009) (31) *Hastings Communications & Entertainment Law Journal* 173 at 179–186.
197 Ibid, 187–191.
198 *Doe v MySpace Inc* 528 F.3d 413, 416 (5th Circuit 2008), referred to in Nelson *et al.*, *op. cit*, 24.

upheld the Communications Decency Act (CDA) immunities[199] and ruled that no duty towards users arose.[200] One court stated that imposing 'a duty under these circumstances for MySpace to confirm or determine the age of each applicant, with liability resulting from negligence in performing or not performing that duty, would of course stop MySpace's business in its tracks and close this avenue of communication'.[201] The CDA exemptions were also upheld in a case where the plaintiff complained of being introduced to an under-age person.[202] Section 30 of the CDA protects the SNs in terms of the defamatory statements of their users. In the case of a prank which went wrong and resulted in death threats, the victim unsuccessfully sued AOL for not taking the prank material down when notified.[203]

There is, however, increasing adverse publicity and pressure on SNs to be more proactive.[204] We now see that there can also be indirect pressure applied to advertisers. One law in Illinois, for example, bans registered sex offenders from using SM.[205] It remains to be seen whether such laws will withstand constitutional challenges.

2.8.22   Child education and awareness

There is increasing awareness of the importance of informing and educating children in relation to internet and SM issues. Education workshop talks are organised for children in schools in relation to internet safety and internet risks.[206] At an EU level, a report was published on 18 April 2011 in relation to children's SM issues and dangers, *Social Networking, Age and Privacy*, which compared comparative research issues across 25 countries.[207] It refers to some of the risks of SM for children, including pornography and sexual images,[208] bullying,[209] 'sexting',[210] meeting contacts offline,[211] sending and or receiving

---

199 *Doe v MySpace Inc* at 420.
200 *Doe v MySpace Inc* 474 F Supp 2d 843, 850–852 (WD Texas 2007), referred to in Nelson *et al.*, *op. cit*, 25.
201 *Doe v MySpace Inc* at 851, as referred to in Nelson *et al.*, *op. cit*, 25.
202 *Doe v Sexsearch.com* 502 F Supp 2d 719, 722 (ND Ohio 2007) 724.
203 Nelson *et al.*, *op. cit*, 25.
204 Ibid, 26.
205 HR 1314, 96th General Assembly, Reg Sessions (Illinois 2009) previously available at www.ilga.gov/legislation/96/HB/09600HB131enr.ht, referred to in Nelson *et al.*, *op. cit*, 26.
206 In Ireland, for example. See 'Safer Internet Day: Talks in Schools', National Centre for Technology in Education, available at http://ncte.ie/, referring to workshops organised for 2011.
207 Livingston *et al.*, *op. cit*. The report is substantial. See reference at Social Networking, Age and Privacy, referred to in EU Kids Online, previously available at www2.lse.ac.uk/media@lse/research/EUKidsOnline/Home.aspx. See also www.eukidsonline.net.
208 Ibid, 6, 49 *et seq.*
209 Ibid, 6, 61 *et seq.*
210 Ibid, 7.
211 Ibid, 7, 85 *et seq.*

sexual images and content,[212] potentially harmful user-generated content (UGC),[213] and misuse of personal data.[214]

2.8.23   The parent gap

One of the problems for many parents is that they are not technology aware and, therefore, are not in a position to assess for themselves the risks that face their children online. This has been referred to as the 'generational divide'.[215] Frequently, parents are not aware of children's (and teenagers') online activities.[216] Parents need to take responsibility in terms of becoming aware of what their children are doing and the technology they are using. However, part of this educational role must also rest with policy makers in assisting and educating parents. Parents must be assisted in keeping or becoming connected.[217]

2.8.24   Child development/child rights

It has been suggested that the number of under-age users of SM provides not just legal issues for SNs, but also moral issues.[218] There are also other issues to consider when we contemplate child protection and children's rights. One of these is the issue of how society should protect children's privacy but without adversely affecting or curtailing their development and learning.[219] What free speech and privacy rights do children possess, and against whom may these rights be enforced?[220] Do children's rights of free speech exist, and do children shed these rights when they go online?[221] These developing concerns are difficult and complex issues.

2.8.25   Child criminals

We often think of those who are infringing privacy and data protection as adults hacking, spamming or seeking to promote their sexual intentions, or as

---

212 Ibid, 73 *et seq.*
213 Ibid, 97–99.
214 Ibid, at 99.
215 Bartoli, *op. cit*, 36.
216 See, for example, Press Release, 'New Study Reveals 14% of Teens Have Had Face-to-Face Meetings With People They've Met on the Internet', National Centre for Missing & Exploited Children (11 May 2006) at http://us.missingkids.com/missingkids/servlet/NewsEventServlet ?LanguageCountry=en_US&PageId=2383, referred to in Stedman, *op. cit*, 373.
217 See generally K Bielenberg, 'Why Parents Must Stay Connected to their Children' *Irish Independent* 31 August 2013.
218 Nelson *et al.*, *op. cit*, 24.
219 Bartoli, *op. cit*, 35.
220 IG Cram 'Minors' Privacy and Freedom of Expression' in *Yearbook of Media and Entertainment Law* (Oxford University Press, Oxford, 1997), 31–52.
221 V Lei, 'Students' Free Speech Rights Shed at the Cyber Gate' (2009–2010) *Richmond Journal of Law & Technology* 1.

organisations, some of which are legitimate but lean a little too much in favour of direct marketing and advertising. However, we infrequently consider that children can commit crimes[222] and acts of infringement too. Children can be victims and perpetrators.[223] These can include a whole variety of activities that can impinge on SM, privacy and data protection.[224] This area gets infrequent attention in the literature and deserves further research. Most laws also fail to differentiate between adult and child perpetrators, include child pornography laws.[225] However, the nature of SM and its increasing popularity with children and young persons will most likely mean that there will be increasing instances of non-adults engaging in activity, such as making, posting or distributing material that on its face offends a specific law. Currently, most laws 'fail to adequately protect juveniles from the harsh penalties'.[226]

2.8.26   Children and defamation

There are already instances where both the parents and the child who made alleged defamatory comments have been sued.[227]

There have also been calls for specific amendments to defamation laws to provide a defence for defamatory statements made by children and juveniles. Such liability could follow them for the rest of their lives.[228] In addition, it is argued that younger people speak in a parlance that is not properly understood by adults[229] and is easily misunderstood by adults,[230] which needs to be acknowledged in defamation law. On this topic, Gurney writes,

> 'Woefully out-of-date defamation law needs to be fundamentally remodelled for an internet world where SN [web]sites dominate other online outlets, including blogs. True reform requires careful consideration of the variety of online speakers as well as their subjects, and of defamation defendants in addition to plaintiffs. Thoughtful change, rather than a quick fix like § 230, will require time.

---

222 CA Lee, 'When Children Prey on Children: A Look at Hawaii's Version of Megan's Law and Its Application to Juvenile Sex Offenders' (Summer/Fall 1998) (1) *University of Hawaii Law Review* 477.

223 JL Barry, 'The Child as Victim and Perpetrators: Laws Punishing Juvenile "Sexting"' (2010–2011) *Vandenberg Journal of Entertainment & Technology Law* 129.

224 In relation to state paternal roles, see, for example, EF Emens, 'Intimate Discrimination: The State's Role in the Accidents of Sex and Love' (March, 2009) (122) *Harvard Law Review* 1307.

225 Barry, *op. cit*, 129.

226 Ibid, 129.

227 See references at KM Gurney, 'MySpace, Your Reputation: A Call to Change Libel Laws for Juveniles Using Social Networking Sites' (2009) (82) *Temple Law Review* 241 at 257. One example is *Draker v Schreiber* 271 SW3d 318 (Texas App 2998).

228 Gurney, *op. cit*, 241.

229 D Boyd, 'Why Youth (Heart) Social Network Sites: The Role of Networked Publics in Teenage Social Life' in D Buckingham, *Youth, Identity and Digital Media* (Cambridge, Mass., 2008) 119 at 134. Referred to in Gurney, *op. cit*, 244.

230 Gurney, *op. cit*, 247.

But the problem of juveniles' activities on SN [web]sites simply cannot wait, as evidenced by the spike in defamation and student speech lawsuits. Teenagers may receive harsh discipline at school for their online speech, and be punished again when the same teachers and school administrators file lawsuits against them. Recent Supreme Court cases authorize, and even encourage, school officials to maximize their oversight of student speech that occurs either on or off campus by minimizing these students' First Amendment rights. Reading this line of Supreme Court precedent in tandem with the Court's much older defamation cases produces a clear call to change the way juveniles are treated in libel lawsuits: Because these students have fewer free speech rights than adults, it is unfair to hold them equally responsible for their speech in a court of law. Out of deference to the Court's direction as well as solicitude for immature teenagers facing dual punishments, judges should implement some simple solutions familiar to the rest of defamation and tort law while awaiting more comprehensive legislative action'.[231]

Also,

'the unique characteristics of SN [web]sites and individuals' behavior there demand a different legal standard in defamation cases. Interactions on the [web]sites are casual and smack more of a spur-of-the-moment conversation than thoughtful prose. SN culture puts a premium on witty, almost boastful, repartee – not accuracy or sensitivity. As Daniel Solove wrote in *The Future of Reputation,* in a passage on blogging that is particularly applicable to SN [web]sites.

One of the main differences between blogs and mainstream media publications is style. Blog posts are edgy, not polished and buffed into the typical prefabricated write-by-the-numbers stock that often gets produced by the mainstream media. Discourse on the internet is pungent. In many respects, this is a virtue ... But blog posts are created with no editors and published with no time delays. There's little time to cool down before sounding off. Just click the Publish button and unleash it to the world ... It goes without saying that this is a recipe for some problems.

The law also needs to consider that readers do not expect the level of care from an obviously juvenile profile on a SN [web]site as they do from the *New York Times.* Although the accuracy of postings on SN [web]sites may be questionable, and defamatory content therefore more likely, readers are also less apt to believe what they see there, reducing reputational damage. As Glenn Reynolds suggested, "[t]he blogosphere ... is a low-trust culture ... Newspapers, on the other hand, used to operating in a higher-trust environment, more commonly require readers to take their word regarding factual assertions." Courts should account for the fact that even though

---

231 Gurney, *op. cit,* 267–268.

content on a SN [web]site might be defamatory, libel law's framework for awarding damages based on limited evidence of injury is inappropriate'.[232]

However, if there is reduced defamatory responsibility for children and or juveniles, might there also be reduced levels of free speech rights for children?[233] Rights and balancing of rights are an issue to be fully considered.

Many argue in favour of net neutrality, especially in relation to free speech online.[234]

However, a school student who posted a false profile and comments about the school principal, and was suspended, was unsuccessful in arguing that the activity was out of school, that it did not disrupt the school and that his *suspension* was unconstitutional.[235] Nelson comments,

> 'The decision to post inappropriate comments is likely tied to the false sense of privacy a user believes to be attached to SN, whether from perceived anonymity or the fact that the individual is communicating with a machine rather than a person. Thus, the rule of thumb, think through each posting and its possible legal implications before posting'.[236]

2.8.27   *Spyware*

Spyware is a form of software program which allows an individual to monitor and see what activities individuals are undertaking on their computers. It is required to be installed on an individual's computer. Spyware is often recommended as a solution for parents concerned about the risks that their children or teenagers may encounter online.

However, if the software is limited to monitoring, by definition it means that the child is not actually protected in the sense of perceived bad websites being blocked. Equally, the same arises in terms of online solicitation and inappropriate pop-up ads, websites, online services, etc. None of these are precluded from being seen or accessed by the child. The risks remain. However, if parents, in subsequently reviewing what their child has been doing, see something they disapprove of, they can caution, reprimand or ban the child as they deem appropriate. They may also seek to use filtering or blocking

---

232 Ibid, 273.
233 Ibid, 268–269. Other organisations, such as CBS, NBC, Universal, BMG and Warner Music, embrace YouTube and upload content, even receiving increased ratings; see *Zeran v America Online Inc* 129 F3d 327, 330–335 (4th Circuit 1997).
234 JL Newman, 'Keeping the Internet Neutral: Net Neutrality and Its Role in Protecting Political Expression on the Internet' (2008) (31) *Hastings Communications & Entertainment Law Journal* 153.
235 See *JS v Blue Mountain School District No 3:07CV585*, 2008 WL 4279517 (MD Pa, 11 September 2008).
236 Nelson, *et al., op. cit*, 31.

technology to prevent access to or from certain websites, which could include (certain) SM. These later solutions are not fool-proof, however, for a tech-savvy teenager. There can frequently be ways to get around such additional technical solutions.[237]

As noted elsewhere, the growing literature in relation to children's rights, free speech and potential rights of access to the internet may mean that, ultimately, there are countering arguments and rights to be balanced against a parent's intention to install spyware monitoring and surveillance software. One could conceivably have a situation where data protection rules are bolstered by these 'new' rights, making it more difficult for parents to seek to restrict or monitor children's access to the internet, websites and/or SM.

2.8.28   Referendum

Recently, children have been expressly recognised as having rights under the Irish Constitution. While there was a lot of discussion at the time, there was an absence of any discussion of the effect of such amendment and the issue of children using SM and related websites. Neither was there discussion of these new children's rights as regards children and content and online abuse on SM and related websites. This is potentially a rich and fruitful area for research and consideration.

2.8.29   Criminal offence of cyberbullying

The Sixth Report of the Irish Special Rapporteur on Child Protection, A Report Submitted to the Oireachtas,[238] by the Special Rapporteur Dr Geoffrey Shannon, recommends that cyberbullying be a criminal offence. The report highlights the advent of online abuse, as well as such issues as the possibility of anonymous reporting by victims. It states,

'The impact and effect of bullying on children has been tragically thrown into the media spotlight ... Whilst bullying has always been an unfortunate aspect of our society, the growth of "Cyber-bullying" has almost overnight created a readily accessible forum for bullies to target children with little or no regulation or sanction. The Irish legal system has been somewhat taken unawares as to the manner and means through which children have fallen victim to cyber-bullying. Whilst there are some legislative provisions in being that might be interpreted in such a manner as to tackle this growing problem, a focused response is required.'[239]

---

237 One example being using proxies or third-party sites to access indirectly the websites that may be blocked directly.

238 G Shannon, *Sixth Report of the Special Rapporteur on Child Protection, A Report Submitted to the Oireachtas*, (Dublin, 23 January 2013).

239 Ibid, p 9.

It adds,

> 'However, in order for a system of legal recourse to be effective victims of such bullying need to be able to feel that they can come forward and express their concerns without fear of retribution. Thus, provision also needs to be made for the protection of child victims of such behaviour, eg the means of retaining their anonymity when making a complaint as to such bullying.'[240]

The report also highlights the issue of potential liability for schools and educational organisations for online abuse, etc. It states that the 'extent of a school's liability arising from an incident of bullying between students is a topic of some considerable debate and one that has been thrown into the fore in recent months'.[241]

It notes recent guidelines published in Ireland, for example, in relation to schools, but cautions that 'in the era of online technology and cyber-bullying a new focus must be brought to bear on this issue. Lessons can be learnt from the developments in New South Wales and Massachusetts in attempting to set a legislative basis to tackle this problem in schools'.[242]

The Recommendations refer to 'Cyber-bullying as a Criminal Offence', and state,

> 'On review of reported cases of harassment involving SN, email and SMS, there appear to be very few criminal prosecutions taken for this type of harassment under the Non-Fatal Offences Against the Person Act, 1997 despite the suitability of that Act. When cyber-bullying is being described as an epidemic, we need to examine why this is the case. Specifically, is there reticence to investigate complaints of cyber-bullying?
>
> Responding to calls for new criminal legislation to tackle cyber-bullying, the Minister for Justice identified our existing laws against harassment as being suitable. However, the Minister has directed the Law Reform Commission to examine difficulties in prosecuting for cyber-bullying and, in particular, the necessity to show persistence in the harassment.
>
> Existing laws regarding harassment can be used to incorporate cyber-bullying incidents. A review of the Post Office (Amendment) Acts should be undertaken with a view to incorporating emerging means of cyber-bullying.'[243]

Anonymity for victims of online abuse, or at least cyberbullying online abuse, is favoured. The Recommendations continue as follows,

> 'The current Irish legal position would appear to suggest that an application for anonymity in the context of cyber-bullying litigation would be

---

240 Ibid, p 9.
241 Ibid, p 9.
242 Ibid, p 9.
243 Ibid, p 20.

unsuccessful. However, it is difficult to be definitive in respect of the legal position because Mr Justice Peart's decision in *McKeogh v John Doe* may well have been different if the applicant had been a child or teenager seeking to rely on the right to privacy of children, and able to invoke the general social interest in protection of children from cyber-bullying. The ideal solution would be an agreement of co-operation to be entered into between ISPs (and potentially other entities such as Facebook) and the Gardaí to provide IP addresses where complaints of cyber-bullying have been received.'[244]

2.8.30 Single body to oversee SM and/or SN

The Irish Oireachtas Joint Committee on Transport and Communications, which held parliamentary hearings and submissions during 2013 *inter alia* in relation to online abuse and cyberbullying, has recommended that a single body should be given responsibility for co-ordinating the regulation of social media content.[245]

Paul C Dwyer of the Irish National Anti-Bullying Coalition told the Committee that just one social network provider received some 100,000 reports or requests per day, but dedicated just 90 staff to process such requests.[246] The Committee and the Report recommend that the online abuse report data be furnished by the SNs to the Irish Data Protection Commissioner.[247]

In Recommendation 3, the Committee supports the recommendation contained in the Action Plan on Bullying that the definition of bullying in the new national procedures for schools should include a specific reference to cyberbullying. Also, guidelines for cyberbullying should be put in place, so that school principals dealing with instances of cyberbullying have a clear protocol to follow.[248] Recommendation 4 refers to employers. It states that employers be made aware of the importance of introducing a social media policy, ie outlining what constitutes cyberbullying and what actions will be taken if there is a breach of such a policy.[249] Employers should be aware that cyberbullying falls under 'harassment', and Section 10 of the Non-fatal Offences Against the Person Act 1997 may apply in such cases.[250] Recommendation 6 states as follows,

> 'The Committee recommends that a single body be given responsibility for co-ordinating the regulation of social media content. Funding and

---

244 Ibid, p 20.
245 Oireachtas Joint Committee on Transport and Communications, *Houses of the Oireachtas, Joint Committee on Transport and Communications Report Addressing the Growth of Social Media and Tackling Cyberbullying*,(Government Publications: Dublin, 18 July 2013).
246 Ibid, p 8.
247 Ibid.
248 Ibid, p 9.
249 Ibid.
250 Ibid.

organisational models for this agency should be agreed with the industry. It is noted that other examples of industry-led partnerships between stakeholders and government have been established in other sectors in recent years.'[251]

2.8.31   Conclusion

The issue of children's use of SM (and other website services) is at the forefront of concerns regarding safety and regard for the personal details of children. This is not just a single neat issue and involves quite a number of problems and concerns, some of which are new and developing. Indeed, SM is not that old itself. It is also the case that there is no one solution to these concerns. A combination of self-regulation, technical solutions as well as more enhanced recognition in the data protection regime for children is likely to be required. As with so many areas involving technology, any solution or combination of solutions cannot be a stand-still endeavour. These matters require constant attention as the underlying technology and its uses change.

2.9   EMPLOYEES/EMPLOYMENT SM LAWS OR CASES

One of the increasingly important and contentious areas of SM is the interface of employees, organisations and SM. For example, many cases can ensue from an employee's use of SM. Organisations must move beyond internet usage policies and email policies to policies which expressly set out what SM the employee can and cannot engage in while in the work environment and while using the organisation's devices.

Laws and cases must also involve themselves with employees/employment SM matters. Organisations can be held legally responsible for what their employees and agents do online.[252] This applies in the US as it does in Ireland and the UK. Caution is needed so that organisations and employees avoid, for example, creating legally binding unintended contracts while online.[253] Organisations also need to be careful that their employees do not engage in creating or distributing defamatory comments online, which can lead to the employer being held directly or contributorily liable for defamation. Many organisations will already be familiar with managing these risks and will have appropriate policies and procedures in place. Employers and organisations now need to

---

251 Ibid, p 10.
252 AJ Bojorquez and D Shores, 'Open Government and the Net: Bringing Social Media into the Light' (2009–2010) (11) *Texas Tech Administrative Law Journal* 45 at 46.
253 Ibid, 50. The article also refers to Florida Attorney General Opinion 9-19 (2009), which refers to a proposed official Facebook page which, if arranged, would need to ensure all records were accessible, and all virtual meetings were open to the public. See ibid, 50 and note 43 at 50.

be aware of SM and how this can affect their liability. Policies will need to be updated and reviewed. Risks need to be monitored on an ongoing basis.

2.9.1 Employer liability issues

Employers and organisations need to understand SM and react to it. They can be held legally responsible for what their employees and agents do online.[254] Risk management for organisations in relation to SM is now 'a major concern'.[255] This is especially so: when adverse comments are being made; when a corporate disaster or data loss strikes;[256] or when corporate resources are used disproportionately or inappropriately and against specific organisational policies.

2.9.2 Viruses, etc

Employees accessing SM can also expose the organisation to viruses and malicious software threats.[257] The means by which unscrupulous third parties seek to get access to, or damage, the computers and network of the employer are ever increasing.

2.9.3 Bandwidth and resources

The use of SM, whether authorised or unauthorised, can use up a large amount of bandwidth resources[258] and time resources of the organisation. Some organisations block access to SM, or alternatively restrict the hours of such access.[259] In the US, it has been suggested that employees generally will have no expectation of privacy in electronic communications transmitted through the employer's network systems.[260] Employers and organisations elsewhere need to be very cautious in adopting this approach. General monitoring of employees is not permissible under EU data protection laws, and the EU Article 29 Working Party has commented as such. Furthermore, it has been acknowledged by

---

254 Ibid, 46.

255 Nelson *et al.*, *op. cit*, 34.

256 Generally see comments in M Boran, 'A Tweet in Time Could Help Save Your Company, How do Firms Stay Afloat When Disaster Strikes and the Story Takes on a Life of its Own in Cyberspace?' *Irish Times*, 1 April 2011.

257 Bojorquez and Shores, *op. cit*, 65. Also note, for example, Miller, 'The Facebook Frontier: Responding to the Changing Face of Privacy on the Internet' (2008–2009) *Kentucky Law Journal* 541 at 551–553.

258 See H Tarrant, 'What Facebook Costs Business', *Moneyweb*, 16 August 2007, previously available at http://moneyweb.co.za/mw/en/page292671?oid=154231&sn=2009%20Detail, now available at www.moneyweb.co.za/moneyweb-broadband/what-facebook-costs-business, referred to in Bojorquez and Shores, *op. cit*, 65.

259 Bojorquez and Shores, *op. cit*, 66, and references therein.

260 Ibid, 67. Note also case of *Pack v Wood County* No 6:08cv198 2009 US District Lexis 57103 (ED Texas 30 July 2009), referred to ibid, where the employee was held not to be able to restrict access to his communications on the employer systems.

national data protection regulators that there can be expectations of privacy in certain contexts. That is to say nothing of what might be argued in terms of privacy and unenumerated privacy expectations under constitutional law, such as the Irish Constitution.[261]

2.9.4 Defamation

Defamation[262] can occur when an employee states something online, or repeats a third-party comment, that is untrue.[263] However, this can create liability for the organisation in a variety of circumstances. Those who author defamatory statements on SM are liable and responsible for them under defamation law.[264] One example is where the statements are posted in the work environment, or even circulated in the work environment electronically.

Traditionally, the concerns related to email. However, employers and organisations need to consider whether they allow the use of SM by employees from the work venue generally. If they do, it is not inconsistent that someone would claim defamation against the employer as well as the irresponsible employee who may have said something alleged to be defamatory on SM. This is particularly so where that employee, or any other employee, regularly mentions work issues on their SM profile pages. Issues in relation to a statement made on instant messaging available on SM should also not be discounted.

A separate example of concern arises where the employer uses content from employee and potential employee SM that later transpires to be defamatory.[265] An organisation may, for example, have a publicity or recruitment campaign and decide to include employee comments from various sources, including SM. Horton states,

> 'The increase in forums and the ability of internet users to publish information – through bulletin boards, chat rooms, and web journals, often referred to as blogs – has created a greater threat of damage to one's reputation on a much larger scale. Defamation, libel, and slander issues in cyberspace have all posed challenges for the law, and in order to better understand the legal

---

261 See, for example, G Hogan and G Whyte, *The Irish Constitution* (Butterworths, Dublin, 1994), 746 and 755.

262 KM Gurney, 'MySpace, Your Reputation: A Call to Change Libel Laws for Juveniles Using Social Networking Sites' (2009) (82) *Temple Law Review* 241 at 249–250 and 254–256; AE Horton, 'Beyond Control? The Rise and Fall of Defamation Regulation on the Internet' (2009) (43) *Valparaiso University Law Review* 1265.

263 Generally, note the new Defamation Act 2009; M McGonagle, *Media Law* (Round Hall, Dublin, 2012); J Maher, *The Law of Defamation* (Round Hall, Dublin, 2011); E Carolan and A O'Neill, *Media Law in Ireland* (Bloomsbury, Dublin, 2010); B McMahon and W Binchy, *Law of Torts* (Tottel, Dublin, 2000).

264 Gurney, *op. cit*, 256.

265 I Byrnside, 'Six Clicks of Separation: The Legal Ramifications of Employers Using Social Networking Sites to Research Applicants' (2008) (10) *Vanderbilt Journal of Entertainment and Technology Law* 445, at 468–469.

issues, one must first understand how the information superhighway, and the growing cyber community, work'.[266]

One of the issues with SM is that statements are frequently posted anonymously or under a made-up user name.[267] This can create problems pursuing or dealing with a particular matter.

2.9.5   Records and information

SN now also has an impact on data preservation and record retention obligations.[268] Organisations need to be aware of whether and how the content of SM may affect their data preservation and record retention obligations.[269] Also, freedom of information (or public access in the US)[270] issues arise in relation to certain SM content.

Issues of public access (in the US)[271] and freedom of information might include certain SM content.[272]

2.9.6   Employee profiles

There is no specific law currently explicitly prohibiting the use by organisations of potential employees' SM profiles.[273] However, other laws may be indirectly applicable, such as privacy, terms of use, terms of service, discrimination and defamation.[274] An organisation needs to consider the legal issues and impact carefully before undertaking equivalent search activities in relation to potential employees.

Given that there is a greater reticence against blanket monitoring in the EU under the data protection regime, caution needs to be employed by organisations in terms of regular searches of employees' online SM, etc. Employers and organisations always need to bear in mind differences between the laws of different jurisdictions, and that a decision from one country may not automatically translate into another jurisdiction. Caution also needs to be maintained when considering decisions of lower-level courts. They may not always be applied by higher-level courts, regardless of jurisdiction.

---

266 Horton, *op. cit*, 1277.
267 Gurney, *op. cit*, 256.
268 Bojorquez and Shores, *op. cit*, 46 and 50 *et seq.*
269 Ibid, 46 and 50 *et seq.*
270 Ibid, 46.
271 Ibid, 46.
272 Generally, see Stephen Mason, gen ed, *Electronic Evidence* (3rd edn, LexisNexis Butterworths, 2012); Bojorquez and Shores, *op. cit*, 50.
273 See Byrnside, *op. cit*, 445; DH Montes, 'Living Our Lives Online: The Privacy Implications of Online Social Networking' (2010) (5) *I/S: A Journal of Law and Policy* 507 at 524.
274 Ibid, 524–525.

A separate issue also arises in terms of employees' profiles. Employment-related websites mean that it is possible for an employer inadvertently to come across a profile that might relate to an existing employee. This 'seeking work' profile might be posted directly by the individual or by an employment agent.

Similar problems may also arise with non-dedicated employment websites. Many general commercial profile websites exist, possibly the most prominent of which is LinkedIn. Individuals upload information and status reports on their academic or professional careers. It can be useful for an employee to advertise their skills on LinkedIn, especially if they are considering a new employment position. However, as LinkedIn, etc are publicly available websites, the risk arises that their employer may also see the posts or comments. One example of this is the case of John Flexman, who claims to have been forced out of his job after the employer saw certain CV details on his LinkedIn profile page.[275] Employees (and, indeed, users generally) should always remember that the comments and materials that they post online can come back and be used against them subsequently.[276]

2.9.7 Telecommuting

The advent of working from home and telecommuting also poses problems for employers. Once at home there is, even according to US commentators, a reasonable expectation of privacy at home.[277] That an employee is working from home during office hours does not mean the normal data protection policies and accepted employee rights are to be ignored. Neither should organisations assume that respect for privacy and data protection of employees disappears after business hours. While (certain) organisational policies and procedures may be argued to extend beyond the physical and temporal confines of the organisation, employees do not abandon their rights on leaving the employer's building. Some may argue that employee privacy and data protection rights are greater at such times. Complexities also arise in relation to mingling of personal data and employment data on the same computer device, as well as device-related issues (eg ownership, control, payment of bills for devices, authority to access).

2.9.8 Employees and blogs

Blogs are frequently viewed by individuals as their personal websites. (Of course, they can be commercially or professionally focused also.) However,

---

275 D Hare, 'Construction Manager "Forced Out" Over LinkedIn CV', *ConstructionWeekOnline. com*, 9 January 2012; C Williams, 'Executive "Forced Out of Job" Over LinkedIn CV', *Daily Telegraph*, 5 January 2012.

276 T Stretton, 'Anything You Tweet or Post Can and Will be Used Against You', *Computers and Law*, Society of Computers and Law, 6 December 2011.

277 Bojorquez and Shores, *op. cit*, 68.

defamation can also arise in the event of employee blogs, official or otherwise. Some of the other dangers of blogs include employees disclosing confidential information, trade secrets or insider information. Privacy as well as intellectual property rights (IPRs) issues are also concerns.[278] Information on blog postings might be used in employee disciplinary actions (up to and including termination) and harassment cases, so employees should always be careful what they say online, including on SM. This is yet another area where organisations may feel the need to ban or restrict employees from using or accessing blogs.

Up to now, many employers may have felt that there were no laws or regulations preventing them from looking at SM in order to vet applicants.[279] In many instances, there is no legal case determining a particular issue.[280] That does not mean that liability cannot arise. Employees as well as employers need to be particularly cautious until such time as the matter is decided in a higher-level court. Even in the US, commentators have raised potential issues of privacy, discrimination, fair credit reporting, violation of website terms and conditions, defamation, etc.[281] SM screening or vetting has also been described as a 'nightmare' for individuals.[282]

Indeed, there are an increasing number of examples where sports clubs are banning, restricting and regulating professional athletes in relation to their SM activities. Recent examples include soccer players' use of Twitter. Regardless of what decisions may be taken by organisations, such decisions should be made available in a written and transparent manner to all employees. This includes detailing the company's position in relation to employee action, communications and devices that may be used off site, if this is permitted.

The extent to which employers may be able to regulate or ban blogs, SM, etc by employees may ultimately depend on the nature of the specific relationship, the business activities, and how regulators and courts may interpret the data protection regime. However, one case suggests that a company may be able to prevent employees from accessing blogs.[283] An organisation may feel, for example, that too much time is wasted online and decide to ban internet access, or restrict access to certain websites and online services.

Where blogs are permitted, one issue facing an organisation is the extent to which it may want to (or be obliged to) maintain a record of employees' blogs.[284]

---

278 G Lastowska, 'User-Generated Content and Virtual Worlds' (2007–2008) (10) *Vanderbilt Journal of Entertainment and Technology Law* 893 at 897.

279 See Byrnside, *op. cit*, 458.

280 See ibid, 459 and references therein.

281 Ibid, 445.

282 C Brandenberg, 'The Newest Way to Screen Job Applicants: A Social Networker's Nightmare' (2007–2008) *Federal Communications Law Journal* 597.

283 *Nicholas v Fletcher*, No 3:06-CV-00043 KKC 2007 WL 1035012, at *1, 9 (ED Ky 30 March 2007), referred to in Nelson *et al.*, *op. cit*, 17.

284 See Nelson *et al.*, *op. cit*, 16–17.

Different issues will also arise in terms of organisations' own official blogs.[285] Some of the issues to be decided are the parameters, content, tone, subjects, etc on which employees are permitted to comment, and indeed which employees are permitted to post the blog.

Recruiters increasingly use SM and mobile messaging to proactively engage and recruit new staff.[286] There are issues in terms of how they obtain contact details in the first instance, but also in terms of what personal data they collect and how they use and store it.

2.9.9   Harassment

Harassment and sexual harassment in the workplace are regulated. SM is a new means for such harassment, including between employees or between former/ estranged partners or spouses.[287] Both can take place in and from the work place, on work equipment and devices.

Harassment is prohibited under various legal regimes. In Ireland, for example, the offence can be committed when a person without lawful authority is persistently following, watching, pestering, besetting or communicating with a subscriber.[288] The harassment may, either 'intentionally or recklessly, seriously interfere' with the subscriber's privacy and the conduct must be 'without lawful authority or reasonable excuse'.[289] Where a person harasses an employee or even a third party on the employer's network, and potentially on SM, the employee and potentially the employer can have issues to answer. In addition, if the employee accesses someone else's emails, passwords, etc, legal issues can arise separately from the harassment offence.

SM, such as Facebook and Twitter, now means that sports stars and celebrities are more accessible to the general public. While sports stars may be able to promote themselves and their brand, for instance, it also opens them up to complaint or unfavourable direct comments from third parties, sometimes anonymously. Stephen Fry is a notable example of a celebrity leaving Twitter after third-party criticism on the website (albeit returning subsequently). So too presenter Ryan Tubridy. A 21-year-old was arrested in connection with allegedly racist statements made on Twitter about the soccer player and commentator Stan Collymore.[290]

---

285 Ibid, 12.
286 M Maher, 'You've Got Messages: Modern Technology Recruiting Through Text-Messaging and the Intrusiveness of Facebook' (2007) *Texas Review of Entertainment & Sports Law* 125.
287 See LL Baughman, 'Friend Request or Foe? Confirming the Misuse of Internet and Social Networking Sites By Domestic Violence Perpetrators' (2010) (19) *Widener Law Journal* 933 and examples therein.
288 Non-Fatal Offences Against the Person Act 1997, s 10.
289 Ibid, s 10(2)(a).
290 'Newcastle Man Arrested Over Racist Tweets Sent to Stan Collymore', *Huffington Post*, 7 January 2012.

In Ireland, the unlawful use of a computer is an offence.[291] The Irish Criminal Damage Act 1991 also creates an offence of unauthorised access to a computer, and it is an offence to damage data.[292] McIntyre states that the Irish legislation creates a 'remarkably broad [offence] [regarding] "damage" [and] modification of any information stored on a computer'.[293]

As the right to privacy is protected by the Irish Constitution, an invasion of privacy in an unlawful manner could open the employer to potential damages. The case of *Herrity v Associated Newspapers* held that there was an invasion of privacy and awarded €60,000 ordinary and aggravated damages and €30,000 punitive damages.[294] This related to the use of a transcript of an illegally recorded telephone conversation regarding private relations.

In the US, there can be specific laws encompassing harassment. For example, section 33.07 of the Texas Penal Code makes it an offence where a person,

'uses the name of persona of another person to create a web page or to post one or more messages on a commercial networking site: (1) without obtaining the other person's consent; and (2) with the intent to harm, defraud, intimidate or threaten any person'.[295]

Under section 33.07(b) of the same Texas law, it is a crime to,

'send an electronic mail, instant message, text message, or similar communication that references … identifying information belonging to any person: (1) without obtaining the person's consent; (2) with the intent to cause the recipient … reasonably believe that the other person authorized … the communication; and (3) with the intent to harm or defraud any person'.[296]

It is also commented that 'with every new technology, there are laws (ie privacy … defamation, and copyright), social norms, and business practices that warrant thoughtful consideration and communication with public officials and employees'.[297]

There have been various attempts at local and federal legislation in the US prohibiting online or cyber-harassment.[298] Many countries do not expressly have a law dealing specifically with SM or online harassment, whether by employees or others. Ireland is one example. There is also no UK law explicitly dealing with online harassment.[299] While there is the Protection

---

291 Criminal Justice (Theft and Fraud Offences) Act 2001, s 9. Section 25 of the Criminal Justice (Theft and Fraud Offences) Act 2001 creates an offence of creating a false instrument.
292 Criminal Damage Act 1991, s 5.
293 TJ McIntyre, 'Computer Crime in Ireland: A Critical Assessment of the Substantive Law' (2005) (15(1)) *Irish Criminal Law Journal* 13 at 14.
294 *Herrity v Associated Newspapers* [2009] 1 IR 316 and 347.
295 Referred to in Bojorquez and Shores, *op. cit*, 68–69.
296 Bojorquez and Shores, *op. cit*, 69.
297 Ibid, 69.
298 See various references and commentary in Montes, *op. cit*, 519–521.
299 N Geach and N Haralambous, 'Regulating Harassment: Is The Law Fit for the Social Networking Age?' (2009) (73) *Journal of Criminal Law* 241.

from Harassment Act 1997, it is questioned how applicable this can be to internet harassment,[300] and hence SM harassment. It is argued in the UK that 'the current overall legislative framework is inaccessible, uncertain and thus inadequate to encompass activities in today's evolving age of online SN'.[301] Online harassment is wide and includes: sending abusive, threatening or obscene email or messages (including via instant messaging or SM); sending friend requests or 'poking' on SM; stalking on Second Life; impersonation (eg fake profiles); spamming; sending malicious emails or email attachments; and subscribing a person to mailing lists, etc.[302] It can also include monitoring communications.[303] Indeed, interception offence issues also arise.

In terms of litigation of these issues, significant evidential issues arise in terms of admissibility of such evidence in court.[304] These include authenticity, hearsay, best evidence rule, fraud and false information.[305] Some cases are illustrative of the expansion of harassment issues. In one example in Kent, a librarian was harassed when a Facebook group was set up called '[f]or those who hate the little fat library man'.[306] Another UK case saw a man cleared of a harassment charge for sending friend request to an ex-girlfriend.[307] The House of Lords has previously held that a silent telephone call can amount to harassment.[308]

Perhaps non-internet-related laws may be used in relation to SM harassment, namely in the UK, the Protection from Harassment Act 1997 (section 2), the Malicious Communications Act 1988 (section 1(1)) and the Communications Act 2003 (section 127).[309] The Public Order Act 1986 (sections 5 and 4A) could also 'theoretically' apply.[310]

However, the range of activity, its severity and its effect vary considerably; and, as with other laws that may now require greater nuancing (eg child criminals), cyber-harassment and cyber-stalking also require the right remedies for the right offence.[311]

---

300 Protection from Harassment Act 1997. ibid.
301 Ibid.
302 Geach and Haralambous, *op. cit*, 242.
303 Baughman, *op. cit*, 940–941.
304 See, for example, ibid, 945–946.
305 Ibid, 946–956.
306 '"Fat Library Man" Bullied Online', *BBC News*, 23 July 2007, available at http://news.bbc.co.uk/2/hi/uk_news/england/kent/6912409.stm, referred to in Geach and Haralambous, *op. cit*, 242.
307 P John, 'Man Cleared of Facebook Harassment', *Birmingham Main*, 27 March 2008, referred to in Geach and Haralambous, *op. cit*, 243.
308 *R v Ireland* and *R v Burstow* [1998] AC 147, referred to in Geach and Haralambous, *op. cit*, 245.
309 Referred to in Geach and Haralambous, *op. cit*, 241.
310 Ibid, 254.
311 M Baer, 'Cyberstalking and the Internet Landscape We Have Constructed' (2010) *Virginia Journal of Law & Technology* 153. Also, C Calvert, 'Fighting Words in the Era of Texts, IMS and Emails: Can a Disparaged Doctrine be Resuscitated to Punish Cyber-Bullies?' (2010–2011) *DePaul Journal of Art, Technology & IP Law* 1; JJ Exum, 'Making the Punishment Fit the (Computer) Crime; Rebooting Notions of Possession for the Federal Sentencing of Child Pornography Offenses' (2009–2010) *Richmond Journal of Law & Technology* 1.

2.9.10   Employee monitoring

Some US commentators suggest that employers are permitted generally to monitor their employees' usage of telephones, emails, internet and work location (via CCTV).[312] In the US, there appears to be a perception that it is legitimate for employers to monitor their employees' electronic activities, including SM. For example, one article states: 'checking the SN [web]sites of potential employees could be wise, as an employer might get some sense of trouble brewing in the future: a lack of discretion, angry entries, a 'TMI' (too much information) proclivity, etc'.[313]

However, there are differences between the US and the EU in terms of data protection and the rights of individual data subjects. EU data protection law does not permit the blanket monitoring of employee activities, including online and electronic communications usage (eg EU Article 29 Working Party). This would most likely include SM. Note also the case of *Herrity v Associated Newspapers*, noted above, which awarded aggravated and punitive damages for invasion of privacy.[314]

Even in the US, there are on occasion cases that support employees' rights of privacy from monitoring, even on employer devices. One example is the case of *Quon v Arch Wireless*.[315]

The Supreme Court in Canada has recognised that employees have rights of privacy and expectations of privacy and data protection at work, which includes internet use and internet browsing history.[316]

The Irish Data Protection Commissioner and the EU Article 29 Working Party also recognise the legitimate expectations of employees in relation to their privacy and data protection rights.

2.9.11   Public organisations and information published

Many public organisations seek to make information available to the public on websites and increasingly on SM. However, it is possible that too much information may be published or posted, or on occasion information that is private, privileged, confidential or otherwise restricted.[317]

There can also be specific rules and regulations pertaining to other issues affecting what may or may not be permitted officially on SM.[318]

---

312 See, for example, Bojorquez and Shores, *op. cit*, 67.
313 Nelson *et al.*, *op. cit*, 19.
314 *Herrity v Associated Newspapers* [2009] 1 IR 316 and 347.
315 *Quon v Arch Wireless* 529 F3d 892 (9th Cir 2008). This related to a public-sector employee.
316 *R v Cole* Supreme Court Canada 2012 SCC 53, available at http://scc.lexum.org/decisia-scc-csc/scc-csc/scc-csc/en/item/12615/index.do.
317 See Bojorquez and Shores, *op. cit*, 50.
318 Ibid, 50.

Difficulties can also arise in relation to distinguishing between which communications and postings are official and which are personal.[319] Some of the relevant factors may include: who prepared the materials; who has control and access; the specific nature of the material; whether it was used in the course of conducting government business; whether public funds were spent to create the material; the purpose of the material; and whether the government entity requires creation of the material.[320]

SM can be summarised as creating additional 'administrative and legal headaches'.[321] It is equally essential that public organisations are aware of the implications of SM and implement appropriate policies and procedures to inform personnel of the correct protocols and to regulate such activity.[322]

2.9.12 *Existing employees*

Organisations should have appropriate policies and contracts in place with their employees, which includes regulating their usage of SM.[323] Given the recent advent of SN, and indeed that many organisations remain unfamiliar with SM, policies dedicated to SM risks are in many instances absent. Frequently, larger organisations will be the first to implement appropriate and dedicated policies. One example is the *IBM Social Computing Guidelines: Blogs, Wikis, Social Networks, Virtual Worlds and Social Media*.[324] It should always be remembered that, regardless of what the policies are, they always need to be reviewed regularly, at least annually.

2.9.13 *Potential employees*

While employers may be equally interested in everything to do with their potential (as well as existing) employees, there may in fact be less of a fair and legitimate entitlement to examine the online and SM activities of such persons. Despite this, many employers, particularly in the US, regularly seek to vet potential employees' SM activities. SM is, therefore, frequently contentious.[325] Potential employers go to the internet as part of their candidate selection and interview process. Caution, however, is required in the EU.

Individuals may be concerned that, when they are applying for a job, the employer may take into account factors that are irrelevant or in breach of

---

319 Ibid, 54.
320 Ibid, 54.
321 Ibid, 65.
322 Ibid, 65.
323 AR Levinson, 'Industrial Justice: Privacy Protection for the Employed' (2009) (18) *Cornell Journal of Law and Public Policy* 609.
324 Available at www.ibm.com/blogs/zz/en/guidelines.html.
325 Brandenberg, *op. cit*, 597.

their data protection rights.[326] Job applicants have been refused employment when the prospective employer found out through their SM that the person smoked cannabis.[327] Even Microsoft has indicated that such searches of SM information is 'fairly typical'.[328]

The use of 'SN [web]sites for gathering applicant information raises several potential legal issues, including invasion of privacy, discrimination, violation of the Fair Credit Reporting Act [1970], violation of terms of service, and defamation ... this is an emerging area of law that is far from settled'.[329]

The main problems with employer searches and decisions based on these searches are (1) inaccurate, irrelevant or indeed false information leading to unfair decisions, (2) illegal decisions being made by employers aided by lack of explicit regulation in this area, and (3) violation of legitimate expectations of privacy.[330]

Some claim that laws must be amended and updated to ensure adequate user protection against 'unfair, illegal or arbitrary employment decisions'.[331]

There is concern that employers may be influenced by the off-duty activities of employees and potential employees.[332] No easy solution exists, but employers and organisations should be proactive as new issues and risks arise, even when a specific issue does not appear to be explicitly referred to in the current legal regime.

In one ExecuNet survey, 75 per cent of recruiters indicated that they used web searches to screen applicants.[333] One view is that, once something is in the public domain, it is 'fair game'.[334] In addition, it can be argued to have been voluntarily posted online by the individual directly.[335] Some commentators even feel that this will be the case where an individual had restricted their privacy settings and a potential employer 'hacks past' them.[336]

---

326 See RB Ecker, 'Comment, To Catch a Thief: The Private Employer's Guide to Getting and Keeping an Honest Employee' (1994) (63) *UMKC Law Review* 251 at 255–261, referred to in Byrnside, *op. cit*, 452.

327 A Finder, 'When A Risque Online Persona Undermines a Chance for a Job', *New York Times*, 11 June 2006, S 1, at 1, referred to in Nelson *et al.*, *op. cit*, 21.

328 Referred to Warren Ashton, Group Marketing Manager, Microsoft, in A Finder, 'When a Risque Online Persona Undermines a Chance for a Job', *New York Times*, 11 June 2006, 1, referred to in I, Byrnside, *op. cit*, 456.

329 Byrnside, *op. cit*, 445.

330 Ibid, 237.

331 Ibid.

332 SD Sugarman, '"Lifestyle" Discrimination in Employment' (2003) (24) *Berkeley Journal of Employment and Labour Law* 377, 378, 407, referred to in Byrnside, *op. cit*, 452.

333 J Greenfoelds and D Haugh, 'When What Happens on MySpace Doesn't Stay on MySpace', *Chicago Tribune*, 28 March 2006, at C1, referred to in Byrnside, *op. cit*, 456.

334 M Irvine, 'When MySpace Becomes Everyone's Space', *Globe & Mail* (Toronto), 30 December 2006, at R12, referred to in Byrnside, *op. cit*, 461.

335 Byrnside, *op. cit*, 461–462.

336 Ibid, 462.

Also,

> 'Although employers have begun using SN [web]sites to assist with hiring decisions, the potential legal ramifications of such a practice are unclear, to say the least. No case has been brought on the basis of such use of these SN [web]sites. However, the increasing popularity of such [web]sites brings with it the potential for numerous legal problems to arise in this "emerging area of law," bolstering the chance that such a case may arise in the not-so-distant future'.[337]

Employers 'are increasingly checking the SN profiles of their applicants and ... those applicants may suffer as a result of the information they have posted on the internet'.[338]

Background checks in the US are indicated not to be illegal, 'so long as employment decisions based on this information are consistent with "business necessity" and do not have a disparate impact on a certain class of applicants'.[339]

Some also argue that an employer's use of SM information in relation to employees and applicants violates the website terms and conditions, which generally refer to personal non-commercial use.[340]

2.9.14 *Identity*

Regardless of whether employers are permitted to use SM for vetting potential employees or existing employees, issues of identity and authenticity arise. While they may find a profile online, they have no guarantee in every instance that the profile they are viewing is that of the applicant/employee.[341] This also arises in relation to comments posted online. Employers may like to use such internet profiling because of the 'wealth of information available from online SN profiles to screen potential employees ... [and because it is] cost-effective ...'.[342] There are many surveys where employers have confirmed that they use such profile information, and also many documented examples of this happening.[343] This trend appears to be increasing, especially in the US.

2.9.15 *Restrictions*

These issues are not always explicitly referred to in the data protection regime, and hence need to be interpreted from the existing provisions by data protection

---

337 Ibid, 447–448.
338 Ibid, 457.
339 Ibid, 450.
340 Ibid, 466–468.
341 Ibid, 470.
342 Montes, *op. cit*, 521.
343 Ibid, 522–523.

regulators. The upcoming reform of the EU data protection regime may add some clarity, if not further regulation, in this area.

The US Credit Reporting Act is aimed at ensuring that decisions are made only on accurate and relevant information.[344] There are claims that the Credit Reporting Act should be expanded to cater properly for SM and employment issues.[345] For example, minor amendments could ensure that information must be accurate but also that users of SM are aware of the information being used in relation to them.[346]

In the US, certain questions may be prohibited by, for example, Title VII of the Civil Rights Act 1964 (prohibiting discrimination on the basis of race, colour, religion, nationality), the Age Discrimination in Employment Act 1967, and Titles I and V of the Americans with Disabilities Act 1990.[347] However, while there may be no,

'direct discrimination or unlawful questioning based on the above, it is very difficult to prove or disprove that this information did not filter into an otherwise lawful decision to not employ, promote, etc, any particular person. Some feel that as yet there is "no adequate protection" against such filtering scenarios.'[348]

Title VII is the main federal statute relating to anti-discrimination, and prohibits employers from discriminating against applicants and employees based on race, colour, religion, sex or national origin.[349]

In order to maintain a claim of invasion of privacy, it is necessary to show that there was a reasonable expectation of privacy.[350]

2.9.16 Redress

If employers do something that they should not do and this has adverse consequences for an employee/potential employee, what sanction should arise? What punishment is appropriate?[351]

Byrnside states,

'Until a definitive judicial decision or legislative decree is announced that addressed these issues, it is safe for applicants to assume that at least some employers will be checking their SN profiles. Therefore, applicants should operate under the assumption that potential employers will see everything

---

344 Davis, *op. cit*, 240.
345 Ibid, 237.
346 Ibid, 241, 251–255.
347 Referred to in Montes, *op. cit*, 523.
348 Ibid, 523.
349 Ibid, 449.
350 *California v Greenwood* 486 US 35, 39–40 (1988), as referred to in Byrnside, *op. cit*, 452.
351 Issue raised in Byrnside, *op. cit*, 472.

they post on their profiles. With this in mind, it is important for applicants to use discretion in deciding in deciding what information to post on their SN profiles and what information to leave out. If applicants insist on putting certain information on their SN profiles, they should, at the very least, adjust the privacy settings to restrict access to their profiles.'[352]

Individuals may face an 'uphill battle' in attempting to prevent employers using their SN information, even if 'password protected'.[353]

Using SM for business

Should a company permit employees to use SNs for business purposes? Such use might,

'include[e] communications with clients and internal communications with coworkers. If employers allow access to SN [web]sites or employees circumvent controls that limit their access, employees may be using the [web]sites to conduct the business of their employers or collaborate with colleagues. As such, the information that relates to the employment of the individual may be relevant to a potential suit. The policy that an employer takes with respect to the use of SN must be specific and detailed but at the same time, cannot be so constraining that the purpose for using the [web] sites to reach clients, consumers, and colleagues is defeated.

IBM has taken the reins and developed guidelines specific to social computing. The company places some responsibility on its employees for monitoring what is said on SN [web]sites and reporting conduct that strays from its guidelines. This would be an important part of any policy relating to SN to ensure that the policy has an enforcement mechanism. Particularly unique to IBM's policy is the requirement that when employees discuss matters related to the company, employees have to identify themselves by name and their role at the company and make it clear that they are speaking for themselves and not on behalf of the company. In addition to this, the company requires employees who post to blogs to use a disclaimer that the views posted do not represent the company's views. The guidelines require employees to be thoughtful with respect to dispersing internal, confidential communications externally via SN [web]sites. Also, the employee may not comment on the business performance of the company or affirm or deny rumors related to the company's business performance. The company makes users personally responsible for the information that is posted on these [web]sites and emphasizes that employees cannot alter previous posts without making it clear that the post has been altered. The policy also requires employees to be respectful with their postings and gently reminds

---

352 Ibid, 473.
353 Ibid, 477.

employees not to let their SN activities interfere with their work-related commitments and duties.

In addition to the IBM guidelines, there are a few additional steps that employers can take with respect to an employee's use of SN in the workplace that may avoid the problems associated with obtaining the information for litigation purposes and maintain a company's reputation on SN [web]sites. First, like IBM has done, companies should make sure that they create a SN policy that is specific and that employees are educated about the policy and the repercussions in the case of violations of the policy. The policy should also be enforced. An umbrella computer usage policy may not be sufficient to encompass the specific concerns related to SN, especially if SN is not mentioned. With respect to enforcement, the company should be consistent and actually follow its own policy guidelines for the policy to have any meaning.[354]

In contrast to a general email policy that usually advises employees that their business email communications should not be considered private, SN [web]sites are usually not viewed in this way because they are personal accounts. A step that employers could take is to require employees who would like to use SN for business purposes to create a separate business account, based on their business email address, as a condition to use the [web]sites in the workplace and on the employer's equipment, including mobile phones, desktops, and laptops. In addition, the company could require that the employee link to the company's fan page or website on his own business page. The employees should also be made aware that the information they post on SN [web]sites, their emails, and conversations may be discoverable. The employer should formulate a written agreement stating that in exchange for the employee's access and use of SN in the workplace, the employee will grant consent for the disclosure of the information from his business profile page, including email, posts, notes, and all features of Facebook or Twitter used for communication purposes, in the event the information is needed for litigation or general auditing purposes. The policy must also make it clear that the employee has no expectation of privacy with respect to communications on SN [web]sites made through the employee's business account, on the employer's computer network, or on the employer's hardware, including desktop computers, laptop computers, and mobile phones'.[355]

Much will depend on the culture of the organisation and what is normally permitted and viewed as acceptable. However, when a particular policy is

---

354 Note, for example, N Lindquist, 'You Can Send This But Not That: Creating and Enforcing Employer Email Policies Under Sections 7 and 8 of the National Labor Relations Act After Register Guard' (2009) *Shidler Journal of Law Communications and Technology* 15.

355 L Thomas, 'Social Networking in the Workplace: Are Private Employers Prepared to Comply with Discovery Requests for Posts and Tweets?' (2010) (63) *SMU Law Review* 1373 at 1398–1401. Internal references omitted.

adopted, it is important to enforce it. If it is not consistently and fairly enforced, it can leave the employer open to claims that the policy does not apply or should not apply because other people were previously permitted to ignore the policy, or were not similarly disciplined.

2.9.17 Education

One author refers to education issues as follows,

> 'In addition to implementing a detailed policy with respect to SN, employees who use the [web]sites must be educated that the same rules that apply with respect to business conversations and communications apply to the use of SN in the workplace. Though SN users generally do not adhere to the rules of formality associated with business communications, it is imperative that employees are educated that communications for business purposes on SN [web]sites should adhere to the same level of formality as email communications and other written communications for business purposes. Thus, employees should be mindful of what they say on such [web]sites and should be educated that what they say could lead to liability, not only for them but also for their employers'.[356]

2.9.18 Policy on SM and SNs

When dealing with policy issues, organisations need to refer to,

> 'the degree of privacy that the employee account should maintain at a minimum. It is unlikely that an employer would want their employees' profiles set to public so that an internet search would reveal information about the employer's business contacts and clients. Depending on the nature of the information and the business of the company, the employer must be explicit regarding what privacy settings the employees' profiles should maintain so that the employers and employees are protected from the unwanted viewing of business profiles on SN [web]sites ... employees [need to be aware of the employer's SN policy'.[357]

2.9.19 Contract consent

Consent issues, as always, raise particular considerations,

> 'By using a contract where the employee agrees to consent to disclosure of the information in exchange for use of SN [web]sites at work for business purposes, a company will be able to ensure that it has the ability to access information so that it retains control of its employees' reluctant actions on SN [web]sites. If a company decides to allow employees to communicate

---

356 Ibid.
357 Ibid.

for business purposes on SN [web]sites, it is imperative that the guidelines be clear with respect to what the employees can and cannot say on the [web] site, the employees' expectations of privacy regarding the communications, the employer's expectations of professionalism, and the penalties for failure to follow the guidelines. And once again, the policy should be enforced to have any merit'.[358]

This is another issue which appears not to have reached a judicial decision as yet in the UK.

2.9.20   Fan pages

Other issues also arise as regards company fan pages,

'The creation of a company fan page may seem like an easy task, but the employer must consider whether the page can be archived or preserved in anticipation of litigation and who has access to the page to act as its administrator. The first issue to consider in creating a company's Facebook page or Twitter account is who is responsible for maintaining and monitoring the [web]site. It has been suggested that a separate email account should be created for all SN [web]site endeavors and account information should be available to all "stakeholders". It is important that the company's Facebook page is viewed as a company-controlled page, rather than any kind of individual asset. As such, the company should limit who posts on these [web]sites as the face of the company. In addition, the individuals in charge of the page should monitor the postings and comments.

An additional consideration regarding who should have access to the page is how to limit access once the employee is terminated or leaves employment. Suppose that an employee in charge of postings on a company's SN page is fired. Assuming that person is the administrator of the company's Facebook page, that employee could still maintain access despite the fact that he is no longer with the company. Because the individual could post to the page and damage the company's reputation, there must be a limit in place to prevent such an occurrence. One source suggests that a company can create a profile page akin to a personal profile page. Once that page is created, a page for the company can be created and additional administrators to the page can be added. These administrators can be readily changed so that when an employee who was in charge of the page leaves the company, he can be deleted as an administrator. Thus, when a company page is created, an employer must decide who will administer the social media [web]sites and transmit information from the company to the public and ensure that upon termination, the ability of the terminated employee to access the [web] sites as an administrator is prevented.

---

358 Ibid.

In addition, employees in charge of the [web]site should have clear guidelines as to what can and cannot be posted on the company's Facebook page. Also, it should be clear that the monitoring of social media and postings on such [web]sites are within the scope of employment of the individual and subject to any limitations and restrictions that the company imposes on such postings. There should be an approval process in place before a posting is made so that upper management in marketing has some oversight in the process. By doing so, the employer maintains a level of control over the postings such that it will be accountable for the content. Because the page should be viewed as a company-controlled asset, it is likely that a court would find that the [web]site is within the company's "possession, custody, or control" and as such, information pertinent to suit must be disclosed to the opposing party and produced by the party in custody of the material. As mentioned previously, there are many problems with the way that SN [web] sites are archived that could lead to problems in obtaining the information.'

2.9.21 Spoliation changes

Thomas states,

'There are a few steps that employers can take to make sure that they do not suffer spoliation sanctions for destruction of information relevant to suit on their SN pages. First, if a company has a reasonable anticipation of litigation, it should issue a litigation hold and a preservation order and contact Facebook and Twitter to make sure they are aware of the preservation order. The preservation order should be specific, relate to the company page for a set period of time, and advise administrators not to delete the postings from the page. In addition to contacting Facebook and Twitter, the administrators of the [web]site for the company should be aware of the holds. Luckily, with Facebook, as long as posters and administrators have not deleted postings on a company's page, older posts can be seen with mere clicks on the company page. But, Facebook does not guarantee that such information will always be available by this method. With Twitter, however, there is approximately a one-and-a half-week window in which the tweets can be retrieved by searching for them using the search engine on Twitter, though they never disappear from a user's Twitter stream. Thus, once again, with a litigation hold, the administrators of a Twitter [web]site should not delete content from the Twitter page during the relevant time period to avoid the extra step of having to retrieve the information from Twitter itself'.[359]

These issues of electronic evidence, maintaining and not damaging potential pertinent electronic evidence, and discovery and electronic discovery are extremely complex. SNs that are outside the normal direct control of the employer or the organisation potentially add costs and issues to be confronted

---

359 Ibid. Discovery is referred to as disclosure in England and Wales.

by them. The Sedona conference and Sedona rules are useful US guides to consider on this issue.[360]

2.9.22   Archives

Thomas states,

> 'Companies that want to be extra cautious with their Facebook or Twitter pages may want to archive the pages themselves and save them locally. There are programs in circulation for archiving tweets that a company's IT department would be able to implement successfully, but this is a task for IT to undertake. The same archiving possibility' may exist for Facebook as well, and it is a good idea for IT to consider whether locally archiving a company's Facebook page would be a viable option. But once again, a company's IT group should formulate the policy regarding the archiving of such [web]sites after discussion with upper management and counsel'.[361]

Employers and organisations need to consider normal archiving and destruction of electronic materials that might be required for litigation. Third-party discovery or disclosure of SM is itself a potential issue. The company's records may, for example, be pertinent where employees access SM via the company's computer network.

2.9.23   Conclusion

Some question whether introducing new laws or expanding regulation would actually solve the problems presented.[362] The issues and concerns for organisations and for employees in terms of privacy and data protection are difficult and complex. The advent of SM, blogging and the like makes it ever more difficult to maintain traditional boundaries. Where these boundaries run, such as when the work day truly ends, and what employees may do as individuals online with expectations of privacy, will remain hotly debated in practice, contracts and policies, as well as in litigation and new laws.

2.10   SCHOOL AND UNIVERSITY STUDENT SM CASES

Obviously, students in schools and universities are heavy users of SM. This particular use raises many issues of law, policy and educational regulation of such activities. Already there are many cases relating to contentious usage of SM by pupils, teachers, university students as well as the issue of potential

---

360 Sedona, available at https://thesedonaconference.org/.
361 Thomas, *op. cit*. Note also, for example, DS Witte, 'Your Opponent Does Not Need a Friend Request to See Your Page: Social Networking Sites and Electronic Discovery' (2010) *McGeorge Law Review* 891 at 895–897.
362 Montes, *op. cit*, 525.

overreach by educational institutions in regulating, monitoring and seeking access and password access to students' SM accounts.

Social network content and communications are beginning to be used as forms of evidence, as highlighted above. This includes both civil cases and criminal cases. Some of these themes are also continued below. We can consider, for instance, a school wishing to litigate in order to protect its computer system or pursue those who may damage its computer system.

However, in the educational sphere we also need to consider the expanding theme of SM content and communications being used as evidence in what might be termed social evidence or social justice; that is, decisions based on evidence obtained from SM that does not reach a court of law.

There is also the sometimes related but separate theme of information and content on SNs focusing on school or college relations and activities. Students can now 'peer into their teachers' personal lives'[363] and create false personas and profiles falsely representing to be a particular student or teacher. Indeed, SNs have particularly focused on student users. When Facebook began, for example, it was restricted to users from university.

2.10.1 Schools

'[P]arents, teachers, and anyone else responsible for the case and safety of children should be aware of the potential dangers of the internet'.[364] Parents and everyone in loco parentis[365] are legitimately concerned that students should not be presented with pornographic websites when they conduct innocent internet search requests. They are also concerned that adverts should not be appearing for medicines and sex websites when they are looking for education-related websites. Some of this may result in technical and organisational-type security measures. However, the need for both parents and educators to teach themselves about what children are doing online should never be underestimated.

2.10.2 Teachers

As indicated above, educator education and familiarity with technology and the activities of children, teenagers, etc are primary considerations. In addition, the actions and safeguards adopted by educators are also important. In reacting and

---

363 AW Estrada, 'Saving Face From Facebook: Arriving at a Compromise Between Schools' Concerns With Teacher Social Networking and Teachers' First Amendment Rights' (2010) (32) *Thomas Jefferson Law Review* 283.

364 MJ O'Connor, 'School Speech in the Internet Age: Do Students Shed Their Rights When They Pick Up a Mouse?' (2009) (11) *University of Pennsylvania Journal of Constitutional Law* 459 at 476.

365 DC Bechstrom, 'Who's Looking at Your Facebook Profile? The Use of Student Conduct Codes to Censor College Students' Online Speech' (2008) (45) *Williamette Law Review* 261 at 279–280.

in being proactive, however, educators also need to be conscious that balance is required. This is very often easy to forget. It is all too easy to overreact, too.

It is also possible to overreact in relation to teacher conduct. There are concerns that what teachers say or do online might conflict with their duties to the school, children, parents, etc. It is also recognised that teachers should not interact online with their pupils. This is a developing area and it is unclear what the attitudes of schools are in the UK in relation to teachers' online contacts with children. How should a teacher react to a Facebook friend request from a student?

Some schools and legislators have even sought to restrict the *use by* teachers of SM.[366] Is this proportionate? Is it overreaction? Is it constitutional? Is there a right to use or have access to the internet? These are obvious issues for future litigation, on both sides of the Atlantic.

Teachers have also been disciplined for particular activities and posted comments online. Examples arise in Florida, Colorado, Tennessee and Massachusetts.[367] One teacher referred to a student as a 'retard' and was disciplined; a kindergarten teacher had a pornographic video on Facebook raising concerns; and another teacher referred to his or her drug use online.[368] Many US schools deal with these issues in accordance with a district-wide school policy.[369] In terms of a proposed California rule regulating teachers' online SM, one commentator suggests that 'the proposed statute withstands constitutional scrutiny. California cannot rely on teachers' common sense alone to guard against irresponsible use of SM. State action on the matter is imperative'.[370] It remains to be seen how a court will decide these issues. It also remains to be seen how these matters will develop at policy level in world jurisdictions, and ultimately in a contested case.

However, while the concerns and implementing safety precautions are legitimate, there is growing concern that the rights of teachers may be overridden or ignored. For example, their rights to free speech (eg US First Amendment) could be infringed.[371] Other rights to be considered include 'associational rights'.[372] One can easily see how these differing standpoints could come into conflict here. Safety is not always a standalone issue, and on occasion must be balanced and proportionate in relation to other legitimate rights that can exist. Fulmer argues for teacher privacy rights, submitting that

---

366 See Estrada, *op. cit*, 284, referring to HR 1314, 94th General Assembly, 2d Reg Sess (Mo 2008), among others.
367 Ibid, 285–286 and references therein.
368 Ibid, 285–286.
369 Ibid, 287–289.
370 Ibid, 311–312.
371 See generally ibid, 283 and 289–297.
372 Ibid, 283 and 297–303. Estrada also analyses a proposed law in California, namely, the California Education Code; ibid, 303–308.

these are needed because there is so little redress available to teachers after the event where an error is made in accusing them.[373]

Conflicts between teacher rights, discovery, disclosure, seizure and official policies are also issues of contention. For example, while there are instances of teachers acting inappropriately or having relationships with their students, and criminal proceedings issuing, the right of the school or college to use evidence of such activities seized or discovered on the teacher's mobile phone, laptop, etc remains unclear. There is a 'vacuum' and 'uncertainty' regarding teachers' devices and their seizure, access, discovery, disclosure and use by third parties such as the school.[374]

2.10.3   Universities

Some of these issues and concerns also exist in higher-level educational establishments. Universities need to consider, perhaps, the more advanced maturity of university students. The concerns arising from SM do need to be carefully considered.

> '[Universities] need guidance on how to appropriately deal with the issue to prevent situations in which students are unfairly punished. [School/ university] officials have admitted to not knowing what students' speech rights are, and the current student speech jurisprudence is not easily applied to postings on MySpace and Facebook. However, the Supreme Court's reasoning in *Tinker*[375] provides a basis for articulating a standard specific to students' use of SN [web]sites. Revising and modifying *Tinker* to factor into consideration the differences between public profiles results in a standard that both protects student speech rights and ensures that the [schools/universities] are able to maintain order and discipline. The final, and perhaps most important, step in this process is to communicate the standard to the [schools/universities], as well as to students and parents, who can then work together to eliminate the problem'.[376]

As has been found by many employers when dealing with these issues, if appropriate and balanced policies do not exist, it is difficult to react in the most appropriate manner. The University of Minnesota Duluth, for example, had difficulties in dealing with students who posted racist SM comments about another student when the policies were not as clear on the issue as they

---

373 EH Fulmer, 'Privacy Expectations and Protections for Teachers in the Internet Age' (2010) *Duke Law & Technology Review*.

374 JO Oluwole, 'Teacher Cell Phone Searches in Light of *Ontario v Quon*' (2010–2011) *Richmond Journal of Law and Technology* 1 at 2. Referring to *Ontario v Quon* 130 Supreme Court 2619 (2010).

375 *Tinker v Des Moines Independent Community School District* 393 US 503.

376 KD Williams, 'Public Schools Vs MySpace: The Newest Challenge to Student Rights' (2008) (76) *University of Cincinnati Law Review* 707 at 730–731.

could be.[377] Twitter has also updated its policies after a number of online abuse incidents in the UK involving threats of rape and bombs.[378] As difficult as these issues are, they are somewhat easier to deal with, and regulate at a policy level, when all the factual issues occur on campus (or at the school). However, what happens when all the activity is out of hours and off premises? Universities in the US are reported to be expanding their conduct and discipline policies to encompass off-campus activities, potentially including activities online.[379] There have already been complaints made in relation to students' off-campus online comments.[380] Examples include the University of Central California, University of Illinois and Valdosta State University.[381]

However, this is still an area fraught with difficulty, and indeed some novelty. These are new issues and new technologies. There have been few cases dealing with these issues and few explicit references in statute laws to these matters. It has, therefore, been commented that, because 'federal courts have remained fairly quiet on this emerging medium of speech, institutions of higher education are more able to continue disciplining students for off-campus cyberspeech that is thought to violate an institution's student conduct code'.[382] The law remains 'underdeveloped'.[383] The comment continues that there may be the glimmer of a tentative recognition of greater respect for students' free speech and First Amendment rights – or, at least, of university students.[384] There are three important cases dealing with college students' free speech rights.[385] The extent to which off-campus student speech may be protected constitutionally may depend on the effect it has on campus.[386] Regard may also be had to reasonableness, interpretations, recipients of the comments, etc.[387]

It has been argued that public universities should be able to discipline students for crimes, and that this can include serious matters such as serious off-campus

---

377 T Strike, 'One Law School's Experience in Creating a Social Networking Policy' (2010) (15) *AALL Spectrum* 24.

378 M Townsent and L Moon, *Guardian*, 'Twitter Clamps Down on Abuse After Rape and Death Threats. Site Will Roll Out "Report Abuse" Button as its Bosses Apologise to Women and Say: "People Deserve to Feel Safe on Twitter"' 3 August 2013.

379 Bechstrom, *op. cit*, 262–263.

380 Ibid, 261–262.

381 Ibid, 263 and 261–263 in relation to the former.

382 Ibid, 264.

383 Ibid, 281. Referring to the US Supreme Court in *Tinker v Des Moines Independent Community School District* 393 US 503 (1969); *Bethal School District No 403 v Fraser* 478 US 675 (1986); *Hazelwood School District v Kuhlmeier* 484 US 260 (1988), referred to ibid, 281–287.

384 Ibid, 281. Referring to the US Supreme Court in *Tinker v Des Moines Independent Community School District, Bethal School District No 403 v Fraser* and *Hazelwood School District v Kuhlmeier*, referred to ibid, 281–287.

385 Ibid, 287–290, namely, *Healy v James* 408 IS 169 (1972); *Papish v Board of Curators of University of Missouri* 410 US 667 (1973); and *Rosenberger v University of Virginia* 515 US 819 (1995).

386 See ibid, 294, and cases referred to at 290–298.

387 See Bechstrom, *op. cit*, 302–303.

harassment, 'such as [online] sexual harassment'.[388] This poses questions, however. If no crime is prosecuted, the student would presumably remain innocent in relation to that accusation from a criminal law perspective. Also, not every conceivable infringement that a college may be concerned with, or that a student, lecturer, etc may complain about, would amount to a criminal act as defined in statute.

This also ignores locus issues. One argument is that 'colleges should not discipline students for their off-campus cyberspeech unless such speech presents a true threat or constitutes a crime ... institutions should also modify their student conduct codes accordingly'.[389] Some would argue that colleges should not be able to discipline for any off-campus speech or activities.

There is a surprising effort to have college students and applicants disclose their SM details to the university or faculty in question.[390] It is questioned how constitutional this may be,[391] and it is seen as an attack on freedom to associate.[392] SM may be argued to be an association or collection of associations.[393] Obviously, free-speech arguments also arise. There could also be a significant chilling effect on what students may be willing to say or post on their SM profiles[394] if they fear that a university or applications committee may access their social network history. Proposals to allow university access to students' and applicants' social network pages may well be reactive and disproportionate when there are other less restrictive mechanisms to deal with the issues.[395] It may also be unlawful. The solution ultimately needs to be nuanced,[396] proportionate and not indiscriminate in relation to the concerns posed. One could also suggest that there is at least some irony that such proposals are coming from supposedly liberal institutions.

There are legitimate concerns in relation to violence and hate speech[397] as well as harassment and sex-related activities. These are legitimate issues for universities to consider and also refer to appropriately in '[s]tudent conduct codes'.[398] However, proportionality is needed, as well as respect for other rights and issues. Off-campus activity is one such issue. Non-statute criminal activity is another. Free speech and free association are significant others also. These

---

388 Ibid, note 20 at 265.
389 Ibid, 310.
390 J Sabin, 'Every Click You Make: How The Proposed Disclosure of Law Students' Online Identities Violates their First Amendment Right to Free Association' (2008–2009) (17) *Journal of Law and Policy* 699 and 701–701.
391 Ibid, 702.
392 Ibid, 721.
393 Ibid, 721–725.
394 Ibid, 725–727.
395 Ibid, 729–733.
396 Ibid, 733.
397 Bechstrom, *op. cit*, 280–281.
398 Ibid, 270–276.

are complex issues, regardless of the legal jurisdiction. One US commentator describes the US situation as follows,

'In *Tinker v Des Moines Independent Community School District*, the Supreme Court definitively established that students do not "shed" their right to free speech "at the [school/college] gate." However, the Court also said that those rights must be "applied in light of the special characteristics of the [school/college] environment ...". Ever since, there has been debate over the exact boundaries of those rights'.[399]

In addition,

'despite discussing student First Amendment rights in at least five significant cases (*Tinker, Fraser, Board of Education, Island Trees Union Free School District No 26 v Pico, Hazelwood, and Morse*), the Supreme Court has thus far only obliquely examined the extent to which the student speech doctrine extends beyond the physical boundaries of the school. Cut adrift without Supreme Court guidance, the lower courts and numerous commentators have attempted to divine the extent to which the [school/university] speech doctrine reaches off-campus conduct, but it is not clear if they have had any success. While I suspect the Court will eventually have to confront this issue head-on and I may therefore be adding my voice to a storm soon to be quelled, I will nevertheless make the attempt because it is an important component of an examination of school speech in the internet age.

The Supreme Court's only examination (if one can call it that) of the off-campus speech issue came recently in *Morse*, where it recognized "some uncertainty at the outer boundaries as to when courts should apply school-speech precedents, but not on these facts." Its determination was based on the fact that Morse's actions were directed towards the [school/university] and visible by its students. They took place across the street, during regular [school/university] hours, at an event sanctioned by the school and supervised by its staff. The Court concluded that "Frederick cannot stand in the midst of his fellow students, during school hours, at a school-sanctioned activity and claim he is not at school"'.[400]

A separate point appears to exist in terms of university researchers using SM for data-mining purposes.[401] The extent to which such details may use

---

399 MJ O'Connor, 'School Speech in the Internet Age: Do Students Shed Their Rights When They Pick Up a Mouse?' (2009) (11) *University of Pennsylvania Journal of Constitutional Law* 459. References omitted.

400 Ibid, 472–473. References omitted.

401 LB Solberg, 'Data Mining on Facebook: A Free Space for Researchers or an IRB Nightmare?' (2010) *Journal of Law, Technology & Policy* 311. In relation to other social networking research possibilities, see, for example, JL Behrens, 'About Facebook. Change at the Social Networking Juggernaut Creates New Opportunities for Law Library Outreach' (April 2008) *AALL Spectrum* 14.

or incorporate identifiable (whether alone or in conjunction with other data) personal data of users remains an issue of concern.

2.10.4   Student awareness

In the US, schools are increasingly using SM to discipline their students – in particular, student athletes.[402] One example is the case of Jessica Schoch in Ohio.[403] She appealed a school decision to expel her based on comments on her MySpace SM profile. She was ultimately reinstated in school after free speech and First Amendment issues were argued.[404] Another student was suspended in Colorado based on comments he made on MySpace.[405] In California, 20 students were suspended for viewing a MySpace post containing threats against another student.[406]

Regardless of legality of statute laws and institutional policies to regulate and discipline some or all SM activities, students need to be aware of the risks. There are dangers online in terms of strangers. Students need to be aware that it is always possible that what they say online may come to the attention of their school or university.

In years to come, an employer or an employment agency may find that embarrassing comment or photograph from the past. As Perlmuter notes,

> '[F]riends can hurt your reputation as much as you can yourself: That embarrassing photo of you at a party, or that impolite quote you made about your department, can be an unguided missile wandering about cyberspace ready to shoot down your good name'.[407]

Students need to be aware that, once they say something online, it can spread quickly and far afield, as well as remaining there perhaps indefinitely.

2.10.5   Public organisations

SM can be summarised as creating additional 'administrative and legal headaches'.[408] It is essential that public organisations are aware of the implications of SM and implement appropriate policies and procedures to inform personnel of the correct protocols and to regulate such activity.[409]

---

402 D Findlay, 'Tag! Now You're "It". What Photographs on Social Networking Sites Mean for the Fourth Amendment' (2008) (10) *North Carolina Journal of Law & Technology* 171 at 179.
403 Referred to in Williams, *op. cit*, 707.
404 Referred to ibid.
405 Referred to ibid.
406 Referred to ibid.
407 DD Perlmuter, 'Facebooking Your Way Out of Tenure', *The Chronicle of Higher Education*, 3 July 2009, available at http://chronicle.com/article/Facebooking-Your-Way-Out-of/46951, referred to in Montes, *op. cit*, 524.
408 Bojorquez and Shores, *op. cit*, 65.
409 Ibid.

Employee access to SM can also expose the organisation to viruses and malicious software threats.[410]

Public organisation must also be cognizant of what they and their employees say and do online, which now includes SM. Many public organisations pursue an interest in making information available to the public on websites and increasingly on SM. However, it is possible that too much information may be published or posted, or information that is privileged, confidential or otherwise restricted.[411] There can also be specific rules and regulations pertaining to other issues, which affect what may be permitted officially on SM.[412]

One of the difficulties for such organisations is deciding what they must seek to regulate and how to achieve that in a prudent and proportionate manner.

Difficulties can also arise in relation to distinguishing between which communications and posts are official and which are personal.[413] Some of the relevant factors may include,

- who creates the materials;

- who has control and access;

- the specific nature of the material;

- whether it was used in the course of conducting government business;

- whether public funds were spent to create the material;

- the purpose of the material; and

- whether the government entity requires creation of the material.[414]

Appropriate and considered policies are necessary. If they are too strong, there is a risk that they may be successfully challenged. The other danger is that it may not be possible to act in the first instance when a problem arises if there is no, or no adequate, policy to deal with a situation.

Further caution is needed. While some US commentators suggest that employers are permitted generally to monitor their employees' usage of telephones, email, internet and work location (via computer or CCTV, for example),[415] this should be cautioned against in Europe. Blanket monitoring is not compatible with the EU data protection regime, unlike the situation in the US, where blanket monitoring by organisations appears to be more accepted.

---

410 Ibid.
411 See ibid, 50.
412 Ibid, 50.
413 Ibid, 54.
414 Ibid, 54.
415 See, for example, ibid, 67.

2.10.6 Conclusion

SM creates many problems for individual students, parents and educational organisations in relation to the use of SNs. Some of these issues are new, but sometimes they bring old rights areas into the conflict once again, such as freedom of speech and of association.

While educational organisations are rightly concerned, there is also a danger of going too far, for example, in blanket monitoring, demanding access to the SM pages of student applicants or seeking to regulate activities outside the educational environment – be that students or teachers. Caution may also be needed, in that one solution may not always fit all; certainly, every US solution may not be an EU solution.

Separately, both students and teachers do need to be aware and prudent in relation to what they say and do online. In the sphere of education, perception can often be as much an issue as actuality.

2.11   RIGHT OR HUMAN RIGHT TO ACCESS THE INTERNET OR SM

There are increasing calls to recognise a right or human right of access to the internet. It is possibly only a matter of time before similar calls arise in relation to such a right encompassing SM access and/or separate calls to recognise a right or human right of access to SM. One text is *Human Rights and the Internet*.[416] Tully also provides a recent analysis.[417] A 2011 UN report has also said that internet access is a human right. The report special rapporteur, Frank La Rue, states that '[g]iven that the Internet has become an indispensable tool for realizing a range of human rights, combating inequality, and accelerating development and human progress, ensuring universal access to the Internet should be a priority for all states'.[418] Finland has stated that it will make a 100Mb broadband connection a legal right by the end of 2015, with a legal right of 1Mb by 2010.[419]

---

416 S Hick, EF Halpin and E Hoskins, eds, *Human Rights and the Internet* (New York: Palgrave Macmillan, 2000).

417 S Tully, 'A Human Right to Access the Internet? Problems and Prospects', *Human Rights Law Review* (14) 2, 175–195. Also section V(5) in Internet: Case-law of the European Court of Human Rights, European Court of Human Rights (ECHR), June 2011, available at www. refworld.org/docid/4ee1d5bf1a.html.

418 United Nations, Report of the Special Rapporteur on the promotion and protection of the right to freedom of opinion and expression, Frank La Rue, 16 May 2011, available at www2.ohchr. org/english/bodies/hrcouncil/docs/17session/A.HRC.17.27_en.pdf.

419 D Reisinger, 'Finland makes 1Mb broadband access a legal right', CNet, 14 October 2009, available at www.cnet.com/uk/news/finland-makes-1mb-broadband-access-a-legal-right/.

2.11.1   Internet access sanctions

It is increasingly recognised that alternative and creative sanctions other than imprisonment can be imposed on convicted persons. These include community service, curfews and electronic tagging. More recently, the issue arises as to whether a court sanction can be imposed to restrict or prevent a person from using and accessing the internet. Already there are examples of cases where such internet access restrictions have been imposed. It is increasingly a trend to try to impose creative sanctions on certain convicted paedophiles and convicted online child sex offenders. For example, a child sex offender could have used SM to make contact with children, solicit them and groom them. Restricting those convicted in relation to online child predatory activities is arguably not without technological precedent.

2.11.2   Hacking internet access sanctions

There are already examples where those convicted of hacking and other computer crimes have had judicial sanctions imposed not to access the internet. This might seem surprising, but there are a number of examples where this has occurred. Under the Irish Criminal Justice (Theft and Fraud Offences) Act 2001, unlawful use of a computer can be an offence, namely, where a person dishonestly operates or causes to be operated a computer within the State with the intention of making a gain for himself or another.[420] An offence of creating a false instrument arises if it is done with the intention that it will be used to induce another person to accept it as genuine and, by reason of so accepting it, to do some act – in this case, to track and profile a subscriber online.[421]

The Irish Criminal Damage Act 1991, for example, creates an offence of unauthorised access to a computer, and it is also an offence to damage data.[422]

2.11.3   Child sex offender internet access sanctions

However, it is a step further again to impose access restrictions against those convicted in relation to child sex crimes emanating from SM.

These can, of course, be 'real' crimes and 'internet crimes'. The former would be where a child is murdered, raped or attacked after meeting with somebody they were introduced to through a social network. An example of the latter is someone convicted of an offence relating to accessing, storing and or creating animation child pornography, which they may have downloaded, uploaded and/or distributed online or electronically.[423]

---

420 Criminal Justice (Theft and Fraud Offences) Act 2001, s 9.
421 Ibid, s 25.
422 Criminal Damage Act 1991, s 5.
423 See the Child Trafficking and Pornography Act 1998 (amended by s 6 of the Criminal Law (Sexual Offences) (Amendment) Act 2007). Note also the harassment offence in s 10 of the Non-Fatal Offences Against the Person Act 1997.

This will be a developing area in many jurisdictions.[424] Some instances do exist. For example, Lori David was banned by a court in Texas from (1) using the internet; and (2) texting anyone other than a family member.[425] She was convicted of an offence which involved sexting, by sending a nude photograph of herself (aged 38) to a 16-year-old boy. He was a friend of her son.

A court in the UK banned an alleged hacker, Jake Davis, from using the internet pending his trial.[426] An Irish court in 2014 also banned an accused from accessing dating websites pending trial. Prosecutors in a US case also demanded that an internet ban be imposed on an alleged hacker, a Mr Cooper, as a bail condition.[427] An original request that he be obliged to install computer and internet monitoring software on his computer was dropped.[428] Jerome Heckenkamp, an alleged US hacker, also had internet bail restrictions imposed pending trial, which he sought to challenge during the long delay between charge and trial.[429] A 17-year-old French hacker (known as DKD) is also reported to have been sentenced with an internet ban for hacking.[430] Four other alleged hackers in the UK were banned from using their online user pseudonyms on the internet or internet relay chat (IRC, a messaging system).[431]

Prime Minister David Cameron indicated that he would like to see rioters, and those planning such activities, banned from SM.[432] There is also a proposed

---

424 Including Ireland, UK, etc.

425 'Katy Mom Banned from Internet After "Sexting" Son's Friend', *CBS Houston*, 14 November 2011, available at http://houston.cbslocal.com/2011/11/14/texas-housewife-banned-from-internet-over-sexting-sons-friend/; 'Mother Banned from the Internet After Pleading Guilty to "Sexting" 16 Year Old Son's Classmate Naked Pictures of Herself', *Daily Mail*, 14 November 2011.

426 E Oswald, 'LulzSec's "Topiary" Released on Bail, Banned from Internet', *Betanews*, 1 August 2011, available at http://betanews.com/2011/08/01/lulzsec-s-topiary-released-on-bail-banned-from-internet/.

427 P Roberts, 'Alleged Anonymous Member Faces Ban, Monitoring Software', *ThreatPost*, 25 July 2011, available at http://threatpost.com/en_us/blogs/anonymous-members-face-internet-bans-monitoring-software-072511.

428 Ibid.

429 K Poulsen, 'Kechenkamp Challenges Computer Ban', *SecurityForces.com*, 3 December 2003, available at www.securityfocus.com/news/7576.

430 'Hacker Banned from the Internet', *GovernmentSecurity.org*, 12 July 2003, available at www.governmentsecurity.org/forum/topic/714-hacker-banned-from-the-internet/. An accused in Ireland was recently banned from accessing dating websites pending trial; see 'Software Designer Banned from Dating Websites After Sex Assault Charge', RTE News, 17 September 2014. A senior barrister has also been suspended from practice for six months as a result of being convicted in relation to harassing text messages; see 'Well Known Barrister Banned from Practising After Harassing Former Girlfriend with Texts', Independent, 8 July 2014, available at www.independent.ie/irish-news/courts/well-known-barrister-banned-from-practising-after-harassing-former-girlfriend-with-texts-30414587.html#sthash.VrBMEnkz.dpuf.

431 G Cluley, 'Anonymous Suspects Bailed – Banned from Using Online Nicknames and IRC', *NakedSecurity.Sophos.com*, 7 September 2011, available at http://nakedsecurity.sophos.com/2011/09/07/anonymous-suspects-bailed-banned-from-using-online-nicknames-or-irc/.

432 'UK Prime Minister Wants to Ban Suspected Rioters From Facebook & Twitter', *TechDirt*, 11 August, 2011, available at www.techdirt.com/articles/20110811/11531615478/uk-prime-minister-wants-to-ban-suspected-rioters-facebook-twitter.shtml.

cyber-security strategy initiative in the UK which, *inter alia*, proposes internet and SM bans for criminals ('criminals who commit offences online') and cyberbullies.[433]

A man in Michigan was charged with hacking after he hacked his wife's Gmail email account (and discovered evidence of her having an affair). The Leon Walker case was predicted to have potential repercussions for investigations that occur in a number of family and divorce cases.[434]

Child conviction internet restriction cases are few in number, but they may grow in frequency. In the US, different courts can take different approaches. Adkins[435] refers to the cases of *United States v Paul*[436] and *United States v Brigham*[437] in the Fifth Circuit, which tend to uphold internet restrictions for convicted child pornography offences, while the Second Circuit is reluctant to impose restrictions on internet usage as a parole or probation restriction, such as in *United States v Peterson*.[438]

2.11.4 Challenges to internet sanctions

If these types of sanctions continue to grow in popularity, it may only be a matter of time before objections are made on the jurisdiction of a court to impose such a restriction or on the enforcement by a court or the police of such a restriction. These objections could conceivably come from a number of constitutional and legal avenues. Exploring these potential avenues is beyond the space and scope of this current work. However, we should explore one such possible avenue: the theory of internet access as a human right.

2.11.5 A human right to internet access

There is an increasing view that access to the internet is, or should be, a human right. To use the words of Adkins, '[i]ncreasingly, being connected to society means being connected to the Internet'.[439] A call has also been made to link data protection rules and the human rights regime.[440] Adkins continues that '[d]ue to recent advances which have caused a surge in Internet popularity

---

433 *The UK Cyber Security Strategy*, CabinetOffice.gov, available at www.cabinetoffice.gov. uk/resource-library/cyber-security-strategy. C Williams, 'Criminals and Cyber Bullies to be Banned from the Web', *Daily Telegraph*, 25 November 2011.
434 C McGreal, 'American Charged With Hacking After Snooping on Wife's Emails', *Guardian*, 27 December 2010.
435 J Adkins, 'Unfriended Felons: Reevaluating the Internet's Role for the Purpose of Special Conditions in Sentencing in a Post-Facebook World' (2011) *Journal of Telecommunications & High Technology Law* 263.
436 *United States v Paul* 274 F3d 155, 169–170 (5th Cir 2001).
437 *United States v Brigham*, 569 F3d 220 (5th Cir 2009).
438 *United States v Peterson*, 248 F3d 79, 83 (2d Cir 2001).
439 Adkins, *op. cit*, 264.
440 C Pounder, 'Why Privacy is at Risk' (2009) (25) *Computer Law & Security Review* 285.

and utility, the Internet is nothing less than essential to our modern way of life'.[441] A growing literature relates to the argument that access by persons to the internet is a human right.[442]

Extensive international jurisprudence and academic literature is devoted to fundamental human rights. In some ways, this can sometimes be argued to take precedence over certain national laws. On occasion, competing rights have to be carefully balanced. This has often been recognised in terms of Irish constitutional rights. There are now suggestions that existing laws and technologies, such as technologies and laws relating to competition law and intellectual property, should be balanced to accommodate human rights.[443]

There has already been a call across jurisdictions to recognise internet access as a human right in this jurisdiction.[444] While this argument and the support for it are growing, it has not generally been linked with the issues and concerns relating to SM, child protection and related statute crimes. It is suggested that it is only a matter of time until these issues become more central.

The increasing use, if not reliance, by individuals on the internet for news, information and communications might enhance the argument for recognition of the internet as an essential technology and, separately, of a human right of access to the internet.

The European Convention on Human Rights has also been relevant in terms of interpreting an associational-type right. For example, the European Court of Human Rights has stated as follows,

'Respect for private life must also comprise to a certain degree the right to establish and develop relationships with other human beings. There appears, furthermore, to be no reason of principle why this understanding of the notion of private life should be taken to exclude activities of a professional or business nature since it is, after all, in the course of their working lives that the majority of people have a significant, if not the greatest, opportunity of developing relationships with the outside world. This view is supported by the fact that, as was rightly pointed out by the Commission, it is not

---

441 Ibid, 284.
442 F La Rue, *Report of the Special Rapporteur on the Promotion and Protection of the Right to Freedom of Opinion and Expression*, United Nations, 16 May 2011. D Kravets, 'UN Report Declares Internet Access a Human Right', *Wired.com*, 2 June 2011. ML Best, 'Can the Internet be a Human Right?' (2004) (4) *Human Rights & Human Welfare* 23–31. 'Top French Court Declares Internet Access "Basic Human Right"', *FoxNews.com*, 12 June 2009, available at www.foxnews.com/story/0,2933,525993,00.html.
443 See, for example, AEL Brown, 'Access to Essential Technologies: The Role of the Interface Between Intellectual Property, Competition and Human Rights' (2010) (24) *International Review of Law Computers & Technology* 51. Brown calls for a draft Access to Knowledge Treaty, ibid.
444 See 'Calls to Make Internet a Human Right Under Irish Law', *Silicon Republic*, 15 April 2011, referring to calls by Ronan Lupton, the chairman of ALTO.

always possible to distinguish clearly which of an individual's activities form part of his professional or business life and which do not.'[445]

2.11.6   *Broadband internet*

In many places, there is ongoing consternation in relation to the slow pace of broadband availability and roll-out. If internet access is recognised as a human right, this may then place an obligation on the state to ensure that it is properly rolled out. This would have obvious political and cost issues.

2.11.7   *Children's rights to access internet*

Just as we are considering expressly enshrining children's rights in the Irish Constitution, the issue of internet access and human rights raises an altogether new issue. Let us assume that there is a human right of access to the internet. The question then arises as to who the recipient of this right is. Is it adults only? Is it children, young persons and teenagers? If we assume that children are recipients of internet access rights, can they assert this right against parents or schools to be allowed to access the internet, SN or other websites? Indeed, can they assert the right in order to access websites without supervision and without internet safety filtering software? These issues have yet to be considered.

2.11.8   *Conclusion*

While the issue of internet restrictions has yet to be considered in the UK, it is only a matter of time. It is to be recommended, however, that any such measures be fully and properly debated and, if implemented, that they be done so in a principled manner. Whether a human right of access to the internet is recognised in particular jurisdictions or not, it may be quite a draconian step regardless to restrict access, whether judicially or via statute. In terms of content, there are developing issues of contention regarding peer to peer (P2P), filtering and 'three strikes'. 'Three strikes' is the concept promoted by the music (and film) industries that an internet access provider should block users when they have been notified for a third time that they are illegally downloading copyright music or film materials. These are sometimes known as graduated responses. Any such step should be considered at a policy level and not in an instant or reactive manner to a hard-case example.

The subject matter of possible internet access sanctions can also differ considerably. Internet restrictions in relation to P2P are quite different from child sex offender restrictions. While copyright infringement is an important issue, P2P infringement issues have, until recently, been viewed more as civil

---

445 *Niemitz v Germany*, ECHR, 23 November 1992, Series A No. 251/B, para. 29.

wrongs than criminal wrongs.[446] In addition, there are many reasons to say that P2P infringement is less serious than physical sex offences arising through sex offenders using SM.

Indeed, in the case of P2P filtering, three strikes and so on, the copyright infringement is only alleged and may never come to court. The telecommunications companies and ISPs are acting on foot of allegations of infringement made by the content industries. The extent to which internet access is recognised as a human right might be more significant in the hierarchy of rights than an allegation of copyright infringement, notwithstanding that copyright is acknowledged now as a property right.[447]

A further issue to be considered, in terms of sentencing restrictions, is the extent to which judicial discretion[448] presently encompasses the scope to impose internet access restrictions. Is there a need for this to be permitted expressly in a new statute? This is not an easy question to answer, and may require an appeal case to decide the point in the absence of a statutory provision arising.

Child safety online is an important issue. However, as we are recognising and expanding the rights of children, there may be an unintended consequence of recognising the human right of internet access. It is always difficult to get the right proportion and balance in sentencing. Clearly, these are also issues which are important and which need to receive greater consideration in future.

2.12 BANS OR RESTRICTIONS ON INTERNET OR SM

This could generally include court orders restricting convicted (or charged) persons prosecuted for hacking, child pornography, etc. This relates to whether there are any literature, cases, rules or laws in relation to bans or restrictions on the use or, of access to, the internet and or SM, eg court orders restricting convicted (or charged) persons prosecuted for hacking, child pornography, etc in respective jurisdictions.

One of the emerging issues in relation to SM is whether it is permissible to impose a ban or sanction against someone convicted that they cannot access the internet, or cannot access certain websites. For example, can someone be banned from SM? Can they be banned from using the internet entirely? This issue applies in the context of, for example, hacking, internet fraud and online child sex offences.

---

446 In relation to copyright offences, see Chapter 13 of the Copyright and Related Rights Act 2000.
447 As provided in s 17(1) of the Copyright and Related Rights Act 2000. See also A Murphy and C Kelly, *Copyright and Related Rights Act 2000* (Round Hall Sweet and Maxwell, Dublin, 2002).
448 See generally A Barak, *Judicial Discretion* (Yale University Press, Yale, 1989); O'Malley, *op. cit.*

Eric P Robinson (in chapter C33) states that,

'Generally, restrictions on speech are suspect under the First Amendment. *Near v Minnesota* 283 US 204 (1919); *New York Times v United States* 403 US 713 (1971); *Nebraska Press Association v Stewart* 437 US 539 (1976). But statutes, regulations, and court orders limiting or restricting speech online have been upheld in certain circumstances.

For example, several states have passed laws barring registered sex offenders from accessing SM sites. See eg 730 Ill Comp Stat 5/3-3-7(a) (7.12); Ky Rev Stat Ann § 17.546; Minn Stat Ann § 244.05(6)(c); NY Penal Law § 65.10(4-a)(b); Tex Gov't Code Ann. § 508.1861. Several of these statutes have been found unconstitutional. See eg *Doe v Jindal* 853 F Supp 2d 596 (MD La 2012); *Doe v Neb* 898 F Supp 2d 1086 (D Neb 2012); *Doe v Prosecutor* 705 F3d 694, 89 ALR 6th 771 (7th Cir 2013) (Indiana statute); *State v Packingham* 748 SE2d 146 (NC Ct App 2013), appeal granted, 749 SE2d 842 (No 366PA13) (NC Nov 7, 2013) (Argued Sept 8, 2014). After its statute barring sex offenders from SM was struck down, Louisiana adopted a new law requiring them to identify themselves as offenders on SM. La Rev Stat § 15:542.1(D) (added by 2012 La Acts chap 385 § 1), while also enacting a modified version of the prior statute. Many SM sites also have their own policies barring registered sex offenders.

But not all courts have ruled against restrictions on use of SM. A New Jersey appeals court upheld restrictions placed on a woman's blogging about her family as a condition of her parole in a criminal case stemming from a custody dispute, because of the limited nature of the restriction. See *State v HLM* No A1257-12, 2014 NJ Super. Unpub. LEXIS 1079 (NJ AppDiv May 13, 2014) (unpublished).

Limitations on attorney speech and advertising can also cover SM. The California Bar recently concluded, for example, that any SM discussion of an attorney's professional qualifications or availability for employment is subject to ethical rules regarding attorney communications. Cal Bar Formal Op 2012-186 (Dec 12, 2012). See also ABA Formal Opinion 10-457 (Aug 5, 2010) (applying advertising rules to attorney web sites). Attorney communication via SM also presents issues regarding the formation of an attorney-client relationship and, if such a relationship exists, client confidentiality. The ABA has proposed a new comment to Model Rule of Ethics 1.18 which would outline the factors in determining whether if she an attorney-client relationship is created via online communication.

Other SM limitations have emerged in the form of contractual provisions restricting customers' online reviews and comments. A new California law prohibits such provisions (Cal Civil Code § 1670.8, added by 2014 Cal Laws chap 308).

Courts now routinely issue protection orders that include SM, and any contact – including an online "like" or "poke" – can lead to an arrest for violating such an order.'

In relation to the UK, Jonathan McDonald indicates as follows,

'There are no rules specifically relating to SM, although there are more general rules in relation to access to the internet.

In relation to sexual offences, where a defendant has committed such offences by use of the Internet, a Sexual Offences Prevention Order under the Sexual Offences Act 2003 may be issued restricting access to the Internet (see C32.11 for further details).

In relation to hacking, in the case of *R v Mangham (Glen Steven)* [2012] EWCA Crim 973, the defendant had committed offences contrary to the Computer Misuse Act 1990 namely by securing unauthorised access to computer material with intent, contrary to section 1 and committing unauthorised modification of computer material contrary to section 3. As these had constituted "serious crimes" under the Serious Crime Act 2007, the lower court had imposed a serious crime prevention order (SCPO, a type of injunction), restricting the defendant to owning and using only one personal computer with internet access. He had to notify the authorities of any employment use and was forbidden to use encryption or data-wiping software on his personal computer. He was also forbidden from deleting any user log or history or from having more than two email accounts. His email accounts also had to be with UK-based service providers. Whilst the Court of Appeal quashed the serious crime prevention order on the grounds that the defendant did not pose a future risk (an SCPO is designed not to punish but is preventive in character), it is possible that an SCPO remains a restriction that may be imposed for computer hacking in the future.'

The Belgium report indicates as follows,

'Legislation

Although there is no specific legal provision in this respect, there exist several provisions that can be used to achieve this objective,

- Article 145 and following of the Act of 13 June 2005 regarding electronic communications enable the confiscation of devices that are used for certain illegal ends as defined in the Act;

- Article 39bis of the Criminal Procedure Code regarding data seizure (compare with Article 19 of the Cybercrime Convention) enables the public prosecutor to restrict access to data; and

- Article 42 of the Criminal Code on special confiscation allows for the confiscation of goods which were used to commit a crime insofar as they belong to the criminal.

Case law

There exists – very limited and non-published – case law according to which an individual condemned in a child pornography case was forbidden access to social media on the basis of the Act of 29 June of 1964 regarding reprieve, suspension and probation (Correctional Court of Veurne, 2 March 2011). In that case, it was a probation measure, but it could for instance also be a measure in the framework of a release from detention before trial.

Another example is a case before the Correctional Court of Mechelen, where the defendant had been harassing girls via the internet, asking them to send nude pictures and movies and then blackmailing them with this material into performing sadomasochistic acts. The Court convicted this defendant to a three-year prison term, accompanied by an internet ban (Correctional Court of Mechelen, 15 June 2012)'.[449]

2.13 IDENTITY THEFT (OR EQUIVALENT)

There are increasing litigation issues and rules or laws relating to identity theft problems. The theft of information, files, etc has always been an issue. However, the advent of digital data, second-generation internet and SM emphasises problems of data theft, password theft, identity theft, hacking and malevolent software such as viruses. A breach in a website's security or a corporate computer system could result in the disclosure of the personal details of millions of individuals. Identity theft is identified as the fastest-growing offence in the US, but equally as one of the most 'daunting set of challenges' to address.[450] As indicated above, Lord Justice Leveson was concerned at the extent of the illicit trade in personal data in the UK.[451]

There is concern that many service apps or applications for SM are easily vulnerable to hackers who use them to vacuum up the personal details of users and to impersonate (some of) those individuals.[452] Facebook has been criticised for not testing and verifying the security of its third-party apps suppliers.[453]

---

449 This case was covered by a Belgian newspaper, and the article is available at: www.demorgen. be/dm/nl/989/Binnenland/article/detail/1454590/2012/06/15/Webpedofiel-krijgt-3-jaar-met-uitstel-en-internetverbod.dhtml.
450 J Winn and K Govern, 'Identity Theft: Risks and Challenges to Business of Data Compromise' (2009) *Temple Journal of Science, Technology & Environmental Law* 49.
451 Leveson Inquiry. *An Inquiry into the Culture, Practices and Ethics of the Press: Report, The Right Honourable Lord Justice Leveson*, November 2012. Available at www.official-documents.gov.uk/document/hc1213/hc07/0780/0780.asp. Also see the main inquiry website at www.levesoninquiry.org.uk/.
452 C Soghoian, 'Hackers Target Facebook Apps', *CNET News*, 27 March 2008, http://news.cnet. com/8301-13739_3-9904331-46.html, referred to in Nelson *et al.*, *op. cit*, 32.
453 J Halliday, 'Facebook Accused of Deceiving Developers Over Security. Social Networking Site Allegedly Did Nothing to Verify Security of Applications It Was Paid Tens of Thousands of Dollars to Review', *Guardian*, 30 November 2012, available at www.guardian.co.uk/technology/2012/aug/13/facebook-developers.

The Federal Trade Commission (FTC) described this as 'deceptive'.[454] The FTC also filed various other privacy complaints against Facebook.[455] In a settlement, Facebook agreed to 20 years of FTC privacy audits.[456] Google was fined \$22.5m in a settlement with the FTC in relation to its having bypassed privacy security settings.[457] The FTC states,

> 'The settlement is part of the FTC's ongoing efforts make sure companies live up to the privacy proms they make to consumers, and is the largest penalty the agency has ever obtained for a violation of a Commission order. In addition to the civil penalty, the order also requires Google to disable all the tracking cookies it had said it would not place on consumers' computers.'[458]

At the time, this was the largest such penalty. SM as well as other websites have also been targeted directly by hackers searching for personal user details.[459]

Personal details such as name, address, date of birth and credit card data are all targets for hackers. There is growing evidence of the vast market involved in the sale of whole databases containing personal details that have been illicitly obtained.

One of the reasons for websites, etc being targeted by hackers is that they can sell the personal data to third parties, seek to blackmail the website company, or use the personal information directly to try to access bank accounts or charge purchases to the accounts of third-party individuals. In another example, as yet unreleased pop songs are hacked and then sold.[460] Attempts to access or charge an individual's bank account using their stolen personal data is known as identity theft. The UK Leveson Inquiry, as well as referring to the illicit trade in personal data, also referred to the press

---

454 Ibid.
455 FTC complaint available at www.ftc.gov/os/caselist/0923184/111129facebookcmpt.pdf.
456 F Lardinois, 'Facebook and FTC Settle Privacy Charges – No Fine, But 20 Years of Privacy Audits', *Techcrunch*, 10 August 2012, available at http://techcrunch.com/2012/08/10/facebook-ftc-settlement-12/. The FTC settlement agreement is available at www.ftc.gov/os/caselist/0923184/111129facebookagree.pdf.
457 F Lardinois, 'Google Settles With FTC, Agrees to Pay \$22.5m Penalty for Bypassing Safari Privacy Settings', *Techcrunch*, 9 August 2012, available at http://techcrunch.com/2012/08/09/google-settles-with-ftc-agrees-to-pay-22-5m-penalty-for-bypassing-safari-privacy-settings/. The FTC settlement is available at http://ftc.gov/opa/2012/08/google.shtm.
458 At http://ftc.gov/opa/2012/08/google.shtm.
459 A Lyly, 'Twitter Hacked, Personal Documents Leak', *Neowin.net*, 17 July 2009, http://neowin.net/news/main/09/07/17/twitter-hacked-personal-documents-leak; Siderr, 'Facebook Applications Revealed' (Winter 2007–2008) (13) *2600: Hacker Quarterly* 32–33, each as referred to in Nelson *et al.*, *op. cit*, 32.
460 J Clark, 'Hackers Convicted of Stealing New Lady Gaga Songs', *ZD Net UK*, 18 June 2011, available at www.zdnet.co.uk/blogs/mapping-babel-10017967/hackers-convicted-of-stealing-new-lady-gaga-songs-10022764/.

blackmailing of a football manager with personal data that was obviously sensitive to him.[461]

There is now also an increasing practice of hacking the closed, or private, SM accounts of well-known individuals such as actors and sports stars. The hackers will then contact and seek to blackmail the individual in order not to make the information, comments, photographs or videos public.

In one of the more recent hacking examples, Sony PlayStation is reported to have been breached, with over 70 million customers' personal details and accounts being illegally accessed.[462] There is also discussion in relation to whether various national data protection authorities will investigate and/or impose sanctions, including monetary sanctions.[463] The UK Information Commissioner (the equivalent of the Irish Data Protection Commissioner) is reported to have contacted Sony to investigate the issues further.[464] Certain US states' Attorneys General are also reported as investigating the breach.[465] The amount of data lost in this instance has been described as 'extraordinary'.[466] It was also reported as including credit card data.[467] The UK Information Commissioner's Office (ICO) has imposed a number of significant fines in relation to data loss. These include fining a police force £150,000 (Greater Manchester Police), a charity £70,000 (Norwood Ravenswood), a health authority £70,000 (Aneurin Bevan Health Board), a council £140,000 (Midlothian Council), hospitals £375,000 (Brighton and Sussex University Hospitals NHS Trust) and a medical entity £225,000 (Belfast Health and Social Care Trust).[468] A spam text marketing

---

461 Leveson Inquiry. *An Inquiry into the Culture, Practices and Ethics of the Press: Report, The Right Honourable Lord Justice Leveson*, November 2012. Available at www.official-documents.gov.uk/document/hc1213/hc07/0780/0780.asp. Also see the main inquiry website at www.levesoninquiry.org.uk/. Note also the case of Daniel Perry in Scotland, who is reported to have committed suicide after online blackmail.

462 See, for example, 'Hacker Steals PlayStation Data', *Irish Times*, 27 April 2011, available at http://irishtimes.com/newspaper/breaking/2011/0427/breaking2.html; 'Sony PlayStation Suffers Breach', *Reuters*, available at www.reuters.com/article/2011/04/26/us-sony-stoldendata-idUSTRE73P6WB20110426.

463 See, for example, 'Sony May Face Legal Action over Data Breach', *Irish Times*, 28 April 2011.

464 Ibid.

465 Ibid.

466 Rory Cellan-Jones and Rupert Goodwins, interviewed on *BBC News*, '"Long Term Damage" from Sony PlayStation Scandal', available at http://news.bbc.co.uk/today/hi/today/newsid_9468000/9468943.stm.

467 See, for example, 'Sony: Credit Data Risked in PlayStation Outage', *Forbes*, available at http://origin.9news.com/money/195455/75/Sony-Credit-data-risked-in-PlayStation-outage-.

468 A Deighton, 'ICO Fines Police and Charity for Data Breaches', *Lexology*, 29 October 2012, available at www.lexology.com/library/detail.aspx?g=7adda7a8-ba0c-4404-adba-1e6121b0824a; S Evans, 'Huge Increase in ICO Fines for Data Breaches', *Computer Business Review*, 13 August 2012, available at www.cbronline.com/news/huge-increase-in-ico-fines-for-data-breaches-130812; 'Data Breaches 10 Times Worse, Say ICO Figures', BBC, 30 August 2012, available at www.bbc.co.uk/news/technology-19424197.

firm was fined £440,000.[469] A local authority was fined £60,000 for sending a child-related report to the wrong person.[470] Separately, the ICO also imposed the first fine for inaccurate and incorrect storage of personal data. Prudential was fined £50,000 for mixing up the account data of customers, which could have resulted in pension-related financial loss for one of the customers.[471]

More recently still, the Leveson Inquiry Report has recommended a more robust approach to implementing (and understanding) the data protection regime, including criticising the UK Information Commissioner for not being more proactive in policing the data protection regime.[472] The report also highlights the needs for a greater appreciation of the data protection regime at judicial level.[473]

2.13.1 *Identity theft and personal name squatting*

Identity theft and using and registering under other people's names are a growing problem. This can be a quasi-personality or IP right. In some instances, in particular in the US, identity theft in relation to financial transactions has been made a specified statute offence.

Many readers will have heard of the problem of parties registering the website domain name (ie website address) of a well-known or famous company. Indeed, the names of celebrities, sports stars and politicians (eg Bertie Ahern) have been registered by third parties. Sometimes, the registrants will then demand a payment from the brand owner.

This latter practice became known as 'domain name squatting' and 'domain name infringement'. There have been numerous important cases around the world in relation to this problem, many of which have resulted in the original entity or individual obtaining an order that the domain name be returned (ie transferred) to them.

---

469 'Spam Texters Fined Nearly Half a Million Pounds as ICO Cracks Down on Illegal Marketing Industry', ICO, 28 November 2012, previously available at www.ico.gov.uk/news/latest_news/2012/spam-texters-fined-nearly-half-a-million-pounds-28112012.aspx; see now www.lawyer-monthly.com/2012/11/spam-texters-fined-nearly-half-a-million-pounds-as-ico-cracks-down-on-illegal-marketing-industry.

470 'Plymouth City Council Fined £60,000 for Sending Child Neglect Report to the Wrong Person', ICO, 22 November 2012, available at www.ico.gov.uk/news/latest_news/2012/plymouth-city-council-fined-60000-for-sending-child-neglect-report-to-wrong-person-22112012.aspx.

471 'Prudential Fined £50,000 for Customer Account Confusion', ICO, 6 November 2012, available at www.ico.gov.uk/news/latest_news/2012/prudential-fined-50000-for-customer-account-confusion-06112012.aspx.

472 Leveson Inquiry. *An Inquiry into the Culture, Practices and Ethics of the Press: Report, The Right Honourable Lord Justice Leveson*, November 2012. Available at www.official-documents.gov.uk/document/hc1213/hc07/0780/0780.asp. Also see the main inquiry website at www.levesoninquiry.org.uk/.

473 Ibid.

Given the growing nature of the problem and the high cost of litigation, a number of specialist arbitration mechanisms were established specifically to deal with these disputes in an efficient and cost-effective manner. The best known of these is the WIPO Arbitration and Mediation Centre's Domain Name Resolution Procedure.[474]

However, given the increase in SM and the increasing incidents of false registrations of profiles in other people's and organisations' names, it is important that this problem be examined.

This problem has already been described as 'username squatting'.[475] It should be noted that, while domain name disputes have included personal names, the issue of SM username squatting is much more likely to involve personal names that commercial names. While SNs increasingly permit organisational users, the vast majority of SM users are individuals.

2.14 HACKING (OR EQUIVALENT)

Hacking is a significant problem, with many different costs. Most jurisdictions are expected to have rules or laws relating to hacking (or equivalent crimes). Unauthorised access to accounts, passwords, etc can involve the offence of hacking. It also, on occasion, does not need to involve someone who is extremely accomplished at computer programming. Some of the revelations in the UK phone hacking scandal and Leveson Inquiry[476] as to the manner of the hacking confirm this. Indeed, the Irish Data Protection Commissioner advised the public to change the generally known default password setting for their mobile phone voicemails.[477] Two Irish students are reported to have pleaded guilty to defacing the Fine Gael political party election website.[478] There have been reports of possible future charges against the students in addition to the Fine Gael incident.[479]

Eric P Robinson (in chapter C33) states that,

'The primary criminal federal statute against computer hacking is the Computer Fraud and Abuse Act 18 USC § 1030 (CFAA), which makes it a crime to obtain information from a computer after accessing it without authorization. The statute also creates a civil action if the unauthorized access causes damage or financial loss. See 18 USC § 1030(g).

---

474 See www.wipo.int/amc/en/domains/.
475 Z Pesochinsky, 'Almost Famous: Preventing Username-Squatting on Social Networking Websites' (2010) (28) *Cardoza Arts & Entertainment Law Journal* 223.
476 The Leveson inquiry, available at www.levesoninquiry.org.uk/.
477 'Commissioner Urges Public to Secure Their Mobile Phones', Data Protection Commissioner, 22 July 2011, available at http://dataprotection.ie/viewdoc.asp?DocID=1160&m=f.
478 M Tighe, 'Student Hackers Face New Charges', *Sunday Times*, 28 August 2013.
479 Ibid.

California and other states have their own versions of this statute. See eg Cal Penal Code § 484-502.9.

Courts disagree on whether use of a computer system or website in violation of the service's terms of use constitutes exceeding authorized access under the statute. Compare *EF Cultural Travel BV v Explorica Inc* 274 F3d 577 (1st Cir 2001) and *United States v Nosal* 676 F3d 854 (9th Cir 2012) (en banc). Congressional efforts to clarify the statute have not succeeded. Unauthorized use of material to which the user legitimately had authorized access is not a violation of the Act. *WEC Caroline Energy Solutions LLC v Miller* 687 F3d 199 (4th Cir 2012) cert denied 133 S Ct 831, 184 L Ed 2d 645 (US 2013); *LVRC Holdings v Brekka* 581 F 3d 1127 (9th Cir 2009).

Aside from the unsuccessful prosecution of Lori Drew for creating a fake MySpace profile that led to a teenage girl's suicide (see C33.7), the most prominent prosecution under CFAA was of Aaron Schwartz, a hacker and activist who downloaded a large portion of the JSTOR database of academic articles. Schwartz committed suicide in 2013, before the case went to trial.'

Jonathan McDonald, referring to hacking in the UK, states that,

'The Computer Misuse Act 1990 criminalises unauthorised access to computer material (s 1), and unauthorised impairment of the reliability of computer systems or data (s 3) may also apply. The Police and Justice Act 2006, section 37, also created new offences relating to the making, supplying and obtaining of tools used in the existing Computer Misuse Act 1990 offences.'

Belgium examples include,

'Legislation

Hacking is criminalised by Article 550bis of the Criminal Code, which criminalises both external (by an outsider) and internal hacking (for example, by an employee). External hacking is described as obtaining (or maintaining) access to a computer system, while knowing that one has no right. Internal hacking is described as overstepping one's rights of access to a computer system. Art. 550bis also criminalizes attempted hacking as well as the development, distribution etc of hacker tools. Art 550ter of the Criminal Code furthermore criminalises system and data interference.

Case law

Correctional Court of Leuven, 15 June 2010

In this case, the Court analysed an attempted hacking of a banking IT-system, whereby the hackers claimed to have good intentions, namely testing the safety of the IT-system in order to increase security. The Court held that people who attempt to hack websites just for the sake of hacking are nevertheless committing computer-related forgery. Furthermore, the court stated that, just because a client gains secured access to internet banking, it does not mean that he becomes an authorized person to access the system within the meaning of Article 550bis.[480]

Correctional Court of Dendermonde, 14 May 2007

In this case, a group of individuals had secretly copied the magnetic strip of payment cards of unaware card holders and used small cameras to capture pin codes. With this information, they withdrew money from the accounts of the card holders. The Court qualified these actions as computer-related forgery (Article 504quater of the Criminal Code) and hacking (Article 210bis of the Criminal Code).[481]

Correctional Court of Dendermonde, 14 November 2008, nr 20.L3.1531/08/26

In this case, a person was caught by the police while using his laptop in his car, parked in front of someone else's house. He confessed that he was chatting via the wireless network of this third person and that he especially drove to this spot because he knew the network did not require a password. The Court ruled that this constituted external hacking (Article 550bis of the Criminal Code).'[482]

2.15   PRIVACY BY DESIGN (PBD) (OR EQUIVALENT)

Privacy by design (PbD) (or equivalent proactive protection policy mechanisms) are an increasing part of protecting SM and other privacy and data protection interests.

Privacy concerns are real, and they are growing as technology grows. Technology also offers solutions in many instances, such as incorporating data protection pre-problem solving into product and service design from the very beginning.

Traditionally, data protection is frequently glossed over from a compliance perspective and looked at in detail only if and when it is necessary to react to a particular issue or complaint arising later on. In effect, it is often the case that organisations do not have to think about data protection in advance in a proactive manner. It is only after an event that detailed compliance is considered. Privacy by design (PbD) seeks to reconfigure the treatment of data protection concerns.

2.15.1   *Privacy by design*

Obviously, there are many data protection concerns posed by SM. Various solutions have been suggested for some of these problems, from legislation to

---

480 This judgment has been published in *Tijdschrift voor Strafrecht* 2011, vol 4, p 270.
481 This judgment has been published in *Tijdschrift voor Strafrecht* 2007, vol 6, p 403.
482 This judgment has been published in *Computerrecht* 2009, vol 2, p 74.

technical solutions to education. One of the new suggested solutions is known as privacy by design (PbD). While this concept could be applied to all data-processing activities, it can also be applied to SM. To date, however, it does not appear to have been.

PbD is relevant to the privacy concerns with SM. This is also a solution applicable in terms of many second-generation internet (Web 2.0) and cloud internet issues. Indeed, others have also been raising the possibility of emphasising privacy as a 'product safety' issue.[483]

The review of the European data protection legal regime, presently being undertaken by the EU Commission, is understood to encompass the promotion of the concept of PbD solutions. It should be recalled that the present EU review is aimed at addressing the problems created by SM and cloud computing, as well as just updating the EU Data Protection Directive 1995.

In Europe the EU Article 29 Working Party expressly recognises the existence and problems posed by SM. As part of dealing with these issues, it proposed greater adoption for the PbD concept.

By making PbD a more explicit legal obligation, 'this would ... bind technology designers and producers and data controllers when using ICT technologies, such that "privacy by default" would become the norm and not the exception'.[484]

Separately, the EU Article 29 Working Party suggests that 'privacy should be embedded into information processing technologies and systems'.[485]

Some have argued that the SNs are in the best position to assist users in dealing with and protecting privacy.[486] There is a criticism that the eCommerce legal defences offer 'intermediaries an incentive to be as little involved as possible in what goes on their web servers'.[487] This includes the EU eCommerce Directive.

---

483 J Grimmelmann, 'Privacy as Product Safety' (2010) *Widener Law Journal* 793.
484 R Wong, 'Data Protection: The Future of Privacy' (2011) (27) *Computer Law & Security Review* 53 at 55.
485 Wong, *op. cit*, 56, referring to Article 29 Working Party, *Opinion 1/2010 on the Concept of 'Controller' and 'Processor'*, adopted on 16 February 2010 at www.cbpweb.nl/dpwnloads_med/med20100219_C.03%20DC-DP_Opinion_Adopted.pdf. Also, M Schmidl and D Krone, 'The EU Art. 29 Working Party's Guidance on Data "Controllers" and "Data Processors"', available at www.bnai.com/EUArticle29/default.aspx.
486 BL Mann, 'Social Networking Websites – A Concentration of Impersonation, Denigration, Sexual Aggressive Solicitation, Cyber-Bullying or Happy Slapping Videos' (2009) (17) *International Journal of Law & Information Technology* 252 at 256.
487 Mann, *op. cit*, 252–257, and referring to C George and J Scerri, 'Web 2.0 and User-Generated Content: Legal Challenges in the New Frontier' (2008) *Journal of Information, Law and Technology* previously at www2.warwick.ac.uk/fac/soc/law/elj/jilt/2007_2/george_scerri; see also www.thefreelibrary.com/Web+2.0+and+user-generated+content%3a+legal+challenges+in+the+new...-a0187327093.

2.15.2   *Pre-problem solving*

At its essence, PbD is about pre-problem solving. It seeks to incorporate the consideration of privacy and data protection issues and concerns into the concept stage of the design of new products and services.

The *Future of Privacy* opinion document addresses PbD, referring to it as a 'new principle' and stating,

'41   The basic concepts of Directive 95/46/EC were developed in the nineteen seventies, when information processing was characterized by card index boxes, punch cards and mainframe computers. Today computing is ubiquitous, global and networked. Information technology devices are increasingly miniaturized and equipped with network cards, WiFi or other radio interfaces. In almost all offices and family homes users can globally communicate via the internet. Web 2.0 services and cloud computing are blurring the distinction between data controllers, processors and data subjects.

42   Directive 95/46/EC has stood well the influx of these technological developments because it holds principles and uses concepts that are not only sound but also technologically neutral. Such principles and concepts remain equally relevant, valid and applicable in today's networked world.

43   While it is clear that technological developments described above are generally good for society, nevertheless they have strengthened the risks for individuals' privacy and data protection. To counterbalance these risks, the data protection legal framework should be complemented. First, the principle of "privacy by design" should be introduced in the new framework; second, as the need arises, regulations for specific technological contexts should be adopted which require embedding data protection and privacy principles into such contexts.'[488]

While the principle of PbD itself is new, similar ideas have been anticipated before. The EU Article 29 Working Party states,

'44   The idea of incorporating technological data protection safeguards in information and communication technologies ("ICT") is not completely new. Directive 95/46/EC already contains several provisions which expressly call for data controllers to implement technology safeguards in the design and operation of ICT. This is the case of Article 17 which lays down the data controllers' obligation to implement appropriate technical and organizational measures. Recital

---

488 *The Future of Privacy*, Joint Contribution to the Consultation of the European Commission on the Legal Framework for the Fundamental Right to Protection of Personal Data, Article 29 Data Protection Working Party, Working Party on Police and Justice, WP 168. Adopted 1 December 2009.

46 calls for such measures to be taken, both at the time of the design of the processing system and at the time of the processing itself. Article 16 establishes the confidentiality of processing, a rule which is mirrored and complemented in regulations regarding IT security. Apart from these Articles, the principles relating to data quality as contained in Article 6 (lawfulness and fairness, purpose limitation, relevance, accuracy, time limit of storage, responsibility) also apply.

45 Whereas the above provisions of the Directive are helpful towards the promotion of privacy by design, in practice they have not been sufficient in ensuring that privacy is embedded in ICT. Users of ICT services – business, public sector and certainly individuals – are not in a position to take relevant security measures by themselves in order to protect their own or other persons' personal data. Therefore, these services and technologies should be designed with privacy by default settings.'[489]

However, it continues,

'46 It is for these reasons that the new legal framework has to include a provision translating the currently punctual requirements into a broader and consistent principle of privacy by design. This principle should be binding for technology designers and producers as well as for data controllers who have to decide on the acquisition and use of ICT. They should be obliged to take technological data protection into account already at the planning stage of information-technological procedures and systems. Providers of such systems or services as well as controllers should demonstrate that they have taken all measures required to comply with these requirements.

47 Such principle should call for the implementation of data protection in ICT (privacy by design or "PbD") designated or used for the processing of personal data. It should convey the requirement that ICT should not only maintain security but also should be designed and constructed in a way to avoid or minimize the amount of personal data processed. This is in line with recent case law in Germany.

48 The application of such principle would emphasize the need to implement privacy enhancing technologies (PETs), "privacy by default" settings and the necessary tools to enable users to better protect their personal data (eg, access controls, encryption). It should be a crucial requirement for products and services provided to third parties and individual customers (eg WiFi-Routers, SNs and search engines). In turn, it would give DPAs more powers to enforce the effective implementation of such measures.

---

489 Ibid.

49 Such principle should be defined in a technologically neutral way in order to last for a long period of time in a fast changing technological and social environment. It should also be flexible enough so that data controllers and DPAs will, on a case by case basis, be able to translate it in concrete measures for guaranteeing data protection.

50 The principle should emphasize, as current Recital 46 does, the need for such principle to be applied as early as possible: "At the time of the design of the processing system and at the time of the processing itself". Safeguards implemented at a late stage are inconsistent and insufficient as regards the requirements of an effective protection of the rights and freedoms of the data subjects.

51 Technological standards should be developed and taken into consideration in the phase of system analysis by hardware and software engineers, so that difficulties in defining and specifying requirements deriving from the principle of "privacy by design" are minimized. Such standards may be general or specific with regard to various processing purposes and technologies.'[490]

PbD is recognised as being important in future data protection compliance and solutions. Various examples are referred to the EU Article 29 Working Party as demonstrating how PbD should enable successful data protection. It states,

- Biometric identifiers should be stored in devices under control of the data subjects (ie smart cards) rather than in external data bases;

- Video surveillance in public transportation systems should be designed in a way that the faces of traced individuals are not recognizable or other measures are taken to minimize the risk for the data subject. Of course, an exception must be made for exceptional circumstances such as if the person is suspected of having committed a criminal offence;

- Patient names and other personal identifiers maintained in hospitals' information systems should be separated from data on the health status and medical treatments. They should be combined only in so far as it is necessary for medical or other reasonable purposes in a secure environment;

- Where appropriate, functionality should be included facilitating the data subjects' right to revoke consent, with subsequent data deletion in all servers involved (including proxies and mirroring)'.[491]

The EU Article 29 Working Party refers to how implementation of PbD may occur in practice. It states,

---

490 Ibid.
491 Ibid.

'53   In practice, the implementation of the privacy by design principle will require the evaluation of several, concrete aspects or objectives. In particular, when making decisions about the design of a processing system, its acquisition and the running of such a system the following general aspects / objectives should be respected,

- Data Minimization: data processing systems are to be designed and selected in accordance with the aim of collecting, processing or using no personal data at all or as few personal data as possible;

- Controllability: an IT system should provide the data subjects with effective means of control concerning their personal data. The possibilities regarding consent and objection should be supported by technological means;

- Transparency: both developers and operators of IT systems have to ensure that the data subjects are sufficiently informed about the means of operation of the systems. Electronic access / information should be enabled;

- User Friendly Systems: privacy related functions and facilities should be user friendly, ie they should provide sufficient help and simple interfaces to be used also by less experienced users;

- Data Confidentiality: it is necessary to design and secure IT systems in a way that only authorised entities have access to personal data;

- Data Quality: data controllers have to support data quality by technical means. Relevant data should be accessible if needed for lawful purposes.

- Use Limitation: IT systems which can be used for different purposes or are run in a multi-user environment (ie virtually connected systems, such as data warehouses, cloud computing, digital identifiers) have to guarantee that data and processes serving different tasks or purposes can be segregated from each other in a secure way.'[492]

2.15.3   *Regulations for specific technological contexts*

However, the 'privacy by design principle may not be sufficient to ensure, in all cases, that the appropriate technological data protection principles are properly included in ICT'.[493] In some cases, there may be a need for a 'more concrete "hands on approach"'.[494] The EU Article 29 Working Party states,

---

492 Ibid.
493 Ibid.
494 Ibid.

'To facilitate the adoption of such measures, a new legal framework should include a provision enabling the adoption of specific regulations for a specific technological context which require embedding the privacy principles in such context.

55   This is not a new concept; Article 14 (3) of the ePrivacy Directive, contains a similar provision: "Where required, measures may be adopted to ensure that terminal equipment is constructed in a way that is compatible with the right of users to protect and control the use of their personal data, in accordance with Directive 1999/5/EC and Council Decision 87/95/EEC of 22 December 1986 on standardization in the field of information technology and communications)".

56   The above would facilitate the adoption, in specific cases, of specific legislative measures embedding the concept of "privacy by design" and ensuring that adequate specifications are provided. For example, this may be the case with RFID technology, SNs, behavioural advertisement, etcetera'.[495]

The EU Article 29 Working Party adds in conclusion that the 'increasing significance of data protection when creating and operating IT systems is posing additional requirements to IT-specialists. This causes the need to firmly incorporate data protection into the curricula of IT-professions'.[496] In addition, the 'technological data protection principles and the ensuing concrete criteria should be used as a basis for awarding labels of quality (certification schemes) in a framework of a data protection audit'.[497]

2.15.4   *Expectations for the future*

There are undoubtedly 'potent, landscape-changing threat[s] to privacy'.[498] Findlay asks the following questions,

- Is it unreasonable to expect privacy in places where such an expectation would have been completely warranted and expected 10 years ago?

- Is it fair to ask people to change their behaviour in the face of such rapid technological change?

- Does the emergence of small, sophisticated and mobile image-capturing devices paired with the explosion of SM expose new privacy risks deserving of protection?

- To what extent must law enforcement standards change and adapt in light of these changes?[499]

---

495 Ibid.
496 Ibid.
497 Ibid.
498 D Findlay, 'Tag! Now You're "It". What Photographs on Social Networking Sites Mean for the Fourth Amendment' (2008) (10) *North Carolina Journal of Law & Technology* 171 at 200.
499 Ibid.

Findlay feels that the choice for solutions to the problem is between individuals' own behaviour and new or reformulated legal protection.[500] Publication in an SM context can have 'severe and dramatic consequences'.[501] The view is expressed that '[c]urrent constructs of privacy law do not prove adept at adequately protecting sensible notions of privacy expectations'.[502]

Garrie, Duffy-Lewis, Wong and Gillespie feel that education, more proactive data protection commissioners and a more enhanced data protection legal regime are required to address the problems with SM.[503] Some authors also suggest that there is not a legally recognised concept of a 'digital identity' in which individuals have, and can seek to protect, rights.[504] This is argued to be evident as a consequence from the UK Identity Cards Act 2006 and what is referred to as 'an individual's transactional identity':[505]

> 'Arguably, a concept of transactional identity which consists of a defined set of information has been evident in commercial practice for several years. However, its presence in legislation which establishes a national identity scheme is a significant development which confirms its emergence as a new legal concept.'[506]

2.15.5   Conclusion

PbD offers a fundamental mind shift in the practical and legal mechanics of privacy and data protection. In the context of SM (and cloud computing, etc) we should embrace it, because these are technologies which affect more individuals, and more rapidly, than any technology before. The scale and pace of growth mean that it is very difficult indeed to stop and think about all the privacy implications. It is commendable, therefore, to engage in pre-problem solving at the early design stage before the new website, product or service goes live.

2.16   TWEETING FROM COURTS, AND ANY RULES/LAWS

Courts are now having to consider whether or not to permit Tweeting from courts and, if so, in what circumstances. Particular rules or laws may be required for the prevention or proper regulation of such SM activities.

---

500 Ibid, 200.
501 Ibid, 201.
502 Ibid, 201.
503 DB Garrie, M Duffy-Lewis, R Wong and RL Gillespie, 'Data Protection: The Challenges Facing Social Networking' (2009–2010) (131) *International Law & Management Review* 127 at 151–152.
504 C Sullivan, 'Digital Identity – The Legal Person?' (2009) (25) *Computer Law & Security Review* 227.
505 Ibid.
506 Ibid, note 11 at 228.

Eric P Robinson (in chapter C33) reports on the US as follows,

'Historically, American courts were reluctant to allow still and audio-video photography and recording equipment (see below). While much of this opposition has waned, it continues regarding newer devices such as smartphones, tablets, and laptops.

Policies vary widely: sometimes from building to building, and sometimes from courtroom to courtroom. Some courts ban the devices from the courthouse entirely, while others allow only selected individuals – usually judges, court personnel, police, and sometimes journalists – to possess and use these devices. Many courts that do allow the devices limit use to the hallways and other areas outside of courtrooms.

An informal survey of federal district courts in 2010 found that 41 of the 92 federal district courts (44 percent) allowed electronic devices into their courthouses, while the other 48 districts (51 percent) banned the devices except for court personnel and probation and pre-trial officers. Among the district courts that allowed the devices in the building, one-third prohibited the public from bringing the devices into courtrooms, while two-thirds allowed the devices in courtrooms but required that they be turned off or silenced.

The best practical advice for those who wish to use new media tools in court is to check local court rules and practice by checking with the court's public information officer, the court's clerk, or (as a last resort) the judge's staff for the procedure in an individual judge's courtroom.

Individuals who use electronic devices, despite court policies against their use, can be held in contempt and jailed. In 2010 a blogger was banned from a Colorado courtroom for using a cell phone in violation of the court's policy, but was permitted to observe the trial in an overflow video room.

Individual state court judges in several states, including California, Colorado, Kansas, Michigan and Ohio, have allowed live Tweeting of proceedings from their courtrooms in recent years. In 2012, the Kansas Supreme Court amended the state's courts rules to explicitly permit Tweeting and texting from courtrooms. 2012 SC 87 (Kan Oct 18, 2012) (order amending Kan Sup Ct R 1001); Iowa did the same in 2014. In the matter of Chapter 25 of the Iowa Court Rules and Amendments to Expanded News Media Coverage Rules (Iowa order Apr 29, 2014) (amending Iowa Ct R 25.1–25.10). Federal judges in Florida, Iowa, Kansas, Massachusetts, Pennsylvania, South Dakota, and Washington DC have also allowed live Tweeting, but in *United States v Shelnutt*, 2009 US Dist LEXIS 101427, 37 Media L Rep 2594 (MD Ga Nov 2, 2009), a federal court denied a media request to send Tweets from the courtroom during trial on the grounds that Federal Rule of Criminal Procedure. 53 bars broadcasting of judicial proceedings (see C33.17).

Even judges who allow electronic devices in their courtrooms may place restrictions on their use, such as prohibiting photography of the jurors or sensitive witnesses. A Kansas state judge declared a mistrial in a 2012 murder case after a reporter Tweeted a photo which inadvertently showed a juror.'

In the UK, Jonathan McDonald states,

'It is permissible for the press, although rules for the general public are more restricted.

For the press, the use of Twitter has been permitted since 2011, when the Lord Chief Justice (head of the judiciary and President of the Courts of England and Wales) issued new Practice Guidance on "The Use of Live Text-Based Forms of Communications (including Twitter) from Court for the Purposes of Fair and Accurate Reporting".

Under the guidance, it is presumed that representatives of the media and legal commentators using live text-based communications from any courts sitting in public session in England and Wales do not threaten the administration of justice and, accordingly, Tweeting is permitted. Permission can be withdrawn by the court, however, at any time.

Ordinary members of the public do not have an automatic right to use Twitter (etc) and must apply to the judge for permission, although this can be done informally.'

Many jurisdictions have no rules or laws that specifically prohibit Tweeting from courts (eg Belgium, Ireland).

2.17 TELEVISION COURTROOM BROADCASTING OR TELEVISION CAMERAS IN COURT, AND RULES OR LAWS

There is also increasing pressure on courts, particularly in certain jurisdictions, to consider permitting television courtroom broadcasting or television cameras in court. If permitted, considered rules or laws may be required, as well as associated effects research.

Eric P Robinson (in chapter C33) refers to the US as follows,

'Most state trial and appellate courts now allow at least some still and video camera coverage of their proceedings. Most federal trial and appeals courts, and the US Supreme Court, generally do not allow such coverage. These policies have also been applied to newer forms of technology, such as smartphones (see C33.16).

The twentieth century saw a long fight over still and video camera access to court proceedings. This fight still continues to some extent today, and the history explains some of the restrictions that still exist on usage of still and video cameras in court.

There were generally no official rules on use of cameras to record court proceedings until the 1930s. In 1934, however, the trial of Bruno Hauptmann in New Jersey state court for the kidnapping and murder of the baby of aviator Charles A Lindbergh attracted extensive media attention, including disruptive flash photography and a snuck-in movie camera. The debacle led the American Bar Association in 1937 to adopt Judicial Canon 35, which recommended that both still and movie cameras be banned from courtrooms. In 1962, the ABA amended Canon 35 to also ban television cameras.

All but two states – Texas and Colorado – adopted bans in their courts. At the same time, Congress banned cameras in federal court. The US Supreme Court endorsed these bans in Estes v Texas 381 US 532 (1965), in which it reversed a conviction for swindling because of the disruptions caused by cameras in the Texas courtroom. The following year, in *Sheppard v Maxwell* 384 US 333 (1966), the Court reversed a murder conviction because of extensive coverage and disruptive behaviour of print, radio and television reporters, even though most of the disruption occurred outside the courtroom.

But even in *Estes* the Court was open to the possibility of allowing cameras if the technology became less obtrusive. "When the advances in these arts permit reporting by printing press or by television without their present hazards to a fair trial," the Court wrote, "we will have another case." *Estes* 381 US at 540.

These changes in technology came in the 1970s, with smaller, less intrusive cameras. In 1978, the ABA considered changing its rule to allow each court to decide for itself, but ultimately decided not to change the 1937 canon. But the same year, the Conference of State Chief Justices voted that each state should create its own policy towards cameras in courts. This led several states to begin experiments allowing such coverage, which the US Supreme Court endorsed in *Chandler v Florida* 449 US 560 (1981), refusing to reverse a murder conviction and holding that *Estes* did not entirely prohibit camera use in courtrooms, as long as they were unobtrusive.

Now, most states allow for some form of cameras in the courtroom. Most states allow camera coverage of trials, but place restrictions on their use. Many states still bar their use in family court and other specialized courts. A few states prohibit camera coverage of trials, and allow coverage in appellate courts only. The Georgia Court of Appeals recently held that the ability to use cameras in trials is not exclusively for the established media, and that individual citizens can use cameras on the same terms. *McLaurin v Ott* 327 GaApp 488, 759 SE2d 567 (Ga App 2014).

The District of Columbia bans cameras entirely from all local court proceedings, although the DC Court of Appeals offers streaming audio and video of its arguments online.

Appellate courts in several states now offer their own live video streams of their proceedings online. In 2011 and 2012, proceedings from a

Massachusetts district court were streamed live and archived online through a project coordinated by Boston public radio station WBUR. The project survived legal challenges, see *Commonwealth v Barnes* 461 Mass 644, 963 NE2d 1156 (2012); and *District Attorney for the Norfolk District v Justices of the Quincy District Court* No SJ-201-0306 (Mass Aug 14, 2012) (single justice order by Botsford J), but stopped streaming when the project's funding ran out.

Camera access to the federal courts is more patchy. The federal courts conducted a limited test of camera coverage of civil trials in several federal district courts from 1991 through 1994. At the conclusion of the test, the committee examining the issue unambiguously recommended that federal courts allow televised proceedings. But the federal Judicial Conference as a whole rejected this recommendation, and concluded in 1994 that "the intimidating effect of cameras on some witnesses and jurors was 'a cause for serious concern'."

Despite this conclusion, in 1996 some judges of the Southern and Eastern districts of New York allowed camera coverage of particular cases. See *Marisol A v Giuliani* 929 F Supp 660 (SDNY 1996); *Katzman v Victoria's Secret Catalogue* 923 F Supp 580 (SDNY 1996); *Sigmon v Parker Chapin Flanau & Kimpl* 937 F Supp 335 (SDNY 1996); *Hamilton v Accu-Tek* 942 F Supp 136 (EDNY 1996).

In reaction to the *Marisol* decision, in March 1996 the Judicial Conference passed a resolution allowing each federal circuit to decide the issue for itself, while strongly urging the circuits to follow the Conference's 1994 policy and to "abrogate any local rules of court that conflict with this decision".

Currently, camera coverage of federal criminal trials is still generally prohibited, except to allow remote viewing by victims under 42 USC § 10608. See Fed R Crim Pro 53; see also *United States v Hastings* 695 F2d 1278, 1279, n 5 (11th Cir 1983), reh'g denied, 704 F2d 559 (11th Cir 1983). The situation regarding civil trials depends on whether the federal appeals court to which a particular district court is assigned has taken action under the Judicial Conference policy to invalidate any district court rules allowing such coverage. If the applicable appeals court has not taken such action, the district court's rule on the issue, if any, applies. The Second and Ninth circuits have not acted to ban cameras in their district courts, so that district courts within these circuits can have their own policies.

In 2011, the federal courts began a second three-year experiment which allowed cameras in 14 federal trial courts to video record civil trials with consent of the judge and both parties, and post the video online. Meanwhile, in a separate program, a total of 32 federal trial and bankruptcy courts offer audio recordings of their proceedings through their websites.

There has been growing pressure for the US Supreme Court to allow still and video cameras to cover its proceedings. The court already posts transcripts of arguments daily, and audio of arguments each week. In February 2014, a video posted to YouTube showed both a portion of the oral argument in the US Supreme Court in a campaign finance case in October 2013 and an activist's interruption of argument before the court in another case a few days before the video was posted. Both portions of the video were apparently shot with hidden cameras in violation of the court's prohibition of cameras.

Several bills have been introduced in Congress in the past several years to require or urge federal courts, including the Supreme Court, to allow cameras. In addition, in 2014 several media organizations began an advertising campaign advocating that cameras be allowed in the Supreme Court.'

In the UK (see chapter C32),

'Since 2013 the Crime and Courts Act 2013 has allowed legal arguments and the final judgment for criminal and civil cases in the Court of Appeal and Supreme Court to be broadcast. Filming is subject to a 70-second delay, allowing offensive language to be screened out.

The Government also intends to extend filming to allow the broadcast of sentencing remarks in the Crown Court. However, victims, witnesses, offenders and jurors will continue to be protected, and will not be part of broadcasts.'

In Belgium, television cameras are in principle not permitted, but exceptions are possible (see chapter C3).

2.18   SM IN COURTROOMS

In addition to Twitter and cameras, courts may have to consider if SM more generally should be permitted or used in courtrooms. This may include, for example, use by the public, journalists, broadcasters, bloggers, jurors, lawyers, witnesses or even judges.

A number of jurisdictions have examples of controversies or cases in relation to the use of SM in courtrooms, whether variously by the public, journalists, broadcasters, bloggers, jurors, lawyers, witnesses or judges.

Eric P Robinson (in chapter C33), in terms of the US, indicates that,

'With the high usage of SM in American society, it is inevitable that Facebook, Twitter and other SM sites and services will increasingly become a factor in legal proceedings. SM can become a problem when used by trial participants in ways that endanger fundamental principles of fairness and impartiality of the courts.

Many of the issues that have arisen from SM have involved jurors using SM to conduct research or communicate with others about a case.

For several years now, courts have been giving jurors more detailed admonitions and jury instructions against educating themselves about cases online. While most courts now have modern jury instructions which tell jurors not to use the internet or SM during trial, it is increasingly apparent that these instructions must specifically mention particular websites and services, and should also include a rationale and explanation for the restrictions that will counteract the habit of "digital natives" to constantly communicate, research and "share" online.

There are numerous instances in which jurors have been found to be using the internet or SM during trial. Several of these have resulted in mistrials or reversals of jury verdicts.

In *Wardlaw v State* 185 Md App 440, 971 A2d 331 (Md Ct Special App 2009), a juror used the Internet to research the definition of "oppositional defiant disorder," a disorder that a therapist testified that she had diagnosed a key witness as having. The appellate court, in a unanimous, three-judge decision, concluded that the trial court's failure to question the jurors about the influence of the Internet research required a reversal.

In another Maryland case – the high-profile prosecution of Baltimore Mayor Sheila Dixon for political corruption charges – the court discovered that five of the jurors had become Facebook friends and communicated during the trial. The issue became moot after Dixon pleaded guilty. *State v Dixon*, Case Nos 109009009, 109210015 and 109210016 (Md Cir Ct, Baltimore County indictments filed Jan 9, 2009).

In *People v Wadle* 77 P3d 764 (Colo App 2003) aff'd, 97 P3d 932 (Colo 2004), the appeals court granted a new trial in a case where a juror did research online about the drug Paxil, which the criminal defendant accused of murdering her step-grandson had taken, and shared that research with other jurors. The Arkansas Supreme Court reversed a murder conviction in a case where one juror Tweeted during the trial, while another fell asleep. *Erickson Dimas-Martinez v State* 2011 Ark 515, 385 S W 3d 238 (Ark 2011). ... A federal judge who found out that a juror had "friended" the plaintiffs in a personal injury and wrongful death case after the trial held that the timing of the online connection meant that the jury verdict for the defence need not be vacated. *Wilgus v F/V Sirius Inc* 665 F Supp 2d 23 (D Me 2009) (denying new trial motion).

A few courts have found jurors in contempt for using SM during trials. A Texas judge sentenced a juror who sent a "friend" request to the defendant in a personal injury case to two days of community service. A Florida court imposed a three-day jail sentence for criminal contempt on a juror who sent a friend request to the defendant in an auto negligence case. After the friend request was discovered and the juror was dismissed, the juror wrote on Facebook, "Score ... I got dismissed!! apparently they frown upon sending a friend request to the defendant ... haha." A New York woman pleaded guilty in 2009 to a misdemeanour charge of attempted unlawful grand jury disclosure after she posted comments to a newspaper website about her experience several months earlier serving on a grand jury that refused to issue an indictment in the 2007 death of a man in police custody.

But courts have not found all juror use of SM to be problematic. In 2006, the New Hampshire Supreme Court rejected a murder convict's effort to overturn a guilty verdict based on a juror's pre-trial blogging, in which the juror said he was going on jury duty and, "now I get to listen to the local riff-raff try and convince me of their innocence." *State v Goupil* 154 NH 208, 908 A2d 1256 (NH 2006). A federal court later rejected the defendant's habeas corpus petition based on a similar argument regarding the juror's blog postings. See *Goupil v Cattell* 2008 DNH 46, 2008 WL 544863, 2008 US Dist LEXIS 14774 (D NH Feb 26, 2008) (unpublished).

In August 2011, California adopted a statute making it a crime for jurors to use SM and the internet to do research or disseminate information about cases. 2011 Cal Laws chap 181 (codified at Cal Penal Code section 166(a) (6)). But two years after the law went into effect the state's Judicial Council recommended that the statute be repealed, saying that the possibility of criminal sanctions actually impeded courts' inquiries into improper online activity by jurors. The criminal provisions were repealed in 2014, 2014 Cal Laws chap 99, although civil penalties remain.

SM use affecting trials is not limited to jurors: other trial participants, including judges, have been found to be using the internet and SM.

An Ohio trial judge was removed from a murder case after comments on the case on a local newspaper's website were traced to her office computer. (His daughter claimed to have made the posts.) *State v Sowell* (Saffold) 134 Ohio St 3d 1204, 2010-Ohio-6723, 981 NE 2d 869 (Ohio 2010) (Pfeifer, Acting CJ). The Second Circuit Court of Appeals upheld a decision by District Judge Denny Chin that relied on internet research in deciding whether a convicted bank robber had violated his terms of supervised release. *US v Bari* 599 F3d 176 (2d Cir 2010). But see *Ibey v Taco Bell Corp* 2012 WL 2401972, 2012 US Dist LEXIS 91030 (June 18, 2012) (court may not take judicial notice of information on LinkedIn profile because its reliability can be questioned).

An ABA ethics opinion concluded that judges may participate in electronic SM, but must avoid any conduct that would undermine the judge's independence, integrity, or impartiality, or create an appearance of impropriety. ABA Formal Op 462 (Feb 21 2013). The Florida Supreme Court's Judicial Ethics Advisory Committee went even further, declaring that judges may not ethically be SM "friends" with lawyers who may appear before the judge in court. Fla Sup Ct Jud Ethics Op 2009-20 (Nov 17 2009). The Massachusetts Judicial Ethics Committee agreed, adding that a judge must recuse him or herself when an SM "friend" appears before the judge. Mass Jud Ethics Comm. Opinion 2011-6 (Dec 28 2011). The Oklahoma Judicial Ethics Advisory Panel concluded that judges may be "friends" with attorneys who do not appear before them. Oklahoma Judicial Ethics Opinion 2011-3 (July 6 2011).

California forged a middle course, concluding that the propriety of judges' online friendships depended on a number of factors. Cal Jud Ethics Comm. Op 66 (Nov 23 2010). Maryland urged judges to "proceed cautiously" in their use of SM. Md Jud Ethics Comm Op 2012-07 (June 12 2012). Other states, while also urging caution, concluded that judges could participate in SM. See NY Jud Ethics Comm. Op 08-176 (Jan 29 2009); Ky Jud Ethics Comm. Op JE-119 (Jan 20 2010); Ohio Jud Ethics Comm. Op 2010-7 (Dec 3 2010); and SC Advisory Comm on Stds of Jud Conduct Op No 17-2009 (Oct 2009).

The Florida District Court of Appeal followed that state's ethics ruling in disqualifying a judge who was Facebook friends with the prosecutor. Domville v Florida, 103 So 3d 184 (Fla App 4 Dist Sept 5 2012), rev denied 110 So 3d 441 (Fla 2013). A North Carolina judge was publicly reprimanded for posting comments on Facebook regarding a pending support and custody hearing, which were visible to the judge's "friends," including one of the lawyers involved in the hearing. B Carlton Terry Jr, Inquiry No 08-234 (NC Jud Stds Comm'n. April 1 2009).

SM usage by trial attendees has also led to problems. In 2010 an Ohio judge found two trial attendees, who separately pointed a Flip camera and a cell phone towards the jury during trial testimony in a murder case, guilty of contempt of court and sentenced them to 30 and 60 days in jail. The judge also declared a mistrial in the murder case. In a New York sex-abuse case, four trial observers were arrested after they used a cell phone to take pictures of the alleged victim as she testified and posted one of the pictures on Twitter.

Another trial participant whose SM use raises questions is counsel. Most of the discussion of attorneys' use of SM has focused on conducting research of trial participants, particularly researching potential jurors during "voir dire".

A 2014 ABA ethics opinion concluded that "a lawyer may review a juror's or potential juror's Internet presence, which may include postings by the juror or potential juror in advance of and during a trial, but a lawyer may not communicate directly or through another with a juror or potential juror." ABA Formal Op Formal Opinion 466 (April 24 2014). This was in accord with earlier opinions of the New York City Bar Association and the New York County Lawyers' Association. NY Cnty Law Ass'n. Formal Op 743 (May 18 2011); NYC. Bar Ass'n Formal Op 2012-02 (2012). The city bar's opinion expanded on what constitutes a "communication," and concluded that "it is an attorney's duty to research and understand the properties of the service or website she wishes to use for jury research in order to avoid inadvertent communications."

Other ethics opinions have considered attorneys' online research about other trial participants. The New York State Bar found it ethical for an attorney to obtain information from an adverse, unrepresented party's public SM page, as long as the attorney does not request access beyond that available to all web users. NYS Bar Ass'n Ethics Op 843 (Sept 10, 2010). But the San Diego County Bar found that sending a "friend" request to an adverse represented party is improper. San Diego County Bar Legal Ethics Opinion 2011–2 (May 24 2011). Similarly, the Philadelphia Bar Association found that it is unethical for an attorney to "friend" a witness with an eye towards impeachment of that witness during trial because such communication is deceptive. Phila. Bar Ass'n Ethics Opinion No 2009-02 (Mar 2009).

This does not mean that all courts will allow online research of jurors. A New Jersey trial court barred the plaintiff's attorney in a medical malpractice case from using a laptop to look up potential jurors via the courthouse's open WiFi, saying that allowing it without advance notice would be unfair to opposing counsel. An appeals court rejected the trial court's reasoning, saying that no court rule required such notice. *Carino v Muenzen* A-5491-08T1, 2010 WL 3448071, 2010 NJ Super. Unpub. LEXIS 2154 (NJ Sup Ct App Div Aug 30 2010) (unpublished), certif denied, 13 A3d 363 (NJ, Feb 1 2011).'

In relation to the UK (see chapter C32),

'In *Attorney General v Fraill*; *R v Knox (Gary)* (Divisional Court, 16 June 2011), a juror in a drugs trial who contacted an acquitted defendant via Facebook, whilst the jury was still deliberating its verdicts in relation to the other defendants, was guilty of contempt of court and was sentenced to eight months' imprisonment.

In *Attorney General v Davey* [2013] EWHC 2317 (Admin), the defendant had been acting as a juror when he posted a message on the internet which set out his view about the case he was trying. Using his Facebook account, he stated that he was a juror in a child sex offence case and thus had the opportunity to lawfully cause problems for a paedophile. He was committed for contempt of court for using the internet to post an opinion regarding a defendant and to research a case.'

In Belgium, an example is,

'a case before the Assize Court of Tongeren, the President of the Court warned the members of the jury about the dangers of using social media like Facebook and Twitter. He urged them to be cautious and asked them not to post any messages on SM about anything that has been said in court. By doing this, their objectiveness and independence as a member of the jury could be threatened and they could be persecuted and removed from the jury (*Assize Court of Tongeren* 3 December 2011).'[507]

SM is increasingly being used by lawyers.[508] One of the areas which is at the forefront of the SM debate is the use of SM in court, and in relation to courts. This might seem surprising at first glance, given the historical stereotype of courts being conservative and traditional.

Yet the legal process in courts is at the cutting edge of the regulation of SM. The first issue arising relates to how courtroom actors or participants may use SM. Are they permitted to? Can a witness, lawyer or even judge Tweet or post comments in relation to a case? Can or should they do so in relation to a case they were involved in? One would think that they should certainly not do so in relation to an active case in which they are participating. Courts are having to deal with all these issues.

2.18.1   In-court: witnesses

In one case, a CEO texted his CFO who was in the witness stand while the judge was distracted with a bench conference.[509] A mis-trial was declared by the judge when he was alerted to what had occurred. The judge stated that the text was,

> 'underhanded and calculated to undermine the integrity of this court and the legal process ... Regretfully, plaintiff through its unacceptable conduct has reached into the court's quiver of sanctions, drawn the bowstring taut and aimed the arrow at the heart of its own case. This court has justifiably released the string.'[510]

Costs were also awarded against the plaintiff company.[511]

2.18.2   In-court: juror postings

It is easy to contemplate how a party in legal proceedings could be prejudiced if one of the jurors was to start posting details of the case, confidential information from the jury room or to solicit opinions or feedback.

---

507 For more information, see: www.hln.be/hln/nl/957/Binnenland/article/detail/1352510/2011/11/23/Voorzitter-assisen-wijst-juryleden-op-gevaren-van-Facebook-en-Twitter.dhtml.
508 See, for example, S Stine and J Poie, 'The Good, the Bad and the Ugly, Blogging, Microblogging and Social Media for Public Lawyers' (2009) (17) *Public Law* 13.
509 DC Espana, 'Judge Tosses Fraud Suit after Witness is Texted by Boss during Trial', *Law. com*, 17 August 2009, http://law.com/jsp/law/LawArticleFriendly.jsp?id=1202433074669, referred to in S Nelson, J Simek and J Foltin, 'The Legal Implications of Social Networking' (2009–2010) (22) *Regent Law Review* 1 at 5.
510 Ibid.
511 Ibid.

In the UK, a woman sitting on a jury polled her Facebook friends to see which way she should vote in the case.[512]

Pennsylvania Senator Vincent Fumo appealed a conviction, arguing that a juror was posting trial details on Twitter, Facebook and blogs.[513]

Another juror posted eight Tweets during a trial, one of which stated 'oh and nobody buy Stoam. Its bad mojo and they'll probably cease to [e]xist, now that their wallet is 12m lighter'.[514]

2.18.3   In-court: lawyers and judges

Lawyers are not immune from the advent of online SM, albeit perhaps a little later than others.[515]

In at least one instance, it has been found unethical to have a friend or colleague purport to make a friend request on your behalf with the intention of obtaining information and details from the SM profile of a witness.[516]

There are even examples now where lawyers and judges themselves have fallen foul of social media. In one instance, a lawyer requested an adjournment in a case due to a family death, but their Facebook account referred to social parties appearing to indicate that they were socialising and that no one had died.[517] The same report refers to other lawyers who posted complaints about clients, lawyers and a judge.[518] In another instance, a lawyer and a client were found to be exchanging text messages while the client was giving a video deposition.[519] There was found to be a breach of Federal Rule of Civil Procedure Rule 30.[520] This issue was discovered because the defence attorney inadvertently sent a text to the plaintiff lawyer saying, 'doing fine'.[521]

---

512 'Juror Dismissed After Asking Facebook Friends How She Should Vote on Trial', *MailOnline*, 25 November 2008, http://dailymail.co.uk/sciencetech/article-1089228/Juror-dismissed-asking-Facebook-friends-vote-trial.html, referred to in Nelson *et al*, *op. cit*, 3.

513 *United States v Fumo*, No 06-319, slip op. 115, 116–116, 125 (ED Pa, June 17 2009), previously available at http://paed.uscourts.gov/documents/opinions/09d0710p.pdf, referred to in Nelson *et al*, *op. cit*, 3–4.

514 J Gambrell, 'Appeal Claims Jurors Bias in "Tweets" Sent During $12 Million Case', *Law.com*, 16 March 2009, www.law.com/jsp/article.jsp/article.?id=1202429071686, referred to in Nelson *et al*, *op. cit*, 4–5.

515 Lawyers are being advised to use social networking for their business. See, for example, C Barnes, 'Social Networking: Not Just for Youngsters Anymore', *Bar Leader*, January–February 2009, at 19.

516 TM Williams, 'Facebook: Ethics, Traps, and Reminders' (2007–2008) (36) *Student Law* 24.

517 M McDonough, 'Facebook Judge Catches Lawyer in Lie, Sees Ethical Breaches', *ABA Journal*, 31 July 2009, http://abajournal.com/news/facebooking_judge_catches_lawyers_in_lies_crossing_ethical_lines_abachicago/, referred to in Nelson *et al.*, *op. cit*, 8.

518 Ibid.

519 *Ngai v Old Navy*, No 07-5653 (KSH) (PS) 2009 WL 2391282, at *1 (DNJ 31 July 2009).

520 Ibid.

521 Ibid.

In Florida, the Judicial Ethics Advisory Committee issued guidance on 9 November 2009 advising that judges should not become SM friends with lawyers who appear in their courts.[522]

A non-practising lawyer was suspended after being found to be blogging during a case when they were serving on a jury.[523] Furthermore, the defendant's conviction was also reversed because of the blogging and the comments made.[524] This would not happen in those many jurisdictions where lawyers are not permitted to act on a jury.

In another example, a judge and a lawyer became Facebook friends during a case in they were both involved, and exchanged comments on the case and when it would conclude, and they speculated on whether one of the parties had had an affair.[525] The judge eventually disqualified himself, and was later found to have breached the judicial code for researching one of the party's websites.[526]

Lawyers also need to be extra vigilant so as not to disclose case or instruction details online or via SM.[527]

Nelson, Simek and Foltin recommend the following rules for law firms in relation to SM:[528]

- Remind lawyers that they should avoid the appearance of establishing a lawyer-client relationship. The rule of thumb should be: do not give legal advice – speak about the issues of law generally and factually instead.

- Confidential information must at all times remain confidential. Firms must have a rule that explicitly forbids any posting of confidential information. Attorneys should be required to request permission to post any information that may even remotely seem private.

- Strict privacy settings should be employed when joining a new social network. Do not rely on the default settings for the social network, which are generally very open and public.

---

522 C Gray, 'The Too Friendly Judge? Social Networks and the Bench' (May–June 2010) (93) *Judicature* 236.
523 M Neil, 'California Lawyer Suspended Over Trial Blogging While Serving as Juror', *ABA Journal*, 4 August 2009, http://abajournal.com/news/calif._layer_suspended_over_trial_blog_while_serving_as_juror/, referred to in Nelson *et al.*, *op. cit*, 9.
524 Ibid.
525 R Jones, 'Judge Reprimanded for Discussing Case on Facebook', *The-Dispatch.com*, 1 June 2009, http://the-dispatch.com/article/20090601/articles/905319995/1005?Title=Judge-reprimanded-for-discussing-case-on-Facebook, referred to in Nelson *et al.*, *op. cit*, 10.
526 Ibid.
527 In relation to one US restriction, see Y Ostolaza and R Pellafone, 'Applying Model Rule 4.2 to Web 2.0: The Problem of Social Networking Sites' (2010) *Journal of High Technology Law* 56.
528 Nelson *et al.*, *op. cit*, 33–34.

- Require lawyers to use disclaimers when publishing any content that relates to work performed by the firm.

- Request good judgment. Ask lawyers to be polite and avoid sensitive subjects.

- Any use of a firm's insignia and logo should be run past the law firm's marketing department.

- Remind lawyers that copyright and financial disclosure laws apply equally to online conduct and offline conduct.

- Firms should take steps to educate their attorneys on these guidelines. Whether through a video presentation or a quick, informal seminar, attorneys should be given an opportunity to learn of these guidelines and ask questions about the guidelines if needed.

2.18.4   Twitter

The UK Press Complaints Commission is considering whether to regulate journalists' Twitter use.[529] A complaint to the Press Complaints Commission in the UK by a blogger, alleging that her privacy was breached by a newspaper article publishing her blog comments, was not upheld.[530] Courts are also debating whether Twitter should be allowed in court for reporting purposes.

2.18.5   Reporting: Twitter in court

A Kansas court permitted a reporter to Tweet from court in a criminal gang-related case, apparently on the basis that it opened the legal process to the public.[531] Other courts have expressly prohibited the use of mobile telephones, smartphones, email, Twitter, etc.[532]

2.18.6   Court reactions: rules, regulations, consultations

How should we deal with such potential problems? Some courts ban mobile telephones in court.[533] Other courts appear to ban electronic devices while in

---

529 D Sabbagh, 'PCC Seeks to Regulate Press Twitter Feeds, Watchdog to Consult on How Tweets can be Brought Under its Remit, Asking Each Newspaper to Draw up a "Twitter Policy"', *Guardian*, 6 May 2011, available at www.guardian.co.uk/media/2011/may/06/pcc-press-twitter-feeds.

530 Adjudication – *Sarah Baskerville v Daily Mail*, available at www.pcc.org.uk/cases/adjudicated.html?article=NjkzNA==.

531 LarrysWorld.com, 'Twitter in the Court: Federal Judge Gets It', www.pcanswer.com/2009/03/09/twitter-in-the-court-federal-judge-get-it/ 9 March 2009, referred to in Nelson *et al.*, *op. cit*, 7.

532 Order Regarding Media Conduct and Electronic Equipment Access, *United States v UBS AG*, No 1:09-cv-20423-ASG (SD Florida 9 July 2009), previously available at www.flsd.uscourts.gov/viewer.asp?file=/cases/pressDocs/109cv20423_106.pdf, referred to in Nelson *et al.*, *op. cit*, 8–9.

533 For example, the United States District Court for the Eastern District of Virginia; see S Nelson and J Simek, 'Three Strikes and You're Out: Judges Talk About Technology in the Courtroom' (July–August 2005) *Law Pract* at 24–25.

the jury box or during case deliberations.[534] Some courts permit certain mobile devices.[535] New Jersey apparently permits jurors to bring mobile telephones to court so long as they are turned off; in one Alaskan court, jurors must 'check' the mobile telephones with the bailiff at the deliberations stage; an Oregon court and the United States District Court for the Western District of Louisiana ban juror mobile telephones.[536] The courts in Ramsey County, Minnesota, prohibit jurors from bringing any wireless device to court, and have even declared two mis-trials when mobile telephones were used during deliberations in breach of the ban.[537]

In Multnomah County courts in Oregon, the juror instruction states: 'Do not discuss this case during the trial with anyone, including any of the attorneys, parties, witnesses, your friends, or members of your family. "No discussion" also means no emailing, text messaging, tweeting, blogging or any other form of communications'.[538] The juror instruction also warns against internet searching,

'In our daily lives we may be used to looking for information on-line and to "Google" something as a matter of routine. Also, in a trial it can be very tempting for jurors to do their own research to make sure they are making the correct decision. You must resist that temptation for our system of justice to work as it should.'[539]

An Arkansas court also issues a juror instruction as follows,

'[D]uring your deliberations, please remember you must not provide any information to anyone by any means about the case. Thus, for example, do not use any electronic device or media, such as the telephone, a cell or smart phone, Blackberry, PDA, computer, the internet, and internet service, any text or instant messaging service, any internet chat room, blog, or website such as Facebook, My[]Space, YouTube or Twitter, to communicate to anyone any information about this case until I accept you verdict.'[540]

---

534 Michigan Supreme Court; see A Ramasastry, 'Why Courts Need to Ban Jurors' Electronic Communications Devices', *FindLaw.com*, 11 August 2009, http://writ.news.findlaw.com/ramasastry/20090811.html, referred to in Nelson *et al.*, *op. cit*, 6.

535 Such as the experimental rules in the United States District Court for the Southern District of New York, referred to in AH Helm, 'Courtrooms All Atwitter', *National Law Journal* (New York City), 10 August 2009, at 34.

536 Ramasastry, *op. cit.*

537 Ibid.

538 'Cell Phone Policies/Instructions for Jurors', JUR-E Bull (National Centre for State Courts, Centre for Jury Studies, Williamsburg, Va.) 1 May 2009, previously available at www.ncsonline.org/WC/Publications/KIS_JurInnJurE05-01-09.pdf, referred to in Nelson *et al.*, *op. cit*, 6.

539 Ibid.

540 This was on 21 April 2009, see 'Ride the Lightening: Web 2.0 Jury Instructions in Arkansas', previously available at http://ridethelightening.senseient.com/2009/05/web-20-jury-instructions-in-arkanss.html, referred to in Nelson *et al.*, *op. cit*, 7.

Apparently, similar such instructions have also been given by judges in individual cases.[541]

Overall, there is no universal norm or consistency of approach to these developing issues. In most instances, there is no defined formal written policy. Where policies do exist, they vary greatly in their form and what they specify. 'We have clearly identified the problem, but we certainly have not standardized a solution'.[542] We might equally say that, where policies do exist, we are not altogether familiar with how successful individual policies are. Are some better defined than others? Are some more appropriate? Are some more successful? Research is needed in this area. The US National Center for State Courts has at least begun the first stage of this research, in terms of gathering the different written policies as may exist in the US into one resource bank.[543] Analysing and comparing these should be the next phase. Researching and monitoring the effectiveness is a further stage still, which may require more complex empirical research, at least in part.

A further point, and one which is critically important, is how user-friendly the policies are. They are aimed at lay jurors and therefore should, as far as possible, be user-friendly and drafted in plain English. This issue does not appear to have been considered expressly in the literature to date.

2.18.7   Tweeting and UK courts

The Contempt of Court Act 1981 prohibits the making of sound recordings in court without judicial permission. It also makes it an offence to take photographs in court. The Constitutional Reform Act 2005 made an amendment whereby cameras are permitted in the Supreme Court.

One commentator states that the 'difference between scribbling notes (published later) and filing copy instantly from the courtroom using an electronic device is self-evidently slight'.[544]

Another commentator states that '[o]f course, despite this development, the same small laptops that may be permitted to be used to live-blog court cases in England and Wales cannot be used to type up notes from the proceedings using a word processor; Notebook and paper is needed for that'.[545] He concludes that

---

541 See Nelson *et al.*, *op. cit*, 7, giving an example of *People v Jamison*, No 8042/06, 2009 WL 2568740, at *6 (NY Supreme Court, 18 August 2009).

542 Nelson *et al.*, *op. cit*, 7.

543 Ibid, 7.

544 S Butterworth, 'Can Live Blogs and Twitter Take Court Reporting into the 21st Century?' *Guardian*, 28 July 2010, available at www.guardian.co.uk/law/afua-hirsch-law-blog/2010/jul/28/live-blogging-tweeting-court-reporting.

545 'Tweeting in Court (With Permission) in England and Wales Only for Now', Slugger O'Toole, available at http://sluggerotoole.com/2010/12/21/tweeting-in-court/.

'Julian Assange's court appearances have brought about one partial thawing of court reporting restrictions, but there are many more ice blocks remaining'.[546]

In announcing the tentative official advent in courts, the Lord Chief Justice is reported as saying that live text-based communications may be permitted so long as the judge feels that it will not interfere.[547] However, Laurence Eastham states that,

> 'Of course Lord Judge is right in principle, but I am not sure he has taken prison overcrowding into account. The history of Twitter is littered with the ill-considered tweet that had unexpected and unfortunate effects – look at poor old Paul Chambers. My immediate reaction to the report is to wonder which profession will end up in prison first – will it be the careless journalist looking for a cheap laugh, the bored barrister awaiting his turn and revealing to his followers what he really thinks about the judge or the trainee solicitor who is supposed to be taking notes but who really doesn't want to be there?'[548]

This was in December 2010. It is very prescient in relation to what was to occur in May 2011 with the Ryan Giggs affair, where details were released, accessed and commented on by approximately 70,000 Twitter users, despite the existence of a super-injunction.

The Paul Chambers case involved a conviction and fine under section 127 of the Communications Act 2003 for Tweeting that he was going to blow up a named airport.[549]

One issue is that Twitter limits Tweets to 140 characters. Therefore, there is a concern that this brevity cannot possibly give a full, fair and accurate report of what has occurred in court.[550]

A concern for journalists is that they should have the full defences available for 'traditional' reporting under normal contempt of court rules when they Tweet from court.[551]

Equally, they want to have defamation defences for fair and accurate court reports available to them.[552] It is recognised that the size restriction of 140

---

546 Ibid.
547 L Eastham, 'Contempt', Editor's Blog, *Society of Computers & Law*, 20 December 2010, available at www.scl.org/site.aspx?i=bp18241.
548 Ibid.
549 L Eastham, 'The Twitter Bomb Joke and the Big Issues', Editor's Blog, *Society of Computers & Law*, 23 November 2010, available at www.scl.org/site.aspx?i=bp18068.
550 D Banks, 'Tweeting in Court: Why Reporters Must be Given Guidelines, A District Judge's Decision to Allow Journalists to Use Twitter in the Julian Assange Hearing Raises Interesting Legal Questions', *Guardian*, 15 December 2010, available at www.guardian.co.uk/law/2010/dec/15/tweeting-court-reporters-julian-assange.
551 Ibid.
552 Ibid.

characters can pose a problem in terms of court Tweets being fair and accurate.[553] This can be an issue generally for all court Tweet reports as well as for particular Tweets. 'Can they fairly sum up what might be complex legal points in 140 characters?'[554] Is a Tweet report of a case fair and reasonable? Equally, is a Tweet on the court process generally also fair and accurate? What educational effects are actually being researched and recorded?

There are certainly real issues as to whether Tweets can be fair and accurate, or indeed whether they can in every instance. However, in certain (but not all) contexts, these issues can perhaps be ameliorated by the technology and setting. For example, the use of links in Tweets, known as Tweetlonger, can enable the reader to click through to more extensive content which, taken as a whole, can provide a much fuller and more detailed explanation of a case. However, this also poses a problem, as there is no guarantee that readers will actually click through to the more extensive content reports. Indeed, depending on the configuration adopted, the likelihood may be reduced that many or any click-throughs will occur. One of the reasons why official music-downloading websites were initially so unsuccessful was that there were too many click-through steps for a user to access and download music. This was in contrast to the more user-friendly unofficial and pirate music websites and peer-to-peer (P2P) services.[555] One commentator suggests that '[i]t might also be solved by the use of liveblogs ... which publish tweets and other material, thus giving adequate context'.[556] The implication appears to be that the full stream or thread of all the Tweets is instantly available for a reader. Thus the reader is not looking at one single post about a case, possibly out of context, but can see a whole stream of Tweets about it.

Another danger is that members of the public, citizen reporters or bloggers may wish to Tweet from court. The risk is that 'the tweeting citizen journalist, unaware of court reporting laws, may include material which should be excluded'.[557]

Other issues arise from the particular hardware being used, such as camera phones.

> '[T]weets will often be sent from a smartphone which has a very good camera. Will the temptation to tweet a picture of someone be too much? While the courts appear to be considering opening up to reporting via use of such technology, there has been no indication that that includes sending pictures or video.'[558]

---

553 Ibid.
554 Ibid.
555 Note separate efforts recently to expand anti-piracy legislative protections in new extra-territorial law. See 'US Firms Back Crackdown on Piracy', *Irish Times*, 26 May 2011.
556 Banks, *op. cit.*
557 Ibid.
558 Ibid.

Soon after Twitter was permitted in the Julian Assange case, the Lord Chief Justice announced interim guidance in relation to the permitting of live, text-based communications in court pending a more detailed formal consultation in relation to the issues presented, and permitting such communications including Twitter.[559]

One could argue that the issuance of the guidelines was appropriate, and even overdue. Alternatively, one can argue that the interim guidelines were premature and unnecessary, and a knee-jerk reaction to one case, as opposed to maintaining a status quo while research and policies are considered.

The President of the UK Supreme Court, Lord Phillips, stated,

> 'The rapid development of communications technology brings with it both opportunities and challenges for the justice system. An undoubted benefit is that regular updates can be shared with many people outside the court, in real time, which can enhance public interest in the progress of a case and keep those who are interested better informed.
>
> We are fortunate that, by the time a case reaches the Supreme Court there is very seldom any reason for any degree of confidentiality, so that questions about what should and should not be shared with those outside the courtroom do not usually arise. This means that we can offer a green light to tweeting and other forms of communication, as long as this does not disrupt the smooth running of the court.'[560]

The Supreme Court guidance is meant to be 'limited to the Supreme Court' in part because it is an appeal court and does not interact with witnesses or jurors, and therefore '[d]ifferent considerations' apply from other courts.[561]

It is noted already that the interim guidelines refer explicitly to only one form of technology service, namely Twitter.[562]

It has been suggested now that the 'default position' is that 'tweeting is allowed'.[563] However, such comments can appear as being overbroad. The guidelines are interim.

A consultation process, in terms of considering the issues in greater detail and in relation to what rules may be applied, was also launched (see below). Regardless of what the finding or recommendations will be, this is undoubtedly

---

559 C Dougan-Bacchus, 'Interim Practice Guidance on Use of Live Text-Based Forms of Communication (Including Twitter) from Court', *All England Reporter* (December 2010) (D) 228.

560 Press Notice, 'Guidance Issued for Tweeting the Twists and Turns of Supreme Court Cases', The Supreme Court of the United Kingdom, Reference Number 02/2011, 3 February 2011, available at www.supremecourt.uk/docs/pr_1102.pdf.

561 Ibid. Also 'Supreme Court to Allow Tweeting', www.loughboroughecho.net.

562 J Griffin, 'Tweeting Allowed in Supreme Court', *Suite 1010*, available at www.suite101.com.

563 'Tweeting Allowed in Supreme Court', http://ukscblog.com/tweeting-allowed-in-supreme-court.

an area that will have to be further developed in practice, research and regulation for some time to come.

2.18.8   UK Supreme Court guidance

The UK Supreme Court also addressed the issue of Tweeting and reporting from its chamber in its own policy, issued in February 2011. The Supreme Court notes that the legislation applicable to it is 'materially different' from other courts, as well as the fact that it is an appeal chamber and does not interact with witnesses or jurors.[564] It is noted that the legislative prohibitions of broadcasting and photography in court were 'specifically exempted' in an amendment to the Act for the new UK Supreme Court.[565] The new rules in relation to the Supreme Court provide that, subject to exceptions, lawyers as well as the public can used text-based communication from the Supreme Court, provided that 'these are silent' and 'there is no disruption'.[566] However, no mobile calls are permitted.[567]

The exceptions referred to above are that the person must observe any reporting restrictions that may apply, and that such communications in cases involving children must maintain anonymity.[568] A 'breach of anonymity will be treated as a contempt of court'.[569] There is also a catch-all-type provision whereby the Supreme Court notes that, on occasion, an order may restrict publication of a judgment so as not to influence current proceedings in lower courts.[570] In terms of such restrictions, these 'will be notified to court visitors by a notice at the door of the courtroom, and, where appropriate, by verbal instructions from a Justice'.[571]

2.18.9   The UK (England and Wales) Twitter consultation

A consultation paper, *Consultation on the Use of Live, Text-Based Communications from Court for the Purposes of Fair and Accurate Reporting*, was issued by the Judicial Office for England and Wales on Behalf of the Lord Chief Justice on 7 February 2011. Respondents were called to direct their views to the Courts Reporting Consultation at the Royal Courts of Justice. It relates

---

564 *The Supreme Court of the United Kingdom Policy on the Use of Live Text-based Communications from Court* (February 2011). Available at www.supremecourt.uk/docs/live-text-based-comms.pdf.
565 Ibid.
566 Ibid.
567 Ibid.
568 Ibid.
569 Ibid. Generally, in relation to contempt law, see Borrie and Lowe, *The Law of Contempt* (LexisNexis, London, 2010); *Arlidge, Eady & Smith on Contempt* (Sweet and Maxwell, London, 2010).
570 Ibid.
571 Ibid.

to the possible use of live text-based communications in court. Therefore, it excludes dealing with non-live Tweeting or text-based communications.

2.18.10   The consultation

The consultation set out some of the issues and considerations, and then invited comments and responses in relation a list of predetermined questions:

'•   Is there a legitimate demand for live, text-based communications to be used from the courtroom?

•   Under what circumstances should live, text-based communications be permitted from the courtroom?

•   Are there any other risks which derive from the use of live, text-based communications from the court?

•   How should the courts approach the different risks to proceedings posed by different websites for live, text-based communications from court?

•   Who should be permitted the use of live, text-based communications from court? Is this reconciled with the blanket prohibition against the use of mobile telephones in court?

•   Should the use of live, text-based communications from court be principally for the use of the media? How should the media be defined? Should persons other than the accredited media be permitted to engage in live, text-based communications from court?'

In December 2011, the UK courts, following the consultation, decided to permit or relax the possibility of Tweeting in court, at the discretion of individual judges.[572]

2.18.11   Contempt consultation

In England and Wales, the Law Commission issued an extensive consultation in 2012 in relation to contempt issues,[573] including,

•   contempt by publication;

•   the impact of new media;

•   contempts committed by jurors; and

•   contempt in the face of the court.

The consultation document stated that various,

---

572 See *Practice Guidance: The Use of Live Text-based Forms of Communications (Including Twitter) from Court for the Purposes of Fair and Accurate Reporting*, Lord Chief Justice of England and Wales, 14 December 2011.

573 Law Commission, Consultation Paper No 209, *Contempt of Court, A Consultation Paper*.

'high profile cases ... underscore the need for this project. These include,

(1) a juror who was found to have researched the defendant on the internet;

(2) the first internet contempt by publication, which concerned the posting of an incriminating photograph of a defendant on a website;

(3) contempt proceedings for the vilification of Chris Jefferies during the investigation into the murder of Joanna Yeates; and

(4) proceedings for contempt by publication following the collapse of the prosecution of Levi Bellfield'.[574]

It adds,

'[s]uch cases illustrate the challenge that is posed by the new media to the existing laws on contempt of court which pre-date the internet age. They also illustrate the continuing need for limits on media coverage in order to protect the administration of justice and the right to a fair trial.'[575]

2.18.12   UK (Scotland) consultation

In October 2013 the Judicial Office for Scotland on behalf of the Lord President and the Review Group issued a consultation in relation to Tweeting from courts. It is entitled *Cameras and Live Text-Based Communications in the Scottish Courts: A Consultation.* The results and or recommendations are awaited.

2.18.13   Conclusion

These issues are only coming to be considered in various courts internationally. What might result from the UK consultation, in terms of policy, has yet to be seen. It may also be the case that the *News of the World* phone hacking scandal, and the police and parliamentary investigations, will have some influence on the ultimate results.[576]

2.19   USE OF SM AS EVIDENCE IN COURTS

Various examples of controversies or cases in relation to the use of SM as evidence in courts are now regularly arising. Online and electronic

---

574 Ibid, 1. Footnotes omitted.
575 Ibid.
576 The final UK policy on these issues may have some influence on the ultimate consideration and discussion of these issues in Ireland, albeit not in any binding way. While there are similarities between Ireland and the UK, there are numerous legal and constitutional differences. It is understood that there may be a forthcoming official consideration of some of these issues at Irish judicial level; no details are currently available.

communications are often no longer a secondary means of communication,[577] but rather the primary means. It is inevitable that SM will increasingly be looked at in terms of providing electronic evidence and electronic discovery. This presents new issues and considerations. '[T]he law provides little guidance on how we should deal with some of the newest sources of evidence … SN [web]sites'.[578] How the law adapts to electronic evidence obtained from SM remains to be fully seen, although there are examples of it already being used. Questions, however, remain as to if and when it should be used. These have yet to be fully contested and considered in superior courts.

Some authors feel that detailed familiarity with social network evidence issues is now a requirement for all lawyers. 'It should now be a matter of professional competence for attorneys to take the time to investigate SN [web]sites. You must pan for gold where the vein lies – and today, the mother lode is often online'.[579] In addition, 'law enforcement, school administrators, opposing legal counsel, and even community vigilantes are actively seeking out'[580] SM – both instances of obtaining information and evidence.

2.19.1   New uses and sources of electronic evidence

Electronic evidence increasingly relies on information obtained from SM. Divorces, separations and family law cases, for example, increasingly use SM information. This includes SM page profiles, comment postings, and photographs and activity on SM, dating websites, etc. There are many instances where SM activity can reveal evidence of infidelity, for example.[581]

Certain pertinent evidence can be easily evident when the opposing parties are direct friends on a social network. However, there are also examples of incriminating details being found out indirectly, when the two parties are not direct friends on a particular social network. In one instance, a wife was able to get access to the incriminating Facebook profile through her friend's account.[582] In some instances now, the first thing to occur in new divorce cases may be respective searches of the SM profiles.[583]

---

577 D Flint, 'Computers and Internet', *Business Law Review*, December 2006, 292.

578 DS Witte, 'Your Opponent Does Not Need a Friend Request to See Your Page: Social Networking Sites and Electronic Discovery' (2010) (41) *McGeorge Law Review* 891.

579 S Nelson, J Simek and J Foltin, 'The Legal Implications of Social Networking' (2009–2010) (22) *Regent Law Review* 1 at 14.

580 D Findlay, 'Tag! Now You're "It". What Photographs on Social Networking Sites Mean for the Fourth Amendment' (2008) (10) *North Carolina Journal of Law & Technology* 171 at 198.

581 See, for example, 'Ride the Lightening, Social Networks: An Avalanche of Evidence', http://ridethelightening.senseient.com/2009/03/social-networks-an-avalanche-of-evidence.html, referred to in Nelson *et al.*, *op. cit*, 13.

582 Ibid.

583 Nelson *et al.*, *op. cit*, 13.

There are additional sources of such evidence in addition to SM. These include activity on online communities[584] and discussion boards. In addition, instant messaging communications can also provide electronic evidence, albeit more difficult to produce. In addition to revealing new smoking guns for litigation, SM might actually be the trigger for litigation. It is clear, however, that SM content is increasingly being sought after in the discovery process and discovery requests,[585] and is often perceived (rightly or wrongly) as being fully available.[586] Many cases will come to test this.

2.19.2 *Individual and organisational liability issues*

Individuals themselves also face significant personal liability issues when they stray beyond the boundaries of what is reasonably permissible, even when they feel they are anonymous. Examples include defamation and harassment.

SM presents many potential problems for employers and organisations, some of which include accessing pornography, sending sexually related or harassing messages, gambling, theft of trade secrets and intellectual property rights.[587] Criminal law liability issues also arise.[588]

There are significant potential liability issues for organisations in relation to what their employees post and upload on their own personal pages, blogs and discussion fora. This will increasingly be an issue in employment disputes and court cases.

Aaron Bland states that '[e]mployees' use of computers now commonly expands the work place well beyond the office walls'.[589] However, data protection laws restrict the extent to which employers can monitor or otherwise utilise employees' email, internet and SM content. (This is despite the widespread availability of software for employee monitoring.)[590] This is increasingly an issue of contention. There is also a perception that US law may permit more employee monitoring than may be permitted elsewhere.

SM electronic evidence can arise in both civil cases and criminal cases. These are highlighted below.

---

584 Highlighted by TZ Zarsky, 'Law and Online Social Networks: Mapping the Challenges and Promises of User-generated Information Flows' (2008) (18) *Fordham Intellectual Property Media & Entertainment Law Journal* 741 at 742.

585 RA Ward, 'Discovering Facebook: Social Network Subpoenas and the Stored Communications Act' (2011) *Harvard Journal of Law & Technology* 563. C Calvert, 'Fighting Words in the Era of Texts, IMS and Emails: Can a Disparaged Doctrine be Resuscitated to Punish Cyber-Bullies?' (2010–2011) *DePaul Journal of Art, Technology & IP Law* 1.

586 EE North, 'Facebook Isn't Your Space Anymore: Discovery of Social Networking Websites' (2010) *Kansas Law Review* 1279.

587 A Blank, 'On the Precipe of E-Discovery: Can Litigants Obtain Employee Social Networking Web Site Information Through Employers?' (2010) (18) *CommLaw Conspectus* 487 at 491.

588 Ibid.

589 Ibid, 494.

590 Ibid, 499.

2.19.3   Civil evidence

The permanence of electronic evidence continues to escape many people. Even President Obama advises users (especially younger users) to 'be careful about what you post on Facebook, because in the YouTube age whatever you do, it will be pulled up again later somewhere in your life'.[591] Oliver North was also partly undone with electronic evidence.

Increasingly, civil litigation relies on electronic evidence. Employee litigation might just as easily seek out employee computers, hard drives[592] and electronic devices as SM content when looking for incriminating evidence.

The Irish Electronic Commerce Act 2000 provides for the equivalence of electronic documents, signatures, etc. In addition, the new electronic discovery rules provide new mechanisms and procedures in relation to electronic discovery in Ireland. These are referred to in the Rules of the Superior Courts (Discovery) 2009.[593] Electronic data or electronically stored information (ESI) became a distinct set of discoverable document under US discovery rules from 2006.[594] There are increasing numbers of electronic evidence cases relating to SM. One example in Ireland is *Net Affinity v Conaghan and Avvio*.[595] This involved, *inter alia*, data claimed by the employer on electronic devices in the possession of the leaving employee. Injunctions restraining the employee who was leaving, as well as the new employer that the employee was moving to, were granted. Various materials were also handed back to the employer containing confidential materials. Non-compete injunctions were also imposed.

A Canadian court in March 2009 permitted access and cross-examination in relation to a plaintiff's Facebook profile.[596] The court stated that it was 'reasonable to infer that his SN [web]site likely contains some content relevant to the issue of how [the plaintiff] has been able to lead his life since the accident'.[597]

---

591 In North, *op. cit*, 1287.
592 Blank, *op. cit*, 501–503. Personal diaries have been discoverable; see *Ramsay v Bailey* 531 F2d 706, 707 (5th Circuit 1976). Referred to in North, *op. cit*, 1280.
593 SI No 93 of 2009. Note also P Lambert, 'The Search for Elusive Electrons: Getting a Sense for Electronic Evidence' (2001) (1:1) *Judicial Studies Institute Journal* 23; and Law Reform Commission, Consultation Paper, *Documentary and Electronic Evidence*, LRC CP 57 – 2009 (Government Publications, Dublin, 2009).
594 Rule 34, Federal Rules of Civil Procedure (1970). Referred to in North, *op. cit*, 1281. Also see JD Frieden and LM Murray, 'The Admissibility of Electronic Evidence Under the Federal Rules of Evidence' (2010–2011) *Richmond Journal of Law and Technology* 1.
595 *Net Affinity v Conaghan and Avvio* IEHC 2011/1574. Dunne J. Interim and Interlocutory injunctions granted against leaving-employee and new employer poaching customer. Available at www.bailii.org/ie/cases/IEHC/2011/H160.html.
596 T Remtulla, 'Canada: Facebook Not So Private? Ontario Court Finds Facebook Profile Discoverable', *Mondaq*, 23 March 2009, www.mondaq.com/article.asp?articleid=76332, referred to in Nelson *et al.*, *op. cit*, 11–12.
597 Ibid.

A US woman lost a custody case after her boyfriend's sexually explicit comments were revealed on his MySpace profile.[598] A US husband was also undermined in a case when his MySpace profile described him as 'single and looking'.[599] A related issue which arises is whether it is ethical for the lawyer to attempt to directly or indirectly bypass an individual's SM privacy settings by getting someone to befriend the party so as to gain access to their SM profile information.[600] This is an issue which does not appear to have been considered in great detail as of yet.

A further issue also arises. Intermediary SNs are increasingly subject to applications to court for orders to identify users,[601] following on from their online activities.

2.19.4   Criminal evidence

Notwithstanding the NSA-Snowden revelations, law enforcement authorities increasingly rely on SM searches.[602] The police are also utilising the information posted on SM, in terms of gathering intelligence, investigations and using this information as evidence at trial. It can also be used at sentencing hearings. The police see many benefits to reviewing SM profiles.[603] However, Wells cautions against invasive police use of the internet and SM. Such privacy-invasive police techniques will 'prove costly, oppressive, and foster a dangerous disrespect for privacy in the digital age'.[604] 'Aggressive' police tactics will rebound and have negative consequences.[605] The police may also be doing so without warrant and any express legal authority, and the question arises as to whether such access violates the right to privacy[606] and data protection.

There are many cases that utilise email evidence.[607] However, this is still often a new consideration in litigation in the UK. Some examples from elsewhere are referred to below.

---

598 V Jaksic, 'Litigation Clues are Found on Facebook', *National Law Journal* (New York City), 15 October 2007, 1, referred to in Nelson *et al.*, *op. cit*, at 12.

599 Ibid.

600 See Nelson *et al.*, *op. cit*, 11 at 15.

601 Blank, *op. cit*, 504–506. Note also EP Stedman, 'MySpace, But Whose Responsibility? Liability of Social-Networking Websites When Offline Sexual Assault of Minors Follows Online Interaction' (2007) (14) *Villanova Sports & Entertainment Law Journal* 363 at 377–394.

602 D Findlay, 'Tag! Now You're "It". What Photographs on Social Networking Sites Mean for the Fourth Amendment' (2008) (10) *North Carolina Journal of Law & Technology* 171 at 179.

603 DH Montes, 'Living Our Lives Online: The Privacy Implications of Online Social Networking' (2010) (5) *I/S: A Journal of Law and Policy* 507 at 526–528.

604 PA Wells, 'Shrinking the Internet' (2010) (5) *New York University Journal of Law & Liberty* 531 at 532.

605 Ibid, 567–568. See also MJ Hodge, 'The Fourth Amendment and Privacy Issues on the "New" Internet: Facebook.com and MySpace.com' (2006) *Southern Illinois University Law Journal* 95.

606 Findlay, *op. cit*, 174.

607 See, for example, S Hickey, 'Ex-Bank Workers Appeal Dismissal for "Porn" Emails', *Irish Independent*, 20 January 2011.

In a US fatal drink-driving case, a defendant may have had her sentence escalated to a custodial sentence after the judge referred to her MySpace photographs, which revealed her in alcohol-related poses, the implication being that these were taken after the drink-driving incident.[608] The judge said that she had not learned her lesson and had shown no remorse.[609]

In a US drink-driving injury case, the defendant was also alleged to have received a higher custodial sentence after a photograph of him wearing a prison uniform emblazoned with the words 'Jail Bird' at a party were posted by a friend on Facebook, and later revealed in court.[610]

At a US sentencing hearing, a person who tried to portray himself as peaceful was met with pictures and comments of himself on MySpace with a gun.[611]

It has also been stated that MySpace pages on which a person had gang tattoo photographs may have partly contributed to a defendant in a US case receiving a death sentence.[612] In one Seattle case, a personal injury claim settled without trial after the defence was able to produce a CD of photographs downloaded from the plaintiff's Facebook and MySpace profile photograph showing him snowboarding and jumping[613] after the disputed injury. A group of Virgin airline employees were fired after posting comments about the company on Facebook.[614] More recently, there have been a number of instances of employees as well as students being disciplined in relation to post on SNs and related websites.[615] The airline Ryanair has also been involved in a number of employee-related disputes where it has sought Norwich Pharmacal court orders to obtain electronic evidence regarding the identity of posters of comments online, as well as disciplining employees in relation to particular comments.

One developing area is the use of SM to assist criminals. They may, for example, find out through online postings that a person is on holiday and that

---

608 Ibid. The case was of Jessica Binkerd.
609 Ibid.
610 'Drinking, Driving, and Facebook Don't Mix', *CBS News*, 18 July 2008, available at http://cbsnews.com/stories/2008/07/18/tech/main4272846.html, referred to in Nelson *et al.*, *op. cit*, 12. This was the case of Joshua Lipton. Also Associated Press, 'Unrepentant on Facebook? Expect Jail Time', CNN, 18 July 2008, previously available at http://cnn.com/2008/crime/07/18/facebook.evidence.ap/index.html, as referred to in Findlay, *op. cit*, 177.
611 E Perez, 'Getting Booked by Facebook', *Milwaukee Journal Sentinel*, 3 October 2007, at 9A, previously available at http://redorbit.com/news/technology/1087625/getting_booked_by_facebook/index.html, referred to in Nelson *et al.*, *op. cit*, 13.
612 J Gormley, 'MySpace and Facebook Becoming Evidence in Court', CBS, 3 February 2009, previously available at http://cbs11tv.com/local/MySpace.Facebook.Evidence.2.926231.html, referred to in Nelson, *et al.*, *op. cit*, 13.
613 Referred to in North, *op. cit*, 1279.
614 S Thiel, 'Virgin Atlantic Fires 13 Cabin Crew Following Facebook Comments', *Bloomberg*, 1 November 2008, available at www.bloomberg.com/apps/news?pid=newsarchive&sid=aObNS7eFKIUY. Referred to in North, *op. cit*, 1287. This may not have been fully tested in court.
615 There are numerous instances in Ireland and other jurisdictions. However, schools and universities are still adopting appropriate policies in this regard.

his or her house is therefore vacant. In one research study, it was found that, in one year in the UK, there were over 100,000 reported crimes with a connection to Facebook.[616]

Material on SM is also increasingly being used in relation to selecting jury members in the US – for example, for finding information on which to challenge prospective jurors.[617] There are also contentious issues in the UK. Jurors have been sentenced for comments and other activities online regarding cases in which they have been involved.

2.19.5 Records

There is debate as to whether SM content can or should be permissible evidence. Some people argue that Tweets, emails and text messages are no different from correspondence.[618] In one sense, that is correct. The Irish Electronic Commerce Act 2000,[619] for example, provides for the equivalence and non-discrimination between electronic documents, writing, etc and traditional hardcopy versions.

Can an employee's Tweets, for example, amount to company record for evidence purposes, record-keeping requirements and ESI electronic evidence preservation purposes? What is a 'record'? What is a company's resource? Is there a BYOD policy? These issues remain unsettled.[620] The management, legal and record-keeping requirements/implications of SM, and the scale of the implications, create a 'Goliath-sized headache'.[621] The technologies are not settled; they are ever fluid and ever expanding. In addition, there can be multiple postings from various authors.[622] 'Your opponents will have trolled the Web for data. Can you claim ignorance? Must you produce … off-site communications by your employees? Can you afford not to know about Web 2.0 data? These are questions that are giving CEOs (and their lawyers) recurring nightmares'.[623]

---

616 'More Than 7,000 Associated Crimes Since January – UK Investigation', *TheJournal.ie*, 20 December 2010, available at www.thejournal.ie. Also S Boggan, 'Facebook: As Offences Linked to Social Networking Sites Increase 7,000%, the Terrifying Truth About Criminals Targeting Your Home', *Daily Mail*, 31 December 2010, available at www.daily mail.co.uk.

617 J Kay, 'Social Networking Sites Help Vet Jurors', *The National Law Journal*, 13 August 2008, referring to *US v Hassoun* No 0:04-cr-60001 (SD Fla 2006), as referred to in Findlay, *op. cit*, 178.

618 SD Nelson and JD Simek, 'Capturing Quicksilver: Records Management for Blogs, Twittering and Social Networks' (June 2009) *Wyoming Law* 1, available at www.wyomingbar.org/pdf/barjournal/barjournal/articles/Twitter.pdf, referred to in Nelson *et al.*, *op. cit*, 16.

619 This Act implements the Electronic Signatures Directive (1999/93/EC) and, in part, the Electronic Commerce Directive (2000/31/EC).

620 Nelson *et al.*, *op. cit*, 16. Also references therein, namely, Nelson and Simek, *op. cit*, 16, and T Baldas, 'Beware: Your "Tweet" on Twitter Could Be Trouble', *National Law Journal* (New York City), 22 December 2008 at 6.

621 Nelson *et al.*, *op. cit*, 16.

622 Ibid, 19.

623 Nelson *et al.*, *op. cit*, 20. References omitted.

The opportunities for a company or its employee to say something that is incriminating or creates legal implications have increased significantly. Defamation and product liability are just two examples. Separately, certain organisations or industry sectors have record-keeping requirements. These are more onerous than before in terms of the scale of the data, their locations, complexity and availability, and when they are required. Equally, the extent to which organisations can control or minimise their risk is made more difficult. Cloud issues may create further headaches to consider.

2.19.6 Discovery/Disclosure

Information on SM can be electronic evidence (or ESI, as it is referred to in the US).[624] SM provides new and 'fertile ground'[625] for relevant discovery of electronic information and materials. However, there are few cases in the US dealing with SM and discovery,[626] and even fewer in Ireland and the UK for example.

Thomas discusses the question of whether SM content can or should be discoverable or disclosed,

> 'The case law regarding email and text messaging could be equally applicable to the use of Facebook accounts with privacy settings in place in the private employment context. If there is a question as to whether the information on a SN [web]site may be discoverable, by analogy to third-party providers of emails and text messaging, it appears that the information on such [web]sites would be discoverable in civil litigation. Though a private employer does not pay for access to a Facebook account, the account is hosted by a third party and could be used for both business and personal use. Thus, applying the principles from *Rozell v Ross-Hoist*, a judge would have discretion to limit production of the information posted to a Facebook account to the extent of the parties' initial disclosures. The use of a SN [web]site at work thus would not give the defendants or plaintiffs free reign to discover anything and everything posted on the [web]site when privacy controls are in place on the account. Allowing discovery of a Facebook profile just because a party has an account would create the situation where counsel would just be fishing for information on the [web] site without any basis. Moreover, considering the networks and numerous friends that a person has on the [web]site, it is economically unfeasible to require production of every posting, email, or conversation on the [web] site for an extended period, because sorting through the information would

---

624 Witte, *op. cit*, 892.
625 Ibid, 893. In relation to US federal rule changes, note, for example, A Peck, 'The December 2006 Federal Rules Amendments Governing Electronic Discovery' (2008) *PLI/Lit* 783; Blank, *op. cit*, 487.
626 L Thomas, 'Social Networking in the Workplace: Are Private Employers Prepared to Comply with Discovery Requests for Posts and Tweets?' (2010) (63) *SMU Law Review* 1373 at 1383.

take too much time to justify the value of the information. It is for this very reason that a request for production from such SN [web]sites may be used strategically against a party to drive up the cost of discovery and push the case toward settlement. Also, because companies are not likely to have encountered numerous requests for production regarding the [web] sites and are unfamiliar with them, it is likely that such requests can be used to distract the party from the real issues of the case, in addition to driving up the costs of discovery.

If a party to a suit has a Facebook account or a Twitter account, a court would be likely to find that such an account is in the possession, custody, or control of the party and, as such, that a party would need to produce relevant information from the [web]site under Rule 34 based on the user agreements in place with Facebook and Twitter. An additional concern is the ability to procure the information for discovery purposes. A recent virtual roundtable by Symantec addressed the problems with obtaining a record of the information from Facebook or Twitter in a useable, understandable format. When users view their profile page on Facebook, it appears to them to be a consolidated page with all information in one place. However, when such user content is archived, information is located in different databases and does not appear in the same format as it appears on a Facebook page Thus, to pull all the information together and decipher how a page appeared takes more time than if the information on a page at any given time were stored as a discrete package of information, like a Word document or an email. This will likely create the biggest e-discovery hassle with respect to compliance with discovery requests.

Another consideration is the Stored Communications Act and the degree that the Act may affect the ability of a party to a suit to obtain information from a third-party provider. It appears that Rule 45 subpoenas issued to third-party providers have limitations that Rule 34 requests for production can overcome. Thus, in the initial interrogatories stage a party should question whether relevant information is present on a Facebook or Twitter page and request that the opposing party produce the information under Rule 34. By going through the party itself to obtain the information, the issues with consent and the Stored Communications Act may be avoided if the information is from the party's own profiles.'[627]

Thomas then refers to SM in the context of employment,

'Considering the problems that may arise with the use of SN in the workplace, private employers and their counsel must consider the benefits and the costs associated with the use of such [web]sites in the workplace. Twitter and Facebook market to employers that they can use the [web] sites to connect with their clients or consumers. But the legal implications

---

627 Ibid, 1394–1395. Internal references omitted.

of the use of such [web]sites and the need to preserve the [web]sites in the anticipation of litigation may lead to headaches for employers, their IT groups, and their counsel. As such, employers who decide to use SN [web]sites for marketing purposes, for internal communications, or for communications with their clients need to take steps to ensure that if the information is ever needed for discovery, they are well-prepared. The first decision to be made by employers is whether to allow their employees the use of SN during business hours while at work. The use of SN in the workplace may be beneficial but may also be problematic due to a loss of productivity in the workplace, the potential for theft of data, liability for the contents of the [web]sites in lawsuits, and damage to the employer's image. Due to these risks, many companies have banned the use of Facebook and Twitter in the workplace, including certain investment banks and law firms. Some employers that do not completely ban the use of Facebook have taken a middle-ground approach to the posting of information on the [web]site. For example, ESPN prohibits its employees from posting onto Facebook or Twitter any content related to sports without its permission. The Associated Press takes an even stronger approach and requires its employees to monitor what they and their friends say on Facebook, and to delete certain posts on their Facebook pages. Assuming that employers allow SN in the workplace, certain steps can be taken to minimize their risk, both with respect to the company's fan page and the employees' personal profiles.'[628]

The UK case of *Hays Recruitment v Mark Irons* in 2008 granted an order requiring the leaving employee to disclose his contact friend list on LinkedIn, as the first employer felt that its client list had been taken to populate the employee's list for the new competing company. The US case of *Ledbetter v Wal-Mart Stores Inc* held that SM content is discoverable once the other side believes there is evidential material.[629]

2.19.7   SM evidential issues

How relevant is SM in terms of discovery?[630] Marsico suggests that SM materials are becoming the new evidential fingerprints of the 21st century.[631] Discovery or disclosure issues generally[632] become more complex with

---

628 Ibid.
629 *Ledbetter v Wal-Mart Stores Inc* No 06-cv-01958-WYD_MJW, 2009 WL 1067018, at *2 (D Colorada 21 April 2009). Referred to in North, *op. cit*, 1279. See also Thomas, *op. cit*, 1391. There appears to be no direct case pronouncing that social network content *per se* can be discoverable evidence in Ireland. Emails and telephone records, however, quite regularly appear in cases here.
630 Blank, *op. cit*, 497–498. Or disclosure in England and Wales.
631 E Marsico, 'Social Networking Websites: Are MySpace and Facebook the Fingerprints of the Twenty-First Century?' (2010) *Widener Law Journal* 967.
632 Blank, *op. cit*, 495–496.

online activity. The scope of discovery[633] or disclosure in 'normal' litigation is expanding because of SM content. In addition, it should be noted that the discovery of SM materials is more complex, as it involves third-party SNs.[634]

Third-party discovery, even normally, is a complex policy issue in litigation. The issues of third-party access and the discovery of employer/employee SM content are set to become hotly contested areas in litigation.[635]

Podolny observes that SM 'friends' (who can be real friends or otherwise) can also become adversaries in litigation.[636] This raises interesting issues in terms of discovery and access to materials that may be sought to be relied on.

The EU Article 29 Working Party refers to cross-border discovery/disclosure issues in civil litigation.[637] SM enhances the potential for disputes that include cross-border content issues. There are also a growing number of examples where proceedings, notice of proceedings and court orders have been served electronically by email and even to the SM pages of individuals.[638]

The internet is no longer restrained and wired. Modern mobile and handheld devices are still proliferating, and invariably it is also possible to access the internet and websites through these devices. This includes Facebook, Google+ and other SM. Various content, comments, photographs, histories, etc can also be maintained on these devices. It is natural, therefore, that mobile electronic discovery is also an evolving area.[639] A note of caution is deserved. A litigator should not be blinkered into thinking that mobile telephones and handheld network telecommunications devices are the only mobile and storage devices that may contain pertinent electronic evidence. Other examples include SIM cards, data storage cards, photographic storage devices, disks, USB keys, etc.

Publicity is always a consideration in litigation, and internet news and SM have increased the potential for publicity. A related sub-issue is that of pre-trial

---

633 Ibid, 496–497.
634 Ibid, 503–504.
635 Ibid at 497.
636 R Podolny, 'When "Friends" Become Adversaries: Litigation in the Age of Facebook' (2009) *Manitoba Law Journal* 391.
637 See Working Document 1/2009 on Pre-Trial Discovery for Cross Border Civil Litigation, Article 29 Data Protection Working Party, 00339/09/EN, WP 158, adopted on 11 February 2009.
638 RA Ward, 'Discovering Facebook: Social Network Subpoenas and the Stored Communications Act' (2011) *Harvard Journal of Law & Technology* 563; AL Shulz, 'Superpoked and Served: Service of Process via Social Networking Sites' (2009) *University of Richmond Law Review* 1497; MM Dan, 'Social Networking Sites: A Reasonable Calculated Method to Effect Service of Process' (2010) *Case Western Reserve Journal of Law, Technology & the Internet* 184; RJ Hedges, KN Rashbaum and AC Losey, 'Electronic Service of Process at Home and Abroad: Allowing Domestic Electronic Service of Process in the Federal Courts' (2010) *The Federal Courts Law Review* 55.
639 See, for example, DB Garrie and YM Griver, 'Mobile Messaging and Electronic Discovery' (2009) *Loyola Law and Technology Annual* 95.

publicity, and prejudicial pre-trial publicity in particular.[640] Internet news and SM increase the potential chance of these issues arising.

2.19.8 Preservation of evidence

Electronic evidence can be easily created. In some instances, it can be easily deleted or altered, too. In litigation, therefore, there can be a duty to preserve[641] and prevent the spoliation[642] of electronic evidence. In relation to e-discovery generally, it is noted that,

> 'In the seminal e-discovery cases of *Zubulake v UBS Warburg LLC*, best known for the judge's 'costshifting' analysis factors, the court held that the duty to preserve evidence attaches, at the latest, on the date an action is filed. In Zubulake IV, Judge Scheindlin wrote that this duty may attach "at the time that litigation [is] reasonably anticipated" if a party has reason to suspect a pending suit.'[643]

The reference to cost-shifting refers, in part, to the fact that dealing with e-discovery can become a very costly exercise.[644] Some cases even settle on the basis not of the merits on either side, but rather on the basis of the anticipated costs of the electronic discovery.

Issues such as preservation might best be considered in advance where possible, as opposed to reacting to an instant contentious situation. In either instance, various internal departmental expertise will be required from management, legal, HR, marketing, etc, as well as appropriate external expertise.[645]

2.19.9 Discovery/Disclosure and privacy

Many discovery and privacy issues arise. For example,

> 'The convergence of social-networking [web]sites and litigation presents a host of complex questions implicating user privacy. This Comment addresses three issues in particular. First, how can a court determine whether there is relevant information contained within a party's private social-networking profiles beyond relying on the requesting party's good-faith

---

640 See generally M Mastromauro, 'Pre-trial Prejudice 2.0: How YouTube Generated News Coverage is Set to Complicate the Concepts of Pre-trial Prejudice Doctrine and Endanger Sixth Amendments Fair Trial Rights' (2010) *Journal of High Technology Law* 289.

641 See Witte, *op. cit*, 895.

642 See Thomas, *op. cit*, 1384–1385. Generally, in relation to the US, note Frieden and Murray, *op. cit*, 1.

643 Rule 34, Federal Rules of Civil Procedure (1970). Referred to in North, *op. cit*, 1282.

644 Note, for example, 'E-Disclosure – Controlling Costs and Reducing Risks', *Society of Computers and Law*, 18 September 2013.

645 Consider, for example, K Grandhi, 'The Discovery Within: Employing E-Discovery Coordinators for Management of Electronic Discovery Processes in Federal and State Cases' (2011) *Temple Journal of Science, Technology & Environmental Law* 1.

assertions? Second, a user who implements Facebook's privacy settings may have a higher expectation of privacy than a user who grants unfettered access to hundreds or even thousands of "friends," and users may expect more privacy with regard to some types of information. How can these expectations be measured for objectivity or reasonableness? Third, the complex interconnectedness of SN [web]sites presents difficult questions surrounding the expectation of privacy in relevant content posted by third parties. When a user is tagged in a third party's photo and that photo is relevant, is the photo discoverable?'[646]

In relation to the US, Thomas states,

'From a discovery standpoint, employees' use of SN for business purposes will greatly increase the realm of discoverable information that a company has to control, and as such, modifications to data retention procedures must be made. If litigation is anticipated, a company and its counsel should issue a litigation hold that encompasses information posted on SN [web]sites – no information should be deleted from the employer's page, the employee's business pages, or archives thereof. As mentioned in Zubulake, a litigation hold does not end the counsel's duty of preservation. The litigation hold with respect to the information on SN [web]sites must be reissued periodically to make sure that employees are aware of their obligations. In addition, employers and counsel must request the information from SN [web]sites or gain access to it from employees who likely have relevant information and be particularly explicit with those employees' obligations of preservation. To save time, employers may also request that employees locally archive their SN [web]site pages to ensure that the data is not lost. There is a caveat with this approach – the stronger the data retention policy, the more data there will be to mine in the event of a discovery request. Companies should be mindful that a policy should be implemented but should also be cautious that in the event of litigation, spoliation does not occur that results in discovery sanctions. Ultimately, companies should be educated about media their employees are using to collaborate with each other, contact clients, conduct business, and should work with their IT groups to formulate retention and archiving policies that are suited for their specific business needs'.[647]

2.19.10   US cases

A US case law commentary states as follows,

'The most complete discussion by an American court on this problem appears in *Mackelprang v Fidelity National Title Agency of Nevada Inc.* In *Mackelprang*, the court denied the defendant's motion to compel the

---

646 North, *op. cit*, 1290.
647 Thomas, *op. cit*, 1398–1401. Internal references omitted.

plaintiff in a sexual harassment lawsuit to consent to the release of her private MySpace messages. The defendant employer initially issued a subpoena to MySpace to learn the profile information and identity behind two accounts that it suspected belonged to the former employee. The employer alleged that the former employee set up dual identities on MySpace, with one account listing her as single with no interest in children and the other listing her as married with six children. The employer believed the plaintiff used the first account to send emails of a sexual nature to colleagues she accused of sexual harassment. MySpace produced some "public" information associated with the account, but it declined to provide any private messages absent a search warrant or a letter of consent from the account holder. The company complied with the defendant's subpoena duces tecum by providing a spreadsheet that confirmed the plaintiff as the user for two accounts on the [web]site. In other cases, MySpace has declined to provide substantive user content in response to subpoenas. In its motion to compel the plaintiff to consent to a release of her MySpace communications, the defendant argued that the private messages could contain evidence that the plaintiff exchanged consensual, sexually charged emails with members of the [web]site. The court agreed with the plaintiff that the request amounted to a "fishing expedition" that "would allow Defendants to cast too wide a net for any information that might be relevant and discoverable" and could result in discovery of irrelevant private communications.

But the court invited a more narrowly tailored request, noting that the 'proper method' would be to serve the plaintiff with "limited requests for production of relevant email communications[,]" including MySpace "private messages that contain information regarding her sexual harassment allegations in this lawsuit or which discuss her alleged emotional distress and the cause(s) thereof." The court invited the defendant to provide "some basis, beyond mere speculation, to support a reasonable belief that Plaintiff engaged in sexually [sic] email communications on her Myspace. com accounts with former coemployees" to warrant reconsideration of the motion. The court denied the defendant's motion without prejudice, leaving the door open for more targeted discovery.

Two recent trial orders involving suits against schools demonstrate the wide usage of Facebook among young people and the potential for relevance to litigation. The procedure followed in *Bass v Miss Porter's School* illustrates a "best practice" for handling Facebook discovery requests. In *Bass*, the defendant school requested production of any text messages or Facebook content related to the teasing and taunting of the plaintiff, a student at the school, or any content related to communications involving the student's allegations. The student, who had since lost access to her Facebook account, served a subpoena on Facebook to obtain content from her former profile to comply with the school's request. When Facebook agreed to provide "reasonably available data" spanning the pertinent time period, the judge ordered the student to provide any responsive documents to the

school and the entire set of documents "to the Court for in camera review
... distinguishing the subset of documents provided to Defendants." The
student provided approximately one hundred pages of content in response
to the school's request, and she provided "more than 750 pages of wall
postings, messages, and pictures" to the court, which represented Facebook's
complete production in response to the subpoena. The court determined that
there was 'no meaningful distinction' between the documents the student
provided to the school and those provided for in camera review. The court
ordered that the entire set of documents be made available to the school
because relevance was "more in the eye of the beholder than subject to
strict legal demarcations," and the student could not unilaterally determine
which documents might be "reasonably calculated to lead to the discovery
of admissible evidence."

In *TV v Union Township Board of Education*, a middle school student sued
her school for emotional distress resulting from a sexual assault allegedly
perpetrated by another student on school grounds. The school attempted
discovery of the plaintiff's private Facebook and MySpace pages to show
evidence of her mental state before and after the incident. The student moved
for a protective order for her private profile information, citing privacy rights
and undue burden. The trial judge granted the protective order "barring the
defendants from seeking or obtaining any discovery or information" from
the plaintiff's online profiles. The court left the door open for later discovery
if the school could make a particularized showing of relevance.

The *Bass* court's creative solution to the defendant's discovery request
indicates both fidelity to the liberal discovery regime under the Federal Rules
and an open-mindedness about the potential relevance of social-networking
information. By way of contrast under similar facts, the state trial court
in TV required an up-front showing of relevance by the requesting party.
The *Bass* approach of serving a subpoena on the social-networking [web]
site and requiring in camera review of all supplied documents removes the
possibility that a responding party will selectively remove damaging photos
or status updates from the discoverable documents. This approach also
permits a responding party to file protective orders for certain documents
after they are provided by the social-networking [web]site but before they
are given to the requesting party. It is sufficiently flexible to ensure that all
relevant SN content is discovered while creating a safety valve to prevent
especially private or prejudicial information from being discovered.'[648]

2.19.11 *Canadian cases*

There are also Canadian cases, described in one review as follows,

'One of the most thorough discussions appears in *Leduc v Roman*, a recent
Canadian personal injury case. In *Leduc*, the plaintiff claimed damages

---

648 North, *op. cit*, 1291–1293. Internal references omitted.

for physical and mental injuries sustained after a traffic accident with the defendant. The defendant moved for production of the entire contents of the plaintiff's private Facebook profile on the basis of a single, publicly accessible profile photo and identifying information on the plaintiff's public Facebook page. After a lower court denied the request, the appellate court reversed in part, reasoning that the private profile "likely contain[ed] some content relevant to the issue of how Mr Leduc has been able to lead his life since the accident".'[649]

The court referred to cases which held that a Facebook profile can contain information relevant to the issues in a particular case,

> Photographs of parties posted to their Facebook profiles have been admitted as evidence relevant to demonstrating a party's ability to engage in sports and other recreational activities where the plaintiff has put his enjoyment of life or ability to work in issue ... In one case the discovery of photographs of a party posted on a MySpace webpage formed the basis for a request to produce additional photographs not posted on the [web]site ....

The *Leduc* court also considered the socialization purpose of Facebook, noting that "Facebook is not used as a means by which account holders carry on monologues with themselves ... [and] Facebook profiles are not designed to function as diaries." The court aptly described the goal of social-networking [web]sites to "enable users to construct personal networks or communities of 'friends' with whom they can share information about themselves, and on which 'friends' can post information about the user." The court explained that Facebook profiles are "data and information in electronic form" producible as "documents" under the Rules of Civil Procedure, and as such, should be disclosed when "relevant to the allegations in the pleadings." Perhaps most importantly, *Leduc* dismissed the idea that public and semi-private profile contents should be treated differently: "A party who maintains a private, or limited access, Facebook profile stands in no different position than one who sets up a publicly-available profile. Both are obliged to identify and produce any postings that relate to any matter in issue in an action."

Leduc correctly recognized that social-networking information provides a wealth of relevant information about a plaintiff's condition before and after an accident in the personal injury litigation context. But despite the court's characterization of the social purpose of Facebook, it had to tackle the issue of the plaintiff's expectation of privacy in some of the information. The *Leduc* court dismissed these concerns rather summarily, but other courts have struggled with the expectations of privacy in various forms of social-networking content.'[650]

---

649 Ibid at 1294–1295.
650 Ibid at 1294–1295.

2.20   PRIVACY, DATA PROTECTION AND SM

It is important to consider examples, controversies and cases in relation to privacy, data protection and SN. The main EU data protection legal measure is the Data Protection Directive 1995. This will be replaced by the proposed EU Data Protection Regulation. In the US, while there is no single general law in terms of data protection comparable to the EU Data Protection Directive 1995, there are a growing number of issue-specific laws, such as in relation to data breach notification, children and revenge porn. Eric P Robinson (in chapter C33), referring to the US, indicates that,

> 'In order to be legally cognizable, privacy claims must be based on a reasonable expectation that information is not public, based on both an individual's perception of privacy and society's standards. See *Katz v United States* 389 US 347 (1967) (because of reasonable expectation of privacy in a closed telephone booth, government must obtain a subpoena to record the phone conversation).

The US Supreme Court recently applied this standard to electronic surveillance by attaching a GPS tracker to a car. *US v Jones* 132 SCt 945, 181 L Ed 2d 911 (US 2012) (warrant required for police to attach GPS tracker). While concurring in this result, Justice Sonya Sotomayor stated that "… it may be necessary to reconsider the premise that an individual has no reasonable expectation of privacy in information voluntarily disclosed to third parties. This approach is ill suited to the digital age, in which people reveal a great deal of information about themselves to third parties in the course of carrying out mundane tasks." Id at 957, 181 L Ed 2d at 926.

Lower courts have applied this "reasonable expectation of privacy" standard in Fourth Amendment contexts involving government access and private claims over unauthorized access and/or disclosure of material from SM. See eg *Guest v Leis* 255 F 3d 325 (6th Cir 2001) (government access to posts on internet bulletin board); *Moreno v Hanford Sentinel Inc* 172 Cal App 4th 1125; 91 Cal Rptr 3d 858 (Cal App 2009) (dismissing privacy suit against newspaper that published plaintiff's MySpace post about her hometown); *US v Meregildo* 883 F Supp 2d 523 (SDNY 2012) (government access to Facebook posts); *People v Harris* 36 Misc 3d 613, 945 NYS 2d 50, 2012 NY Slip Op 22109 (NYC Crim Ct 2012) (government access to Twitter posts), aff'd, 43 Misc 3d 136(A), 2014 NY Slip Op 507670(U) (NY App Term, Apr 24, 2014); *Ehling v Monmouth-Ocean Hospital Service Corp* 872 F Supp 2d 369 (2012) (declining to dismiss privacy claim against employer who accessed employee's Facebook posts); *US v Lustig* 3 F Supp 3d 808 (SD Cal Mar 11, 2014) (government access to Craigslist post).

Traditional privacy claims, such as intrusion or public disclosure of private facts, can also be asserted against someone who posts the information to SM, just as if the information was disclosed on any other medium. See eg *Zimmerman v Barr Case* No 2014CA000613 (Fla Cir Ct Seminole County filed Mar 10, 2014) (privacy suit over Tweeting of plaintiff's home address).

Users of SM sites and services may also assert privacy expectations based on the sites' stated privacy policies. The Federal Trade Commission recommends that all SM sites and services have a privacy policy, and will initiate proceedings against sites and services without such policies as well as those that do not act in accordance with such policies. The FTC reached settlements with Google in 2011 and Facebook in 2012 over allegations that the sites made users' information available in ways that were contrary to the assurances of the sites' own privacy policies. See eg *In re Google* FTC No 102-3136 (2011); *In re Facebook* FTC No 092-3184 (2012). Google also reached settlements with the FTC and 37 states and the District of Columbia over its circumvention of users' "do not track" settings. *US v Google* No CV 12-04177 SI (ND Cal dismissed pursuant to settlement Nov 16, 2012); *In re Google Cookie Placement Consumer Privacy Litigation* Case No 1:12-md-02358-SLR (D Del settled 2013).

The FTC has also taken action against entities whose databases of users' and customers' personal and financial information have been stolen because of inadequate security, on the grounds that weak protection of such databases is an unfair trade practice and violates the Fair Credit Reporting Act, if applicable to the organization. The first of these cases involved an email sent to customers which included all customers' email addresses, visible to all recipients, in the To: field. The case was settled with an agreement that the company would change and report to the FTC on its data practices for 20 years. See In the Matter of Eli Lilly and Company, Docket No C-4047 (FTC 2002).

Private parties have also filed lawsuits making privacy claims over SM. A suit over privacy issues on Google Buzz ended with the company paying $8.5 million to cover attorney fees and costs and to create a fund dedicated to Internet privacy policy or privacy education. *In re Google Buzz User Privacy Litigation*, Case No 5:10-cv-00672-JW (ND Cal June 2, 2011) (approving settlement). A class action suit over Facebook's "sponsored stories" program, which placed users' photographs and information in advertisements directed at their friends, ended with a settlement in which Facebook agreed to change its terms of service and pay $10 million in *cy pres* restitution. *Fraley v Facebook* Case No CV 11-01726 RS (ND Cal final judgment Sept 19, 2013) (approving settlement).

Among the revelations by former National Security Administration (NSA) contractor Edward Snowden was the PRISM program, which was reported to have directly tapped into the servers of major American internet companies to collect information, including SM data, of non-Americans flowing through the US-based systems. The program, which was reportedly approved by the classified Foreign Intelligence Surveillance Court (known as the FISA Court), was reported to also collaterally collect and store information about United States citizens. In response, US-based technology companies were reportedly taking steps to make their systems inaccessible to government surveillance.'

In the UK, there are 'numerous incidents of controversy with respect to data protection and SM in the UK; however, there have been no cases in which a breach of the law has been cited. In 2014, it was reported that the ICO was going to investigate Facebook for a possible breach of the UK Data Protection Act 1998 for conducting a psychology study on up to 700,000 of its users, during which their news feeds were manipulated without their knowledge' (see chapter C32).

2.21   SM AND FAMILY LAW CASES

Family law cases increasingly involve SM. These may not always be reported, however, as some jurisdictions place reporting restrictions on family cases in order to protect the parties and sensitive familial relationship details, and in particular any children involved. Eric P Robinson (in chapter C33), summarising the US position, indicates as follows,

'As in other types of cases, SM postings can be used as evidence in family law cases, particularly those involving child custody or distribution of assets. In a 2010 survey of members of the American Academy of Matrimonial Lawyers, 81 percent said that they had seen an increase in use of SM evidence in divorce cases since 2005.

In *Caples v Caples* No 2002-1758 (La Dist Ct 2011), aff'd, 103 So 3d 437 (La App 2012) a father unsuccessfully tried to use the fact that the grandmother allowed a 10-year-old to have a Facebook profile as grounds for taking custody of the child. While the court rejected this argument, it did order that the Facebook profile be deactivated.

In *New Jersey v HLM* No A-1257-12T3 (NJ App Div May 13 2014) (unpublished), the appeals court affirmed a lower court order barring a mentally disturbed woman from blogging about her ex-husband and children.'

Jonathan McDonald indicates (in chapter C32) in relation to the UK as follows,

'In the case of *Re J (A Child)* [2013] EWHC 2694 (Fam) the High Court granted a contra mundum (against the world) injunction preventing the naming of a baby whose father had posted information about the child on Facebook in breach of an undertaking to the court. The judge said that, in principle, an English court can grant a contra mundum injunction against the world including a foreign-based internet website provider, ie Facebook. Among other things, it had to be shown that the person being injuncted could be properly served and that there was a real possibility that the order would be enforceable. Whilst the case involved family law, a key principle discussed was the right to privacy, namely the child's privacy. The court said that the injunction would only be justified if it was necessary to protect the child's right to privacy under Article 8 of the European Convention on Human Rights (the right to privacy) which had to be balanced against the public interest in discussing the workings of the family justice system. The court then granted the injunction more narrowly than was requested. The party requesting the injunction had also asked the court to prevent publication of images of the baby, but the court declined to grant this.

There is also anecdotal evidence to suggest that SM material is increasingly being cited in divorce proceedings (ie with flirtatious messages sent on SM cited as evidence of unreasonable behaviour), however, such cases rarely reach the higher courts and so there have been no examples reported in the law reports.'

An example in Belgium is,

'*Justice of the Peace (Vredegerecht) Ninove 3 mei 2012, case nr AR 12A356*

In this case, the divorce parties were ordered by the court to refrain from spreading libellous statements or insults through public fora, including Facebook. One spouse complained that the other had been posting insulting comments on his own Facebook profile after she had left him. The Justice of the Peace prohibited both parties (even though the husband was the only one that had been posting insulting remarks) from spreading any libellous or insulting comments towards each other or the children on public fora like social media, this for a period of almost a year, subject to payment of 100 euro per infringement.[651]'

2.22   SPORTS PERSONS, SPORTS CLUBS AND SM

Sports, sports persons and their respective clubs, universities or organisations must increasingly consider SM issues. For example, this may include sports players being disciplined by sports clubs for comments they may make on Twitter, etc. There is a growing issue and conflict in relation to athletes and SM. This relates in particular to whether athletes can be stopped from using SM such as Facebook and Twitter. There are growing instances where organisations seek to stop and even discipline athletes for using and posting on SM. It is, perhaps, surprising to learn that this includes not only professional sports organisations but also college and amateur organisations.

---

651 This case has been annotated by G Verschelden, 'Vrederechter censureert Facebookpagina van echtgenoten', *Juristenkrant* 2012, afl 252, p 1.

2.22.1   SM and sport

Given the popularity of SM, it was inevitable that sports organisations would seek to exploit it for advertising, marketing and other commercial purposes. However, it is also used for other activities, in particular in relation to the athletes themselves. Some of these examples include the recruitment of students to sports through SM websites and text messages.[652] The use and content of text messaging between athletes and their coaches is receiving increased attention.[653] Obviously, there are advantages, such as ease of contact, training time updates, cost, group texts, etc, to the use by athletes of SM.[654] Some of the evolving concerns, however, are highlighted below. Some concerns centre on the safety of athletes. Safety dangers can arise from unruly fans[655] threatening athletes on the latter's social network pages, or otherwise threatening them as a result of something that the athlete may have said online. Equally, clubs, organisations, schools and colleges can be concerned that their athletes and sports stars may say or do something controversial online, whether in a post, photograph, etc.[656]

2.22.2   Issues and concerns

There are evolving issues in terms of the ability of organisations to regulate and monitor their athletes' online activities. For example,

- Do colleges have a right to stop their student athletes posting on Facebook?

- Do professional sports clubs have the right to control the use by athletes of SM and what they may post?[657]

- Is there a right to regulate?

- Is there a right to monitor?

- What rights do athletes have in terms of personal privacy to post to their own private and public SM pages?

- Do athletes have free-speech rights (such as under the US First Amendment,[658] for example) that encompass Facebook and Twitter

---

652   M Maher, 'You've Got Messages: Modern Technology Recruiting Through Text-Messaging and the Intrusiveness of Facebook' (2007) (8) *Texas Review of Entertainment and Sports Law* 125 at 127.
653   Ibid, 127.
654   Ibid, 127.
655   Ibid, 147.
656   One instance of a controversial sports star Tweet at the time of writing was that of Joey Barton referring to another soccer player made on 9 January 2012. Referred to on the Newstalk sports show, 10 January 2012.
657   Maher, *op. cit*, 127.
658   Ibid, 127. See also D McLaren, 'Freedom of Speech for Sports Stars on Social Media?' *UK Sports Network*, Social Media and Sport, 26 August 2010, available at www. theuksportsnetwork.com/freedom-of-speech-for-sports-stars-on-social-media.

postings and may outweigh the purported claims of colleges and sporting organisations?

- What privacy and data protection rights do athletes retain in relation to their online private and online public postings, and which rights may be breached by their organisation in terms of monitoring or, indeed, in terms of seeking to regulate and prevent them entirely?

These issues will be increasingly contested and are evolving.[659]

2.22.3   SM and professional/amateur athletes

Sporting organisations have been increasingly expressing concerns about what their sports stars may be saying via SM.

One American football player, Chad Ochocino, was fined $25,000 for Tweeting during a game.[660] The NFL now bans players from using SM up to 90 minutes before games and during games.[661] The UK under-19 cricketer Azeem Rafiq criticised a coach in an online post and was dropped as a result.[662]

On occasion, players have been reprimanded for photographs that are leaked or taken by third parties, sent on to friends, retweeted, etc. American Football player Matt Stafford was reprimanded over a photograph of him lifting a beer keg.[663] Other American Football players have been criticised for recording a song with sexual references.[664] Some players are also reported as being dismissed, such as at the Big 12 teams Texas and Oklahoma.[665]

This is an increasing issue in UK sports.[666] Liverpool Football Club is reported as investigating Nathan Ecclestone in relation to a Tweet in bad taste which referred to 9/11.[667]

---

659 While there are recent examples in Ireland of athletes' litigation in relation to sporting issues, such as a boxing case regarding which boxer should be deemed to qualify for competition, there does not appear to be a case involving these SN issues. *O'Reilly v Irish Amateur Boxing Association*, High Court, 19 August 2011, Cooke J.

660 McLaren, op. cit.

661 Ibid.

662 Ibid.

663 See, for example, C Robinson, 'Social Networking a Potential Trap for Prospects', *Yahoo Sports Tuesday*, 7 April 2009, available at http://sports.yahoo.com/news/social-networking-potential-trap-prospects-193500837--nfl.html.

664 Ibid.

665 Ibid.

666 S Rice, R Rai and J Charlton, 'Silly Twits: Sports Stars in Social Networking Controversy', *Independent on Sunday*, 14 September 2011.

667 'Liverpool Investigate Nathan Eccleston Over Controversial 9/11 Tweet', *Independent*, 14 September 2011.

The Football Association in the UK is having to concern itself with social media comments by soccer players. Rio Ferdinand, for example, was fined £45,000 for a particular Tweet perceived as being racist.[668]

The issue of social media controversies has also affected Gaelic Athletic Association (GAA) athletes. The GAA president responded to certain comments on Twitter as follows,

> 'I wouldn't call it banter, it was one-sided and it was outrageous to suggest that a draw would be rigged ... They called into question the honesty of the entire TV3 crew, the games section in Croke Park ... They called into question my honesty and the honesty of Liam Hayes and the two cameras and that is outrageous, absolutely outrageous ... It's not a random chat. If you want a random chat you pick up your mobile – those players put it on record, it was done for effect and done to suggest that in some way we would collude to be dishonest ... I can't see how they can justify their actions.'[669]

The concern from the club (and organisational) perspective is that the comments, innocent or otherwise, can adversely reflect on the player and the club. Revenue, sponsorship and fan goodwill can all be jeopardised. This is also an issue for individual athletes. Australian Olympic swimmer Stephanie Rice lost a sponsorship contract with Jaguar after Tweeting 'Suck on that faggots!' after Australia scored a try against South Africa in a rugby game.[670]

Another aspect of concern relates to athletes looking to be signed by professional teams. Many such individuals will naturally have their own private SM profiles. However, there are reports that certain sports clubs in the US regularly use false profiles of pretty girls to make friend requests to these unsigned athletes.[671] This is known as 'ghosting'.[672] Therefore, good prospective athletes may have lost contracts and been de-selected as a result of what clubs feel about their SM comments, friends, etc. One should be aware that, while regular or blanket monitoring of employees appears to be permissible in the US, this is not permitted under EU data protection law. It may be that blanket monitoring and false-profile friend requests in relation to athletes may also be in breach of EU data protection.

---

668 J Jackson, 'Rio Ferdinand Warned by Sir Alex Ferguson After $45,000 Twitter Fine', *Guardian*, 17 August, 2012, available at www.guardian.co.uk/football/2012/aug/17/rio-ferdinand-alex-ferguson-warned-twitter. There was also a second fine in 2014.

669 Referred to in 'GAA President Liam O'Neill Rejects "Fix" Allegations', *Joe.ie*, 4 July 2012, available at www.joe.ie/gaa/gaa-news/gaa-president-liam-oneill-rejects-fix-allegations-0026545-1.

670 M Cowley, 'Twitter Turns into Anti-Social Networking Trap for Sport Stars', *Sydney Morning Herald*, 9 September 2010.

671 See, for example, C Robinson, 'Social Networking a Potential Trap for Prospects', *Yahoo Sports* Tuesday, 7 April 2009, available at http://sports.yahoo.com/news/social-networking-potential-trap-prospects-193500837--nfl.html.

672 Ibid.

2.22.4   SN and college athletes

The prevalence of text messages, etc from sports coaches to potential and actual athletes has growing issues. Some of these are seen as negative. The disadvantages include imposing unjustified pressures on students, interfering with students' education and threats to student privacy.[673] Effectively, students are seen by some coaches as being available to contact 24/7.

Some academic institutions have banned student athletes from using SM.[674] Others are actively monitoring these issues as they come to an organisational policy position on these communications. Some also keep an eye on student and athlete postings.[675]

Once an age issue (ie an under-age user issue) is triggered for the website, there may arguably be a legal or duty of care issue.[676] One suggestion has been that there should be two versions of a social network, one for children and one for adults.[677]

Obviously, athletes must take responsibility for own postings.[678] However, it is quite a different thing to say that an organisation has a right *per se* to regulate or prevent an athlete from accessing and posting via SM. It can be argued, for example, that in the US the First Amendment[679] rights of the individual present a constitutional bar to organisations preventing an individual from making statements online. This opens up a new line for First Amendment litigation. Privacy rights are also an issue if the organisation seeks to routinely monitor the athlete online. Issues that may also be considered are the extent to which such rights can be contracted away, for example, in a contract of engagement or playing contract. Does a professional playing contract have the same status as a student athlete's scholarship or student playing agreement? Are there legitimate reasons for saying that student athletes have more concern in protecting the private aspects of their being, including online postings, than commercial professional players? Should students' privacy and free-speech interests be protected more so than those of older famous professionals who may have professional agents and lawyers?

2.22.5   SM and journalists

Journalists also have to consider SM. Ethical issues arise in terms of what they may use from SM, Twitter, etc as sources for sports news stories. Not all

---

673 Maher, *op. cit*, 129–131.
674 Ibid, 139–140, and examples therein.
675 Ibid, 140.
676 EP Stedman, 'MySpace, But Whose Responsibility? Liability of Social-Networking Websites When Offline Sexual Assault of Minors Follows Online Interaction' (2007) (14) *Villanova Sports & Entertainment Law Journal* 363 at 395.
677 Ibid, 395.
678 Maher, *op. cit*, 144.
679 Ibid, 142–143.

Twitter accounts are bona fide who they say they are. The Irish presidential election debate turned into controversy when an unverified Tweet was read out live but subsequently turned out to be incorrect. Can a journalist use a comment from a source that he or she has not verified?

The range of Facebook and other SM channels vastly escalates the potential scale of news sources available to the sports journalist. However, authenticity is again an issue. So too is news values and news judgments. Is there real news quality to a Facebook comment they may read? Are quality and professionalism affected? Some SM profile pages may be set to private or have a restricted set of friends. Issues of ethics, hacking, privacy and data protection arise.[680]

Sometimes there is a reluctance in certain organisations to fully or appropriately engage with social media which can cause particular problems.[681]

2.22.6 Competing rules

One of the problems also to be considered is that there may be competing or complementary rules, codes, etc applicable to the same incident. There may be the club or college rules as well as the rules of the national sports representative organisation.[682] This is in addition to certain activities being potentially criminal while others potentially breach civil law.

2.22.7 Transparency

Also, from the athletes' point of view, it is reasonable for them to expect that, if certain matters are officially deemed to be inappropriate or otherwise not permissible, these matters should be clearly and transparently set out in advance. They need to be able to know what is and is not permitted.

Separately, in deciding whether a particular penalty or sanction is enforceable, it can be a factor that the 'offence' was made known in a transparent and explicit manner.

---

680 See generally, S Reed, 'Sports Journalists' Use of Social Media and Its Effects on Professionalism' (2011) *Journal of Sports and Media* 43 at 57 and *passim*.

681 In the case of RTE, the Irish national broadcaster, scandals such as the fake presidential debate Tweet and the Fr Reynolds scandal (where a priest was defamed) have perhaps led to the adoption of a more cautious approach. Media organisations also have to develop social media policies. One newspaper indicated to its journalists that they should not comment via social media on the Leveson Report at the time of the report's release. The BBC told its staff not to refer to any of its difficulties and investigations on social media or in the press. See M Hennessy, 'BBC Chief Tells Staff Not to Air Its Difficulties in Press and Social Media', *Irish Times*, 14 November 2012.

682 A Tracy, 'Athletic Discipline for Non-Sport Player Misconduct: the Role of College Athletic Department and Professional League Discipline and the Legal System's Penalties and Remedies' (2009) *Virginia Sports & Entertainment Law Journal* 254 at 255–256.

Tracy notes these issues when stating that '[f]or athletes engaging in non-sport misconduct, there is no baseline penalty scheme. Punishments run the gamut, without deference to type of conduct, sport, level, gender, or even existing policy'.[683]

2.22.8   Conclusion

These issues are only coming to be contested presently. The final outcome remains to be seen. Particular nuances may mean that there are different results between college students and professionally paid sports stars; between public and private internet spaces; and between the particular jurisdictions involved. Indeed, a further unresolved point relates to whether something that can be viewed or accessed worldwide can be restricted in terms of the law that may apply in one particular jurisdiction.

The Olympic Games in London showed that national icons and sporting heroes are not immune from online abuse, including death threats. While certain abusers have already been identified and prosecuted, the Crown Prosecution Service in the UK has indicated that it is willing to appeal unduly lenient sentences for such online abuse where deemed appropriate.[684] It remains to be seen whether similar prosecutions will arise in most jurisdictions. Separately, a High Court Judge in Ireland has called for further criminal offences for online abuse.

2.23   PERSONAL RELATIONS AND RELATIONSHIPS

Personal relations and relationships incorporate an important aspect of SM and legal issues. This may include, for example, personal relations, revenge porn, private images, etc. These examples are increasingly controversial. As well as being the subject of controversy and cases, there is also increasing pressure for new specific laws. Alex Cochrane defines revenge porn as follows,

'Revenge porn is the increasingly common problem faced by individuals, usually women, on the break-up of a relationship during which they had shared intimate photographs or videos of themselves with their former lover (consensually) and which are then published online (without their consent) in an act of revenge.'[685]

Cochrane indicates that the UK government, like other jurisdictions, is considering criminalising revenge porn activities, and that 'Liberal Democrat peers Lord Marks and Baroness Grender have put forward an amendment to

---

683 Tracy, *op. cit,* 270.
684 E Davey, 'London 2012: Stiffer Sentences Possible for Olympic Criminals', BBC, 25 July 2012, available at www.bbc.co.uk/news/uk-england-london-18957632.
685 A Cochrane, 'Legislating on Revenge Porn: An International Perspective', SCL, 24 July 2014, available at www.scl.org/site.aspx?i=ed38027.

the Criminal Justice and Courts Bill, which would allow for a one-year jail term for publishing intimate images without consent. The offence would only be committed where a reasonable expectation of privacy existed at the time the photographs were taken'.[686]

Referring to Australia, Cochrane states,

'The South Eastern Australian state of Victoria became the first in Australia to make revenge porn illegal by updating its existing laws. The new law will make it an offence to partake in "non-consensual sexting," ie the deliberate sending of naked pictures of another person without that person's consent.'[687]

Referring to Brazil, Cochrane states,

'The suicide of 17 year old Julia Rebecca in November 2013 sparked pressure on the government to pass legislation outlawing revenge porn. In April 2014, the "Marco Civil" Internet Civil Rights Bill was signed into law. Internet providers delivering content generated by third parties will be held secondarily liable for infringement of privacy resulting from the disclosure, without consent of its participants, of photos, videos or other material containing nudity or acts of a sexual private character when, after receipt of notification by the participant or legal representative, they fail (within the technical limits of its service) to remove the content. Some have argued the decision to remove content upon receipt of notification should be left to the court. Moreover, the effectiveness of the legislation, it would seem, is limited to domestic publication. Claims brought against internet providers outside the Brazilian jurisdiction are likely to face enforceability issues.'[688]

Referring to Canada, Cochrane states,

'The Protecting Canadians from Online Crime Act (known as Bill C-13) was introduced in November 2013 to address criminal behaviour associated with cyberbullying. Now at the Report stage, the Bill creates the new offence of non-consensual distribution of intimate images, punishable by a maximum penalty of five years' imprisonment on indictment or six months' imprisonment on summary conviction.'[689]

Referring to Germany, Cochrane states,

'In May 2014, the German Higher Court of Koblenz ruled that ex-partners must delete explicit photographs taken of their former partners when the relationship ends. The woman in question had consented to all of the material being taken but demanded that all of the images and videos in

---

686 Ibid.
687 Ibid.
688 Ibid.
689 Ibid.

165

which she appeared be deleted. The Court agreed, but held that her partner did not need to delete photographs of her fully clothed which had little, if any, capacity to compromise her.'[690]

Referring to Israel, Cochrane states,

'In January 2014, the Knesset criminalised the posting of sexually explicit media content without the depicted person's knowledge or content. The offence covers content shared on social media and is punishable by up to five years in prison. It is the first country to prosecute as "sexual offenders" those found guilty of posting such content.'[691]

Referring to Japan, Cochrane states,

'The increase in revenge porn cases (around 318 cases involving minors reported in 2013) has spurred consideration by Japan's Liberal Democratic party of legislation to criminalise such acts. The Bill proposal, however, is still in the early stages.'[692]

Referring to the Philippines, Cochrane states,

'The Anti-Photo and Video Voyeurism Act 2009 carries the most severe penalty created to date. Those taking, copying, reproducing, selling, distributing, publishing or broadcasting photo or video coverage of sexual acts or private images without the consent of the person(s) involved can face a prison sentence of up to seven years and a fine up to five hundred pesos (around £6709).'[693]

Referring to the US, Cochrane states,

'New Jersey and California were the first states to enact specific criminal offences for revenge porn. According to the National Conference of State Legislature (NCSL), so far nine other states have enacted revenge porn laws (Arizona, Colorado, Georgia, Hawaii, Idaho, Maryland, Utah, Virginia and Wisconsin), with Pennsylvania and New York seemingly set to follow. In total, Bills have been introduced and are pending in at least 27 states. A number of these, however, have failed or been adjourned.

The Californian provision has already been criticised as failing to address the 'selfie' situation, where the victim takes the photograph or makes the recording him or herself (which, according to a survey conducted by Cyber Civil Rights Initiative, make up 80 percent of photographs published in 'revenge porn' cases). The provision only applies to the person making the recording, leaving anyone who might redistribute the recording, including operators of websites, not covered by the law. Moreover, the defendant must

---

690 Ibid.
691 Ibid.
692 Ibid.
693 Ibid.

have intended to cause the victim severe emotional distress and this motive-based approach has been criticised as being too onerous on the claimant.'[694]

2.24   SM AND PERSONAL DATA OF DECEASED PERSONS

Issues relating to the SM personal data of deceased persons is increasingly highlighted. Everyone dies. What happens to the personal information on an individual's SM page when someone dies? What happens to the SM ghost or, as some computer commentators might say, the SM 'ghost in the machine'?

Do privacy and data protection rights extend beyond death? Until relatively recently, most data protection practitioners would have said 'no'. However, some comments on one EU Article 29 Working Party Opinion[695] raise for discussion the possibility that data protection should extend post mortem, at least in certain circumstances. The current consensus remains in favour of data protection ceasing upon death, but we may be entering a period where we will encounter a number of hard cases where 'interests' exist post mortem and deserve 'informational' protection. It may be that there will be an increasing case for the data protection regime to step in as the most appropriate legal mechanism to protect these interests.

In such an instance, there may be a need to re-interpret the Data Protection Directive 1995, or to expand it in the current EU data protection review. In other instances, such as the Irish Data Protection Acts, which are more explicitly restrictive in terms of accommodating post-mortem informational data protection, specific amendments may be required. The Irish Data Protection Acts refer explicitly to a 'living individual', while the Data Protection Directive 1995 does not.[696]

From Belgium (see chapter C3), there is the following example,

'Journalistic Council ("Raad voor de Journalistiek"), Decision regarding the complaint of Mr Paul de Vloo against the Newspaper "De Krant van West-Vlaanderen" and Pieter-Jan Breyne, journalist, ("Beslissing van de over de klacht van de heer Paul De Vloo tegen De Krant van West-Vlaanderen en Pieter-Jan Breyne, journalist"), 24 June 2010

In this case, the father of a victim of a traffic accident filed a complaint against a Belgian newspaper for using pictures they found on the victim's Facebook profile, without asking consent. The newspaper published two pictures of the victim, one that was publicly accessible on the Facebook

---

694 Ibid.

695 Article 29 Working Party, *Article 29 Working Party Opinion 4/2007 on the Concept of Personal Data*, WP 136, at 22–23.

696 See definition of 'personal data' in the Data Protection Act 1988, as amended by the Data Protection (Amendment) Act 2003.

profile of the victim, whereas the other one was found on a Facebook page for which access was limited due to privacy settings. The Council decided that the second picture was not public and therefore should not have been published without consent. The fact that the journalist had access to the non-public Facebook pages of the victim does not justify him publishing the picture without consent. In consequence, the journalist did not fulfil his usual duty of care and the Board declared the complaint valid.'[697]

2.24.1 The SM ghost

We are growing familiar with the growth and popularity of SM. Some issues are immediately obvious; others come to light only over time. Now SM is beginning to reveal one of the areas that may enhance calls for informational protection post mortem, and some may argue for having such protection on a regulatory footing. Again, the data protection regime may well be the most appropriate legal sphere for such explicit rights. In the interim, there may be increasing arguments to extend current definitions and interpretations of the data protection regime.

Billions of people have SM profile pages containing a host of personal data in relation to themselves personally and also their friends and family. However, as the timeline of SM advances, increasing numbers of members inevitably pass away. Their personal data remains a lingering ghost in the SM machine. This will become an increasingly important issue.

The question, therefore, arises as to who owns and controls social network profiles and personal data of deceased people.

According to interpretations of data protection laws until now, personal data related only to living individuals. Does that mean that personal data, as defined in legislation, automatically ceases to be personal data once the data subject has passed away? Alternatively, does it mean that only the data protection rights of the dead individual cease to exist?

The main concern is that there is great personal interest in the informational ghost that remains on the system. While the individual data subject may be dead, he or she may have friends, partners, children and other family relations. They will obviously be concerned with, and interested in, what happens to the ghost personal data. Indeed, let us not forget the person who has died. During their lifetime, individuals may be concerned as to what happens to their personal data once they have died. These individuals may be few and far between as yet, but it is not difficult to anticipate that they may have certain wishes and intentions as to what should happen to their data afterwards.

---

697 The full text of the decision is available (in Dutch) at http://rvdj.be/sites/default/files/pdf/
      beslissing201009.pdf.

Notwithstanding that there may be difficulties in deciding which family member is the most appropriate person to control the data, the family arguably have many legitimate interests in gaining access to and control of the personal profile. They may wish to get access; post an announcement in case friends and acquaintances are unaware of the death; post a memorial or appreciation; delete the profile; or copy photographs or materials from the profile.

It must be acknowledged that the SNs are beginning to react. Some websites have a policy in place to begin addressing these ghost access issues. This is not universally the case and, even where there is a policy or notice on the website, it is not always transparent or available in a user-friendly manner. However, these are self-regulating measures.

What happens if the matter is not addressed, or is not addressed to the extent that the next of kin, etc would like? What happens when there is a conflicting claim? What is the specific claim?

Indeed, a longstanding partner may also be greatly concerned as to what happens to the SM profile and information. This gets even more complicated when we consider married, estranged, separated, divorced, partner and same-sex issues.

While the legal position may be uncertain, there is a legitimate argument that data protection or other privacy laws are the more appropriate mechanism to address these emerging SM ghost issues. That there may not be a policy in place with all SM, or that they are not, on occasion, user-friendly, only emphasises this concern.

Indeed, there is separate point to be made. Data protection rights and obligations frequently mean that data processing for new purposes, and new data transfers, will turn on how transparent and fair the new purposes and transfers may be. Would the data subjects reasonably expect or envisage the new activities at the time of their original consent to processing? If these concepts of reasonable and legitimate expectations are expanded to SM ghost data, what would these people envisage would happen to their personal data after they pass away? Do SNs need to engage users with these issues while people are alive?

As indicated above, SM and data protection laws may have to deal with competing claims of access. Is a son more entitled than a widow to access and control the deceased's SM profile? What happens if one relative wants to delete but another wants to make a post on the SM profile?

What happens in the case of difficult personal relationships such as estranged parties, mistress, wife, separated and divorced partners, etc? Courts will have to decide these issues in future.

In these and other instances, should people anticipate these problems, like they may do when they contemplate a will? Are SNs obliged to respect a preference made in a will in respect of what should happen to a profile after the person dies?

While succession law is well established,[698] it is an altogether different problem to decide whether SM profiles are a recognised form of property, or some other recognised category which may legitimately be included in a traditional will.

Yet further difficulties arise. How will a dispute be adjudicated if the person specified in a will is not the natural next of kin, or is different from the person recognised by an SN in its policy? These issues are far from resolved. Indeed, they are only just beginning to come into consideration in data protection and informational rights discussions. Soon these issues will be contested in courts.

2.24.2 The health analogy

While succession law may provide some analogies, as referred to above, we might also be able to look at the analogy with health personal data. While health data is recognised as the more important form of sensitive personal data, it is not referred to in the content of SM or post-mortem data in data protection law. Yet, certain laws and policies in relation to health data may provide an analogy. Indeed, this is not a fanciful concern, as Google has proposed the online storage of certain health-related data in the Google Health and HealthVault services.[699]

The Access to Health Records Act 1990 in the UK refers to the regulation of access to medical data after a patient dies.[700] This relates mostly to disclosure by medical practitioners and medical institutions. These access issues can be quite complicated. An insurance company, for example, may make an access request where the individual previously expressed an objection to disclosure.[701] The next of kin might also object to such disclosure.[702] How is a doctor, hospital or nursing home meant to resolve these issues? The legal concept underlying the protection of the file is the common law duty of confidentiality, which is stated to extend beyond the date of death.[703] The Irish Medical Council also refers to confidentiality obligations.[704] Confidentiality was examined in *Coco v AN Clark (Engineers) Limited*;[705] *House of Spring Gardens v Point Blank*;[706] and

---

698 In Ireland, this is governed by the Succession Act 1965. UK succession law is governed by the Administration of Estates Act 1925. (Note that other laws will also apply in terms of most questions of succession law and practice.)

699 Referred to in J Caldarella, 'Privacy and Security of Personal Health Records Maintained by Online Health Services' (2010) *Alb Law Journal of Science & Technology* 203. Note also LB Jacques, 'Electronic Health Records and Respect for Patient Privacy: A Prescription for Compatibility' (2010–2011) *Vandenberg Journal of Entertainment & Technology Law* 441.

700 See 'Confidentiality After Death', Wessex Local Medical Committees, available at www.wessexlmcs.com/confidentialityafterdeath.

701 Ibid.

702 Ibid.

703 Ibid.

704 Medical Council, *Guide to Professional Conduct and Ethics for Registered Medical Practitioners*, 7th Edition 2009, Section 24 General Principles of Confidentiality, at 26–27.

705 *Coco v AN Clark (Engineers) Limited* [1969] FSR 415.

706 *House of Spring Gardens v Point Blank* [1984] IR 611.

Mahon v Post Publications;[707] and in the UK in *Campbell v MGN Ltd.*[708] One factor to be considered is what detriment will be suffered if there is a disclosure of the data.[709] However, these authorities do not deal with the personal data of deceased persons.[710] New considerations arise.

The British Medical Association (BMA) also provides some guidance in relation to health data in its *Access to Health Records, Guidance for Health Professionals in the United Kingdom.*[711] The types of situations that may be specified are who may apply for access,[712] and what happens where somebody lacks capacity[713] (as might a child who engages in SM), etc. It states,

'The ethical obligation to respect a patient's confidentiality extends beyond death. The Information Tribunal in England and Wales has also held that a duty of confidence attaches to the medical records of the deceased under section 41 of the Freedom of Information Act. The Freedom of Information Act in Scotland contains an exemption to the disclosure of medical records of the deceased patients. However, this duty of confidentiality needs to be balanced with other considerations, such as the interests of justice and of people close to the deceased person. Health professionals should therefore counsel their patients about the possibility of disclosure after death and solicit views about disclosure where it is obvious that there may be some sensitivity. Such discussions should be recorded in the records.'[714]

The BMA guidance continues,

'Statutory rights of access are set out in the access to Health Records Act 1990 or Access to Health Records (Northern Ireland) Order 1993. The Access to Health Records Act 1990 covers manual health records made since 1 November 1991. In Northern Ireland the corresponding legislation, the Access to Health Records (Northern Ireland) Order 1993, covers manual records from 30 May 1994. Access must also be given to information recorded before these dates if this is necessary to make a later part of the records intelligible'.[715]

It is also noted that the BMA refers to the practice whereby it was recommended not to reply to insurance company requests for duration certificates partly on

---

707 *Mahon v Post Publications* [2007] IESC 15.
708 [2004] 2 WLR 1232.
709 AA Sheikh, 'The Data Protection Acts 1988 and 2003, Some Implications for Public Health and Medical Research', *Health Research Board*, 84–85.
710 Ibid, 85.
711 British Medical Association, 'Access to Health Records, Guidance for Health Professionals in the United Kingdom', December 2008. Also see 'Confidentiality', General Medical Council, available at www.gmc-uk.org/guidance/ethical_guidance/confidentiality.asp.
712 BMA Guidance, Section 4.1 (Who May Apply For Access?), at 3.
713 Ibid, Section 4.1.4, at 4.
714 Ibid, Section 5 (Deceased Patients), at 8.
715 Ibid, Section 5.1 (Are There Any Rights of Access to a Deceased Patient's Records?), at 8.

the basis that the deceased person is no longer in a position to give informed consent.[716]

Of course, there are various business cases for access to medical records for research purposes, which can also be post mortem.[717] Generally, the Irish Data Protection Commissioner has issued guidance on health research, in its *Data Protection Guidelines on Research in the Health Sector*.[718] It states, *inter alia*,

> 'The Data Protection Acts require that where access to patient identifiable information is not accompanies by an explicit consent that it be undertaken for medical purposes and be undertaken by a health professional or a person who, in the circumstances, owes a duty of confidentiality to the data subject that is equivalent to that which would exist if that person were a health professional. The term health professional is defined in the appendix to this document and is intentionally broad to ensure all appropriate health professional can access patient data for medical purposes which also include research.
>
> Questions as to whether a staff member, who is not a health professional and is to access patent identifiable information without consent, can be considered to owe an equivalent duty of confidentiality to the patient, need to be assessed on a case by case basis. As a general guide such persons would need to have a contractual duty of confidentiality that would carry an appropriate penalty would there be a breach of confidentiality.'[719]

There is also proposed legislation in California to protect an individual's genetic health data.[720] Among other things, the proposed law seeks to ensure that there is written consent before use; and that genetic data cannot be the basis of employment or housing discrimination (which would append to existing anti-discrimination).[721] Another US Bill, in Vermont, defines genetic data as forming 'real property' and the 'exclusive property' of the individual.[722] In addition, in recognition of the value of such data even post mortem, the proposed law provides that individuals can include instructions in their will as

---

716 Ibid, Annex 2.
717 A Withers, 'Archiving and Storing Patients' Health Records After Death Can Help with Medical Research', ArticlesOnline, 29 August 2010, available at http://articlesonlinedirectory. com.
718 Data Protection Commissioner, *Data Protection Guidelines on Research in the Health Sector*, available at http://dataprivacy.ie.
719 Ibid, Section 2.8 'Persons Accessing Patient Identifiable Data', at 12.
720 T Ray, 'Vermont, California Follow Massachusetts in Introducing Genetic Data Protection Bills', 9 March 2011, *Genome Web, Pharmacogenomics Reporter*, available at www. genomeweb.com/dxpgx/vermont-california-follow-massachusetts-introducing-genetic-data-protection-bill?utm_source=twitterfeed&utm_medium=twitter. In relation to the UK generally, see *Inside Information: Balancing Interest in the Use of Personal Genetic Information* (Human Genetics Commission, UK, 2002), in particular at 85–87, as referred to in Sheikh, *op. cit*, 81.
721 Ibid.
722 Ibid.

to what should happen (or not happen) with their genetic data.[723] There is also the concept of primary and secondary uses in relation to medical and health data.[724] Can the next of kin decide what to do with the SM profile data? The question arises as to whether (and, if so, what) personal health data of deceased persons can be disclosed. One commentator suggests that this health data issue 'is a complex area of law and it cannot be said that there exists a clear answer to the query'.[725]

2.24.3   Personal data

The EU Data Protection Directive 1995 defines personal data as,

> 'any information relating to an identified or identifiable natural person ("data subject"); an identifiable person is one who can be identified, directly or indirectly, in particular by reference to an identification number or to one or more factors specific to his physical, physiological, mental, economic, cultural or social identity.'[726]

However, the Irish Data Protection Acts defines personal data as data relating to a 'living individual' who is or can be identified either from the data or from the data in conjunction with other information that is in, or is likely to come into, the possession of the data controller.[727]

In the UK, personal data is defined as,

> 'data which relate to a living individual who can be identified–
>
> (a)   from those data, or
>
> (b)   from those data and other information which is in the possession of, or is likely to come into the possession of, the data controller,
>
> and includes any expression of opinion about the individual and any indication of the intentions of the data controller or any other person in respect of the individual.'[728]

The EU PRIVIREAL Project discusses what amounts to personal data, and states as follows,

> 'This is not a question of "rights" for the dead. The central issue is whether the Directive covers data that relates to a person who has dies. It concerns whether duties apply to the personal data that was obtained from living

---

723 Ibid.

724 Sheikh, *op. cit*, 76, referring to BMA Guidance on Secondary Uses of Patient Information, Ethics Department BMA, 2007, at 5.

725 Sheikh, *op. cit*, 81 *et seq.*

726 Article 2.

727 Section 2 of the Data Protection Act 1988, as amended by the Data Protection (Amendment) Act 2003.

728 Data Protection Act 1998 (as amended).

people who are now dead. Clearly, some of the duties of the Directive do not apply. It is not possible to inform the dead person about the processing of the data or to seek their consent for new processing. However, if the data was collected from the dead person when alive for specific purposes, do duties in relation to the processing of that data continue for those stated aims? Must the processing remain lawful and fair? Must the data be kept securely? Is the effect of the death of the data subject that of removing the data from the scope of the Directive. The implementation of the Directive by Member States shows a variety of approaches to this area.'[729]

The PRIVIREAL Project recommends that the Commission should seek to clarify whether or not the personal data of deceased persons falls within the definition of 'personal data'.[730]

2.24.4   EU Article 29 Working Party

The EU Article 29 Working Party has also touched on these issues in its Opinion 4/2007 on the Concept of Personal Data. It states,

> 'Information relating to dead individuals is therefore in principle not to be considered as personal data subject to the rules of the Directive, as the dead are no longer natural persons in civil law. However, the data of the deceased may still indirectly receive some protection in certain cases.

> On the one hand, the data controller may not be in a position to ascertain whether the person to whom the data relate is still living or may be dead. Or even if he may do so, the information on the dead may be processed under the same regime as that on the living without distinction. As the data controller is subject to the data protection obligations imposed by the Directive as regards the data on living individuals, it will probably be easier for him in practice to process also the data on the dead in the way imposed by the data protection rules, rather than to separate the two sets of data. On the other hand, the information on dead individuals may also refer to living persons. For instance, the information that the dead Gaia suffered from haemophilia indicates that her son Titius also suffers from the same disease, as it is linked to a gene contained in the X-chromosome. Thus, where the information which is data on the dead can be considered to relate at the same time also to the living and be personal data subject to the Directive, the personal data of the deceased may indirectly enjoy the protection of data protection rules.

---

729 Sheikh, *op. cit*, 81, referring to www.privireal.org/content/recommendations/#Refc, the PRIVIREAL Project, which is an EU body dedicated to examining Directive 95/46/EC of the European Parliament and of the Council of 24 October 1995, on the protection of individuals with regard to the processing of personal data and on the free movement of such data, in the context of the medical research issues.

730 Sheikh, *op. cit*, 82.

Thirdly, information on deceased persons may be subject to specific protection granted by sets of rules other than data protection legislation, drawing the lines of what some call 'personalitas praeterita.' The obligation of confidentiality of medical staff does not end with the death of the patient. National legislation on the right to one's own image and honour may grant also protection to the memory of the dead.'[731]

However, it adds that,

'nothing prevents a Member State from extending the scope of the national legislation implementing the provisions of [EU Data Protection Directive 1995] to areas not included in the scope thereof provided that no other provision of Community law precludes it, as the ECJ has recalled.[732] It is possible that some national legislator may decide to extend the provisions of national data protection law to some aspects concerning processing data on deceased persons, where a legitimate interest may justify it.'[733]

2.24.5 UK

Some guidance on disclosures is provided by the UK General Medical Council regarding disclosures after death, which include factors such as,

- whether the disclosure of information may cause distress to, or be of benefit to, the patient's partner or family;

- whether disclosure of information about the patient will in effect disclose information about the patient's family or other people;

- whether the information is already public knowledge or can be anonymised;

- the purpose of the disclosure.[734]

2.24.6 Ireland

It has been suggested that the Irish Data Protection Acts 'are not applicable to the dead'.[735] The Data Protection Directive 1995 also refers to 'living individuals'.

Sheikh, however, raises a separate point. 'The protection of the Acts may arise in the case where there is joint personal data in relation to both the dead and a living person'.[736]

---

731 *Opinion 4/2007 on the Concept of Personal Data*, Article 29 Working Party, at 23.
732 Judgment of the European Court of Justice C–101/2001 of 06/11/2003, Lindqvist, § 98.
733 *Opinion 4/2007 on the Concept of Personal Data*, Article 29 Working Party, at 23–24.
734 *Confidentiality: Protecting and Providing Information*, UK General Medical Council (April 2004), para 30, referred to in Sheikh, *op. cit*, 83.
735 Sheikh, *op. cit*, 82.
736 Ibid, 82.

While some rights are recognised in law as existing post mortem, other laws are less explicit, while others are clear in providing that rights are extinguished on death.

The Irish Civil Liability Act 1961 provides that causes of action can continue to the benefit of a person's estate where the person dies.[737]

An example of where rights cease on death is US defamation law.[738] A similar provision in the Civil Liability Act 1961 in Ireland provides that Irish defamation actions also cease on death.[739]

2.24.7 *(Living) third-party interests*

One commentator concludes that, for the moment, it seems that privacy interests do not survive death 'except where disclosure of a certain type of information would cause distress to families if released. In these cases, it seems that such information has been protected from disclosure as it may affect the privacy of the existing family'.[740] There has been an example of a case where this was successfully argued.

In the US case of *New York Times Company v National Aeronautics and Space Administration (NASA)*,[741] the families of astronauts on the fatal space shuttle Challenger were objecting to recordings of their deceased family members being released to the media. The media were requesting access to the black box recordings. The court stated,

'the Challenger families' privacy interest in the tape in question outweighs the public interest such that release of the tape would constitute a clearly unwarranted invasion of the families' personal privacy.'[742]

The media also requested access to photographs of a deceased legal counsel to President Clinton. The case, *National Archives and Records v Favish*,[743] held that,

'[t]he right to personal privacy is not confined ... to the "right to control information about oneself" ... To say that the concept of personal privacy must "encompass" the individual's control of information about himself does not mean it cannot encompass other personal interests as well.'[744]

---

737 See section 7(1). As referred to in Sheikh, *op. cit*, 86.
738 Sheikh, *op. cit*, 86.
739 See section 7(1). As referred to ibid.
740 Sheikh, *op. cit*, 86.
741 *New York Times Company v National Aeronautics and Space Administration* 782 F Supp 628 (12 December 1991) (affirmed on appeal to the Supreme Court).
742 Ibid.
743 *National Archives and Records v Favish*, United States Court of Appeals for the Ninth Circuit, 30 March 2004.
744 Ibid, referred to in Sheikh, *op. cit*, 87.

The court also said: 'In addition this well-established cultural tradition acknowledging a family's control over the body and death images of the deceased has long been recognised at common law'.[745] The decision was upheld on appeal to the US Supreme Court.[746]

The comment is made in Ireland that,

'[w]here aspects of the deceased may affect the living person by causing, especially family members, him/her harm, such connection has been recognised by the law of privacy and protected. Where private information about the deceased will affect the living individual and case him/her harm, the public interest in disclosure will be examined and disclosure may be prohibited if harm will be caused to the living individual.'[747]

However, it is acknowledged that there is no law in Ireland equivalent to that in other jurisdictions on this issue.[748] Furthermore, the Irish Data Protection Acts are limited to living individuals.[749] 'In the absence of relevant legislation, there exists only common law and ethical guidelines that might guide medical practitioners'.[750] The data protection principles in the UK appear similar.

Ultimately, this is an issue which has yet to be properly dealt with in legislation, and may have to be dealt with at the EU level. 'While some of the national laws strictly define the personal data as only such that identify a living person, some of the laws including the harmonisation directive do not solve the problem and leave the question open'.[751]

2.24.8 Conclusion

While the solutions and, indeed, full parameters of what should happen to the SM personal data of deceased persons are far from clear, it is inevitable that this problem will have to be considered much more frequently. Certain comfort may come through self-regulation and self-administered social network policies. However, these policies will arguably not be able to deal with each and every data ghost problem that arises. Ultimately, some of the solutions may have to come from the data protection regime. In that regard, there may be increasing pressure to recognise that personal data, as protected under the data protection regime, needs to be reinterpreted or expanded post mortem. It will also need to be considered what interest or value is actually being protected. Data protection variously refers to privacy and fundamental rights, while the

---

745 Ibid.
746 See *The Oyez Project, National Archives and Records Administration v Favish*, 541 US 157 (2004) www.oyez.org/cases/2000-2009/2003/2003_02_954.
747 Sheikh, *op. cit*, 88.
748 Ibid.
749 Ibid.
750 Ibid.
751 R Polcak, 'Aims, Methods and Achievements in European Data Protection' (November 2009) (23) *International Review of Law, Computers & Technology* 179 at note 16 at 187.

Constitution, constitutional (property) rights and succession law may refer to other interests. The concept and interests grounding expanded data protection need to be considered.

2.25   SM, WEBSITE, SERVICE PROVIDER OR ISP DEFENCE RULES/LAWS

This refers to and includes laws that may be similar to the EU eCommerce Directive or US Digital Millennium Copyright Act (DMCA) eCommerce defences. These generally comprise of mere conduit, caching and hosting-style defences. Other jurisdictions now consider rules or laws providing SM, website, service provider or ISP defences (similar to EU eCommerce Directive or US DMCA eCommerce defences). In the US, the position is summarised by Eric P Robinson (in chapter C33), as follows,

'An important federal law regarding the internet generally is section 230 of the Communications Decency Act, 47 USC § 230. This statute provides that "interactive computer services," including SM websites and services, are generally immune from civil or criminal liability – except for federal criminal and intellectual property laws – for material posted by users of the site or service. Courts have interpreted this statute broadly, dismissing virtually all types of claims against websites and services for content posted by individuals and entities other than the operator of the site or service.

While general screening and minor editing of material posted by users is permitted, a website or service operator editing the material to add a basis for liability – for example, adding a defamatory statement – can waive the immunity by making the operator the provider of the content. Courts have also held that immunity may be waived if a website or service is structured in such a way that users are compelled to post material that violates the law. See eg *Fair Housing Council of San Fernando Valley v Roommates. com* LLC 521 F3d 1157 (9th Cir 2008) (no immunity for roommate site that included illegal housing restrictions amongst listing choices), *MCW Inc v badbusinessbureau.com*, 2004 WL 833595, 2004 US Dist LEXIS 6678, Civ No 3:02-CV-2727-G (ND Tex April 19 2004). But when such information is posted by users with no prompting from the site operator, section 230 immunity applies. *Chicago Lawyers' Committee for Civil Rights Under Law Inc v Craigslist Inc* 519 F3d 666 (7th Cir 2008).

While promoters of the internet and SM defend section 230 immunity as important protection that supports the creation and adoption of new [websites] and technologies, the provision has also been criticized for being too broad. In 2013 the attorneys general of 47 states sent a letter to the leaders of the Congressional commerce committees urging that the statute be amended to specifically exempt obscenity, sexual exploitation of children, and state criminal laws from the immunity.

Another statute, the Digital Millennium Copyright Act, Pub L 105–304, 112 Stat. 2860 (1998), includes numerous provisions regarding copyright in the digital era. Title II of the Act, separately known as the Online Copyright Infringement Liability Limitation Act, 17 USC § 512, provides that online service providers (OSPs) are protected under a 'safe harbour' for copyright infringement claims over infringing material posted by users, as long as the OSP implements prescribed 'notice and takedown' procedures to block or remove infringing material upon notification by a copyright owner. The statute also allows copyright owners to subpoena records in order to determine the identity of infringers who post such material.'

In the UK (see chapter C32), Jonathan McDonald indicates,

'Under the Electronic Commerce (EC Directive) Regulations 2002, a service provider (which may include a website and, by extension, an SN provider) is generally not liable for any material where it: (a) acts as a mere conduit; (b) caches the material; or (c) hosts the material. The most relevant of these for SNs is the hosting defence, which has been interpreted broadly by the courts. The defence may be lost, however, where the service provider has performed an "active role" in an unlawful activity or has gained an awareness of the unlawful activity or content (*L'Oreal v eBay* Case C-324/09).'

The EU eCommerce Directive 2000/31/EC was implemented in Belgian Law by way of the Law of 11 March 2003 concerning certain legal aspects of information society services (Official State Gazette 17 March 2003). It provides for liability exemptions for 'mere conduits', 'hosting' and 'caching' (see chapter C3).

2.26   ECOMMERCE DEFENCE CASES

In Belgium (see chapter C3), the following extract gives a flavour of EU and national cases,

'*Court of Cassation, 3 February 2004, case n° P031427N*

In this case, an operator of a website displaying links to child pornography was found liable for distribution of child pornography. The webmaster argued that he, as an operator of a website, could rely on the liability exemption for hosting service providers and therefore was not liable for content of the linked websites. The Court, however, judged that the exemption was not applicable in this case, as the webmaster's activities did not have a merely technical, automatic or passive character. The latter had purchased, developed and economically exploited the website and had offered a collection of hyperlinks that led to child pornography images. The Court decided that the process of collecting these hyperlinks had happened under supervision and with the knowledge of the webmaster.[752]

---

752 The full text of this judgment is available at http://jure.juridat.just.fgov.be/view_decision. html?justel=F-20040203-3&idxc_id=197925&lang=nl.

179

Chairman of the Court of Antwerp, 5 October 2006, nr. 06/3006/A

In this case, an operator of a website for seniors was accused of copyright breach. The website had certain mailing groups, via which people could discuss certain topics, such as music. The members of these mailing groups were able to send messages to one another, even with attachments, which were then stored in an electronic archive. The issue here was that, through one of these mailing groups, sound recordings were distributed without the consent of the rights holders, resulting in a breach of copyright. The Court judged that the website operator's activities did not have a merely technical, automatic or passive character, since the operator actively took measures to allow these infringements, like the archiving or the fact that the administrators of the mailing group received consent of the operator.[753]

Court of Commerce of Brussels (7th Chamber) 31 July 2008

Lancôme complained that eBay allowed advertisements which violated their trademarks and did not take any measures to prevent counterfeited goods from appearing amongst genuine online sales advertisements. The Court clarified that the liability exemption is not limited to a specific type of service provider, but to specific and clearly defined actions. The Court held that the complaint only concerned eBay's activities of distributing advertisements of candidate sellers, to which it considered the 'hosting' exemption to be applicable.[754]

Court of Appeal of Liège (7th Chamber), 22 October 2009

A manager of a construction company had read negative comments about his company on the website of a consumer organization. He decided to sue the consumer organization in order to obtain the personal data of the persons who had posted the negative comments. The construction company based its claim on Article 21 of the E-Commerce Law of 23rd of March 2003 concerning the legal aspects of certain information society services, which states that intermediary service providers are obliged to provide any information that is useful for the detection of breaches of law to certain judicial and administrative authorities. The Court of Appeal of Liège, however, ruled that Article 21 should not be understood as an objective right for a physical or legal person to receive this information, either directly by an immediate injunction against the provider, or indirectly via a handover of the information by the judicial or administrative authority.[755]

---

753 The full text of this judgment is available at www.ie-forum.nl/getobject.php?id=2172.
754 The full text of this judgment is available at http://jure.juridat.just.fgov.be/view_decision. html?justel=F-20080731-12&idxc_id=225620&lang=nl.
755 This judgment was reproduced in *Revue du Droit des Technologies et de l'Information* 2010, n° 1, p 95 (and annotated by J Feld, 'Forums de discussion: espaces de libertés sous haute responsabilité', *RDTI* 2010, p 106–120).

Court of Appeal of Brussels, (9th Chamber), 25 November 2009

(This case is the continuation of the previously described case.)

The construction company sued the consumer organization for the damages they had suffered from the defamatory statements. The Court decided that moderators of website fora are arbiters in the conflict between freedom of expression and the rights of third parties, like protection of reputation. A moderator that has a right to control the messages of the internet users accepts civil liability, based on Article 1382 of the Civil Code. Therefore, the activities of moderators do not merely have a technical, automatic and passive character, so the exemption of the eCommerce Directive is not applicable.[756]

European Court of Justice, (3rd Chamber), Sabam v Netlog, Case nr. C-360/10, 16 February 2012

In this case, the Court of Justice was asked to assess the legality of a request by a Belgian copyright society (SABAM), to direct a Belgian SN (Netlog) to implement a general filtering system to prevent unlawful use of musical and audio-visual work by its users. The Court considered Netlog as a hosting service provider, which led to its conclusion that the implementation of a general filtering system would collide with the eCommerce Directive, more specifically the prohibition for Member States to impose a general obligation to monitor on service providers conducting activities of mere conduit, caching and hosting.[757]'

In the US, Eric P Robinson (in chapter C33), indicates the position as follows,

'Forty-seven states and the District of Columbia have adopted the Uniform Electronic Transactions Act (UETA), which provides a set of standard state laws for eCommerce transactions, including use of electronic signatures and records. The three remaining states – Illinois, New York and Washington – each have their own statutes regarding these issues. See 5 Ill Comp Stat § 175/1-101; NY State Tech Law § 301, *et seq*; and Wash Rev Code § 19.34.300, *et seq.*

In addition, Congress has enacted the Electronic Signatures in Global and National Commerce Act (E-SIGN), which establishes the validity of electronic records and signatures, although it does not mandate their use. Pub L No 106-229, 114 Stat 464 (2000), 15 USC §§ 7001–7006. The Act

---

756 This judgment was reproduced in *RDTI* 2010, n° 38, p 102 (and also annotated by J Feld).
757 The full text of this judgment is available at http://curia.europa.eu/juris/liste. jsf?language=en&num=C-360/10. For a commentary, see F Coudert, '*SABAM v Netlog*: ECJ confirms general filtering systems installed for the prevention of copyright infringements are disproportionate', time.lex Blog, 16 February 2012, available at www.timelex.eu/nl/blog/ detail/sabam-v-netlog-ecj-confirms-general-filtering-systems-installed-for-the-prevention- of-copyright-infringements-are-disproportionate.

also applies when states have either not adopted a law on the subject or have enacted provisions that are inconsistent with the E-SIGN Act. The statute's requirements must be met for an electronic signature to be valid; the mere fact that a document is electronic is not in and of itself sufficient. *Campbell v Gen Dynamics Gov't Sys Corp* 407 F3d 546 (1st Cir 2005).'

2.27 LAWS PROTECTING PERSONAL DATA/ PERSONALLY IDENTIFIABLE INFORMATION

The Data Protection Act 1998 is the main piece of legislation that governs the protection of personal data in the UK (see chapter C32). The Data Protection Act and Data Protection (Amendment) Act govern data protection in Ireland. Eric P Robinson (in chapter C33) indicates that,

'Unlike Europe, the United States has adopted only a few laws placing limits on disclosure of personal data and personally identifiable information. Examples of such laws include the Fair Credit Reporting Act, Pub L 91–508, 84 Stat 1114 (1970), codified at 15 USC § 1681 *et seq*, the Right to Financial Privacy Act, Pub L 95–630, 92 Stat 3641 (1978), codified at 12 USC §§ 3401-3402, and the Fair and Accurate Credit Transactions Act, Pub L 108–159, 117 Stat 1952 (2003) (amending 15 USC § 1681 *et seq*), which place limitations of disclosure and use of personal financial information. The Health Insurance Portability and Accountability Act (HIPAA) includes provisions that restrict disclosure of personal health information. See 42 USC § 1320d, *et seq*; see also 45 CFR § 160 101, *et seq* (implementing regulations). And the Family Educational Rights and Privacy Act of 1974 (FERPA, also known as the Buckley Amendment), Pub L No 93-380, 88 Stat 484 (1974), codified at 20 USC § 1232, restricts disclosure of educational records.

Several states have adopted their own laws regarding online privacy. California's Online Privacy Protection Act of 2003, codified at Cal Bus & Prof Code §§ 22575–22579, requires entities such as web sites and SM services that collect information to have and conspicuously display a privacy policy disclosing how they use the information that they collect, including whether the information is sold to other entities or used for web tracking. Utah requires disclosure if personal information will be sold. Connecticut requires disclosure regarding the use of Social Security numbers. Conn Stat § 42-470. Massachusetts, Minnesota, and Nevada have laws that require collectors of personal information to safeguard that information. See Mass Gen'l L chap 93H; Minn Stat chap 325M; Nev Rev Stat chap. 603A.'

In Belgium (see chapter C3), examples are,

'*Law of 8 December 1992 for the protection of private life in relation to the processing of personal data, Official State Gazette, 18 March 1993*

This Law was amended in 1998 by the Law of 11 December 1998 transposing EU Directive 95/46/EC of 24 October 1995 of the European Parliament and the Council on the protection of individuals with regard to the processing of personal data and on the free movement of such data, Official State Gazette, 3 February 1999.

This law applies to any processing of personal data by (wholly or partially) automatic means (Article 3(1)). Article 1 of the Act defines personal data as "any information concerning an identified or identifiable natural person".

The basic principles of the Law are that any processing of personal data needs to have a legitimate basis (Article 5), a legitimate and well-defined purpose (Article 4(1)2), the processing needs to be relevant (Article 4(1)3), as precise as possible (Article 4(1)4), transparent (Article 9) and adequately secured (Article 16). Furthermore, the data retention period should be minimized (Article 4(1)5), and personal data can only be transferred to countries that offer an adequate level of protection (Article 21 etc).

Law of 13 June 2005 on electronic communications, Official State Gazette, 20 June 2005

This law implemented EU Directive 2002/58/EC of the European Parliament and of the Council of 12 July 2002 concerning the processing of personal data and the protection of privacy in the electronic communications sector (Directive on privacy and electronic communications).'

2.28   DATA BREACH LAWS AND CUSTOMERS/ USERS/ REGULATORS NOTIFIED OF HACKING OR DATA LOSS

Certain jurisdictions now recognise the need for data breach laws. Such laws provide for customers, users and/or regulators to be notified if an organisation's data and/or systems have been hacked or data has otherwise been lost. Many organisations, both official and private, have suffered data security and data protection breaches. Some examples involve the organisation directly losing particular personal data sets, such as laptops or media storage devices. Other examples involve the security of the organisation being breached by third parties, eg hackers in deliberate attacks. While the latter electronic threats have always been an issue, they are increasing in frequency. The increasing scale and regularity of these breaches is alarming and is now increasingly recognised as an important official policy concern.

Eric P Robinson (in chapter C33) notes that,

'All but three states – Alabama, New Mexico, and South Dakota – have adopted statutes creating a duty to disclose breaches of personal financial information. Many of these statutes follow the model set by California's law, 2002 Cal Laws chap 915. In 2008, California expanded this law to cover medical information. 2007 Cal Laws chap 699. But these laws still vary somewhat on what entities and what personal information are covered, what constitutes a breach, and form and recipients of the notice.

While there is no federal statute regarding disclosure of data breaches, several federal government entities have adopted regulations on the subject. The Federal Reserve has adopted guidelines for banks, thrifts and other financial entities to follow regarding disclosure of breaches of financial data. See Interagency Guidance on Response Programs for Unauthorized Access to Customer Information and Customer Notice, 12 CFR Part 30, app B (Office of the Comptroller of the Currency); 12 CFR Part 208, app D-2 and Part 225, app F (Federal Reserve Board); 12 CFR Part 364, app B (FDIC); and 12 CFR Part 570, app B (Office of Thrift Supervision). The Federal Department of Health and Human Services (HHS) and Federal Trade Commission have adopted similar rules regarding breaches of health information. 45 CFR §§ 164.400-414 (HHS); 16 CFR Part 318 (FTC). The FTC also acts against data breaches that occur because of lapses in companies' privacy policies.

Some data breaches have resulted in litigation. A study of such federal cases from 2005 to 2011found suits including 86 causes of action, most commonly unfair business practices claims, claims under the Fair Credit Reporting Act, and breach of contract claims. About half of these cases settled, with slightly less ended by the courts' grant of either a motion to dismiss or a motion for summary judgment. S Romanosky, D Hoffman, and A Acquisti, "Empirical Analysis of Data Breach Litigation", 11 J Empirical L Studies 74 (2014).'

The position in Belgium (see chapter C3) is as follows,

'Such an obligation exists for operators of an electronic communications network and providers of electronic communications services on the basis of Article 114(1) and following of the Act of 13 June 2005 on electronic communications. These operators and providers must notify the national telecoms authority (BIPT) as well as the individual users when the breach causes adverse effects on the users' privacy.

The Belgian Data Protection Act currently does not provide for a general data security breach notification duty for all data controllers. A Bill introduced in Parliament for amending said Act aims to introduce a general security breach notification. The Belgian DPA (Privacy Commission) further recommended, in a recent recommendation on security measures and data breaches, that companies should notify any security breaches in case of "public incidents". The DPA said that notification procedures for data security breach incidents should be documented by companies. If a "public incident" occurs, the DPA should receive information about the causes and damage within a period of 48 hours. Unfortunately, the Belgian Privacy Commission did not specify what was meant by the term "public incident".'[758]

---

758 The full text of this document is available (in Dutch) at www.privacycommission.be/sites/ privacycommission/files/documents/aanbeveling_01_2013.pdf.

2.28.1 Breaches, data loss and threats

Over the last number of years, there have been some breath-taking examples of data loss and data breach. In some single instances, the personal data of millions of users or customers has been put at risk. This has involved commercial entities such as banks and utilities, and also official agencies from health to revenue agencies. These breach instances can involve general personal data as well as sensitive personal data.

There are now attacks not just on particular websites or organisations, but also on infrastructure-related companies such as computer security firms RSA and Comodo and also Google in China.[759] These are entities that provide technology infrastructure and security to others. Defence and security-related entities are also attacked by hackers, despite the perception that these would be more secure.[760]

2.28.2 SNs

On occasion, regulators also warn SNs to enhance their privacy security and privacy practices, even in the US which is perceived as having less data protection laws than in the EU.[761] For example,

'US lawmakers told Facebook today they were concerned about changes in its privacy policy that would allow personal information to be viewed by more than friends, and options on other websites that would allow third parties to save information about Facebook users and friends.'[762]

The Irish Data Protection Commissioner has recently told Facebook to delay and to amend proposed changes to its privacy policies.[763] There is perhaps an irony as this is after the audit report and re-audit report of Facebook by the Data Protection Commissioner when any expected improvements at that point in time would have occurred.[764]

---

759 D O'Brien, 'Web Security Breaches Show Better Solutions Are Necessary', *Irish Times*, 25 March 2011.

760 E Pilkington, 'Hackers Expose Defence and Intelligence Officials in US and UK, Security Breach by "Hactivists" Reveal Email Addresses of 221 British Military Staff and 242 NATO Officials', *Guardian*, 8 January 2012.

761 See 'Facebook Told to Tighten Privacy', *Irish Times*, 27 April 2010, available at www.irishtimes.com/newspaper/breaing/2010/0427/breaking72.html?via=rel.

762 See ibid.

763 P Flanagan, 'Data Protection Group Seeking Change to Facebook Privacy Policy', *Irish Independent*, 29 November 2012, available at www.independent.ie/business/technology/data-protection-group-seeking-change-to-facebook-privacy-policy-3309757.html.

764 See *Facebook Ireland Limited, Report of Audit*, Data Protection Commissioner, 21 December 2011, available at www.dataprotection.ie; and *Facebook Ireland Limited, Report of Re-Audit*, Data Protection Commissioner, 21 September 2012, available at www.dataprotection.ie.

SNs, as well as other data controllers, have to be constantly on guard against security attacks and security lapses.[765] They also share the same obligation as other organisations in terms of implementing appropriate security measures.

The importance of security in SNs is important in a number of respects. SNs now collect and store personal data in relation to billions of users. This crosses both general and sensitive personal data. While users may be uploading comments, materials, photographs, etc, they frequently would not expect that some, or all, of their personal details would be freely available on the internet for anyone to access.

In addition, a significant number of SM users are children and young people. Many view this type of personal data as deserving particular sensitivity and protection above that of adult personal data. Indeed, children raise personal physical safety as well as psychological safety issues.

There is a proportionality requirement in data protection, which requires that only so much personal data as is legitimately required in relation to a stated processing purpose needs to be collected. Equally, proportionality applies to data protection security measures. The same level of security protections proportionate and applicable to a bank is not needed for a corner grocery store. A window-cleaning company does not necessarily need the same level of security as may be needed for a doctor or hospital dealing with sensitive medical data.

One can argue, therefore, that stronger and more proportionate security measures need to be applied to SNs than many other organisations and websites, given,

- the scale of membership and users;

- the vast quantities of different types of personal data collected;

- that sensitive personal data as well as general personal data is involved;

- that visual as well as text-based content is involved; and

- that children's personal data is a significant category of the user database.

2.28.3   UK

There are numerous examples of data breaches in the UK. In November 2007, for example, an official body lost the personal details of 25 million UK citizens.[766] Personal details of 84,000 UK prisoners were also lost on

---

765 See, for example, story in relation to Facebook security issues and upgrades, 'Facebook Rolls Out Tighter Security', *Irish Times*, 14 May 2010, available at www.irishtimes.com/newspaper/breaking/2010/0510/breaking30.html?via=rel.

766 Referred to in, for example, JA Cannataci and JPM Bonnici, 'The UK 2007–2008 Data Protection Fiasco: Moving on From Bad Policy and Bad Law?' (March–July 2009) (23) *International Review of Law Computers and Technology* 47.

an unencrypted memory stick device.[767] The UK government terminated its contract with a company as a result of one data loss incident.[768] In addition, it announced a review of all official contracts in order to ensure that they were adequate in terms of dealing with data protection, security and data loss issues.[769]

2.28.4 *Ireland*

Ireland also has a growing number of data breaches. Laptops with customer data were stolen from Bord Gáis, involving the personal data of 75,000 customers.[770] Ten laptops were also stolen from the Revenue Commissioners, albeit later recovered.[771] Trinity College had to apologise for a breach whereby a file containing student and staff names, addresses, identifications and emails was inadvertently available on the college network.[772] What is most surprising is the length of the breach: the material was available apparently from August 2009 to March 2011.[773] Insurance companies also breached data protection rules when employees inappropriately looked at claims histories of families, friends and well-known personalities, as well as quoting policies after reviewing an industry claims database.[774] Ultimately, large-scale prosecutions are expected in Ireland[775] as well as other countries. This potentially includes SNs in the event of breach (both of security and data protection compliance obligations).

2.28.5 *Consequences*

The consequences of loss or breach can include loss of users, damage, lawsuits, adverse publicity and investigation from the Irish Data Protection Commissioner, the Information Commissioner's Office (ICO) in the UK, the Federal Trade Commission (FTC) in the US, etc.

---

767 See A Rigby, 'Government Review of Data Processing Contracts', *Society of Computers and Law*, 10 September 2008, available at www.scl.org/site.aspx?i=ed1099.
768 The contract with PA Consulting was reported as being terminated on 10 September 2008, as referred to in Rigby, *op. cit.*
769 Ibid.
770 See Bord Gáis, 'Statement from Bord Gáis Energy on Laptop Theft', 17 June 2009, available at www.bordgaisenergy.ie/news/?d=20090617.
771 'Revenue's 10 Laptops Recovered', *Irish Times*, 12 February 2011.
772 University correspondence dated 29 April 2011. Copy with author.
773 Ibid.
774 See D Labanyi, 'Insurers Breached Data Rules', *Irish Times*, 27 April 2011, available at http://irishtimes.com/newspaper/breaking/2011/0427/breaking11.html.
775 Referred to in Cannataci and Bonnici, *op. cit*, 52. In relation to loss claims generally arising from data loss, see for example Rigby, 'Government Review of Data Processing Contracts', *op. cit*; and A Rigby, 'Terminating the PA Consulting Contract', *Society of Computers and Law*, 31 October 2008, available at www.scl.org/site.aspx?i=ed1110. Also see R Preston-Jones, 'Civil Liability for Mass Data Loss: Lessons from the USA', *Society for Computers and Law* February/March 2010 at 21.

While there have been some cases in the US in terms of data loss and damage, there are relatively few in the EU.[776] This is set to change, given the increasing level of losses and breaches, both in terms of claims for damage and official penalties imposed. Sometimes, different rights can clash; for example, data protection and privacy rights can, on occasion, conflict with copyright.[777] This can relate to service disclosures regarding users, to online tracking, injunctions and litigation.[778] There are also suggestions that the presentation of the data protection regime, especially to industry, should be reformulated into a business case for data protection rights.[779] This includes privacy by design (PbD).[780]

2.28.6   *Data security obligations: DPA*

The data security obligations apply to SNs as they do to other data controllers. These are contained in the Irish Data Protection Acts (and representative of data protection laws in each of the EU nations). Primarily, the 1998 Act states that those collecting and processing personal data must take,

> 'appropriate security measures shall be taken against unauthorised access to, or unauthorised alteration, disclosure or destruction of, the data, in particular where the processing involves the transmission of data over a network, and against all other unlawful forms of processing.'[781]

Section 2C states that, in determining what are appropriate security measures, in particular where the processing involves the transmission of data over a network, a data controller may have regard to the state of technological development and the cost of implementing the measures, and shall ensure that the measures provide a level of security appropriate to,

● the harm that might result from unauthorised or unlawful processing, accidental or unlawful destruction or accidental loss of, or damage to, the data concerned; and

● the nature of the data concerned.[782]

---

776 Preston-Jones, *op. cit*, 21.
777 OB Vincents, 'When Rights Clash Online: The Tracking of P2P Copyright Infringements Vs the EC Personal Data Directive' (2007) (16) *International Journal of Law and Information Technology* 270.
778 Ibid.
779 'Privacy Protection: Discussion Document on the Business Case', *Society for Computers and Law*, 26 August 2009, available at www.scl.org/site.aspx?i=ne12800. It also refers to privacy by design (PbD).
780 Ibid.
781 Section 2(1)(d) of the Data Protection Act 1988, as amended by the Data Protection (Amendment) Act 2003.
782 Section 2C, as amended by the Data Protection (Amendment) Act 2003.

Data controllers must take all reasonable steps to ensure that persons employed by them, and other persons at the place of work concerned, are aware of and comply with the relevant security measures.[783]

2.28.7   Data breach/loss notification rules

Certain jurisdictions are now introducing or considering specific rules obliging employers and other data controllers to report any instance of data security breach to the relevant regulator. Sometimes the users also have to be notified, for example so that they may take their own security precautions in the event of loss or breach by the organisation. This may include changing PINs, passwords, etc. Some examples include reporting laws in New York and California.[784] The US Department of Health and Human Services has also made proposals that certain loss and breaches in relation to health personal data must be notified within one hour.[785] There are proposals in relation to the data loss and breach notification obligation in the proposed EU Data Protection Regulation.

The Irish Data Protection Commissioner has also issued a Code of Practice, dated 29 July 2011, whereby incidents of personal data loss or breach by organisations should be notified to the Data Protection Commissioner.[786] It reiterates,

'The Data Protection Acts 1988 and 2003 impose obligations on data controllers to process personal data entrusted to them in a manner that respects the rights of data subjects to have their data processed fairly (Section 2(1)). Data controllers are under a specific obligation to take appropriate measures to protect the security of such data (Section 2(1)(d)).'[787]

The Irish Data Protection Commissioner states that the Code of Practice is to address incidents where 'personal data has been put at risk of unauthorised disclosure, loss, destruction or alteration'.[788] In such incidents, the focus of the Data Protection Commissioner will be 'on the rights of the affected data subjects in relation to the processing of their personal data'.[789]

In the event of a data loss, or potential loss, incident,

'the data controller must give immediate consideration to informing those affected. Such information permits data subjects to consider the

---

783   Ibid.
784   Each as referred to in T Smith, 'New York State Information Security Breach and Notification Act: State Breach Notification Requirement' (2010) *Albany Law Journal of Science and Technology* 399.
785   J Roman, 'One Hour to Report Breach: Possible? HSS Proposal Could Impact Health Data Exchanges' *GovInfoSecurity*, 19 August 2013, available at www.govinfosecurity.com/one-hour-to-report-breach-possible-a-5999.
786   *Personal Data Security Breach Code of Practice*, Data Protection Commissioner. Available at www.dataprotection.ie/docs/7/7/10_-_Data_Security_Breach_Code_of_Practice/1082.htm.
787   Ibid.
788   Ibid.
789   Ibid.

consequences for each of them individually and to take appropriate measures. In appropriate cases, data controllers should also notify organisations that may be in a position to assist in protecting data subjects including, where relevant, An Garda Síochána, financial institutions etc.'[790]

Advice is given in relation to incidents where the data lost may be protected by encryption technology,

'If the data concerned is protected by technological measures such as to make it unintelligible to any person who is not authorised to access it, the data controller may conclude that there is no risk to the data and therefore no need to inform data subjects. Such a conclusion would only be justified where the technological measures (such as encryption) were of a high standard.'[791]

An outsourced data processor must immediately report any incidents to the data controller,[792]

'[a]ll incidents in which personal data has been put at risk should be reported to the Office of the Data Protection Commissioner as soon as the data controller becomes aware of the incident, except when the full extent and consequences of the incident has been reported without delay directly to the affected data subject(s) *and* it affects no more than 100 data subjects *and* it does not include sensitive personal data or personal data of a financial nature. In case of doubt – in particular any doubt related to the adequacy of technological risk-mitigation measures – the data controller should report the incident to the Office of the Data Protection Commissioner'.[793]

Contact should be made 'within two working days of becoming aware of the incident' and 'outlining the circumstances surrounding the incident'.[794] There are also obligations in terms of maintaining reports, etc.[795] The Commissioner may then investigate the incident and issue recommendations, as well as enforcement proceedings if necessary.[796]

2.28.8   UK penalties

The UK ICO has imposed a number of significant fines recently in relation to data loss in the UK, including,

● a police force £150,000 (Greater Manchester Police);

● a charity £70,000 (Norwood Ravenswood);

---

790 Ibid.
791 Ibid.
792 Ibid.
793 Ibid. Original emphasis.
794 Ibid.
795 Ibid.
796 Ibid.

- a health authority £70,000 (Aneurin Bevan Health Board);

- a council £140,000 (Midlothian Council);

- a hospital £375,000 (Brighton and Sussex University Hospitals NHS Trust); and

- a medical entity £225,000 (Belfast Health and Social Care Trust).[797]

A spam text marketing firm was fined £440,000.[798] A local authority was fined £60,000 for sending a child-related report to the wrong person.[799]

Prudential was fined £50,000 for inaccurate records when it mixed up the account data of customers.[800]

2.28.9   Leveson

More recently still, the Leveson Inquiry Report has recommended a more robust approach to implementing (and understanding) the data protection regime, including criticising the UK Information Commissioner for not being more proactive in policing the data protection regime.[801] The report also highlights the need for a greater appreciation of the data protection regime, in particular at judicial level.[802] This may also be the case in Ireland and other jurisdictions.

2.28.10   Criminal and custodial sentences for breach

The Leveson Report also recommends legal amendment to introduce custodial sentences in the UK for breach of the data protection regime.[803] This

---

797 A Deighton, 'ICO Fines Police and Charity for Data Breaches', Lexology, 29 October 2012, available at www.lexology.com/library/detail.aspx?g=7adda7a8-ba0c-4404-adba-1e6121b0824a; S Evans, 'Huge Increase in ICO Fines for Data Breaches', *Computer Business Review*, 13 August 2012, available at www.cbronline.com/news/huge-increase-in-ico-fines-for-data-breaches-130812; 'Data Breaches 10 Times Worse, Say ICO Figures', BBC, 30 August 2012, available at www.bbc.co.uk/news/technology-19424197.
798 'Spam Texters Fined Nearly Half a Million Pounds as ICO Cracks Down on Illegal Marketing Industry', ICO, 28 November 2012, available at www.lawyer-monthly.com/2012/11/spam-texters-fined-nearly-half-a-million-pounds-as-ico-cracks-down-on-illegal-marketing-industry.
799 'Plymouth City Council Fined £60,000 for Sending Child Neglect Report to the Wrong Person', ICO, 22 November 2012, available at www.ico.gov.uk/news/latest_news/2012/plymouth-city-council-fined-60000-for-sending-child-neglect-report-to-wrong-person-22112012.aspx.
800 'Prudential Fined £50,000 for Customer Account Confusion', ICO, 6 November 2012, available at www.ico.gov.uk/news/latest_news/2012/prudential-fined-50000-for-customer-account-confusion-06112012.aspx.
801 Leveson Inquiry. *An Inquiry into the Culture, Practices and Ethics of the Press: Report, The Right Honourable Lord Justice Leveson*, November 2012. Available at www.official-documents.gov.uk/document/hc1213/hc07/0780/0780.asp. Also see the main inquiry website at www.levesoninquiry.org.uk/.
802 Ibid.
803 Ibid.

recommendation has been welcomed by the ICO.[804] Importantly, there appears to be full political support for this.[805]

2.28.11 Conclusion

Given the nature of the activities of SNs, there will inevitably be increased scrutiny of the security measures employed. Where these prove to be inadequate, the potential for liability arises. It is hoped that SNs and regulators will assess the risk and proportionality of SNs prior to an event of serious data loss or data breach.

---

804 A Travis and O Bowcott, 'Leveson Data Protection Proposals Unite Cameron and Clegg in Concern', *Guardian*, 30 November 2012, available at www.guardian.co.uk/media/2012/ nov/30/leveson-data-protection-proposals-concern.
805 Ibid.

Section C
Country Reports

Chapter C1

Argentina

J Darío Veltani
AVOA – Attorneys at Law

C1.1 INTRODUCTION

Argentina is a civil law jurisdiction.

C1.2 SPECIFIC SM AND SN LAWS

No specific laws, but the Personal Data Protection Law, No 25,326 (hereinafter, the 'PDPL') provides comprehensive protection for personal data stored in files, records, databases, or other technical means of data processing, either public or private, in order to guarantee the privacy rights of people.

It is important to point out that, according to the PDPL: (i) any information about a person, whether an individual or a legal entity, is considered as 'personal data' and, therefore, protected; and (ii) the definitions of 'database' and 'data processing' are not limited to electronic or digital means, so the traditional processing and storage of data (for example, in paper files) are also within the scope of the PDPL. Social networks can be considered as big databases, with personal data, in terms of the PDPL.

The recently enacted Grooming Law, No 26,904, which amended the Criminal Code, establishes grooming as a specific crime. As well as the PDPL, this is not specifically an SN law, because it punishes child molestation through the internet using not only SNs, but it applies to SNs.

C1.3 SM CRIMINAL LAW CASES

It is difficult to define a case as an 'SM criminal law' case. But we are seeing an increase in cases in which SM communications are being offered as evidence of crimes. Usually, these crimes are common crimes (such as fraud, harassment, threats, etc), but they are committed, at least partially, by using SM. An example of this is a recent decision regarding a woman, who was threatened by an ex-boyfriend. In this decision, the court considered a Facebook chat between the accused man and the victim as evidence of the threats.[1]

C1.4   SM CIVIL LAW CASES

The civil law cases related to SM are mostly concerned with the protection of privacy and/or honour and/or trademarks. However, there has been a court decision that addresses another interesting issue: when SM is used to organize illegal or forbidden activities, or activities engaging minors. In this case, some students created a 'group' on Facebook, in which they planned to miss school on particular days and then celebrate that action. All the members of the group should not attend school on the indicated days, and instead go to another place to meet and celebrate. In this scenario, a consumer association filed a suit against Facebook, Inc, requesting the immediate closing of the group. A Lower Court of the Province of Mendoza (in which the facts took place) admitted the action and ordered Facebook to close the group.[2]

C1.5   CASES WHERE SM-RELATED EVIDENCE USED OR ADMISSIBLE

According to our procedural codes, SM-related evidence is admissible in court. However, we do not have specific rules or proceedings for the collection of digital evidence (like e-discovery rules or similar), so in each case the judge has plenty of options to admit or dismiss the evidence. Therefore, the attorney's skills are essential for the correct incorporation of the digital evidence. An example of this situation happened on a labour case in 2013, in which a man was dismissed from his job when the employer – a corporation – found pictures of him on Facebook in which he was allegedly drinking alcohol in the workplace and during work time. The worker sued the company for wrongful termination and won, because the court considered that the evidence was not conclusive because, among other things, there were no descriptions of the time and circumstances in which the pictures were taken.

C1.6   SPECIFIC ONLINE ABUSE/ONLINE BULLYING/ CYBERBULLYING LAWS

Argentina has not yet enacted a regulation concerning bullying and/or cyberbullying. There are some Bills regarding this topic in Congress, but they

---

1   See case 'R, J C, Cámara Nacional de Apelaciones en lo Criminal y Correccional, sala IV 08/07/2013', AR/JUR/36144/2013.
2   See case 'Protectora Asociación Civil de Defensa del Consumidor c Facebook Inc, Juzgado de 1a Instancia en lo Civil, Comercial y Minas Nro 2 de Mendoza • 11/05/2010', AR/JUR/13887/2010.

have not been approved. Therefore, in cases of bullying, the courts apply the general civil and/or criminal rules that forbid – and even punish – any causation of damages.

C1.7   OTHER LAWS APPLIED TO ONLINE ABUSE/ ONLINE BULLYING/CYBERBULLYING

None. In these situations, the courts have applied (see C1.6) the general civil and/or criminal rules, according to the case.

C1.8   CHILDREN AND SM LAWS OR RULES

There are no specific laws or rules regarding children and SM. However, it is important to mention that children under the age of 14 are not legally authorized to execute any agreement and, therefore, cannot have an account of their own on SM websites. In effect, in Argentina an individual attains full legal capacity at the age of 18. Before that time, there is a period between the age of 14 and the age of 18, in which the individual is considered an 'adult minor'. 'Adult minors' can execute 'little agreements' of day-to-day life (the commonly used book example is that they can buy their bus tickets to go to school). In the criminal field, we can point out that the Computer Crime Law No 26,388 amended the Criminal Code with regard to the distribution of child pornography. Even though this criminal offence does not relate exclusively to SNs, it certainly applies to them. Section 128 of the Criminal Code punishes with imprisonment of six (6) months to four (4) years any person who produces, finances, offers, trades, publishes, facilitates, discloses or distributes, by any means, any representation of a child under the age of eighteen (18) years old dedicated to explicit sexual activities or any representation of their genitals for predominantly sexual purposes. The same punishment goes to the person who organizes live shows of explicit sexual representations where minors participate. It also punishes with imprisonment of four (4) months to two (2) years any person who is in possession of the representations described with the undoubtable purpose of distribution or marketing. Finally, it punishes with imprisonment of one (1) month to three (3) years any person who facilitates access to pornographic performances or provides pornographic material to minors under 14 years.

C1.9   EMPLOYEES/EMPLOYMENT SM LAWS OR CASES

In Argentina, there is no specific law related to the use of SM at work. Therefore, the general provisions of Labour Law N° 20,744 apply to any conflict that such use might generate.

In this connection, there have been several cases regarding the possibility of monitoring email communications by the employer. In such cases, the courts have held that the employer can monitor email communications of its employees if: (i) the email account had been provided by the employer for working purposes only; (ii) the employer had notified the employee of a policy regarding the use of corporate email; (iii) the employee has no privacy expectations regarding the use of its email account (that is, he/she was notified that the employer might have access to the email messages); (iv) the monitoring criteria are general and not intended to discriminate against or harass any particular worker or group of workers; and (v) the sanctions in case of a breach of the policy are reasonable and comply with the general provisions regarding working sanctions.

Since SM has a clearly different nature than email, the conclusions regarding email monitoring cannot be applied directly to the use of SM at work. However, there is a particular case regarding email monitoring that might be relevant in SM cases. In this case, a company's director requested an employee for access to her emails. This request was witnessed by a notary public, who verified the authorization given by the employee and left notice of such authorization in a public deed. After that, the director found that the employee had used the email to send sensitive information of the company and, therefore, the employee was dismissed. The employee sued the company for wrongful termination, but the court held that the authorization given by the employee was enough for the company to verify her emails (in this case, there was no policy), so the claim was rejected.[3]

C1.10 SCHOOL AND UNIVERSITY STUDENT SM CASES

There does not appear to be any published case law related to this matter.

C1.11 RIGHT OR HUMAN RIGHT TO ACCESS THE INTERNET OR SM

The Law No 26,032 establishes that the activities of seeking, receiving and imparting information or ideas through the internet are included within the constitutional right that protects freedom of speech. Also, there was a case in which a judge granted an indemnification for moral damages to a man who could not access the internet due to the failure of the internet service provider. The judge stated that it was reasonable to assume that an individual can experience changes and disturbances in his or her mood if restricted in the use of a service that is taking an increasingly important role in social communication.[4]

---

3   See case 'Garcia, Delia c YPF s / despido' CNTrab, Sala X, 13/08/2003, elDial, AA1AC2.
4   See case 'Richelme, Luis Pablo c Telecom Argentina SA Arnet s/ordinario' CNCom, Sala D, 20/05/2010. [ED, (11/03/2011, nro 12.708)].

C1.12   BANS OR RESTRICTIONS ON INTERNET OR SM

There does not appear to be any published case law related to this matter yet. Any such orders should pass strict constitutional scrutiny because they would restrict constitutional rights. It is possible that, in the near future, our prosecutors might request orders of this kind in cases of grooming (that is, online child molestation).

C1.13   IDENTITY THEFT (OR EQUIVALENT)

There have been several Bills addressing this issue, but none of them has been approved. However, if the identity theft is committed in order to commit a crime (for example, to transfer money from a bank account), general rules regarding fraud apply. So the problem is when the identity theft is not a means to committing a crime but an action itself. In this case, though, there might be a sanction if the 'thief' makes contact with friends and/or family of the victim, in which case we could have a violation of privacy rights, honour and data protection rights. Finally, in some cases, the trademark law might be suitable if the identity that has been impersonated matches with a registered trademark.

C1.14   HACKING (OR EQUIVALENT)

First, we should define the term 'hacking', because at first this term was related to the actions of certain people who were 'curious' for technology and just wanted to break into computers and computer systems. But lately, this 'romantic' version of the hackers has changed, since they have turned into real criminals who are paid for obtaining private information and/or for attacking systems, in a way that they could generate not only digital but also physical damage. This distinction is necessary because, some years ago, 'hacking' was punished only if real damage was caused (which had to be proved in court). So we did not sanction the actions that consisted only in trespassing technological barriers, for curiosity or similar. Following this criteria, in 2002 a Criminal Court considered that the hacking of the Supreme Court of Argentina website was not a criminal offence, since that action did not cause any actual damage (because it was more like a 'deface' in which the hackers only showed a picture with a political message when you entered the website, but did not affect the website performance).[5]

However, today the scenario has changed, and 'hacking' is punished even when no actual damage is caused. In effect, the Computer Crime Law N° 26,388 introduced 'hacking' as a specific criminal offence into the Criminal Code. It is regulated in section 153 bis, which punishes with 15 days' to 6 months'

---

5   See case 'Gornsetin, Marcelo H y otros', Juzgado Nacional de Primera Instancia de en lo Criminal y Correccional Federal No 12, 20/03/2002, AR/JUR/3267/2002.

imprisonment anyone who knowingly gains access by any means, without authorization or exceeding such authorization, to any computer system or data which is restricted. Also, section 157 of the Criminal Code, as amended by Computer Crime Law No 26,388, imposes a punishment of 1 month's to 2 years' imprisonment on any person who knowingly and unlawfully, or violating security and confidentiality systems, gains access by any means to a database containing personal data. These two crimes do not require actual damage or the commission of other crimes, so we can say that, currently, the mere 'hacking' is a criminal offence. However, if the person not only accesses but also causes damages to the computers, or copies, alters or deletes information, they commit other crimes that have different punishments. Finally, from the civil point of view, the 'hacking' shall be illicit itself. However, in our legal system, to obtain a civil indemnification, you have to prove the damages, and – with the exception of the Consumer Defence Law – we do not have 'punitive damages'.

C1.15   PRIVACY BY DESIGN (PBD) (OR EQUIVALENT)

Not applicable.

C1.16   TWEETING FROM COURTS, AND ANY RULES/LAWS

In Argentina, there is no specific ban for Tweeting from courts. However, our procedural system is not based on juries. In the few cases in which the proceedings include the participation of juries (for example, in the Province of Buenos Aires), they are restrained from any contact with the outside world when they are deliberating. So they cannot Tweet.

C1.17   TELEVISION COURTROOM BROADCASTING OR TELEVISION CAMERAS IN COURT, AND RULES OR LAWS

In Argentina, the civil procedure is mostly written, so there are not public hearings. In criminal law cases, instead, the procedure has a first part which is written, and a second part, which is oral. In this second part, the general rule is that anyone can witness the hearing. However, in cases of public interest, the court has the power to authorize the broadcasting (whether live or recorded). Recently, the Supreme Court decided to hold some public hearings in a case that involved Google and Yahoo. In these hearings, the Supreme Court called a group of experts, as 'amicus curiae' (friends of the court) to explain their positions regarding the kind of responsibility system that should be applied to the internet intermediaries (currently, in Argentina we are discussing if the intermediaries should be held responsible by application of the subjective theory, which is based on guilt, or by the objective theory, in which they should respond only for delivering a service that is 'dangerous' to society).

C1.18 SM IN COURTROOMS

This could generally include SN use in courtrooms by the public, journalists, broadcasters, bloggers, jurors, lawyers, witnesses or Judges.

There does not appear to be any published case law related to this matter.

C1.19 USE OF SM AS EVIDENCE IN COURTS

In Argentina, the general principle regarding evidence in court is admissibility. This principle has its particularities in the case of criminal proceedings, in which the concept of chain of custody is more relevant. But in civil cases, the judge has plenty of options to admit any kind of evidence, as long as it is related to the case. So there is no much to discuss regarding evidence collected on SM.

However, there might be some difficulties to prove the authorship of a post or comment. This is because, in order to do so, it is necessary to obtain the IP address of the author, and then track such IP address to a final user. We do not have a specific rule in our Proceedings Code regarding this matter, so in many cases it is difficult to identify the author of a comment or post on SM.

So, currently, the main problem regarding the use of SM comments as evidence in court is related to procedure – or lack of procedure – to collect them and file them in an adequate way.

C1.20 PRIVACY, DATA PROTECTION AND SM

There has been a case in which a Judge from the Province of Salta ordered Twitter, Google, Facebook and Whatsapp to refrain from spreading a video of a minor and delete from their database all kinds of records concerning the little girl. The decision was issued after the mother of the child asked for an urgent measure that guarantees her daughter's constitutional right to intimacy, privacy and honour.[6]

It is important to point out that, based on the Personal Data Protection Law No 25,326, companies like Google or Yahoo are facing lots of claims in Argentina. This is because of the allegedly illegitimate use of personal data and/or images in these companies' web searchers. Our courts have different views on the kind of responsibility that should apply to these companies, so currently we are waiting for a precedent from our Supreme Court on the matter. This discussion

---

6   See case 'M L P en representación de la menor F C c/redes sociales Twitter, WhatsApp, Facebook, Google, Yahoo y/ousuarios de Twitter s/medida autosatisfactiva' – Juzg Civ y Com Salta – No 8 – 14/03/2013.

on the kind of responsibility that should apply to web searchers might later be extended to SM.

C1.21   SM AND FAMILY LAW CASES

In family cases, there is an increase rate of claims regarding infidelities that are proved by messages and/or pictures that can be seen on SM. But there are also other types of conduct that are proved by pictures posted on SM. In a recent divorce case, for example, one of the parties alleged that the pictures that the other uploaded to Facebook were offensive. However, the court found that such pictures just showed that the party who uploaded them was enjoying some moments and that it cannot be expected that whoever is processing a divorce needs to limit his/her recreational and social activities, adding more troubles to the painful moment that he/she is already going through.[7]

C1.22   SPORTS PERSONS, SPORTS CLUBS AND SM

There does not appear to be any published case law related to this matter.

C1.23   PERSONAL RELATIONS AND RELATIONSHIPS

There have been several cases involving public figures, mostly from show business (e.g. actresses, singers, etc.) whose intimate videos were published on the internet without consent. However, since our laws are not clear regarding 'revenge porn', we have not had a conviction for this crime yet. Indeed, 'revenge porn' itself is not a crime. What might be a crime is the stealing of such videos or the extortion that usually comes along in these cases. The author's firm is currently involved in a case accusing a man for 'revenge porn', and has obtained an indictment for extortion. If the man is convicted, it might be the first conviction in the country on a 'revenge porn' case.

C1.24   SM AND PERSONAL DATA OF DECEASED PERSONS

There does not appear to be any published case law related to this matter.

C1.25   SM, WEBSITE, SERVICE PROVIDER OR ISP DEFENCE RULES/LAWS

None.

---

7   See case 'B, L G R c/ S, O N s/ Divorcio' – Cámara Nacional de Apelaciones en lo Civil – SALA H – 03/12/2013 (elDial.com – AA84BE).

C1.26   ECOMMERCE DEFENCE CASES

Not applicable.

C1.27   LAWS PROTECTING PERSONAL DATA/ PERSONALLY IDENTIFIABLE INFORMATION

In Argentina the protection of personal data is regulated by a complex legal system, composed of: (i) a constitutional provision – which is a special judicial remedy known as 'habeas data'; (ii) the Personal Data Protection Law No 25,326 (hereinafter, the 'PDPL'); (iii) Decree No 1558/2001 (hereinafter, the 'Decree'); and (iv) several rules issued by the National Data Protection Authority (Dirección Nacional de Protección de Datos Personales), regarding the collection, storage and use of personal data.

The concepts of 'personal data' and 'database' are defined by the PDPL in a way that is more extensive than other regulations around the world. In effect, in Argentina, 'personal data' means any information about an individual (including legal entities), whether such individual is identified or identifiable, and 'databases' are defined as any compilation of personal data that is stored with any kind of order criteria, regardless of the storage media (which means that, according to Argentine law, the concept of 'database' is not necessarily related to computers and information technology).

In this context, the PDPL and the Decree set forth several principles, that any owner and/or user of databases with personal data must comply with. Such principles are, basically, the following: (i) the legality principle; (ii) the data quality principle; (iii) the finality principle; (iv) the confidentiality principle; and (iv) the informed consent principle. Also, they establish a very strict procedure for the international transfer of personal data.

The Authority for the application of the PDPL is the National Data Protection Authority (see above), which depends of the National Ministry of Justice and has several inspection and sanction powers. The National Data Protection Authority also has regulation powers and is in charge of the National Registry of Databases (Registro Nacional de Bases de Datos).

C1.28   DATA BREACH LAWS AND CUSTOMERS/ USERS/REGULATORS NOTIFIED OF HACKING OR DATA LOSS

None.

Chapter C2

Australia

Dr David Rolph
Faculty of Law, University of Sydney

C2.1   INTRODUCTION

Australia is a Common Law jurisdiction.

C2.2   SPECIFIC SM AND SN LAWS

There is a decided policy preference in Australia against technology-specific laws, so there are no specific SM and SN laws, as such. However, there are a range of legislative provisions that apply to SM communications.

C2.3   SM CRIMINAL LAW CASES

There have been a number of criminal law cases involving SM. Criminal defamation is still an offence in every State and Territory throughout Australia. However, it is rarely prosecuted, as it requires the written consent of the Director of Public Prosecutions in the relevant jurisdiction prior to the commencement of proceedings.[1] In November 2009, in one of the first criminal defamation prosecutions in Australia in several decades, a South Australian teenager was found guilty of criminal defamation arising from postings on a Facebook page, which was a 'hate site' for a local police officer. The Kadina Magistrates' Court placed the offender on a two-year good behaviour bond.[2]

Contempt of court has also arisen through the use of SM. Prominent Australian broadcaster, Derryn Hinch, was found guilty of contempt of court by the Supreme Court of Victoria. Hinch was punished for contempt of court for

---

1   Crimes Act 1900 (ACT) s 439; Criminal Code (NT) ss 203–08; Crimes Act 1900 (NSW) s 529; Criminal Code (Qld) s 365; Criminal Law Consolidation Act 1935 (SA) s 257; Criminal Code (Tas) s 196; Wrongs Act 1958 (Vic) Pt I; Criminal Code (WA) s 345.
2   Nigel Hunt, 'Teen guilty of Facebook slur', *Sunday Mail* (Adelaide), 22 November 2009. See further Patrick Lim, 'You Have 3 Friend Requests and 1 Criminal Conviction: Tackling Defamation on Facebook' (2010) 12(10) *Internet Law Bulletin* 169.

breaching suppression orders, which had been imposed on reporting in relation to the high-profile murder trial of Adrian Bayley for the brutal rape and murder of Irish woman, Jill Meagher, who was living and working in Melbourne at the Australian Broadcasting Corporation. SM websites, like Twitter and Facebook, were instrumental in the criminal investigation that led up to the arrest of Adrian Bayley. Following Bayley's arrest and charge, politicians, police and even Jill Meagher's widower, Tom, publicly pleaded with SM users to act responsibly so as not to prejudice Bayley's right to a fair trial. Suppression orders were imposed to prevent the reporting of Bayley's extensive criminal record for sexual violence against women, as well as other pending proceedings against Bayley.[3] Hinch published an article on his website, www.humanheadline. com.au, breaching these suppression orders, which had been made by the Magistrates' Court of Victoria.[4] He then Tweeted the article.[5] Having been found guilty of contempt of court for breaching the suppression order by Kaye J, Hinch was fined $100,000. He refused to pay the fine and was sentenced to 50 days' imprisonment.[6] He was released in March 2014.[7]

C2.4 SM CIVIL LAW CASES

Outside the subject-specific contexts outlined below, there have been a number of areas of law in which SM issues have arisen in civil litigation in Australia. The volume of civil litigation involving an aspect of SM is substantial and constantly increasing.

Defamation cases have started to be brought based on SM publications. In November 2013, the District Court of New South Wales handed down the first judgment based on Twitter defamation. In *Mickle v Farley*, Elkaim DCJ awarded the plaintiff $105,000 damages (including a component of $20,000 aggravated damages).[8] In his assessment of damages, His Honour gave particular emphasis to the special harm caused by defamation via SM, stating that,

> 'when defamatory publications are made on social media it is common knowledge that they spread. They are spread easily by the simple manipulation of mobile phones and computers. Their evil lies in the grapevine effect that stems from the use of this type of communication.'[9]

This is not the first Twitter defamation case in Australia. The case that was expected to become Australia's first Twitter defamation case, *Crosby v Kelly*, is

---

3   *R v Hinch* [2013] VSC 520, [6] (Kaye J).
4   Ibid, [8].
5   Ibid, [9].
6   *R v Hinch (No 2)* [2013] VSC 554, [48].
7   Tom Minear, 'Derryn Hinch freed from jail after serving 50 days for breaching Jill Meagher order', *The Herald Sun*, 8 March 2014.
8   [2013] NSWDC 295.
9   Ibid, [21].

still on foot before the Federal Court of Australia. The respondent, Mike Kelly, was a Labor parliamentarian. The applicants, Lynton Crosby and Mark Textor, were the operators of a polling company which was affiliated with the opposing party, the Liberal Party. Kelly Tweeted that Crosby and Kelly 'introduced push polling to Aus'.[10] At the time of writing, the proceedings have not been settled.

There have been other earlier, high-profile Twitter defamation lawsuits in Australia, which have been settled. The most prominent case involved Melbourne writer and critic, Marieke Hardy, who had to pay undisclosed damages and apologise to Joshua Meggitt, a man she had incorrectly identified on Twitter as the author of 'hate blogs' directed towards her.[11] In addition, Chris Mitchell, the editor of the major national broadsheet newspaper, *The Australian*, threatened to sue a journalism academic from the University of Canberra, Julie Posetti, over a Tweet in which Posetti claimed that a journalist on the newspaper, Asa Wahlqist, had been increasingly told what to write in the lead-up to the 2010 Federal election.[12]

Defamation cases have also started to be commenced arising out of Facebook publications. Thus, in *Polias v Ryall*, the plaintiff commenced defamation proceedings over comments posted on Facebook by his former fellow poker players, as well as conversations that occurred in various gambling venues.[13] In *Ives v Lim*, the plaintiff brought defamation proceedings against his former partner, claiming that he had been defamed by her in the course of obtaining an interim violence restraining order against him. He subsequently attempted to hold her liable for comments about the proceedings and the allegations against him made by third parties on SM websites, Facebook and LiveJournal.[14]

Social media and their norms and etiquette have the potential to change the way in which courts approach the issue of defamatory meaning. In another defamation case, Corboy J of the Supreme Court of Western Australia made some general observations about defamation, in the course of which he observed that,

> '[e]mails, SMS messaging, Twitter, blogs and other forms of social media such as Facebook impact on the way people communicate and the language they use. Communications through those media often lack the formality and the careful consideration that was once thought to make the difference between the written and spoken word. The very purpose of the media is to enable people to communicate instantaneously, often in a language which is

---

10   For interlocutory decisions in this litigation, see *Crosby v Kelly* (2012) 203 FCR 451; [2012] FCAFC 451; *Crosby v Kelly* [2013] FCA 1343.

11   Michelle Griffin, 'Man sues Twitter over hate blog', *The Sydney Morning Herald*, 17 February 2012.

12   Geoff Elliott, '*The Australian*'s Chris Mitchell to sue Julie Posetti for defamation', *The Australian*, 26 November 2010; Tim Dick, 'The editor and the twitterer', *The Sydney Morning Herald*, 29 November 2010.

13   [2013] NSWSC 1267.

14   [2011] WASC 122.

blunt in its message and attenuated in its form. That will affect both what is regarded as defamatory and the potential for harm.'[15]

There have also been cases of civil contempt involving SM publications. For instance, in *Australian Competition and Consumer Commission v Allergy Pathway Pty Ltd (No 2)*, the respondent gave an undertaking to the regulator in relation to contraventions of the Trade Practices Act 1974 (Cth) ss 52, 53 and 55. By its undertaking, the respondent promised not to make or publish certain statements about its products. However, on its YouTube and Facebook pages and its Twitter feed, members of the public posted statements which contravened this undertaking. Finkelstein J found that the respondent became liable for these statements published by third parties when it became aware of the postings and when, within a reasonable period of time, it took no steps to take them down. The respondent was therefore liable for contempt of court.[16]

C2.5 CASES WHERE SM-RELATED EVIDENCE IS USED OR ADMISSIBLE

SM-related evidence is becoming increasingly important across both civil and criminal litigation. It is not possible to deal comprehensively with all the cases in Australia in which such evidence has been relied upon, so the following examples serve as a representative selection.

In *Schilg v Saltmarsh*, the offender was prosecuted for doing a 'burnout' in his motor vehicle, contrary to the Road Transport (Safety and Traffic Management) Act 1999 (ACT) s 5B. The 'burnout' was recorded in a video, which was uploaded to Facebook and subsequently brought to the attention of the police. The offender was convicted and had his car impounded for three months.[17]

Evidence gleaned from SM has been used in personal injury claims. In *Reitano v Shearer*,[18] the plaintiff was a 17-year-old girl who was injured in a rear-end motor vehicle collision. From the time of the accident until the time of the trial, some five years later, she cultivated a false persona through various SM sites, with a view to increasing the damages she was awarded for future economic loss. In particular, the plaintiff sought to suggest that her career ambition had always been to be a foreign correspondent. Dealing with the evidence when assessing the plaintiff's damages, North J found that the plaintiff's evidence in relation to her career ambitions, but more generally about her level of pain and suffering, was not to be accepted.[19] His Honour ultimately awarded the

---

15 *Prefumo v Bradley* [2011] WASC 251, [43].
16 (2011) 192 FCR 34, 42; [2011] FCA 74.
17 [2013] ACTSC 181.
18 [2014] QSC 44.
19 Ibid, [11].

plaintiff only \$139,026, with a component of \$8,600 general damages and \$75,000 damages for future economic loss.[20]

C2.6 SPECIFIC ONLINE ABUSE/ONLINE BULLYING/ CYBERBULLYING LAWS

There are, as yet, no specific online abuse / online bullying / cyberbullying laws in any Australian jurisdiction. Periodically, there have been attempts at a media campaign to introduce cyberbullying laws. The Sydney tabloid newspaper, *The Daily Telegraph*, for example, ran a 'Stop the Trolls' campaign after a series of unpleasant Twitter incidents involving high-profile celebrities.[21] No legislative change resulted from the campaign. Nonetheless, cyberbullying has continued to be an important political, social and policy issue in Australia. In January 2014, the Federal Government released a discussion paper, *Enhancing Online Safety for Children*.[22] It proposed the establishment of a Children's e-Safety Commissioner, who would have responsibility for implementing a scheme for the rapid removal of harmful content from large-scale SM sites, as well as working with industry on improving technological mechanisms to allow parents to control children being exposed to harmful content, developing guidelines for parents about appropriate SM content, funding research into the effects of internet use on children, and supporting schools to provide education and training for students about internet use.[23] In addition, the discussion paper canvassed whether specific cyber-bullying offences needed to be introduced into Commonwealth law, either as a criminal offence or a civil wrong or both.[24]

C2.7 OTHER LAWS APPLIED TO ONLINE ABUSE/ ONLINE BULLYING/CYBERBULLYING

In the absence of specific cyberbullying laws, more general offences have been used to deal with offensive online behaviour. Under the Criminal Code (Cth) s 474.14, it is an offence to use a telecommunications network with an intention to commit a serious offence; under the Criminal Code (Cth) s 474.15, it is an offence to use a carriage service to make a threat; and under the Criminal Code (Cth) s 474.17, it is an offence to use a carriage service to menace, harass or cause offence.

---

20   Ibid, [32].
21   Gemma Jones and Holly Byrnes, 'Time is up for Twitter trolls and bullies', *The Daily Telegraph* (Sydney), 11 September 2012; Gemma Jones, Amanda Lulham and Carleen Frost, 'Our campaign – for whom the bell now trolls', *The Daily Telegraph* (Sydney), 13 September 2012.
22   At www.communications.gov.au/online_safety_and_security/cyber_safety/Discussion_ Paper_Enhancing_Online_Safety_for_Children.
23   Ibid, 5.
24   Ibid, 20–25.

These provisions have been used in prosecutions arising out of SM activity. For instance, in *Agostino v Cleaves*, the offender pleaded guilty to using postings on the victim's Facebook wall in order to menace her in contravention of the Criminal Code (Cth) s 474.17. The offender had been in a relationship with the victim and was upset when the victim terminated the relationship. He was sentenced to six months' imprisonment, which was upheld on appeal.[25]

In *R v McDonald and Deblaquiere*, the offenders were found guilty of using a carriage service in a manner which would cause offence in contravention of the Criminal Code (Cth) s 474.17. McDonald and Deblaquiere were cadets at the Australian Defence Force Academy. McDonald engaged in consensual sexual activity with the complainant. However, McDonald and Deblaquiere had organised a Skype connection in order to allow Deblaquiere and five other cadets to observe the sexual encounter. This occurred without the complainant's knowledge. McDonald and Deblaquiere were convicted and placed on 12-month good behaviour bonds.[26]

In every State and Territory, there are also criminal laws preventing harassing, threatening and intimidatory behaviour, through offences such as assault, which could extend to conduct occurring through SM websites. In every State and Territory, there are also stalking laws, some of which specifically extend to include the sending of electronic messages.[27]

C2.8   CHILDREN AND SM LAWS OR RULES

The Criminal Code (Cth) has a number of criminal offences affecting children and SM websites. It is an offence to use a carriage service for child pornography or child abuse material,[28] as well as to possess, control, produce, supply or obtain child pornography or child abuse material for use through a carriage service.[29] It is also an offence to use a carriage service to engage in sexual activity with a child under the age of 16 years,[30] to use a carriage service to procure sexual activity with a child under the age of 16 years[31] and to use a carriage to 'groom' a child under the age of 16 years.[32] In relation to these latter

---

25   [2010] ACTSC 19.

26   Christopher Knaus and Michael Inman, 'ADFA Skype scandal cadets sentenced, avoid jail', *The Canberra Times*, 23 October 2013. See *R v McDonald and Deblaquiere* [2013] ACTSC 122 (Refshauge J); *R v McDonald and Deblaquiere* SCC 346 of 2011; SCC 405 of 2011 (Nield AJ).

27   Crimes (Domestic and Personal Violence) Act 2007 (NSW) s 13; Domestic and Family Violence Act 2007 (NT) s 7; Criminal Code (WA) s 338E. As for those jurisdictions which specifically include internet communications, see Criminal Code (Qld) s 359B; Criminal Law Consolidation Act 1935 (SA) s 19AA; Criminal Code (Tas) s 192; Crimes Act 1958 (Vic) s 21A.

28   Criminal Code (Cth) ss 474.19, 474.22.

29   Ibid, ss 474.20, 474.22.

30   Ibid, s 474.25A.

31   Ibid, s 474.26.

32   Ibid, s 474.27.

offences, the offender has to be at least 18 years old. It is also an offence to use a carriage service to transmit indecent communications to a child under the age of 16 years, again where the offender is at least 18 years old.[33]

There have already been successful prosecutions for these offences. For example, in *Rodriguez v The Queen*, the offender set up a fake Facebook profile and began communications with a person he thought was a 14-year-old girl but who was in fact an undercover police officer. Over the course of four months, the offender cultivated a sexualised relationship with the person he thought was a young girl, sending sexually explicit messages and images and asking for the same to be returned to him. In addition to the offence of using a carriage service to cause offence in contravention of the Criminal Code (Cth) s 474.17, the offender was found guilty and sentenced to six months' imprisonment.[34]

Although there has been widespread concern about the risks posed to children by SM technologies, this has yet to manifest itself in legislative change. The most significant development has been the report of the Law Reform Committee of the Parliament of Victoria, following its inquiry into sexting. The impetus for this inquiry was an awareness of the prevalence of sexting amongst young people and concern about the application of child pornography laws to consensual peer-to-peer sexting. Young people between the ages of 15 and 18 years had found themselves charged with and convicted of child pornography offences and placed on the child sex offenders register, with long-term adverse consequences for employment, *inter alia*.[35] The Law Reform Committee recommended the creation of a defence to any prosecution for child pornography, where the film or photograph depicted only the accused person and that, at the time of the making, taking or being given the film or photograph, the accused person was no more than two years older than the minor and the film or photograph depicted the accused person engaged in lawful sexual activity, either by himself or herself or with others with whom he or she could lawfully engage in sexual activity.[36] It also recommended the creation of a specific summary offence of non-consensual sexting, whereby a person intentionally distributes, or threatens to distribute, an intimate image of another person. An 'intimate image' is defined as a photograph or footage in which a person or persons are engaged in sexual activity, in an indecent sexual manner or context or in a state of partial or complete nudity.[37] In December 2013, the Victorian Government announced that it intended to legislate these changes, thereby creating the first specific sexting laws in Australia.[38]

---

33   Ibid, s 474.27A.
34   [2013] VSCA 216.
35   Nicole Brady, '"Sexting" youths placed on sex offenders register', *The Age* (Melbourne), 24 July 2011.
36   Parliament of Victoria, Law Reform Committee, *Inquiry into Sexting*, May 2013, Recommendation 6.
37   Ibid, Recommendation 7.
38   Farrah Tomazin, 'New Victorian law to crack down on malicious sexting', *The Age*, 15 December 2013.

C2.9 EMPLOYEES/EMPLOYMENT SM LAWS OR CASES

Employment law is one of the most significant areas in which SM publications have been considered by courts, tribunals and commissions. It is common for employers to implement SM policies governing their employees' conduct. The extent to which such policies can or should regulate employees' conduct outside their workplace is a controversial issue.

There have been two high-profile and significant cases in relation to unfair dismissal of employees for SM use. In *Linfox Australia Pty Ltd v Fair Work Commission*, the employee made racially and sexually discriminatory, as well as generally derogatory, comments about two of his managers on his Facebook wall. He thought his Facebook profile was on the highest privacy setting, the account having been set up by his wife and his daughter. However, his Facebook profile was viewable by the public and was seen by one of his managers. His employer sought to terminate his employment on the grounds of his SM publications. The Full Court of the Federal Court of Australia upheld the decision of the Fair Work Commission that his dismissal had been unfair and ordered his reinstatement. In particular, the court accepted the right of an employee to exercise freedom of speech, particularly in circumstances where he was labouring under a misapprehension as to how private or public his speech was.[39]

To a different effect was the decision of the Federal Circuit Court of Australia in *Banerji v Bowles*. Michaela Banerji Tweeted under the handle, 'La Legale'. Under her pseudonym, she Tweeted, often in critical or mocking terms, about the immigration policies of the then Labor Government, the Prime Minister, the Opposition Leader, the Minister for Foreign Affairs, the Opposition Spokesman on Immigration and the company which operated the Commonwealth immigration detention centres. She was also an employee of the Department of Immigration and Citizenship. Banerji commenced proceedings before Fair Work Australia, seeking an injunction to restrain her employer from taking adverse action against her based on her SM use. She anticipated that her employer was intending to sack her. Banerji attempted to argue that she had the protection of the implied freedom of political communication, which arose from the text and structure of the Commonwealth Constitution. Her argument was rejected on the basis that the constitutional jurisprudence did not recognise an absolute right to freedom of speech on government and political matters and that it was legitimate to encroach upon that freedom, so long as the encroachment was reasonably appropriate and adapted. The decision of the Federal Circuit Court thus left her exposed to dismissal from her position.[40]

---

39 [2013] FCAFC 157.
40 [2013] FCCA 1052.

The use of SM during working hours can also be used as grounds for dismissal. In *O'Connor v Outdoors Creations Pty Ltd*, Gooley C of Fair Work Australia held that '[e]xcessive use of social media during work hours may constitute a valid reason for the termination of employment', although in this case, the evidence did not establish that the landscape architect who was challenging his unfair dismissal had in fact used a Google chat service excessively during work hours.[41]

Cases involving unfair dismissal for SM use, both during and outside working hours, are becoming increasingly common.[42] There have also been cases in which a sexual harassment claim has been brought by a plaintiff against a co-worker. Thus, in *Styles v Clayton Utz (No 3)*, the plaintiff was a solicitor who was suing her former firm for sexual harassment, *inter alia*, by her fellow solicitors. One of the grounds was that Clayton Utz had failed to ban some of those solicitors from maintaining a Facebook page entitled 'Clayton Utz Workplace Relations (Sydney) Whorebags'.[43]

C2.10   SCHOOL AND UNIVERSITY STUDENT SM CASES

Most, if not all, universities in Australia have codes of conduct governing student behaviour. These now extend to include SM use. Thus, misconduct on SM sites can be used as a ground for discipline, suspension or exclusion of a student. For example, in *X v University of Western Sydney*, one of the grounds which the university used to suspend a first year medical student was a Facebook conversation he had with the victim of his offending conduct. Ultimately, Hall J found that X had not been afforded procedural fairness in the handling of the disciplinary proceedings because the decision-maker failed to disclose allegations raised by the complainant in her interview to the student, thereby depriving him of an opportunity to respond, but there was no argument that the Facebook conversation fell outside the ambit of the university's policy.[44]

C2.11   RIGHT OR HUMAN RIGHT TO ACCESS THE INTERNET OR SM

There has not been much detailed discussion of a right or a human right to access the internet in Australia. The most detailed consideration of internet use in the human rights context has been the Australian Human Rights Commission's

---

41   [2011] FWA 3081, [42]–[43].
42   See also *O'Keefe v Williams Muir's Pty Ltd t/a The Good Guys* [2011] FWA 5311 (no unfair dismissal based on Facebook use); *Holcim (Australia) Pty Ltd v Serafini* [2011] FWAFB 7794 (unfair dismissal based on employee's photographing and videoing of traffic accidents and uploading to Facebook and YouTube).
43   [2011] NSWSC 1452.
44   [2014] NSWSC 82.

background paper, *Human Rights in Cyberspace*, which was released in September 2013.[45] In this document, the AHRC canvasses whether there is, or should be, a right to internet access and, if so, whether this right arises under international human rights law or under domestic law. The AHRC notes that the right of internet access, and ensuring equitable and effective internet access, is particularly important for people with disabilities and for elderly people.[46]

C2.12   BANS OR RESTRICTIONS ON INTERNET OR SM

In five Australian States, courts have the power to make supervision orders in respect of serious sex offenders on application by the relevant Attorney-General. In New South Wales, Queensland, Victoria and Western Australia, the Supreme Court may order that a serious sex offender, at the expiry of his or her sentence, be released from custody subject to conditions.[47] In South Australia, the Supreme Court has the power to release a serious sex offender on licence, which enables the Parole Board or the Training Centre Review Board to make conditions with which the offender must comply.[48] In New South Wales, the Supreme Court also has the power to make such an order in relation to the release of a high-risk violent offender.[49] In New South Wales, there have been a number of cases in which a specific order has been made, restricting a serious sex offender's access to SM websites.[50] In all those jurisdictions where the court is authorised to impose conditions itself upon the release of a serious sex offender, orders have been made restricting serious sex offenders' use of the internet generally.[51]

C2.13   IDENTITY THEFT (OR EQUIVALENT)

There is no offence at the Commonwealth level dealing specifically with identity theft. There are 'financial information' offences under the Criminal

---

45 At www.humanrights.gov.au/publications/background-paper-human-rights-cyberspace.

46 Ibid, 27–30. See also Carolyn Dalton and Emma Keir, 'Addressing the digital divide: should universal access to broadband be considered a human right?' (2011) 20(2) *Human Rights Defender* 16–18.

47 Crimes (High Risk Offenders) Act 2006 (NSW) s 5C; Dangerous Prisoners (Sexual Offenders) Act 2003 (Qld) s 13(5)(b); Serious Sex Offenders (Detention and Supervision) Act 2009 (Vic) ss 9, 15; Dangerous Sexual Offenders Act 2006 (WA) s 17(1)(b).

48 Criminal Law (Sentencing) Act 1988 (SA) s 24.

49 Crimes (High Risk Offenders) Act 2006 (NSW) s 5F.

50 See, for example, *State of New South Wales v Cruse (No 2)* [2014] NSWSC 128; *State of New South Wales v Scott* [2014] NSWSC 276; *State of New South Wales v Atkins* [2014] NSWSC 292.

51 *Fletcher v Secretary to the Department of Justice* (2006) 165 A Crim R 569; *TSL v Secretary to the Department of Justice* (2006) 14 VR 109; *State of New South Wales v Green* [2013] NSWSC 1003; *Attorney-General for the State of Queensland v Fardon* [2013] QSC 264; *Attorney-General for the State of Queensland v Eades* [2013] QSC 266; *Director of Public Prosecutions (WA) v Dick (No 5)* [2013] WASC 357; *Director of Public Prosecutions v Dunn* [2013] WASC 359.

Code (Cth): it is a crime dishonestly to obtain or deal in personal financial information without the consent of the person to whom the information relates.[52] There are further provisions relating to obtaining property or financial advantage by deception, which can be used to prosecute incidents of identity theft.[53] In some States and Territories, there are legislative provisions dealing with identity theft or analogous offences.[54] It is an offence to deal with or supply identification information with an intent to commit a criminal offence, with a maximum penalty ranging between five to ten years' imprisonment. It is also an offence to possess identification information with intent, as well as possessing equipment to make identification documents.

C2.14   HACKING (OR EQUIVALENT)

There are laws in relation to 'computer trespass' and unauthorised access of data in every State and Territory, as well as at a Commonwealth level in Australia.[55] The legislation in the Australian Capital Territory, New South Wales, the Northern Territory, South Australia and Victoria has been amended to reflect substantially the Commonwealth offences. There are four levels of criminal liability, with the gradations depending upon the defendant's intent or the way the data was secured on a computer. The legislative regimes in Queensland, Tasmania and Western Australia do not follow the Commonwealth legislation. In Queensland, the offence is limited to the use of a 'restricted computer' without the consent of the computer's controller. In Tasmania, the offence requires an intention and a lack of 'lawful excuse' in relation to damaging computer data or accessing a computer without authority. However, the legislation does not define what constitutes 'lawful excuse' for the purposes of the offence, creating uncertainty. In Western Australia, it is an offence for a person to access information stored in a restricted system without authorisation.

C2.15   PRIVACY BY DESIGN (PBD) (OR EQUIVALENT)

No details.

---

52   Criminal Code (Cth) s 480.4.
53   Ibid, ss 134.1 (obtaining property by deception), 134.2 (obtaining financial advantage by deception), 135.1 (general dishonesty), 135.2 (obtaining financial advantage), 135.4 (conspiracy to defraud).
54   Criminal Code (Cth) ss 370.1–370.3, 372.1–372.6; Crimes Act 1900 (NSW) ss 192I–192M; Criminal Code (Qld) s 408D; Criminal Law Consolidation Act 1935 (SA) ss 144A–144F; Crimes Act 1958 (Vic) ss 192A–192E; Criminal Code (WA) ss 489–494.
55   Criminal Code (Cth) ss 477.1–477.3, 478.1–478.4; Criminal Code (ACT) ss 412–421; Criminal Code (NT) ss 276–276F; Crimes Act 1900 (NSW) ss 308C–308I; Criminal Code (Qld) s 408E; Summary Offences Act 1953 (SA) s 44; Criminal Code (Tas) ss 257A–257F; Crimes Act 1958 (Vic) ss 247A–247I; Criminal Code (WA) s 440A.

C2.16   TWEETING FROM COURTS, AND ANY RULES/LAWS

There are contradictory developments in Australia in relation to the regulation of the use of Twitter in courtrooms. Judges have an inherent power to control the proceedings in their courts. For a number of years now, courts and tribunals have allowed Tweeting in the exercise of this inherent power. The first case in which Tweeting was permitted was *iiNet*, when the trial judge, Cowdroy J, permitted the use of Twitter, given the public interest in the proceeding. Also, given the importance of the technological issues in the case, it was apposite to that this was the first case in which live Tweeting was permitted.[56] Subsequently, hearings of many high-profile cases and commissions of inquiry have been live Tweeted by journalists. For example, in New South Wales in 2013, the Independent Commission Against Corruption hearings into substantial allegations against two former State Labor Party Ministers were live Tweeted over the several weeks for which the proceedings ran.[57]

A number of jurisdictions permit journalists to live Tweet during proceedings. In South Australia, an amendment to the Supreme Court Rules 2006 (SA), which came into effect on 1 October 2013, permits a 'bona fide member of the media' to 'communicate by means of an electronic device to and from a court room during the conduct of proceedings'.[58] In Western Australia, the Chief Justice of the Supreme Court announced on 31 January 2014 that journalists would be able to live Tweet from West Australian courtrooms.[59] The relevant Practice Direction, which came into effect on 4 February 2014, permits 'bona fide members of the media' to use electronic devices within the courtroom while the court is in session to record, transmit or receive.[60] In Victoria, the Supreme Court has published a document titled 'Media Policies and Practices', which states that 'accredited journalists' can 'use electronic equipment for the publication of material on the internet (blogging, twittering and similar)'.[61] By contrast, in New South Wales, the relevant legislation prohibits the transmission

---

56   Sally Jackson, 'Judges have final decision after Twitter enters court', *The Australian*, 19 October 2009; Leanne O'Donnell, 'Court Reporting All A Twitter', *Gazette of Law and Journalism*, 5 May 2014.

57   The following journalists have been live Tweeting from the ICAC: Kate McClymont (@Kate_McClymont) (*The Sydney Morning Herald*); Michaela Whitbourn (@MWhitbourn) (*The Sydney Morning Herald*); Sarah Gerathy (@sarahgerathy) (ABC News); Katie Kimberley (@KatieKimberley) (2GB News); and Michael Safi (@safimichael) (*The Guardian Australia*).

58   Supreme Court Civil Rules 2006 (SA) r 9B(3).

59   Supreme Court of Western Australia, 'Live Tweeting from WA Courts Allowed' (Media Statement), 31 January 2014.

60   Supreme Court of Western Australia, *Consolidated Practice Directions – Practice Direction 3.1*, 30 January 2014. [11].

61   Supreme Court of Victoria, *Media Policies and Practices* (2014).

of 'information that forms part of the proceedings of a court' by posting the information on SM sites.[62]

A number of courts themselves Tweet, such as the Supreme Court of New South Wales (@NSWSupCt), the Supreme Court of Victoria (@SCVSupremeCourt), the Family Court of Australia (@FamilyCourtAU), the County Court of Victoria (@CCVMedia) and the Magistrates' Court of Victoria (@MagCourtVic).

C2.17 TELEVISION COURTROOM BROADCASTING OR TELEVISION CAMERAS IN COURT, AND RULES OR LAWS

From 1 October 2013, the High Court of Australia made public audio-visual recordings of its hearings. The recordings are available online through the High Court's website, www.hcourt.gov.au/cases/recent-av-recordings. No other Australian court as yet records or streams its hearings on a routine basis. However, in New South Wales, the then Attorney-General, Greg Smith SC, issued a press release on 25 March 2014 which stated that the government was 'proposing new legislation to encourage greater media access to broadcast sentencing proceedings in criminal trials'.[63] The proposal would create a presumption in favour of allowing filming and broadcasting of final proceedings, such as verdicts and sentences in criminal cases, subject to a number of exceptions. Broadcasting would not be allowed where: filming would reveal the identity of jurors, protected witnesses or victims; the proceedings contain significant material subject to suppression orders; or material which would prejudice other trials or police investigations, or reveal police methodology; or filming would put the safety and security of a person at risk.

C2.18 SM IN COURTROOMS

Thus far, there have been few controversies or cases involving SM in courtrooms. In *R v Wills*, it came to the trial judge's attention that a juror had been posting material to Facebook, which might be prejudicial to the fraud trial they were sitting on or would otherwise constitute a contravention of the Jury Act 1977 (NSW). Haesler DCJ instructed a court officer to examine the juror's Facebook page and to interview the juror. The court officer uncovered that the juror had fellow jurors as Facebook friends but that the jurors had not discussed anything

---

62 Court Security Act 2005 (NSW) s 9A(1)(b). The Court Security Act 2005 (NSW) provides that people have the right to enter and remain in an area of court premises that is open to the public, and that journalists have a right to enter and remain in an area that is located outside a building in which the court is housed or is sitting for the purpose of making a media report: ibid, s 6. The legislation also prohibits the use of a recording device to record sound or images in court premises: ibid, s 9.

63 Greg Smith, 'Courts to Open Doors to Camera' (Media Release, 25 March 2014).

about the evidence in the trial. The material posted on Facebook included a Photoshopped picture of the juror in a wig and gown, as well as general observations about the trial, such as the type of the proceedings, the unusual nature of the proceedings, the length of the proceedings, concerns about how long the trial might last and 'joy at having a weekend off'.[64] Haesler DCJ held that nothing on the Facebook page rose to a *prima facie* level requiring him to examine the jurors on oath. His Honour observed that,

> '[i]t is clear in a modern world where there are social media sites that the opportunity for discussing matters pertaining to a trial has been increased beyond that which occurred before there was ready access to the Internet and such sites.'[65]

In November 2011, Victorian magistrate, Peter Mealy, told journalist, Margaret Simons, that her live Tweeting of committal proceedings was inappropriate and that any live Tweeting would constitute a contempt of court.[66]

Controversies involving the use of SM in courtrooms are bound to eventuate but, fortunately, in Australia, there have not been many so far.

C2.19 USE OF SM AS EVIDENCE IN COURTS

There has been a controversy about the service of originating process via Facebook or other SM websites. The first unreported example of this occurred in the Supreme Court of the Australian Capital Territory, when Harper M ordered that notice of default judgment could be served on the defendants via Facebook.[67] In *Byrne v Howard*, Brown FM of the Federal Magistrates Court of Australia held that substituted service of documents in family law proceedings via Facebook and MySpace was acceptable.[68] However, in *Flo Rida v Mothership Music Pty Ltd*, the New South Wales Court of Appeal (MacFarlan JA, Ward and Gleeson JJA agreeing) set aside the service of originating process for breach of contract via Facebook. The District Court of New South Wales had ordered substituted service against United States rapper, Flo Rida, on the day before he was due to leave Australia. The District Court of New South Wales had no power to serve originating process outside Australia. There was no evidence that Flo Rida left Australia to evade service of the originating process. The New South Wales Court of Appeal was also not satisfied that the Facebook page was an effective means of substituted service,

---

64 [2012] NSWDC 285, [5].
65 Ibid, [4].
66 Chip le Grand and Pia Akerman, 'No tweeting edict a "timely reminder" for journalists', *The Australian*, 5 November 2011.
67 Nick Abraham, 'Australian court serves documents via Facebook', *The Sydney Morning Herald*, 12 December 2008.
68 (2010) 239 FLR 62.

given the absence of any evidence suggesting that the page in question was Flo Rida's personal one or was otherwise likely to come to his attention.[69]

C2.20 PRIVACY, DATA PROTECTION AND SM

No details.

C2.21 SM AND FAMILY LAW CASES

Distressingly, SM activity now features routinely in family law litigation. In *Lackey v Mae*, Neville FM observed that,

> '[a]n unfortunate and increasing feature of modern litigation, particularly but not exclusively in family law, is the use of "social media". While it can be used for good, often it is used as a weapon, either by one or both of the parties, and or by their respective supporters. It is a veritable "Aladdin's Cave" which parties (and lawyers) readily and regularly explore for (invariably incriminating) "evidence" to be used for litigation. As a weapon, it has particularly insidious features. Unfortunately, in the context of this matter, "netiquette" was not on display, and in fact, it could only be a nothing more than a euphemism for outlandish electronically-fomented conduct.
>
> For example, it often seems to be the case that people will put on such media (particularly but not only Facebook) comments that I suspect they would not say directly to the person against or about whom such remarks are directed. In this regard, such remarks are, in my view, a form of cyber-bullying. Often, they are very cowardly, because those who "post" such derogatory, cruel and nasty comments (regularly peppered with disgusting language and equally vile photographs) appear to feel a degree of immunity; they think they are beyond the purview or accountability of the law, and that they need not take any responsibility for their remarks. They inhabit the cyber-sphere and operate as "Facebook rangers" who "hit and run" with their petty and malicious commentary, and seem to gloat (or be encouraged) by the online audience that waits to join the ghoulish, jeering crowd in the nether-world of cyber-space. To a significant degree, such conduct has been on display here.'[70]

C2.22 SPORTS PERSONS, SPORTS CLUBS AND SM

There have been a large number of controversies in Australia involving sportspeople and their use of SM. In 2010, Olympic gold medal-winning

---

69   [2013] NSWCA 268.
70   [2013] FMCAfam 284, [9]–[10].

swimmer, Stephanie Rice, created controversy with a homophobic Tweet during a rugby match between the Wallabies (the Australian national rugby team) and the Springboks (the South African national rugby team). Not only did she have to hold a teary media conference, at which she apologised profusely for any offence caused by her Tweet, Rice also lost a lucrative sponsorship with luxury car company, Jaguar, and had to return the car she had received from it.

Also in 2010, a rugby league player, Joel Monaghan, was forced to leave Australia to take up playing in England, after a photograph of him simulating a lewd sex act with a dog at an end-of-season 'Mad Monday' celebration was circulated via Twitter. The police and the RSPCA launched investigations into Monaghan's conduct. Monaghan was forced to resign and eventually to leave the country, signing to play with the Warrington Wolves.[71]

In 2012, another rugby league player, Robbie Farah, featured prominently in a campaign by a Sydney tabloid newspaper, *The Daily Telegraph*, to 'Stop the Trolls'. The reason for his participation was that he received a 'vile' Tweet about his recently deceased mother. However, his position as one of the faces of the campaign was undermined when it was revealed that he himself had Tweeted that the then Prime Minister, Julia Gillard, should be given 'a noose' for her 50th birthday.[72]

In 2013, yet another rugby league player, George Burgess, found himself at the centre of a nude photo drama. Burgess took two full-frontal 'selfies'. These came into the possession of a young woman, who enlisted the assistance of a friend in an attempt to sell the photographs to mainstream media outlets. Unsurprisingly, no mainstream media outlet was interested. The photographs then began to circulate widely on Twitter and were then given to a gay website. The wide circulation of the images through SM was then reported as a news story by tabloid newspapers.[73]

C2.23 PERSONAL RELATIONS AND RELATIONSHIPS

Controversies about the dissemination of private images and the phenomenon of 'revenge porn' have started to occur with increasing regularity in Australia. Cases have now started to be brought in relation to this type of material. For

---

71 Chris Dutton and John-Paul Moloney, 'Disgraced Monaghan's career on line as prank goes viral', *The Canberra Times*, 5 November 2010; Adrian Proszenko, 'Shamed Raider looks to UK: I don't want to lose my livelihood over a stupid prank, Monaghan says', *The Canberra Times*, 7 November 2010.

72 Stephen Brook, 'Farah sorry for hang PM tweet', *The Australian*, 13 September 2012; James Manning, 'Farah regrets PM "noose" tweet', *The Sydney Morning Herald*, 13 September 2012.

73 'Nude pics of NRL and South Sydney Rabbitohs star George Burgess end up online', 'Sydney Confidential', *The Daily Telegraph* (Sydney), 11 July 2013; '"Gorgeous" George Gift', 'Sydney Confidential', *The Daily Telegraph* (Sydney), 12 July 2013.

example, in *Police v Usmanov*,[74] the accused uploaded six nude photographs of his ex-girlfriend to Facebook without her permission. She asked him to take them down, which he did, but he later reposted them and sent them to her roommate. Usmanov was prosecuted in the Local Court of New South Wales for the offence of publishing an indecent article in contravention of the Crimes Act 1900 (NSW) s 578C. This was a landmark case because it was the first time that a prosecution under this statutory provision had been based on an SM publication. Usmanov pleaded guilty. Mottley DCM sentenced Usmanov to six months' imprisonment. In the course of sentencing Usmanov, Mottley DCM observed that,

> 'Facebook gives instant access to the world … [I]ncalculable damage can be done to a person's reputation by the irresponsible posting of information through that medium. With its popularity and potential for real harm, there is a genuine need to ensure the use of this medium to commit offences of this type is deterred.'[75]

C2.24 SM AND PERSONAL DATA OF DECEASED PERSONS

There have been a number of high-profile instances of Facebook tribute pages for deceased persons being defaced by online trolls. For example, in *R v Hampson*, the offender pleaded guilty to using a carriage service in an offensive way, in contravention of the Criminal Code (Cth) s 474.17, as well as knowingly possessing and distributing child exploitation material. The offender engaged in Facebook trolling. He defaced two Facebook tribute pages, which were established to commemorate two children who had died in separate incidents, by repeatedly posting offensive comments and child pornography. He was sentenced to two years' imprisonment with a non-parole period of eight months.[76]

C2.25 SM, WEBSITE, SERVICE PROVIDER OR ISP DEFENCE RULES/LAWS

Under the Broadcasting Services Act 1992 (Cth) Sch 5 cl 91, there is a broad-based immunity for internet service providers (ISPs) and internet content hosts (ICHs). An ISP or an ICH cannot be subject to civil or criminal liability, directly or indirectly, arising under a State or Territory law or any principle of common law or equity, in respect of hosting internet content where it was not aware of the nature of the internet content. In addition, an ISP or an ICH cannot

---

74 [2011] NSWLC 40.
75 Ibid, [19].
76 [2011] QCA 132.

be subject to a requirement, whether direct or indirect, arising under a State or Territory law or any principle of common law or equity, to monitor, make inquiries about, or keep records of internet content that it hosts.

Notwithstanding its importance and its potentially broad application, this immunity is not widely known. Its judicial consideration is quite limited. Its most important application has been in the decision of the New South Wales Court of Criminal Appeal in *Fairfax Digital Australia and New Zealand Pty Ltd v Ibrahim*. Three media organisations challenged nationwide suppression orders which had been made pursuant to State legislation, the Court Suppression and Non-Publication Orders Act 2010 (NSW). The orders purported to prevent 'disclosure, dissemination or provision of access' by means of book, newspaper, magazine, radio, television or the internet of material relating to other criminal proceedings against the defendants. The court concluded that the orders were futile and ineffective, so set them aside. In the course of judgment, Basten JA, with whom Whealy JA agreed, held that the effect of the immunity under the Broadcasting Services Act 1992 (Cth) Sch 5 cl 91 was that a media outlet could only be held liable for internet content that it hosted which contravened those orders where the media outlet was unaware of the internet content.[77]

There are important limitations to this immunity, notwithstanding its apparent breadth. The immunity can be displaced once the ISP or the ICH is made aware of the internet content. In order to deprive the ISP or the ICH of the immunity, a plaintiff simply needs to notify the ISP or the ICH of the presence of the internet content and, if the ISP or the ICH does not deal with the internet content within a reasonable time, it cannot rely on the immunity. In practical terms, this happens routinely. This means that the statutory immunity is neither broader, nor more than useful, than the common law defence of innocent dissemination. Thus, the Supreme Court of Victoria has found that the search engine, Google, could be held liable as a publisher of defamatory matter, created by a third party and searched for by a user over whom the search engine had no control, after Google had been made aware of the existence of the defamatory matter and had taken no steps to take it down. In reaching this conclusion, Beach J did not need to deal with the Broadcasting Services Act 1992 (Cth) Sch 5 cl 91. It was sufficient to deal with the case on the basis of the defence of innocent dissemination. The plaintiff succeeded in his claim against Google and was awarded $200,000 damages.[78] In separate proceedings against another search engine, Yahoo!, in respect of a similar matter, the search engine did not take the point that it was not a publisher for the purposes of defamation law. It was ordered to pay the plaintiff $225,000 damages.[79]

---

77   (2012) 83 NSWLR 52.
78   *Trkulja v Google Inc (No 5)* [2012] VSC 533.
79   *Trkulja v Yahoo! LLC* [2012] VSC 88.

C2.26   ECOMMERCE DEFENCE CASES

No details.

C2.27   LAWS PROTECTING PERSONAL DATA/ PERSONALLY IDENTIFIABLE INFORMATION

At the Commonwealth, State and Territory levels in Australia, there is legislation providing protection for information privacy.[80] At a Commonwealth level, the Privacy Act 1988 (Cth) governs the protection of personal data. The legislation identifies 13 Australian Privacy Principles ('APPs') which regulate how entities subject to the legislation (so-called 'APP entities') manage personal information.[81] The term, 'personal information', is defined in the Act as information or an opinion about an identified or reasonably identifiable individual, whether the information or opinion is true, and whether the information or opinion is recorded in a material form.[82] The State and Territory legislation mirrors this.

In addition to general privacy legislation, there are also specific statutory provisions dealing with privacy, regulating certain types of information which have been of particular concern. The most prominent one is the protection of health information. The Privacy Act 1988 (Cth) defines 'sensitive information' to include health information.[83] Stronger protections under the APPs apply to 'sensitive information'.[84] There are also separate Commonwealth Acts which protect healthcare identifiers[85] and electronic health records.[86] There is also State and Territory legislation which specifically protects health information.[87]

Another prominent category of information specifically protected by legislation is the disclosure of certain information by telecommunications providers.[88] The recording or storage of a private conversation without the other party's

---

80   Information Act (NT); Privacy and Personal Information Protection Act 1998 (NSW); Information Privacy Act 2009 (Qld); Personal Information Protection Act 2004 (Tas); Information Privacy Act 2000 (Vic).

81   Privacy Act 1988 (Cth) sch 1. An 'APP entity' is defined to include Commonwealth government agencies, as well as organisations with a turnover exceeding $3 million, and some small business (including those provides health services or disclosing personal information for a benefit, service or advantage).

82   Ibid, s 6(1).

83   Ibid, s 6(1).

84   Ibid, sch 1 cl 3.

85   Healthcare Identifiers Act 2010 (Cth).

86   Personally Controlled Electronic Health Records Act 2012 (Cth).

87   Health Records (Privacy and Access) Act 1997 (ACT); Information Act (NT); Health Records and Information Privacy Act 2002 (NSW); Information Privacy Act 2009 (Qld); Health Records Act 2001 (Vic).

88   Telecommunications Act 1997 (Cth) pt 13.

consent is prohibited under State and Territory legislation.[89] There is also a Commonwealth Act, applying to Commonwealth government agencies and their employees, criminalising the use of surveillance devices without the consent of the target.[90]

C2.28 DATA BREACH LAWS AND CUSTOMERS/ USERS/ REGULATORS NOTIFIED OF HACKING OR DATA LOSS

Currently, there is no requirement under the Privacy Act 1988 (Cth) for entities to report a data breach. The Australian Privacy Principle 11 requires APP entities to take such steps as are reasonable in the circumstances to protect the information from misuse, interference and loss, and from unauthorised access, modification or disclosure.[91] Australia's regulatory body for privacy, the Office of the Australian Information Commission ('OAIC'), takes the view that notification to the person affected and to itself may constitute a 'reasonable step' where a data breach has occurred.[92] The OAIC's data breach guide recommends notification as one of the four steps which should occur when an entity responds to a data breach.[93] The States and the Territories have not enacted any data breach notification laws.[94]

In 2013, the then Federal Labor Government introduced the Privacy Amendment (Privacy Alerts) Bill 2013 (Cth). This Bill would have introduced mandatory data breach notification provisions for APP entities. It was passed by the House of Representatives but lapsed when the Parliament of Australia was prorogued for the 2013 election.

In the context of health information, there is a mandatory data breach notification requirement relating to the Personally Controlled Electronic Health Records system.[95]

---

89 Listening Devices Act 1992 (ACT); Surveillance Devices Act (NT); Surveillance Devices Act 2007 (NSW); Invasion of Privacy Act 1971 (Qld); Listening and Surveillance Devices Act 1972 (SA); Listening Devices Act 1991 (Tas); Surveillance Devices Act 1999 (Vic); Surveillance Devices Act 1998 (WA).

90 Surveillance Devices Act 2004 (Cth).

91 Privacy Act 1988 (Cth) sch 1 cl 11.

92 Office of the Australian Information Commissioner, 'Data Breach Notification: A Guide to Handling Personal Information Security Breaches' (April 2012), at www.oaic.gov.au/images/ documents/privacy/privacy-resources/privacy-guides/Data_breach_notification_guide_ April2012FINAL.pdf.

93 Ibid, 17–26.

94 Commonwealth Attorney-General's Department, *Australian Privacy Breach Notification: Discussion Paper* (October 2012), at www.ag.gov.au/Consultations/Documents/ AustralianPrivacyBreachNotification/AustralianPrivacyBreachNotificationDiscussionPaper. PDF.

95 Personally Controlled Electronic Health Records Act 2012 (Cth) s 75.

Chapter C3

Belgium

**Brendan Van Alsenoy, Valerie Verdoodt, Eva Lievens, Ruben Roex,
Ellen Wauters and Els Kindt**
Centre for Law and ICT (ICRI), KU Leuven, iMinds

C3.1 INTRODUCTION

Belgium is an EU member state and is a Civil Law jurisdiction.

C3.2 SPECIFIC SM AND SN LAWS

No details.

C3.3 SM CRIMINAL LAW CASES

For example,

*Correctional Court of Leuven, 8 November 2010, Case n° AR nr LE53.
L7.4816-09*

This case involved a dispute between two police officers and a private
individual. The individual had been handcuffed by the officers after a traffic
accident for being recalcitrant. Following this event, the individual repeatedly
sent provocative and insulting personal messages via Facebook. The court
decided that these messages severely disturbed the peace of mind of the police
inspectors and that this constituted 'stalking' within the meaning of Article
442bis of the Criminal Code.[1]

Council Chamber (Raadkamer) of Nijvel, 4 December 2013, Case n° 75/11

This case concerned an animal rights activist who had insinuated through
SM that a certain company that sold puppies had broken the Belgian Animal
Welfare Law of 14 August 1986. According to the activist, the company sold
fake dog passports and illegally ended the lives of unsold puppies. However,

---

1   This judgment was annotated by J Ceuleers, 'Belaging via Facebook is Ernstig Misdrijf',
    Auteurs & Media 2011, Issue 1, p 115.

the activist did not have any real evidence to back up these statements. The Council Chamber considered that the distribution of these kind of libellous statements on a Facebook discussion forum constituted a press offence (Article 150 of the Belgian Constitution).[2]

For more examples of SN criminal law cases, see C3.13 (on identity theft) and C3.14 (on hacking).

C3.4   SM CIVIL LAW CASES

For example,

Court of Brussels (20th Chamber), 20 June 2011

As indicated earlier, the publication of libellous remarks on social media can constitute a so-called 'press offence' in Belgium. In practice, many cases involving such press offences are brought before civil courts. In the case of 20 June 2011, the Civil Court of Brussels decided that the unnecessary use of hurtful and insulting words can constitute a tort, especially if there is no public interest. According to the Court, it is unlawful to purposely degrade someone's honour or reputation, for merely subjective reasons, by using unacceptably sharp language which is clearly disproportionate and unnecessary to express the opinion. The fact that the victim of the defamatory comments did not try to react directly to the weblog did not prevent a claim for civil liability.[3]

For more examples of SN civil law cases, see C3.9 (on employment) and C3.21 (on family law).

C3.5   CASES WHERE SM-RELATED EVIDENCE USED OR ADMISSIBLE

For example,

Court of Appeal of Antwerp, 22 February 2011, Case n° 2009/AR/1908

The Antwerp Court of Appeal accepted that the Belgian treasury could rely on information made public by taxpayers through social media as a way to help demonstrate tax fraud. In this case, a taxpayer had submitted certain costs relating to his Land Rover Defender as deductible expenses. The tax controller, however, decided to take a look at the SM page of the taxpayer, on which he discovered that the car was actually regularly used for the taxpayer's alpinism

---

2   This judgment was annotated by A Godfroid and A Vandecasteele, 'Kritiek op grootschalige hondenfokkerij zindert na', *Juristenkrant* 2014, afl. 283, p 3. The full text of this judgment is available (in French) at www.kluwer.be/files/communities/legalworld/rechtspraak/RK%20Nijvel%204%20december%202013.pdf.

3   A Dutch summary of this judgment can be found in *Auteurs & Media* 2012, Issue 5, p 463.

and diving trips, as well as for foreign travel. Therefore, the tax controller lowered the amount of deductible expenses, a reasoning which was accepted by the Court.

For more examples of cases where SN-related evidence has been used or been admissible, see C3.9 (on employment) and C3.21 (on family law).

C3.6   SPECIFIC ONLINE ABUSE/ONLINE BULLYING/ CYBERBULLYING LAWS

Article 145 §3bis of the Law of 13 June 2005 on electronic communications[4] criminalises 'harassment by electronic communication means' and states the following:

> 'A person who is liable for using an electronic communications network, service or other electronic means with the purpose of causing nuisance to its correspondent or to inflict damage on him as well as the person who prepares any device whatsoever intended to commit the above offence, as well as the attempt to commit the latter, will be penalized with a fine of 50 EUR to 300 EUR and by a jail sentence of fifteen days to two years or one of these penalties.' (free translation)

For this article to be applicable, a number conditions must be met. First, the harassment must be carried out by electronic means (this includes the internet and SM). Second, the perpetrator must have the intention to harass. Third, the harassment must be done vis-à-vis a 'correspondent'. This implies that there must be some form of interaction between the perpetrator and the target, for example via the sending of emails, texting, posting messages on the victim's website, etc.

C3.7   OTHER ONLINE ABUSE/ONLINE BULLYING/ CYBERBULLYING LAWS

The Criminal Code contains a number of provisions that may be applicable to bullying in SM.

First, Article 422bis of the Criminal Code, which punishes persons who menace an individual, while they knew or should have known that through their behaviour they would seriously disturb the peace of that individual (see also C3.3).

---

4   Law of 13 June 2005 on electronic communications, Official State Gazette, 20 June 2005. The full text of the Act can be accessed at www.bipt.be/en/operators/telecommunication/compilation-of-consolidated-legislation/national-framework/basic-legislation.

Secondly, Articles 443–444 of the Criminal Code criminalise defamation and libel. Cyberbullying through SM may, under certain conditions, be classified as libel or defamation.

Thirdly, Article 448 of the Criminal Code punishes persons who offend or insult someone by means of writings or images. The perpetrator must have a malicious intent and the insult must be public. These Articles could also be applied in the context of SM.

Article 383 of the Criminal Code criminalises the display, sale or distribution of writings or images that are indecent. If this is done in the presence of minors below the age of 16, more severe sentences are imposed according to Article 386. In addition, Article 384 stipulates that the production of indecent writings or images is also a criminal offence. In cases of cyberbullying where sexually explicit images are used ('sexting'), these provisions may be relevant.[5]

If the cyberbullying involves the spreading of images of the victim without his or her consent, it could be covered by Article 10 of the Belgian Copyright Law which protects the right to one's image. Moreover, this type of harassment could qualify as the processing of personal data, for which a person may need the consent of the data subject, according to Article 5 of the Belgian Data Protection Law.

All the aforementioned provisions are formulated in a broad and technology-neutral manner, so in theory they could be applied in the SM context. Not all of these provisions have already been applied in case law. However, several instances do exist, which are discussed below. See C3.3 (on criminal law cases), C3.14 (on hacking) and C3.13 (on identity theft).

C3.8 CHILDREN AND SM LAWS OR RULES

No details. However, a recently approved legislative proposal aims to protect minors against 'grooming' practices, including on SM.[6]

C3.9 EMPLOYEES/EMPLOYMENT SM LAWS OR CASES

This could generally include employee use of SM.

---

5 Child pornography is addressed in Article 383bis of the Criminal Code. This Article criminalises the display, sale, rental, distribution, transmission, delivery, possession or (knowing) obtainment of access of or to images that depict poses or sexual acts with a pornographic character which involve or depict minors.

6 Legislative proposal of 24 March 2014 concerning the protection of minors against being approached with a view of committing punishable acts of a sexual nature ('Wetsontwerp betreffende de bescherming van minderjarigen tegen benadering met als oogmerk het plegen van strafbare feiten van seksuele aard'), De Kamer, 5de zitting van 53ste zittingsperiode, Doc 53 3449/003. The full text of the current version of the proposal is available (in Dutch) at www.senate.be/www/?MIval=/dossier&LEG=5&NR=1823&LANG=nl.

Legislation

Article 8 of the European Convention on Human Rights and Article 22 of the Belgian Constitution protect the right to privacy and private communication, which also protects employee privacy. Software that enables the recording of SM use or otherwise traces user activity can only be used if there is a legal basis, for a legitimate purpose and in a proportionate way. Furthermore, the Belgian Data Protection Act will apply in cases where an employer monitors employee use of SM in an automated fashion.

There is no specific legislation concerning the use of SNs or SN data by employees/employers. Under Belgian Labor law, an employer has the right to unilaterally set up a social media policy concerning the use of Information Technology. This means that an employer can, for instance, block access to certain websites in the work environment or only allow these sites to be accessed during certain periods (breaks).[7] Furthermore, the employer can, in certain circumstances, monitor employee use of SM, but several regulatory instruments impose certain limits on the ability of employers to use SM data or monitor employees' usage of SM. For example,

Collective Labor Agreement (Collectieve Arbeidsovereenkomst – 'CAO') no 38 of 6 December 1983

This instrument requires employers to respect the private life of job applicants. Only information which is pertinent to the position may be collected. This may restrict employers' ability to use data available on SM.[8]

Collective Labor Agreement (Collectieve Arbeidsovereenkomst – 'CAO') no 81 of 26 April 2002

This instrument regulates the monitoring of electronic communications at work, and restricts employers' ability to monitor the use of ICTs by employees, including their visits to SM websites. It states that,

> 'The employer can only monitor behavior in order to prevent unlawful or inappropriate acts that can damage a person's dignity; to protect confidential economic, commercial or financial interests of the undertaking; to safeguard the operation of network systems; or subsidiary to sustain the respect for the principles and rules concerning online technologies of the undertaking.' (free translation)[9]

Also relevant in this context is Article 124 of the Belgian Electronic Communications Law which prohibits someone intentionally taking note of the existence of private communication, as well as the storing, making

---

7   Rousseau, J & Plets, I, 'Een praktische leidraad voor socialemediarichtlijnen' in Valcke, P, Valgaeren, PJ and Lievens, E (eds), *Sociale media. Actuele juridische aspecten*, Antwerpen, Intersentia, 2013, 268p.

8   CAO nr. 38 is available at www.cnt-nar.be/CAO-COORD/cao-038.pdf.

9   CAO nr. 81 is available at www.cnt-nar.be/CAO-COORD/cao-081.pdf.

public or using information that one has received intentionally or not. Finally, Article 314bis of the Belgian Criminal Code protects the secrecy of electronic correspondence and punishes the discovery of the content of private communication, but only during the transfer process of the information.

Case law

Labor Court of Appeal (Arbeidshof) of Brussels, 29 May 2013, Case nr 2011/ AB/817

In this case, an employee of a security company was dismissed after someone else posted a video of him on his Facebook profile. This video shows the employee demonstrating his physical competences (combat sport) during work hours, in the buildings of the European Commission, on a floor that is only reserved for commissioners. Once they discovered the video, the security company terminated his employment for urgent cause. The Court, however, decided that the facts of this case were not sufficiently grave to justify immediate termination.[10]

Labor Court of Appeal (Arbeidshof) of Brussels, 3 September 2013, case nr 2012/AB/104

A board member of a publicly traded company had posted sceptical and critical comments about the company's financial performance. These comments were accessible to the public at large. Once found out, his employment contract was instantly terminated. The Court decided that, since the comments were posted on the public part of the profile, the employee knew that 'non-friends' could also have access to them and this was sufficient grounds for immediate termination.[11]

Labor Court (Arbeidsrechtbank) of Namen (2nd Chamber), 10 January 2011, case nr 10/563/A

In this case, an employee had been dismissed for posting racist and derogatory statements regarding one of her colleagues. Although the profile (where the comments were posted) was not accessible to the public, the employer had asked another colleague who did have access to the profile to communicate these statements to him. The Court did not take issue with this approach. In its view, the fact that an employee who had access to the communications, voluntarily or after injunction of the employer, decides to hand them over to the latter is not sufficient to render the evidence unlawful.[12]

---

10   The full text of this judgment is available at: http://jure.juridat.just.fgov.be/view_decision. html?justel=F-20130529-2&idxc_id=274510&lang=nl.

11   A French summary of this judgment is available at http://jure.juridat.just.fgov.be/view_ decision.html?justel=F-20130903-11&idxc_id=276376&lang=nl. This case has been annotated by D Casaer, 'Kritiek op werkgever via Facebook verantwoordt ontslag om dringende reden', *Juristenkrant* 2013, afl 278, 6.

12   This case has been annotated by K Rosier, 'Réflexions sur le droit au respect de la vie privée et la liberté d'expression sur Facebook dans le cadre des relations de travail' RDTI 2012, afl 46, 90–99.

Labor Court of Appeal (Arbeidshof) of Brussels (8th Chamber), 13 June 2012, case nr 2011/AB/326

This case dealt with the use of SN statements as evidence of co-habitation, which was a relevant issue in the determination of unemployment benefits. A woman had mentioned on Facebook that she was living with someone, and she was spotted in male company both outside and inside her place of residence. The Court considered that the mere statement on Facebook of 'living with someone' did not constitute evidence of co-habitation, if both persons keep their separate addresses and pay their own rental and energy costs (ie there is no evidence of 'economical co-habitation').[13]

C3.10 SCHOOL AND UNIVERSITY STUDENT SM CASES

For example,

Council for disputes concerning decisions regarding educational advancement ('Raad voor betwistingen inzake studievoortgangsbeslissingen'), 13 August 2009, Decision (Besluit) Nr 2009/059

In this case, several students were found guilty of cheating during exams. While taking the exams, the students in question had received several verbal warnings. The suspicion of cheating was later further corroborated on the basis of SM posts (these SM posts had been communicated to the university staff by a fellow student).[14]

C3.11 RIGHT OR HUMAN RIGHT TO ACCESS THE INTERNET OR SM

In 2012, a member of Parliament introduced a legislative proposal for a constitutional amendment which would introduce a fundamental right of access to the internet. This proposal is currently still pending.[15]

C3.12 BANS OR RESTRICTIONS ON INTERNET OR SM

Legislation

Although there is no specific legal provision in this respect, there exist several provisions that can be used to achieve this objective,

---

13 A summary of this judgment is available in *Sociale Kronieken*, 2012, Issue 8, p 444.

14 The full text of this decision is available in Dutch at www.ond.vlaanderen.be/hogeronderwijs/raad/uitspraken2009/2009-059.htm.

15 The full text of the proposal can be accessed at www.dekamer.be/FLWB/PDF/53/2046/53K2046001.pdf. Its current status can be monitored at www.dekamer.be/kvvcr/showpage.cfm?section=flwb&language=nl&leftmenu=none&cfm=/site/wwwcfm/search/fiche.cfm?ID=53K2046&db=FLWB&legislat=53.

- Article 145 and following of the Act of 13 June 2005 regarding electronic communications enable the confiscation of devices that are used for certain illegal ends as defined in the Act;

- Article 39bis of the Criminal Procedure Code regarding data seizure (compare with Article 19 of the Cybercrime Convention) enables the public prosecutor to restrict access to data; and

- Article 42 of the Criminal Code on special confiscation allows for the confiscation of goods which were used to commit a crime insofar as they belong to the criminal.

Case law

There exists – very limited and non-published – case law according to which an individual condemned in a child pornography case was forbidden access to social media on the basis of the Act of 29 June of 1964 regarding reprieve, suspension and probation (Correctional Court of Veurne, 2 March 2011). In that case, it was a probation measure, but it could for instance also be a measure in the framework of a release from detention before trial.

Another example is a case before the Correctional Court of Mechelen, where the defendant had been harassing girls via the internet, asking them to send nude pictures and movies and then blackmailing them with this material into performing sadomasochistic acts. The Court convicted this defendant to a three-year prison term, accompanied by an internet ban (Correctional Court of Mechelen, 15 June 2012).[16]

C3.13 IDENTITY THEFT (OR EQUIVALENT)

At the time of writing, Belgian law does not explicitly criminalize identity theft. However, identity theft may involve several activities which are punishable on the basis of other provisions.[17] In this regard, a distinction needs to be made between (1) the act of stealing someone's identity, and (2) the use of this stolen identity. The first component is not explicitly criminalized under Belgian law, but the identity of a person in principle amounts to 'personal data' as defined by the Belgian Act on the Processing of Personal Data of 8 December 1992. Article 4(1) of this Act, for example, requires that personal data be processed fairly and lawfully. Naturally, the processing of personal data for criminal purposes would constitute a violation of this provision. Violating this provision may entail a fine under Article 39.

---

16 This case was covered by a Belgian newspaper, and the article is available at www.demorgen. be/dm/nl/989/Binnenland/article/detail/1454590/2012/06/15/Webpedofiel-krijgt-3-jaar-met-uitstel-en-internetverbod.dhtml.

17 Roex, R, 'Identiteitsdiefstal via sociale media. Een juridische benadering van een maatschappelijk fenomeen' in Valcke, P, Valgaeren, PJ and Lievens, E (eds), *Sociale media. Actuele juridische aspecten*, Antwerpen, Intersentia, 2013, 268p.

The use of a stolen identity is punishable under the Belgian Criminal Code, specifically by Article 193 (fraud in information technology). This provision states that the manipulation of data in an IT system with malicious or fraudulent intent is a criminal offence. The term 'IT system' is interpreted very broadly, which means that it would also include SM sites. A specific example can be found in a case before the Correctional Court of Ghent (see C3.2), where the Court decided that 'the setting up of a Facebook account in the name of another person *and* the posting of fake messages on this account, which is publicly accessible, should constitute manipulation of relevant legal computer data'.[18]

The use of a stolen identity can also be punishable under Article 550ter of the Criminal Code (sabotage of information technology). The latter punishes a person who 'knowing he is not allowed to, directly or indirectly enters, changes or deletes data in an IT system, or with any other technological means changes the normal application of data in an IT system ...'. This provision does not require malicious or fraudulent intent. Other computer crimes that can be relevant are computer-related forgery (Art 210bis of the Criminal Code, compare with Art 7 of the Cybercrime Convention) and computer-related fraud (Art 504quater of the Criminal Code, compare with Art 8 of the Cybercrime Convention) or causing nuisance through means of electronic communications (Art 145 of the Act of 13 June 2005 on electronic communications). Furthermore, certain use of a stolen identity might, depending on the circumstances, also amount to stalking (Article 442bis of the Belgian Criminal Code), slander (if certain slanderous statements are made) (Article 443 et seq of the Belgian Criminal Code) or wrongful pretence (Article 231 of the Belgian Criminal Code).

Case law

Correctional Court of Ghent, 21 September 2011

In this case, a woman was convicted for setting up a fake Facebook account using the name of her former employer after she had been dismissed. On this profile she posted fake messages, giving the impression that her employer was having an affair. She also used a picture of him that she had found on the internet as the profile picture. The court determined that she was guilty of computer-related forgery (Article 210bis of the Belgian Criminal Code), stalking (Article 442bis of the Belgian Criminal Code), defamation (Article 443 et seq of the Belgian Criminal Code) and wrongful pretence (Article 231 of the Belgian Criminal Code).[19]

18　See below: Corr Gent 21 September 2011, *Tijdschrift voor Strafrecht* 2012, Issue 2, 104 (annotation by E Baeyens).

19　This judgment was published in *Nullum Crimen* (NC) 2014, issue 1, pp 68–75 (annotation by F Delbar), accessible at www.nullumcrimen.be (13 February 2014). This case was also annotated by E Kindt, B Bruyndonckx and H Kaspersen, 'Veroordeling van identiteitsdiefstal op Facebook "avant la lettre" van de wet?' *Computerrecht* 2012, pp 161–170.

C3.14   HACKING (OR EQUIVALENT)

Legislation

Hacking is criminalised by Article 550bis of the Criminal Code, which criminalises both external (by an outsider) and internal hacking (for example, by an employee). External hacking is described as obtaining (or maintaining) access to a computer system, while knowing that one has no right. Internal hacking is described as overstepping one's rights of access to a computer system. Article 550bis also criminalizes attempted hacking as well as the development, distribution etc of hacker tools. Art 550ter of the Criminal Code furthermore criminalises system and data interference.

Case law

Correctional Court of Leuven, 15 June 2010

In this case, the Court analysed an attempted hacking of a banking IT-system, whereby the hackers claimed to have good intentions, namely testing the safety of the IT-system in order to increase security. The Court held that people who attempt to hack websites just for the sake of hacking are nevertheless committing computer-related forgery. Furthermore, the court stated that, just because a client gains secured access to internet banking, it does not mean that he becomes an authorized person to access the system within the meaning of Article 550bis.[20]

Correctional Court of Dendermonde, 14 May 2007

In this case, a group of individuals had secretly copied the magnetic strip of payment cards of unaware card holders and used small cameras to capture PIN codes. With this information, they withdrew money from the accounts of the card holders. The Court qualified these actions as computer-related forgery (Article 504quater of the Criminal Code) and hacking (Article 210bis of the Criminal Code).[21]

Correctional Court of Dendermonde, 14 November 2008, nr 20.L3.1531/08/26

In this case, a person was caught by the police while using his laptop in his car, parked in front of someone else's house. He confessed that he was chatting via the wireless network of this third person and that he especially drove to this spot because he knew the network did not require a password. The Court ruled that this constituted external hacking (Article 550bis of the Criminal Code).[22]

---

20   This judgment has been published in *Tijdschrift voor Strafrecht* 2011, vol 4, p 270.
21   This judgment has been published in *Tijdschrift voor Strafrecht* 2007, vol 6, p 403.
22   This judgment has been published in *Computerrecht* 2009, vol 2, p 74.

C3.15 PRIVACY BY DESIGN (PBD) (OR EQUIVALENT)

In Belgium, there are no rules or laws relating to PbD as such. This topic has received some discussion in academic literature.[23]

Article 23 of the European Commission's 2012 proposal for a General Data Protection Regulation mentions the principle of PbD, together with the principle of privacy by default, and places the responsibility to implement these principles on the data controller. Once this Regulation is adopted, it will have direct effect in all European countries.

C3.16 TWEETING FROM COURTS, AND ANY RULES/ LAWS

In Belgium, there are no rules or laws that specifically prohibit Tweeting from courts. According to Articles 148 and 149 of the Belgian Constitution, Court sessions have a public nature, so there is an openness vis-à-vis the public. Furthermore, Article 19 of the Constitution protects the right of freedom of expression, which could be applied to Tweets about court sessions. However, in some courts, the chair demands that mobile phones or other electronic devices are switched off during court sessions, which makes Tweeting from courtrooms impossible.[24] This competence can be derived from Article 281 of the Code of Criminal Proceedings, according to which the chair has 'the power to take any measures which they find useful to discover the truth'.[25]

C3.17 TELEVISION COURTROOM BROADCASTING OR TELEVISION CAMERAS IN COURT, AND RULES OR LAWS

Television cameras are, in principle, not permitted, but exceptions are possible.

C3.18 SM IN COURTROOMS

In a case before the Assize Court of Tongeren, the President of the Court warned the members of the jury about the dangers of using social media like Facebook and Twitter. He urged them to be cautious and asked them not to post any messages on SM about anything that has been said in court. By doing

---

23 See, for example, Hans Graux, 'Privacybescherming op sociale netwerken: heeft u nog een privéleven?', in P Valcke, PJ Valgaeren and E Lievens (eds), *Sociale media – Actuele juridische aspecten*, 2013, Antwerpen, Intersentia, pp 1–27.
24 For example, Vredegerecht van Zomergem – see www.vredegerechtzomergem.be/ vredegerecht_zomergem/Hoe_verloopt_mijn_proces_op_het_vredegerecht.html.
25 See Article 281 of the Code of Criminal Proceedings.

this, their objectiveness and independence as a member of the jury could be threatened and they could be persecuted and removed from the jury. (*Assize Court of Tongeren, 3 December 2011*).[26]

C3.19   USE OF SM AS EVIDENCE IN COURTS

Particularly in divorce and employment cases. See C3.9 (on employment) and C3.21 (on family law) and C3.2 and C3.3.

C3.20   PRIVACY, DATA PROTECTION AND SM

Not specifically.

C3.21   SM AND FAMILY LAW CASES

For example,

Justice of the Peace (Vredegerecht) Ninove 3 mei 2012, case nr AR 12A356

In this case, the divorce parties were ordered by the court to refrain from spreading libellous statements or insults through public fora, including Facebook. One spouse complained that the other had been posting insulting comments on his own Facebook profile after she had left him. The Justice of the Peace prohibited both parties (even though the husband was the only one that had been posting insulting remarks) from spreading any libellous or insulting comments towards each other or the children on public fora like social media, this for a period of almost a year, subject to payment of 100 euro per infringement.[27]

C3.22   SPORTS PERSONS, SPORTS CLUBS AND SM

A Belgian goalkeeper was suspected of having created fake posts on an internet forum of his team, leading to disciplinary sanctions. He was disciplined for 'repeatedly unprofessional behaviour', after allegedly insulting the management of his football team and his competitor for the number one keeper spot. He had also allegedly posted anonymous messages on an unofficial fan club webpage, questioning the skills of the management and his competitor, while glorifying himself. However, the messages were linked to his IP address and a news reporter exposed the trolling activities of the goalkeeper. As a

---

26   For more information, see www.hln.be/hln/nl/957/Binnenland/article/detail/1352510/2011/11/23/Voorzitter-assisen-wijst-juryleden-op-gevaren-van-Facebook-en-Twitter.dhtml.

27   This case has been annotated by G. Verschelden, 'Vrederechter censureert Facebookpagina van echtgenoten', *Juristenkrant* 2012, afl 252, p1.

result, the football team removed him from the first team and his contract was subsequently terminated.[28]

C3.23 PERSONAL RELATIONS AND RELATIONSHIPS

In 2013, and again in 2014, there was much controversy about Facebook 'hate' pages (eg called 'Antwerp whores') which showed (sometimes sexually suggestive) images of girls, accompanied by insulting comments. Law enforcement authorities took this phenomenon very seriously, and founders of the pages have been brought before the (youth) courts.[29] Other cases mentioned in the news have referred, for example, to threats of blackmail related to doctored naked images.[30]

C3.24 SM AND PERSONAL DATA OF DECEASED PERSONS

For example,

Journalistic Council ('Raad voor de Journalistiek'), Decision regarding the complaint of Mr Paul de Vloo against the Newspaper 'De Krant van West-Vlaanderen' and Pieter-Jan Breyne, journalist, ('Beslissing van de over de klacht van de heer Paul De Vloo tegen De Krant van West-Vlaanderen en Pieter-Jan Breyne, journalist') 24 June 2010

In this case, the father of a victim of a traffic accident filed a complaint against a Belgian newspaper for using pictures they found on the victim's Facebook profile, without asking consent. The newspaper published two pictures of the victim, one that was publicly accessible on the Facebook profile of the victim, whereas the other one was found on a Facebook page for which access was limited due to privacy settings. The Council decided that the second picture was not public and therefore should not have been published without consent. The fact that the journalist had access to the non-public Facebook pages of the victim does not justify him publishing the picture without consent. In consequence, the journalist did not fulfil his usual duty of care and the Board declared the complaint valid.[31]

---

28 See, for example, 'Onthulling: Stijnen bestookte anoniem internetfora', *Sporza* 20 February 2011, available at http://sporza.be/cm/sporza/voetbal/Jupiler_Pro_League/1.967369.
29 For more information, see VRT News, '"Antwerp whores" Facebook fan page under investigation', FlandersNews.be, 3 January 2013, available at www.deredactie.be/cm/vrtnieuws.english/News/1.1517219.
30 See eg F Vranckx, 'Facebook-afperser dreigt met verspreiden getrukeerde naaktfoto's', *Gazet van Antwerpen* 27 August 2009, available at www.gva.be/nieuws/binnenland/aid858428/facebook-afperser-dreigt-met-verspreiden-getrukeerde-naaktfoto-s.aspx/.
31 The full text of the decision is available (in Dutch) at http://rvdj.be/sites/default/files/pdf/beslissing201009.pdf.

C3.25 SM, WEBSITE, SERVICE PROVIDER OR ISP DEFENCE RULES/LAWS

The EU eCommerce Directive 2000/31/EC was implemented in Belgium by way of the Law of 11 March 2003 concerning certain legal aspects of information society services (Official State Gazette, 17 March 2003). It provides for liability exemptions for 'mere conduits', 'hosting' and 'caching'.

C3.26 ECOMMERCE DEFENCE CASES

For example,

Court of Cassation, 3 February 2004, case n° P031427N

In this case, an operator of a website displaying links to child pornography was found liable for distribution of child pornography. The webmaster argued that he, as an operator of a website, could rely on the liability exemption for hosting service providers and therefore was not liable for content of the linked websites. The Court, however, judged that the exemption was not applicable in this case, as the webmaster's activities did not have a merely technical, automatic or passive character. The latter had purchased, developed and economically exploited the website and had offered a collection of hyperlinks that led to child pornography images. The Court decided that the process of collecting these hyperlinks had happened under supervision and with the knowledge of the webmaster.[32]

Chairman of the Court of Antwerp, 5 October 2006, nr 06/3006/A

In this case, an operator of a website for seniors was accused of copyright breach. The website had certain mailing groups, via which people could discuss certain topics, such as music. The members of these mailing groups were able to send messages to one another, even with attachments, which were then stored in an electronic archive. The issue here was that, through one of these mailing groups, sound recordings were distributed without the consent of the rights holders, resulting in a breach of copyright. The Court judged that the website operator's activities did not have a merely technical, automatic or passive character, since the operator actively took measures to allow these infringements, like the archiving or the fact that the administrators of the mailing group received consent of the operator.[33]

Court of Commerce of Brussels (7th Chamber) 31 July 2008

Lancôme complained that eBay allowed advertisements which violated their trademarks and did not take any measures to prevent counterfeited goods from

---

32   The full text of this judgment is available at http://jure.juridat.just.fgov.be/view_decision. html?justel=F-20040203-3&idxc_id=197925&lang=nl.

33   The full text of this judgment is available at www.ie-forum.nl/getobject.php?id=2172.

appearing amongst genuine online sales advertisements. The Court clarified that the liability exemption is not limited to a specific type of service provider, but to specific and clearly defined actions. The Court held that the complaint only concerned eBay's activities of distributing advertisements of candidate sellers, to which it considered the 'hosting' exemption to be applicable.[34]

Court of Appeal of Liège (7th Chamber), 22 October 2009

A manager of a construction company had read negative comments about his company on the website of a consumer organization. He decided to sue the consumer organization in order to obtain the personal data of the persons who had posted the negative comments. The construction company based its claim on Article 21 of the E-Commerce Law of 23 March 2003 concerning the legal aspects of certain information society services, which states that intermediary service providers are obliged to provide any information that is useful for the detection of breaches of law to certain judicial and administrative authorities. The Court of Appeal of Liège, however, ruled that Article 21 should not be understood as an objective right for a physical or legal person to receive this information, either directly by an immediate injunction against the provider, or indirectly via a handover of the information by the judicial or administrative authority.[35]

Court of Appeal of Brussels, (9th Chamber), 25 November 2009

(This case is the continuation of the previously described case.)

The construction company sued the consumer organization for the damages they had suffered from the defamatory statements. The Court decided that moderators of website fora are arbiters in the conflict between freedom of expression and the rights of third parties, like protection of reputation. A moderator that has a right to control the messages of the internet users accepts civil liability, based on Article 1382 of the Civil Code. Therefore, the activities of moderators do not merely have a technical, automatic and passive character, so the exemption of the E-Commerce Directive is not applicable.[36]

European Court of Justice, (3rd Chamber), Sabam v. Netlog, Case nr C-360/10, 16 February 2012

In this case, the Court of Justice was asked to assess the legality of a request by a Belgian copyright society (SABAM), to direct a Belgian SN (Netlog) to implement a general filtering system to prevent unlawful use of musical and audio-visual work by its users. The Court considered Netlog as a hosting

---

34 The full text of this judgment is available at http://jure.juridat.just.fgov.be/view_decision. html?justel=F-20080731-12&idxc_id=225620&lang=nl.
35 This judgment was reproduced in *Revue du Droit des Technologies et de l'Information* 2010, n° 1, p 95 (and annotated by J Feld, 'Forums de discussion: espaces de libertés sous haute responsabilité', *RDTI* 2010, pp 106–120).
36 This judgment was reproduced in *RDTI* 2010, n° 38, p 102 (and also annotated by J Feld).

service provider, which led to its conclusion that the implementation of a general filtering system would collide with the E-Commerce Directive, more specifically the prohibition for Member States to impose a general obligation to monitor on service providers conducting activities of mere conduit, caching and hosting.[37]

C3.27 LAWS PROTECTING PERSONAL DATA/ PERSONALLY IDENTIFIABLE INFORMATION

In particular,

Law of 8 December 1992 for the protection of private life in relation to the processing of personal data, Official State Gazette, 18 March 1993

This Law was amended in 1998 by the Law of 11 December 1998 transposing EU Directive 95/46/EC of 24 October 1995 of the European Parliament and the Council on the protection of individuals with regard to the processing of personal data and on the free movement of such data, Official State Gazette, 3 February 1999.

This law applies to any processing of personal data by (wholly or partially) automatic means (Article 3(1)). Article 1 of the Act defines personal data as 'any information concerning an identified or identifiable natural person'.

The basic principles of the Law are that any processing of personal data needs to have a legitimate basis (Article 5), a legitimate and well-defined purpose (Article 4(1)2), the processing needs to be relevant (Article 4(1)3), as precise as possible (Article 4(1)4), transparent (Article 9) and adequately secured (Article 16). Furthermore, the data retention period should be minimized (Article 4(1)5), and personal data can only be transferred to countries that offer an adequate level of protection (Article 21 etc).

Law of 13 June 2005 on electronic communications, Official State Gazette, 20 June 2005

This law implemented EU Directive 2002/58/EC of the European Parliament and of the Council of 12 July 2002 concerning the processing of personal data and the protection of privacy in the electronic communications sector (Directive on privacy and electronic communications).

---

37   The full text of this judgment is available at http://curia.europa.eu/juris/liste. jsf?language=en&num=C-360/10. For a commentary, see F Coudert, '*SABAM v Netlog*: ECJ confirms general filtering systems installed for the prevention of copyright infringements are disproportionate', time.lex Blog, 16 February 2012, available at www.timelex.eu/nl/blog/ detail/sabam-v-netlog-ecj-confirms-general-filtering-systems-installed-for-the-prevention- of-copyright-infringements-are-disproportionate.

C3.28   DATA BREACH LAWS AND CUSTOMERS/USERS/ REGULATORS NOTIFIED OF HACKING OR DATA LOSS

Such an obligation exists for operators of an electronic communications network and providers of electronic communications services on the basis of Article 114(1) and following of the Act of 13 June 2005 on electronic communications. These operators and providers must notify the national telecoms authority (BIPT) as well as the individual users when the breach causes adverse effects on the users' privacy.

The Belgian Data Protection Act currently does not provide for a general data security breach notification duty for all data controllers. A Bill introduced in Parliament for amending said Act aims to introduce a general security breach notification. The Belgian DPA (Privacy Commission) further recommended, in a recent recommendation on security measures and data breaches, that companies should notify any security breaches in case of 'public incidents'. The DPA said that notification procedures for data security breach incidents should be documented by companies. If a 'public incident' occurs, the DPA should receive information about the causes and damage within a period of 48 hours. Unfortunately, the Belgian Privacy Commission did not specify what was meant by the term 'public incident'.[38]

FURTHER READING

Lievens, Eva, 'Bullying and sexting in social networks: Protecting minors from criminal acts or empowering minors to cope with risky behaviour?', *International Journal Crime, Law & Justice* 2014 (in press).

Lievens, Eva, 'Children and Peer-to-Peer Risks in Social Networks: Regulating, Empowering or a Little Bit of Both?', in Simone van der Hof, Bibi van den Berg, and Bart Schermer (eds) *Minding Minors Wandering the Web: Regulating Online Child Safety* TMC Asser Press, The Hague, 2014, 191–209.

Valcke, Peggy, Valgaeren, Pieter Jan and Lievens, Eva (eds), *Sociale media. Actuele juridische aspecten* Antwerpen, Intersentia, 2013, 268p.

Wauters, Ellen, Lievens, Eva and Valcke, Peggy, 'Towards a better protection of social media users: a legal perspective on the terms of use of SN sites', *International Journal of Law and Information Technology* 2014.

www.emsoc.be (http://emsoc.be/academic-community)

www.spion.me

---

38   The full text of this document is available (in Dutch) at www.privacycommission.be/sites/privacycommission/files/documents/aanbeveling_01_2013.pdf.

Chapter C4

Brazil

Roberto Fragale Filho (PPGSD-UFF, Brazil)
Socio-Legal Researcher
José Carlos de Araújo Almeida Filho (SPP-UFF, Brazil)
Civil Procedure and Electronic Law Researcher

Sonia Barroso (ICM-UFF, Brazil)
Law and Economics Researcher

Bernardo Menicucci Grossi
Attorney at Law, Intellectual Property and Cyber Law Researcher

Marcus Vinícius Brandão Soares (Audit-Susep, Brazil)
Information Technology and Electronic Procedure Researcher

C4.1   INTRODUCTION

Brazil is a Civil Law jurisdiction.

C4.2   SPECIFIC SM AND SN LAWS

There are no specific SM and SN laws in Brazil. Yet, there is an ordinance related to the public sector issued by the National Council of Defense (Portaria CSN n 38/2012) which requires different public agencies to establish criteria and responsibilities for the safe use of new media, as well as define teams, always led by civil servants, to coordinate their use. The ordinance takes into account the 'new reality of interaction and communication between people, companies, agencies and public and private entities', but maintains that 'when not used with well-defined criteria (it) can bring risks to Information Security and Communications'. Although not expressly determining the content of the rules to be adopted by each agency, the ordinance provides for general guidelines on the matter. It requires institutional profiles in social networks to be preferably managed by integrated teams exclusively composed by public servants or federal employees. Thus, it bans outsourcing of management of agencies and public administration profiles.

243

C4.3 SM CRIMINAL LAW CASES

Most of the SM criminal law cases in Brazil are related to libel and/or defamation usually made on blogs. Recently, the Brazilian Supreme Court has authorized the opening of a criminal procedure for libel and defamation against former governor of Rio de Janeiro State and federal representative, Anthony Garotinho, for a post made on his personal blog four years ago (June, 2010) suggesting that a fraud was committed by Rio de Janeiro Water and Sewer State Company in one of its contracts (see www.conjur.com.br/2014-jun-25/ stf-aceita-queixa-calunia-difamacao-anthony-garotinho, retrieved August 7, 2014). Likewise, journalist and blogger Paulo Henrique Amorim has been convicted several times for libel and defamation for his posts (see www.conjur. com.br/2014-abr-28/paulo-henrique-amorim-condenado-injuria-merval-pereira, retrieved August 7, 2014).

C4.4 SM CIVIL LAW CASES

There are no such cases that we are aware of.

C4.5 CASES WHERE SM-RELATED EVIDENCE USED OR ADMISSIBLE

The use of SM-related evidence is still very controversial, especially when it is not introduced by the parties. Saskia Elisabeth Schwanz, a family judge from Campo Grande in the State of Mato Grosso, uses Facebook as evidence in alimony cases and explains that, once such evidence is introduced, conciliation rates are around 90% (see www.campograndenews.com.br/lado-b/ comportamento-23-08-2011-08/facebook-vira-dedo-duro-e-entrega-o-ouro-durante-brigas-na-vara-de-familia, retrieved August 7, 2014).

C4.6 SPECIFIC ONLINE ABUSE/ONLINE BULLYING/ CYBERBULLYING LAWS

There are no such laws in Brazil.

C4.7 OTHER LAWS APPLIED TO ONLINE ABUSE/ ONLINE BULLYING/CYBERBULLYING

There are no such other laws that we are aware of.

C4.8 CHILDREN AND SM LAWS OR RULES

There are no such laws that we are aware of, although the internet and SM have been used to combat paedophilia, as police experts monitor suspects and pretend to be children to meet these criminals.

C4.9 EMPLOYEES/EMPLOYMENT SM LAWS OR CASES

There are no specific laws on the matter and case law is scarce, although it seems to point to a restricted use of SM on employment matters. Thus, offending one's employer on Facebook (see www.conjur.com.br/2013-jul-08/comentario-ofensivo-facebook-quebra-confianca-permite-demissao, retrieved August 27, 2014), publishing pictures wearing one's employer uniform (see www.conjur.com.br/2013-nov-20/seguranca-divulgou-fotos-expos-empresa-rede-social-recebe-justa-causa and www.conjur.com.br/2012-jun-12/tst-mantem-demissao-enfermeira-divulgou-fotos-colegas-uti, both retrieved August 29, 2014), liking on Facebook a criticism made by someone else over one's employer (see http://g1.globo.com/tecnologia/noticia/2014/06/justica-julga-valida-demissao-com-justa-causa-por-curtida-no-facebook.html, retrieved August 29, 2014) or commenting on an employer decision on a blog (see www.vermelho.org.br/noticia/124024-6, retrieved August 28, 2014) are examples of employee behaviour that constitute grounds for dismissal on a just cause basis.

C4.10 SCHOOL AND UNIVERSITY STUDENT SM CASES

Even though there is no law or legal cases related to the use of SM in schools and universities, cyberbullying has become a real problem for such institutions (see http://g1.globo.com/educacao/noticia/2014/08/64-de-professores-relatam-bullying-entre-alunos-na-internet-diz-pesquisa.html, retrieved August 15, 2014). Whenever authorities are compelled to act, they use legal dispositions from the Civil Code or the Criminal Code accordingly.

C4.11 RIGHT OR HUMAN RIGHT TO ACCESS THE INTERNET OR SM

Despite many articles and papers suggesting the right of access to the internet as a human right, especially after its recognition by the United Nations, there is no case regarding that matter. However, it is important to mention that Federal Act 12,965 (April 23, 2014), which is commonly referred to as the Internet Bill of Rights, recognizes that the use and access to the internet in Brazil shall observe its importance to the concepts of human personality and citizenship.

C4.12 BANS OR RESTRICTIONS ON INTERNET OR SM

There is no specific case regarding bans or restrictions on the use or of access to the internet and/or SM. Due to the legality principle, widely adopted by the Constitution, there can only be a conviction upon prior law that defines the conduct as an offence and sets the penalties to be served.

C4.13   IDENTITY THEFT (OR EQUIVALENT)

Brazilian laws are not that specific regarding this kind of practice or conduct. Identity theft, or similar, is proscribed and prosecuted under Article 171 of the Brazilian Criminal Code [Federal Act 2,848 (December 7, 1940)], which assigns the penalty of imprisonment from one to five years and a fine.

C4.14   HACKING (OR EQUIVALENT)

There is a severe concern to ensure data integrity in the Public Administration and, as a result, many behaviours were defined as crimes in the Criminal Code. Its Articles 313-A and 313-B define as a crime the act of entering false information on a system or database, as well as inserting or facilitating, authorizing the insertion of false data, changing or wrongly deleting correct data in computerized systems or databases with the purpose of obtaining an undue advantage for himself or another or to cause harm. It is equally a crime to modify or alter the official information system or computer without authorization or request by the competent authority. The penalties for those crimes vary according to the prevailing Acts, and range from imprisonment for three months to 12 years. It is important to note that these acts are defined as crime only for the purposes of modifying or harming computer systems and databases owned by the State. Federal Act 12,737 (November 30, 2012), commonly referred to as the Carolina Dieckmann Act, introduced Articles 154-A and 154-B into the Criminal Code, which provide that the invasion of another's computer device, connected or not to a network due to a breach of security, in order to obtain, tamper with or destroy data or information without express or implied consent of the owner, and even to install vulnerabilities to gain unlawful advantages, shall lead to a sentence of imprisonment from three months to one year and a fine.

C4.15   PRIVACY BY DESIGN (PBD) (OR EQUIVALENT)

There are no cases or discussions regarding privacy by design in Brazil.

C4.16   TWEETING FROM COURTS, AND ANY RULES/LAWS

The use of the internet during trials is not regulated by Brazilian law and is left to the discretion of the courts. It is common, however, to see Tweets and blog posts made in real time from inside the courtroom, especially in famous cases.

C4.17   TELEVISION COURTROOM BROADCASTING OR TELEVISION CAMERAS IN COURT, AND RULES OR LAWS

Courtroom broadcasting is done by TV Justiça (http://www.tvjustica.jus.br/) for most of the High Courts (Federal Supreme Tribunal, Electoral Superior

Tribunal Labor Superior Tribunal) and for its administrative body, the National Council of Justice. The broadcast sessions and some other TV programmes are also available on YouTube (www.youtube.com/user/TVJustica). At their discretion, some State Courts broadcast their sessions on their institutional websites on live streaming.

C4.18   SM IN COURTROOMS

The use of SM in courtrooms has not yet emerged as a problem, even though some controversy arose years ago as the Federal Supreme Court members were photographed while chatting in their intranet during a trial (see www. conjur.com.br/2007-ago-23/globo_capta_conversa_ministros_supremo, retrieved August 19, 2014). Regardless of such event, it is recommended that any material or photograph to be taken inside courtrooms should have been previously authorized by the judging body due to a lack of regimental formalization.

C4.19   USE OF SM AS EVIDENCE IN COURTS

The use of SN as evidence in courts follows the general rules for the distribution of the burden of proof and of the admissibility of electronic evidence. Article 225 of the Civil Code [Federal Act 10,406 (January 10, 2002)] states that photographic, cinematographic reproductions, phonographic records and, in general, any other mechanical of electronic reproduction of facts shall make full proof of their content if the party against whom they appear does not challenge or deny them. It has become common for the use of documents issued in the Public Record Office to prove facts in social networks and on the internet so as to exclude the possibility of denial by the other party, as regulated by Federal Act 8,935 (November 18, 1994). In any case, Federal Act 4,657 (September 4, 1942) states that, where the law is silent, the judge must decide the case in accordance with the general principles of law and observing daily practices equivalent to the nature and complexity of business. Thus, it is possible to conclude that the use of SM as evidence in courts is admitted in Brazil and widely observed in lawsuits.

C4.20   PRIVACY, DATA PROTECTION AND SM

Most of the cases related to privacy matters deal with public personalities (actors, singers, politicians), as was the case for actress Carolina Dieckmann whose case was the trigger for the enactment of legal regulation (see C4.14). Also, there is some legal discussion and scarce case law over a right to oblivion/ anonymity/forgetting on the internet. As for labour matters, controversy arose from an employee's personal use of computers owned by the employer. Case law has settled the issue establishing that employees do not have any expectation of privacy on computers provided by one's employer. Recently, a major Brazilian telecoms provider has been fined for recording and selling its subscriber browser data. Yet, the fine was based on consumer law rather than Brazil's recent internet law mentioned in C4.11 (see www.privacylaws.com/ Publications/enews/International-E-news/Dates/2014/8/Brazil-issues-fine-of-12-million-euros-under-new-Internet-privacy-law/ and www.privacylaws. com/Publications/enews/International-E-news/Dates/2014/8/Brazil-CORRECTION/, retrieved August 29, 2014).

C4.21 SM AND FAMILY LAW CASES

Answers for this matter have been provided at C4.5 and C4.19.

C4.22 SPORTS PERSONS, SPORTS CLUBS AND SM

There are no cases related to the use of SM in sports.

C4.23 PERSONAL RELATIONS AND RELATIONSHIPS

Cases related to SM misuse, especially revenge porn, have come to the courts. Besides the Carolina Dieckmann case (referred to at C4.14 and C4.20), another prominent case deals with journalist Rose Leonel, a victim of revenge porn who won one of the first legal cases on the matter and now devotes her time to run a Non-Governmental Organization that helps victims of revenge porn (for her personal story, see http://revistamarieclaire.globo.com/Revista/ Common/0,,ERT259500-17737,00.html and http://g1.globo.com/pr/norte-noroeste/noticia/2014/03/fui-assassinada-diz-mulher-que-criou-ong-contra-vinganca-porno.html; for the NGO work, see www.mariasdainternet.org, all retrieved August 17, 2014).

C4.24 SM AND PERSONAL DATA OF DECEASED PERSONS

There is no legal regulation or case law on the use of SM personal data of deceased persons. Yet, there is a Bill Proposition being discussed in the House of Representatives (Proposition 4,099/2012) that modifies Article 1.788 of the Brazilian Civil Code to establish a right of digital heritage (see www.ibdfam. org.br/noticias/5118/Projeto+de+Lei+garante+aos+herdeiros+acesso+%C3% A0+heran%C3%A7a+digital, retrieved August 20, 2014). On the other hand, there are some legal discussions over the 'immortalization' of dead people on SM, as seems to be the case with the Facebook profile of Priest José Carlos Medeiros Nunes. Despite his death on January 18, 2013, his profile remains active, as people continue to post comments and ask for blessings (see www. facebook.com/josecarlos.medeirosnunes, retrieved August 29, 2014).

C4.25   SM, WEBSITE, SERVICE PROVIDER OR ISP DEFENCE RULES/LAWS

Recently approved Federal Act 12,965 (see C4.11) sets rules for all internet relations.

C4.26   ECOMMERCE DEFENCE CASES

Most of the case law on e-commerce, similarly to the situation described at C4.20, is based on Brazilian consumer law. A change may be expected with the recent approval of Federal Act 12,965, as mentioned in C4.11 and C4.25.

C4.27   LAWS PROTECTING PERSONAL DATA/ PERSONALLY IDENTIFIABLE INFORMATION

See C4.20.

C4.28   DATA BREACH LAWS AND CUSTOMERS/USERS/ REGULATORS NOTIFIED OF HACKING OR DATA LOSS

There are no such laws that we are aware of.

Bulgaria

Rossitsa Voutcheva, Donika Ilieva and Teodor Milev
BWSP Ilieva, Voutcheva & Co Law Firm

C5.1 INTRODUCTION

Bulgaria is an EU member state and is a Civil Law jurisdiction.

C5.2 SPECIFIC SM AND SN LAWS

There are no specific SM and SN laws; however, for the provision of SM and SN services, the Data Protection Directive 95/46/EC and the Bulgarian Personal Data Protection Act (PDPA)[1] may be applicable in certain situations. In other situations, the Cybercrimes chapter of the Bulgarian Criminal Code (CC)[2] is applicable.

C5.3 SM CRIMINAL LAW CASES

There are criminal law cases related to the use of SM. In penal case No 630/2011 of District Court Ruse, Resolution No 173, the court found the prosecuted guilty in breach of Article 319a of the CC because of access obtained to computer data (SM accounts) without the permission of its owner. The crime is penalized with a fine of up to BGN 3000. This is also the court practice which can be seen from Resolution No 26 on penal case No 15/2013 of District Court Dobrich, which adjudicated in a similar way.

Other criminal law cases involve situations when individuals who use SM propagate or incite discrimination, violence or hatred on the grounds of race, nationality or ethnic origin. Such individuals are penalized by imprisonment from one to four years and a fine from BGN 5,000 to BGN 10,000, as well as public censure according to Article 162, par 1 of the CC.[3] In a specific case,

---

1   Promulgated in State Gazette No 1/04.01.2002, last amended in SG No 15/15.02.2013.
2   Promulgated in SG No 26/2.04.1968, last amended in SG No 84/27.09.2013.
3   Verdict No 430 of 13.10.2011 on penal case No 5980/2011 by Regional Court Varna.

an individual created an event on an SN with a name which incited violence towards an ethnic group in Bulgaria. Due to this fact, the judge panel sentenced him to 10 months' imprisonment, applying Article 162, par 1 of the CC. But, due to the fact that the individual had a clean criminal record, by applying also Article 66, par 1 of the CC, the sentence of imprisonment was replaced with a three-year probation period.

C5.4 SM CIVIL LAW CASES

The civil law cases available are not directly related to SM. Some civil law cases, however, involve SM. In all of the cases below, various Bulgarian and EU regulations were violated by the use of SM.

Breach of IP rights

Use of a photograph published on SM without authorization by a third party. In cases where the photograph is under the protection of the Copyright and Neighbouring Rights Act (CNRA),[4] the owner of the copyrights can seek compensation when his rights have been infringed pursuant to Article 94 of the CNRA. According to Article 18 of the CNRA the author is entitled to exclusive rights to use his work and to permit its use by others. In addition, the user of the photograph can be obliged by the author to mention his name and the author can seek compensation, if this has not been done according to Article 15, par 1, point 4 of the CNRA. Resolution No 2025 of 21.11.2012, No 5673/2012, Sofia City Court is on the issue above. In this case, a newspaper used a professional photograph from the SM account of an individual. The court decided that this was a copyright infringement. Although the individual had made this image public by using it as a profile picture, the photograph's copyright belonged to the photographer, so any proliferation of the image had to be done with the author's consent. In this case, the judge panel applied Article 94 of the CNRA, because of infringement of copyrights, and fined the delinquent BGN 3500.

Breach of the general prohibition not to cause any damage to third parties

When an individual uses SM in order to cause detriment to an individual, the latter can seek compensation, when there is a statement of untrue facts which leads to detriment according to Article 45 of the Obligations and Agreements Act (OAA)[5]. In this sense ruled Resolution No 257 of 13.01.2012, on civil case No 8318/2011, by the Sofia City Court. In this case, an individual made a comment on SM regarding a tourist agency by evaluating negatively the trip in

---

4   Promulgated in SG No 56/29.06.1993, last amended in SG No 25/25.03.2011.
5   Promulgated in SG No 2/05.12.1960, last amended in SG 50/30.05.2008.

which she participated and had been organized by the agency. According to the claimant (the touring agency), the individual's comment has caused damage to the company by ruining the image of the agency and pushing away potential new customers. The claimant sought compensation on the grounds of Article 45 of the OAA. The claim was overruled because the illegal behaviour should be a statement of untrue facts and the personal evaluation cannot be considered as illegal.

Another case is Resolution No 458 of 05.03.2013, No 1719/2011, by the Sofia City Court. In this case, an individual had been hired by a company to participate in an event in which she was informed that only private photographs and video would be taken, and that they would not be proliferated. After a few weeks the individual found out that a video taken from that night had been uploaded on SM. The claimant in this case (the individual) wanted to be compensated according to Article 94 of the CNRA for infringed copyrights. But the judge panel decided that there had been no copyrights created that could have been infringed. In order to create a copyright work, an intentional behaviour is required, while in this case the individual had not even been aware that she was being filmed. Due to this fact, the judge panel declined the claim and advised the claimant to seek compensation through Article 45 of the OAA for damage caused.

C5.5   CASES WHERE SM-RELATED EVIDENCE USED OR ADMISSIBLE

The court practice in Bulgaria is rather controversial. Some of the judges and court panels are of the opinion that SM-related evidence is not admissible.[6] However, there are a lot of other cases where judge panels have resolved differently. In this sense are the following resolutions and verdicts,

- Resolution No 257 of 13.01.2012 on civil case No 8318/2011 by the Sofia City Court: the SN publication was accepted after being protocoled and certified by a notary.

- Verdict No 430 of 13.10.2011 on penal case No 5980/2011 the Regional Court Varna and Resolution 202 on penal case No 491/2013 of the Regional Court Botevgrad: SM was found admissible as evidence in the form of computer forensics expertise.

- Resolution No 1137 of 18.09.2013 on case No 290/2013 of the Competition Protection Commission: an extract from SM may be provided by either side in a litigation case.

---

6   Resolution No 5660 from 10.12.2013 on civil case No 11146/2013 of Varna's Regional Court.

C5.6 SPECIFIC ONLINE ABUSE/ONLINE BULLYING/ CYBERBULLYING LAWS

There are no specific online abuse laws.

C5.7 OTHER LAWS APPLIED TO ONLINE ABUSE/ ONLINE BULLYING/CYBERBULLYING

Although there are no specific laws on cyberbullying, the PDPA and the EU Data Protection Directive 95/46/EC are applicable for most of these cases. From the practice of the European Court of Justice we can see that, in situations where cyberbullying involves posting information about a certain individual, this is considered as personal data processing, because in such cases personal information (such as real name, address etc) is being disclosed to a wide public. By posting this information, the cyberbullies become data controllers. So they cannot disclose this information without consent or without informing the individual whose personal information is being disclosed, depending on the case. This has been confirmed by the European Court of Justice's resolution in 2003 in the so-called 'Lindquist case'. There is no particular practice in Bulgaria regarding the above. However, in the absence of a special law on cyberbullying, by the rules of the generally applicable law, Article 45 of the OAA can be applicable and compensation can be sought upon any damage caused in relation to use of SM.[7]

C5.8 CHILDREN AND SM LAWS OR RULES

There are no specific laws or rules regarding children and SM in our jurisdiction. However, there are specific provisions which may be applicable for the protection of children's personal data in SM. According to Article 11a, par 1 of the Child Protection Act (CPA),[8] there are specific requirements when disclosing child-related information. In case of infringement of the statutory requirements the sanctions are between BGN 1000 and BGN 3000 pursuant to Article 45, par 12 of the CPA. Another provision which may be applicable for child protection and SM is that of Article 45, par 15 of the CPA, according to which any parent, tutor, curator or another person taking care of a child who has allowed the participation of a child in broadcasts and thus poses threats to his/her physical, psychological, moral and/or social development shall be liable to a fine of between BGN 1000 and BGN 2000.

---

7 For example, Resolution No 257 of 13.01.2012 on civil case No 8318/2011 by the Sofia City Court and Resolution No 458 of 05.03.2013 No 1719/2011 by the Sofia City Court.

8 Promulgated in SG No 48/13.06.2000, last amended in SG No 84/27.09.2013.

C5.9 EMPLOYEES/EMPLOYMENT SM LAWS OR CASES

There are cases involving SM and employment, but generally they do not envisage the use of SM in breach of employment duties and as redundancy ground. Under Resolution No 3831 of 04.10.2011 on civil case No 8921/2011 of the Varna Regional Court, an employee was dismissed because of systematic disciplinary offences and one of them involved continuous surfing in the internet, including SM sites. This act is considered as failure to utilize working time efficiently, which is a disciplinary offence according to Article 187, par 1, point 1 of the Bulgarian Labour Code (LC).[9] In a different case, an employee of a Municipality used the internet, including SM, in order to make a statement which ridiculed a member of the Municipal assembly, for which the former was dismissed. According to Article 187, par 1, point 8 of the LC, this behaviour represents a disciplinary offence which ruins the enterprise's reputation. According to the court resolution, the dismissal act was unlawful, because the disciplinary offence was not specified enough. However, we can conclude that, if the dismissal act had specified the disciplinary offence sufficiently, the dismissal would have been lawful.[10]

C5.10 SCHOOL AND UNIVERSITY STUDENT SM CASES

There are no law cases involving students in schools and universities.

C5.11 RIGHT OR HUMAN RIGHT TO ACCESS THE INTERNET OR SM

There are no specific rules or laws in relation to the right of access to internet and SM.

C5.12 BANS OR RESTRICTIONS ON INTERNET OR SM

The only applicable restrictions on the use of internet and SM is according to the list of permitted items, possessions and food products which can be received, used or kept by individuals who have been sentenced to prison or correctional facility which is issued by the Minister of Justice in accordance with Article 122, par 2 of the Enforcement of Penalties and Detention Act.[11] This list includes no items which may provide access to the internet or SM, so we may consider this as an implicit ban on the use of the internet and SM in prison. However, in some prisons, computers have been installed in certain

---

9   Promulgated in SG No 26/1.04.1986, last amended in SG No 1/03.01.2014.
10   Resolution No 4240 of 28.11.2011 on civil case No 10209/2011 of Regional Court Plovdiv.
11   Promulgated in SG No 25/03.04.2009, last amended by SG No 68/02.08.2013.

rooms and the prisoners have limited access to them. The computers have an internet connection, but the prisoners can visit a limited amount of websites and under the supervision of a prison guard. This is at least the case in Varna prison.

C5.13 IDENTITY THEFT (OR EQUIVALENT)

According to the Personal Data Protection Commission's Ordinance on the Minimal Level of Technical and Organizational Measures and Admissible Type of Protection, identity theft is recognised as high (and extremely high) level of interference when processing personal data, which means that this is unlawful processing. In accordance with the PDPA, individuals can claim compensation for the damage incurred when their information has been processed in an unlawful manner. For identity theft, so-called 'hacking' is also applicable because, in most cases, identity theft is done by hacking. The latter is a crime according to Article 319a, par 1 of the CC.

C5.14 HACKING (OR EQUIVALENT)

There are such laws. According to Article 319a, par 1 of the CC: 'Anyone who copies, uses or obtains access to computer data in a computer system without permission, where such is required, shall be punished by a fine of up to BGN 3,000'. According to Article 319a, par 4 of the CC, 'where the hacking has been committed with regard to information that is qualified as state secret the punishment is imprisonment from one to three years'. Where grave consequences have occurred from hacking of a state secret, the punishment is imprisonment of one to eight years according to Article 139a, par 5 of the CC. Other applicable laws regarding hacking are when this involves a data breach. According to Directive 2009/136/EC in the case of a personal data breach, the provider of publicly available electronic communications services shall, without undue delay, notify the personal data breach to the competent national authority. When the personal data breach is likely to adversely affect the personal data or privacy of a subscriber or individual, the provider shall also notify the subscriber or individual of the breach without undue delay.

C5.15 PRIVACY BY DESIGN (PBD) (OR EQUIVALENT)

There are no rules or laws in our jurisdiction regarding privacy by design.[12] However, there is a discussion between the EU's institutions regarding

---

12 Privacy by design means that businesses should build privacy protections into their everyday business practices. This idea is guided by its 7 principles: 1. Proactive not Reactive; 2. Privacy as Default Settings; 3. Privacy Embedded into Design; 4. Full Functionality; 5. End-to-End Security; 6. Visibility and Transparency; 7. Respect for User Privacy.

privacy by design. In a communication from the Commission to the European Parliament, the Council, the European Economic and Social Committee and the Committee of the Regions called 'Smart Grids: from innovation to deployment', privacy by design is considered as a principle which shall be implemented in the near future in EU legislation.

C5.16　TWEETING FROM COURTS, AND ANY RULES/LAWS

There are no rules or laws in connection with Tweeting from courts, so we can consider there are no restrictions.

C5.17　TELEVISION COURTROOM BROADCASTING OR TELEVISION CAMERAS IN COURT, AND RULES OR LAWS

Video cameras and ordinary cameras are explicitly forbidden by the internal rules of every court. However, it is possible to bring in such devices, but only after the explicit preliminary consent of the judge panel.

C5.18　SM IN COURTROOMS

There are no such examples.

C5.19　USE OF SM AS EVIDENCE IN COURTS

The court practice in Bulgaria is rather controversial. Some of the judges and court panels are of the opinion that SM-related evidence is not admissible in Bulgarian court cases.[13] However, there are a lot of other cases where judge panels have resolved differently. In this sense are the following resolutions and verdicts,

- Resolution No 257 of 13.01.2012 on civil case No 8318/2011 by the Sofia City Court: the SN publication was accepted after being protocoled and certified by a notary.

- Verdict No 430 of 13.10.2011 on penal case No 5980/2011 the Regional Court Varna and Resolution 202 on penal case No 491/2013 of the Regional Court Botevgrad: SM was found admissible as evidence in the form of computer forensics expertise.

13　Resolution No 5660 of 10.12.2013 on civil case No 11146/2013 of Regional Court Varna.

- Resolution No 1137 of 18.09.2013 on case No 290/2013 of the Competition Protection Commission: an extract from SM may be provided by either side in a litigation case.

C5.20 PRIVACY, DATA PROTECTION AND SM

Resolution of 28.07.2011 of the Personal Data Protection Commission (PDPC) on complaint No 1586/05.04.2011 dismissed the individual's claim for a breach of his rights. The latter placed a comment on a website. After that, his name and photo remained on the website. The individual considered this as an infringement of his rights according to the PDPA and filed a complaint to the PDPC. The PDPC dismissed the complaint on several grounds. First, the particular SN's General Terms and Conditions permitted the link between the user profile and other websites. The website on which the individual made the comment had asked upon entry that the user logs in, either with a registered profile or with an SM profile. The individual used the second option, so actually the individual had expressed his explicit consent to processing of his personal data, which means that this is legal processing according to Article 4, par 1, point 2 of the PDPA. The website even permitted an individual who makes a comment to limit the possibility of his information to be seen. These are the motives which the PDPC used in order to dismiss the complaint.

C5.21 SM AND FAMILY LAW CASES

In cases related to family law generally, SM is used as a source of information. A particular example is a claim for an increase of the child support paid by the father. The claim is grounded by the use of SM as evidence for the father's place of work and standard of living. However, the juridical panel concludes that the extract from the SM is not enough to make the presumption about the father's salary.[14] But the judge panel determines an increase in child support, because of the well-known fact that the standard of living is higher in that other country of the father's residence.

In various divorce cases, one of the spouses has also used SM as a source of information for the other spouse's behaviour (eg extramarital relationships, or extramarital children); after that, the fact is confirmed by the other spouse and this leads to divorce.

C5.22 SPORTS PERSONS, SPORTS CLUBS AND SM

There have been such cases. In one of them a footballer has been fined BGN 1000 by his coach because of a photo posted on an SM website. The photograph

---

14 For example, Resolution No 246 of 27.01.2011 on civil case No 16600/2010 of Regional Court Varna.

drew media attention because it demonstrated the footballer's homosexual orientation. The coach reacted immediately by fining the footballer, saying that this photograph undermined the club's image, because the players represent not only themselves, but the club as well.

C5.23 PERSONAL RELATIONS AND RELATIONSHIPS

The proliferation of pornographic material on the internet is a crime recognised by Article 159, par 2 of the CC. There have been such cases and the penalty for such actions is imprisonment of up to three years and a fine of between BGN 1000 and BGN 3000. A person's private images are considered as private data, because through them a person can be identified. This means that uploading such images on the internet without the person's consent is an unauthorized proliferation of personal data. This statement has been gathered from the practice of the PDPC.[15]

C5.24 SM AND PERSONAL DATA OF DECEASED PERSONS

No such examples are available.

C5.25 SM, WEBSITE, SERVICE PROVIDER OR ISP DEFENCE RULES/LAWS

The EU eCommerce Directive was transposed through the Bulgarian Electronic Commerce Act (ECA) in 2006. According to Article 4 of the ECA, the provider of information society services must provide, to the service recipients and the competent authorities, direct and permanent access to certain information. Pursuant to Article 6 of the ECA, a service provider who sends unrequested commercial messages by electronic mail without prior consent of the recipient must provide clear and unambiguous identification of the commercial communication as an unrequested one. According to Article 10 of the ECA, the service provider provides appropriate, efficient and accessible technical means for detecting and correcting input errors, before the service recipient makes a statement on the conclusion of the contract.

C5.26 ECOMMERCE DEFENCE CASES

There are cases when information service providers have been sanctioned, because they have not provided direct and permanent access of statutory

---

15   For example, Resolution No 54/23.01.2008 of the Personal Data Protection Commission.

information. Such sanctions are imposed by the Bulgarian Consumer Protection Commission. There are also numerous cases where the service providers send unrequested commercial messages by email without providing clear identification of the unrequested commercial communication. For this, the Consumer Protection Commission has imposed monetary sanctions, as foreseen in the Bulgarian ECA (see C5.25).

C5.27 LAWS PROTECTING PERSONAL DATA/ PERSONALLY IDENTIFIABLE INFORMATION

Relevant laws in Bulgaria are the Bulgarian Personal Data Protection Act which transposes the EU Data Protection Directive (Directive 95/46/EC). The PDPA regulates the protection of rights of individuals with regard to the processing of their personal data. The objective of the PDPA is to guarantee the inviolability of personality and privacy by ensuring protection of individuals in case of unauthorised processing of personal data relating to them, in the process of free movement of data.

C5.28 DATA BREACH LAWS AND CUSTOMERS/ USERS/REGULATORS NOTIFIED OF HACKING OR DATA LOSS

According to Directive 2009/136/EC in the case of a personal data breach, the provider of publicly available electronic communications services shall, without undue delay, notify the personal data breach to the competent national authority. When the personal data breach is likely to adversely affect the personal data or privacy of a subscriber or individual, the provider shall also notify the subscriber or individual of the breach without undue delay. Article 319a of the CC is also applicable here. Such crimes are penalized with a fine of up to BGN 3000.

Chapter C6

China

Eric Su (Su Jianfei)
HFG

C6.1 INTRODUCTION

China is a Civil Law mixed system.

C6.2 SPECIFIC SM AND SN LAWS

There does not appear to be any specific SM or SN law; however, the general rules can be found in Article 36 of the Tort Law, which reads that,

> 'The internet users and internet service providers shall assume tort liability if they utilize the internet to infringe upon civil rights and interests of others. If an internet user commits tortious acts through internet services, the infringer shall be entitled to inform the internet service provider to take necessary measures, including, inter alia, deletion, blocking and unlinking. If the internet service provider fails to take necessary measures in a timely manner upon notification, it shall be jointly and severally liable with the said internet user for the extended damage. If an internet service provider is aware that an internet user is infringing on the civil rights and interests of others through its internet services and fails to take necessary measures, it shall be jointly and severally liable with the said internet user for such infringement.'

Also, because the contents that emerge or are created on SM may constitute works, so the Copyright Law can be applied to the affairs concerning SM, and the most relevant right may be the right of dissemination via the internet.

Besides, because the users have disclosed/registered their private information on the SN, due to many kinds of reasons, these information can be acquired or provided to other parties, which can result in some criminal offences, such as fraud causing the Criminal Law to be applied to. Meanwhile, the Standing Committee of the National People's Congress (NPC) has issued a Decision on Strengthening Information Protection on Networks on 28 December 2012, which consists of 12 Articles and aims to strengthen information protection.

C6.3   SM CRIMINAL LAW CASES

There is a criminal case concerning SM reported by the press; in this case, the suspect, a junior school student, issued three Weibo (similar to Tweets) expressing his doubt about a criminal case in Gansu, and the police charged him with aggravated assault, based on the fact that his Weibo had been forwarded up to 500 times. And the recent news is that the junior school student has been released.

C6.4   SM CIVIL LAW CASES

There is a civil case concerning the Huagai Company, which claimed copyright infringement against the defendant based on the unauthorized use of a copyright picture forwarded on Weibo. The Baiyun People's Court in Guangzhou City made awards in relation to the plaintiff's claims.

C6.5   CASES WHERE SM-RELATED EVIDENCE USED OR ADMISSIBLE

Theoretically, SM-related evidence can disclose some technology as prior art under the patent law. I have not found a case about SN related evidence, however, there is a case concerning the internet evidence admitted to prove some technology constituted prior art in invalidation announcement by Patent Re-examination Board. The case number is 161161.

C6.6   SPECIFIC ONLINE ABUSE/ONLINE BULLYING/ CYBERBULLYING LAWS

There does not appear to be any specific online abuse law; however, such activity can be subject to liability of infringement against the right of reputation or freedom of the person and, if severely, it can be charged with libel.

C6.7   OTHER LAWS APPLIED TO ONLINE ABUSE/ ONLINE BULLYING/CYBERBULLYING

Online abuse can be subject to liability of infringement against the right of reputation or freedom of the person according to civil law and, if severely, it can be charged with libel under criminal law.

C6.8   CHILDREN AND SM LAWS OR RULES

There is no law or rule specific to children and SM.

C6.9   EMPLOYEES/EMPLOYMENT SM LAWS OR CASES

There do not appear to be any laws involving SM and employees. However, the employer can make its internal regulations with respect to employee use of SM; if violated by the employee, Article 39 of the Labour Law applies, which allows the employer to terminate the contract in case the employee violates the internal regulations.

C6.10   SCHOOL AND UNIVERSITY STUDENT SM CASES

There does not appear to be any law or case involving students in schools and universities in relation to the use of SM. The only relevant rule we can find is a principled provision addressed in Article 48 of the University Regulation System Governing Students, which reads that the students shall comply with the competent regulations made by the country or universities to use internet, and shall not log on to illegal websites or disseminate harmful information.

C6.11   RIGHT OR HUMAN RIGHT TO ACCESS THE INTERNET OR SM

There does not appear to be any literature, case, rule or law in relation to a right or human right of access to the internet and/or SM in our country. However, actually, people in our country are entitled to access the internet regardless of an express right embedded in the constitution or law, which can be deemed as a right originating from natural law.

C6.12   BANS OR RESTRICTIONS ON INTERNET OR SM

There are some rules in relation to bans or restrictions on the use of access to the internet. In the civil law field, specifically, copyright law allows the copyright holder to establish technology measures to protect their copyright or copyright-related rights in case some other parties access or use their works without authority. In the criminal law field, there are charges against offences concerning the internet, eg trespass on computer information system or illegal destruction of computer information system, which are specified in Articles 255 and 256 of the Criminal Law.

C6.13   IDENTITY THEFT (OR EQUIVALENT)

There is a specific law relating to identity theft (or equivalent), which is addressed in Amendment VII to the Criminal Law of the People's Republic of China. Article 253 (A) is added after Article 253 of the Criminal Law, and reads as follows,

'Any staff member of a State body, or an organization of finance, telecommunication, transportation, education, or health care, etc, violates the State regulations, by selling or illegally providing the citizens' personal information obtained during the course of performing duties or providing services, and in such cases if the circumstances are serious, then such staff member shall be sentenced to a fixed-term imprisonment of not more than three years or criminal detention with a fine imposed concurrently or shall be only subject to a fine.

Whoever illegally obtains the above-mentioned information by theft or through other means, and in such cases if the circumstances are serious, then such person shall be punished in accordance with the provisions of the preceding paragraph.

Where an organization commits any of the crimes mentioned in the preceding two paragraphs, a fine shall be imposed on the organization, and the persons who are directly in charge of the organization and such other persons who are directly responsible for the crime shall be punished respectively in accordance with provisions of the preceding two paragraphs.'

C6.14   HACKING (OR EQUIVALENT)

As stated in C6.13, if someone conducts hacking, he/she shall be subject to civil or criminal liability.

C6.15   PRIVACY BY DESIGN (PBD) (OR EQUIVALENT)

Privacy by design is an approach to system engineering which takes privacy into account throughout the whole engineering process. There does not appear to be any rule, law or discussion relating to privacy by design.

C6.16   TWEETING FROM COURTS, AND ANY RULES/LAWS

There does not appear to be a clear rule about whether it is permissible to Tweet/Weibo from court. The actual facts are that many courts themselves have been using Weibo to broadcast their trial, and the typical one is the Bo Xilai case in Jinan Intermediate People's Court. However, whether the law allows Tweeting from court is controversial.

C6.17   TELEVISION COURTROOM BROADCASTING OR TELEVISION CAMERAS IN COURT, AND RULES OR LAWS

In our jurisdiction, there may be television courtroom broadcasting or television cameras in court which can be conducted by the court themselves (see C6.16) and the press invited or allowed by the court. And there is a concrete rule addressed in 'Trial Rule of People's Court' issued by the Supreme People's Court in 1993, of which Article 9 reads that the auditors could not take sound, camera or video recording during the trial.

C6.18 SM IN COURTROOMS

In a criminal case, some lawyers try to, and actually do, broadcast the trial and express their comment on the trial. This has caused opposition from the court, which banned internet access so that lawyers could not use Weibo. However, the court's action has been criticized by some lawyers, who allege that it is based on no legal grounds.

C6.19 USE OF SM AS EVIDENCE IN COURTS

There does not appear to be a law regulating electronic evidence. However, some infringement or offence could be proved by the SM evidence, especially which may be critical or important evidence; for example, the Supreme Court has interpreted that, if the libel information on a website has been scanned, clicked 5,000 or more times, or forwarded up to 500 or more times, this constitutes the severe circumstances provided in Article 246(1) of the Criminal Law. So the charge depends largely on the SM evidence, which also will be adopted by the court.

C6.20 PRIVACY, DATA PROTECTION AND SM

There are some news reports about the private information leak on RenRen Website (SN) and Weibo. But, due to the lack of a specific law regulating the problem, it is difficult to protect privacy or personal data. The legal ground that can be relied on is the privacy right protected by Tort Law and the Decision of the Standing Committee of the NPC on Strengthening Information Protection on Networks (see C6.2).

C6.21 SM AND FAMILY LAW CASES

There does not appear to be any example of controversies or cases in relation to SM and family law cases.

C6.22 SPORTS PERSONS, SPORTS CLUBS AND SM

Generally, China has an open attitude towards the sports persons and SM, and until now there is not any regulation about SM use by sports persons and sports clubs. There exist some famous Weibo accounts of sports persons, such as Fangzhe, the gold medal gymnast at the London Olympic Games in 2012.

C6.23   PERSONAL RELATIONS AND RELATIONSHIPS

There are some examples in relation to personal relations and relationships. One famous party in the controversies is called Fangzhouzi, who is keening on pointing out some famous persons' embarrassment or unfaithfulness, and his opponents include Hanhan, a famous writer of liberalism and Cui Yongyuan, the famous independent TV media person. Recently, Fang and Cui have been arguing about genetically modified food (GMF), which is the hottest topic on Weibo.

C6.24   SM AND PERSONAL DATA OF DECEASED PERSONS

There do not appear to be any particulars about the SM personal data of deceased persons; the account of the deceased person can be taken charge by his relatives or friends, or be cancelled. And the most common circumstance is the account will be kept the same status as the date of last updating before death, which attracts fewer people to visit.

C6.25   SM, WEBSITE, SERVICE PROVIDER OR ISP DEFENCE RULES/LAWS

The safe-harbour defence is available to website service providers, which is embedded in Articles 22 and 23 of the Regulations on the Protection of Right of Dissemination via Information Network, which specify as follows,

'Article 22: A Web service provider shall be exempted from liability for compensation when providing those who receive its services with information storage space so as to enable them to make works, performances, or sounds or visual recordings available to the public via information network, provided that the following conditions are met,

(1)   The information storage space is clearly indicated as having been provided for use by those who receive its services, accompanied by an announcement on the name, contact person, and Web address of the Web service provider;

(2)   It has not altered the works, performances, or sound or visual recordings provided by those who receive its services;

(3)   It is unaware of, and has no justified reason to be aware of, the infringement of a work, performance, or sound or visual recording provided by anyone who receives its services;

(4)   It has gained no economic benefits directly from works, performances, or sound or visual recordings provided by those who receive its services; and

(5)   It has, pursuant to these Regulations, deleted the work, performance, or sound or visual recording regarded by the right owner as involving infringement after receiving the right owner's written notice.

Article 23: A Web service provider that provides a search or link service to those who receive its services shall be exempted from liability for compensation if it has disabled, in accordance with these Regulations, the link to an infringing work, performance, or sound or visual recording after receiving the right owner's written notice, unless it is aware of or should be aware of the infringement of that work, performance, or sound or visual recording, in which case it shall bear joint liability for the infringement.'

C6.26   ECOMMERCE DEFENCE CASES

There are many cases relating to the safe harbour defence, eg *Sohu vs Tudou* (2010), whose registered users uploaded a movie copyrighted by Sohu, and Tudou raised safe-harbour defence against Sohu's claim. However, the Shanghai First Intermediate People's Court did not support Tudou's defence, based on the fact that Tudou was aware of the infringing works on its website and did not take actions to stop it, which had constituted contributory infringement. The case citation is (2010) 沪一中民五(知)终字第130号.

C6.27   LAWS PROTECTING PERSONAL DATA/ PERSONALLY IDENTIFIABLE INFORMATION

As stated in C6.26, there is not any special law provided for the protection of personal data or personally identifiable information, but there are some scattered rules embedded in civil law and criminal law. Besides, the Decision of the Standing Committee of the NPC on Strengthening Information Protection on Networks applies when dealing with the protection of privacy or data protection.

C6.28   DATA BREACH LAWS AND CUSTOMERS/ USERS/REGULATORS NOTIFIED OF HACKING OR DATA LOSS

There does not appear to be any data breach law providing for customers, users and regulators to be notified if an organization's data and/or systems have been hacked or data otherwise lost. Whether to notify when the data is disclosed or hacked depends on the organization.

Chapter C7

Czech Republic

Ronald Given, Partner
Katerina Kulhankova, Associate
Wolf Theiss

C7.1 INTRODUCTION

The Czech Republic is an EU member state and is a Civil Law jurisdiction.

C7.2 SPECIFIC SM AND SN LAWS

There are no specific SM and SN laws in the Czech Republic.

C7.3 SM CRIMINAL LAW CASES

In general, SN criminal law cases in the Czech Republic deal mainly with the following: cyberbullying; cyber-grooming; cyber-stalking; sexting; identity theft; procuring and possessing passwords to computer systems; unauthorized access to a computer system; defamation; and distribution of child pornography.

In the Czech Republic, only the court decisions deemed by judges to be significant and essential are publicly available in the online database. The public usually does not become aware of a specific case unless the case reaches a court of higher instance or if it is made public by the media. Like in most countries, certain sensational cases capture the public interest and gain media attention. Please see a few examples below:

Supreme Court: case no 5 Tdo 641/2012 dated 26 July 2012

The defendant was accused of committing the crime of production and other handling of child pornography as well as sexual abuse and a misdemeanour for endangering a child's upbringing. In this case, the defendant agreed via the online SN 'lide.cz' to meet with an under-age girl with whom he subsequently had consensual sex. The court established that the defendant knew the girl was less than the consensual age of fifteen. The defendant recorded the above-mentioned acts on his mobile phone and also took photos which he sent to her SN private profile mailbox on 'lide.cz'. The girl opened the message and stored its content on the desktop of her friend's computer. It was later discovered there by other adults.

An initial question before the court was whether the defendant had 'made an image of sexual nature depicting a child publicly accessible'. In the opinion of the Supreme Court the actual sending of pornographic work existing in electronic form, via electronic mail to the private storage space used by a particular person, did not constitute 'making the image publicly accessible'. It therefore did not meet the requirements for the special criminal offence of 'making an image depicting a child publicly accessible'. The court stated that 'making the image publicly accessible' would mean, for example, posting it on an SM website. This decision of the Supreme Court was also supported by the Constitutional Court decision in case no. I.ÚS 1428/13 dated 20 August 2013.

Regional Court in Plzeň: case no 50 To 30/2014 – 474 dated 10 March 2014

A well-known court expert witness was accused of taking consensual naked photos of his former girlfriend during intercourse. After the relationship ended and without her knowledge, he created a Facebook profile under her given name and surname where he published the photos and then made them available to specifically selected users. Moreover, he wrote at least eight letters on behalf of his ex-girlfriend without her knowledge, in which he described her personality in a disparaging way and sent these humiliating letters, including the copies of the Facebook page with the intimate photographs, to her employer, colleagues and ex-boyfriend.

In court, the conduct was found to be a misdemeanour for damage to another person's rights. The court imposed a fine of approximately EUR 1,095 on the defendant. The court ordered that, if the fine was not paid within the stipulated deadline, an alternative penalty of three months' imprisonment would be enforced.

C7.4   SM CIVIL LAW CASES

The civil law cases usually concern defamation, which does not have to be qualified as a criminal offence and therefore can only have civil law consequences. The legal basis for civil law cases usually arises from the Act No 262/2006 Coll, Labour Code, as amended (the 'Labour Code') or the Act No 89/2012 Coll, Civil Code, as amended (the 'Civil Code').

Cases based on the Labour Code usually arise when an employee criticizes their employer on an SM website. If the criticism is extensive, the employment relationship with the employee may be terminated immediately or the employee may be persuaded to sign an agreement on termination of employment. To our knowledge, there are no higher-court decisions in this regard.

A more common case would be a breach of an employee's duty not to use an employer's computer for non-working purposes. In case the breach is extensive, the employment relationship may be terminated immediately, as stated in the decision of the following case:

Supreme Court: case no 21 Cdo 1771/2011 dated 16 August 2012:

In this case, the employee visited online news and SM websites with questionable or sensitive content, violating agreed employment rules. His employment was immediately terminated. The employee, as plaintiff, argued that, although he used the computer for surfing that was not part of his work obligations, it did not affect his working duties and there was no serious breach of his work obligations. The plaintiff also argued that the employer secretly monitored his internet use in violation of the Labour Code. The court determined that employees may use the resources of the employer including computer technology or phones for their personal use, but only with the consent of the employer. The court decided that immediate termination of employment was justified in this case, as the employer had created rules that employees were not allowed to use computers during working hours for personal purposes. The employee had been notified of the rules.

C7.5 CASES WHERE SM-RELATED EVIDENCE USED OR ADMISSIBLE

SM-related evidence would generally be admissible, provided that the content is sufficiently protected from abuse. Czech law does not contain restrictions regarding the non-permissibility of objects serving as evidence. It is therefore up to the court's sole discretion to determine whether a piece of evidence submitted will be allowed to serve as evidence. In order to determine the genuineness of evidence, courts may require direct access to the SM account in question, rather than settling for a simple screenshot, as screenshots can easily be manipulated and modified. We would recommend asking a notary public to officially record the content on an SM site using the notary stamp, prior to the court proceeding. This procedure would be faster and may be accepted by court even if the content on the SM site has been deleted afterwards. Again, all this depends on the court's discretion and the particular circumstances of the case.

There have been cases of Facebook messages serving as evidence, and a friendship on Facebook was proposed as evidence for the exclusion of a judge for bias.

Supreme Court: case no 7 Tdo 1289/2011 dated 16 November 2011

In this case, the district court judge (ruling as a single judge of 1st instance) was a 'Facebook friend' with another judge of the same court. The second judge was a 'Facebook friend' with the victim and witness to the case under consideration. The district court issued a decision in October 2010 which was followed by an appeal. In January 2011, after the judgment of the district court, the judge deciding in the 1st instance became a 'Facebook friend' with the witness as well. At the appeal, the appellant objected that the 1st instance judge was biased. The appellate court rejected the argument, although it admitted that the fact that the judge is a 'Facebook friend' with the witness may cause legitimate concerns. However, since the friendship occurred three months after the verdict and the judge testified that, at the time of the decision, he did not know the witness, the appellate court did not accept the objection and upheld the decision of the district court.

The Supreme Court upheld the decisions of the previous instances and added that the judge could not be responsible for the other relationships of his 'Facebook friends'. The fact of such electronic friendship does not constitute a basis for bias. Finally, the court noted that it is always necessary to assess the true nature of the friendship, not its mere presence on a social network.

C7.6 SPECIFIC ONLINE ABUSE/ONLINE BULLYING/ CYBERBULLYING LAWS

There are no such laws in the Czech Republic.

C7.7 OTHER LAWS APPLIED TO ONLINE ABUSE/ ONLINE BULLYING/CYBERBULLYING

The Act No. 40/2009 Coll, Criminal Code, as amended (the 'Criminal Code') and the Act No 101/2000 Coll, on personal data protection (the 'Personal Data Protection Act') would serve as legal grounds for dealing with cases of online abuse, online bullying and cyberbullying cases.

Online abuse, online bullying and cyberbullying cases are not classified as criminal offences, but they may be subsumed by the Criminal Code under the following criminal acts:

- complicity in suicide (Article 144),

- restriction of personal freedom (Article 171),

- blackmailing (Article 175),

- unauthorized use of personal data (Article 180),

- damage to another person's rights (Article 181),

- breach of the confidentiality of transmitted information (Article 182),

- breach of the confidentiality of papers and other documents retained in privacy (Article 183),

- defamation (Article 184),

- spreading of pornography (Article 191),

- production and other handling of child pornography (Article 192),

- endangerment of child's upbringing (Article 201),

- criminal fraud (Article 209),

- unauthorized access to computer systems and data carrier (Article 230),

- provision and possession of an access device and the password to a computer system and other such data (Article 231),

- damage to the record in the computer system and the information medium and interference in computer equipment from negligence (Article 232),

- violence against a group of people or an individual (Article 352),

- dangerous threating (Article 353),

- stalking (Article 354),

- incitement to hatred against a group of individuals or restriction of their rights and freedoms (Article 356), and

- spreading false news (Article 357).

The Personal Data Protection Act ensures the fundamental rights of a citizen to be protected against unauthorized interference into their private and personal life, and unauthorized collection, disclosure, or other misuse of personal data.

C7.8   CHILDREN AND SM LAWS OR RULES

There are no laws or rules specific to children and SM in the Czech Republic.

However, Czech law in general provides greater protection to children (ie persons under 18 years of age). Furthermore, the Criminal Code establishes certain specific offences protecting children, such as: endangerment of child's upbringing (Article 201); tempting a child to sexual intercourse (Article 202); abuse of a child when producing pornography (Article 193); and production and other disposition with children's pornography (Article 192).

C7.9   EMPLOYEES/EMPLOYMENT SM LAWS OR CASES

There are no specific laws relating to employees using SM in the Czech Republic. As mentioned at C7.4, the Labour Code provides the employer with the authority to forbid the use of work property by employees for personal purposes. The Labour Code also entitles the employer to, within reason, control whether the employees obey such rule; however, the employer may not, without a serious reason, breach the employee's right to privacy.

There have been some cases when the employer terminated the employment relationship with the employee on the grounds of the employee's misuse of working devices, namely spending time on SM websites (see C7.4). However, certain limitations regarding the extent of control apply, and the admissibility of termination of an employment relationship without notice will be assessed in each case individually with regard to the particular circumstances. Please note that termination without previous notice is considered an extreme measure and shall be used only in the most serious situations. In other cases, the employer may, for example, claim damages for lost profits due to the inactivity of the employee while on SM or issue a warning to the employee.

The employer may monitor the activities of the employee to a certain extent. The most common practice for doing so, mainly in larger companies due to the financial constraints, is to assess data about SM usage in an anonymous manner. If the employer finds an issue with the data collected, he can then connect the anonymous data back to the individual employee.

C7.10 SCHOOL AND UNIVERSITY STUDENT SM CASES

In the Czech Republic, there are no laws or cases involving students in schools and universities in relation to SM use. Students are required to comply with the school's internal rules and regulations which may, for example, cover the usage of cell phones, wireless internet connections (if applicable) regarding SM websites or block SM websites completely. Some schools (but not universities) have opted to block SM websites. Unfortunately, no statistical data regarding the percentage is available. As to individual criminal cases concerning school students, there are cases of production and other disposition with child pornography, sexual abuse, blackmailing, tempting to sexual intercourse, rape, online abuse, online bullying and cyberbullying in which under-age students were involved.

C7.11 RIGHT OR HUMAN RIGHT TO ACCESS THE INTERNET OR SM

There is no literature, cases, rules or laws regarding the right or human right to access SM websites. There are only some materials regarding the right and human right to access the internet in general.

Constitutional Court: case no I ÚS 22/10 dated 7 April 2010

The Constitutional Court declared that people are not obliged to limit their personal expenses in order to be able to allow an attorney for court representation. In particular, the Constitutional Court ruled that each individual has a right to a private life and access to the internet is a part of this privacy.

C7.12 BANS OR RESTRICTIONS ON INTERNET OR SM

To our knowledge, there are no cases or laws restricting the use of SN or internet to persons convicted for particular types of criminal offences.

Under Act No 480/2004 Coll, on some services of information society, as amended, it is prohibited for legal entities or persons carrying out business to advertise (eg via email) unless such messages comply with legal requirements. Such messages: (i) may not be sent without the consent of the addressee; (ii) must be clearly and distinctly marked as commercial communications; (iii) cannot hide or conceal the identity of the sender; (iv) must contain a valid address to which the recipient may send a request for termination of such communications; or (v) must provide the opportunity to clearly, simply and free of charge refuse consent to the use of electronic contact details. If the legal entities or persons carrying out business do not comply with the requirements, they can be fined up to CZK 1,000,000 (approx EUR 36,500) by the Data Protection Office (the 'DPO').

In the Czech Republic, there is no law prohibiting an internet connection provider from entering into an agreement which allows the provider to, for example, limit the user's access to certain information or reduce the speed of data transfer after exhausting a data limit. Based on this, some internet providers block traffic on some ports, limit the data transfer speed or block access to certain websites. Currently, some of the largest internet connection providers (such as Telefónica O2 Czech Republic, Vodafone Czech Republic and T-Mobile Czech Republic) restrict or limit access to certain websites that contain illegal content. Providers offering such incomplete connection must clearly indicate and present the service as limited and not as a full service with access to the internet.

C7.13 IDENTITY THEFT (OR EQUIVALENT)

Each individual has a right for protection of personality (identity). This right is embedded in many laws, mainly the Constitutional Act No 2/1992 Coll, Charter of fundamental rights and freedoms, as amended (the 'Charter'), the Civil Code, the Labour Code, the Criminal Code, the Data Protection Act, and the Act No 46/2000 Coll, on rights and obligations for publishing periodic press and on amendments to other Acts (Printing Press Act).

In case an unlawful breach occurs, the person suffering damage may ask the court to order: (i) that the intruder must cease the unlawful breach; (ii) a remedy of the unlawful breach; and (iii) adequate compensation.

In civil proceedings, adequate compensation is usually provided in the form of public apology (moral satisfaction), unless a mere apology would not suffice due to the intensity of the breach. In such a case, the person suffering damage may demand financial compensation.

Moreover, for extreme cases, the Criminal Code offers the following offences which may be applicable in case of identity theft:

- Unlawful access to a computer system and data storage device (Article 230) provides protection in cases where a third person gains unlawful access to one's computer (or data storage device) by breaking a safety measure. In this case, mere breach of a simple password suffices; it is not necessary that the intruder actually steals and uses the data.

- Procuring and processing of an entry device and a password to a computer system and other such data (Article 231) covers whatever processing (eg also possession) of a device, software, database of passwords, which allows the offence to be committed. In this case, it is necessary to prove the intent of the intruder. This provision aims to minimize any attempts to acquire such data by broadening the circle of responsible persons.

- Damage to another person's rights (Article 181) consists of causing serious harm to someone by leading him/her into error; or by using someone's mistake.

C7.14 HACKING (OR EQUIVALENT)

Hacking mainly falls within the scope of three criminal offences in the Criminal Code:

- unlawful access to a computer system and data storage device (Article 230);

- breach of the confidentiality of transmitted information (Article 182); and

- breach of the confidentiality of papers and other documents retained in privacy (Article 183).

Also, a completely new Act on Cyber Security is currently in the legislative process. The contemplated effective date is set as of 1 January 2015. The final wording of the Act is not yet determined, as there are extensive discussions over the proposal, mostly concerning the scope of authority of the national regulator, the National Security Authority ('NSA'). The Act aims to create rights and responsibilities necessary for ensuring security in cyberspace. Its purpose is to ensure protection against targeted attacks on information infrastructure and national IT systems. The Act shall impact only service providers (ie website operators, web hosting providers) and not common users. Under this Act, service providers will be obliged to notify the NSA about events and incidents which could potentially endanger the safety of the services. The NSA will be entitled to adopt countermeasures in order to remove the danger. Also, the proposed Act allows declaring a state of cyber emergency in case the safety of informational systems or networks of electronic communications is endangered and the interests of the Czech Republic could be damaged as a result of the potential incident. The Act does not create civil or criminal liability, as it is covered by the Civil and Criminal Codes, but establishes a system of safety measures which are intended to ensure that cyber safety incidents do not occur, or to moderate the fallout in case they do.

C7.15 PRIVACY BY DESIGN (PBD) (OR EQUIVALENT)

The PbD concept is not very well known in the Czech Republic. There are only general rules for processing and controlling personal data in the Data Protection Act and a rule in the Legislative Rules of the Government, which obliges the government to consider and assess the impact of proposals of new laws in relation to one's protection of privacy and personal data.

The general data protection rules are harmonized on the EU level. Therefore, the Czech Republic is obliged to ensure a certain level of personal data protection. The European Data Protection Directive has been transposed into Czech law. According to unofficial information acquired from the DPO in an anonymous telephone conversation, PbD in the Czech Republic is guaranteed merely on the basis of the Data Protection Act. In addition, the DPO does not plan any further legislative modifications or new laws regarding the PbD concept.

The clause in the Legislative Rules of the Government regarding obligatory consideration and assessment of the impact of proposals of new laws was added in 2012. The addition has not become known to the general public; however, professional commentators praised the addition of the new provision, as well as the DPO in its annual report.

C7.16 TWEETING FROM COURTS, AND ANY RULES/LAWS

There are three regimes in the Czech court proceedings: civil proceedings, as well as criminal proceedings against adults, may be generally broadcast (ie Twitter can be used during such proceedings). Judges can, however, in exceptional cases suspend the broadcasting of the proceedings. Criminal proceedings against people younger than 18 years of age cannot, under any circumstances, be broadcast. See further details below.

Accessibility of the public to court proceedings is one of the basic requirements of the Czech judiciary system (with the exception of criminal proceedings against people younger than 18 years of age – see details below).

First, public accessibility is the principal attribute that can ensure the right to a fair trial, which is embedded in the Charter. By making the proceedings public, the parties to the proceedings are protected from arbitrary and uncontrolled decision-making of courts. Public accessibility therefore helps to ensure public

277

trust in the judiciary, makes it transparent and is one of the guarantees of the impartiality of the judges, because the public can see for itself whether the judge makes his decisions under visible supervision or pressure.

Secondly, public access to trials helps to discourage criminal behaviour. By making the proceedings accessible to the public, the individuals (mostly in criminal cases) can be subject to public censure and hence are less likely to commit offences or crimes in the future.

Act No 99/1963, Civil Procedure, as amended (the 'Civil Procedure Code') states that court sessions are public. Members of the public can be excluded only in cases: (i) where classified information regarding interests of the Czech Republic is concerned; (ii) where business secrets are concerned; (iii) where important interests of the parties to the case are concerned; and (iv) where decency and morals could be endangered. In cases where members of the public are excluded, judges can allow certain individuals to be present at the sessions, while ensuring that they are obliged to maintain secrecy about everything they find out about the categories of information mentioned in (i) to (iii) above. Furthermore, judges can exclude minors and persons that could disturb the peaceful process of the proceedings. Act No 6/2002 Coll, on courts and judges, as amended (the 'Act on Courts and Judges') reiterates the public nature of the proceedings, while adding that, although the public can be excluded from the sessions, the judgments are always promulgated publicly.

The Act on Courts and Judges states that the audio and video broadcasting and procurement of video recordings may be carried out only with the previous consent of the judge (senate of judges). The judge (senate) may disallow the broadcasting or recording of the sessions where such broadcasting or recording could negatively affect the actual proceedings. In order to ensure the principle of publicity is preserved, though, judges should disallow recording or broadcasting of the proceedings only in rare cases. In the case of audio recording, mere notification of the judge (senate) is sufficient. For criminal proceedings against adults under Act No 141/1964 Coll, Criminal Procedure, as amended (the 'Criminal Procedure Code'), identical conditions apply.

Generally, the public is excluded from legal proceedings concerning minors under the age of 18, under Act No 218/2003 Coll, on judiciary in delinquency of minors (the 'Juvenile Delinquency Act'). The intention of the Act on Juvenile Delinquency is to limit the negative impact on the minors connected with excessive public attention, to eliminate defamatory influences, and to protect the privacy of the minor. At the request of the minor and where the court does not find it to be against the interests of the minor, the judge can allow for the proceedings to be public. Even if the judge allows for the proceedings to be public, no one can make public any information (including the given name and the surname of the minor) which would enable identification of the minor in any way. In addition, it is prohibited to make public any text or any depiction regarding the identity of the minor (eg even sketched portraits).

C7.17 TELEVISION COURTROOM BROADCASTING OR TELEVISION CAMERAS IN COURT, AND RULES OR LAWS

Television courtroom broadcasting or television cameras in court are allowed, provided that certain conditions are met. See C7.16 for more details.

C7.18 SM IN COURTROOMS

There are no examples of controversies in relation to the use of SM in courtrooms *per se*. However, see below for details of recent notable cases regarding television broadcasting.

Supreme Court: case no 8 Tdo 972/2011 dated 15 December 2011

One of the most closely watched proceedings was a case involving the so-called 'Vítkov arsonists', who threw Molotov cocktails into the windows of a Romani (the Anglophonic exonym is 'gypsy') house and caused severe burns to a Romani girl. Public television broadcast live from the court sessions including the closing speeches and the judgment. The first arsonist received a sentence of 22 years' imprisonment, and the second was sentenced to 20 years' imprisonment, in addition to paying compensation for damages. The decision of the chief judge to allow the live broadcasting inspired an online discussion on whether to allow live broadcasting or not, with valid arguments on both sides.

According to the arguments, the direct audio or video broadcasting could, depending on the circumstances of the case, have a negative impact on the proceedings and cause (i) a change in the conditions in the courtroom, (ii) negative pressure on the participants and witnesses or even unduly influence their behaviour, and (iii) thus impair the proper administration of justice.

Constitutional Court: case no I ÚS 2208/13 dated 11 December 2013

This case concerned the Central Bohemian governor (in Czech *hejtman*) and member of the Parliament, David Rath. Mr Rath was arrested for allegedly accepting a bribe for manipulating public procurement, when he was caught with a wine box containing CZK 7 million in cash (approx EUR 255,000). The case attracted the attention of the media and the public from the very beginning. Potentially, negative media influence was considerable. The main witness (and co-accused) in this case, Ivana Salačová, testified that the media played an important role. Although the court did not allow video broadcasting during the trial, journalists wrote online reports. One of the journalists Tweeted during the trial that he was surprised that Salačová was not hit by a car yet. Upon hearing the news of this Tweet, Salačová had an emotional breakdown and the court had to be interrupted, as she was concerned for her own and her family's safety. This might prove that online Tweeting and reports may have the same or similar effects as live broadcasting.

High Court in Prague: case no 7 To 121/2006 dated 12 December 2006

The possibility of live broadcasting was also subject to a dispute in 2004. The chief judge of the court of appeals allowed live broadcasting in the murder case preparation of the journalist Sabina Slonková by a group of lawyers. Five TV cameras were supposed to be present in the court. Many public figures, including the then president, Václav Klaus, voiced their concern over the decision, generally stating that the broadcasting could cause the proceedings to become politicized. After further discussion, the chief judge prohibited the live broadcasting.

C7.19 USE OF SM AS EVIDENCE IN COURTS

See C7.5.

C7.20 PRIVACY, DATA PROTECTION AND SM

Minor breaches of privacy and data protection happen quite often. Only a small percentage, however, reach the relevant authorities. Here are some specific examples from different privacy and data protection areas.

Cyber-stalking

The defendant (in case no 8 Tdo 1503/2011 dated 30 November 2011, tried by the Municipal Court in Prague) was a woman employed as a janitor in a company, where the plaintiff was an associate. The defendant repeatedly contacted the plaintiff via Facebook and continuously expressed her affection towards the plaintiff, even though he repeatedly asked her to stop doing so. Furthermore, the defendant tried to force the plaintiff to arrange a meeting in person and, using threats and verbal assaults, she tried to create a sense of guilt for her feelings in the plaintiff. Due to the long-term and repeated harassment, the plaintiff sustained insomnia and could not concentrate, which he argued had harmed his mental health. The defendant was convicted of the offence of stalking and misdemeanour for assault.

Cyber-bullying

There have been two notable cases of cyberbullying in the Czech Republic. Both of them happened at schools – an elementary school in Klobouky near Brno, and a high school in Olomouc. In both cases, Facebook was used. As the cases concern minors and the decisions are not public, we could obtain only information reported by the media.

In the first case, the victim was a 6th grade female student. Her schoolmates created a false Facebook account in her name in order to cyberbully her. Before long, she had 84 friends, both children and adults. On her profile, her schoolmates then bullied the girl, threatened to kill her, her mother and discussed how to do so. When the girl found out about the Facebook account, she had a nervous breakdown and had to start taking medication.

The second case is not dissimilar from the first. The victim was again a girl. Her schoolmates cyberbullied her, threatened to harm her physically and kill her and discussed what to do with the cadaver in order for it to be impossible to identify.

Sexting

A 15-year-old girl from Moravia got into contact with a 16-year-old boy from France. They began exchanging increasingly revealing pictures. Finally, the girl sent the boy a picture of her naked body from the waist up, including her face. Afterwards, she refused to send him additional, even more revealing, pictures. As a reaction, the boy began to blackmail her, saying that he would contact her family and friends. After more arguments with the girl, the boy made three pictures of her public.

C7.21   SM AND FAMILY LAW CASES

We are not aware of any examples, controversies or cases in relation to SM and family law cases.

C7.22   SPORTS PERSONS, SPORTS CLUBS AND SM

We are not aware of any notable examples of controversies or cases in relation to sports persons, sports clubs and SM. In general, Czech athletes do not use social media as extensively as, for example, athletes in the United States. Based on internal research, athletes usually post non-contentious content on their SM accounts. However, we cannot exclude the possibility that sports clubs might have disciplined the players internally without making the information public.

Usually, players use Twitter and/or Facebook. Other SM websites are not that commonly used in the Czech Republic.

C7.23   PERSONAL RELATIONS AND RELATIONSHIPS

Online media, usually tabloid, as well as other websites, refer to revenge porn and other similar cases quite often. See the decision of the Regional Court in Plzeň no 50 To 30/2014 – 474 dated 10 March 2014, as described at C7.2.

C7.24   SM AND PERSONAL DATA OF DECEASED PERSONS

To our knowledge, there has been no such example of any controversy or case in relation to SM regarding personal data of a deceased person.

The statement of the DPO no 4/2012, on data processing of deceased persons, clarifies how personal data of deceased persons should be handled. The Data Protection Act, contrary to the Civil Code, does not establish rules for the transfer of rights and obligations arising from legal relationships after one's death. That means that, after the death of a person, provisions of the Data Protection Act regarding personal data, where the data subject acts as a party to civil law relationships, lose their validity. Specifically concerned are provisions on (i) consent with data processing, (ii) consent with personal data processing, (iii) informational duty of the data controller, and (iv) protection of rights of the data subject and compensation for damages.

Data controllers are obliged by law to examine whether the personal data they control is true and accurate with regard to the objective of data processing and controlling. Upon discovering that the person is deceased, data controllers are obliged to store the personal data for a necessary period of time, depending on the nature of the data (eg to fulfil statutory obligations regarding maintaining accounting records). If the objective (eg offering trade and services) vanishes together with the death of the individual, data controllers are obliged to destroy the data.

C7.25 SM, WEBSITE, SERVICE PROVIDER OR ISP DEFENCE RULES/LAWS

The Czech Republic transposed the EU eCommerce Directive (2000/31/EC) primarily by Act No 480/2004 Coll, on certain services of the information society, as amended (the 'Act on Certain Services of the Information Society'). The provisions of the Act on Certain Services of the Information Society reflect the provisions of the EU eCommerce Directive. Articles 12 to 15 of the eCommerce Directive regarding defences have been transposed almost *verbatim* into Articles 3 to 6 of the Act on Certain Services of the Information Society.

C7.26 ECOMMERCE DEFENCE CASES

High Court in Prague: case no 3 Cmo 197/2010 dated 2 March 2011

The High Court in Prague has dealt with an eCommerce case regarding hosting providers. In this case, the court specified the rules by which specific information should be assessed and potentially marked as illegal as well as an obligation for the provider to remove such information. The case concerned a thread in a discussion forum, where uncomplimentary phrases had been published on the account of a certain company. The court stated that the provider is obliged to prevent committing crimes and prevent distribution of posts that are apparently illegal. It is necessary to consider posts 'apparently illegal' that aim to defame another person and are only vulgarities without any attempts for factual conversation. The provider can thus relieve himself of the liability only if he proves that he could not have been aware of the illegality of the information.

C7.27 LAWS PROTECTING PERSONAL DATA/ PERSONALLY IDENTIFIABLE INFORMATION

In the Czech Republic, privacy and data protection are regulated in the Data Protection Act. Under this Act, personal data is any information regarding an established or determinable data subject. A data subject is deemed to be established or determinable if it can be directly or indirectly identified especially based on a number, a code or on more components specific to the physical, physiological, psychic, economic, cultural or social identity.

The Data Protection Act then states that data controllers can process data solely with the consent of the data subject. The Act then provides several exceptions when consent is not necessary – eg the processing is necessary in order to comply with statutory obligations, or when it is necessary to protect highly important interests of the data processor.

The Data Protection Act provides special rules for sensitive personal data, for transmitting personal data to third parties (different rules apply for EU member states and third parties), for notification of the DPO and the exceptions from the notification obligation, and the authority of the DPO to sanction offences under the Data Protection Act.

C7.28 DATA BREACH LAWS AND CUSTOMERS/ USERS/REGULATORS NOTIFIED OF HACKING OR DATA LOSS

The proposal of the Act on Cyber Security states that service providers will be obliged to report a cyber security incident. A cyber security incident means a breach of security of information in information systems or breach of security or integrity of networks. The service providers will be obliged to notify the NSA, which will enter them into evidence and will be entitled to take necessary steps in order to reduce the damage.

Chapter C8

Denmark

Alexandra Huber/Karina Emmertsen
Lead Advokatpartnerselskab

C8.1   INTRODUCTION

Denmark is an EU member state and is a Civil Law jurisdiction.

C8.2   SPECIFIC SM AND SN LAWS

In line with the Scandinavian law system, we do not have any specific SM and SN laws, but the usage of SM will be regulated by the applicable laws in Denmark, for instance the Criminal Code, the Marketing Practices Act and the Employment Act.

C8.3   SM CRIMINAL LAW CASES

There are a number of cases relating to actions online that are covered by the Criminal Code. Primarily, they involve actions of threat against other persons in open debate fora.

In 2010, for instance, a person was convicted for threatening a prominent politician and sentenced to 20 days of jail on probation for having threatened to kill the politician in an open debate forum on Facebook (see U.2010.2085Ø).

C8.4   SM CIVIL LAW CASES

None.

C8.5   CASES WHERE SM-RELATED EVIDENCE USED OR ADMISSIBLE

We see a number of cases in which the usage of SM sites has been used as evidence. For instance, in matrimonial cases, it might be used to document the type of relationship between the parties, or to document the behaviour of one party (see V2012.B.1633.12). Mostly Facebook posts are used as evidence to prove whether a specific statement in question was made or where a person was located.

C8.6 SPECIFIC ONLINE ABUSE/ONLINE BULLYING/ CYBERBULLYING LAWS

Denmark has not passed a parliamentary law regarding online bullying, even though it has been proposed several times in the last years by different political parties. But, so far, no actual initiative has been brought before the parliament. Where the bullying issue is located in the school environment, it is the general view that this issue is dealt with on the school level. However, certain organisations, such as Red Barnet (part of Save the Children), are focusing on the problem, and many schools have implemented anti-bullying action plans. Likewise, employers are advised to implement such plans if necessary to ensure a safe working environment.

C8.7 OTHER LAWS APPLIED TO ONLINE ABUSE/ ONLINE BULLYING/CYBERBULLYING

Any case of bullying may be covered by the Criminal Code, if applicable. Where the bullying issue is located in the work environment, the employer may face damages if he does not provide for a safe and sound work environment.

C8.8 CHILDREN AND SM LAWS OR RULES

The consumer ombudsman has provided for guidelines regarding the usage of SM in relation to advertising, including advertisements directed to children and teenagers. These guidelines are based on the EU Directives and prohibit any advertisement that makes use of the simple-mindedness of young people. Additionally, it will be regarded as misleading if the advertisement directly invites the recipient to go to the store and purchase the product or if it suggests convincing the parents to make the purchase.

Additionally, the Media Council for Children and Young People as part of the Danish Film Institute is monitoring the usage of digital media by young people and provides for parental guidelines and, for instance, age limits in films and computer games.

C8.9 EMPLOYEES/EMPLOYMENT SM LAWS OR CASES

There are no specific laws or rules, but we have seen cases. There are three main areas within the topic of SM and employment: the first issue is the case of an employee's declarations and status updates on work-related matters; the second issue is the usage of SM for private reasons during work hours; and the third issue is the usage of professional SM (such as LinkedIn or Xing) after termination of an employment contract, specifically in relation to contact with customers of a previous employer.

Declarations and status updates on work-related matters

The employee is obliged to be loyal to the employer. If an employee makes statements via SM that are disloyal, it will be necessary to determine whether these statements are private or public. Especially if statements are made in groups, it may be possible to argue that the statement was made in a private setting. If a statement can be shared by other users, the statement will be regarded as public, because the employee has no control over whether or not this statement is published to an unlimited number of people. The larger the group and the lesser the group members can be tied together with a personal bond, the more difficult it will be to argue that the statement was made merely in private. Additionally, we see a tendency that employers implement SM policies for the personal use of Facebook. If a policy is in place, determining that any declaration on SM is regarded as public, this will be taken into account when determining whether or not the statement is public and therefore can form grounds for termination of the employment.

Personal usage of SM during working hours

If a policy is in place regulating the personal usage of SM during working hours, this must be respected by the employee. The excessive personal usage of SM during working hours can form grounds for termination.

Contact with clients of a previous employer via professional SM

A rather difficult issue is the usage of professional SM (such as LinkedIn or Xing) after termination of employment. If the employee has signed an obligation not to contact any customers of the previous employer, it is still to be clarified whether a simple status update on LinkedIn regarding a new job or the sharing of posts and advertisement of the new employer constitutes a contact to previous customers, if the employee is linked to the customers on LinkedIn. As LinkedIn is tied to the individual, it is possible that nothing much can be done in order to prevent such future LinkedIn contact to the customers.

C8.10   SCHOOL AND UNIVERSITY STUDENT SM CASES

There are a number of cases involving young people, who still go to school, in relation to their usage of Facebook. However, none of these involve the school or university system specifically.

C8.11 RIGHT OR HUMAN RIGHT TO ACCESS THE INTERNET OR SM

There are a number of e-articles regarding this topic; however, no specific literature has been published on this specific matter in Denmark.

C8.12 BANS OR RESTRICTIONS ON INTERNET OR SM

Persons convicted for sexual offences in relation to children may be convicted in accordance with the Danish Criminal Code § 236 and may, under such conviction, not seek any contact to minors via the internet. If they disregard this ruling and seek contact via the internet, this action in itself will be deemed as a criminal offence and will lead to new criminal charges.

C8.13 IDENTITY THEFT (OR EQUIVALENT)

A proposal for such a law was brought forward in the Parliament in 2012; however, due to a hacking incident of an IT system of a municipality, the process of adopting any laws in this area has been put on hold until the investigations in relation to the specific incident have been finalised.

C8.14 HACKING (OR EQUIVALENT)

There are no specific hacking laws in place. Hacking is a crime under the Danish Criminal Code § 263, stk.2. This paragraph regulates offences in relation to privacy of correspondence and privacy of information.

C8.15 PRIVACY BY DESIGN (PBD) (OR EQUIVALENT)

The approach of PbD is used regarding a preliminary approval of very large IT systems, but this is based on the general demand under Danish rules on data protection that the IT system must safeguard the privacy of data. Some scholars argue that the PbD approach is already covered by the data protection rules in force, as the IT system must be safe and proper for the handling of the data.

C8.16 TWEETING FROM COURTS, AND ANY RULES/LAWS

If the court hearing is open to the public (which is generally the case), the right to transmit any text messages from the court hearing is limited to certain persons, namely lawyers, prosecutors, court personnel and journalists; see Danish Code on Court Procedure (retsplejeloven) § 32, sec. 3. Other persons may not transmit text, including Tweets or any other written communication, from the hearing. The courts can prohibit the aforementioned persons from transmitting text.

C8.17 TELEVISION COURTROOM BROADCASTING OR TELEVISION CAMERAS IN COURT, AND RULES OR LAWS

It is prohibited to take pictures or record sound in the court unless granted by the judge. The president of the court may even prohibit cameras in general within the court building. Permission will only be granted if the case has significance for the public. The court will determine the specifics in relation to when the recordings may be published etc.

Parties to a criminal court hearing may not be photographed, or in any other way recorded, when entering the court building, unless they have given their consent thereto.

C8.18 SM IN COURTROOMS

In 2005 a journalist was sentenced to payment of DKK 10,000 (approx. 1,400 EUR) for having taken a picture of a defendant when approaching the court building without the consent of the defendant.

C8.19 USE OF SM AS EVIDENCE IN COURTS

By far the major role of SM in court cases is as evidence for statements made or geographical placement of a person, or regarding pictures taken. SM is often used when it is necessary to determine the nature of a relationship between two parties. There are no restrictions on providing SM material as documentary proof in court. However, the person whose profile is published will typically have to be heard as a witness in relation to the documents at hand.

C8.20 PRIVACY, DATA PROTECTION AND SM

There have been cases regarding the right of authorities to check data on Facebook. It was deemed that information on Facebook is public, as long as the user does not restrict the content to a limited group of people (FOM2011.2011-2657-2091).

C8.21 SM AND FAMILY LAW CASES

In Denmark, it is very typical that SM evidence is used in family law cases. No major family law cases have been seen in relation to the usage of SM.

C8.22 SPORTS PERSONS, SPORTS CLUBS AND SM

In 2012 the Danish Football League (DBU) agreed with the players on the national team not to use any SM sites during the Euro Cup. Basically, this meant a prohibition for the team members to produce anything on SM sites during the Euro Cup. This was discussed in the Danish media, as it was seen as a violation of the right of free speech. A year later, the DBU abolished the ban and instead issued a few guidelines for the team members to think of when posting status updates online. The communication department closely watched the updates of the players, but no large controversy has appeared in the media in this regard since the ban was abolished in 2013.

C8.23 PERSONAL RELATIONS AND RELATIONSHIPS

None published. These matters most likely do exist and are solved under the Criminal Code and data protection rules.

C8.24 SM AND PERSONAL DATA OF DECEASED PERSONS

None to our knowledge.

C8.25 SM, WEBSITE, SERVICE PROVIDER OR ISP DEFENCE RULES/LAWS

The eCommerce Directive is implemented in Denmark under the E-Handelsloven.

C8.26 ECOMMERCE DEFENCE CASES

None in relation to SM.

C8.27 LAWS PROTECTING PERSONAL DATA/ PERSONALLY IDENTIFIABLE INFORMATION

The Personal Data Act (persondataloven) is in force and provides for the general level of protection as under the EU data protection rules and regulations. When working with highly sensitive data, registration with the data authority (datatilsynet) is required.

C8.28 DATA BREACH LAWS AND CUSTOMERS/USERS/ REGULATORS NOTIFIED OF HACKING OR DATA LOSS

There are no special rules regulating this incident. However, under the general rule of fair practices in relation to data protection, the Danish Data Protection

Agency has issued these four steps that should be complied with, in case of a breach of security:

- All data should be deleted or eventually returned by the unauthorised user.

- It should be ensured that the data is deleted from the internet and search engines.

- The persons whose data has been affected by the breach should be notified as quickly as possible.

- On a long-term basis, it should be secured that this breach cannot occur again, possible guidelines need to be adapted and improved, and a thorough systematic check should be undertaken.

Chapter C9

El Salvador

Morena Zavaleta
Arias & Muñoz

C9.1 INTRODUCTION

El Salvador is a Civil Law system.

C9.2 SPECIFIC SM AND SN LAWS

There are no specific SM and SN laws.

C9.3 SM CRIMINAL LAW CASES

We do not have knowledge of these types of cases.

C9.4 SM CIVIL LAW CASES

We do not have knowledge of these types of cases.

C9.5 CASES WHERE SM-RELATED EVIDENCE USED OR ADMISSIBLE

We do not have knowledge of court decisions (criminal, civil or any other kind) in which SM was used as evidence; however, we have knowledge of a current case in which there was a mobile phone theft and the defendant took a picture with the stolen telephone camera and it was automatically uploaded to the Facebook page of the victim, but this case is in the early stages yet, so it is not certain that the SM uploaded photo will be accepted as proof.

We consider, however, that, even if there are no specific regulations that admit SM evidence, there are forms to gather evidence related to SM through permitted channels, such as notary affidavits and expert reports.

C9.6 SPECIFIC ONLINE ABUSE/ONLINE BULLYING/ CYBERBULLYING LAWS

There are no specific laws, but there are laws that protect minors and adults against general extortion, abuse and other types of personal threatening behaviour by any means including electronic, such as a law of protection of infants (LEPINA) and the Criminal Code.

C9.7 OTHER LAWS APPLIED TO ONLINE ABUSE/ ONLINE BULLYING/CYBERBULLYING

We do not have knowledge of such laws; however, we consider that there are certain laws that protect minors (LEPINA) and criminal laws (Criminal Code) that may be applied in these types of cases.

C9.8 CHILDREN AND SM LAWS OR RULES

There are no laws or rules that specifically apply to children and SM.

C9.9 EMPLOYEES/EMPLOYMENT SM LAWS OR CASES

There are no laws involving SM and employees/employment.

C9.10 SCHOOL AND UNIVERSITY STUDENT SM CASES

There are no laws involving students in schools and universities in relation to the use of SM.

C9.11 RIGHT OR HUMAN RIGHT TO ACCESS THE INTERNET OR SM

We do not have knowledge of these types of cases.

C9.12 BANS OR RESTRICTIONS ON INTERNET OR SM

There are no rules or laws in relation to bans or restrictions on the use of, or access to, the internet and/or SM.

C9.13 IDENTITY THEFT (OR EQUIVALENT)

Our Constitution provides as an essential right the protection of personal and familiar intimacy and personal image. Our Criminal Code contains provisions that consider identity theft as a crime, if used for journalistic, advertisement, commercial or artistic reasons.

C9.14 HACKING (OR EQUIVALENT)

There are no rules or laws relating to hacking.

C9.15 PRIVACY BY DESIGN (PBD) (OR EQUIVALENT)

There are no rules or laws relating to privacy by design (PbD) or equivalent.

C9.16 TWEETING FROM COURTS, AND ANY RULES/LAWS

From the start of any hearing, it is prohibited to use a mobile phone, or to do anything that disrupts the order of the hearing in the court. These rules are given specifically by the judge before the hearing, such instructions are given before the beginning of the same, but there are no written rules or laws that regulate this subject.

C9.17 TELEVISION COURTROOM BROADCASTING OR TELEVISION CAMERAS IN COURT, AND RULES OR LAWS

There are no specific rules. Although a hearing is public (with some exceptions, due to special circumstances), it is most likely that the judge will prohibit its TV broadcasting (we do not know of any case in which this was permitted). In the family jurisdiction, and to some extent in criminal matters when a minor is involved, the hearings are held privately because the law protects the integrity of the minor. The laws that establish these rules can be found in the Family Code and the Criminal Code.

C9.18 SM IN COURTROOMS

Not applicable.

C9.19 USE OF SM AS EVIDENCE IN COURTS

We do not have knowledge of court decisions in which SM was used as evidence; however, we have knowledge of a current case in which there was a mobile phone theft and the defendant took a picture with the stolen telephone camera and it was automatically uploaded to the Facebook page of the victim, but this case is in the early stages yet, so it is not certain that the SM uploaded photo will be accepted as proof.

C9.20   PRIVACY, DATA PROTECTION AND SM

There have been decisions in relation to privacy and data protection, but we do not have knowledge of cases about SM.

There is a specific and important case in which a person filed a claim against a company, dedicated to compiling private data related to financial and banking data, in order to sell the information to banks and other financial institutions to use, for example, in the financial classification and good standing of clients or prospective clients.

C9.21   SM AND FAMILY LAW CASES

We have knowledge of family law cases in which SM has been mentioned, but only as a secondary matter and not as a central motive of the controversy.

C9.22   SPORTS PERSONS, SPORTS CLUBS AND SM

We do not have knowledge of these types of cases.

C9.23   PERSONAL RELATIONS AND RELATIONSHIPS

We do not have knowledge of these types of cases.

C9.24   SM AND PERSONAL DATA OF DECEASED PERSONS

We do not have knowledge of these types of cases in our jurisdiction.

C9.25   SM, WEBSITE, SERVICE PROVIDER OR ISP DEFENCE RULES/LAWS

There are no rules or laws providing SM, website, service provider or ISP defences.

C9.26   ECOMMERCE DEFENCE CASES

No details.

C9.27   LAWS PROTECTING PERSONAL DATA/ PERSONALLY IDENTIFIABLE INFORMATION

There are no privacy or data protection or similar laws providing for the protection of personal data or personally identifiable information.

C9.28   DATA BREACH LAWS AND CUSTOMERS/ USERS/REGULATORS NOTIFIED OF HACKING OR DATA LOSS

There are no specific laws providing that customers, users or regulators should be notified if an organization's data or systems have been hacked or lost.

Chapter C10

Estonia

Professor Katrin Nyman-Metcalf

C10.1 INTRODUCTION

Estonia is an EU member state and is a Civil Law jurisdiction.

C10.2 SPECIFIC SM AND SN LAWS

None. Generally, access to information is secured by the Public Information Act 2000 (RT I 2000, 92, 597 as amended). See www.riigiteataja.ee/en/eli/ee/Riigikogu/act/514112013001/consolide (includes official translation into English).

Communications principles, access, etc are regulated by the Electronic Communications Act 2004 (RT I 2004, 87, 593 as amended). See www.riigiteataja.ee/en/eli/ee/Riigikogu/act/507012014001/consolide (includes official translation into English).

Legislation is generally technology-neutral. As Estonia has a very wide use of e-governance as well as private e-services, many transactions covered by various laws are in fact performed using ICTs, but the laws enable and allow this rather than stipulate special rules based on the technology used.

Estonia is ranked second in the world in the Freedom House index for internet freedom (2013).

C10.3 SM CRIMINAL LAW CASES

Not known.

C10.4 SM CIVIL LAW CASES

Not known.

C10.5   CASES WHERE SM-RELATED EVIDENCE USED OR ADMISSIBLE

It is important to note that, in Estonia, digital signatures are widely used and have the same legal validity as regular signatures, for private and public transactions. It is thus not unusual to have electronic evidence of various kinds and special SM issues are not singled out.

See   www.riigiteataja.ee/en/eli/ee/Riigikogu/act/530102013080/consolide (includes official translation into English).

C10.6   SPECIFIC ONLINE ABUSE/ONLINE BULLYING/ CYBERBULLYING LAWS

None. There are special 'web constables' with whom it is possible to interact online (via email, through different portals) and they can also advise on online crime, like cyberbullying. This is not just aimed at young people or against online abuse etc, but reactions against such happenings are important parts of what the web constables should deal with and inform about. See www.politsei. ee/en/nouanded/veebikonstaablid/ (in English).

C10.7   OTHER LAWS APPLIED TO ONLINE ABUSE/ ONLINE BULLYING/CYBERBULLYING

The Penal Code has no special rules for online activities. There is a Child Protection Law 1992 (as amended), but it does not contain specific online provisions.

C10.8   CHILDREN AND SM LAWS OR RULES

There are no specific SM laws or rules, but a lot of attention is given to the issue in education, awareness campaigns etc. Estonia ranks a shared second in the EU for children's use of the internet (93% of all 6- to 17-year-olds use the internet regularly) and 57.7% of children claim to have been in some risk situation on the internet (as compared to 30.8% EU average) – which can also indicate a high degree of awareness of what such dangerous situations are. (Source http://www.unicef.ee/page/91 - in Estonian).

In 2013 the Penal Code was amended in a few places to strengthen provisions against child pornography, to facilitate reaction against persons accessing, sharing, etc such material.

C10.9   EMPLOYEES/EMPLOYMENT SM LAWS OR CASES

There is no special legislation. There is a discussion on the use of SM information by prospective employers to look into candidates; and, in the absence of special legislation, the Employment Law together with the Data Protection Law must be interpreted, the Data Protection Inspectorate having given clarifications on its interpretation. Basically, information that is in the public domain can be accessed, but the candidate for employment should be informed of the searches that the prospective employer undertakes.

C10.10   SCHOOL AND UNIVERSITY STUDENT SM CASES

None. Schools can make their own rules on any limiting of use of laptops etc, although such rules are very rare, as the use of ICT in education at all levels in Estonia is very high.

C10.11   RIGHT OR HUMAN RIGHT TO ACCESS THE INTERNET OR SM

Access to the internet is regarded as a fundamental right.

C10.12   BANS OR RESTRICTIONS ON INTERNET OR SM

There are almost no restrictions on using/accessing the internet in Estonia. Since a few years ago, there has been one restriction: the Gambling Act of 2008 requires that gambling servers for gambling websites must be located physically in Estonia, resulting in DNS filtering of remote gambling sites. As for depriving persons of access to internet as a sanction, this is not foreseen in the Penal Code.

The Prisons Law restricts access to internet in prisons unless there are special reasons to grant it. However, prisoners should have access to the database of laws and some other websites that they may need to make complaints, etc (such as the Chancellor of Justice, the European Court of Human Rights, etc); and restricting access to such sites must be motivated by special circumstances – this was also confirmed by the Supreme Court. It can be difficult to find examples of legitimate *limitations* on internet use by prisoners, but one important case, where the right to have access to certain websites like the Council of Europe was considered, is Case Number 3-3-1-5-09 on 7 December 2009; see www. nc.ee/?id=11&tekst=222520885 (in Estonian). General information on the Estonian Supreme Court is found at www.nc.ee/?lang=en.

C10.13   IDENTITY THEFT (OR EQUIVALENT)

This is a crime in the Penal Code – Article 157 (Illegal use of another person's identity); also, Article 213 on computer-related fraud. Provisions on the abuse of identity documents and similar also explicitly show that digital as well as paper documents/signatures are covered by the provisions (eg Art 349-350). Estonia has a very high usage of electronic identity documents and electronic signatures.

See www.riigiteataja.ee/en/eli/ee/Riigikogu/act/511032014001/consolide (includes official translation into English).

C10.14   HACKING (OR EQUIVALENT)

A number of provisions of the Penal Code are relevant, especially Articles 206 (Interference in computer data), 206¹ (Unlawful removal and alteration of means of identification of terminal equipment), 207 (Hindering of operation of computer system), 208 (Dissemination of spyware, malware or computer viruses), 216¹ (Preparation of computer-related crime), 217 (Unlawful use of computer system) and 217¹ (Use of terminal equipment with unlawfully removed or altered means of identification).

See www.riigiteataja.ee/en/eli/ee/Riigikogu/act/511032014001/consolide (includes official translation into English).

C10.15   PRIVACY BY DESIGN (PBD) (OR EQUIVALENT)

Not known.

C10.16   TWEETING FROM COURTS, AND ANY RULES/LAWS

Judges may give permission to broadcast from court sessions; before this can be done, permission should be requested according to guidelines for media and court relations, published on the court's website. There is no mention of Tweets etc, so the guidelines would have to be interpreted accordingly; the main element is that the judge should give permission in each case.

See www.kohus.ee/et/ajakirjanikule/kohtute-haldamise-noukoja-soovitused-kohtute-meediasuhtluseks (in Estonian).

C10.17   TELEVISION COURTROOM BROADCASTING OR TELEVISION CAMERAS IN COURT, AND RULES OR LAWS

Broadcasting from courtrooms is permitted, if the judge in the individual case allows it, and he/she can stipulate exact rules. It is quite common to have broadcasts from courtrooms. It is normally prevented only if a case is held behind closed doors, for which specific reasons are needed (like cases involving children or state secrets) or there are other reasons why filming is particularly disruptive. Guidelines exist and are public (see C10.16).

C10.18   SM IN COURTROOMS

No major considerations, as the principle of openness of trials and the right to film, etc is widely applied, and SM has not changed this much.

C10.19   USE OF SM AS EVIDENCE IN COURTS

See above on digital signatures and the use of electronic information; nothing special on SM.

C10.20   PRIVACY, DATA PROTECTION AND SM

Not directly applicable, but of relevance on related matters: see *Delfi AS v Estonia*, ECtHR Application number 64569/09. This case concerns online comments of a defamatory nature and the question whether the website (news portal) should be responsible for the anonymous comments. The European Court of Human Rights found in favour of Estonia which had ruled that, even if the website had a takedown system, this was not sufficient. The very small fine imposed was mentioned in the case as a relevant matter, as the Estonian as well as the European court stressed the desire not to punish but to ensure that more effective takedown procedures are introduced when a website enables defamatory comments to be posted.

C10.21   SM AND FAMILY LAW CASES

Not known.

C10.22   SPORTS PERSONS, SPORTS CLUBS AND SM

Not known.

C10.23   PERSONAL RELATIONS AND RELATIONSHIPS

The web constables (see C10.6) have identified cases of apparent revenge, calling ex-husbands paedophiles, etc. This evidence is anecdotal, from media articles, but it is clear that the web constables deal with information about such issues and the possibility of turning to the court or to the Data Protection Inspectorate if there is a case of misuse of personal data and/or a case of defamation or some other act covered by legislation.

C10.24   SM AND PERSONAL DATA OF DECEASED PERSONS

No cases.

C10.25   SM, WEBSITE, SERVICE PROVIDER OR ISP DEFENCE RULES/LAWS

Estonia is an EU member state and all EU Directives are implemented in the country.

C10.26   ECOMMERCE DEFENCE CASES

The case of *Delfi v Estonia*, that was decided by the European Court of Human Rights in October 2013 (see C10.20), mentions the EU e-commerce provisions and some commentators have stated that they feel the Court did not properly take such rules into account, or it could not have agreed with the verdict of the Estonian courts that found Delfi (the web portal) liable for damages for defamation. However, the European Court of Human Rights and many commentators agree that the EU provisions in the given case are not clear enough to point to one definitive outcome.

C10.27   LAWS PROTECTING PERSONAL DATA/ PERSONALLY IDENTIFIABLE INFORMATION

The Personal Data Protection Act 2007 (RT I 2007, 24, 127 as amended) – see www.riigiteataja.ee/en/eli/ee/Riigikogu/act/512112013011/consolide (official translation into English).

C10.28   DATA BREACH LAWS AND CUSTOMERS/ USERS/REGULATORS NOTIFIED OF HACKING OR DATA LOSS

The Personal Data Protection Act (see C10.27). One additional key issue is that Estonia relies to a large extent on e-governance for all public and many private services, so that any access to any personal data leaves a footprint. The person concerned can access all databases via one portal, using the ID card and digital signature that everyone possesses, to look at his/her data, including to see if anyone has accessed (that is, used or looked at) the data. Authorities must be ready to explain any use of data. This system ensures that unauthorised access of personal data are very difficult and most likely will be detected. The Data Protection Inspectorate can also ask authorities to explain any unusual or extensive accessing of personal data.

Chapter C11

Finland

Markus Myhrberg
Lexia Attorneys Ltd

C11.1   INTRODUCTION

Finland is an EU member state and is a Civil Law jurisdiction.

Please note that cases from the district courts are not published in the internet database (finlex.fi), and the official versions of Acts are only the ones in Finnish and Swedish. Only some of the Acts have English translations and even those are not always up to date.

C11.2   SPECIFIC SM AND SN LAWS

None, but all other laws are applicable also to SM and SN.

C11.3   SM CRIMINAL LAW CASES

In the Kouvola Court of Appeal, there was a case which was about Habbo Hotel (habbo.fi) and petty theft (Criminal Code, Chapter 28, Section 3). Habbo Hotel is a virtual hotel, where the users can meet their friends, spend some time and chat. The defendant was prosecuted for stealing furniture worth 465 euros from another person's account in the virtual Habbo Hotel. The problem with the case was that theft is bound to the concept of movable property (Criminal Code, Chapter 28, Section 1). In the government Bill (HE 66/1988 vp page 34), it is mentioned that movable property in the case of theft would not include intellectual property, the right to claim or electronic funds. Illegal moving of those kinds of funds could be punishable depending on the circumstances as fraud or embezzlement. So movable property in this case is considered as concrete objects, which the virtual furniture in Habbo Hotel is not. The district court had sentenced the defendant, but for the rule of law the Kouvola Court of Appeal dismissed the charge for petty theft.[1]

---

1   See www.finlex.fi/fi/oikeus/ho/2011/kouho20110284.

C11.4   SM CIVIL LAW CASES

No details yet.

C11.5   CASES WHERE SM-RELATED EVIDENCE USED OR ADMISSIBLE

In the Labour Court and in the Market Court, there have been cases where extracts from a Facebook page have been used as written evidence.[2]

C11.6   SPECIFIC ONLINE ABUSE/ONLINE BULLYING/ CYBERBULLYING LAWS

Nothing specific, but in the recent amendment (879/2013) to the Criminal Code, online abuse was specially mentioned in the government Bill to be applying to the new section.

To Chapter 24 (Offences against privacy, public peace and personal reputation), Section 1a was added, which is about invasion of communication privacy (peace). The section states that, if a person repeatedly sends messages to or calls someone, so that the act could cause the victim considerable disturbance or harm, the person shall be sentenced for an invasion of communication privacy to a fine or to imprisonment for up to six months. According to the government Bill, communication includes private messages in SM services, real-time discussions/chats, online games and forums. Invasion through these kinds of message services can cause the same kind of anxiety and fear as other kinds of communication envisaged in the section. Therefore, it can even prevent people using the service.

To Chapter 25 (Offences against personal liberty), Section 7a was added, which is about stalking. One of the ways in which stalking can be done is repeatedly contacting someone. According to the government Bill, contacting might even be leaving a message to that person in a public forum on the internet. The sentence for stalking is a fine or imprisonment for up to two years.

C11.7   OTHER LAWS APPLIED TO ONLINE ABUSE/ ONLINE BULLYING/CYBERBULLYING

No details yet.

---

2   See, for example, finlex.fi/fi/oikeus/tt/2013/20130129, finlex.fi/fi/oikeus/tt/2012/20120052, finlex.fi/fi/oikeus/mao/2013/20130450, finlex.fi/fi/oikeus/mao/2012/20120121, finlex.fi/fi/oikeus/mao/2012/20120381, finlex.fi/fi/oikeus/mao/2011/20110032 and finlex.fi/fi/oikeus/mao/2013/20130198.

C11.8 CHILDREN AND SM LAWS OR RULES

Nothing specific to SM, but normal legislation applies. For example, if a fee is charged for the service, a child as an incompetent person may only enter into transactions which, in view of the circumstances, are usual and of little significance (Guardianship Services Act (442/1999),[3] Chapter 4 'Status of the incompetent person', Section 24).

C11.9 EMPLOYEES/EMPLOYMENT SM LAWS OR CASES

There are some cases, such as the Bijou Brigitte case in 2011, and the Hesburger case in 2014.

In the Bijou Brigitte case, the shop, which sells fashion jewellery and other accessories, sued its employee for 5000 euros for damages. A part-time employee had founded a group in Facebook. The group's purpose was to urge people to boycott the company. The employee had criticised the employer for both ending the employments and poor terms. From the employer's aspect, these writings damaged the company's reputation as an employer. According to the decision given by the district court of Helsinki on 22 February 2011, the employee had broken the loyalty obligation, but the employer could not show the actual damage caused by the writings. Therefore the lawsuit was dismissed. There was no appeal against the decision.[4] The loyalty obligation can sometimes restrict the freedom of speech, but the limit should be decided on a case-by-case basis, as the position of the employee also has an effect. The loyalty obligation is based on Chapter 3, Section 1 in the Employment Contracts Act.[5] That section is about an employee's general obligations.

In the Hesburger case, two managers from one of the hamburger chain's places of business were found guilty of message interception, contrary to the Criminal Code,[6] and were sentenced to a fine by the district court of Helsinki. They had read private messages from an employee's Facebook account. They were accused of hacking into the employee's Facebook account to read those private messages, but they claimed that the Facebook account was open on the work computer. The messages were between the Facebook account holder and another employee. The messages were also forwarded to a staff manager. Both

---

3   See www.finlex.fi/en/laki/kaannokset/1999/en19990442.pdf.
4   See   www.digitoday.fi/yhteiskunta/2011/02/22/haukkui-yhtiota-facebookissa---selvisi-ilman-korvauksia/20112614/66;   www.iltasanomat.fi/kotimaa/art-1288370995640.html; www.uusisuomi.fi/kotimaa/109063-nainen-boikotoi-facebookissa-joutuu-oikeuteen-%E2%80%93-%E2%80%9Dharskia%E2%80%9D;   and   www.holtta.fi/sitenews/view/-/nid/146/ngid/1/.
5   See www.finlex.fi/en/laki/kaannokset/2001/en20010055.pdf.
6   See Criminal Code 39/1889, Chapter 38 (Data and Communication offences), Section 3 (Message interception) at www.finlex.fi/en/laki/kaannokset/1889/en18890039.pdf.

managers were sentenced to fines equivalent to 30 days' earnings, so the shift manager's fine was 1200 euros and the field manager's fine was 990 euros.[7]

C11.10   SCHOOL AND UNIVERSITY STUDENT SM CASES

Not to our knowledge.

C11.11   RIGHT OR HUMAN RIGHT TO ACCESS THE INTERNET OR SM

Section 60 c of the Communications Market Act regulates universal service obligation concerning the provision of universal telephone services, which includes internet connection. The Act's English translation can be found at www.finlex.fi/en/laki/kaannokset/2003/en20030393.pdf.

C11.12   BANS OR RESTRICTIONS ON INTERNET OR SM

There is an Act (1068/2006) related to blocking certain websites which have child pornography or which otherwise fulfil the requirements for blocking, eg are portals to child pornography websites. But this is not a punishment for a single person for their crime, but blocks those sites for everyone. In the Supreme Administrative Court, there was a case (KHO 2013:136) related to this Act. Matti Nikki (A in the case), who is an internet activist, requested to have his parody website, which aimed to prove the current problems with filtering, removed from the list, which is updated by the National Bureau of Investigation (NBI). When NBI refused, he appealed to the administrative court. The administrative court of Helsinki overturned NBI's decision. Then NBI appealed to the Supreme Administrative Court, where the ruling of the administrative court of Helsinki was overturned. Therefore, Nikki's website was blocked. At least Nikki's lawyer, Ville Oksanen from Turre Legal, said in an interview that his client would appeal to the European Court of Human Rights.[8]

C11.13   IDENTITY THEFT (OR EQUIVALENT)

Identity theft is not criminalized, but some crime might be committed while doing it, like defamation, dissemination of information violating personal privacy, fraud, unauthorised use, computer break-in or message interception.[9]

---

7   See www.hs.fi/kotimaa/a1395975626244.
8   See www.mpc.fi/kaikki_uutiset/kho+poliisi+toimi+oikein+estaessaan+paasyn+
    lapsipornoinfosivustolle/a924270.
9   See www.poliisi.fi/poliisi/helsinki/home.nsf/pages/4AA4B4D403026EC2C2257A7E0034F
    614?opendocument.

C11.14 HACKING (OR EQUIVALENT)

Many sections in Chapter 38 (Data and communications offences) of the Criminal Code are related to hacking, eg interference in a computer system ('basic' in Section 7a and 'aggravated' in Section 7b) and computer break-in ('basic' in Section 8 and 'aggravated' in Section 8a).

C11.15 PRIVACY BY DESIGN (PBD) (OR EQUIVALENT)

None.

C11.16 TWEETING FROM COURTS, AND ANY RULES/ LAWS

There is no specific regulation but, for example, in closed proceedings there is the secrecy obligation which affects everyone present there (Section 18 of the Act on the Publicity of Court Proceedings in General Courts).

C11.17 TELEVISION COURTROOM BROADCASTING OR TELEVISION CAMERAS IN COURT, AND RULES OR LAWS

There is no television courtroom broadcasting. However, recording is regulated by the Act on the Publicity of Court Proceedings in General Courts.[10]

Even though it has the principle of publicity (Section 1), Section 21 regulates the recording of oral proceedings. In open proceedings (proceedings can be closed, if one of the requirements listed in the Section 15 is fulfilled), someone other than the court may take a photograph, tape record and (in another manner) record and transfer video and audio signals by technical means only with the permission of the chairperson and in accordance with his or her instructions. Permission for recording before the beginning of consideration of the case, or when the decision of the court is pronounced, may be granted if the recording does not cause significant detriment to the protection of privacy of a party or another person and it does not endanger his or her safety and there are no other weighty reasons comparable to those for refusing permission. Permission to record other parts of the court proceedings may be granted if the conditions provided in the previous sentence have been met and, in addition, the recording causes no detriment to the undisturbed progress of the oral proceedings and the

---

10   See www.finlex.fi/en/laki/kaannokset/2007/en20070370.pdf.

participants in the court proceedings consent to the recording. It would be very rare to have the whole proceedings recorded.

There is separately the Act on the Publicity of Administrative Court Proceedings.[11] Section 14 is about the recording of oral proceedings. In open proceedings (proceedings can be closed, under Section 11), someone other than the administrative court may take a photograph, tape record and (in another manner) record and transfer video and audio signals by technical means only with the permission of the administrative court and in accordance with its instructions. Permission may be granted unless: the recording or transfer would cause significant detriment to the protection of the privacy of a witness, other person to be heard or a party or it endangers his or her safety; the recording or transfer would impede the undisturbed progress of the oral proceedings; or there are other weighty reasons comparable to those earlier mentioned for refusing permission.

Please note that there is always an oral proceeding in the district courts, but not always in the administrative courts.

C11.18 SM IN COURTROOMS

No details yet.

C11.19 USE OF SM AS EVIDENCE IN COURTS

No details yet.

C11.20 PRIVACY, DATA PROTECTION AND SM

No details yet.

C11.21 SM AND FAMILY LAW CASES

No details yet.

C11.22 SPORTS PERSONS, SPORTS CLUBS AND SM

No details yet.

C11.23 PERSONAL RELATIONS AND RELATIONSHIPS

No details yet.

---

11   See www.finlex.fi/en/laki/kaannokset/2007/en20070381.pdf.

C11.24   SM AND PERSONAL DATA OF DECEASED PERSONS

No details yet.

C11.25   SM, WEBSITE, SERVICE PROVIDER OR ISP DEFENCE RULES/LAWS

The EU eCommerce Directive has been implemented in the Act on Provision of Information Society Services.[12] Chapter 4 is about 'Exempting service providers, acting as intermediaries, from liability'.

The Finnish Copyright Act (Act 404/1961),[13] and in particular Section 60 c §, implements the Information Society Directive and the Enforcement Directive. As for website blocking, Section 60 c of the Copyright Act (as amended by Act 21.7.2006/679 to implement Directive 2004/48/EC) provides the legal grounds for issuing blocking orders.

C11.26   ECOMMERCE DEFENCE CASES

For example, the District Court of Helsinki ordered Elisa Corporation, under the penalty of a fine, to stop making copyright-infringing material publicly available through Pirate Bay. The court decision says that Elisa must remove the Pirate Bay service's domain names from Elisa's name servers and to block traffic to the IP addresses that the service uses. Elisa appealed the decision to the Helsinki Court of Appeal, which did not change the court decision.[14]

C11.27   LAWS PROTECTING PERSONAL DATA/ PERSONALLY IDENTIFIABLE INFORMATION

For example, the Personal Data Act[15] and the Act on the Protection of Privacy in Electronic Communications.[16]

C11.28   DATA BREACH LAWS AND CUSTOMERS/USERS/ REGULATORS NOTIFIED OF HACKING OR DATA LOSS

For example, the Act on the Protection of Privacy in Electronic Communications,[17] Chapter 5 (Information security in communications),

---

12   See www.finlex.fi/en/laki/kaannokset/2002/en20020458.pdf.
13   See www.finlex.fi/en/laki/kaannokset/1961/en19610404.pdf.
14   See http://elisa.fi/ir/pressi/?o=5130.00&did=17728 and http://elisa.fi/ir/pressi/?o=5120.00& did=18126.
15   See www.finlex.fi/en/laki/kaannokset/1999/en19990523.pdf.
16   See www.finlex.fi/en/laki/kaannokset/2004/en20040516.pdf.
17   Ibid.

Section 21 (Information security notifications to the Finnish Communications Regulatory Authority) and Section 21a (Information security notifications to subscribers and users).

Commission Regulation (EU) No 611/2013[18] on the measures applicable to the notification of personal data breaches under Directive 2002/58/EC of the European Parliament and of the Council on privacy and electronic communications is directly applicable to all Member States, including Finland.

The Regulation applies to the notification of personal data breaches by providers of publicly available electronic communications services. Article 2 is about notification to the competent national authority and Article 3 is about notification to the subscriber or individual. The competent national authority in Finland is the Finnish Communications Regulatory Authority (Viestintävirasto).

18　See http://eur-lex.europa.eu/LexUriServ/LexUriServ.do?uri=OJ:L:2013:173:0002:0008:EN: PDF.

Chapter C12

France

Florence Chafiol Chaumont
August & Debouzy

C12.1 INTRODUCTION

France is an EU member state and is a Civil Law jurisdiction.

C12.2 SPECIFIC SM AND SN LAWS

There are no specific SM and SN laws. Nevertheless, SNs, as online public communication services, are subject to French general rules of law and more particularly to,

- Act no 2004-575 on Confidence in the Digital Economy of June 21, 2004 (Loi pour la confiance dans l'économie numérique, also referred to as 'LCEN');

- the Act on the Freedom of the Press of January 29, 1881; and

- the French Data Protection Act, dated January 6, 1978, amended by an Act dated August 6, 2004 (referred to as the 'Loi Informatique et Libertés' or the 'LIL').

C12.3 SM CRIMINAL LAW CASES

Many criminal offences can be committed on SM. In the past, French courts have punished breaches of the Act of July 29, 1881 relating to the Freedom of the Press which took place on SM, such as defamation, insults against individuals, incitement to discrimination, violence, hatred, apology of crimes and offences, and endangerment of minors. French courts have applied these provisions in several cases, some of which are mentioned below,

- On October 18, 2013, the Court of Appeal of Nimes sentenced a French politician to pay a fine of €4,000 for incitement to discrimination, violence and hatred, after he had published racist comments on his Facebook wall. Access to his wall was unrestricted and therefore deemed public by the court. This ruling was issued on the basis of Article 24 of the Act of July 29, 1881 on the Freedom of the Press.[1]

- On January 17, 2012, the Criminal Court of Paris sentenced a trade union delegate for having publicly insulted the management of his company on Facebook. The court ruled that, due to their outrageous and insulting nature against human dignity, his remarks exceeded acceptable criticism.

- In 2012, after the publication of anti-Semitic comments on Twitter, several Jewish associations brought a legal action before courts in order for Twitter to disclose the connection data enabling the authors of the litigious comments to be identified. On January 24, 2013, the Court of First Instance of Paris (*Tribunal de Grande Instance*) ordered Twitter to disclose the data.

Under French law, additional provisions involving criminal offences committed on the internet exist (see C12.5, where the vast majority of those provisions are dealt with). In addition to the cases already mentioned, on March 13, 2012, the French Supreme Court (*Cour de cassation*) upheld the decision handed down by the Court of Appeal of Lyon convicting the accused of the rape of a minor. Such minor had been brought into contact with the perpetrator through the use of a communication network (an online discussion website). The ruling was issued on the basis of Articles 222-23[2] and 222-24[3] of the French Criminal Code.

C12.4   SM CIVIL LAW CASES

In France, there are several SM civil law cases which relate to breach of privacy, data protection, unfair competition or intellectual property rights (for further details, see C12.8 and C12.19).

Furthermore, in a decision handed down by the Commercial Court of Paris on July 6, 2011, the CEO of a company was sentenced to pay compensation for the disparaging comments he posted on Twitter towards one of his competitors. The ruling states, 'Remarks by the CEO of Zlio [which were posted on Twitter] denigrate the quality of Référencement's services. The court deemed that such

---

1 Article 24 of the Act of July 29, 1881 states that individuals guilty of incitement to discrimination, hatred and violence against a person or a group of persons due to their origin, membership or non-membership of an ethnic group, nation, race or religion, can be sentenced to a one-year prison term and to a fine of €45,000.

2 Article 222-23 of the French Criminal Code provides 'Any act of sexual penetration, whatever its nature, committed against another person by violence, constraint, threat, or surprise, is rape. Rape is punished by fifteen years' criminal imprisonment'.

3 Article 222-24, 8° of the French Criminal Code provides 'Rape is punished by twenty years' criminal imprisonment where the victim has been brought into contact with the perpetrator of these acts through the use of a communications network, for the distribution of messages to a non-specified audience'.

acts of unfair competition resulted in damages in the amount of €10,000 ... the court sentenced Zlio to take all the necessary technical measures to erase all content harming Référencement's image'.

C12.5 CASES WHERE SM-RELATED EVIDENCE USED OR ADMISSIBLE

In France, only evidence obtained fairly,[4] that is to say in compliance with the privacy and confidentiality of correspondence,[5] is deemed admissible by the courts.

Nevertheless, respect of privacy and confidentiality do not apply when information is public.

Indeed, French judges differentiate content that is freely accessible to anyone, and content protected by confidentiality. When setting up their SM accounts, users define a certain level of confidentiality, upon which courts rely when deciding if information is public or not.

Therefore, the provision of SM content before courts, when its author wished it to be kept private, does not constitute admissible evidence in court.

SM-related evidence has been used and held admissible by courts on several occasions,

- *Industrial Court (Conseil de Prud'hommes) of Boulogne Billancourt, – November 19, 2010:*

  In this case, three employees were dismissed by their employer for having posted on their Facebook walls messages insulting him. The court held that such content could be lawfully produced in court, and did not infringe the employees' rights to privacy.

  In this case, SM-related evidence was admissible because the messages posted on Facebook were accessible to 'friends of friends' and, accordingly, were deemed public by the court.

- *Court of Appeal of Poitiers – January 16, 2013:*

  The court relied upon messages posted on Facebook by an employer to demonstrate the existence of an employment contract.

  In this case, the court held that messages were public, constituting admissible evidence, because they were posted without any restrictions regarding their recipients, and everyone could see them.

---

4   This principle stems from a decision of the *Cour de cassation* of January 15, 1970.
5   This principle is mentioned in Articles 226-15 and 423-2 of the French Criminal Code.

Several similar cases exist (see, in particular, decisions handed down by the Court of Appeal of Reims on June 9, 2010 and by the Court of Appeal of Besançon on November 15, 2011).

It should be noted that courts deem SM evidence admissible because it is accessible to the public through settings enabling content to be seen by 'friends of friends', for instance. Accordingly, the settings of SM accounts regarding confidentiality are crucial to determine whether messages are intended to be publicly posted or not. Disclosing SM content, when its author wished it to be private, cannot constitute admissible evidence in court.

C12.6 SPECIFIC ONLINE ABUSE/ONLINE BULLYING/ CYBERBULLYING LAWS

Under French law, there are different laws that incriminate criminal offences committed on, and through the use of the Internet,

1) The Act of July 29, 1988 on the Freedom of Press, incriminates offences such as defamation (Article 29), incitement to discrimination, libel and racial insult (Articles 24 bis and 32).

2) Different provisions of the French Criminal Code punish offences committed on the internet and aimed specifically at protecting minors. The following offences, committed through the use of the internet, are particularly sanctioned: circulation of pornographic content (Article 227-24), recourse to child prostitution (Article 225-12-1), sexual abuse and rape of a minor (Articles 222-23 and 222-24), and sexual provocation (Article 227-22-1).

See below several of these provisions,

- Articles 225-12-1 and 225-12-2 of the French Criminal Code punish the recourse to child prostitution. Article 225-12-1 paragraph 1 provides that 'Soliciting, accepting or obtaining, in exchange for remuneration or a promise of remuneration, relations of a sexual nature with a minor who engages in prostitution, even if not habitually, is punished by three years' imprisonment and a fine of €45,000'. And Article 225-12-2 provides that 'the penalty is increased to five years' imprisonment and to €75,000 where the person was put in contact with the offender by the use, for the dissemination of messages to an unrestricted public, of a communication network'.

- Article 227-23 of the French Criminal Code punishes the endangerment of minors, and provides that 'Taking, recording or transferring a picture or representation of a minor with a view to circulating it, where that image or representation has a pornographic character, is punished by three years' imprisonment and a fine of €45,000. Attempting to do so is subject to the same penalties. The same penalty applies to offering or distributing such a picture or representation by any means, and to importing or exporting it, or causing it to be imported or exported. The penalties are increased to five years' imprisonment and a fine of €75,000 where use was made of a communication network for the circulation of messages to an unrestricted public in order to circulate the image or representation of a minor'.

- Article 227-22-1 of the French Criminal Code punishes an adult who makes sexually oriented requests to a minor via the internet by two years' imprisonment and a fine of €300,000.

- Article 227-24 of the French Criminal Code punishes acts of 'happy slapping' and provides that 'The manufacture, transport, distribution by whatever means and however supported, of a message bearing a pornographic or violent character or a character seriously violating human dignity, or encouraging minors to play games that could physically endanger them, or the trafficking in such a message, is punished by three years' imprisonment and a fine of €75,000, where the message may be seen or perceived by a minor. Where the offences under the present article are committed through the press or by broadcasting or by a communication network, the specific legal provisions governing those matters are applicable to define the persons who are responsible'.

The fight against offences committed on the internet is carried out by different means. For instance, the Internet Service Providers Association (AFA), backed by the European Commission, created a French online service enabling the reporting of abusive content.[6] Upon receipt of the report, the AFA verifies if the content is prohibited under French law, and if so, submits the file to the police, and more specifically to the Central Office for the Fight Against Crime Linked to Information and Communication Technology (*Office Central de la Lutte contre la Criminalitée liée aux Technologies de l'Information et de la Communication*, or 'OCLCTIC').

C12.7 OTHER LAWS APPLIED TO ONLINE ABUSE/ ONLINE BULLYING/CYBERBULLYING

See above.

C12.8 CHILDREN AND SM LAWS OR RULES

There are no specific rules that apply to children and SM.

---

6   Available at www.pointdecontact.net/qui_sommes_nous.

However, certain provisions of the French Criminal Code (see C12.5) concern children and offences committed on the internet (See Articles 225-12-1, 225-12-2, 227-23 and 227-24 of the French Criminal Code).

C12.9 EMPLOYEES/EMPLOYMENT SM LAWS OR CASES

There have been several cases involving SM and employees in France.

Employees have been dismissed for having posted malicious messages about their employers on SN.

Decision handed down by the Industrial Court (Conseil de Prud'hommes) of Boulogne Billancourt – on November 19, 2010

In this case, three employees were dismissed by their employer for having posted on Facebook pages, and more particularly on their walls, different messages insulting and criticizing the employer. The court deemed that the content posted on the Facebook walls justified the dismissal of the employees, as it was public and therefore not protected by message confidentiality.

Decision handed down by the Court of Appeal of Reims – on June 9, 2010

The court ruled that the dismissal of an employee was justified because the latter had posted abusive and slanderous messages about his employer on his Facebook wall. Such messages were deemed public, for they were posted on a wall which was accessible to everyone.

Decision handed down by the Court of Appeal of Besançon – on November 15, 2011

The court held that the dismissal of an employee was justified as he had posted messages that strongly criticized his company on the wall of one of his colleagues.

Decision handed down by the Court of Appeal of Reims on November 15, 2011

The court ruled that the dismissal of an employee was not justified because the latter's employer intentionally accessed the employee's Facebook messages which were directed at certain individuals only. Thus, the court emphasized that those messages were not publicly accessible to 'friends of friends', and were therefore protected by message confidentiality.

Decision handed down by the Criminal Court of Paris on January 17, 2012

The Criminal Court of Paris convicted a trade union delegate for public insult as he had published on Facebook outrageous and insulting remarks towards the management of the company he worked for. The court pointed out that his remarks exceeded acceptable criticism.

Finally, in 2013 a television host was dismissed following comments he had made on Twitter, which were qualified as 'not acceptable' by the Director of the TV channel.

C12.10 SCHOOL AND UNIVERSITY STUDENT SM CASES

If using SM disturbs the school/university community, the board of education may take disciplinary measures against a student that could lead to exclusion from the school/university.

For instance, in 2006, the exclusion of a student from his school was challenged by his parents who brought an action before the Administrative Court of Clermont-Ferrand. The parents claimed that the school could not sanction extracurricular behaviour. On April 6, 2006, the Court dismissed the parents' claim on the ground that, even if the alleged act was committed outside the school, it could disturb the smooth running of the public service, thus justifying the exclusion from school.

More recently, on February 8, 2013, following the creation of false teacher Facebook accounts accompanied by insults and obscene photo-montages, five students were expelled from their school. There are currently criminal proceedings pending relating to the public insult of a civil servant.

C12.11 RIGHT OR HUMAN RIGHT TO ACCESS THE INTERNET OR SM

In an important decision dated June 10, 2009, the French Constitutional Council[7] (*Conseil Constitutionnel*) ruled that access to the internet was a necessary right for the exercise of freedom of expression and communication, as specified in Article 11 of the Declaration of the Rights of Man and of the Citizen. It highlighted that, as the internet is an important means of communication, the freedom to access these services must be protected.

Nevertheless, this decision must not be overestimated, as it does not consecrate the right of internet access as a 'human right' or a 'fundamental right'.[8]

---

7   The French Constitutional Council is the highest constitutional authority in France. Its main activity is to rule on whether proposed statutes conform with the Constitution, after they have been voted by Parliament and before they are signed into law by the President of the Republic.

8   *Francillon, J.,* Téléchargement illégal. Heur et malheur de la loi « Création et Internet »: la loi Hadopi censurée par le Conseil constitutionnel, Rev. Sc. crim. 2009, p 617 ; *Boubeker I.,* De la « Hadopi » à la loi « Hadopi 2 ». Analyse de la décision du Conseil Constitutionnel n°2009-580 DC et de ses conséquences, RLDI 2009/51, p. 108.

In a nutshell, the right to internet access is protected as a means for each individual to exercise their freedom of expression, but the right to internet access does not exist, as such, in France.

C12.12 BANS OR RESTRICTIONS ON INTERNET OR SM

The Act of June 12, 2009 introduced an obligation for each internet user to secure their internet connection. In other words, provisions introduced by the law aimed to fight against illegal downloading, by requiring that each internet user ensure that their internet connection is not used for illegal downloading.

Each internet user is required to monitor uses of their internet connection and to secure its access. If they fail to secure it, they may be liable for negligence and to pay a fine of €1,500 (Article R 335-5 of the French Intellectual Property Code).

Before July 8, 2013, internet users who were liable for illegal downloading (that is to say, if they failed to secure their internet connection) could also have their internet connection cut for a period of a month. Nevertheless, Decree No 2013-596 of July 8, 2013 cancelled this penalty. Therefore, to our knowledge, there are no more laws that restrict access to the internet in France.

C12.13 IDENTITY THEFT (OR EQUIVALENT)

Identify theft is a criminal offence. The 'Loppsi 2' Act of March 14, 2011 created the offence of 'digital identity theft' through Article 226-4-1 of the French Criminal Code.

Article 226-4-1 of the French Criminal Code provides that '[t]he taking of an individual's identity on the Internet, or the use of data of any kind enabling the identification of said person in order to cause him trouble or to affect his honour, is punishable by a one-year prison sentence and a fine of €15,000.00.'

Furthermore, civil liability may be incurred for digital identity theft on the ground of breach of privacy or image rights.

On November 24, 2010, the Court of First Instance (*Tribunal de grande instance*) of Paris sentenced the author of a Facebook account who passed himself off as a famous French comic, Omar Sy. He was sentenced to pay €1,500 compensation for sustained damage.

It is important to note that, prior to bringing actions, the victims of identity theft need to obtain, by a court decision, the disclosure of data enabling the author of the identity theft to be identified by the SN or internet service provider. For instance, on April 4, 2013, the Court of First Instance (*Tribunal de grande instance*) of Paris ordered Twitter to disclose all information relating to the identity of an individual who had created a false Twitter account.

C12.14   HACKING (OR EQUIVALENT)

There are laws relating to hacking in France,

Article 323-1 of the French Criminal Code provides 'Fraudulently accessing or remaining within all or part of an automated data processing system is punishable by two years' imprisonment and a fine of €30,000. Where this behaviour causes the suppression or modification of data contained in that system, or any alteration of the functioning of that system, the sentence is three years' imprisonment and a fine of €45,000'.

Article 323-3 of the French Criminal Code provides 'The fraudulent introduction of data into an automated data processing system or the fraudulent deletion or modification of the data that it contains is punishable by five years' imprisonment and a fine of €75,000'.

For instance, in 2012, a student was sentenced by a French court to pay €400 compensation for damage caused to his former teacher after having hacked the latter's Facebook account. In that case, the student had cracked his teacher's password and drew a Chinese hat and moustache on his profile picture (Court of First Instance of Angers, May 22, 2012).

In some cases, hacking is intended to harm others. In January 2013, the Court of First Instance of Avignon convicted a 38-year-old man for hacking his girlfriend's Facebook account and posting nude pictures of her. He was sentenced to a one-year prison term, ordered to refrain from contacting her and sentenced to pay €2,000 compensation for the moral damage she sustained.

C12.15   PRIVACY BY DESIGN (PBD) (OR EQUIVALENT)

In France, there are discussions relating to PbD. For instance, the data protection authority, the CNIL, delivers labels to products and procedures complying with the French Data Protection Act (Article 11 thereof). Labels become a tool of a PbD policy.

According to the CNIL, PbD is an 'interesting concept'. The CNIL is actually waiting for more clarifications and underlines the necessity to have more details about its implementation.

C12.16   TWEETING FROM COURTS, AND ANY RULES/LAWS

There is no law prohibiting Tweets from courts, but images and cameras are banned in courts, and therefore Tweeting pictures of individuals attending hearings can be considered as a breach of Article 308 of the French Code of Criminal Procedure and Article 38 ter of the Act of July 29, 1881 which provides that 'As soon as the hearing has begun, the use of any type of device enabling the recording, fixation or transmission of sound or image is prohibited.

The president of the court is entitled to seize any device used in violation of this prohibition'.

Nevertheless, many professionals deem that writings and, accordingly, Tweets from courts are allowed.[9]

It should be noted that, pursuant to Article 309 of the French Code of Criminal Procedure and Article 438 of the French Code of Civil Procedure, the President of the court must conduct hearings and ensure that there is no disruption. Therefore, he is entitled to ban the use of Twitter in courts.

C12.17 TELEVISION COURTROOM BROADCASTING OR TELEVISION CAMERAS IN COURT, AND RULES OR LAWS

To guarantee the serenity of justice, sound recording and audio-visual recording in courts are prohibited pursuant to Article 308 of the French Code of Criminal Procedure and Article 38 ter of the Act of July 29, 1881 (see C12.16).

Accordingly, any recording or sound recording equipment, television or cameras or photographic equipment is prohibited in courts. Any breach of this prohibition is punishable by a fine of €4,500.

Nevertheless, there are two exceptions:

- Paragraph 2 of Article 308 of the French Code of Criminal Procedure provides that: 'the president of the criminal court (*Cour d'assises*) may order that all or part of the hearing be sound-recorded under his supervision. Under the same conditions, he may also order that an audiovisual recording of the hearing or the evidence of the victim or the civil party be made, if either requests this';

- According the Act of July 11, 1985, audio-visual recordings or sound recordings are authorized for historical purposes, and more particularly for the constitution of historical archives (Article 1 of Act No 85-699 of July 11, 1985). Accordingly, due to their historical interest, several cases have been recorded in France, such as the Klaus Barbie case in 1987, the Paul Touvier case in 1994, or the case relating to the explosion of the industrial plant AZF in Toulouse in 2009.

C12.18 SM IN COURTROOMS

A case has recently been referred to the High Council for the Judiciary (*Conseil Supérieur de la Magistrature*) regarding the use of Twitter by two judges during hearings.

---

9   *E Derieux, A Granchet,* Réseaux sociaux en ligne, Aspects juridiques et déontologiques, Lamy Axe Droit, 2013.

The case began in 2012 when a journalist revealed that two judges shared approximately 20 messages on Twitter during hearings.

On April 29, 2014, the High Council for the Judiciary recommended that the Ministry of Justice take disciplinary measures, and that the judges be reassigned to another court.

This decision has been highly commented on in France.

C12.19   USE OF SM AS EVIDENCE IN COURTS

There do not appear to have been any examples of controversies or cases in relation to the use of SM as evidence in courts, except those mentioned in C12.4 and C12.8.

C12.20   PRIVACY, DATA PROTECTION AND SM

First of all, it should be noted that many cases relating to the violation of privacy rights on SM result from data processing. Threats relating to privacy rights are related to (i) data collection which may be carried out without the knowledge of the individuals concerned, and (ii) the nature and content of data collected and stored. Therefore, users may bring a claim for violation of their privacy rights due to an unlawful data processing on SN.

For instance, Facebook was sentenced on April 2013 to remove images of a bishop which were deemed to be a violation of his right to privacy on the basis of Article 9 of the French Civil Code, which provides that: 'Everyone has the right to respect for his private life. Without prejudice to compensation for injury suffered, the court may prescribe any measures, such as sequestration, seizure and others, appropriate to prevent or put an end to an invasion of personal privacy; in case of emergency, those measures may be provided for by interim order'.

On December 6, 2013, the Court of First Instance of Paris ordered Google to remove nine pictures of Max Mosley which were on Google Images. The pictures in question represented sexual scenes with Max Mosley and were taken without the latter's knowledge and consent. The court ruled that the publication of such images violated his right to privacy on the basis of Article 9 of the French Civil Code.

On December 15, 2012, the Court of First Instance of Paris ordered the removal of pornographic movies which appeared in Google's results lists when using the name of a woman. Given that data were irrelevant (the movies were produced a long time ago), the court ruled that the publication of such movies was a violation of the woman's privacy rights, and that she must benefit from the right to be forgotten.

In June 2012, the French data authority, the CNIL, issued a warning against the company Yatedo which collected and exploited personal data from Facebook to create online curricula vitae. The CNIL deemed that such data processing, because it referred to irrelevant and outdated data, could undermine the reputation of users and violate their private life.

The French Supreme Administrative Court (*Conseil d'Etat*) upheld the CNIL's sanction against the company Pages Jaunes in a ruling dated March 12, 2014. In this case, the CNIL issued a warning against Pages Jaunes which collected personal data of SM users, and added them to its online directories. The *Conseil d'Etat* upheld the CNIL's decision and held that the company Pages Jaunes had proceeded to an unfair and illicit data collection, as the SM users had never been informed that their personal data could be extracted and collected by Pages Jaunes. The *Conseil d'Etat* stressed that fundamental rights and privacy of users must be respected.

C12.21 SM AND FAMILY LAW CASES

There do not appear to be any particular cases related to this matter.

C12.22 SPORTS PERSONS, SPORTS CLUBS AND SM

In April 2013, footballer Joey Barton, who was playing for 'Olympique de Marseille' at the time, insulted another footballer on Twitter. Nevertheless, he was not sanctioned by the French Sports Federation.

More recently, a Tweet made headlines in France after the girlfriend of footballer Samir Nasri insulted the French national football team and its manager. The French Sports Federation did not punish him for his girlfriend's Tweet, but made a public announcement condemning her words.

It should be noted that, as an employee, a sports player may be dismissed for having insulted his hierarchy on Twitter. Nevertheless, an employee cannot be dismissed for making comments on Twitter if his account has restricted access or can only be seen by 'followers' (Decision No 11-19530 handed down by the *Cour de cassation* on April 10, 2013).

C12.23 PERSONAL RELATIONS AND RELATIONSHIPS

There do not appear to be any particular cases relating to this matter, except the ruling of the Court of First Instance of Avignon (see C12.13).

C12.24 SM AND PERSONAL DATA OF DECEASED PERSONS

There are no particular cases or controversies in France related to the SM personal data of deceased persons.

Article 40 of the French Data Protection Act deals with this issue and enables heirs to request that the personal data of a deceased person be updated. It provides that: 'If a deceased person's heirs are made aware that the personal data of the deceased person have not been updated, said heirs may ask the data processor to proceed to the update that should be done taking into account the death'.

C12.25 SM, WEBSITE, SERVICE PROVIDER OR ISP DEFENCE RULES/LAWS

Pursuant to the Act on Confidence in the Digital Economy of June 21, 2004, and specifically to Article 6-I-2 thereof, in order to avoid liability, host providers have an obligation to withdraw certain material from the websites they host.

In order to benefit from a limitation of liability, upon obtaining actual knowledge or awareness of illegal activities, the service provider has to act expeditiously to remove or to disable access to the information concerned.

Article 6-I-2 of the Act on Confidence in the Digital Economy states that,

> 'natural persons or legal entities who undertake, even free of charge, in order to render accessible to the public via online public communication services, the hosting of signals, writings, images, sounds or messages of any kind, supplied by the recipients of those services, cannot be held liable because of those activities or of the data stored on request of a recipient of those services, if they did not have actual knowledge of their unlawful nature, or of facts and circumstances disclosing this unlawful nature, or if, as from the moment they acquired such knowledge, they acted promptly to withdraw this data or bar access to this data.'

Thus, there is an obligation which is subject to a number of conditions. First of all, the host/service provider must have actual knowledge of the contentious facts. Such knowledge must result from a notice, the content of which is precisely defined by Article 6-I-5 of the Act.

Article 6-I-7 specifies that neither the ISPs nor the host providers are under a general obligation to monitor the information they transfer or store, nor are they under a general obligation to search for facts or circumstances that disclose copyright infringing content.

Moreover, Article 6.II provides that, 'host providers/service providers must keep and store data enabling the identification of anyone who contributed to the creation of the contents of services they provided'.

C12.26 ECOMMERCE DEFENCE CASES

The question of whether some websites can be qualified as 'host providers' has been hotly debated and has raised different issues for the courts.

For instance, courts have had to address whether websites such as YouTube or Dailymotion qualify as hosts or editors.

- On May 6, 2009, the Court of Appeal of Paris deemed that a difference should be made between a host who as 'a technical provider makes accessible to the public stored content supplied by the recipient of this service, and as an editor is the one who determines the content made accessible to the public, so that the criterion to distinguish between the two resides in the service's capacity to act on the content put online'.

  Therefore, the Court of Appeal held that the website of exchange Dailymotion, which does not have control over the content made accessible to the public, benefits from the status of technical intermediary, and therefore is not liable for the information stored (Paris Court of Appeal, judgment of May 6, 2009, Dailymotion /Ch. Carion).

- As such, the Court of Appeal of Paris ruled that 'exploiting a website through the selling of advertising space, as long as it does not entail the capacity to act on the content online, does not justify qualifying the person running this website as editor' (Court of Appeal of Paris, October 13, 2010, Roland Magdane c/ Dailymotion).

- The *Cour de cassation*, in an important decision dated February 17, 2011, ruled along the same lines and held that the person running a website which sells advertising spaces qualifies as a host.

- The Court of First Instance of Créteil ruled that YouTube qualifies as a host because the website only makes accessible to the public the stored content supplied by the recipient of the service, by providing a technology enabling the storage and viewing of videos. Hence, YouTube does not determine the content made accessible to the public (decision handed down by the Court of First Instance of Créteil on December 14, 2010, *Institut national de l'audiovisuel v Youtube*).

Regarding SNs, it can be assumed that they qualify as hosts. Indeed, Facebook was required by the court to remove a litigious picture and to provide connection data enabling the identification of its author. Judges rendered this decision on the basis of Article 6 of the LCEN and deemed that Facebook was not the editor of the website but the host, and accordingly must store personal data of users in order to enable their identification if needed (Court of First Instance of Paris, April 13, 2010).

C12.27 LAWS PROTECTING PERSONAL DATA/ PERSONALLY IDENTIFIABLE INFORMATION

Data protection matters are regulated under French law by Act no 78-17 dated January 6, 1978, amended by an Act dated August 6, 2004[10] (referred to as the 'Loi Informatique et Libertés' or the 'LIL').

---

10 The purpose of the LIL dated August 6, 2004 was to implement in France the European Directive 95/46/EC dated October 24, 1995.

Several decrees were enacted, amongst which a Decree dated October 20, 2005 further amended on March 25, 2007 (hereafter the 'Decree'). Amongst other items, this Decree defines the level of information which must be provided to a data subject.

Data protection privacy is enforced both by a French independent authority called the 'Commission Nationale Informatique et Libertés' (or the 'CNIL')[11] and by the criminal courts.[12] It should be noted as a preliminary that French law does not distinguish penalties applicable to data collected from individual consumers versus business-to-business situations: all the penalties apply, irrespective of the nature of the data subject at stake.

Pursuant to Article 2 of the LIL, it shall apply to 'automatic processing of personal data ...'.

According to the LIL, 'personal data' is defined as 'any information relating to a natural person who is or can be identified, directly or indirectly, by reference to an identification number or to one or more factors specific to him'.[13]

It should be noted that this definition is extremely broad as it encompasses any information which can identify a person,

- directly (name, surname, email address, pictures, etc) or

- indirectly (social security number, IP address (although French courts do not have a unified position on this), phone number, etc) or

- only in conjunction with other information which the data controller may have (for instance, a nationality is not *per se* personal data, but it becomes personal data if associated with any other information which allows one to clearly identify the person concerned by such nationality).

C12.28   DATA BREACH LAWS AND CUSTOMERS/USERS/ REGULATORS NOTIFIED OF HACKING OR DATA LOSS

Under Article 34 bis of the French Data Protection Act, electronic communication service providers are required to notify any breach of personal data they encounter. Typically, this provision is directed at telecom providers

---

11   CNIL penalties: a financial penalty not exceeding €150,000 for the first breach and €300,000 in the event this breach occurs again within five years of the first sentence for the same facts; an injunction to stop the processing. In addition, in case of bad faith of the data controller, the CNIL is entitled to order to make available to the public, through any media (website etc), the other penalties it has ordered.

12   As per Articles 226-16 to 226-24 of the French Criminal Code, there are numerous criminal conducts concerning data protection which may be sanctioned by French criminal courts by five years' imprisonment and a fine of €300,000.

13   Article 2 of the LIL further provides that 'In order to determine whether a person is identifiable, all the means that the data controller or any other person uses or may have access to should be taken into consideration.'

and internet service providers (please note that other industries are not required to notify any data breach).

Article 34 bis of the Data Protection Act defines data protection breaches as breaches of security leading to the accidental or unlawful destruction, loss, alteration, unauthorised disclosure of, or access to, personal data transmitted, stored or otherwise processed in connection with the provision of a publicly available communications service.

In these cases, all personal data breaches shall be notified to the French Data Authority, the CNIL, no later than 24 hours after the detection of the personal data breach.

The service provider shall notify personal data breaches to subscribers or individuals where a personal data breach is likely to adversely affect their personal data or privacy. The notification to the subscriber or individual shall be made without undue delay after the detection of the personal data breach.

Notification of a personal data breach to a subscriber or individual concerned shall not be required if three cumulative conditions are met,

- the provider has demonstrated to the satisfaction of the competent national authority that it has implemented appropriate technological protection measures;

- that those measures were applied to the data concerned by the security breach; and

- that such technological protection measures render the data unintelligible to any person who is not authorised to access it.

Chapter C13

Germany

Dr Ingo Schöttler
GAD eG

C13.1   INTRODUCTION

Germany is an EU member state and is a Civil Law jurisdiction.

C13.2   SPECIFIC SM AND SN LAWS

None.

C13.3   SM CRIMINAL LAW CASES

For example,

AG Wolfratshausen, 25 March 2013, 2 CS 11 js 27699/12

This case concerned the question whether the announcement of an (unspecified) gun rampage on Facebook may be punishable by law. The court decided that the announcement of such running amok is suitable to disturb the public peace within the meaning of section 126 of the German Criminal Code (StGB).[1] However, the accused was acquitted, because he assumed that only his closest circle of friends, which included 25 to 35 people, would read the posting with the announcement on Facebook. So, according to the court, he had no intent to disturb the public peace (that is, a significant number of people).

OLG Celle, 2. Criminal Chamber, 14 March 2013, 32 SS 125/12

The court of appeal had to deal with the question whether an entry in a list of online supporters can already represent a public incitement to crime under section 111 of the German Criminal Code.[2]

---

1   Criminal Code in the version promulgated on 13 November 1998, Federal Law Gazette [*Bundesgesetzblatt*] Part I p 3322, last amended by Article 3 of the Law of 2 October 2009, Federal Law Gazette Part I p 3214; an English translation is available at www.gesetze-im-internet.de/englisch_stgb/englisch_stgb.html#p1149.
2   Section 111 states that a person who publicly incites the commission of an unlawful act shall be held liable as an abettor (Section 26).

The court decided that, with the entry into a freely accessible and viewable list of supporters for a criminal campaign in the internet, the undersigned pursuant to section 111 of the German Criminal Code incites the commission of an unlawful act, if the call for an impartial third party is to be understood, through its detailed description, as a seriously intentioned appeal to commit the criminal offence described closer in the call.

C13.4   SM CIVIL LAW CASES

For example,

LG Berlin, 33. Civil Chamber, 13 August 2012, 33 O 434/1

This case involved a well-known rapper who had to pay compensation because of derogatory statements made on various SM websites. According to the court, comments on SM websites, which focus on the defamation of a person and deliberately malicious exaggerated criticism, and not on the factual dispute, entitle the person concerned to demand compensation (in this case €8,000) for a serious breach of personal rights.

AG Munich, 15 June 2012, 158 C 28716/11

The AG Munich had to decide in a case in which private Facebook photos, which showed the girlfriend of a convicted sexual offender, were leaked to a newspaper. The court decided that, if a person in a full body photograph despite pixelation is visible (and is also recognisable), the publication of this private photo on the front page of a newspaper is a violation of the general personality right of the person concerned and of the right to one's own image. The girlfriend was awarded damages of €1,200.

See also C13.9.

C13.5   CASES WHERE SM-RELATED EVIDENCE USED OR ADMISSIBLE

For example,

AG Reutlingen, 31 October 2011, 5 DS 43 js 18155/10 jug

The court decided that, if a defendant is sufficiently suspicious to have aided a burglary and to have exchanged evidentiary information with the main culprit via the chat and Messenger function of his Facebook account, his account is to be confiscated, if it is expected that earlier sent messages and chat messages are still stored in the database of the provider.

C13.6   SPECIFIC ONLINE ABUSE/ONLINE BULLYING/ CYBERBULLYING LAWS

None.

C13.7 OTHER LAWS APPLIED TO ONLINE ABUSE/ONLINE BULLYING/CYBERBULLYING

The German Criminal Code contains a number of provisions that may be applied in this context, especially:

- Section 185: Insult;

- Section 186/187: (Intentional) defamation;

- Section 201a: Violation of intimate privacy by taking photographs;

- Section 238: Stalking, especially Section 238 (1) No. 2 which punishes individuals who stalk persons by trying to establish contact with them by means of telecommunications or other means of communication and thereby seriously infringes their lifestyle;

- Section 240: Using threats or force to cause a person to do, suffer or omit an act.

C13.8 CHILDREN AND SM LAWS OR RULES

None.

C13.9 EMPLOYEES/EMPLOYMENT SM LAWS OR CASES

For example,

ArbG Duisburg, 26 September 2012, 5 CA 949/12

In this case the court decided that insults of the employer or colleagues, which constitute a significant defamation of the person concerned, can justify an extraordinary dismissal for reasons of conduct without a previous warning. According to the court, this shall also apply to entries on SNs like Facebook and even if the entry is only visible for so-called 'Facebook friends' and their friends.

Landesarbeitsgericht Hamm (Westfalen),10 October 2012, 3 SA 644/12

The court ruled that, if an apprentice describes his employer on his Facebook page as 'slave-driver' and 'exploiter' and his work as 'stupid shit', these massive defamatory statements can justify an extraordinary termination of the apprenticeship relationship without a previous warning.

C13.10 SCHOOL AND UNIVERSITY STUDENT SM CASES

For example,

BGH, 23 June 2009, VI ZR 196/08

The BGH decided that the evaluation of teachers on the internet using a school grading system is not in breach of the general right of personality, if the evaluation only concerns the professional activity of teachers. According to the court, the reviews are not inadmissible because they can be given anonymously, since the possibility to use the internet anonymously is legally and technically provided. In such circumstances, as a rule, the freedom of expression and the legitimate interest in information outweigh the teachers' right of informational self-determination.

OVG Lüneburg, 26 January 2010, 2 ME 444/09

According to the court, it is not objectionable if a school refers a student to another school of the same type, who is responsible for the announcement (not seriously meant) of a gun rampage on SM. The court argued that it has to be made clear to the students that such behaviour will not remain without serious regulatory measures, because the announcement of a gun rampage, even as a joke, is not acceptable.

C13.11   RIGHT OR HUMAN RIGHT TO ACCESS THE INTERNET OR SM

There are a number of cases that deal with the question whether prison inmates have the right to use a computer within the scope of their fundamental right to information and communication. As a result, the actual case law does not allow for individual computer use by prisoners.[3]

C13.12   BANS OR RESTRICTIONS ON INTERNET OR SM

Examples are limited,

A 21-year-old was sentenced to six months of not using SMs such as 'Facebook' and 'WhatsApp' (AG Munich, 24 March 2014, 1013 LS). He had harassed female students on these SNs and had compelled them to send him nude pictures, which he had posted on the internet. Due to the mental age of the offender, the court operated in its decision with the sanctions of juvenile justice.

C13.13   IDENTITY THEFT (OR EQUIVALENT)

The German Criminal Code contains a number of provisions that may be applied in this context, especially,

- Section 202a (Data espionage);

---

3   See BVerfG, 31 March 2003, 2 BvR 1848/02; OLG Hamm, 17 August 2010, 1 Vollz (Ws) 255/10.

- Section 202b (Phishing): Under this section, individuals who unlawfully intercept data not intended for them by technical means from a non-public data processing facility (or from its electromagnetic broadcast) shall be liable to imprisonment not exceeding two years or a fine;

- Section 202c (Acts preparatory to data espionage and phishing);

- Section 263 (Fraud);

- Section 263a (Computer Fraud);

- Section 269 (Forgery of data intended to provide proof): Under this section, individuals who, for the purposes of deception in legal commerce, store or modify data intended to provide proof in such a way that a counterfeit document would be created upon their retrieval, or uses such data, shall be liable to imprisonment not exceeding five years or a fine;

- Section 303a (Data tampering);

- Section 303b (Computer sabotage).

C13.14 HACKING (OR EQUIVALENT)

Similar to the cases of identity theft, the German Criminal Code contains a number of provisions that may be applied in this context, especially,

- Section 202a (Data espionage): Under this Section, persons who unlawfully obtain data, which were not intended for them and which were especially protected against unauthorized access, if they have circumvented this protection, shall be liable to imprisonment not exceeding three years or a fine;

- Section 202c (Acts preparatory to data espionage and phishing);

- Section 303a (Data tampering): This section states that individuals who unlawfully delete, suppress, render unusable or alter data shall be liable to imprisonment not exceeding two years or a fine;

- Section 303b (Computer sabotage).

C13.15 PRIVACY BY DESIGN (PBD) (OR EQUIVALENT)

Currently, there are no regulations relating to PbD as such. PbD is mentioned in Article 23 of the EU proposal for a General Data Protection Regulation.[4]

---

4   Proposal for a regulation of the European Parliament and of the Council on the protection of individuals with regard to the processing of personal data and on the free movement of such data (General Data Protection Regulation) /* COM/2012/011 final - 2012/0011 (COD) */, available at http://eur-lex.europa.eu/legal-content/EN/TXT/?uri=CELEX:52012PC0011.

If this Regulation is adopted, it will have direct effect in Germany too. The concept is also discussed in academic literature.[5]

C13.16 TWEETING FROM COURTS, AND ANY RULES/LAWS

There are no regulations that specifically prohibit Tweeting from courts. However, some judges have imposed such a ban within the framework of their 'maintenance of order'[6] in the sitting.[7] This topic has also received some discussion in academic literature.[8]

C13.17 TELEVISION COURTROOM BROADCASTING OR TELEVISION CAMERAS IN COURT, AND RULES OR LAWS

Television courtroom broadcasting is prohibited by Section 169 of the German Constitution Act.[9] The second sentence states that live audio, television or radio recordings, as well as audio and film recordings intended for public presentation or for publication of their content, shall be inadmissible.

C13.18 SM IN COURTROOMS

See C13.16.

C13.19 USE OF SM AS EVIDENCE IN COURTS

Both in criminal and in civil cases, information published on SM has been used as evidence in courts (see C13.3 and C13.4).

---

5   See eg *Boehme-Neßler*, Privacy by Design - Der EU-Datenschutz als Modell moderner Gesetzgebung, ZG 2013, 242–249; *Schulz*, Privacy by Design, CR 2012, 204–208 (all in German).

6   Section 176 of the German Courts Constitution Act states: 'The maintenance of order in the sitting shall be incumbent on the presiding judge'.

7   See eg a press release of the German Federal Constitutional Court (*Bundesverfassungsgericht*), available at www.bundesverfassungsgericht.de/pressemitteilungen/bvg12-060.html.

8   See eg *von Coelln*, Justiz und Medien, AfP 2014, 193–202; *Krieg*, Twittern im Gerichtssaal – The revolution will not be televised, K&R 2009, 673–678 (all in German).

9   Courts Constitution Act in the version published on 9 May 1975 (Federal Law Gazette [*Bundesgesetzblatt*] Part I p 1077), last amended by Article 1 of the Act of 2 July 2013 (Federal Law Gazette Part I p 1938). An English translation is available at www.gesetze-im-internet.de/englisch_gvg/englisch_gvg.html#p0813.

C13.20 PRIVACY, DATA PROTECTION AND SM

For example,

Schleswig-Holstein Administrative Court, 9 October 2013, 8 A 218/11

In this case the court decided that the operator of a fan page on Facebook is not the responsible 'controller' under section 3 (7) of the German Federal Data Protection Act.[10] Therefore the operation of such a fan page may not be prohibited by the data protection supervisory authority.

Oberverwaltungsgericht Schleswig-Holstein, 14 February 2013, 8 B 61 / 12

In this case the court decided that Irish data protection law does apply to Facebook Ireland Limited.

Therefore, Facebook may require registration under a real name from its users (contrary to section 13 (6) of the German Telemedia Act).

C13.21 SM AND FAMILY LAW CASES

Examples are limited,

Persons who receive insults or threats via Facebook may obtain a contact and approach ban under the German Protection Act (OLG Hamm, 23 April 2013, 2 UF 254/12).

C13.22 SPORTS PERSONS, SPORTS CLUBS AND SM

Examples are, again, limited,

The footballer Ryan Babel was fined €3,000 by the Sport Court of the German Football Federation (DFB), because after a game he commented on Twitter, 'I don't know, the ref was on drugs'.[11]

C13.23 PERSONAL RELATIONS AND RELATIONSHIPS

For example,

OLG Koblenz, 20 May 2014, 3 U 1288/13

The court decided that, after the end of a love relationship, an ex-partner may be required to delete image and video files that have been previously made by

---

10 Federal Data Protection Act in the version promulgated on 14 January 2003 (Federal Law Gazette Part I p 66), as most recently amended by Article 1 of the Act of 14 August 2009 (Federal Law Gazette Part I p 2814). An English translation is available at www.gesetze-im-internet.de/englisch_bdsg/index.html.
11 See the corresponding statement of his club, TSG 1899 Hoffenheim, available at www. achtzehn99.de/babel-fined-by-dfb/.

consensus. But, according to the court, this should only apply to images of the genital area. There is no equivalent cancellation claim regarding photos and films that show everyday or holiday situations.

C13.24   SM AND PERSONAL DATA OF DECEASED PERSONS

For example,

LG Saarbrücken, 14 February 2014, 13 S 4/14

The court decided that, in principle, the widow of a deceased is not entitled to injunctive relief against the publication of a 'virtual tomb' on the internet with condolence entries. Nevertheless, in this case the injunctive relief was granted, because the condolence entries wrongly suggested that the deceased had had an affair.

Furthermore, there is discussion in academic literature about what happens with the 'digital inheritance' (emails, data etc) after the death of an account holder.[12]

C13.25   SM, WEBSITE, SERVICE PROVIDER OR ISP DEFENCE RULES/LAWS

The German Telemedia Act serves to implement Directive 2000/31/EC of the European Parliament and of the Council of 8 June 2000 on certain legal aspects of information society services, in particular electronic commerce, in the internal market ('Directive on electronic commerce'). It provides corresponding liability exemptions/limitations for 'mere conduit' (Section 8), 'caching' (Section 9) and 'hosting' (Section 10).

C13.26   ECOMMERCE DEFENCE CASES

For example,

BGH, 14 May 2013, VI ZR 269/12-, BGHZ 197, 213-224

This case concerned the conditions of the liability of the operator of an internet search engine (Google) for rights-infringing search suggestions produced by the (automatic) keyword addition function. According to the court the liability

---

12   See eg *Brinkert/Stolze/Heidrich*, Der Tod und das soziale Netzwerk, ZD 2013, 153–157; *Brisch/Müller-ter Jung*, Digitaler Nachlass – Das Schicksal von EMail- und De-Mail-Accounts sowie Mediencenter-Inhalten, CR 2013, 446–455; *Dopatka*, Digitaler Nachlass – Der Umgang mit elektronischen Daten nach dem Tod, NJW 2010, NJW-aktuell Nr 49, 14–16 (all in German).

of the operator requires the breach of reasonable inspection duties. However, the operator is always responsible if he becomes aware of an unlawful infringement of personal rights. If an affected party gives the operator notice of an unlawful infringement of his personality, the operator is obliged to prevent such violation in the future.

VG Cologne, 15 December 2011, 6 K 5404/10

In this case the court decided that liability of an access provider can only be considered if the access provider intentionally works together with a user of his service to commit unlawful acts (in this case, organizing unlawful online gaming).

C13.27   LAWS PROTECTING PERSONAL DATA/ PERSONALLY IDENTIFIABLE INFORMATION

Section 1 (1) of the German Federal Data Protection Act states that the purpose of this Act is to protect individuals against their right to privacy being impaired through the handling of their personal data. The Act serves to implement Directive 95/46/EC of the European Parliament and of the Council of 24 October 1995 on the protection of individuals with regard to the processing of personal data and on the free movement of such data (OJ EC L 281, p 31 *et seq*).

Furthermore, there are data protection regulations in a variety of special Acts, for example in the German Telemedia Act (TMG, sections 11–15a) and the German Telecommunications Act (TKG, sections 91–107).

C13.28   DATA BREACH LAWS AND CUSTOMERS/ USERS/REGULATORS NOTIFIED OF HACKING OR DATA LOSS

Section 42a of the German Federal Data Protection Act states that, if a private or a public body determines that,

- special types of personal data (as defined in Section 3 (9));

- personal data subject to professional secrecy;

- personal data related to criminal offences or administrative offences or the suspicion of punishable actions;

- or personal data concerning bank or credit card accounts,

have been unlawfully transferred or revealed to third parties, with the threat of serious harm to the data subject's rights or interests, the body shall notify the responsible supervisory authority and the data subject without delay.

Greece

Dr Marina Perraki (Partner)
Gerry Kounadis (Associate)
Maria Chaidou, Elina Kefala, Katerina Kontolati, Ioanna Tapeinou
(Trainee Lawyers)
Tsibanoulis & Partners Law Firm

C14.1   INTRODUCTION

Greece is an EU member state and is a Civil Law jurisdiction.

C14.2   SPECIFIC SM AND SN LAWS

SNs can be defined, in general terms, as online communication websites which allow people to create networks of users with similar ideas or to join these already existing networks. Despite the absence of a specific legal framework governing the use and function of SNs in Greece, certain articles of special laws, the Greek Civil Code, the Greek Penal Code and the Hellenic Data Protection Authority's decisions, as well as the Constitution of Greece, apply *mutatis mutandis*.

Law 2472/1997 on the Protection of Individuals with regard to the Processing of Personal Data (hereafter the 'Personal Data Law') implementing Directive 95/46/EC constitutes the primary legislative tool as far as the protection of citizens' rights related to their personal data is concerned. Processing of personal data is considered as any operation which is performed upon personal data by the public administration or by a public law entity or private law entity or an association or a natural person, whether or not by automatic means. Furthermore, Laws 2867/2000 on 'Organisation and Operation of Telecommunications', 2774/1999 and 2472/1997 on 'Privacy Statement', and 2225/1994 on the 'Protection of Freedom of Response and Communication' include a number of provisions associated with protection of privacy in telecommunications. In addition, pursuant to Article 22 of L 3471/2006 ('Protection of personal data and privacy in the electronic telecommunications sector and amendment of law 2472/1997', hereinafter the 'Protection of Personal Data and Privacy in the Electronic Telecommunications Sector Law'), the Hellenic Data Protection Authority issued directive No 2994/29.4.2011 referring to the process of declaration of consent for processing of personal data through electronic means. What is more, Article 4 of the Protection of Personal Data and Privacy in the Electronic Telecommunications Sector Law introduces the principle of confidentiality, and Article 5 lays down rules on the data process.

Additionally, by virtue of Articles 57 and 59 of the Greek Civil Code, personality includes all goods which are integrally related to the person to whom they belong as having physical, mental, spiritual and social individuality. In case of unlawful infringement of personality and in particular of the honour or the reputation of the individual, with insulting or aggravated defamation, the offended person has the right to demand that the infringement is waived and not repeated in the future (Supreme Court, case no 854/2002).[1] Moreover, provisions with respect to cybercrime are included in the Presidential Decree 131/2003 ('Adjustment to Directive 2000/31 of the European Parliament and Council regarding certain legal aspects of the services of the information society, especially of electronic trade, to the internal market, 'Directive on electronic trade'), which, *inter alia*, governs spamming and the liability of internet service providers for actions of users or subscribers.

What is more, the Greek Penal Code includes provisions, which might apply to SM-related cases, such as the breach of sexual dignity under Article 337, the facilitation of others' debauchery under Article 348, child pornography under Article 348A, and the attraction of children for sexual reasons under Article 348B.[2] Finally, Articles 370 *et seq* on crimes relating to confidentiality might also apply *mutatis mutandis*.

Last but not least, the Constitution of Greece includes a number of provisions on the protection of the privacy of individuals. The fundamental provision of Article 2 para 1 states that 'the respect and the protection of human dignity are paramount duty of the state'. Important provisions are also included in Articles 9 and 19; Article 9 states, *inter alia*, that 'private and family life of the individual is inviolable', thus prohibiting the public disclosure of an individual's life, and Article 19 protects the secrecy of letters and the freedom of correspondence and communication.

C14.3 SM CRIMINAL LAW CASES

There are no relevant rulings of the Greek courts yet, apart from the ones mentioned specifically below.

---

1   Article 57 of the Greek Civil Code provides that, 'A person who has suffered an unlawful infringement on his personality has the right to claim the cessation of such infringement as also the non-recurrence thereof in the future. A claim for compensation, according to the provisions about tort, is not excluded'.

2   See also C14.6 regarding the Greek penal code provisions for cybercrime.

C14.4   SM CIVIL LAW CASES

A number of cases relating to SM have been examined by the Greek civil courts. The following ones have been chosen as the most indicative of the way in which courts have implemented the relevant legislation in Greece,

(A)   A teacher offended the personality of a director of secondary education, insulting him via emails and posts on SM. He accused him of being liable for illegal appointments and mismanagement. The director submitted an application for interim measures and the court accepted it, forcing the teacher to refrain from sending insulting emails or posting on SM, otherwise it would impose a pecuniary penalty of €500 and imprisonment of one month (Decision No 520/2012 First Instance Court of Rhodes).

(B)   The biological mother of an adopted child uploaded photos of the minor on Facebook containing his full personal information, without the consent of the foster parents. This action was found to infringe L 2472/1997 (Personal Data Law) as a minor's photos containing his full personal information constitute personal data and, consequently, their uploading requires the foster parents' consent. Furthermore, the uploading of the photo infringes the minor's right to his image, which is a manifestation of the right to personality (Article 57 of the Greek Civil Code). The First Instance Court of Thiva (Decision No 363/2012) ordered the biological mother to delete the picture within a period of five days. In addition, in case of non-compliance, the court would also impose a pecuniary penalty of €1,000 and imprisonment of one month.

(C)   A case was heard before the First Instance Court of Thessaloniki (Decision No 16790/2009) where the defendant had made derogatory comments in a group on Facebook about the claimant with the purpose of damaging her reputation, as they were both candidates for a university employment. The court ruled that the man should delete the comments and also ordered interim measures.

(D)   Pursuant to Decision No 4980/2009 of the Piraeus Multimember Court of First Instance, the alleged infringement of the personality of the claimant caused by a signed article accompanied by a photograph of the claimant under the title 'Who will put a leash on the Illegal Prefect?', compiled and uploaded by the defendant on his blog, was not an infringement made by publication on the electronic press. Similar decisions were adopted by the Salonika Multimember Court of First Instance (Decision Nos 22228/2011 and 25552/2010).

C14.5   CASES WHERE SM-RELATED EVIDENCE USED OR ADMISSIBLE

One example that has been heard before the Court of Appeal of Kerkira (Decision No 95/2013) concerns a man who had communicated with a minor girl via Facebook and had a relationship with her. In the court, printouts of the messages were adduced and the man was eventually convicted.

C14.6   SPECIFIC ONLINE ABUSE/ONLINE BULLYING/ CYBERBULLYING LAWS

Despite the dramatic extent of this phenomenon worldwide, the term 'cyberbullying' has not been legally defined under Greek law yet, and therefore no laws governing online abuse (or online bullying or cyberbullying) have been enacted. Such offences may be punished – by analogy – according to the provisions of the Greek penal law.

C14.7   OTHER LAWS APPLIED TO ONLINE ABUSE/ ONLINE BULLYING/CYBERBULLYING

According to the EU Commission,

> 'Cyberbullying is repeated verbal or psychological harassment carried out by an individual or group against others. It can take many forms: mockery, insults, threats, rumours, gossip, "happy slapping", disagreeable comments or slander. Interactive online services (email, chat rooms, instant messaging) and mobile phones have given bullies new opportunities and ways in which they can abuse their victims'.[3]

Since there is no legal definition of cyberbullying under the Greek legal framework, such conduct may fall under certain provisions of the Greek Penal Code establishing a similar harassment.

By virtue of L 3727/2008, paragraphs 3 and 4 were added to Article 337 of the Greek Penal Code in order to protect the legal right to sexual freedom and dignity of persons under the age of 18 and to implement the Council of Europe Convention on the Protection of Children against Sexual Exploitation and Sexual Abuse. The provisions of paragraphs 3 and 4 specify as follows:

> '3.   Any adult who intentionally comes into contact, through the Internet or other information and communication technologies, with a child under the age of fifteen (15) years and offends his or her sexual freedom and dignity by indecent gestures or proposals shall be punished by imprisonment from 2 to 5 years. If the perpetrator habitually commits the aforementioned crime or in the event that a meeting with the child takes place following the said crime, he shall be punished by imprisonment from 3 to 5 years.

---

3   See http://europa.eu/rapid/press-release_MEMO-09-58_en.htm?locale=FR.

4.   Any adult who intentionally comes into contact, through the internet or other information and communication technologies with a child appearing to be under the age of (fifteen) 15 years and offends his or her sexual freedom and dignity by indecent gestures or proposals shall be punished by imprisonment from 1 to 5 years. If the perpetrator habitually commits the aforementioned crime or in the event that a meeting with the child takes place following the said crime, he shall be punished by imprisonment from 3 to 5 years.'

Moreover, paragraphs 4 and 6 of Article 22 of the Personal Data Law read as follows:

'4.   Any person that unlawfully interferes in any way whatsoever with a personal data file or takes notice of such data or extracts, alters, affects, destroys, processes, transmits, discloses, renders accessible to unauthorized persons or allows such parties to take notice of such data or anyone who exploits such data in any manner whatsoever, shall be punished by imprisonment together with a financial penalty and, where such data is sensitive, by imprisonment for a period of at least one year together with a penalty amounting between €2,900 and €30,000, subject to more serious sanctions provided under other provisions.

...

6.   if the perpetrator committing the acts referred to in paragraph 4, purported to gain unlawful benefit on his/ her behalf or on behalf of another person or to cause harm to a third party then she/he shall be punished by imprisonment for a period of up to 10 years and a penalty amounting between €6,000 and €30,000.'

The basic forms of the said offence are the unlawful interfering with personal data and the unlawful acts of data processing as described under paragraph 4, Article 22 of the Personal Data Law. Pursuant to Article 7 para 2 (e) of the Personal Data Law, the competent judicial authorities are granted the power to collect and process personal data, if such measure is required for the investigation of any criminal case.

C14.8   CHILDREN AND SM LAWS OR RULES

Although Greece has not yet concluded a specific law concerning the use of SM by children, the rights of minors are protected by the provisions of the Greek Penal Code, set in implementation of European Conventions. Cyberbullying, trafficking, child pornography, sexual harassment and child grooming via the internet constitute criminal offences related to SM and children.

Article 348A of the Penal Code on child pornography punishes those who, with the purpose of gaining profit, produce, distribute, make public, possess, or sell child pornographic material on any medium, by imprisonment of at least one year and a penalty of €10,000 up to €100,000. An aggravating circumstance is established if the pornographic materials include exploitation of the need or mental incapacity, deafness, or inexperience of an under-age person or involve the use of violence against the minor. In such cases, perpetrators are punished by imprisonment of up to ten years and a penalty of €50,000 up to €100,000. In the event that the victim is seriously injured, the punishment shall be imprisonment of at least ten years and a penalty of €100,000 up to €500,000.

In order for Greece to ratify and implement the Council of Europe Convention on the Protection of Children against Sexual Exploitation and Sexual Abuse, L 3727/2008 was introduced. More specifically, by virtue of Article 4 of L 3727/2008, a new Article 348B was added to the Penal Code,

> 'Any person who intentionally suggests to an adult, through information and communication technology, to meet a child under the age of 15 years, with the purpose of committing against him/ her the offences mentioned in paragraphs 1 and 2 of Article 339 and 348A, where such proposal is followed by further acts leading to the commitment of the said offences, shall be punished by imprisonment of at least two years and a penalty of €50,000 up to €200,000'.

Additionally, in accordance with Article 349 of the Penal Code, persons who encourage child prostitution are also punished by imprisonment of up to ten years and a penalty of €10,000 up to €50,000. The punishment shall be more severe and the penalty shall reach the amount of €50,000 if the crime involves a minor under the age of 15 or if the crime is committed by parents or step-parents, relatives, guardians, custodians, or teachers or if it is committed with the use of electronic means of communication.

As provided under Article 351A of the Penal Code on trafficking, adults who commit indecent acts against minors in exchange for money or other material exchange, or adults who engage with minors in indecent acts between minors before themselves or other people, shall be punished as follows: if the victim is under the age of ten years, by imprisonment of at least ten years and a penalty of €100,000 up to €500,000; if the victim is between ten and fifteen years old, by imprisonment of up to ten years and a fine of €50,000 up to €100,000; if the victim has passed the age of 15 years, by imprisonment of at least one year and a penalty of €10,000 up to €50,000. Finally, if the offence results in the death of the victim, life imprisonment is imposed. In addition, Article 339 of the Penal Code punishes any person who commits the offence of seduction on a person younger than fifteen 15 years old. More severe punishment is provided for if the victim is younger than ten years.

C14.9 EMPLOYEES/EMPLOYMENT SM LAWS OR CASES

There is no specific law governing the use of SM at work, but the question raised is whether the employer has the power to prohibit employees from accessing SM websites. The particular treatment of the use of SM depends on each employer. The current view of the Greek case law in the above matter is reflected in the following decision. The Athens Court of First Instance (Decision No 34/2011) ruled that the termination of the employment agreement by the employer (an airport company) was legal and justified by a significant reason. The facts considered by the court were as follows. An airport company had banned its personnel from the access to SNs. However, a female employee violated this policy by visiting SM sites on a daily basis for her personal use. Such daily use of SM affected her productivity and thus the company decided to terminate the employment relationship with the woman. The court rejected the employee's claim for unfair dismissal, and ruled in favour of the termination of the employment agreement on valid grounds.

C14.10 SCHOOL AND UNIVERSITY STUDENT SM CASES

The Computer Technology Institute and Press (CTI), which operates under the supervision of the Greek Ministry of Education and Religious Affairs, made a policy recommendation in November 2011 for the proper use of SM in schools. In order to reduce the risks associated with the online environment, the CTI made certain proposals for the safe use of SN services in Greek schools. Some of these proposals are the following,

(A)   The school network shall include SM (Facebook, etc) in its filters and therefore prevent nursery and primary schools from access thereto.

(B)   Students of secondary schools shall be informed on the responsible use and the risks posed in the excessive use of SM during the course of informatics.

The Greek Ministry of Education and Religious Affairs issued a circular under the online input number BOZΣ9-3AΔ and protocol number 13247/Γ7/7.2.2012 on the 'Access of Primary Education students to SN via the Internet'. The circular provides that, in order for the students of primary education to be protected from serious online risks, the access to SM via the accounts of the Greek School Network (which is the educational intranet of the Ministry of Education and Religious Affairs interlinking all schools and providing basic and advanced telematics' services) shall not be provided in an unmonitored manner. Primary school headmasters may request, in writing, access to an SN for a specified time in the context of their participation in a specific educational programme, properly justifying such necessity.

C14.11 RIGHT OR HUMAN RIGHT TO ACCESS THE INTERNET OR SM

The rights to expression, information, communication and personal development, as well as the right to privacy, are some of the core civil rights and therefore directly guaranteed by the Constitution of Greece under Articles 5, 5A and 9A. Restrictions on these rights may be imposed by law only insofar as they are absolutely necessary and justified for reasons of national security, such as combating crime or protecting rights and interests of third parties.

Under Article 5A para 2 of the Constitution of Greece, all persons have the right to participate in the Information Society. Facilitation of access to electronically transmitted information, as well as of the production, exchange and diffusion thereof, constitutes an obligation of the State, always in observance of the guarantees under Articles 9, 9A and 19 of the Constitution of Greece. Article 9 provides that the private and family life of the individual is inviolable and, with respect to Article 9A, all persons have the right to be protected from the collection, processing and use (especially by electronic means) of their personal data, as specified by law. The protection of personal data is ensured by an independent authority, the Hellenic Data Protection Authority, which has been established and operates as regulated by the relevant legislation (Article 19 para 2). In addition, according to Article 19 para 1 of the Constitution of Greece, the secrecy of letters and all other forms of free correspondence or communication shall be absolutely inviolable. The guarantees, under which the judicial authority shall not be bound by this secrecy for reasons of national security or for the purpose of investigating extremely serious crimes, shall be specified by law. Finally, under Article 19 para 3 of the Constitution of Greece, evidence that has been obtained in violation of Articles 9 and 9A cannot be used in court.

The right to information, which is constitutionally established through the revision of Article 5A of the Constitution of Greece and contributes to the effective exercise of the right to free development of personality, may be subject to restrictions if affecting the rights of others.

C14.12   BANS OR RESTRICTIONS ON INTERNET OR SM

To the best of our knowledge, no cases have been reported.

C14.13   IDENTITY THEFT (OR EQUIVALENT)

A fundamental provision, on which the protection of personality is based, is Article 58 of the Greek Civil Code, pursuant to which,

> 'If the right of a person to bear a given name has been challenged by another person or if anyone made an unlawful use of a given name, the person entitled to the name or any person who suffers prejudice may claim the cessation of the offence as also the non-recurrence thereof in the future. A further claim for damages based on the provisions governing unlawful acts shall not be excluded.'

Furthermore, the main legal framework which governs the protection of personal data and, hence, identity theft consists of the Personal Data Law and the Protection of Personal Data and Privacy in the Electronic Telecommunications Sector Law.

C14.14 HACKING (OR EQUIVALENT)

L 2121/1993 (the 'Intellectual Property Law'), as amended and currently in force, regulates intellectual property rights on computer programs (Articles 40–45) and provides preventive measures for potential infringement in addition to civil and criminal penalties (Articles 65–67).

C14.15 PRIVACY BY DESIGN (PBD) (OR EQUIVALENT)

Article 5 para 4 of the Protection of Personal Data and Privacy in the Electronic Telecommunications Sector Law provides,

> 'The design and selection of technical means and IT systems as well as the equipment for the provision for electronic communication services should be done in such way that they fulfil their purpose using the minimum possible data.'

C14.16 TWEETING FROM COURTS, AND ANY RULES/LAWS

There is no specific law to permit or to prohibit Tweeting from courts. As a result, the existing general legal framework applies to the issue under discussion. Pursuant to Article 93 para 2 of the Constitution of Greece, 'The hearings of all courts shall be public, except when the court decides that publicity would be to the detriment of the good usages or that special reasons call for the protection of the privacy or family life of the litigants'. The above provision establishes the principle of publicity, which is divided into direct and indirect publicity.[4] The 'direct publicity' grants to any person the right to access the courtroom and attend the hearing as a third party. 'Indirect publicity' grants – to third parties who are absent from the courtroom – the right to receive notice of the facts that took place during the trial and, in parallel, the expression of relevant views and comments.[5] Although indirect publicity applies to citizens and to the media, its concept has been connected mainly with the latter.[6]

---

4   See Argyris Karras, 'Criminal Procedural Law' (in Greek), Ant N Sakkoula Publications, Athens-Komotini, 1998, p 671.
5   Ibid.
6   Ibid.

Nonetheless, the principle of publicity is waived 'if publicity of the hearing is detrimental to bona mores or there are special circumstances regarding the protection of the private or family life of parties'.[7] Moreover, functions of Twitter allow the uploading of photographs from the court and personal data of the parties participating in the trial. However, according to Article 8 of L 3090/2002, it is prohibited to take photos of the people that are brought before courts. In addition to the above, pursuant to Article 4 of the Protection of Personal Data and Privacy in the Electronic Telecommunications Sector Law,

> 'any use of electronic communications services rendered through a publicly available electronic communications network, as well as the pertinent traffic and location data, as described in Art 2 of the present Law shall be protected by the principle of confidentiality of telecommunications. The withdrawal of confidentiality shall be allowed only under the procedures and conditions provided for in Art 19 of the Constitution.'

C14.17 TELEVISION COURTROOM BROADCASTING OR TELEVISION CAMERAS IN COURT, AND RULES OR LAWS

Pursuant to Article 8 of L 3090/2002, broadcasting is prohibited and television broadcasting may be allowed only by virtue of a decision of the court or of the prosecutor, or where there is substantial public interest.[8]

C14.18 SM IN COURTROOMS

There is no relevant ruling of the Greek courts in relation to the use of SM in courtrooms yet. However, a case that has been decided by the Hellenic Data Protection Authority is the following: a journalist posted on an SN website verbatim information regarding the personal data of the plaintiff as it was written in the suit. According to the Hellenic Data Protection Authority (Decision No 140/2012), the above action constitutes infringement of plaintiff's right to personal data, as the publication of such information cannot be justified as being absolutely necessary, for exclusively journalistic purposes, on issues which the public has a right to information on. The Hellenic Data Protection Authority ordered the journalist to delete the post and pay a pecuniary penalty of €10,000.

---

7   Article 330 of the Greek Code of Criminal Procedure.
8   On a more general level, according to Article 330 of the Greek Code of Criminal Procedure. 'If publicity of the hearing is detrimental to bona mores or there are special circumstances regarding the protection of the private or family life of parties, especially if publicity in a trial regarding crimes against sexual freedom and economic exploitation of sexual life may lead to particular distress or vilification of the victim and, in particular, of the minor, the court shall order the conduct of the trial, or part of it, without publicity'.

C14.19 USE OF SM AS EVIDENCE IN COURTS

For example, a case examined by the First Instance Court of Thessaloniki (Decision No 16823/2010) had the following facts: a former employee of a company had posted on several SM sites (including Facebook and MySpace) an unusual number of photographs and videos of the products and the facilities of the company where they had worked in the past, in such a way as to create the impression that they were posted by the company where they used to work. They also created an account on both Facebook and MySpace under the name of the company. Moreover, the defendant used the name and the distinctive title of the plaintiff on the internet, showing them as a user of an online SM tool. On that website there was also a link, showing the plaintiff as the operator of a facility. The material was of inferior quality. The plaintiff's attorney submitted to the court printed pages with the above elements to prove the dispute. The court concluded that the defendant's conduct infringed the rights of the plaintiff company to the name, the brand and its distinctive features, and gave an unlawful nature to the acts, causing a risk of confusion in the general public, which might be mistaken as to the origin of these entries on the web, and it ordered them to stop the infringement.

C14.20 PRIVACY, DATA PROTECTION AND SM

Apart from those mentioned above, indicatively, the following case was examined before the First Instance Court of Thessaloniki (Decision No 34697/2010): a photograph of a minor child was published on Facebook by its father without the prior consent of his ex wife (mother of the child) who had custody of it. The father posted also comments that were offensive for the personality of the child. According to the legal grounds of the Court Decision, a person's photographs are included in the definition of 'personal data' of Article 2a of Personal Data Law (L 2472/1997) while publication online meet the definition of 'processing personal data' of Article 2d of the same law. The Court ordered the father to delete the photograph and the comments from its profile on Facebook as well as to refrain from posting and publishing such information or anything that is related to the dispute. In the event of non-compliance, a pecuniary penalty of €1,000 and imprisonment of one (1) month would be imposed.

C14.21 SM AND FAMILY LAW CASES

The Greek courts are dealing with an ever-increasing number of such cases resulting from the use of SM sites, such as the following,

The biological mother of an adopted child uploaded photos of the minor on Facebook containing his full personal information, without the consent of the foster parents. This action infringes L 2472/1997 (Personal Data Law) as a minor's photos containing his full personal information constitute personal data and, consequently, their uploading requires the foster parents' consent. Furthermore, the uploading of the photo infringes the minor's right to his image, which is a manifestation of the right to personality (Article 57 of the Greek Civil Code). The First Instance Court of Thiva (Decision No 363/2012) ordered the biological mother to delete the picture within a period of five days. In addition, in case of non-compliance, the court would also impose a pecuniary penalty of €1,000 and imprisonment of one month.

C14.22 SPORTS PERSONS, SPORTS CLUBS AND SM

A few days before the opening of the 30th Olympic Games in 2004, a Greek triple jumper made a racist comment on Twitter saying, 'With so many Africans in Greece, at least the West Nile mosquitoes will eat homemade food'. Within a few hours, the athlete's comment became known all over Greece through SM. The athlete apologised, claiming that she made the comment for fun, having no intention to belittle anyone. The athlete was eventually excluded from the Olympics. The relevant announcement of the Hellenic Olympic Committee stated that the athlete's comment was contrary to the values and ideals of Olympism.

C14.23 PERSONAL RELATIONS AND RELATIONSHIPS

There are two main categories of revenge porn: the first relates to videos and photos that are taken by the victims themselves or by their lovers, always with their consent; and the second category relates to the deceitful acquisition of these videos and photos.[9]

Although there are no court rulings relating to revenge porn, a number of revenge porn incidents have been published in the press, such as the following,[10]

(A) In December 2013, a 23-year-old man was arrested because he asked a 35-year-old woman to send him nude photos of a minor relative of hers, or else he would post personal photos of her on Facebook.

(B) In August 2013, a 25-year-old man was arrested because, while having in his possession a video of sexual content involving a 17-year-old girl, he threatened her that he would post it online.

C14.24 SM AND PERSONAL DATA OF DECEASED PERSONS

In 2009, a complaint was submitted before the Hellenic Data Protection Authority, according to which a person uploaded a private document issued by

---

9   See Giannis Andritsopoulos, 'E-pornography revenge: in the years of Internet revenge is...naked', Ta Nea (in Greek), available at www.tanea.gr/news/science-technology/article/5070231/pornografia-ths-ekdikhshs/.

10   Ibid.

the Division of Criminal Investigation of the Hellenic Police. The document included the genetic code (DNA) of three persons, one of them deceased, as well as his autopsy report. The Authority mentioned that the processing of personal data of the deceased person falls outside the scope of L 2472/1997 (Personal Data Law) and therefore declined competence to rule.

C14.25 SM, WEBSITE, SERVICE PROVIDER OR ISP DEFENCE RULES/LAWS

Greece has implemented the Directive on electronic commerce (2000/31/EC) by virtue of Presidential Decree 131/2003. The scope of the Decree includes any information society service provided in Greece or another member state by a service provider established in Greece (Article 2 para 1). The information society service is defined as any service normally provided for remuneration, at a distance, by means of electronic equipment, and at the individual request of a recipient of a service (Article 1 (a)).

The entities in the eCommerce area, providing services to the recipients, consist of the 'service provider' (Article 1 (b)), defined as any natural or legal person providing an information society service and the 'established service provider' (Article 1 (c)), namely a service provider who effectively pursues an economic activity using a fixed establishment for an indefinite period. The presence and use of the technical means and technologies required to provide the service do not, in themselves, constitute an establishment of the provider (Article 1 (c), ind 2). Pursuant to Article 1 (d) a 'recipient of the service' is defined as any natural or legal person who, for professional ends or otherwise, uses an information society service, in particular for the purposes of seeking information or making it accessible.

Where the provider undertakes the transmission on a communication network of information provided by the recipient of the service, or the provision of access to a communication network ('mere conduit'), and as long as the provider does not initiate the transmission, does not select the recipient of the transmission and does not select or modify the information contained in the transmission, such provider cannot be held liable for the information transmitted (Article 11 para 1). Article 11 para 2 provides that the acts of transmission and of provision of access (referred to above) include the automatic, intermediate and transient storage of the information transmitted, insofar as this takes place for the sole purpose of carrying out the transmission on the communication network, and provided that the information is not stored for any period longer than is reasonably necessary for the transmission.

Furthermore, where the service of the intermediary consists of the transmission on a communication network of information provided by the recipient of the service, the provider shall not be held liable for the automatic, intermediate and temporary storage of that information, performed for the sole purpose of making more efficient the onward transmission of the information to other recipients of the service, upon their request ('caching'), on the conditions set out in Article 12 para 1 (a)–(e) of the Decree.[11] Pursuant to Article 12 para 2, 'This Article shall not affect the possibility for a court or administrative authority ... of requiring the service provider to terminate or prevent an infringement'.

When the intermediary is responsible for the storage of information provided by the recipient of the service ('hosting'), the service provider shall not be held liable for the information stored at the request of the recipient, provided that such provider does not have actual knowledge of the illegal activity or information and that, upon obtaining such knowledge, acts expeditiously to remove or disable access to the information (Article 13 para 1). According to Article 13 para 2, 'paragraph 1 shall not apply when the recipient of the service is acting under the authority or the control of the provider'. Article 13 shall not affect the possibility for a court or administrative authority of requiring the service provider to terminate or prevent an infringement (Article 13 para 3).

Lastly, Article 14 para 2 provides for obligations for information society service providers to inform promptly the competent authorities of alleged illegal activities undertaken or information provided by recipients of their service, or to communicate to the competent authorities, at their request, information facilitating the identification of recipients of their service with whom they have storage agreements.

C14.26   ECOMMERCE DEFENCE CASES

To the best of our knowledge, no cases have been reported.

C14.27   LAWS PROTECTING PERSONAL DATA/ PERSONALLY IDENTIFIABLE INFORMATION

The protection and processing of personal data in Greece are principally regulated by L 2472/1997 (Personal Data Law), by virtue of which the Data Protection Directive 95/46/EC has been incorporated into Greek law (see

---

11 Pursuant to Article 12 para 1 (a)–(e), '... on condition that: (a) the provider does not modify the information; (b) the provider complies with conditions on access to the information; (c) the provider complies with rules regarding the updating of the information, specified in a manner widely recognised and used by industry; (d) the provider does not interfere with the lawful use of technology, widely recognised and used by industry, to obtain data on the use of the information; and (e) the provider acts expeditiously to remove or to disable access to the information it has stored upon obtaining actual knowledge of the fact that the information at the initial source of the transmission has been removed from the network, or access to it has been disabled, or that a court or an administrative authority has ordered such removal or disablement'.

C14.1). The Personal Data Law sets forth the basic terms and conditions in relation to data collection and processing, while imposing essential obligations on data controllers regarding all categories of activities relating to data, such as collection, processing and transfer. Furthermore, the Personal Data Law introduces the fundamental rights of data subjects, namely the right to information, access, rectification or deletion, as well as enforcement provisions and sanctions. What is more, it provides for the establishment of the competent supervisory authority, namely the Hellenic Data Protection Authority. Lastly, Article 4 of the Protection of Personal Data and Privacy in the Electronic Telecommunications Sector Law introduces the principle of confidentiality, and Article 5 lays down rules on the data process.

C14.28   DATA BREACH LAWS AND CUSTOMERS/ USERS/REGULATORS NOTIFIED OF HACKING OR DATA LOSS

Pursuant to Article 10 of L 2472/1997 (Personal Data Law), the controller must implement appropriate organisational and technical measures with a view to securing data and protecting it against accidental or unlawful destruction, accidental loss, alteration, unauthorised disclosure or access, as well as any other form of unlawful processing. Such measures must ensure a level of security that is appropriate for managing the risks posed by processing and the nature of the data that is subject to processing. However, there is no rule on the provision of official information to the data subjects in the event of hacked or lost data.

Chapter C15

Hungary

Szabolcs Szentléleky dr.
Hungarian Competition Authority

C15.1   INTRODUCTION

Hungary is an EU member state and is a Civil Law jurisdiction.

C15.2   SPECIFIC SM AND SN LAWS

No details.

C15.3   SM CRIMINAL LAW CASES

Mostly libel cases occur in Hungary. Perpetrators often says disparaging statements about the insulted person on SM websites. We cannot mention specific cases, because court decisions are not available due to the lack of anonymity.

C15.4   SM CIVIL LAW CASES

No details.

C15.5   CASES WHERE SM-RELATED EVIDENCE USED OR ADMISSIBLE

In cases where the tax authority is conducting an investigation into presumed tax evasion, SM posts of photos could be used as evidence for further investigation.

C15.6   SPECIFIC ONLINE ABUSE/ONLINE BULLYING/ CYBERBULLYING LAWS

There are no such laws in Hungary.

C15.7 OTHER LAWS APPLIED TO ONLINE ABUSE/ ONLINE BULLYING/CYBERBULLYING

Not yet.

C15.8 CHILDREN AND SM LAWS OR RULES

There are no laws or rules specific to children and SM, but Section 149/A of the Act C of 2003 on Electronic Communication requires internet access providers to provide free content filtering software for their subscribers in order to protect minors.

C15.9 EMPLOYEES/EMPLOYMENT SM LAWS OR CASES

No details.

C15.10 SCHOOL AND UNIVERSITY STUDENT SM CASES

Currently there are no such laws or cases in Hungary.

C15.11 RIGHT OR HUMAN RIGHT TO ACCESS THE INTERNET OR SM

There have not yet been any cases in relation to a human right of access to the internet or SM.

C15.12 BANS OR RESTRICTIONS ON INTERNET OR SM

No details.

C15.13 IDENTITY THEFT (OR EQUIVALENT)

No details.

C15.14 HACKING (OR EQUIVALENT)

No details.

C15.15 PRIVACY BY DESIGN (PBD) (OR EQUIVALENT)

No details.

C15.16 TWEETING FROM COURTS, AND ANY RULES/LAWS

No details.

C15.17 TELEVISION COURTROOM BROADCASTING OR TELEVISION CAMERAS IN COURT, AND RULES OR LAWS

In civil cases, television cameras are allowed in courtrooms if the participating parties give their permission. Section 5(1) of the Act III of 1952 on the Code of Civil Procedure states that the court shall adjudge civil cases in public hearing. The court may declare – in a reasoned statement – that the whole or certain sections of the hearing will be closed from the public, where it is deemed absolutely necessary for the protection of classified information, trade secrets or any other information that is rendered confidential by specific other legislation. The court may shut out the public for reasons of morality, for the protection of minors, or upon the party's request if justified with a view to protecting the party's personal rights. Furthermore, in particularly justified cases, the court may bar the public from the hearing when examining witnesses with a view to keeping their data confidential, and where holding the hearing in closed session is absolutely necessary for the protection of the life and safety of the witness and his family. The court shall deliver the decision on the closed hearing publicly.

In criminal cases, Section 74/A (2) of the Act XIX of 1998 on Criminal Proceedings states that the press shall be entitled to provide information on public court hearings. Section 74/B stipulates that any sound or video recording of the court hearings shall be subject to the permission of the presiding judge, and sound or video recordings of persons present at the hearing – with the exception of the members of the court, the keeper of the minutes, the prosecutor and counsel for the defence – shall be subject to the consent of the person concerned. The presiding judge may refuse to grant permission, or may withdraw the permission at any stage of the court procedure, in order to ensure an uninterrupted and undisturbed trial. The press shall not provide information, and no information may be disclosed to the press, of hearings or parts of hearings conducted in camera, unless the publicity of a hearing was denied due to repeated disturbance of the order or regular course of the trial.

In criminal cases, minors under the age of 14 cannot be present among the audience of the trial, and the presiding judge may exclude persons under the age of 18.

C15.18   SM IN COURTROOMS

In the *Rezesova*[1] and *Szita Bence*[2] cases, journalists were posting the latest news to Facebook[3] and to other websites[4] live from the courtroom.

C15.19   USE OF SM AS EVIDENCE IN COURTS

No details.

C15.20   PRIVACY, DATA PROTECTION AND SM

In 2006, an extreme right-wing website[5] published the names, addresses and phone numbers of judges who were hearing cases against protesters in Budapest.[6]

C15.21   SM AND FAMILY LAW CASES

In family law cases, photos and SM posts could be used as evidence when the judge is trying to estimate alimony, or when one party is trying to prove the other's disloyalty.

C15.22   SPORTS PERSONS, SPORTS CLUBS AND SM

No details.

C15.23   PERSONAL RELATIONS AND RELATIONSHIPS

In the last few years, some websites (such as excsajok.tk or tundermacko. info) have been established in order to publish photos of under-age girls or ex-girlfriends with their names. In some cases, their phone number, email address, Facebook account name and Skype or MSN ID were also published.

---

1   See   http://dailynewshungary.com/slovak-driver-rezesova-who-caused-fatal-accident-back-in-prison/.
2   See http://budapesttimes.hu/2012/11/09/boys-murder-too-horrific-to-describe/.
3   See https://hu-hu.facebook.com/hvghu/posts/10152998468103532.
4   See   http://hvg.hu/itthon/20131119_Rezesova_per_targyalas   or   www.sonline.hu/somogy/kek-hirek-bulvar/szita-bence-gyilkossag-online-tudositas-pecsrol-533181.
5   See http://kuruc.info/r/2/6277/.
6   See www.theguardian.com/world/2006/sep/19/1.

C15.24   SM AND PERSONAL DATA OF DECEASED PERSONS

No details.

C15.25   SM, WEBSITE, SERVICE PROVIDER OR ISP DEFENCE RULES/LAWS

No details.

C15.26   ECOMMERCE DEFENCE CASES

There are defences which are similar to the EU eCommerce Directive. Section 8 of the Act CVIII of 2001 on Electronic Commerce and on Information Society Services stipulates that the mere conduit and network access provider shall not be held liable for the information transmitted, on condition that the provider,

a)   did not initiate the transmission;

b)   did not select the receiver of the transmission; and

c)   did not select or modify the information contained in the transmission.

Section 9 states that a caching service provider shall not be held liable for damages resulting from the automatic, intermediate and transient storage of the information transmitted on condition that,

a)   the provider did not modify the information;

b)   access to the stored information was provided in compliance with conditions on access to the information;

c)   the provider complies with rules regarding the updating of the information, specified in a manner widely recognized and used by industry;

d)   the intermediate storage did not interfere with the lawful use of technology, widely recognized and used by industry, to obtain data on the use of the information; and

e)   the provider acted expeditiously to remove or to disable access to the information it has stored upon obtaining actual knowledge of the fact that the information at the initial source of the transmission has been removed from the network, or access to it has been disabled, or that a court or any other authority has ordered such removal or disablement.

Section 10 stipulates that a hosting service provider shall not be held liable for the information stored at the request of a recipient of the service, on condition that,

a)   the provider does not have actual knowledge of illegal activity in connection with the information and is not aware of facts or circumstances from which the illegal activity or information is apparent; or

b)   the provider, upon obtaining knowledge or awareness of what is contained in paragraph a), acts expeditiously to remove or to disable access to the information.

Finally, Section 11 says that a location tool services provider shall not be held liable for damages resulting from allowing access to the information on condition that,

a)   the provider does not have actual knowledge of illegal activity in connection with the information and is not aware of facts or circumstances from which the illegal activity or information is apparent; or

b)   the provider, upon obtaining knowledge or awareness of what is contained in paragraph a), acts expeditiously to remove or to disable access to the information.

C15.27   LAWS PROTECTING PERSONAL DATA/ PERSONALLY IDENTIFIABLE INFORMATION

No details.

C15.28   DATA BREACH LAWS AND CUSTOMERS/ USERS/REGULATORS NOTIFIED OF HACKING OR DATA LOSS

No details.

India

Raghunath Ananthapur
Tatva Legal, Bangalore

C16.1 INTRODUCTION

India is a Civil Law jurisdiction.

C16.2 SPECIFIC SM AND SN LAWS

Although there is no specific legislation or regulations governing SM and SN web-based services, certain provisions of the Information Technology Act, 2000 (IT Act) and the Copyright Act, 1957 (Copyright Act) impose certain obligations on intermediaries.

C16.2.1 Intermediary

The term 'intermediary' is widely defined under the IT Act. Section 2(w) of the IT Act defines 'intermediary' as any person who on behalf of another person receives, stores, transmits or provides any service with respect to an electronic record[1] and includes telecom service providers, network service providers, internet service providers, web-hosting service providers, search engines, online payment sites, online-auction sites, online-market places and cyber cafes. SM websites, such as Facebook and Orkut, that receive, store and transmit information uploaded by their users, qualify as 'intermediaries' for the purposes of the IT Act.

C16.2.2 Obligations of Intermediary under the IT Act

Retention of records

Section 67C of the IT Act requires an intermediary to retain such information, and for such period of time, as shall be prescribed by the Central Government.

---

1   Section 2(ta) of the IT Act defines 'electronic record' as data, record or data generated, image or sound stored, received or sent in an electronic form or micro film or computer generated micro fiche.

The Central Government has yet to frame rules implementing the retention provision. Therefore, the nature of data that is to be preserved and retained by the intermediary, and duration of retention, is not known. However, under the Interception Rules, Monitoring & Collection of Traffic Data or Information Rules and the Intermediaries Guidelines, the intermediary is required to maintain certain records for the prescribed duration.

Interception, monitoring or decryption of information

Section 69 of the IT Act empowers the Central Government or a State Government or any of its authorised officers to intercept, monitor or decrypt any information generated, transmitted, received or stored in any computer resource.[2] The rights of interception, monitoring or decryption may be exercised in the interests of the sovereignty or integrity of India, the defence of India, security of the State, friendly relations with foreign States or public order or for preventing incitement to the commission of any cognizable offence relating to the foregoing, or for investigation of any offence. The reasons for ordering interception, monitoring or decryption should be recorded in writing.

An intermediary is required to provide all facilities and technical assistance to the authorised officers of the Government to: (a) provide access to or secure access to the computer resource generating, transmitting, receiving or storing information; (b) intercept, monitor or decrypt the information, as the case may be; or (c) provide information stored in the computer resource.[3]

Any intermediary who fails to assist the authorised agency of the Government in interception, monitoring or decryption of information is liable to be punished with imprisonment for a term up to seven years and a fine.[4]

The Central Government has published rules regarding the procedure and safeguards to be followed for interception, monitoring and decryption of information[5] (Interception Rules).[6]

Interception Rules

Intermediary to provide assistance for interception, monitoring or decryption

a)   The intermediary is required to provide technical assistance and the equipment, including hardware, software, firmware, storage, interface

---

2   Section 2(k) of the IT Act defines 'computer resource' as computer, computer system, computer network data, computer database or software.
3   Section 69(3) of the IT Act.
4   Section 69(4) of the IT Act.
5   Section 2(v) of the IT Act defines 'information' as including data, message, text, images, sound, voice, codes, computer programmes, software and databases or micro film or computer generated micro fiche.
6   Information Technology (Procedure and Safeguards for Interception, Monitoring and Decryption of Information) Rules, 2009. Ministry of Communications and Information Technology (Department of Information Technology), Notification No GSR 780 (E), dated October 27, 2009, published in the Gazette of India, Extraordinary, Part II, Section 3(i).

and access to the equipment, wherever requested by the authorised officer of the Government, for performing interception, monitoring or decryption of information;[7]

b)   If a decryption direction is made, the subscriber of an electronic signature or intermediary, as the case may be, is required to disclose the decryption key, or provide the decryption assistance;[8]

c)   The intermediary is required to designate officers with specific responsibilities to receive and handle requisition for interception, monitoring or decryption under the Interception Rules;[9]

d)   The intermediary is required to acknowledge receipt of any requisition for interception, monitoring or decryption under the Interception Rules within two hours of receipt of such requisition.[10]

Intermediary to maintain records

A designated officer of the intermediary is required to maintain proper records containing the following details: intercepted or monitored or decrypted information, the particulars of the persons, computer resource, email account, website address etc subject to interception, monitoring or decryption; details of the officer to whom the information was disclosed; number of copies of the information that were made, including the method by which such copies were made and the date of destruction of such copies, and the duration within which the directions remained in force.[11] Records should be destroyed by the intermediary within two months of the discontinuance of the interception, monitoring or decryption of such information.[12]

Fortnightly submission of interception requisitions

The intermediary is required to submit, once every 15 days, a list of interception, monitoring or decryption of information requisitions received by it in the preceding fortnight to the authorised officer.[13]

Intermediary to implement effective controls to prevent unauthorised access, proper handling of requisitions

The intermediary is required to implement effective controls to prevent unauthorised interception of information and ensure that extreme secrecy is maintained and utmost care and precaution is taken in the matter of interception, monitoring or decryption of information. Only the designated officers of the

---

7   Rule 19 of Interception Rules.
8   Rule 17 of Interception Rules.
9   Rule 14 of Interception Rules.
10   Rule 15 of Interception Rules.
11   Rule 16 of Interception Rules.
12   Rule 23(3) of Interception Rules.
13   Rule 18 of Interception Rules.

intermediary should be involved in interception, monitoring or decryption of information.[14]

Unauthorised interception

Any person who intentionally without authorisation intercepts or attempts to intercept, or authorizes or assists any other person to intercept, any information in the course of its occurrence or transmission at any place within India would be liable to punishment under the relevant provisions of the law.[15]

Any interception, monitoring or decryption of information by an employee of the intermediary performing the functions of installation, operation and maintenance of a computer resource or accessing stored information, in limited circumstances in the course of his duty, would not amount to violation of the law.[16] However, an employee of the intermediary is required to maintain strict secrecy and confidentiality of the information that comes into his knowledge while performing such duties.[17]

Disclosure of intercepted, monitored or decrypted information

a)   The contents of intercepted, monitored or decrypted information should not be disclosed by the intermediary or any of its employees except to the authorised officer;[18]

b)   The contents of intercepted, monitored or decrypted information should not be disclosed or reported in public by any means without the prior order of the competent court in India;[19]

c)   If the intermediary or its employee discloses intercepted, monitored or decrypted information in violation of the Interception Rules, it will be liable to be punished in accordance with the relevant provisions of the law.[20]

The intermediary is responsible for any action of its employees that is in violation of the Interception Rules.[21]

Blocking access to information by the public

Section 69-A of the IT Act empowers the Central Government or its authorised officers to direct any agency of the Government or intermediary to block access to any information generated, transmitted, received, stored or hosted in any computer resource. The rights of blocking access to information may be

---

14   Rule 20 of Interception Rules.
15   Rule 24(2) of Interception Rules.
16   Rule 24(4) of Interception Rules.
17   Rule 24(3) of Interception Rules.
18   Rule 25(1) of Interception Rules.
19   Rules 25(3) of Interception Rules.
20   Rules 25(5) of Interception Rules.
21   Rule 21 of Interception Rules.

exercised in the interests of the sovereignty and integrity of India, the defence of India, security of the State, friendly relations with foreign States or public order, or for preventing incitement to the commission of any cognizable offence relating to the foregoing. The reasons for issuing directions for blocking of access to information should be recorded in writing.

Any intermediary who fails to comply with the directions of the Central Government is liable to be punished with imprisonment for a term up to seven years and a fine.[22]

The Central Government has notified rules regarding the procedure and safeguards to be followed for blocking of access to information (Blocking of Information Rules).[23]

Blocking of Information Rules

a)   Any person may send a complaint to the authorised officer of the Central Government, State Government or authorised agency of the Government for the blocking of access by the public to any information generated, transmitted, received, stored or hosted in any computer resource;[24]

b)   The authorised officer, prior to issuing blocking directions, is required to provide notice to the intermediary or any person who has hosted the objectionable information to appear and submit their reply and clarifications.[25] However, in case of an order from a competent court in India for the blocking of any information, the designated officer is required to act immediately through the Secretary, Department of Information Technology in implementing the directions of the court;[26]

c)   In the event the intermediary fails to comply with the blocking directions issued to it, the designated officer is empowered, with the prior approval of the Secretary, Department of Information Technology, to initiate action against the intermediary to impose punishment with imprisonment for a term up to seven years and a fine;[27]

d)   The intermediary is required to designate officers with specific responsibilities to receive and handle directions for the blocking of information under the Blocking of Information Rules;[28]

---

22   Section 69A(3) of the IT Act.
23   Information Technology (Procedure and Safeguards for Blocking for Access of Information by Public) Rules, 2009. Ministry of Communications and Information Technology (Department of Information Technology), Notification No GSR 781 (E), dated October 27, 2009, published in the Gazette of India, Extraordinary, Part II, Section 3(i).
24   Rule 6 of Blocking of Information Rules.
25   Rule 8 of Blocking of Information Rules.
26   Rule 10 of Blocking of Information Rules.
27   Rule 12 of Blocking of Information Rules.
28   Rule 13 of Blocking of Information Rules.

e)   The intermediary is required to acknowledge receipt of any requisition for blocking of information under the Blocking of Information Rules within two hours of receipt of such requisition;[29]

f)   The intermediary is required to maintain strict confidentiality of all requests and actions taken regarding the blocking of information.[30]

In the period from January 31, 2010 to June 30, 2013, Google received 673 requests from the Government of India and the courts to remove objectionable content; 88 of these requests were from the courts in India, and 555 were from the Government of India (Executive, Police etc).[31]

Monitoring and collection of traffic data or information

Section 69-B of the IT Act empowers the Central Government to authorize any agency of the Government to monitor and collect traffic data[32] or information generated, transmitted, received or stored in any computer resource. The rights of monitoring may be exercised to enhance 'cyber security'[33] and for identification, analysis and prevention of intrusion or spread of 'computer contaminant'[34] in the country.

The intermediary is required to provide technical assistance and extend all facilities to the Government agency to enable online access or to secure and provide online access to the computer resource.

If an intermediary intentionally or knowingly fails to provide assistance to the agency of the Government, it shall be liable to be punished with imprisonment for a term up to three years and a fine.

The Central Government has published rules regarding the procedure and safeguards to be followed for the monitoring and collection of traffic data or information (Monitoring and Collection of Traffic Data or Information Rules).[35]

---

29   Rule 13(2) of Blocking of Information Rules.
30   Rule 16 of Blocking of Information Rules.
31   Google Transparency Report may be downloaded from www.google.com/transparencyreport/removals/government/.
32   Explanation to Section 69-B of the IT Act defines 'traffic data' as any data identifying or purporting to identify any person, computer system or computer network or location to or from which the communication is or may be transmitted and includes communications origin, destination, route, time, date, size, duration or type of underlying service and any other information.
33   Section 2(nb) of the IT Act defines 'cyber security' as protecting information, equipment, devices, computer, computer resource, communication device and information stored therein from unauthorised access, use, disclosure, disruption, modification or destruction.
34   'Computer contaminant' is defined in Section 43 of the IT Act and means any set of computer instructions that are designed: (a) to modify, destroy, record, transmit data or program residing within a computer, computer system or computer network; or (b) by any means to usurp the normal operation of the computer, computer system, or computer network.
35   Information Technology (Procedure and Safeguard for Monitoring and Collecting Traffic Data or Information) Rules, 2009. Ministry of Communications and Information Technology (Department of Information Technology), Notification No GSR 782(E), dated October 27, 2009, published in the Gazette of India, Extraordinary, Part II, Section 3(i).

Monitoring and Collection of Traffic Data or Information Rules

Intermediary to provide assistance and extend all facilities

a)   The intermediary is required to extend all facilities, co-operation and assistance in installation, removal and testing of equipment and also enable online access or to secure and provide online access to the computer resource for the monitoring and collection of traffic data or information.[36]

b)   The intermediary is required to acknowledge receipt of requisition for assistance from the authorised officer within two hours from the receipt of such requisition.[37]

c)   The intermediary is required to maintain proper records of monitoring requisitions received by it, and is required to destroy the records within six months of the discontinuance of the monitoring or collection of traffic data or information.[38]

Intermediary to implement effective controls to prevent unauthorised access, proper handling of requisitions

The intermediary should implement effective controls to prevent unauthorised monitoring or collection of traffic data or information and ensure extreme secrecy is maintained and proper care is taken in the matter of monitoring or collection of traffic data or information. Only the designated officers of the intermediary should be involved in the monitoring or collection of traffic data or information.[39]

Unauthorised monitoring or collection of information

Any person who intentionally without authorisation monitors or collects any information, or authorizes or assists any other person to monitor or collect any information in the course of its occurrence or transmission at any place within India, would be liable to punishment under the relevant provisions of the law.[40]

Any monitoring or collection of any information by an employee of the intermediary performing the functions of installation, operation or maintenance of computer resource or accessing information, in limited circumstances in course of his duty, would not amount to violation of the law.[41] However, an employee of the intermediary is required to maintain strict secrecy and confidentiality of the information that comes into his knowledge while performing such duties.[42]

---

36   Rule 4(7) of Monitoring and Collection of Traffic Data or Information Rules.
37   Rule 4(8) of Monitoring and Collection of Traffic Data or Information Rules.
38   Rules 4(9) and 8 of Monitoring and Collection of Traffic Data or Information Rules.
39   Rule 5 of Monitoring and Collection of Traffic Data or Information Rules.
40   Rule 9(1) of Monitoring and Collection of Traffic Data or Information Rules.
41   Rule 9(2) of Monitoring and Collection of Traffic Data or Information Rules.
42   Rule 9(3) of Monitoring and Collection of Traffic Data or Information Rules.

Disclosure of monitored or collected information

Details of monitored or collected traffic data or information should be disclosed by the intermediary or its employees only to the authorised officer of the Government.[43] The intermediary is required to maintain strict confidentiality of the directions issued for the monitoring or collection of information and the monitored or collected information.[44]

The Indian Computer Emergency Response Team

The Central Government has designated the Indian Computer Emergency Response Team[45] to perform the following functions in the area of 'cyber security':[46]

a)   Collection, analysis and dissemination of information on cyber incidents;

b)   Forecast and alerts of cyber security incidents;

c)   Emergency measures for handling cyber security activities;

d)   Coordination of cyber incidents response activities;

e)   Issue guidelines, advisories, vulnerability notes and white papers relating to information security practices, procedures, prevention, response and reporting of cyber incidents;

f)   Other functions relating to cyber security prescribed by the Central Government.

The intermediary is required to provide the necessary information and comply with the directions issued by the Indian Computer Emergency Response Team.[47] Intermediaries failing to provide the information sought, or to comply with the directions issued, would be liable to punishment with imprisonment for a term up to one year or a fine of up to INR1,00,000 (Rupees One Lakh), or both.[48]

C16.3   SM CRIMINAL LAW CASES

Google India Private Limited v Visaka Industries Limited[49]

a)   Google India Private Limited approached the High Court of Andhra Pradesh at Hyderabad seeking dismissal of a criminal case filed against it before the XI Additional Chief Metropolitan Magistrate, Secunderabad;

---

43   Rule 9(4) of Monitoring and Collection of Traffic Data or Information Rules.
44   Rule 11 of Monitoring and Collection of Traffic Data or Information Rules.
45   See www.cert-in.org.in/.
46   Section 70-B(4) of the IT Act.
47   Section 70-B(6) of the IT Act.
48   Section 70-B(7) of the IT Act.
49   Criminal Petition No 7207 of 2009.

b)   In the criminal case filed before the Magistrate Court the complainant has accused Google India Private Limited of offences punishable under Sections 120-B (criminal conspiracy), 500 (defamation) and 501 (printing or engraving matter known to be defamatory) of the Indian Penal Code, 1860;

c)   It is the case of the complainant that defamatory articles having reference to it were published by the Google Groups website that is owned by Google India Private Limited. Google India Private Limited pleaded exemption from liability arising from passive hosting of information on the Google Groups website. It relied on the provisions of the IT Act that exempt intermediaries from liabilities arising from passive hosting of third party information;

d)   The High Court observed that, although the complainant issued a take-down notice to Google India Private Limited regarding dissemination of defamatory material and unlawful activity through its websites, Google India Private Limited did not initiate any action. Therefore, the High Court held that Google India Private Limited could not claim exemption from liability under the IT Act;

e)   Google India Private Limited has now approached the Supreme Court of India for quashing of criminal proceedings.[50] The matter is pending.

Vinay Rai v Facebook India, Google India Private Limited, Orkut, Youtube, Blogspot, Yahoo India Private Limited and Others[51]

a)   The complainant accused Google and others of publishing objectionable content, and therefore to be punishable under Sections 153-A (promoting enmity between different groups on grounds of religion, race, place of birth, residence, language etc, and doing acts prejudicial to the maintenance of harmony), 153-B (imputations, assertions prejudicial to national integration), 292 (sale of obscene book), 109 (abetment), 500 (defamation) and 120-B (criminal conspiracy) of the Indian Penal Code, 1860;

b)   The trial court, while observing that there is prima facie material against the accused persons for committing offences under the Indian Penal Code, 1860, summoned them to face trial under Sections 292, 293 and 120B of the Indian Penal Code, 1860;

c)   The trial court also directed a copy of the order to be sent to the Government of India for taking appropriate steps regarding the violations;

---

50   No 5238 of 2011.
51   Complaint Case No 136 of 2011. Metropolitan Magistrate Patiala House Courts, New Delhi.

d)   Google India Private Limited[52] and Facebook India Online Services Private Limited approached the High Court of Delhi to stay the proceedings of the trial court;[53]

e)   Facebook India argued that the term 'document', as defined under the Indian Penal Code, 1860, does not include an electronic document. It was also contended that the documents submitted by the complainant containing the objectionable content, downloaded from the website www.facebook.com, was not supported by a certificate/affidavit as required under the Evidence Act, 1872 in order for it to be acceptable as evidence. Facebook India also contended that it is not liable as per the provisions of the IT Act that exempt intermediaries for hosting third party information. Facebook India has made a distinction between the Facebook India entity and Facebook Inc that owns and controls the website. It is the case of Facebook India that, since it does not own or control the website, it should not be liable for the content posted on the website;

f)   It is reported that Google India Private Limited also made a distinction between Google Inc and Google India Private Limited. Google Inc is the service provider and not Google India Private Limited. Therefore, Google India Private Limited cannot be made liable for the actions of its holding company, Google Inc;[54]

g)   According to the news reports, the Delhi High Court did not stay the proceedings of the trial court.

C16.4   SM CIVIL LAW CASES

C16.4.1   Civil cases involving internet intermediaries

Posting defamatory content on blogs, websites etc.

In *Vyakti Vikas Kendra, India Public Charitable Trust through Trustee Mahesh Gupta and Others v Jitendra Bagga and Another*,[55] it was alleged that the first defendant had posted defamatory content having references to a spiritual guide on www.blogger.com, a blog publishing service operated by Google. The plaintiffs provided to the court the 'URLs' of the blog that contained the defamatory content. The Delhi High Court passed an ex-parte interim order directing Google to remove all defamatory content about the plaintiffs on the

---

52   *Google India Private Limited v Vinay Rai*, Criminal MC 100/2012.
53   *Facebook India Online Services Private Limited v Vinay Rai*, Criminal MC 102/2012.
54   'Can block websites like China, Delhi High Court warns Facebook, Google': article available at   www.ndtv.com/article/india/can-block-websites-like-china-delhi-high-court-warns-facebook-google-166383.
55   CS (OS) No 1340/2012.

blog within 36 hours from the date of receiving knowledge of the court order. The Delhi High Court also restrained the first defendant (user of the blog service and the person responsible for posting the defamatory content) from sending any emails or positing any defamatory content that may have a direct or indirect reference to the plaintiffs. By further order of the court, Google was directed to remove all the defamatory content posted by the person responsible for posting defamatory content from its website www.blogger.com and all other country-specific domains owned by Google Inc.

In *Nirmaljit Singh Narula v Indijobs at Hubpages.com and Others,*[56] it was alleged that the first defendant had published defamatory articles having reference to the plaintiff, a spiritual guide. Defamatory articles were published on the website, www.hubpages.com, a web hosting service that provides to its users web space to publish content written by them. Prior to initiating the legal action, the plaintiff had provided notice to the second defendant, the owner of the website www.hubpages.com, to take down the defamatory articles and also to provide contact details of the person responsible for posting such content. Despite the take-down notice, the owner of the website did not remove the content, on the ground that the articles merely projected a difference of opinion about a public figure. The designated officer of the Government under the Blocking of Information Rules and the Registrar of the domain www.hubpages. com were also impleaded in the case. The Delhi High Court passed an interim order restraining the person responsible for posting defamatory content from writing or publishing any content that is defamatory about the plaintiff on the website and in any other print or electronic media. The owner of the website was also required to remove defamatory content about the plaintiff written by any person, including the first defendant, within 36 hours from the date of the order. The Delhi High Court also issued directions to the Registrar of Domains, www.hubpages.com to block the website from public access within India if the website failed to remove the defamatory content. The owner of the website was also directed to provide complete details of the identity of the first defendant, including contact details, author log-in data, registration data, residence address and IP address to the court in a sealed cover.

In *Gospel for Asia and Others v Google Inc and Others,*[57] the Delhi High Court issued notices to Google India Private Limited, YouTube, Blogger and Facebook pursuant to a petition filed by Gospel for Asia and Believers Church that defamatory and derogatory articles against them were available on the internet. The matter is pending.

In *Visaka Industries Limited v Gopal Krishna, Google India Private Limited and Google Inc,*[58] the plaintiff claimed that certain content posted on the Google Groups website was defamatory and sought a mandatory injunction of

---

56 CS (OS) No 871/2012.
57 CS (OS) No 3297/2012.
58 OS No 143 of 2010.

the court directing Google India Private Limited and Google Inc to remove the message posted on certain identified 'URLs'.

The lower court, while dismissing the suit, made the following observations:

a)   On the question of jurisdiction, the court observed that mere website access could suffice for a court to assume jurisdiction. Since the plaintiff company had access to the alleged defamatory articles from the place of its corporate office in India, part of the cause of action arose within the territorial limits of the court;

b)   The court, while deciding whether the suit discloses any cause of action against the corporate defendants, observed that there was a cause of action against the corporate defendants which needed to be established by adducing evidence. It is because, although the defendants were not directly involved in the publication, it is only through the medium supplied by the defendants that the alleged defamatory articles were published;

c)   The court did not grant mandatory injunction for removal of the articles from the Google Groups website because the plaintiff had failed to prove that the alleged articles were defamatory and have affected its reputation and business;

d)   The court, in accordance with the provisions of Section 79 of the IT Act, held that Google Inc could not be made liable, because it was not doing any editorial functions and, on a website like Google, it would be impossible to monitor the content on each and every group.

Cause of action in case of defamation on internet: single publication rule v multiple publication rule

In *Khawar Butt v Asif Nazir Mir & Others*,[59] the plaintiff's claimed that the defendant posted false allegations against the plaintiff on the Facebook page of another person (also a party in the case). The plaintiff claimed compensation for libellous posting and a mandatory injunction. The question that came to be decided by the Delhi High Court was whether defamatory material on the internet (that is, Facebook) gives rise to a fresh cause of action every moment the offending material remains on the webpage, or whether the cause of action arises only when the offending material is first posted on the webpage. The Delhi High Court considered the two legal positions followed in other jurisdictions, namely the single publication rule and the multiple publication rule in relation to defamatory content contained in online publications. In the case of the single publication rule, the publication has a single cause of action that arises on first publication of the online material. While, in the case of the multiple publication rule, each 'hit' on a webpage creates a new publication giving rise to a separate cause of action. The Delhi High Court was of the view

---

59   CS (OS) No 290/2010. Order delivered on November 7, 2013.

that the single publication rule is more appropriate and pragmatic to apply for online material. The Delhi High Court notes that the legislative policy would be defeated if the mere continued residing of the defamatory material on the website were to give a continuous cause of action to the plaintiff to sue for defamation. The Delhi High Court notes, however, that, if there is re-publication by the defendant with a view to reaching a different or larger section of the public in respect of the defamatory material, such re-publication would amount to a fresh cause of action. In the current case, the alleged defamatory article was said to have been posted around October 26, 2008, October 27, 2008 and December 25, 2008. Since the suit to claim damages had not been filed within the period of limitation of one year, ie before the expiry of December 25, 2009, the court dismissed the claim for being barred by limitation.

Blocking of access to websites

In *Reliance Big Entertainment v Multivision Network and Others*,[60] the High Court of Delhi granted a 'John Doe' interim injunction restraining identified defendants and other unnamed persons from communicating, making available, distributing, duplicating, displaying, releasing, showing, uploading, downloading, exhibiting or playing the movie 'Singham' in any manner without authorization from the petitioner, and in any manner violating the plaintiff's copyright in the movie through media such as CD, DVD, Blu-ray, VCD, cable TV, DTH, Internet, MMS, tapes and conditional access systems.

In *RK Productions Private Limited v BSNL, Bharati Airtel Limited and Others*, the High Court of Madras granted a 'John Doe' interim injunction restraining several ISPs, TSPs and other unnamed persons from:

a) infringing plaintiff's copyright in the movie '3' in any manner, including by copying, recording, communicating or allowing others to communicate uploading, downloading; and

b) infringing copyright in movie '3' through different mediums including CD, DVD, Blu-ray disc, VCD, cable TV, Direct to Home services, internet services, multimedia messaging services, pen drives, hard drives, tapes and conditional access systems.

In *Multi Screen Media Private Limited v Sunit Singh and Others*,[61] the High Court of Delhi granted an interim ex-parte 'John Doe' order as follows:

a) Order restrains certain websites (around 472) from engaging in any conduct that would infringe the plaintiff's broadcast reproduction rights in relation to 2014 FIFA World Cup matches and content related thereto;

b) Order directs certain defendants to ensure and secure compliance with the order;

---

60   CS (OS) No 1724/2011.
61   CS (OS) No 1860/2014.

c)   Order directs certain defendants to ensure and secure compliance with the order by calling upon the various internet service providers registered under it to block access to the websites identified by the plaintiff (around 472) and such other websites that may be subsequently notified by the plaintiff that are infringing its copyright.

By a further order dated July 1, 2014, the number of websites to be blocked was reduced to 219.

In *Star India Private Limited and Another v Haneeth Ujwal & Others*,[62] the Delhi High Court granted an ad-interim order restraining 107 websites, referring to them as 'rogue websites', from in any manner hosting, streaming, broadcasting, rebroadcasting, retransmitting, exhibiting, making available for viewing and downloading, providing access to the public (including its subscribers) through the internet, the plaintiff's broadcast contained in its Channels Star Sports 1, Star Sports 2, Star Sports 3, Star Sports 4, Star Sports HD1, Star Sports HD2 in relation to the 2014 India–England Cricket Series content.

The Delhi High Court also, through its order, directed the Department of Telecommunications and the Department of Electronics and Information Technology to ensure and secure compliance of the order by directing the various internet service providers to the websites identified by the plaintiff (107 websites) and such other websites that the plaintiff may subsequently notify. The order also directs the Domain Name Registrar of each of the 107 websites to disclose the contact details and other details about the owner of the websites.

Regulating content over WhatsApp

It is reported that the Indian Government is finding it difficult to regulate content over WhatsApp. It is also reported that WhatsApp was recently used to incite communal violence in the State of Uttar Pradesh. It is the concern of the Government that WhatsApp servers or offices are not located in India, so the response is not timely. Also, unlike other SM websites, the WhatsApp application is a peer-to-peer application, making it difficult to block specific content. The Government will have to block the entire application if it has to stop offensive content from spreading. WhatsApp has over 40 million subscribers in India.[63]

C16.5   CASES WHERE SM-RELATED EVIDENCE USED OR ADMISSIBLE

There may be several cases involving SM-related evidence considered by the lower courts in India. Orders of the lower courts are not normally reported in the law reports.

---

62   CS (OS) No 2243/2014.
63   See   www.rediff.com/news/slide-show/slide-show-1-india-struggle-with-hate-on-whatsapp/20140813.htm#1.

C16.6 SPECIFIC ONLINE ABUSE/ONLINE BULLYING/ CYBERBULLYING LAWS

None.

C16.7 OTHER LAWS APPLIED TO ONLINE ABUSE/ ONLINE BULLYING/CYBERBULLYING

None.

C16.8 CHILDREN AND SM LAWS OR RULES

None.

C16.9 EMPLOYEES/EMPLOYMENT SM LAWS OR CASES

None.

C16.10 SCHOOL AND UNIVERSITY STUDENT SM CASES

None.

C16.11 RIGHT OR HUMAN RIGHT TO ACCESS THE INTERNET OR SM

None.

C16.12 BANS OR RESTRICTIONS ON INTERNET OR SM

None.

C16.13 IDENTITY THEFT (OR EQUIVALENT)

Any person who fraudulently or dishonestly makes use of the electronic signature, password or any other unique identification feature of any other person is liable to be punished with imprisonment up to three years and a fine up to Rs. 1,00,000 (Rupees One Lakh).[64]

---

64 Section 66-C of the IT Act.

Any person who by means of any communication device or computer resource cheats by personation is liable to be punished with imprisonment up to 3 years and fine up to INR1,00,000 (Rupees One Lakh).[65]

C16.14 HACKING (OR EQUIVALENT)

The IT Act contains provisions relating to unauthorised access and tampering of source code.

Any person who, without authorisation of the owner of a computer, computer system or computer network ('System'), commits any of the following actions is liable to pay damages by way of compensation to the affected person:[66]

a)   Gains unauthorised access to such System;

b)   Downloads, copies or extracts any data, computer database[67] or information from such System, including information stored in any removable storage medium of such system;

c)   Introduces or causes to be introduced any computer contaminant[68] or computer virus[69] into any System;

d)   Damages[70] such system, data or database, or programmes residing in such System;

e)   Disrupts any System;

f)   Denies or causes the denial of access to any person authorised to access any System by any means;

g)   Provides assistance to any person to facilitate access to a System in contravention of the provisions of the IT Act;

h)   Charges the services availed of by a person to the account of another person by tampering with or manipulating any System;

i)   Destroys, deletes or alters any information residing in any System or diminishes its value or utility or affects it injuriously by any means;

---

65   Section 66-D of the IT Act.
66   Section 43 of the IT Act.
67   Explanation to Section 43 defines 'computer database'.
68   Explanation to Section 43 defines 'computer contaminant' as any set of computer instructions that are designed: (a) to modify, destroy, record, transmit data or program residing within a computer, computer system or computer network; or (b) by any means to usurp the normal operation of the computer, computer system, or computer network.
69   Explanation to Section 43 defines 'computer virus' as any computer instruction, information, data or program that destroys, damages, degrades or adversely affects the performance of a computer resource or attaches itself to another computer resource and operates when a program, data or instruction is executed or some other event takes place in that computer resource.
70   Explanation to Section 43 defines 'damages' as means to destroy, alter, delete, add, modify or rearrange any computer resource by any means.

j)   Steals, conceals, destroys or alters any computer source code used for a System with an intention to cause damage.

While adjudging the quantum of compensation payable by the offender, the adjudicating officer is required to take into consideration the following factors:

a)   The amount of gain of unfair advantage, wherever quantifiable, made as a result of the default;

b)   The amount of loss caused to any person as a result of the default;

c)   The repetitive nature of the default.

If any offence (listed in a to j above) is committed by any person dishonestly[71] or fraudulently,[72] he is liable to be punished with imprisonment for a term up to three years or a fine up to INR5,00,000 (Rupees Five Lakhs), or both.

Tampering with source code

Any person who knowingly or intentionally tampers with computer source code[73] that is required to be kept or maintained by the law is punishable with imprisonment up to three years or a fine of INR2,00,000 (Rupees Two Lakhs), or both.

While, on the face of it, it could be interpreted that this provision applies only when 'source code is required to be maintained by law', the court in *Syed Asifuddin and Others v The State of Andhra Pradesh and Others*[74] has held that the disjunctive word 'or' is used by the legislature between the phrases 'when the computer source code is required to be kept' and the other phrase 'maintained by law for the time being in force' and, therefore, both the situations are different.

C16.15   PRIVACY BY DESIGN (PBD) (OR EQUIVALENT)

Nothing specific.

C16.16   TWEETING FROM COURTS, AND ANY RULES/LAWS

No specific rules or laws, as long as such publication of information does not amount to 'criminal contempt' within the meaning of Section 2(c) of the

---

71   The word 'dishonestly' has the meaning given to it in Section 24 of the Indian Penal Code, 1860. Whoever does anything with the intention of causing wrongful gain to one person or wrongful loss to another person is said to do that thing 'dishonestly'.

72   The word 'fraudulently' has the meaning given to it in Section 25 of the Indian Penal Code, 1860. A person is said to do a thing fraudulently if he does that thing with intent to defraud but not otherwise.

73   'Computer source code' is defined as the listing of programs, computer commands, design and layout and program analysis of computer resource in any form.

74   2006 (1) ALD Cri 96.

Contempt of Courts Act, 1971. In this context, 'criminal contempt' means publication of any matter which:

a)   Scandalizes or lowers the authority of any court;

b)   Prejudices or interferes with the due course of any judicial proceedings;

c)   Interferes with or obstructs the administration of justice in any other manner.

Relevant provisions:

a)   Innocent publication of any matter which interferes with or obstructs the course of justice in connection with any civil or criminal proceedings pending at the time of publication is not contempt of court;[75]

b)   Fair and accurate publication of judicial proceedings is not contempt of court.[76] 'Judicial proceedings' means day-to-day proceedings;[77]

c)   Fair criticism on the merits of any case which has been heard and finally decided is also not contempt of court;[78]

d)   Publication of a fair and accurate report of judicial proceedings before any court sitting in chambers or *in camera* is not contempt of court, unless publication is restricted by the court or the information relates to a secret process or an invention.[79]

C16.17   TELEVISION COURTROOM BROADCASTING OR TELEVISION CAMERAS IN COURT, AND RULES OR LAWS

Audio/video recording of court proceedings is not permitted.

In *Deepak Khosla v Union of India and Others*,[80] the Delhi High Court observed that there is no legal right available to any person under any enactment, common law or rules for the recording of proceedings in open court by way of audio/video proceedings. In this case the petitioner had approached the Delhi Court to declare that the petitioner is entitled to non-intrusively audio-record judicial proceedings that involve his participation before the court.

The Company Law Board, a quasi-judicial body that governs all companies, introduced an amendment to the Company Law Board Regulations, 1991 on

---

75   Section 3 of the Contempt of Courts Act, 1971.
76   Section 4 of the Contempt of Courts Act, 1971.
77   1984 CriLJ 481.
78   Section 5 of the Contempt of Courts Act, 1971.
79   Section 7 of the Contempt of Courts Act, 1971.
80   AIR 2011 Delhi 199.

February 20, 2014 restricting audio or video recordings of the proceedings by the parties before any bench of the Company Law Board.[81]

C16.18   SM IN COURTROOMS

No details.

C16.19   USE OF SM AS EVIDENCE IN COURTS

No details.

C16.20   PRIVACY, DATA PROTECTION AND SM

No details.

C16.21   SM AND FAMILY LAW CASES

No.

C16.22   SPORTS PERSONS, SPORTS CLUBS AND SM

No details.

C16.23   PERSONAL RELATIONS AND RELATIONSHIPS

According to the news reports:

- A student was arrested for uploading obscene pictures of a girl on Facebook in an attempt to humiliate her. The accused is reported to have met the girl at the college and pretended to be in love with her. It is also reported that he offered her drugged juice and, while she was unconscious, took obscene pictures of her with him. He is later said to have blackmailed her with threats of circulating the pictures on the internet if he was not paid INR10,00,000 (Rupees Ten Lakhs);[82]

- A youth was arrested for uploading edited vulgar photos of a girl on Facebook after she rejected his marriage proposal;[83]

---

81 File No 10/36/2001-CLB, Government of India, Company Law Board dated February 20, 2014.
82 See http://tulunadunews.com/tag/arrest/page/2/.
83 See   http://spotnewsindia.com/2013/11/25/facebook-crime-youth-uploaded-edited-vulgar-photo-girl-fb-arrested-computer-siezed/.

- A Unani doctor was arrested for posting obscene photos of his ex-wife on the internet. The accused had created a fake Facebook profile of his ex-wife and posted some obscene comments and her morphed photographs.[84]

C16.24   SM AND PERSONAL DATA OF DECEASED PERSONS

No details.

C16.25   SM, WEBSITE, SERVICE PROVIDER OR ISP DEFENCE RULES/LAWS

C16.25.1   *Exemption from liability*

IT Act

Subject to satisfaction of certain conditions, an intermediary is not liable for any third party information, data or communication link made available or hosted by it.[85] The exemption provided under the IT Act does not shield an intermediary from liability under the Copyright Act and the Patents Act, 1970.[86]

Exemption from copyright liability is provided under Section 52(b) and (c) of the Copyright Act from any liability arising from storage of work in which copyright subsists.

The conditions to be satisfied for exemption from liability arising under any law except the Copyright Act and the Patents Act, 1970 are as follows:

a)   The intermediary is only providing access to a communication system over which information made available by third parties is transmitted or temporarily stored or hosted;[87] or

b)   The intermediary does not initiate the transmission, select the receiver of the transmission, and select or modify the information contained in the transmission;[88] and

c)   The intermediary has observed due diligence while discharging its duties under the IT Act[89] and has complied with the rules framed under

---

84   See www.business-standard.com/article/pti-stories/unani-doctor-arrested-for-slandering-ex-wife-on-internet-113110801093_1.html.
85   Section 79(1) of the IT Act.
86   Section 81 of the IT Act.
87   Section 79(2)(a) of the IT Act.
88   Section 79(2)(b) of the IT Act.
89   Section 79(2)(c) of the IT Act.

the Information Technology (Intermediaries Guidelines) Rules, 2011[90] (Intermediaries Guidelines);

d) The intermediary has not conspired or abetted or aided or induced, whether by threats or promise or otherwise, in connection with the commission of the unlawful act;[91]

e) The intermediary expeditiously removes or disables access to objectionable or unlawful content that is being transmitted or published through its services soon after receiving actual knowledge or on being notified by the appropriate Government.[92]

C16.25.2 *Due diligence to be observed by intermediary*

The intermediaries Guidelines prescribe the due diligence to be observed by intermediaries.

The intermediary should publish terms of usage and a privacy policy for access to or usage of its services,[93] and should retain the right to terminate the access rights of users who fail to comply with them.[94]

Terms of usage should prohibit an intermediary's users from hosting, displaying, uploading, modifying, publishing, transmitting, updating or sharing any information that:[95]

1. belongs to another person and to which the user does not have a right;

2. is grossly harmful, harassing, blasphemous, defamatory, obscene, pornographic, paedophilic, libellous, invasive of another's privacy, hateful, or racially, ethnically objectionable, disparaging, relating or encouraging money laundering or gambling, or otherwise unlawful in any manner whatever;

3. harms minors in any way;

4. infringes any patent, trademark, copyright or other proprietary rights;

5. violates any law;

6. is deceiving or misleading as regards the origin of such message or communicates any information which is grossly offensive or menacing in nature;

7. impersonates another person;

---

90 Ministry of Communications and Information Technology (Department of Information Technology), Notification No 341(E), dated April 11, 2011, published in the Gazette of India, Extraordinary, Part II, Section 3(i), available at http://deity.gov.in/sites/upload_files/dit/files/GSR314E_10511(1).pdf.
91 Section 79(3)(a) of the IT Act.
92 Section 79(3)(b) of the IT Act.
93 Rule 3(1) of Intermediaries Guidelines.
94 Rule 3(5) of Intermediaries Guidelines.
95 Rule 3(2) of Intermediaries Guidelines.

8. contains a software virus or other program that destroys or limits the functionality of any computer resource;

9. threatens the unity, integrity, defence, security or sovereignty of India, friendly relations with foreign states, or public order, or causes incitement to the commission of any cognizable offence or prevents investigation of any offence or is insulting any other nation.

The Intermediaries Guidelines prohibit an intermediary from knowingly hosting or publishing any information listed in 1 to 9 above. An intermediary is also prohibited from initiating the transmission, selecting the receiver of the transmission and editing the information listed in 1 to 9 above.[96]

Temporary, transient or intermediate storage of information and timely removal of objectionable content after receiving actual knowledge is not regarded as hosting, publishing, editing or storing objectionable content.[97]

The intermediary is required to initiate action to remove objectionable content within 36 hours of obtaining knowledge, either by itself or through the affected party. The intermediary is required to preserve objectionable or unlawful information and associated records for at least 90 days, for investigation purposes.[98]

The Central Government has clarified that, where the intermediary has obtained actual knowledge of objectionable content through the affected party, it is required to respond or acknowledge to the complainant within 36 hours of receiving the complaint and, accordingly, initiate appropriate action.[99]

The intermediary is required to secure its system by implementing security measures prescribed in the Information Technology (Reasonable Security Practises and Procedures and Sensitive Personal Information) Rules, 2011.[100]

The intermediary is required to designate a grievance officer to address complaints under the Intermediaries Guidelines. Details of the grievance officer should be published on the intermediary's website. The intermediary is required to redress the complaint within one month from the date of receipt of the complaint.[101]

C16.25.3 Copyright Act

The Copyright Amendment Act, 2012 introduced provisions to exempt intermediaries from liability for copyright infringement arising from transient or incidental storage in the following cases:

---

96   Rule 3(3) of Intermediaries Guidelines.
97   Ibid.
98   Rule 3(4) of Intermediaries Guidelines.
99   Clarification on the Information Technology (Intermediary Guidelines) Rules, 2011 under Section 79 of the Information Technology Act, 2000, March 18, 2013.
100 Rule 3(8) of Intermediaries Guidelines.
101 Rule 3(11) of Intermediaries Guidelines.

a) The transient or incidental storage of a work or performance purely in the technical process of electronic transmission or communication to the public;

b) The transient or incidental storage of a work or performance for the purpose of providing electronic links, access or integration, subject to the following conditions:

- such links, access or integration has not been expressly prohibited by the rights holder,

- the intermediary is unaware or has no reasonable grounds for believing that such storage is of an infringing copy, and

- the intermediary has disabled access to the work on being notified by the owner of the work. If the intermediary does not receive – within 21 days from the date of receipt of notification from the owner of the work – the orders of the competent court that the 'transient or incidental' storage of the alleged work is infringement of copyright, it may continue with providing access to such work.

Rule 75 of the Copyright Rules, 2013 provides the procedure to be followed by the copyright owners to issue a take-down notice and by the intermediary to avail exemption from liability. The copyright owner should give a written complaint to the intermediary, notifying the infringing copy of the work.[102] The written complaint should include details of the 'URL' of the website,[103] and the details of the person, if known to the complainant, responsible for uploading the work.[104] The owner of the copyright is also required to provide an undertaking that it will procure an order of the court within 21 days from the date of complaint against the person responsible for uploading the infringing copy and furnish the order to the intermediary.[105]

The intermediary is required to disable access to the infringing work within 36 hours from receipt of the complaint.[106]

If the owner of the copyright fails to obtain the order of the court, the intermediary may restore the storage of such work,[107] and further is not obliged to respond to any further notice sent by the same copyright owner with respect to the same work in the same location.[108]

C16.26 ECOMMERCE DEFENCE CASES

See C16.3 and C16.4.

---

102 Rule 75(1) of Copyright Rules.
103 Rule 75(2)(d) of Copyright Rules.
104 Rule 75(2)(e) of Copyright Rules.
105 Rule 75(2)(f) of Copyright Rules.
106 Rule 75(3) of Copyright Rules.
107 Rule 75(5) of Copyright Rules.
108 Rule 75(6) of Copyright Rules.

C16.27   LAWS PROTECTING PERSONAL DATA/ PERSONALLY IDENTIFIABLE INFORMATION

C16.27.1   Data privacy

On 11 April 2011, the Indian Ministry of Communications and Technology published rules implementing certain provisions of the IT Act dealing with the protection of sensitive personal data: security practices and procedures that must be followed by organisations dealing with sensitive personal data (Data Privacy Rules).[109]

Following the introduction of the Data Privacy Rules, there was confusion amongst outsourcing companies regarding compliance with certain provisions of the Data Privacy Rules, particularly the consent provisions.

To address the concerns of the outsourcing industry, the Department of Information Technology, Ministry of Communications and Technology published clarifications to the Data Privacy Rules.[110]

C16.27.2   Personal information and sensitive personal data

The overall scheme of the Data Privacy Rules – including the brief description in the preamble, and the provision of the IT Act under which they are enacted – appears to seek to protect Sensitive Data. The Data Privacy Rules refer consistently to 'sensitive personal data or information' ('Sensitive Data') as the subject of protection, but also refer, with respect to certain obligations, to 'personal information'. Sensitive Data is defined as a subset of 'personal information'. The use of the terms 'information' and 'personal information' are general usages and are thus not intended to expand the scope of the Data Privacy Rules. 'Personal information' is any information that relates to a natural person, which either directly or indirectly, in combination with other information available or likely to be available within a body corporate, is capable of identifying such a person.[111]

Sensitive Data[112] is defined as personal information that relates to:

a)   passwords;

b)   financial information, such as a bank account or credit card or debit card or other payment instrument details;

c)   physical, psychological and mental health condition;

---

109 Notification no GSR 313(E), dated 11 April 2011, published in the Gazette of India, Extraordinary, Part II, Section 3(i).
110 Press Note, Government of India, Ministry of Communications and Information Technology, August 24, 2011.
111 Rule 2(i) of Data Privacy Rules.
112 Rule 3 of Data Privacy Rules.

d) sexual orientation;

e) medical records and history;

f) biometric information;

g) any detail relating to (a)–(f) above received by the body corporate for the provision of services; or

h) any information relating to (a)–(g) that is received, stored or processed by the body corporate under a lawful contract or otherwise.

Sensitive Data is broadly defined to include data obtained by any method, including lawful contract. Information that is freely available, accessible in the public domain, or furnished under the Right to Information Act 2005[113] is excluded from the ambit of the above definition.[114]

Further, the Data Privacy Rules do not cover Sensitive Data that is available in non-digital form.[115]

C16.27.3 Key terms in the Data Privacy Rules

Body corporate

The term 'body corporate' is defined as any company and includes a firm, sole proprietorship or other association of individuals engaged in commercial or professional activities.[116] The Department of Information Technology has clarified that the Data Privacy Rules apply only to a body corporate that is located in India ('Indian Body Corporate').

Any person on behalf of body corporate

The term 'any person on behalf of body corporate' is not defined in the Data Privacy Rules. It most likely refers to another Indian Body Corporate that collects, stores or processes Sensitive Data on behalf of the Indian Body Corporate.

Provider of information

The term 'provider of information' is not defined in the Data Privacy Rules but the Department has clarified that the term, as referred to in the Data Privacy Rules, refers to natural persons who provide sensitive personal data to an Indian Body Corporate ('Provider').

---

113 Government of India, Right to Information Act 2005, No 22 of 2005.

114 Rule 3 of Data Privacy Rules.

115 Section 43A of the IT Act, under which the Data Privacy Rules are enacted, provides as follows: 'where a body corporate, possessing, dealing or handling any sensitive personal data or information in a computer resource which it owns, controls or operates, is negligent in implementing and maintaining reasonable security practices and procedures and thereby causes wrongful loss or wrongful gain to any person, such body corporate shall be liable to pay damages by way of compensation to the person so affected'.

116 Section 43A(i) of the IT Act.

Applicability

The Data Privacy Rules appear to apply to the Sensitive Data of any individual collected, processed or stored in India via computer resources by an Indian Body Corporate. The application of the Data Privacy Rules is not limited to Sensitive Data belonging to Indian residents.

The Department has clarified that, if an Indian Body Corporate is performing the functions of collection, storage or processing of Sensitive Data pursuant to a contract directly with the Provider (residing in any jurisdiction), the Data Privacy Rules in their entirety become applicable to such Indian Body Corporate ('Principal Indian Body Corporate'). However, if an Indian Body Corporate is performing the functions of collection, storage or processing of Sensitive Data under a contract with any organization in India or outside India, Rules 5 and 6 of the Data Privacy Rules relating to consent and disclosure requirements do not apply to such Indian Body Corporate ('Processor Indian Body Corporate'). Processor Indian Body Corporate would therefore be governed by the provisions of the contract that it has entered into with the Principal Indian Body Corporate or a foreign body corporate. While the consent and disclosure requirements are made inapplicable to the Processor Indian Body Corporate, other obligations under the Data Privacy Rules, such as publication of privacy policy, transfer conditions, and security standards (discussed below), appear to remain applicable to the Processor Indian Body Corporate.

Essentially, for the purposes of compliance under the Data Privacy Rules, the Indian Body Corporate is divided into two categories: Principal Indian Body Corporate and Processor Indian Body Corporate. A Principal Indian Body Corporate is an Indian Body Corporate that performs the functions of collection, storage or processing of Sensitive Data under a contract directly with the Provider. The Provider can be resident in any country. A Processor Indian Body Corporate is an Indian Body Corporate that performs the functions of collection, storage or processing of Sensitive Data under a contract with a Principal Indian Body Corporate or a foreign body corporate.

The Data Privacy Rules contain detail procedures that need to be followed by the Principal Indian Body Corporate while collecting the Sensitive Data. The Principal Indian Body Corporate is required to obtain prior written consent from the Provider regarding the usage of the information. Consent may be obtained through letter, fax, email or by any mode of electronic communication. Sensitive Data should be collected only for the lawful purpose of the Principal Indian Body Corporate.[117]

The Provider should be provided with an option of declining to provide Sensitive Data and, in the case of a Provider who has already consented to the

---

117 Rule 5 of Data Privacy Rules.

collection of Sensitive Data, should be provided with an option to withdraw such consent.[118]

Sensitive Data should not be used for purposes other than the purpose for which it is collected. Further, the Principal Indian Body Corporate should not retain Sensitive Data for a period longer than it is required.[119]

The Provider has a right of access to information about himself that is being held, and to review such information. The Provider is also entitled to require the Principal Indian Body Corporate to correct or amend any inaccuracies in the information.[120]

The Data Privacy Rules contain independent conditions for the disclosure (Rule 6) and transfer of Sensitive Data (Rule 7), but fail to clarify which actions constitute 'disclosure' and which amount to 'transfer'; the disclosure of Sensitive Data could also qualify as 'transfer' of Sensitive Data. Conditions for 'transfer' are higher than the conditions applicable for 'disclosure' of information.[121]

The disclosure of Sensitive Data is not permitted without the consent of the Provider of the information, unless it is made pursuant to a contract with the Provider or to Government agencies or pursuant to an order under the law.[122]

The Principal Indian Body Corporate or Processor Indian Body Corporate may transfer Sensitive Data to any other organization or a person in India or outside India if the Provider has agreed to such transfer of Sensitive Data. If no such consent is obtained from the Provider, information may be transferred subject to the recipient agreeing to treat the information with the same level of protection that is provided under the Data Privacy Rules and such transfer is necessary for the performance of the lawful contract between the transferor and the Provider.[123]

The Data Privacy Rules require that the Principal Indian Body Corporate and the Processor Indian Body Corporate implement reasonable security practices and standards, and that they have a comprehensively documented information security program, and security policies. These must contain managerial, technical, operational and physical security control measures that are commensurate with the information assets being protected and with the nature of the business.[124]

---

118 Rule 5(7) of Data Privacy Rules.
119 Rule 5(5) of Data Privacy Rules.
120 Rule 5(6) of Data Privacy Rules.
121 The recipient body corporate (whether in India or outside) has to ensure protection of Sensitive Data on the same levels as adhered to by the transferor under the Data Privacy Rules. However, the disclosure of Sensitive Data to a third party contains no such express condition if it is with the consent of the Provider of the information or in accordance with the contract entered with the Provider of the information.
122 Rule 6(1) of Data Privacy Rules.
123 Rule 7 of Data Privacy Rules.
124 Rule 8(1) of Data Privacy Rules.

Under the Data Privacy Rules, a 'body corporate' or 'any person acting on its behalf' is not under an obligation to notify its customers or employees of data security breaches. However, although not expressly specified in the Data Privacy Rules, it may be argued that, if the data security breach is of a serious nature or if the data is of such a nature that, if compromised, it is likely to cause wrongful loss or wrongful gain to any person, the 'body corporate' could be under an obligation to notify the data security breach to the affected individuals.

C16.28 DATA BREACH LAWS AND CUSTOMERS/ USERS/REGULATORS NOTIFIED OF HACKING OR DATA LOSS

Under the Data Privacy Rules, a body corporate is not under an obligation to notify its customers or employees of data security breaches. However, although not expressly specified in the Data Privacy Rules, it may be argued that, based on a reading of Section 43A of the IT Act, if the data security breach is of a serious nature or if the data is of such a nature that, if compromised, it is likely to cause wrongful loss or wrongful gain to any person, the 'body corporate' could be under an obligation to notify the data security breach to the affected individuals.

Ireland

Patrick Carrol, Barrister at Law
Paul Lambert, Solicitor, Adjunct Lecturer

C17.1 INTRODUCTION

Ireland is an EU member state and is a Common Law jurisdiction.

C17.2 SPECIFIC SM AND SN LAWS

Many laws affect SM and SN, but there are no express SM and SN laws.

C17.3 SM CRIMINAL LAW CASES

There are no express SM criminal laws.

However, there are a growing number of criminal cases involving SM and SN abuse and SM evidence.

A woman was remanded in custody from July to October 2014 for repeatedly Tweeting online abuse about the wife of a former colleague. It was also directed by Judge McCartan that she should not have access to electronic devices, equipment or phones.[1]

A man was fined €2,000 for sexual innuendo-type comments made on a woman's Facebook SM profile, similar to a 'fraping' incident (that is, accessing a person's computer or mobile device to place 'joke' content on their SM profile if they momentarily leave their computer or device 'open' and unattended).[2] The defendant was charged under the Criminal Damage Act

---

1   The case of Gráinne O'Toole; see 'Woman Remanded for Tweeting Abuse About Wife of Former Colleague,' RTE, 11 July 2014, available at www.rte.ie/news/2014/0710/629876-tweeting-abuse/.
2   'Man fined €2000 for first Facebook "fraping" criminal case – Judge says "reprehensible offence seriously damaged woman's good name"', Independent, 20 June 2014, available at www.independent.ie/irish-news/courts/man-fined-2000-for-first-facebook-frapingcriminal-case-30394813.html#sthash.j5FeiImD.dpuf.

1991 which carries a maximum penalty of ten years in prison and a €10,000 fine. It is understood that this is the first prosecution for criminal damage to an SM profile account.

C17.4 SM CIVIL LAW CASES

One of the first cases directly involving an SM or related website in Ireland is understood to relate to fake Facebook profile accounts. Takedown, damages and other reliefs were reported as being sought.[3] However, the case involving international businessman JP McManus and Facebook was settled at an early stage.

The biggest Irish SM case involves an innocent student, who was defamed and abused over a taxi fare evasion video on various SM and related websites.[4] Interim and contested interlocutory injunctions were granted to the student. Various Norwich Pharmacal orders were also granted.

Another Facebook case occurred in Belfast. This case was *HL (a minor) v Facebook Incorporated, Facebook Ireland Limited, The Northern Health and Social Care Trust, Department of Justice for Northern Ireland, Department of Health and Social Services and Public Safety for Northern Ireland, the Home Office, Department of Culture, Media and Sport, Attorney General for Northern Ireland, Advocate General for Northern Ireland and Attorney General for England and Wales*.[5]

A number of cases involve contentious comments on SM and related websites and resulting Norwich Pharmacal orders to assist plaintiffs to identify the persons behind the comments. Examples include the student case above,[6] various Ryanair cases[7] and criminal and family cases.

A related development is the complaint to the Data Protection Commissioner to investigate Facebook on foot of the Snowden revelations, and the Irish High Court's referral of the matter to the CJEU.[8] This is one of the privacy and data protection cases taken by Max Schrems and Europe Against Facebook.

---

3   *JP McManus v Facebook*, referred to in 'JP McManus Facebook Action Struck Out,' RTE News, 30 May 2011, available at www.rte.ie/news/2011/0530/301729-mcmanusjp/.

4   See *McKeogh v Doe and Others*, [2012] IEHC 95 (26 January 2012), available at www. bailii.org/cgi-bin/markup.cgi?doc=/ie/cases/IEHC/2012/H95.html&query=eoin+and+mckeogh&method=boolean.

5   [2013] NIQB 25 (1 March 2013), McCloskey J, available at www.bailii.org/cgi-bin/markup. cgi?doc=/nie/cases/NIHC/QB/2013/25.html&query=facebook&method=boolean.

6   See *McKeogh v Doe and Others* [2012] IEHC 95 (26 January 2012).

7   See eg *Ryanair Ltd v Unister GmbH and by order Aeruni GmbH* [2013] IESC 14 (13 March 2013); *Ryanair v Johnson* IEHC 2005/514P.

8   *Schrems v Data Protection Commissioner* [2014] IEHC 310 (18 June 2014); *Schrems v Data Protection Commissioner (No 2)* [2014] IEHC 351 (16 July 2014).

The Digital Rights Ireland data retention case also began in the Irish courts and was subsequently referred to the CJEU by the Irish courts for the ultimate momentous decision.[9]

In 2010, the Irish Red Cross sought orders against Google in order to identify a whistleblower.[10]

Family law cases commonly use SM-related evidence.

C17.5   CASES WHERE SM-RELATED EVIDENCE USED OR ADMISSIBLE

There are cases, both criminal and civil, in Ireland where SM-related evidence has been used or has been admissible.

Family law cases also commonly use SM-related evidence.

As with other jurisdictions, SM issues become most pronounced during national examples of SM-related online abuse and suicide.

C17.6   SPECIFIC ONLINE ABUSE/ONLINE BULLYING/ CYBERBULLYING LAWS

A Revenue employee was convicted in Ireland of sending sexual messages to his female supervisor, some of which indicated that he was threatening to rape and kill women.[11]

A German national was convicted in Ennis Circuit Court in Ireland for sending 'chilling, disturbing and ominous' text messages and emails to a psychologist.[12] He received a three-year suspended sentence.

The Communications Minister Pat Rabbitte, TD, warns that there may be a gap in the country's legislation when it comes to online abuse, bullying and defamation via SM.[13]

---

9   *Digital Rights Ireland Ltd v Minister for Communication & Ors* [2010] IEHC 221 (5 May 2010); C-293/12 *Digital Rights Ireland and Seitlinger and Others.*
10   See 'High Court Order to Hand Over "Red Cross" Blogger ID', PoliticalWorld.org, available at www.politicalworld.org/archive/index.php/t-3180.html.
11   'Meath Man to be Sentenced for Text Harassment,' Breaking News, available at www. breakingnews.ie/ireland/meath-man-to-be-sentenced-for-text-harassment-503520.html.
12   G Deegan, 'Man Sent "Ominous" Texts to Psychologist,' *Irish Times*, 24 February 2011, available at www.irishtimes.com/newspaper/ireland/2011/0224/1224290732379.html.
13   'Irish Govt Looking to Plug Gaps in Laws Over Social Media Bullying – Rabbitte,' Silicon Republic, 6 March 2013, available at www.siliconrepublic.com/comms/item/31759-irish-govt-looking-to-plug/.

In a report to the Government, the Internet Content Governance Advisory Group has recommended amending laws to cater for SM and online abuse. Some of the key recommendations to be implemented include,

- '• Amending the laws so that the "sending of grossly offensive, indecent, obscene, or menacing" messages relates to electronic communications;

- • Overhauling disclosure and discovery rules for the courts for cases involving online media or abuse;

- • A national council for child internet safety industry representatives and government which will co-ordinate online safety plans and education measures;

- • The teaching of internet safety and digital literacy skills in schools;

- • Further support for parents dealing with cyberbullying.' [14]

The Report of the Internet Content Governance Advisory Group was published in May 2014. [15]

Schools in Ireland are now required to implement an anti-bullying programme, including in relation to online abuse, and to record instances of online abuse. Online abuse has also been a concern for the Minister of Education. [16]

C17.7 OTHER LAWS APPLIED TO ONLINE ABUSE/ ONLINE BULLYING/CYBERBULLYING

There are a number of instances where the police (Gardai) have investigated online abuse and traced online abusers and trolls. It is understood that certain individuals have been cautioned.

A man was fined €2,000 for sexual innuendo-type comments made on a woman's Facebook SM profile, similar to a fraping incident. [17] The case was taken and prosecuted under the Criminal Damage Act 1991. This carries a maximum penalty of ten years in prison and a €10,000 fine. It is understood to be the first prosecution for criminal damage to an SM profile account.

---

14 Juno McEnroe and Conall Ó Fátharta, 'Online Abuse Victims Will be Able to Use Facebook Posts as Evidence,' Examiner, 25 June 2014, available at www.irishexaminer.com/ireland/online-abuse-victims-will-be-able-to-use-facebook-posts-as-evidence-273197.html.

15 The report is available at www.dcenr.gov.ie/NR/rdonlyres/0BCE1511-508E-4E97-B1A9-23A6BE9124AA/0/InternetContentGovernanceAdvisoryGroup.pdf.

16 Katherine Donnelly, 'Schools Ordered to Get Tough on Bullying Epidemic,' Independent, 21 January 2013.

17 'Man fined €2000 for first Facebook "fraping" criminal case – Judge says "reprehensible offence seriously damaged woman's good name"', Independent, 20 June 2014, available at http://www.independent.ie/irish-news/courts/man-fined-2000-for-first-facebook-frapingcriminal-case-30394813.html#sthash.j5FeiImD.dpuf.

The Sixth Report of the Special Rapporteur on Child Protection, A Report Submitted to the Oireachtas[18] by the Special Rapporteur Dr Geoffrey Shannon, recommends that cyberbullying should be a criminal offence. The report highlights the advent of online abuse, as well as such issues as the possibility of anonymous reporting by victims. It states,

> 'The impact and effect of bullying on children has been tragically thrown into the media spotlight ... Whilst bullying has always been an unfortunate aspect of our society, the growth of "Cyber-bullying" has almost overnight created a readily accessible forum for bullies to target children with little or no regulation or sanction. The Irish legal system has been somewhat taken unawares as to the manner and means through which children have fallen victim to cyber-bullying. Whilst there are some legislative provisions in being that might be interpreted in such a manner as to tackle this growing problem, a focused response is required.'[19]

It adds,

> 'However, in order for a system of legal recourse to be effective victims of such bullying need to be able to feel that they can come forward and express their concerns without fear of retribution. Thus, provision also needs to be made for the protection of child victims of such behaviour, eg the means of retaining their anonymity when making a complaint as to such bullying.'[20]

The report also highlights the issue of potential liability for schools and educational organisations for online abuse, etc. It states that the 'extent of a school's liability arising from an incident of bullying between students is a topic of some considerable debate and one that has been thrown into the fore in recent months'.[21]

It notes recent guidelines published in Ireland for schools, but cautions that 'in the era of online technology and cyberbullying a new focus must be brought to bear on this issue. Lessons can be learnt from the developments in New South Wales and Massachusetts in attempting to set a legislative basis to tackle this problem in schools'.[22]

The recommendations refer to 'Cyber-bullying as a Criminal Offence', and state,

> 'On review of reported cases of harassment involving social networking, email and SMS, there appear to be very few criminal prosecutions taken for this type of harassment under the Non-Fatal Offences Against the Person Act, 1997 despite the suitability of that Act. When cyber-bullying is

---

18   G Shannon, *Sixth Report of the Special Rapporteur on Child Protection, A Report Submitted to the Oireachtas*, (Dublin, 23 January 2013).
19   Ibid, p 9.
20   Ibid, p 9.
21   Ibid, p 9.
22   Ibid, p 9.

being described as an epidemic, we need to examine why this is the case. Specifically, is there reticence to investigate complaints of cyber-bullying?

Responding to calls for new criminal legislation to tackle cyber-bullying, the Minister for Justice identified our existing laws against harassment as being suitable. However, the Minister has directed the Law Reform Commission to examine difficulties in prosecuting for cyber-bullying and, in particular, the necessity to show persistence in the harassment.

Existing laws regarding harassment can be used to incorporate cyber-bullying incidents. A review of the Post Office (Amendment) Acts should be undertaken with a view to incorporating emerging means of cyber-bullying.'[23]

Anonymity for victims of online abuse, or at least cyberbullying online abuse, is favoured. The recommendations continue as follows,

'The current Irish legal position would appear to suggest that an application for anonymity in the context of cyber-bullying litigation would be unsuccessful. However, it is difficult to be definitive in respect of the legal position because Mr Justice Peart's decision in *McKeogh v John Doe* may well have been different if the applicant had been a child or teenager seeking to rely on the right to privacy of children, and able to invoke the general social interest in protection of children from cyber-bullying. The ideal solution would be an agreement of co-operation to be entered into between ISPs (and potentially other entities such as Facebook) and the Gardaí to provide IP addresses where complaints of cyber-bullying have been received.'[24]

The Oireachtas Joint Committee on Transport and Communications, which held parliamentary hearings and submissions during 2013 *inter alia* in relation to online abuse and cyberbullying, has recommended that a single body should be given responsibility for co-ordinating the regulation of SM content.[25]

Paul C Dwyer of the National Anti-Bullying Coalition told the Committee that just one SN provider received some 100,000 reports or requests per day but dedicated just 90 staff to processing such requests.[26] The Committee and the Report recommend that the online abuse report data be furnished by the SNs to the Irish Data Protection Commissioner.[27]

In Recommendation 3, the Committee supports the recommendation contained in the Action Plan on Bullying that the definition of bullying in the new national

---

23   Ibid, p 20.
24   Ibid, p 20.
25   Oireachtas Joint Committee on Transport and Communications, *Houses of the Oireachtas, Joint Committee on Transport and Communications Report Addressing the Growth of Social Media and Tackling Cyberbullying*, (Government Publications: Dublin, 18 July 2013).
26   Ibid, p 8.
27   Ibid.

procedures for schools should include a specific reference to cyberbullying. Also, guidelines for cyberbullying should be put in place, so that school principals dealing with instances of cyberbullying have a clear protocol to follow.[28]

Recommendation 4 refers to employers. It states that employers should be made aware of the importance of introducing an SM policy, ie outlining what constitutes cyberbullying and what actions will be taken if there is a breach of such a policy.[29] Employers should be aware that cyberbullying falls under 'harassment', and Section 10 of the Non-fatal Offences Against the Person Act 1997 may apply in such cases.[30]

Recommendation 6 states as follows,

'The Committee recommends that a single body be given responsibility for co-ordinating the regulation of social media content. Funding and organisational models for this agency should be agreed with the industry. It is noted that other examples of industry-led partnerships between stakeholders and government have been established in other sectors in recent years.'[31]

In 1999 a man was gaoled for spreading libel on the internet.[32]

A mother told a coroner's court that she found 'horrific' text and Facebook online abuse messages on her son's mobile phone after his suicide.[33] She said that 'I feel if it were not for those messages, he would still be here'.[34] There have been a number of suicides in Ireland associated with online abuse and particular SNs.

A German national was convicted in Ennis Circuit Court in Ireland for sending 'chilling, disturbing and ominous' text messages and emails to a psychologist.[35] He received a three-year suspended sentence.

Potential laws include,

- Post Office (Amendment) Act 1951
    - s 13 refers to offensive telephone messages;

---

28 Ibid, p 9.
29 Ibid.
30 Ibid.
31 Ibid, p 10.
32 'Man Jailed for Spreading Libel on the Internet,' RTE News, 20 December 1999.
33 Gareth Naughton, 'Mother Links Son's Suicide to Cyberbullying, Woman Tells Coroner's Court She Found "Horrific" Messages on Phone,' Irish Times, 4 March 2014, available at www.irishtimes.com/news/crime-and-law/courts/mother-links-son-s-suicide-to-cyberbullying-1.1712029.
34 'Mother of 17 year-old Who Died by Suicide Found "Horrific" and "Threatening" Messages on His Phone, Inquest Hears. "I Feel If It Were Not for Those Messages, He Would Still be Here" Mother Says,' Independent, 3 March 2014, available at www.independent.ie/irish-news/mother-of-17-yearold-who-died-by-suicide-found-horrific-and-threatening-messages-on-his-phone-inquest-hears-30057924.html.
35 G Deegan, 'Man Sent "Ominous" Texts to Psychologist,' Irish Times, 24 February 2011, available at www.irishtimes.com/newspaper/ireland/2011/0224/1224290732379.html.

- Data Protection Acts 1988 and 2003
    - s 2 refers to fair obtaining and processing of personal data;
    - s 6A refers to the right to object to processing likely to cause distress;
    - s 8 refers to permitting disclosure for investigation of crime;
- Prohibition of Incitement of Hatred Act 1989;
- Non-Fatal Offences Against the Person Act 1997
    - s 5 refers to threats to kill or cause serious harm;
    - s 9 refers to coercion;
    - s 10 refers to harassment;
- Norwich Pharmacal orders have been used since at least 2005 to help identify internet users and online abusers;
- Defamation Act 2009;
- Data Protection Directive 1995;[36]
- ePrivacy Directive;[37]
- Electronic Commerce Act 2000;
- European Communities (Directive 2000/31/EC) Regulations 2003;
- European Communities (Protection of Consumers in Respect of Contracts made by Means of Distance Communication) Regulations 2001;
- European Communities (Unfair Terms in Consumer Contracts) Regulations 2000;[38]
- European Communities (Unfair Terms in Consumer Contracts) Regulations (SI 27/1995);
- Child Pornography Prevention Act 1996;
- Child Trafficking and Pornography Acts 1998 and 2004;
- Child Trafficking and Pornography (Amendment) Act 2004;

---

36 Data Protection Directive 1995 (Directive 95/46/EC of the European Parliament and of the Council of 24 October 1995 on the protection of individuals with regard to the processing of personal data and on the free movement of such data).
37 Directive on privacy and electronic communications 2002 (Directive 2002/58/EC of the European Parliament and of the Council of 12 July 2002 concerning the processing of personal data and the protection of privacy in the electronic communications sector, as amended by Directives 2006/24/EC and 2009/136/EC).
38 SI No 307/2000.

- Children Act 2001;

- Consumer Credit Act 1995;

- Consumer Information Act 1978;

- Copyright and Related Rights Act 2000 (as amended);

- Criminal Damage Act 1991;

- Criminal Evidence Act 1992;

- Criminal Justice Acts 1993, 1994 and 2006;

- Criminal Justice (Theft and Fraud Offences) Acts 1991 and 2001;

- Education Act 1998;

- Employment Equality Acts 1998 (as amended);

- European Convention on Human Rights Act 2003;

- Evidence rules;

- Freedom of Information Acts 1997 and 2003;

- Human Rights Act 1998;

- Interception of Postal Packets and Telecommunications Messages (Regulation) Act 1993;

- Minimum Notice and Terms of Employment Acts 1973 and 2001;

- Civil Liability Act 1961;

- Safety, Health and Welfare at Work Act 2005;

- Sale of Goods and Supply of Services Act 1980;

- European Convention on Human Rights;

- ePrivacy Regulations/Privacy and Electronic Communications Regulations.

In addition, issues of theft law, fraud law, computer fraud and misuse and hacking may also apply, depending on the circumstances.

C17.8   CHILDREN AND SM LAWS OR RULES

There are no such express laws, although a recent Constitutional amendment has expressly recognised legal Constitutional rights for children. It has been suggested that this may have implications for children, SM and online abuse, none of which were considered at the time of the Constitutional amendment itself.[39]

---

39   P Lambert, *Social Networking: Law, Rights and Policy* (Clarus Press, 2014).

In a recent case, a teacher was convicted in connection with a relationship, both physical and via Facebook and texts, with a 14-year-old student.[40]

The draft EU Data Protection Regulation refers to children expressly for the first time.

C17.9 EMPLOYEES/EMPLOYMENT SM LAWS OR CASES

There are no laws specific to SM and employees. However, existing employment rules and legislation will apply in the online environment. Many employment cases occur in employment tribunals as opposed to courts and may therefore not be reported or otherwise widely highlighted.

In one interesting case in February 2014, a bank manager who was sacked after 'forwarding lewd pornography' received compensation when he appealed.[41]

Employers and organisations must be increasingly conscious of employee SM issues.[42] Cyber-crime costs are also an issue for organisations.[43]

C17.10 SCHOOL AND UNIVERSITY STUDENT SM CASES

The issue of online abuse is a very prominent issue, as a problem, in terms of dealing with students engaged in online abuse and also in terms of recording instances of reported online abuse.

Schools are increasingly obliged to have policies in place to deal with online abuse and also to record instances of such abuse.

Recommendation 3 of the Oireachtas Joint Committee on Transport and Communications Report supports guidelines for cyberbullying for schools,

---

40 S Maguire, 'Assistant Teacher Jailed for Having Sex With 14-Year-Old Pupil After Facebook Relationship,' Independent, 16 July 2014, available at www.independent.ie/irish-news/courts/assistant-teacher-jailed-for-having-sex-with-14yearold-pupil-after-facebook-relationship-30436792.html#sthash.IUBrJvCE.dpuf.
41 'Bank Manager Sacked After "Forwarding Lewd Pornography" Gets Compensation,' Independent, 18 February 2014, available at www.independent.ie/irish-news/courts/bank-manager-sacked-after-forwarding-lewd-pornography-gets-compensation-30020832.html.
42 P Lambert, 'Five Ways to Stop Your Company Getting Stung Over Social Media Gaffes,' Independent, 13 March 2014, available at www.independent.ie/business/technology/five-ways-to-stop-your-company-getting-stung-over-social-media-gaffes-30087652.html.
43 R Riegel, 'Cyber-crime Cost Irish Economy €350m in 2013,' Independent, 12 March 2014, available at www.independent.ie/business/technology/cybercrime-cost-irish-economy-350m-in-2013-30084104.html.

so that school principals dealing with instances of cyberbullying have a clear protocol to follow.[44]

There are a number of examples where students have been disciplined in relation to online abuse activities. There is at least one report where a parent of a tragic victim of online abuse was considering suing the school in question.

C17.11   RIGHT OR HUMAN RIGHT TO ACCESS THE INTERNET OR SM

There is human rights jurisprudence but not yet in relation to the internet and SM.

C17.12   BANS OR RESTRICTIONS ON INTERNET OR SM

As elsewhere, there are developing examples of restrictions being applied for and applied by the courts. There does not appear to be any appeal jurisprudence as yet.

The Director of Public Prosecutions in a recent case asked for an order preventing a convicted sex offender from contacting children online after a court heard that he was using Twitter to claim he worked for the band One Direction.[45]

C17.13   IDENTITY THEFT (OR EQUIVALENT)

No explicit laws. However, a number of laws (see C17.3 and C17.6) may apply.

C17.14   HACKING (OR EQUIVALENT)

Section 9 of the Criminal Justice (Theft and Fraud Offences) Act 2001 provides for an offence of dishonest operation of a computer with the intention of making a gain for oneself or another or of causing loss to another.

The Criminal Damage Act 1991 provides an offence in relation to unauthorised access to a computer. Section 5 provides that 'A person who without lawful

---

44   Oireachtas Joint Committee on Transport and Communications, *Houses of the Oireachtas, Joint Committee on Transport and Communications Report Addressing the Growth of Social Media and Tackling Cyberbullying*, (Government Publications: Dublin, 18 July 2013), p 9.
45   C Gallagher and A NicArdghail, 'Convicted Sex Offender Claimed He Worked for One Direction,' Irish Times, 28 July 2014, available at www.irishtimes.com/news/crime-and-law/convicted-sex-offender-claimed-he-worked-for-one-direction-1.1880796.

excuse operates a computer … with intent to access any data … shall, whether or not he accesses any data, be guilty of an offence'.

There is also an offence of threatening to damage property, per the Criminal Damage Act 1991, providing that 'A person who … makes … a threat, intending that that other would fear it would be carried out … to damage any property belonging to that other or a third person, or … shall be guilty of an offence'.

Organised crime and organised cyber-theft may involve conspiracy-type offences, such as the Criminal Justice Act 2006.

The Criminal Justice (Theft and Fraud Offences) Act 2001 can also be relevant in relation to the creation of a false instrument (section 25(1)). The Electronic Commerce Act 2000 creates offences such as in relation to electronic signatures. Potentially the Official Secrets Act 1963 may also be relevant. Data protection offences are also very important. Cyber and official terror issues are increasing in prominence. There is a history of terror-related legislation in Ireland, eg Criminal Justice (Terrorist Offences) Act 2005.

C17.15   PRIVACY BY DESIGN (PBD) (OR EQUIVALENT)

There is no specific law, but the Data Protection Commissioner has referred to and endorsed PbD on a number of occasions. General data protection laws apply, eg security.

C17.16   TWEETING FROM COURTS, AND ANY RULES/LAWS

There are instances of this occurring, but there are no explicit rules or laws as such.

It may be that courts will come to distinguish media Tweets and public Tweets. Public Tweets are often more restricted in other jurisdictions, if permitted.

C17.17   TELEVISION COURTROOM BROADCASTING OR TELEVISION CAMERAS IN COURT, AND RULES OR LAWS

Not permitted. However, cameras have been permitted into empty courts to take background footage, and on a few occasions to take footage before a particular case commences, such as the judge entering the courtroom and sitting down at the judge's bench.

C17.18   SM IN COURTROOMS

Not expressly permitted as yet, but this is a developing area.

C17.19   USE OF SM AS EVIDENCE IN COURTS

See variously above.

The Rules of the Superior Courts (Discovery) 2009 relate to and provide for issues of electronic discovery in Ireland.[46] While not contemplated at the time, they potentially encompass forms of electronic discovery where SM content is relevant, necessary, discoverable and permissible.[47]

One of the developments in this sector in Ireland has been the launch by Owen O'Connor of Cernan of the now annual eDiscovery Ireland conference. It comprises a large number of headline speakers and break-out sessions from recognised experts in Ireland and internationally.

A number of interested parties in the eDiscovery and forensic sector in Ireland have sought to deal with perceived issues and problems with the eDiscovery rules (SI 93 of 2009) in Ireland. They have drafted a best practice guide which, with judicial endorsement, it is hoped will provide guidance to practitioners and, indeed, to the courts.

While there are relevant provisions in the Electronic Commerce Act 2000 and now in the eDiscovery rules, it is perhaps the activity of SM and its interface with intellectual property and with the employment sphere that will really bring electronic evidence issues to the fore in Ireland. The forecast search for elusive electrons[48] is increasingly social.

C17.20   PRIVACY, DATA PROTECTION AND SM

An innocent student, who was defamed and abused over a taxi fare evasion video on various SM and related websites,[49] obtained interim and interlocutory injunctions.

A man was fined €2,000 for sexual innuendo-type comments made on a woman's Facebook SM profile, similar to a fraping incident.[50]

As a result of the controversial Facebook psychological manipulation study, involving approximately 700,000 users, the Irish Data Protection Commissioner has written to Facebook seeking more details. The Information

---

46   SI No 93/2009.
47   Generally, see S Mason (ed) *Electronic Evidence, Disclosure, Discovery & Admissibility* (Lexis Nexis Butterworths, London, 2007).
48   P Lambert, 'The Search for Elusive Electrons: Getting a Sense for Electronic Evidence' (2001) (1) *Judicial Studies Institute Journal* 23–49. In terms of the US, see eg Frieden and Murray, *op. cit*, 1.
49   See *McKeogh v Doe and Others* [2012] IEHC 95 (26 January 2012)
50   'Man fined €2000 for first Facebook "fraping" criminal case – Judge says "reprehensible offence seriously damaged woman's good name"', Independent, 20 June 2014, available at http://www.independent.ie/irish-news/courts/man-fined-2000-for-first-facebook-fraping criminal-case-30394813.html#sthash.j5FeiImD.dpuf.

Commissioner in the UK is also considering this matter and is liaising with the Irish Commissioner. It is understood that regulators and privacy groups elsewhere are similarly concerned.

Personal data was removed from the Irish Genealogy website over security fears, and the Irish Data Protection Commissioner is reported as ordering the closure of civil records search over fears that it may expose too much personal information.[51]

C17.21 SM AND FAMILY LAW CASES

Traditionally, Ireland has adopted a highly restrictive approach to the media's reporting of family law and childcare cases. The sensitivity of such matters, and the generally accepted public interest in such an austere approach to such reportage, have been reflected in the rigidity of the relevant laws in the area. Ultimately, this has had the knock-on effect of preventing publication and the generation of awareness of jurisprudential matters relevant to family law and SM. However, as a result of newly promulgated legislation, it is likely that there will be an exponential and rapid development of legal discourse in the area.

In January 2014, the Minister for Justice, Alan Shatter signed into law the Courts and Civil Law (Miscellaneous Provisions) Act 2013 (Part 2). This provided a qualified prerogative to the media to report on family law and childcare matters. Although this legislation has served to relax the once highly rigid rules in relation to the reportage of family law matters, it is important to note that there remain key restrictions which serve the public interest, and reflect the sensitive and private nature of family law proceedings.

First, a discretion has been granted to the court to exclude representatives of the press, or to restrict reporting, under certain circumstances. Furthermore, the public interest in ensuring the anonymity of the parties has been retained, as the legislation prohibits members of the press from publishing information which may identify the parties involved in the case. In the event that a member was to publish details identifying parties to a case, they are now liable to be convicted of a criminal offence, fined up to €50,000, and/or imprisoned for up to three years.

C17.22 SPORTS PERSONS, SPORTS CLUBS AND SM

Gaelic Athletic Association (GAA) athletes are not immune to the issue of SM controversies. The GAA president responded to certain comments on Twitter as follows,

---

51   A Hern, 'Personal Data Removed From Irish Genealogy Site Over Security Fears, Irish Data Protection Commissioner Orders Closure of Civil Records Search Over Fears That It Exposes Too Much Information,' Guardian, 21 July 2014, available at www.theguardian.com/technology/2014/jul/21/ireland-shuts-government-genealogy-personal-data-concerns.

'I wouldn't call it banter, it was one-sided and it was outrageous to suggest that a draw would be rigged ... They called into question the honesty of the entire TV3 crew, the games section in Croke Park ... They called into question my honesty and the honesty of Liam Hayes and the two cameras and that is outrageous, absolutely outrageous ... It's not a random chat. If you want a random chat you pick up your mobile – those players put it on record, it was done for effect and done to suggest that in some way we would collude to be dishonest ... I can't see how they can justify their actions.'[52]

Cork selector Ronan McCarthy also criticised the online abuse of the players as 'disgusting'.[53]

The concern from the club (and organisational) perspective is that the comments, innocent or otherwise, can adversely reflect on the player and the club. Revenue, sponsorship and fan goodwill can all be jeopardised. This is also an issue for individual athletes. Australian Olympic swimmer Stephanie Rice lost a sponsorship contract after an imprudent Tweet.[54]

Another aspect of concern relates to athletes looking to be signed by professional teams. Many such individuals will naturally have their own private SM profiles. However, there are reports that certain sports clubs in the US regularly use false profiles of pretty girls to make friend requests to these unsigned athletes.[55] This is known as 'ghosting'.[56] Therefore, good prospective athletes may have lost contracts and been de-selected as a result of what clubs feel about their SM comments, friends, etc. One should be aware that, while regular or blanket monitoring of employees appears to be permissible in the US, this is not permitted under EU data protection law. It may be that blanket monitoring and false-profile friend requests in relation to athletes may also be in breach of EU data protection.

C17.23 PERSONAL RELATIONS AND RELATIONSHIPS

These issues are increasingly important and topical. Various legal, policymaker and interest groups, as well as victims, have been concerned. It is predicted that the importance will only increase, as will the need for meaningful solutions.

---

52 Referred to in 'GAA President Liam O'Neill Rejects "Fix" Allegations', Joe.ie, 4 July 2012, available at www.joe.ie/gaa/gaa-news/gaa-president-liam-oneill-rejects-fix-allegations-0026545-1.
53 J Fogarty, 'McCarthy Hits Out at "Disgusting" Online Abuse of Players,' Examiner, 22 July 2014, available at www.irishexaminer.com/sport/gaa/football/mccarthy-hits-out-at-disgusting-online-abuse-of-players-276281.html.
54 M Cowley, 'Twitter Turns into Anti-Social Networking Trap for Sport Stars,' *Sydney Morning Herald*, 9 September 2010.
55 See eg C Robinson, 'Social Networking a Potential Trap for Prospects,' *Yahoo Sports* Tuesday, 7 April 2009, available at http://sports.yahoo.com/nfl/news?slug=cr-socialnetowrking040709.
56 Ibid.

Many voice the concern that, specifically in terms of revenge porn and sexual image online abuse, the existing laws are not sufficient. Other jurisdictions are already enacting such laws. These issues are also being highlighted in the US, UK and Germany, for example.

We know at least one solicitor who was consulted in relation to such an instance, but understand no civil case has been taken. No doubt such cases can be taken.

A man was fined €2,000 for sexual innuendo-type comments made on a woman's Facebook SM profile, similar to a fraping incident.[57] The case is reported in the media as follows,

> 'Mr Justice Garrett Sheehan asked how he was supposed to assess the damage if nothing had physically been broken. Counsel for the Director of Public Prosecutions replied that the offence had more in common with harassment than criminal damage and that the harm was reputational rather than monetary.'[58]

The defendant was charged under the Criminal Damage Act 1991 which carries a maximum penalty of ten years in prison and a €10,000 fine. It is understood that this is the first prosecution for criminal damage to an SM profile account.

In another case in March 2014, a man was convicted but avoided jail for 'vile' internet sexual messages about his ex-girlfriend.[59]

There is no express revenge porn law per se, similar to the growing trend of explicit revenge porn laws elsewhere.

C17.24   SM AND PERSONAL DATA OF DECEASED PERSONS

This is a developing area.

C17.25   SM, WEBSITE, SERVICE PROVIDER OR ISP DEFENCE RULES/LAWS

The relevant laws are the Electronic Commerce Act 2000 and the European Communities (Directive 2000/31/EC) Regulations 2003 (the 'eCommerce

57   'Man fined €2000 for first Facebook "fraping" criminal case – Judge says "reprehensible offence seriously damaged woman's good name"', Independent, 20 June 2014, available at http://www.independent.ie/irish-news/courts/man-fined-2000-for-first-facebook-frapingcriminal-case-30394813.html#sthash.j5FeiImD.dpuf.
58   Ibid.
59   J Fallon, 'Man Avoids Jail for 'Vile' Internet Messages About Ex-girlfriend, Childcare Worker Says Ex-boyfriend Ruined Her Life by Posting Sexual Messages,' Irish Times, 20 March 2014, available at www.irishtimes.com/news/crime-and-law/courts/man-avoids-jail-for-vile-internet-messages-about-ex-girlfriend-1.1731368.

Regulations').[60] The eCommerce Regulations implement the remainder of the eCommerce Directive[61] not already implemented by the Electronic Commerce Act 2000.

The eCommerce defences are implemented in the eCommerce Regulations. Regulation 16 refers to mere conduit, Regulation 17 refers to caching and Regulation 18 refers to hosting.

Regulation 16 provides for mere conduit as follows,

'16(1) An intermediary service provider shall not be liable for information transmitted by him or her in a communication network if —

(a) the information has been provided to him or her by a recipient of a relevant service provided by him or her (being a service consisting of the transmission in a communication network of that information), or

(b) a relevant service provided by him or her consists of the provision of access to a communication network,

and, in either case, the following conditions are complied with —

(i) the intermediary service provider did not initiate the transmission,

(ii) the intermediary service provider did not select the receiver of the transmission, and

(iii) the intermediary service provider did not select or modify the information contained in the transmission.

(2) References in paragraph (1) to an act of transmission and of provision of access include references to the automatic, intermediate and transient storage of the information transmitted in so far as this takes place for the sole purpose of carrying out the transmission in the communications network, and provided that the information is not stored for any period longer than is reasonably necessary for the transmission.

(3) This Regulation shall not affect the power of any court to make an order against an intermediary service provider requiring the provider not to infringe, or to cease to infringe, any legal rights.'

Regulation 17 provides for caching as follows,

'17(1) An intermediary service provider shall not be liable for the automatic intermediate and temporary storage of information which

---

60 SI No 68/2003.
61 Directive 2000/31/EC on certain legal aspects of information society services, in particular electronic commerce, in the internal market.

is performed for the sole purpose of making more efficient that information's onward transmission to other users of the service upon their request, if —

   (a)   that storage is done in the context of the provision of a relevant service by the relevant service provider consisting of the transmission in a communication network of information provided by a recipient of that service, and

   (b)   the following conditions are complied with —

      (i)   the intermediary service provider does not modify the information,

      (ii)   the intermediary service provider complies with conditions relating to access to the information,

      (iii)   the intermediary service provider complies with any rules regarding the updating of the information that have been specified in a manner widely recognised and used by industry,

      (iv)   the intermediary service provider does not interfere with the lawful use of technology, widely recognised and used by industry to obtain data on the use of the information, and

      (v)   the intermediary service provider acts expeditiously to remove or disable access to the information it has stored upon obtaining actual knowledge of the fact that the information at the initial source of the transmission has been removed from the network or access to it has been disabled, or that a court or an administrative authority has ordered such removal or disablement.

   (2)   This Regulation shall not affect the power of any court to make an order against an intermediary service provider requiring the provider not to infringe, or to cease to infringe, any legal rights.'

Regulation 18 provides for hosting as follows,

   '18(1) An intermediary service provider who provides a relevant service consisting of the storage of information provided by a recipient of the service shall not be liable for the information stored at the request of that recipient if —

   (a)   the intermediary service provider does not have actual knowledge of the unlawful activity concerned and, as regards claims for damages, is not aware of facts or circumstances from which that unlawful activity is apparent, or

   (b)   the intermediary service provider, upon obtaining such knowledge or awareness, acts expeditiously to remove or to disable access to the information.

(2)   Paragraph (1) shall not apply where the recipient of the service is acting under the authority or the control of the intermediary service provider referred to in that paragraph.

(3)   This Regulation shall not affect the power of any court to make an order against an intermediary service provider requiring the provider not to infringe, or to cease to infringe, any legal rights.'

C17.26   ECOMMERCE DEFENCE CASES

The *Betfair* case involves issues pertaining to the eCommerce defences.[62] It was open to Betfair to argue and prove on the facts at trial that one of the eCommerce defences may apply in relation to a chatroom on its website.

The *McKeogh* case raises interesting eCommerce defence issues, including whether the defences apply per se and also, if they apply, whether they are lost.[63] For example, an interesting issue is presented if employees of a service provider (as opposed to users generally) may be involved in online abuse.

C17.27   LAWS PROTECTING PERSONAL DATA/ PERSONALLY IDENTIFIABLE INFORMATION

The relevant laws are the Data Protection Act 1988 and the Data Protection (Amendment) Act 2003 (as amended). The 2003 Act implements the Data Protection Directive (95/46/EC). The secondary legislation includes the the ePrivacy Regulations 2011[64] which deals with data protection for phone, email, SMS and internet usage. They implement the EU ePrivacy Directive (2002/58/ EC (as amended by Directive 2006/24/EC and 2009/136/EC)).

C17.28   DATA BREACH LAWS AND CUSTOMERS/ USERS/REGULATORS NOTIFIED OF HACKING OR DATA LOSS

The Data Protection Commissioner has approved a Personal Data Security Breach Code of Practice[65] under Section 13(2)(b) of the Data Protection Acts, 1988 and 2003. The Data Protection Acts 1988 and 2003 impose obligations

---

62   *Mulvaney & Ors v The Sporting Exchange Ltd trading as Betfair* [2009] IEHC 133 (18 March 2009), available at www.bailii.org/cgi-bin/markup.cgi?doc=/ie/cases/IEHC/2009/H133.html &query=betfair&method=boolean.
63   See *McKeogh v Doe and Others* [2012] IEHC 95 (26 January 2012).
64   European Communities (Electronic Communications Networks and Services) (Privacy and Electronic Communications) Regulations 2011 (SI No 336/2011).
65   Personal Data Security Breach Code of Practice, 29 July 2011, available at www. dataprotection.ie/docs/Data_Security_Breach_Code_of_Practice/1082.htm.

on data controllers to process personal data entrusted to them in a manner that respects the rights of data subjects to have their data processed fairly (Section 2(1)). Data controllers are under a specific obligation to take appropriate measures to protect the security of such data (Section 2(1)(d)). Where an incident gives rise to a risk of unauthorised disclosure, loss, destruction or alteration of personal data, in manual or electronic form, the data controller must give immediate consideration to informing those affected. Such information permits data subjects to consider the consequences for each of them individually and to take appropriate measures. In appropriate cases, data controllers should also notify organisations that may be in a position to assist in protecting data subjects including, where relevant, An Garda Síochána, financial institutions etc. All incidents of loss of control of personal data in manual or electronic form by a data processor must be reported to the relevant data controller as soon as the data processor becomes aware of the incident.

All incidents in which personal data has been put at risk should be reported to the Office of the Data Protection Commissioner as soon as the data controller becomes aware of the incident, except when the full extent and consequences of the incident have been reported without delay directly to the affected data subject(s) *and* it affects no more than 100 data subjects *and* it does not include sensitive personal data or personal data of a financial nature. In case of doubt – in particular, any doubt related to the adequacy of technological risk-mitigation measures – the data controller should report the incident to the Office of the Data Protection Commissioner.

Data controllers reporting to the Office of the Data Protection Commissioner in accordance with this Code should make initial contact with the Office within two working days of becoming aware of the incident, outlining the circumstances surrounding the incident.

Should the Office of the Data Protection Commissioner request a data controller to provide a detailed written report of the incident, the Office will specify a timeframe for the delivery of the report based on the nature of the incident and the information required. Such a report should reflect careful consideration of the following elements,

- the amount and nature of the personal data that has been compromised;

- the action being taken to secure and/or recover the personal data that has been compromised;

- the action being taken to inform those affected by the incident or reasons for the decision not to do so;

- the action being taken to limit damage or distress to those affected by the incident;

- a chronology of the events leading up to the loss of control of the personal data; and

- the measures being taken to prevent repetition of the incident.

This Code of Practice applies to all categories of data controllers and data processors to which the Data Protection Acts 1988 and 2003 apply.

The Code of Practice does not apply to providers of publicly available electronic communications networks or services. The ePrivacy Regulations 2011 place specific obligations on providers of publicly available electronic communications networks or services to safeguard the security of their services.

There are a growing number of data breach incidents in Ireland, as elsewhere, one of the more notable ones involving Loyalty Build.[66] There is no general breach notification law as yet.

---

66 E Keogh, 'Inquiry Launched into Data Breach at CIT,' Examiner, 8 April 2014, available at www.irishexaminer.com/ireland/inquiry-launched-into-data-breach-at-cit-264616.html. See also 'Data Breaches Up in 2013 Says Symantec,' Independent, 10 April 2014, available at www.independent.ie/business/technology/data-breaches-up-30171676.html.

Chapter C18

Italy

Giovanni Maria Riccio
(with the kind assistance of Ms Silvia Surano and Maria Laura Salvati)
Professor of Comparative Law, University of Salerno
Attorney at law, founder and partner at E-Lex – Belisario Scorza Riccio &
Partners (Rome, Italy)

C18.1   INTRODUCTION

Italy is an EU member state and is a Civil Law jurisdiction.

C18.2   SPECIFIC SM AND SN LAWS

The Italian legal framework does not currently include any specific regulation on SM and SN. Regulating the use of SM and SNs is, however, advocated by many. In particular, some politicians have often remarked on the necessity of a regulation for some specific issues, such as the use of SM by children and teenagers, the privacy issues, as well as the peculiarities of the commission of crimes through SM websites.

Moreover, many companies and public administration are increasingly drafting internal policies on the use of SM by their employees during business hours.

C18.3   SM CRIMINAL LAW CASES

Over the last few years, there have been several decisions by criminal courts (including the Court of Cassation) about criminal offences made through SM. The most common offences were defamation, copyright infringements, stalking and identity theft.

The Criminal Court of Cassation held, in decision No 32404/2010, that the repeated sending of mobile texts and SM messages is stalking, named persecutory acts by Article 612-bis of the Italian Criminal Code (this criminal offence was introduced by Law Decree No 11 of February 23, 2009).

On 2012, the Office of Preliminary Investigations of Livorno recognized that SM should be considered a means of publicity for aggravating the crime of defamation pursuant to Article 595, par 3 of the Italian Criminal Code.

Again in 2012, the Court of Teramo held an interesting decision stating that, in the case of a minor accused of a crime committed through SM, the parents, in order to avoid parental responsibility, are required to demonstrate that they have limited the minor's access to and use of the internet.

Moreover, the Criminal Court of Appeal, in judgment No 25774 of April 23, 2014, held that the conduct of a person who creates a fake Facebook profile by using the picture of another person, associated with a fancy nickname, commits the offence of replacement of a person pursuant to Article 494 of the Italian Criminal Code. The court noted that the description of an unflattering profile on SM highlights both the end of the benefit, which consists in facilitating communication and exchange of content on the network, and the purpose of damaging the third person whose picture has been unlawfully used.

C18.4   SM CIVIL LAW CASES

The cases of civil lawsuits generally concern the claim for non-pecuniary and pecuniary damages suffered by the victims of illegal acts committed by means of SM.

The first decision was held on March 3, 2010 by the Court of Monza, which granted compensatory damages amounting to €15,000 to a person defamed via Facebook by another user.

C18.5   CASES WHERE SM-RELATED EVIDENCE USED OR ADMISSIBLE

A very interesting decision concerns a case dealing with the revision of the conditions of separation between spouses.

The applicant, claiming she was fired and, therefore, no longer having the means of livelihood, had asked to be put against the former husband to pay alimony. The latter was opposed to the request because, considering the state and sentimental photos on Facebook, it was clear that the ex-wife had a stable relationship and had a standard of living higher than she used to have during the marriage.

The judgment of the Court of Santa Maria Capua Vetere, dated June 13, 2013, stated that everything published by the user on his Facebook profile can be used in court as proof and is not covered by the Data Protection Code (Legislative Decree No 196 of 2003). The decision remarks, in fact, that, even if the access to the content of a profile is governed by privacy settings chosen by the user, all the content (text, pictures, etc) published does not have a privacy expectation.

A privacy expectation, according to the court, can be granted exclusively to the messages sent via messaging and chat services.

In fact, only these latter communications can be considered as private correspondence (pursuant to Article 616 of the Italian Criminal Code), receiving the maximum protection under the terms of their disclosure. The other posts, as already known by other users, even if within the circle of so-called 'friends', cannot be similarly protected.

In other words, when a user publishes content on his profile, he implicitly accepts the risk that this content can be known by third parties, other than so-called 'friends'.

C18.6 SPECIFIC ONLINE ABUSE/ONLINE BULLYING/ CYBERBULLYING LAWS

There is no specific legislation for online abuse and cyberbullying. In 2009, however, Article 612-bis of the Criminal Code was introduced, regulating the crime of stalking. According to the second paragraph of the above mentioned article, the penalty is increased if the offence is committed through electronic tools.

In light of the increase in cases of bullying through the internet and SM, the need to introduce specific legislation has been one of the topics at the centre of the political debate.

In January 2014, Senator Elena Ferrara has filed a Bill containing provisions aiming at preventing the phenomenon of cyberbullying towards minors. Currently, the Bill is waiting for the approval of the Constitutional Affairs Committee of the Parliament.

C18.7 OTHER LAWS APPLIED TO ONLINE ABUSE/ ONLINE BULLYING/CYBERBULLYING

In the Italian system, since there is no specific legislation, Articles 594 (insult) and 595 (defamation) of the Criminal Code can be applied. The latter, as already mentioned, provides for a specific aggravating in case of use of 'form of publicity'.

The aforementioned Article 612-bis of the Criminal Code (stalking) and the provisions of the Data Protection Code can also be applied.

C18.8 CHILDREN AND SM LAWS OR RULES

There is no specific rule for the use of SM by children.

According to a strict interpretation of the Data Protection Code – in particular, Article 23 – minors under 18 may not independently give consent to the processing of their personal data and, therefore, could not sign up to and use SM without the supervision of a parent.

In many cases, the Data Protection Authority has promoted the responsible use of SM, addressing not only children but also parents and companies (see, for instance, the provision of May 23, 2014).

C18.9   EMPLOYEES/EMPLOYMENT SM LAWS OR CASES

There is no specific legislation, but both private companies and public administrations are adopting internal policies and guidelines in order to regulate the use of SM, and access to the internet in general, in the workplace. In many companies, access to certain websites, including Facebook, is blocked.

In addition, there have been numerous cases of suspension from work for employees who, during working hours, used SM for personal purposes, as well as cases of dismissal for having published offensive statements against the employer on SM.

One of the first cases dates back to 2011, when an employee of the National Social Security Fund and Service of Certified Public Accountants was dismissed, after numerous letters of warning and suspension, for using SM sites during working hours, editing and posting personal photos and making propaganda against the security fund.

C18.10   SCHOOL AND UNIVERSITY STUDENT SM CASES

There is no specific legislation. However, the Data Protection Authority has organised several courses for schools, in order to raise the awareness of teachers and young people on the use of SM.

In order to comply with this purpose, the Authority has prepared some leaflets with recommendations and guidelines in order to make clear to children, in simple terms, the risks of using the internet as well as SM.

C18.11   RIGHT OR HUMAN RIGHT TO ACCESS THE INTERNET OR SM

In 2010, a strong debate was sparked in Italy on the possibility of including the right of access to the internet among the fundamental rights of citizens. The proposal, put forward by Professor Stefano Rodotà, former Data Protection

Commissioner, was formalized with the presentation of a Bill that was intended to introduce Article 21-bis into the Italian Constitution.

Article 21-bis should have had this text: 'Everyone has the right of access to the internet network, on equal terms, in technologically appropriate ways, and to remove all obstacles to economic and social order'.

The Bill has not been approved. It should be noted, however, that another similar Bill was introduced in 2013 by the deputy Ms Veronica Tentori. The proposal has not been examined yet.

C18.12   BANS OR RESTRICTIONS ON INTERNET OR SM

According to Article 276 of the Criminal Procedure Code, any person who is under house arrest cannot 'communicate with people other than family members living together'. According to the Criminal division of the Court of Cassation, the prohibition is not only on talking to people not of the family and not living together but also on getting in touch with other people via communications methods including the internet or SM (decision No 4064 of December 6, 2011).

C18.13   IDENTITY THEFT (OR EQUIVALENT)

Article 494 of the Criminal Code punishes 'anyone who, in order to procure for himself or others an advantage or to cause damage to others, induces someone in error, unlawfully replacing himself to another person, or attributing to himself or others a false name, or a false state, which is a quality to which the law attaches legal effects'.

Recently, Decree No 933 of 2013 introduced into the Criminal Code for the first time the notion of 'digital identity'. Article 640-ter of the Criminal Code (computer fraud) was added to the aggravating circumstance in cases where the offence is committed with improper use of digital identity theft or damage to one or more subjects.

C18.14   HACKING (OR EQUIVALENT)

The Criminal Code punishes anyone who gains unauthorized access to a computer or telecommunications system protected by security measures (Article 615). The penalty is imprisonment up to three years. The offence was introduced in 1993 to protect the so-called 'informatics domicile', ie the virtual space within which the holder carries on its activities or maintains a personal relationship and with respect to which he has the right to prevent or restrict access.

The unauthorized access is realized as soon as the security measures of the system are overcome. Article 615-ter of the Criminal Code punishes the mere intrusion, even before considering the possibility of damages or theft of personal data.

A computer system is considered as any hardware or software that is able to store, generate and process data relevant to the user and whose access is protected by a device, which can also consist of a simple password.

There is no doubt, therefore, that an SM account falls within the notion of computer system to which the abovementioned rule can be applied.

C18.15 PRIVACY BY DESIGN (PBD) (OR EQUIVALENT)

There are no laws governing privacy by design. The Data Protection Authority has repeatedly remarked on the need for measures for the protection of privacy since the time of the design of computers and electronic systems or devices.

C18.16 TWEETING FROM COURTS, AND ANY RULES/LAWS

The Italian legal system does not provide for the figure of the 'jury', as understood in common law countries. Thus it has never been necessary to provide rules for the use of SM during trials.

By analogy, the use of Twitter, as well as the use of any means of communication and distribution of the news, is permitted under the law of the press and, therefore, is subject to the same limitations. Obviously, documents that are expected to be kept secret (for example, the records of the preliminary investigation before they are communicated to the subject under investigation) cannot be spread via Twitter or through SM.

C18.17 TELEVISION COURTROOM BROADCASTING OR TELEVISION CAMERAS IN COURT, AND RULES OR LAWS

The Italian legal system regulates the use of cameras in courtrooms during criminal proceedings.

Article 147 of the enacting provisions of the Code of Criminal Procedure provides that, where the trial may be a public hearing, in order to exercise the right to record, the court may authorize, if the parties permit, TV coverage or recordings, provided there is no prejudice to the peaceful and smooth conduct of the hearing or decision.

The authorization may be given without the consent of the parties when there is a social interest particularly relevant to the knowledge of the trial.

In any case, it is forbidden to film or record parties, witnesses, experts, consultants, technicians, performers, and so on, if these persons do not allow it.

The Data Protection Authority has ruled on the legality of filming people, other than the parties, who are present during the hearing (Provision July 5, 2005).

In this case, a cameraman took images of a subject who, at the time of the trial, was having a relationship with one of the defendants, and was present in the courtroom during the trial and was portrayed in vivid emotional reactions during the process.

On this occasion, the Data Protection Authority held that the dissemination of images was unlawful because the subject in question, who was clearly identifiable, was not directly related to the court case.

C18.18   SM IN COURTROOMS

The Criminal division of the Court of Cassation (judgment No 2887 filed January 24, 2014) convicted a national evening news broadcast for having aired a clip depicting child victims of sexual offences without parental consent.

In this case, the defendants were convicted pursuant to Article 734-bis of the Criminal Code, which forbids the disclosure of particulars or images of persons injured by acts of sexual violence.

C18.19   USE OF SM AS EVIDENCE IN COURTS

See C18.4.

C18.20   PRIVACY, DATA PROTECTION AND SM

One of the most important cases that took place in Italy in terms of invasion of privacy and SM is the Vividown case, which involved Google Video. The case was about a disabled boy bullied by his school-mates, who filmed these acts and published the video on Google Video.

The case has had tremendous media coverage since, in the first instance (April 12, 2010), in addition to the authors of the video, three Google executives were held liable.

The judgment of the Court of Appeal of Milan (February 27, 2013) was later overturned on appeal, and the acquittal of the managers of Google has been confirmed by the Court of Cassation (December 17, 2013, No 5107).

C18.21 SM AND FAMILY LAW CASES

See C18.4.

C18.22 SPORTS PERSONS, SPORTS CLUBS AND SM

The use of Twitter and SM in general by sport players has had a significant increase, especially in football. Many were the stories that have created controversy among sports clubs and their players.

It is worth mentioning the case of Wesley Sneijder, a former Inter player, who is prohibited from using Twitter, having been found guilty of publishing critical comments about the team.

C18.23 PERSONAL RELATIONS AND RELATIONSHIPS

Even in Italy, in recent times, there have been cases of 'revenge porn'.

In one of these cases, decided by the District Judge of Chieti, the judge convicted the defendant and ordered him to pay almost €60,000 in costs and fines in favour of the injured party. The ruling was later upheld by the Court of Appeal of Chieti.

C18.24 SM AND PERSONAL DATA OF DECEASED PERSONS

Although this is a topic that is debated in Italy, there are no cases yet.

C18.25 SM, WEBSITE, SERVICE PROVIDER OR ISP DEFENCE RULES/LAWS

The eCommerce Directive (2000/31/EC) has been implemented in Italy by Legislative Decree No 70 of 2003. Articles 12 and 13 of the Directive has been implemented verbatim by the Legislative Decree (in Articles 14 and 15).

The second paragraph of Article 16 of the Legislative Decree contains a significant difference from Article 14 of the Directive (while the first paragraph of this latter article has been implemented verbatim). The Directive holds that ISPs are not liable 'if upon obtaining such knowledge or awareness, acts expeditiously to remove or disable access to the information'. By contrast, Article 16 of the Legislative Decree states that the obligation to remove is triggered only by a 'communication of the competent authorities'. It means that ISPs cannot remove or disable access before receiving this communication.

Anyway, a notice and take-down procedure is not provided by the Legislative Decree.

C18.26 ECOMMERCE DEFENCE CASES

Probably the most important case, which involved YouTube, was decided by the Court of Rome on October 20, 2011. According to the court, in order to comply with the request of the law, a generic 'cease and desist' letter is not sufficient, and rights-owners are expected to report all of the individual URLs where the infringing content is published.

C18.27 LAWS PROTECTING PERSONAL DATA/ PERSONALLY IDENTIFIABLE INFORMATION

The relevant law is the Privacy Code (Legislative Decree No 196 of 2003), which grants the right, for any individual, to protect his personal data.

C18.28 DATA BREACH LAWS AND CUSTOMERS/ USERS/REGULATORS NOTIFIED OF HACKING OR DATA LOSS

Legislative Decree No 70 of 2003 has implemented the so-called ePrivacy Directive (Directive 2002/58/EC) and modified the Privacy Code. According to Article 32-bis of the Privacy Code, the telecom operator must communicate the infringement to the Data Protection Authority without undue delay, ie at the moment when it becomes aware of the infringement (see also the Data Protection Authority's provision on data breach of April 4, 2013).

Malta

Dr Antonio Ghio
Fenech & Fenech Advocates

C19.1   INTRODUCTION

Malta is an EU member state and is a mixed Common Law and Civil Law jurisdiction.

C19.2   SPECIFIC SM AND SN LAWS

At present, Malta does not have any specific SM and SN laws; however, the absolute majority of laws in Malta, including criminal and civil laws, are to a large extent technology neutral and therefore can encapsulate activities carried out through SM and SN.

C19.3   SM CRIMINAL LAW CASES

The number of criminal law cases regarding, directly or indirectly, SM sites is increasing. Most of these cases relate to racist or similar comments made on Facebook, as well as alleged hacking and/or unauthorised use of third party Facebook accounts.

Noteworthy criminal case law relating to SM is listed below,

In *Il-Pulizija v Karl Farrugia* (2010) decided by Mr Justice Silvio Meli, Farrugia was accused under the Press Act (Chapter 248 of the Laws of Malta) of inciting violence through his comment on the Facebook group 'No to the Pope in Malta'. The comment outlined the author's wishes that someone would shoot the Pope (Benedict XVI) in both hands, feet, and in his side in order to mimic the injuries sustained by Jesus Christ. The defendant argued through a preliminary plea that the Facebook comments could not fall under the definitions of 'printed matter' or 'broadcast' found in the Press Act. The court noted, however, that recent amendments to the law have widened the scope of these definitions, so that they could also be used in relation to comments posted on Facebook. Farrugia was given a one-month sentence suspended for a year and a fine of €500.

In *Il-Pulizija v Joseph Taliana* (2014) decided by Magistrate Dr Neville Camilleri, Taliana was accused of various computer misuse offences under the Criminal Code (Chapter 9 of the Laws of Malta), notably that he was accessing without authorisation and making use of a Facebook account belonging to third parties. The court, however, dropped the charges on the basis that the evidence provided by the Police was not the best evidence and was circumstantial, emphasising that, in criminal proceedings, the law requires the presentation of the best evidence and that such evidence should be confirmed under oath by the person providing such evidence. In this case, information provided to the Police by Facebook as well as local ISPs was held to be inadmissible as it was not confirmed by oath by representatives of Facebook and the local ISPs respectively.

C19.4   SM CIVIL LAW CASES

The majority of civil law cases relating to SM revolve around defamatory libel arising from posts or comments and/or Tweets made through Facebook or Twitter. Case law relating to defamatory libel in SM is increasing. However, a number of proceedings are still ongoing.

In *Richard Cachia Caruana v Joe Grima* (2014) decided by Magistrate Dr Francesco Depasquale, Grima was sued for defamatory libel and was ordered to pay €5,000 in libel damages under Article 28 of the Press Act, following certain statements regarding Cachia Caruana that he posted on his Facebook profile. In the separate posts, Grima stated that the plaintiff, who in the past held senior governmental positions, was selling his villa for €5 million, and that the villa also came with a pool, which was created with exclusive grants. Grima also commented on the large salary of the plaintiff, arguing that the income he made was a result of the corrupt politics of prior governments.

Between 5 and 6 August 2014, Daphne Caruana Galizia, a prominent journalist and blogger, together with Andrew Borg Cardona and Peter Caruana Galizia, instituted a number of defamatory libel proceedings against Tony Abela and Aaron Farrugia, claiming that various posts and Tweets written by the defendants were defamatory. These cases are still ongoing, but tend to indicate that defamatory libel proceedings can be instituted not only in relation to Facebook, but also Twitter.

C19.5   CASES WHERE SM-RELATED EVIDENCE USED OR ADMISSIBLE

In *Il-Pulizija v Naomi Pace* (2014) decided by Magistrate Dr Marseann Farrugia, Pace was accused of causing grievous bodily harm to the victim Sonia Sammut, and that the offender subsequently boasted about her criminal actions on Facebook. These posts were used as evidence against Pace, leading to her being found guilty and sentenced to a two-year jail term suspended for four years.

In *Il-Pulizija v Leslie Pace, Dave Delia, Axel Zammit and Paul Muscat* (2014) decided by Magistrate Dr Carol Peralta, the four young men caused grievous bodily harm to the victim Ryan Vella, after Zammit stated that the latter had spoken against him with a foreign girl on Facebook. The relevant Facebook posts were presented as evidence during the proceedings. The defendants were conditionally discharged and placed on probation for three years.

C19.6 SPECIFIC ONLINE ABUSE/ONLINE BULLYING/ CYBERBULLYING LAWS

Malta does not presently have any such laws.

C19.7 OTHER LAWS APPLIED TO ONLINE ABUSE/ ONLINE BULLYING/CYBERBULLYING

Criminal proceedings in relation to online abuse and online bullying are instituted under the provisions relating to harassment found in Article 251A of the Criminal Code (Chapter 9 of the Laws of Malta). Harassment is very widely defined in our law. The Criminal Code stipulates that a person who pursues a course of conduct which amounts to harassment of another person, and which he knows or ought to know that such course of conduct amounts to harassment, shall be guilty of an offence. Maltese law makes use of the 'reasonableness' test whereby such offence would only subsist if a reasonable person in possession of the same information would think that such course of conduct would amount to harassment. It is also interesting to note that Article 251C of the Criminal Code states that reference to 'harassing a person' also includes alarming the person or causing the person distress. The Criminal Code, however, remains silent on the nature of any tools used in connection with the harassment, and one is led to assume that the intention of the legislator was to criminalize the action, irrespective of whether any technology such as computers or mobile phones was used to carry out such action. Offences under Article 251A carry a maximum imprisonment term of up to three months and a fine of up to €5,000.

Furthermore in these cases, the Police regularly make use of and refer to a generic criminal law provision found in Article 49 of the Electronic Communications (Regulation) Act (Chapter 399 of the Laws of Malta) which provides that whoever makes 'improper' use of an electronic communications network or apparatus may be found guilty and fined up to €24,000.

C19.8 CHILDREN AND SM LAWS OR RULES

No such laws or rules presently exist.

C19.9 EMPLOYEES/EMPLOYMENT SM LAWS OR CASES

No such laws or cases presently exist.

C19.10 SCHOOL AND UNIVERSITY STUDENT SM CASES

See C19.5.

In December 2006, the Police commenced investigations into four videos uploaded on YouTube showing cases of 'happy slapping', where the victims were repeatedly hounded, kicked and punched and verbally abused at the Malta College of Arts, Science and Technology (MCAST).

C19.11 RIGHT OR HUMAN RIGHT TO ACCESS THE INTERNET OR SM

The Government of Malta, led by the Nationalist Party, in late 2012 published a White Paper (available at www.gov.mt/en/Government/Press%20Releases/Documents/pr2223a.pdf) for general consultation proposing the introduction of four distinct 'digital rights' within the Constitution of Malta. These proposed digital rights, intended as mere declaratory principles and so non-enforceable in a court of law, were,

1.   the right to internet access;

2.   the right to informational access;

3.   the right to informational freedom; and

4.   the right to digital self-determination.

The White Paper clearly identified that any right to internet access (both access to the infrastructure as well as any information found online) could never be deemed to be a human right but merely a tool for the enjoyment of existing human rights, including the right to freedom of opinion and expression.

In 2014, the Nationalist Party, now in opposition, presented a Bill in Parliament to entrench these 'digital rights' in the Constitution but this time as enforceable rights, unlike the proposals contained in the White Paper. It is expected that this Bill will start to be discussed in Parliament in Q4 2014.

C19.12 BANS OR RESTRICTIONS ON INTERNET OR SM

No specific laws or rules exist in relation to restrictions on the use of the internet or SM. However, certain Magistrates, when issuing protection orders under Article 412C of the Criminal Code, and by which they restrict an accused person from making contact with the injured party or other individuals, have sometimes included specific references to SM, thereby prohibiting the accused from making any contact with such third parties using SM.

In relation to prohibiting internet access, the latest Bill to amend the Constitution and introduce 'digital rights' presented in front of the Maltese Parliament (see C19.11) specifically lists, as one of the major guiding principles behind the Bill, that any restriction on access to and use of the internet, including SM, should be as little as possible and that any such restrictions should be transparent, legitimate, necessary and proportional in a democratic society.

C19.13   IDENTITY THEFT (OR EQUIVALENT)

No specific laws or rules relating to identity theft currently exist in Malta, and traditionally the courts look at identity theft merely as a preparatory act for the commission of other offences such as fraud. However, the general provisions found in the Data Protection Act (Chapter 440 of the Laws of Malta) could be indirectly applicable in situations of identity theft.

C19.14   HACKING (OR EQUIVALENT)

The Criminal Code contains a specific sub-title relating to computer misuse, which is mostly modelled on the Council of Europe Convention on Cybercrime. Whilst no direct reference is made to hacking, such activity would still fall foul of Articles 337C and 337D of the Criminal Code which relate to the unlawful or unauthorised access and use of any data software or other information, as well as computer equipment.

C19.15   PRIVACY BY DESIGN (PBD) (OR EQUIVALENT)

At present, no rules, laws or local discussion have been initiated in relation to privacy by design issues, with the exception of limited discussions regarding the impact that the new EU General Data Protection Regulation would have on the local data protection legal landscape.

C19.16   TWEETING FROM COURTS, AND ANY RULES/ LAWS

While there exists no specific legislative provision prohibiting Tweeting from the courts, the presiding judge or Magistrate has the legal authority to prohibit any activity which affects 'good order' during court proceedings. To our knowledge, no such order has ever been given by the courts specifically limiting Tweeting. In fact, it is quite common in a number of high-profile cases such as murder trials (unless the presiding judge or Magistrate would have issued a gagging order relating to the proceedings) for journalists to update the general public of the ongoing proceedings through Tweets as well as real-time posts on their websites.

C19.17 TELEVISION COURTROOM BROADCASTING OR TELEVISION CAMERAS IN COURT, AND RULES OR LAWS

Article 26(1)(g) in Subsidiary Legislation 12.09 issued under the Code of Organization and Civil Procedure (Chapter 12 of the Laws of Malta) provides that, during the hearing of any case, no person is allowed to take or attempt to take any photograph or film, by any means whatsoever, except when the taking of such photograph or film has been ordered or authorised by a court or tribunal in connection with any proceedings before it. Typically, cameras are allowed in courtrooms for the official opening of the legal year, as well as during the official speech made during the inaugural sitting of a new judge or magistrate, or during the last sitting of a retiring judge or magistrate.

C19.18 SM IN COURTROOMS

No details.

C19.19 USE OF SM AS EVIDENCE IN COURTS

See the *Taliana* case (cited in C19.3).

C19.20 PRIVACY, DATA PROTECTION AND SM

During the past months, various publicised controversies have arisen in light of the growing number of registered Maltese users on the SN site, Ask.fm. These controversies were further fuelled following the death of Lisa Marie Zahra, a 15-year-old girl who was found dead at the bottom of Dingli Cliffs in April 2014, and who was a victim of cyberbullying on the very same site; Erin Tanti has been charged with her murder and is currently undergoing criminal proceedings.

C19.21 SM AND FAMILY LAW CASES

The use of SM evidence, as well as matters related to the unauthorised use of Facebook accounts, has featured in a number of separation and custody cases. However, such cases are not traditionally reported and are not easily accessible.

C19.22   SPORTS PERSONS, SPORTS CLUBS AND SM

A recent controversy (2014) arose in relation to the publication of a photo of TVM Sports Presenter Sandro Micallef on Facebook under a page entitled 'Zbalji tal-Kummentaturi Maltin' (Errors by Maltese Commentators), which poked fun at his choice of words during the commentary of a 2014 World Cup match. The photo was accompanied by the phrase used by Mr Micallef himself: 'Jaqbez wiehed, jaqbez tnejn, qisu sikkina tahraq diehla fil-butir' (He goes past one, two players like a hot knife through butter). In return, however, Mr Micallef threatened the administrators of that specific Facebook page with legal action if the photo was not taken down, and that he would be holding them responsible for any moral and financial damages he could suffer in his employment in the near future.

In 2013, the Malta Football Association (MFA) carried out investigation into several allegations regarding Maltese referee Marco Borg's personal 'likes' on Facebook. The case arose when screenshots were taken showing that Borg had 'liked' a page/post on Facebook in reference to football games and football teams related to the BOV Premier League. The MFA dropped the investigation when it concluded through a technical report that the screenshots had been fabricated.

C19.23   PERSONAL RELATIONS AND RELATIONSHIPS

In January 2014, there was a highly publicised controversy in relation to the leaking of private indecent images of various Maltese women and young girls on a page entitled 'Maltese girls caught on camera' on the SN site, Tumblr.com.

Between December 2013 and January 2014, another highly publicised incident relating to the leaking of a private video of a young Maltese actress engaging in oral sex was reported. The alleged perpetrator was the ex-boyfriend of the victim who published the private video on Facebook.

In the criminal appeal case, *Il-Pulizija v Cyrus Engerer*, decided by Mr Justice Michael Mallia in April 2014, Engerer was found guilty of revenge porn after he had taken compromising images from his former partner's computer and set up an email address to distribute such images amongst the work colleagues of his former partner. Mr Engerer was sentenced with a two-year jail term suspended for two years.

In early 2014, a French photographer, domiciled in Malta, was sentenced to a two-year jail term suspended for four years after being found guilty of leaking photos and a video of himself performing oral sex on a young Maltese male model and distributing them on Facebook and other SM sites.

C19.24   SM AND PERSONAL DATA OF DECEASED PERSONS

In November 2013, a public controversy arose following the death of teenage boy Igor Scicluna, especially when hateful comments were posted on the SN site, Ask.fm, instigating the idea that the death was a result of personal drug use.

See also the Lisa Marie Zahra case (referred to in C19.20).

C19.25   SM, WEBSITE, SERVICE PROVIDER OR ISP DEFENCE RULES/LAWS

The Electronic Commerce Act (Chapter 426 of the Laws of Malta) transposes, inter alia, Directive 2000/31/EC on Electronic Commerce, including the mere conduit provisions found therein. Articles 19, 20 and 21 of the Act also provide defences to information society service providers in relation to caching, hosting and transmission of information.

C19.26   ECOMMERCE DEFENCE CASES

There are presently no cases in Malta where such defences or pleas have been raised.

C19.27   LAWS PROTECTING PERSONAL DATA/ PERSONALLY IDENTIFIABLE INFORMATION

The Data Protection Act (DPA) (Chapter 440 of the Laws of Malta) transposes Directive 95/46/EC. Several pieces of subsidiary legislation have also been promulgated under the Data Protection Act, mostly relating to (i) the processing of personal data in the electronic communications sector; (ii) the processing of personal data by the Police; and (iii) the processing of personal data relating to minors. The Information and Data Protection Commissioner is presently drafting new subsidiary legislation relating to the processing of personal data in the education sector.

Following the declaration of invalidity of the EU Data Retention Directive by the Court of Justice of the European Union in April 2014, the Maltese Government is presently considering the amendment and/or revocation of certain provisions found in the Processing of Personal Data (Electronic Communications Sector) Regulations (SL 440.01), and which transpose the EU Data Retention Directive into Maltese law.

C19.28   DATA BREACH LAWS AND CUSTOMERS/ USERS/REGULATORS NOTIFIED OF HACKING OR DATA LOSS

Various reporting obligations arise through different legislative instruments in relation to data breaches. Whilst the Data Protection Act does not include any regulatory reporting obligation in relation to data breaches, the Processing of Personal Data (Electronic Communications Sector) Regulations (SL 440.01), which, amongst others, implements Commission Regulation (EU) 611/2013 on the measures applicable to the notification of personal data breaches under Directive 2002/58/EC, introduces a number of data breach reporting obligations on the providers of publicly available electronic communications services. In cases of personal data breaches, such service providers must, without delay, notify the personal data breach to the Information and Data Protection Commissioner. Subject to certain limitations, when the personal data breach is likely to adversely affect the personal data or privacy of a subscriber or individual, the provider must also notify the subscriber or individual of the breach without undue delay. SL 440.01 defines 'personal data breach' as a breach of security leading to the accidental or unlawful destruction, loss, alteration, unauthorised disclosure of, or access to, personal data transmitted, stored or otherwise processed in connection with the provision of a publicly available electronic communications service.

Providers of remote gambling services under the Maltese Remote Gaming Regulations (SL 438.04) also have an obligation to report any security-related incidents, including data breaches, by means of an Incident Report to the Maltese Lotteries and Gaming Authority.

Chapter C20

Mexico

Jose Luis Ramos-Zurita, Javier Uhthoff-Rojo, Saul Santoyo, Ignacio Dominguez-Torrado
Uhthoff Gomez Vega & Uhthoff, SC

C20.1   INTRODUCTION

Mexico is a Civil Law jurisdiction.

C20.2   SPECIFIC SM AND SN LAWS

Within the Mexican legal system, there are no specific SM and SN laws, ie there are no Acts or Codes that are directed to specifically regulate the structure, conduct and/or activities performed by individuals or entities within an SM or SN electronic environment.

Having said this, there are several different legal instruments, both at Federal and State level, that are applicable to SM concerning the conduct of individuals or entities participating in them, the services provided on them, the privacy and security of the information posted, such as the Federal Criminal Code, the Federal Law for the Protection of Data in Possession of Private Parties, the Federal Telecommunications Law, the Advance Electronic Signature for Tax Purposes Law, and several State Acts such as the Federal District (Mexico City) Law for the Promotion of a Free-of-Violence Living Within the School Environment; and several others State laws are applicable to SM and SN.

Furthermore, within the Mexican legal system there is no formal 'case law', as we are a country under a Roman Tradition Legal System, so the primary and most important source of the law is what is formally enacted by Congress, with some minor participation concerning Administrative Regulations issued by the Executive Branch through the different government agencies.

However, there is a specific system concerning the different criteria adopted by the courts and judges, which are the same criteria that are collectively called '*jurisprudencias*' which, according to the Organic Law of the Federal Judicial Power (LOPJF), can only be created by the higher Federal courts (either the Supreme Court of the Nation and/or the Federal Circuit Courts)

431

when the criteria adopted originates in the resolution of at least five different cases involving similar rights or matters, and such criteria can be invoked in subsequent matters that fall into the scope of that particular criteria, as lesser courts are obliged to follow '*jurisprudencia*'; nevertheless, this does not replace the formal enacted laws, nor there is so much emphasis on case law, in contrast to Common Law systems, nor there is a systematization of the relevant case information, such as the one made by the American Bar Association in the US.

C20.3   SM CRIMINAL LAW CASES

To the best of our knowledge, there have been very few criminal cases involving the use of SM and fewer that have gained enough notoriety (see C20.2) in order to be documented and made available to the general public.

Considering this, what may be the most notorious case happened in August 2011 and involved two school teachers, Gilberto Martínez Vera and María de la Luz Bravo Pagola, who used Twitter and Facebook to allegedly 'broadcast' and spread false rumours about alleged attacks involving gunmen of the organized crime syndicates that operate in the State of Veracruz against the civilian population, conduct that provoked a serious response from the State Government and resulted in the indictment of both Martinez Vera and Bravo Pagola under charges of terrorism and sabotage, and also resulted in the enactment of an amendment (in November 2012) to the Criminal Code of the State of Veracruz: the creation of Article 373 of that Code, which establishes 'breach and disturbance of the public peace' as a felony.

On 25 August 2011, Martinez Vera posted several messages on Twitter to report an alleged kidnapping of five school children, which led to a shooting and a 'grenade attack' on the 'Alfonso Reyes Elementary School' located in downtown Veracruz, while on the same date Bravo Pagola used her Facebook account (which had over 4,500 friends at that moment) to report an alleged shooting 'on a school located in Buenavista, behind one of Pemex's main facilities – called 'Activo Integral Veracruz' – at Boca del Rio, Veracruz, and afterwards that same day she continued to 'confirm' other similar violent acts on the wall of her Facebook account, despite multiple messages of the State Governor and government officials discrediting her postings.

See   www.samachar.com/Mexico-Two-accused-of-terrorism-via-Twitter-Facebook-ljhkJLfcgec.html.

C20.4   SM CIVIL LAW CASES

There have been very few civil cases involving the use of SM and fewer that have gained enough notoriety (see C20.2) in order to be documented and made available to the general public.

However, on 21 June 2012, Javier Lozano, a senator of the National Action Party (PAN), filed a defamation and moral damage civil claim against Manuel Bartlett, who was at the time a Senator for the opposing Labour Party (PT), because Bartlett had used his Twitter account in past weeks to post several affirmations accusing Lozano of illicit enrichment, trafficking with privileged information and using his position to cover up the 'murderous' activities of then president Felipe Calderon. As a result of the claim, on 1 October 2013, the 10th Civil Judge of Puebla, State of Puebla ruled that Bartlett did commit an illicit action by sustaining his private opinions as if they were true and proven facts, which was augmented by the use of public means of communication (including his Twitter account), thus provoking moral damage against Lozano, and ordered the mandatory repair of such damage by paying Lozano $67,300 MXP (approximately US$5,125) and the publication of the ruling in the largest circulation newspaper ('el Sol de Puebla') in Puebla.

At the moment, Bartlett has appealed such decision before the State of Puebla Superior Tribunal and is pending resolution. See http://articulos2011.blogspot. mx/2013/10/sentencia-contra-manuel-bartlett-por.html.

C20.5   CASES WHERE SM-RELATED EVIDENCE USED OR ADMISSIBLE

Besides several highly publicized cases of child pornography, in which different electronic media over the internet (although not specifically involving Facebook, Twitter or other similar SM) have been used as evidence, according to press reports a judge in the State of Tabasco accepted as valid evidence several Facebook, Twitter and Whatsapp messages in order to sustain divorce claims, provided such information has been 'either legally obtained and/or made public by the owner of the SN account'. This condition follows what the Mexican Supreme Court established on June 2011 concerning the extent of private communications (specifically concerning electronic mail), thus the acceptance of SM-generated evidence would depend on whether it can be considered as being 'public' content, as opposed to the reserved nature of emails and/or restricted-access information that can be part of SM. See http://miabogadoenlinea.net/el-derecho-y-mexico/4428-correo-electronico-y-adulterio.

C20.6   SPECIFIC ONLINE ABUSE/ONLINE BULLYING/ CYBERBULLYING LAWS

While there are no such Federal laws, Article 33 section V of the 'Federal District (Mexico City) Law for the Promotion of a Free-of-Violence Living Within the School Environment' establishes what can be considered as cyberbullying and foresees guidelines to combat this phenomenon.

It states the following,

> '33. For the purposes of this Law, the different kind of abuse among students are:
>
> ...
>
> V. performed through information technologies and communications: all psico-emotive violence implemented through the use of technology of virtual [websites] and tools, such as chats, blogs, SNs, email, and text messages sent by mobile devices, forums, video servers that store or photographs, websites, telephones and other technological means, including "spoofing" (identity falsely impersonating someone else) by using such communications means.
>
> This kind of violence is usually anonymous and massive as usually most members of the educational community learn of the use of such violence and; ...'

C20.7 OTHER LAWS APPLIED TO ONLINE ABUSE/ ONLINE BULLYING/CYBERBULLYING

While there are no other State laws that specifically deal with this issue, in June 2013 the Congress of the State of Nuevo Leon passed a Bill that amended Articles 344 and 345 of the Criminal Code of the State of Nuevo Leon, establishing what should be considered as 'defamation' in the following terms: 'to wilfully communicate to one or more persons, any true or false information and/or about a determined or undetermined facts, about another person, which may result in disgrace, disrepute, tort, or contempt for that person'. It also established penalties of up to five years' imprisonment for any person who commits this felony, including when such conduct is performed using telecommunications and/or 'technologically advanced' means such as SM.

As a result of the strong protests of several influential sectors of the population (including journalists and media artists), the Bill that contained the amendments to the above-mentioned dispositions of the Criminal Code of the State of Nuevo Leon were vetoed by the Governor, and the Local Congress is yet to review the Bill in compliance with such veto.

C20.8 CHILDREN AND SM LAWS OR RULES

While there are no Laws or Regulations specific to children and the use of SM, Mexico was a participant in and signed the 'Memorandum on the protection of personal data and privacy in Internet SNs, specifically in regard to children and adolescents' ('Montevideo Memorandum'), which in 2009 established several guidelines concerning these subjects in a conference sponsored by the ITU. See www.iijusticia.org/docs/MemoMVD_En.pdf.

Consequently, it is supposed that all future legislation and general policies issued by the Mexican Federal Government concerning SM and telecommunications should include the guidelines and recommendations contained in such document, but so far the only formal Bill that has actually been passed to be published as a Law is the 'Federal District (Mexico City) Law for the Promotion of a Free-of-Violence Living Within the School Environment' (see C20.6).

C20.9 EMPLOYEES/EMPLOYMENT SM LAWS OR CASES

The Federal Labour Law governs employee-employer relations, and it does not contain specific rules concerning the use of SM in the workspace; however, it does allow the employer to establish regulations and limitations concerning work tools and use of the employer's property, which may be used to limit the access of employees to SM and/or establish guidelines for the conduct of employees in connection with SM.

C20.10 SCHOOL AND UNIVERSITY STUDENT SM CASES

There are no specific laws or regulations addressing SM in schools or universities, but there are press reports that involve students and SM,

'On July 2, 2013, the bodies of Luis Antonio Ortiz Guerra and Andrés Barba Oliva were found in "La Cebada" Ranch, outside the city of Guadalajara, State of Jalisco, after being reported as missing since June 21, 2013, on what appears to be a vengeance murder case provoked by the bullying that the two assassinated teenagers performed against the teenager son of Jose Angel Charrasco Coronel, a prominent member of the Sinaloa Cartel (who has been in prison since his arrest on January 2013); while the investigations of this case are still ongoing, it appears that the two murdered teenagers were contacted via SNs by members of the Cartel, who lured them into a meeting held at a "The Citadel" shopping mall and then were kidnapped and assassinated.'

See www.reporteindigo.com/reporte/guadalajara/asesinados-por-hacer-bullying.

C20.11 RIGHT OR HUMAN RIGHT TO ACCESS THE INTERNET OR SM

Article 6 of the Mexican Constitution was amended, on 11 June 2013, to establish that access to the internet is a human right guaranteed by the State,

'Article 6

Expression of ideas shall not be submitted to judicial or administrative inquiry, except for the cases when such expression of ideas goes against the moral or third party's rights, or causes perpetration of a felony, or disturb law and order. The right of reply shall be exercised according to law. The State shall guarantee the right to information.

Every person has the right to free access [to] timely information, and to seek, receive and impart information and ideas of all kinds by any means of expression.

The State shall guarantee the right of access to information technologies and communications, as well as broadcasting and telecommunications, including the broadband and internet. To this end, the State shall establish conditions for effective competition in the provision of such services ...'

C20.12 BANS OR RESTRICTIONS ON INTERNET OR SM

While there are recently enacted laws and regulations that establish penalties for hacking and child pornography, there are no recent cases involving these subjects; one of the most notable criminal matters concerning child abuse and pornography were known to the public in 2003 through press reports that involved Jean Succar Kuri, who was convicted of being a child molester and operating a child pornography network that used the internet and other means to distribute its illegal contents. See www.eluniversal.com.mx/notas/340926.html and www.jornada.unam.mx/2007/09/23/index.php?section=politica&article=012n1pol.

As a result of this highly publicized case, the Mexican Government created the Federal Cyber Police, a branch of the Federal Police that is tasked to combat cybercrimes such as fraud and child pornography; shortly after its creation, many States also created local cyber police task forces that deal with the same sort of crimes at a local level.

Considering this, there are a few press reports that mention scattered child pornography cases in which the Police (federal or local) intervened: see www.ssp.gob.mx/portalWebApp/wlp.c?__c=1d4c5, http://jcarreto.blogspot.mx/2013/11/pornografia-infantil-en-la-web-y-redes.html, www.vanguardia.com.mx/pornografiainfantilymasdelitosconstruidosenredessociales-1159764.html, and www.eluniversal.com.mx/nacion-mexico/2014/policia-federal-detiene-a-pornografos-infantiles--988125.html.

C20.13 IDENTITY THEFT (OR EQUIVALENT)

A few States have amended their Criminal Codes in order to expressly foresee this illicit conduct, as follows,

'Federal District (Mexico City) Criminal Code (Chapter III – Identity Theft)

Article 211 Bis. Anyone who by any means assumes, for illicit purposes, the identity of another person, or gives his or her consent to carry out the usurpation of their identity, shall be punished by penalty of one to five years in prison and a fine of four hundred to six hundred days.

State of Mexico Criminal Code (Chapter V – Identity Theft)

Article 264. A penalty of one to four years in prison and a fine of one hundred to five hundred days shall be imposed to anyone who, with unlawful intent, exercises a right or uses any data, information or documents that rightfully belongs to another and by means of such individualizes that person before society and allowing a natural or legal person to be identified or identifiable between collective, to impersonate him or her.

It equates to such identity theft and the same penalties will be imposed in the preceding paragraph under this Article to anyone who:

I.- Commits a wrongful act provided for in the laws by reason of the identity theft;

II.- Use personal data without the consent of whom must grant;

III.- Giving consent to carry out identity theft; and

IV.- Availing themselves of homonymy to commit any crime.

The penalties provided for in this Article shall be imposed regardless of the corresponding one for committing other crimes.

State of Colima's Criminal Code (Chapter III – Fraud)

Article 233. It is equivalent to fraud, and will be punished by the penalties provided in the preceding article those who:

...

VII. By the use of the computer, telematics or electronic media, obtain an undue profit for himself, or using some other computer manipulation, code instructions, prediction, data interception, data modification, use the information networks and/or mounting "mirrors" and/or "trap sites" aimed to capture crucial information for unauthorized use of such data, impersonate identities and/or modify the data gathered by automated programs, pictures, operating systems vulnerability or any principal, secondary and tertiary operating system file that affects reliability and variation of web browsing or use such a device to obtain undue profit ...'

C20.14 HACKING (OR EQUIVALENT)

The provisions mentioned in C20.13 in some cases also cover hacking. Articles 211 Bis 1 to 211 Bis 7 of the Federal Criminal Code refer to specific provisions concerning 'hacking', such as the following,

'Article 211 Bis 1.- Whoever without authorization modified, destroyed or cause loss of information contained in systems or equipment protected by a security mechanism computer, ... six months to two years in prison and a fine of one hundred to three hundred days.

When you access or make an unauthorized copy information in computer systems or equipment protected by a security mechanism ... three months to one year in prison and fifty to one hundred and fifty days' fine.

Article 211 Bis 2.- Whoever without authorization modified, destroyed or cause loss of information contained in electronic or computer equipment state, protected by some mechanism security will be imposed from one to four years in prison and a fine of two hundred to six hundred days.

When you know or unauthorized copy information in computer systems or equipment property of the state that is protected by a security mechanism, will be imposed from six months to two years of imprisonment and a fine of one hundred to three hundred days.

Who knows without authorization, obtain, copy or use information in any system, computer or computer storage medium of public safety, protected by some means of security, will face a penalty of four to ten years in prison and a fine of five hundred to one thousand days general minimum wage in the Federal District. If the offender is or has been a public servant in a law enforcement institution, the penalties include dismissal and disqualification from four to ten years to work in another occupation, office, position or public commission.

Article 211 Bis 3.- When it is authorized to access computer systems and equipment of State improperly modify, destroy or cause loss of information it contains, is impose two to eight years in prison and a fine of three hundred to nine days.

Who being authorized to access systems, equipment or computer storage media in public safety take unfair copy or use information contained therein, will face a penalty of four to ten years in prison and a fine of five hundred to one thousand days general minimum wage in the Federal District. If the offender is or has been a public servant in a law enforcement institution, shall also be imposed, up more than half the sentence, dismissal and disqualification for a period equal to the resulting penalty to work in another occupation, office, position or public commission.

Article 211 Bis 4.- Whoever without authorization modified, destroyed or cause loss of information in computer systems or equipment of the institutions of the financial system, protected by a security mechanism, will be imposed six months to four years imprisonment and a fine of one hundred to six hundred days.

When you know or unauthorized copy information in computer systems or equipment of the institutions of the financial system, protected by a security mechanism, it shall be subject to three months to two years in prison and a fine of fifty to three hundred days.

Article 211 Bis 5.- Whoever is authorized to access computer systems and equipment of the institutions of the financial system, unduly modify, destroy or cause loss of information they contain will be imposed from six months to four years in prison and a fine of one hundred to six hundred days.

To him who is authorized to access computer systems and equipment of the institutions of the financial system, unduly copy information they contain will be imposed from three months to two years in prison and a fine of fifty to three hundred days.

The penalties provided for in this Article shall be increased by one half when behaviors are committed by officials or employees of the institutions of the financial system.

Article 211 Bis 6.- For the purposes of Articles 211 Bis Bis 211 4 and 5 above, the term institutions in the financial system, those identified in Article 400 Bis of this Code.

Article 211 Bis 7.- The penalties provided in this chapter shall be increased by one-third when the information obtained is used to benefit themselves or others.'

C20.15 PRIVACY BY DESIGN (PBD) (OR EQUIVALENT)

Although there are no specific rules or laws including this concept, the Federal Law for the Protection of Data in Possession of Private Parties includes some provisions that loosely incorporate a similar concept; however, from a strict legal point of view, there is no obligation or requirement for information systems to be engineered or designed from the outset with this concept in mind.

C20.16 TWEETING FROM COURTS, AND ANY RULES/ LAWS

Although there are several provisions that not only allow, but also require, that most if not all judicial procedures should be deemed public, with the possible exceptions being when the matter of the process may result in irreparable damage to one of the involved parties (concerning confidential information) and/or cases that disturb the public order (essentially criminal matters) and/or can affect the image or well-being of a minor (civil/family matters), the courts and trial system in Mexico is fundamentally different from that in the US and other common law systems. There have been several modifications to State and Federal Procedure Law, but nowadays the vast majority of trials are still in a written form rather than oral procedures, so it would be quite difficult, if not outright impossible, to actually 'Tweet' something during the course of a trial, as the trial itself is only reflected in the ruling or sentence that is handed down, in written form, when it is finished.

With the above in mind, there is no prohibition on using SM and/or any other form of public dissemination of the rulings issued by courts, with the exceptions noted above.

C20.17 TELEVISION COURTROOM BROADCASTING OR TELEVISION CAMERAS IN COURT, AND RULES OR LAWS

The Mexican Supreme Court (SCJN) owns and operates 'El Canal Judicial' (or 'The Judicial Channel') in which, several times a week, live sessions from the court are directly broadcast over cable networks and the internet. See www. sitios.scjn.gob.mx/canaljudicial/.

C20.18 SM IN COURTROOMS

We are not aware of any reports that specifically involve the use of SM in courtrooms.

C20.19 USE OF SM AS EVIDENCE IN COURTS

Besides several highly publicized cases of child pornography, in which different electronic media over the internet (although not specifically involving Facebook, Twitter or other similar SM) have been used as evidence, according to press reports a judge in the State of Tabasco accepted as valid evidence several Facebook, Twitter and Whatsapp messages in order to sustain divorce claims, provided such information has been 'either legally obtained and/or made public by the owner of the SN account'. This condition follows what the Mexican Supreme Court established on June 2011 concerning the extent of private communications (specifically concerning electronic mail), thus the acceptance of SM-generated evidence would depend on whether it can be considered as being 'public' content, as opposed to the reserved nature of emails and/or restricted-access information that can be part of SM. See http://miabogadoenlinea.net/el-derecho-y-mexico/4428-correo-electronico-y-adulterio.

C20.20 PRIVACY, DATA PROTECTION AND SM

The Federal Law for the Protection of Data in Possession of Private Parties grants legal powers to the Federal Institute for Information Access and Data Protection (IFAI) to impose sanctions and oblige private parties concerning privacy and data protection issues (similar to the laws applied to the case of *Max Schrems v Facebook* in the EU), but there are no recorded cases involving controversies on this subject in Mexico.

C20.21 SM AND FAMILY LAW CASES

There are no recorded cases involving controversies on this subject in Mexico, mainly due to the fact that procedural law allows an exception from the public nature of judicial procedures, so they are to be kept restricted to protect the right and interests of the parties involved due to the sensitive nature of matters involved in such procedures.

C20.22 SPORTS PERSONS, SPORTS CLUBS AND SM

In September 2012, the Mexican Soccer Team of Pachuca imposed a fine and a suspension on its then star attacker Nery Castillo, due to the inappropriate comments made via his Twitter account concerning the owner of Guadalajara Soccer Team, Jorge Vergara.

Further to the media coverage, this was possible from a legal point of view because it is common practice for professional soccer teams to include several provisions that regulate the conduct of its players in the contracts and agreements of such teams.

See http://deportes.terra.com.mx/sanciona-pachuca-a-nerycastillo,ae8de34cd 691a310VgnVCM3000009acceb0aRCRD.html and www.futbolsapiens.com/ actualidad/nacional/pachuca-sanciona-a-nery-castillo-por-burlarse-de-vergara/.

C20.23 PERSONAL RELATIONS AND RELATIONSHIPS

Press reports document several cases where 'public persons' (mainly media personalities such as actresses or singers) have been involved in the unwanted disclosure of private information (nude or pornographic photographs or videos) using the internet, although not specifically SM.

Notable cases involved the late Tex-Mex singer Jenny Rivera, Noelia, Michelle Vieth and others. See www.elgrafico.mx/farandula/14-07-2013/videos-eroticos-de-las-famosas.

Notwithstanding the above, there have not been any reports concerning formal legal actions in connection with such media 'scandals'.

C20.24 SM AND PERSONAL DATA OF DECEASED PERSONS

We are not aware of any reports that involve the use of SM personal data of deceased persons and any controversy and/or notable case involving similar issues.

C20.25   SM, WEBSITE, SERVICE PROVIDER OR ISP DEFENCE RULES/LAWS

Although not directed specifically at SM, websites and ISPs, there are several laws, such as the Federal Law for Consumer Protection, the Federal Telecommunications Law and the Federal Commerce Code that apply when dealing with services and transactions carried out in the digital domain (cyberspace), which also cover the defences and rights of both consumers and providers.

C20.26   ECOMMERCE DEFENCE CASES

We are not aware of any reports that involve eCommerce defences and any controversy and/or notable case involving similar issues.

C20.27   LAWS PROTECTING PERSONAL DATA/ PERSONALLY IDENTIFIABLE INFORMATION

The Federal Law for the Protection of Data in Possession of Private Parties foresees several mechanisms for the safekeeping and assurance of the privacy concerning data and private information. As an example, Articles 6 to 9 of such law establish the following,

Article 6. Managers in the processing of personal data must comply with the principles of legality, consent, information, quality, purpose, loyalty, proportionality and accountability under the Act.

Article 7. Personal data must be collected lawfully and in accordance with the provisions established by this Law and other applicable regulations.

Obtaining personal data should not be done through deceptive or fraudulent means.

In the processing of personal data, it is assumed that there is a reasonable expectation of privacy, understood as the trust you place any other person in respect of the personal information provided by them will be treated according to what the parties agreed on the terms set by this Act.

Article 8. Any processing of personal data is subject to the consent of the owner, unless otherwise provided by this Act.

Express consent is when the will is manifested verbally, in writing, by electronic, optical or other technology, or by unmistakable signs.

It is understood that the owner consents to the of your data, when having made available the privacy notice, it is not opposed.

Financial or economic data will require the express consent of the owner, except as provided for in Articles 10 and 37 of this Law.

Consent may be revoked at any time and will be retroactive. To revoke consent, the data controller must, in the privacy notice, establish mechanisms and procedures for this.

Article 9. In the case of sensitive personal data, the data controller must obtain the express written consent of the owner for treatment, through their written signature, electronic signature, or authentication mechanism established for that purpose.

Databases containing sensitive personal data without creating them for legitimate purposes and consistent with specific activities or explicit aims of the regulated party is justified.

C20.28   DATA BREACH LAWS AND CUSTOMERS/ USERS/REGULATORS NOTIFIED OF HACKING OR DATA LOSS

Articles 19 and 20 of the Federal Law for the Protection of Data in Possession of Private Parties foresee this particular obligation for the people responsible for handling such data, in the following terms,

Article 19. Anyone responsible for carrying out the processing of personal data shall establish and maintain appropriate administrative, technical and physical measures which will be designed to protect personal data against damage, loss, alteration, destruction, and also against unauthorized use, access or treatment.

Those responsible shall take measures that shall be never less than those taken to ensure the safety of their own information security. In the above-mentioned measures the responsible shall also take into account the existing risk, the sensitivity of the data involved, the constant technological development and the consequences to the information owners.

Article 20. Violations of safety occurring at any stage that significantly affect the economic or moral rights of the owners or data subjects require that the data subjects will be informed immediately by the data holder or host, so that the owners or data subjects can take appropriate measures to defend their rights.

New Zealand

Judge David Harvey

C21.1   INTRODUCTION

New Zealand is a Common Law jurisdiction.

C21.2   SPECIFIC SM AND SN LAWS

No specific laws that address SM or SN are provided in the statute books; however, when the Harmful Digital Communications Bill (presently before a Select Committee) becomes law, what constitute harmful digital communications will include communications in the SM and SN space.

C21.3   SM CRIMINAL LAW CASES

There are a number of criminal cases where SM has featured as part of the background or as an element of offending or of relevance in sentencing. Examples follow,

R v Derrick-Hardie [2012] NZHC 2833. Sentencing murder case where offender met then girlfriend (A) on Facebook – between Feb and Apr 2011 they exchanged Facebook messages in which offender in various messages stated thought he was born to kill or be killed, referred to 'stabbing', stated was going to kill someone.

R v Hulme [2012] NZHC 1766. Offender threatened to post explicit pictures of victim on Facebook.

R v Vaux-Phillips [2012] NZHC 1119. Sentencing case regarding culpable homicide murder of teenager Hayden Miles. Hayden contacted defendant by Facebook – defendant invited Hayden to meet.

Police v Harris-Reardon [2012] DCR 568. Criminal law – defendant charged with harassment, knowing that the harassment was likely to cause that person, given his personal circumstances, to reasonably fear for his safety. Defendant sent the complainant nine requests to be a friend on Facebook in one day and had also created a fictitious Facebook page – defendant stated that his repeated friend requests on Facebook did not qualify as harassment.

R v Cooper [2013] NZHC 2713. Sentencing manslaughter; attempting to pervert course of justice – appropriate sentence – C killed J with blow to head by elbow (single punch) – C wrapped J in duvet and put under shed in C's garden – several days later, C buried J in shallow grave in garden – over next year, C used J's bank card to withdraw J's WINZ benefit and created fictitious Bebo account.

R v Pillai HC Auckland CRI-2006-092-002766 Mar 24, 2010. P met 11 of victims on social internet sites and made contact using false identities – P asked victims to send naked photos of themselves.

Mills v Police HC Auckland CRI-2009-404-000355 Nov 20, 2009. Bail case – diagnosed as HIV positive 25 May 2007 – M received counselling and was urged to follow 'safe sex' practices – M made sexual contacts through SM sites – police alleged between May 2007 and March 2009 that M had unprotected intercourse with 14 complainants.

R v Grygoruk HC Auckland CRI-2006-092-012831 May 23, 2008. Blackmail under ss 237(1)(b) and 238 Crimes Act 1961; altering documents with intent to defraud – conducting series of internet frauds or 'phishing scams' over five-year period.

Police v Joseph [2013] DCR 482. Created a video clip which contained messages of threats to the Government accompanied by images linking that language with terrorism – defendant then uploaded this video clip to YouTube (via an Internet cafe), subtitled it 'Operation 911 New Zealand', and linked it to 21 separate media websites – Police traced the source of the video. [This case involved the interpretation of a very complex section of the Crimes Act which contained elements of a public disruption/quasi terrorist offence. The case turned on the issue of intention and contained similarities to the so-called Twitter Joke Trial (*Chambers v DPP*) in England.]

R v Milne HC Nelson CRI-2010-042-1429. Criminal offences – threatening victim saying that unless the debt was paid you would reveal the facts of the sexual abuse on Facebook. The texts were threatening and abusive.

R v Feng HC Auckland CRI-2008-004-27372. Blackmail and sexual offences. Email and postings on MSN and Bebo.

R v Patel [2009] NZCA 102. Trying to get the complainant to give him a copy of a photograph that he had seen on the complainant's Bebo website.

R v H [2009] NZCA 77. Judge had remanded the appellant in custody after viewing material apparently sent by the appellant to the complainant through Bebo, an SM website.

Mead v Police HC Auckland CRI-2011-404-320. Online dating site – bail case.

Van Helmond v Community Probation Service [2013] NZHC 990. Criminal offences blackmail – complained about his lawyer, 'he complained about me, alleging that I called him a cyber-bully, he complained about others cyber-bullying him'.

R v Nightingale [2013] NZHC 877. Criminal offences blackmail – very ease of communication through texting and SM and its prevalence in our society has sparked a rise in cyber bullying and similar types of offending.

Keesing v Police [2012] NZHC 422. Virtual creation of police employee; unsuccessful appeal against conviction for personation of a police employee contrary to s 48(1) Policing Act 2008 – conviction following defended hearing – appellant created profile of police officer from his Facebook account using a photograph of the then Deputy Commissioner and got a name (H) off the internet after carrying out a search using references such as 'drugs' and 'police' – appellant used profile to send a message to complainant stating that had contacted CYFS regarding her child being exposed to methamphetamine and advised victim to contact Auckland Central Police Station – friend of appellant wanted to exact some kind of revenge on complainant – complainant did an internet search and found H was an actual detective involved in drug investigations – complainant received no response from her reply and made a complaint to the Police Complaints Authority – whether elements of s 48(1) had been met – mens rea essential ingredient of offence of personation (*Keesing v Police*) – purposive approach to legislation taken. HELD: no doubt but that appellant acted without reasonable excuse, intention clearly to be mischievous – circumstances were likely to lead victim to believe sender of Facebook message was police employee – clear that appellant was pretending to be a police employee as used a photograph of a police officer in uniform and took and used the name of a serving officer involved in drug-related offending – nothing to suggest phrase 'words, conduct or demeanour' limited to when uttered or undertaken by one person in the physical presence of another – words used by officer not required to be spoken to complainant – s 48 intended to create an offence where a person personated police employees, regardless of whether pretence maintained at a distance or in person – clear intention of Parliament to prohibit any words or conduct by which people, by whatever means, pretended to be police employees – appeal dismissed.

R v Stewart Court: High Court, Wellington. Judgment Date: 29/11/2013. Sentencing – Blackmail – targeting young girls on SM.

R v Nicholls: High Court, Nelson. Judgment Date: 13/6/2012. Sentencing – Blackmail in the context of the use of intimate photos and the use of Bebo.

R v HDSN: High Court, Auckland. Judgment Date: 21/10/2013. Blackmail – prosecution alleged that Mr N threatened to publish intimate photographs of the complainants on the internet. That can fairly be regarded as a threat to disclose.

R v Boyd: Court of Appeal. Judgment Date: 11/10/2014. Appeal raised some relatively novel questions relating to the sentencing of an adult male who met young girls via Internet chat rooms, and subsequently formed relationships with them, which in turn led to unlawful (albeit consensual) sexual activity. Court noted that this sort of thing, or so it seems, is one unfortunate aspect of the ubiquitous rise of the Internet phenomenon. The court endorsed the recent observations of the English Court of Appeal in *Wheeler*, that: 'The use by older men of Internet chat rooms used by young girls can have no acceptable justification'.

C21.4   SM CIVIL LAW CASES

Two cases I decided dealt with the application of the Harassment Act to the blogosphere and were civil proceedings,

MJF v Sperling [2013] NZFLR 715, [2013] DCR 567, Harvey J. Respondent posted messages about the applicant on an online blog – whether the blog posts can fall within the ambit of the Harassment Act.

Brown v Sperling [2012] DCR 753 (extract), Harvey J. Respondent posted messages about the applicant on an online blog and also posted messages on Facebook and Twitter.

Rodriguez v Osborne CIV-2009-004-000028. Harassment – application for a restraining order pursuant to s 9 Harassment Act 1997 – the parties met one another in the course of employment and, following resolution of a conflict between the parties in the Disputes Tribunal, the respondent sought more compensation from the applicant – forms of harassment included text messages, establishing a fake Facebook profile – no evidence of harassment for the month prior to making her application – whether the applicant was in need of ongoing protection with reference to: (1) the fact the applicant was harassed and in the circumstances this was enough to cause distress; (2) the degree of distress, actual or threatened; (3) the harassment was a specified act pursuant to ss 3 and 4 – 'personal safety' given a liberal interpretation. HELD: proceedings adjourned for 6 months.

Wishart v Murray [2013] NZHC 540. Defamation – substantively unsuccessful application to strike out defamation claims; unsuccessful application for security for costs – plaintiff wrote a book called *Breaking Silence* which M, the mother of three-month old twins Chris and Cru Kahui, collaborated on – the twins died from non-accidental injuries in 2006 – the father C of the twins had during his trial suggested M had inflicted the fatal injuries – when the book's impending release became known in June 2011 the first defendant established a Facebook page called 'Boycott the Macsyna King Book' and used Twitter to publicise it – Twitter statements had links to the main Facebook page and acted as a headline or teaser, encouraging people to go to the Facebook page – first defendant posted comments on Twitter and on the Facebook page criticising the plaintiff and M – *currently on appeal*.

Karam v Fairfax New Zealand Ltd [2012] NZHC 887 (civil procedure) and [2012] NZHC 887 (defamation).

Karam v Parker HC Auckland CIV-2010-404-3038 29/7/2011.

About Health Supplements Ltd v Charnley [2013] NZHC 2004. Civil procedure, discovery.

N v M [2014] NZHC 239. Harassment case.

McDonald v Williams HC Auckland CIV-2011-404-4420. Harassment case – W director of TradeMe Ltd (TML) which owned and operated eponymous online auction site; TML maintained community message board on which members conversed on wide range of general interest topics.

Muzz Buzz Franchising PTY Ltd v JB Holdings (2010) Ltd High Court, Auckland. Judgment Date 28/6/2013. Passing off – misleading and deceptive conduct – market presence – the plaintiff adapted the sales and marketing activities of the business to take advantage of the internet and the growth in SM such as Facebook.

C21.5   CASES WHERE SM-RELATED EVIDENCE USED OR ADMISSIBLE

In the family court, evidence has been used derived primarily from Facebook pages (see C21.21).

C21.6   SPECIFIC ONLINE ABUSE/ONLINE BULLYING/ CYBERBULLYING LAWS

No specific laws, although see the application of the Harassment Act to the blogosphere in the cases of *MJF v Sperling*, *Brown v Sperling* and *Rodriguez v Osborne* (referred to in C21.4). However, a comprehensive Bill – the Harmful Digital Communications Bill – is working its way through the legislative process. It is planned that this Bill should be enacted by the time the House rises at the end of July 2014. It deals with both the civil and criminal aspects of harmful digital communications and provides a civil enforcement regime which uses a 'fast-track' process to address and, if appropriate, order takedown of harmful digital communications.

C21.7   OTHER LAWS APPLIED TO ONLINE ABUSE/ ONLINE BULLYING/CYBERBULLYING

The Harassment Act (see above).

C21.8   CHILDREN AND SM LAWS OR RULES

No specific laws or rules.

C21.9   EMPLOYEES/EMPLOYMENT SM LAWS OR CASES

No specific statutory provisions, although there have been cases involving employers/employees and SM or the use thereof.

Taiapa v Te Runanga O Turanganui A Kiwa Trust t/a Turanga Ararau Private Training Establishment [2013] NZEmpC 38 (2013) 10 NZELR 378. Employment case where employee took family to Rotorua and attended Waka Ama Championships – manager was informed that employee was at championships and found photograph on Facebook showing employee at event – manager suspected employee was misusing sick leave.

Hook v Stream Group (NZ) Pty Ltd [2013] NZEmpC 188. Unsuccessful challenge in EmpC to determination of Employment Relations Authority dismissing personal grievance for constructive dismissal – H employed by FGNZL – FGNZL merged with SG – H disenchanted with initiatives of SG after merger – H emailed other staff and made derogatory comments – late in 2010 issues arose in relation to H being absent from office without notifying supervisor and with tardiness, H's use of email system and H recording disciplinary process without seeking permission of attendees in advance – 8 Feb 2011 SG gave H formal written warning – warning expressed to be current for 12 months – H signed warning – H absent from office 26 Jul 2011 without prior notice or approval – H eventually said he had attended work interview – 27 Jul manager spoke to H – H made clear he was looking for alternative employment – manager offered to accommodate H in terms of time off work for interviews – manager set meeting for 2 Aug to discuss absence from office – meeting held and another rescheduled to discuss outcome (the follow up meeting) – H did not attend follow up meeting – manager told H meeting would go ahead in H's absence – 11 Aug manager resolved to issue final written warning – H did not challenge warning – 19 Aug H advised manager he was resigning and intended to work out 2 weeks' notice – manager accepted resignation – H went on short period of sick leave and returned to work – H disruptive on return to work – manager advised H, H not required to work out notice period and GS would instead pay him out as provided under employment agreement – H raised no concerns – H raised personal grievance and alleged GS had constructively dismissed him and had breached implied term not, without reasonable and proper cause, to conduct itself in a manner calculated or likely to destroy or seriously damage relationship of trust and confidence – after H left work GS undertook search of Facebook and found H's page in public domain – on page H advised he was 'going to quit tomorrow' and referred to his boss as a 'dickhead' – GS said Facebook entries went to

H's credibility and undermined H's version of events and supported GS's contention that H resigned of own free will – Authority dismissed personal grievance – H challenged determination of Authority in EmpC – EmpC considered: (i) whether H was issued with ultimatum by GS; (ii) proper use of material from Facebook in employment disputes. HELD: GS did not issue ultimatum to H – GS' final warning gave H no cause to resign – GS had acted in moderate even lenient manner – no breach of duty by GS that caused H to resign – well established that conduct outside workplace can give rise to disciplinary action and that Facebook posts (even those with privacy setting) not necessarily to be regarded as protected communications beyond reach of employment processes – Australian case law made it clear that in Australia posting of derogatory, offensive and discriminatory comments or statements about managers or other employees on Facebook might provide valid reason for termination of employment – those cases recognised Facebook was not strictly private forum and posted comments could vitiate claim of constructive dismissal – challenge dismissed – costs reserved – costs to be agreed – failing agreement as to costs memoranda to be filed according to timetable set.

Wellington Free Ambulance Service Inc v Adams [2010] NZEmpC 59 [2010] ERNZ 128, (2010) 9 NZELC 93,512. Successful challenge by de novo hearing to the determination by the Employment Relations Authority pursuant to s 127 Employment Relations Act 2000 that the respondent be reinstated in her employment as a dispatcher with the plaintiff – duration of the interim order for reinstatement was uncertain with a scheduled investigation into the respondent's personal grievance alleging unjustified dismissal for which remedies including reinstatement was sought pending before the Authority – the Authority was to apply 3 tests in its determination being: (1) whether the respondent had an arguable case for determination by the Authority that she had been unjustifiably dismissed; (2) where the balance of convenience lay; (3) the overall justice of the position – the Court considered that the Authority effectively decided the application for interim reinstatement on the overall justice of the case after highlighting the unusual features of the application of tests by the Authority: (1) it was unclear whether the Authority considered the respondent had an arguable case and that she had been dismissed unjustifiably, but also an arguable case for reinstatement in employment upon that finding; (2) in determining the balance of convenience, the Authority could not decide whether the disadvantages to the respondent if not reinstated outweighed the disadvantages to the plaintiff of an interim order for reinstatement in the event that the plaintiff was ultimately successful in establishing justification for dismissal – dismissal followed an investigation into complaints against the respondent from colleagues relating to abuse, rudeness and aggression of the colleagues personally and on Facebook – where the Court determined that there was an arguable case of unjustifiable dismissal, what was the appropriateness and likelihood of an order for reinstatement in employment in terms of its practicability – in considering the practicability of reinstatement, the Court considered that any interim reinstatement would require gradual implementation with retraining and counselling. HELD: finding that the respondent had an arguable case of unjustified dismissal under s 103(A) because the plaintiff never disclosed to the respondent substantial and significant information sought and obtained by it in the course of its inquiry – balance of convenience favoured suspension of the respondent – the Authority's determination was set aside and replaced by the current judgment which declined the application for reinstatement – costs reserved.

Bettany v Masonry Design Solutions Ltd AA 154-08, 5076560 Apr 24, 2008. Employment case for unjustifiable dismissal where employer considered B's timekeeping had got worse and considered that B's use of internet (900 visits to internet sites in 12 days) was unreasonable and amounted to serious misconduct.

Nelson v Katavich Employment Relations Authority, Christchurch. Judgment Date: 19/2/2013. N had no clear role but performed tasks as directed including maintenance of false blogs to influence internet searches; N created one blog titled hitlerhatesbabies@gmail.com with ilovehitler as password; N took on management responsibilities for Invercargill and Nelson offices at K's direction. K knew N had used blog title and internet password some weeks before dismissal and had not treated it as significant.

C21.9.1 A selection of news media articles

Toby Manhire, 'Turkish Twitter ban backfires spectacularly' 25 March 2014. The Listener Online http://www.listener.co.nz/commentary/the-internaut/turkish-twitter-ban-backfires-spectacularly/.

Toby Manhire, 'Turkey and the Twitter menace' 26 June 2013 and 'French voters defy election blackout with #radiolondres' 24 April 2012.

'Air NZ wins access to sacked flight attendant's Facebook, bank accounts' 11 August 2013 www.nbr.co.nz/article/air-nz-wins-access-sacked-flight-attendants-facebook-bank-accounts-ck-144207.

'Sour ex-staff cook up bad eatery reviews' www.nzherald.co.nz/wairarapa-times-age/news/article.cfm?c_id=1503414&objectid=11180091 Wednesday Jan 1, 2014 Cassandra Mason.

'Fast-food workers fired on Facebook' Paul Easton 27/01/2014, www.stuff.co.nz/dominion-post/news/9652173/Fast-food-workers-fired-on-Facebook.

Joe Potter-Butler, 'Shouting at the world on Facebook and Twitter' www.employment-law.co.nz/blog/Shouting-at-the-world-on-Facebbook-and-Twitter. In March 2010 Tania Dickinson, an employee of the Ministry of Social Development, described herself in a Facebook post as a 'very expensive paperweight' who is 'highly competent in the art of time wastage, blame shifting and stationary [sic] theft'. Unsurprisingly, Ms Dickinson no longer works for the Ministry of Social Development

'Burger King worker keeps her job despite Facebook slag' by MSN NZ Money staff 9/02/2011, http://money.msn.co.nz/marketandbusinessnews/8208558/burger-king-worker-keeps-her-job-despite-facebook-slag. Dunedin Burger King worker, who was given a final warning after complaining about her job on Facebook, says she stands by her online posts.

C21.9.2   *Tribunals cases*

Our employment disputes are dealt with by a specific Employment Court. The following cases involve complaints not specifically relevant to employment but involve complaints to Tribunals including the Broadcasting Standards Authority and the Advertising Standards Authority. The cases below involved SM issues in one form or another,

Middleton and Television New Zealand Ltd – 2013-040 [2013] NZBSA 63 (3 September 2013).

Bennett and RadioWorks Ltd (More FM) – 2011-119 [2011] NZBSA 152 (22 November 2011).

Ruawai College Board of Trustees and TVWorks Ltd – 2013-003 [2013] NZBSA 34 (7 May 2013).

New Zealand Law Students Association Magazine Advertisement [2013] NZASA 12659 (30 January 2013).

Hohaia v New Zealand Post Limited AA362/10 (Auckland) [2010] NZERA 670 (17 August 2010). Employment case regarding Facebook.

C21.10   SCHOOL AND UNIVERSITY STUDENT SM CASES

There are no specific statutes, although there have been some cases where SM has been involved. Schools and universities have developed acceptable use policies, and the NGO Netsafe (www.netsafe.org.nz) has been responsible for developing policies, guidelines and advice for educational institutions.

Some examples of cases involving students and young people follow,

R v Nicholls [2012] NZHC 1334 – pair met on Bebo, nude pictures sent – blackmail case.

Re Curry Health Practitioners Disciplinary Tribunal (HPDT) 386-Nur11-174P. Defendant created identity of 18-year-old male on Bebo SM site and established contact with two victims aged 15 and 14 respectively.

R v Curry DC Whangarei CRI-2009-088-005739 13 May 2010. Defendant, a 46-year-old man, sought out young females using SM websites with the intent of forming a sexual relationship.

C21.11 RIGHT OR HUMAN RIGHT TO ACCESS THE INTERNET OR SM

For example, see the following articles,

Joy Liddicoat 'Human Rights and the Internet' Human rights research (Online), 2011 http://ndhadeliver.natlib.govt.nz.ezproxy.auckland.ac.nz/delivery/ DeliveryManagerServlet?dps_pid=FL17056946.

DJ Harvey 'Free Public Access to Law and Primary Legal Information as an Aspect of Internet Freedom' 31 May 2013, The ITCountrey Justice http:// theitcountreyjustice.wordpress.com/category/internet-rights/.

C21.12 BANS OR RESTRICTIONS ON INTERNET OR SM

A large number of cases that go on appeal, on issues involving admissibility of evidence at a subsequent trial, have a specific direction that publication on the Internet is not to take place until the trial has been completed. There are numerous examples and the practice is quite common. The following was a pre-emptive attempt to prevent internet publication but maintain traditional media publication, having regard to the permanency of internet information, its searchability and retrievability,

Police v PIK [2008] DCR 853, Harvey J. Criminal procedure – the Judge discussed the development of Google software that used advanced searching processes to make accurate searching far more possible for the average internet user – the Judge noted that once information is on the web it very rarely ever dies – the internet challenges the current law on publication in that a person with traditional media may remember some general information about a story but will not remember the details – with the internet, however, the viewer may go back and research in detail the news.

C21.13 IDENTITY THEFT (OR EQUIVALENT)

No specific laws at the moment, although the Harmful Digital Communications Bill (see C21.2) makes provision for the misuse of the identity of another.

The following cases have elements of 'identity theft', although the case was not decided on that point,

R v Cooper [2013] NZHC 2713. Sentencing manslaughter; attempting to pervert course of justice – appropriate sentence – C killed J with blow to head by elbow (single punch) – C wrapped J in duvet and put under shed in C's garden – several days later, C buried J in shallow grave in garden – over next year, C used J's bank card to withdraw J's WINZ benefit and created fictitious Bebo account.

R v Pillai HC Auckland CRI-2006-092-002766 Mar 24, 2010. P met 11 of victims on social internet sites and made contact using false identities – P asked victims to send naked photos of themselves.

C21.14   HACKING (OR EQUIVALENT)

Sections 248–252 of the Crimes Act 1961 – inserted by an amendment to the Act in 2003 – specifically apply to computer misuse, including damaging computer systems, using computer systems to obtain a financial advantage and associated issues such as Denial of Service attacks, the possession of and dealing in 'hacking' software and s 252 which criminalises the unauthorised access of a computer system (without any gain or damage element. See www. legislation.govt.nz/act/public/1961/0043/latest/DLM330415.html.

C21.15   PRIVACY BY DESIGN (PBD) (OR EQUIVALENT)

Not to my knowledge.

C21.16   TWEETING FROM COURTS, AND ANY RULES/LAWS

In New Zealand the judges have developed a suite of Media Guidelines (see below) for use in the courts. These Guidelines are currently being reviewed. The prime directive at the moment is that no 'live feeds' will be communicated from the court room. The first mention of a matter of evidence or the like must wait for 10 minutes after the event. There have been cases where accredited journalists have 'Tweeted' subject to that 10-minute restriction. In normal cases, one would ask the judge.

C21.17   TELEVISION COURTROOM BROADCASTING OR TELEVISION CAMERAS IN COURT, AND RULES OR LAWS

The court Media Guidelines provide the rules for the use of broadcast equipment in court (see www.justice.govt.nz/media/publications/global-publications/m/ media-guide-for-reporting-the-courts-and-tribunals-edition-3.1/media-guide-for-reporting-the-courts-and-tribunals-edition-3.1).

C21.18   SM IN COURTROOMS

There have been a couple of cases where it has come to the attention of the trial judge that there had been juror research on the internet. The jurors in question were discharged. At the moment, the Law Commission is looking at the current law relating to contempt of court and is focusing one line of enquiry upon juror misconduct.

Police v Slater [2011] DCR 6 Harvey DCJ. The defendant had operated a blog and was charged with breaching non-publication orders made under s 140 of the Criminal Justice Act 1985 in respect of certain individuals who were the subject of criminal proceedings and, in one instance, of publishing particulars from which a victim of crime was identifiable, in breach of s 139. In some cases, the name of the individual concerned was published in the form of a pictogram or code; in others, the name was published, under the heading of 'interesting name', separately from a discussion of the proceedings in question. The defendant raised a number of technical defences to the individual charges, but his general defences to the charges included the following,

(1)   that there was no publication in New Zealand; and

(2)   that he had not published a report or an account of the proceeding in each case, but merely commentary or opinion which was not caught by a non-publication order.

Specifically, the defendant argued that the terms 'report or account' used in s 140 had to be given a restrictive interpretation and referred to a report or an account of a proceeding by a person present in Court, and that s 140 was directed to the news media who reported on what occurred in court as the surrogates of the public. For the Crown, it was argued that s 140 applied to any person who had the ability to disseminate information in a public forum.

Held (convicting the defendant),

1   The reality was that the blog was available free of charge to internet users in New Zealand who accessed it from time to time. The availability of the material from a server located in the United States was irrelevant. The evidence was that the material was able to be read and comprehended in New Zealand, and was uploaded on the blog by the defendant present in New Zealand at the time. Thus the acts necessary for publication – the creation of the material, the posting of the material, and the availability of the material to be comprehended by readers in New Zealand – all took place within the jurisdiction. Accordingly, there was publication in New Zealand;

2   Section 140 was a justifiable limitation upon the right to free speech and had to be given a purposive interpretation. The terms 'report' or 'account' were to be interpreted as any narrative or information relating to proceedings in respect of an offence;

3   The law had to be seen to be always speaking [purposeful] and to encompass and recognise new technologies. Conceptually, a blog was no different from any other form of mass media communication, especially since it involved the internet. Blogging was made to a wide audience

and went beyond a private conversation, and accordingly constituted publication;

4   Section 140 captured the publication of pieces of information that, when taken together, identified a person. It was immaterial that the information was contained in a code or pictogram: the information could be decoded in the same way that an aggregation of information might lead to the identification of a person by a process of elimination.

Mussa v R Court of Appeal. Judgment Date: 1/4/2010. Issue – sufficiency of judge's directions regarding juror use of the internet.

C21.19   USE OF SM AS EVIDENCE IN COURTS

The following cases seem to be relevant to the question.

R v Pillai HC Auckland CRI-2006-092-002766 Jul 29, 2009. Evidence – ruling as to admissibility of evidence of AB at trial of accused on 34 counts primarily of sexual offending against six alleged victims – meeting the accused on SM website, development of relationship between text messages and chatting on site, use of false name coupled with posting photograph on site.

Corbett v Western HC Auckland CIV-2010-404-001495 May 25, 2010. Sufficient in material to raise at least the possibility that plaintiff was an 'incapacitated person' but reliance on a Wikipedia definition and views of a lawyer and a family representative were insufficient.

Police v PIK [2008] DCR 853, Harvey J. Criminal procedure – the Judge discussed the development of Google software that used advanced searching processes to make accurate searching far more possible for the average internet user – the Judge noted that once information is on the web it very rarely ever dies – the internet challenges the current law on publication in that a person with traditional media may remember some general information about a story but will not remember the details – with the internet, however, the viewer may go back and research in detail the news.

Police v Casino Bar (No 3) Ltd [2013] NZHC 44. Use of Facebook as evidence re liquor licence. CGML cited other aspects of Mr Samson's Facebook page which contained what it described as 'volatile commentary' about existing businesses. The objection stated that Mr Samson had been banned from attending the objector's business.

C21.20   PRIVACY, DATA PROTECTION AND SM

The case of *Police v PIK* (see C21.19) indirectly involves privacy protection for the purposes of the integrity of a subsequent trial.

Back Country Helicopters Ltd v Minister of Conservation [2013] NZHC 982. A clip showing Mr Dunne (Minister of the Crown) addressing a camera was posted on YouTube.

Koyama v New Zealand Law Society [2012] NZHC 2853. Counsel Mr Koyama had recorded covertly and placed in-chambers discussions on YouTube.

The Solicitor-General of New Zealand v Krieger (CIV-2013-425-000273, Panckhurst J) High Court, Invercargill. Feb 17, 2014. Contempt of court – breach of High Court injunction – disseminating via the internet private and confidential information belonging to EQC – $5,000 fine.

See also the following article,

John Edwards 'The potential impact of the Internet on privacy rights' 1996 2(1) *Human Rights Law and Practice* 15.

The Crimes Act contains specific provision for 'crimes against personal privacy', but this is directed to the interception of communications, the use of and dealing in interception devices, etc. See www.legislation.govt.nz/act/public/1961/0043/latest/DLM329802.html.

C21.21 SM AND FAMILY LAW CASES

There have not been controversies, but the use of SM such as Facebook as evidence is routine and unremarkable. Interestingly enough, the admissibility of this evidence as emanating from a machine device or technical process (s 137 Evidence Act 2006) has not been challenged and, in some cases, it should be, because the steps that have to be undertaken to render machine-based evidence admissible are little understood by lawyers. The challenge in *R v Pillai* above could have been on technological grounds, but there may have been compelling evidence that obviated that.

See the following examples,

Re R (Children) FAM-2003-092-000317, 25 October 2006. In assessing the father's parenting capacity, the court had regard to factors including SM.

AJD v SED [2013] NZHC 3154. Posted threats and accusations on Facebook – S applied to FC for protection order.

Clark v Coles FAM-2007-003-000153, 30 September 2013. Domestic violence – cross-applications for protection order – internet psychological abuse – harassment – Facebook, email, blogs, text messages, phone calls.

Chapman v Hughes FAM-2012-085-000938, 11 September 2013. Allegations of psychological abuse – harassment – intimidation – humiliation – personal information taken from applicant's home – distributed via internet – persistent stalking – threatening text messages – numerous breaches of previous undertaking by respondent to not contact applicant – contact made with applicant's daughters since temporary protection order made – accessed Facebook account.

R v F [2013] NZHC 2498. Later posted some of the photographs on the internet.

Clark v Coles (FAM-2007-003-000153, Judge L de Jong) Family Court, Christchurch, Sep 30, 2013. Domestic violence – cross-applications for protection order – internet psychological abuse – harassment – Facebook, email, blogs, text messages, phone calls.

JLE v JAR-B (FAM-2000-032-000644, Judge JF Moss) Family Court, Wellington, Oct 24, 2012. Domestic violence – successful application by father for protection order against mother – successful application for order suspending mother's future contact – parties parents of 12-year-old child (KA) – KA lived with mother until Mar 2011 – contact with father persistently blocked by mother – KA appointed ward of Court Mar 2011 – lived with father from Jul 2011 – limited supervised contact with mother – father alleged ongoing psychological abuse by mother – unauthorised contact with KA by Facebook and email – pressured child to conceal social media contact – laid false complaints – posted abusive material on public internet websites – undermined relationship between father and KA – no substance to mother's belief that father posed risk to child – whether domestic violence occurred in form of psychological abuse – whether protection order necessary to exclude risk of ongoing domestic violence – no indication of mother's behaviour changing – child accepted past manipulation by mother – building resiliency – wished for ongoing contact – whether appropriate for child to give evidence – approaches to children giving evidence in family proceedings – signs of shift in thinking – whether continued wardship order required. HELD: protection order necessary for safety of father and KA – duration and intensity of ongoing psychological domestic violence – wardship order to continue – extreme nature of alienation – father appointed Court's agent – no contact with mother before start of KA's year 10 school year – settled year necessary for KA – limited supervised Skype contact – KA's legal name amended to include father's name and to exclude surname R.

AW v AM (FAM-2008-092-001385, Judge DA Burns) Family Court, Auckland. Sep 18, 2012. Care of children – successful application to relocate a child from NZ to Germany – child was born in Jul 2008 – parents' relationship ended when the child was 6 weeks old – father had not seen the child since – father convicted of male assaults female where the mother was the victim and the child was present – father was imprisoned – mother had a protection order against the father – German mother arrived in NZ aged 19 and now wished to return to Germany – mother struggled financially in NZ – in Germany, mother could live with her parents rent free, would have her parents' support, receive a higher benefit and be eligible for student loans – mother proposed to ensure on-going contact between the child, his father and whanau through Skype, photographs and email – mother agreed to add father's family members on Facebook but not the father – mother offered 3 occasions for contact before departure – mother unlikely to return to NZ in the foreseeable future primarily due to financial reasons – mother enrolled the child at Kohanga Reo and facilitated contact with the father's family – father opposed the application but reluctantly consented to relocation at the hearing – father sought to establish a relationship with the child before his departure – father had convictions for driving offences, dishonesty crimes, crimes of violence and had compliance issues with sentences – father was under an intensive supervision sentence – father acknowledged he had ongoing anger issues – application carefully reviewed as the father lacked legal advice, was under mixed feelings and was operating under pressure. HELD: pursuant to s 44 Care of Children Act 2004 (the Act), the court directed the mother could relocate the child to Germany and that his life could be in Germany thereafter – final parenting order made in favour of the mother providing her day-to-day care of the child – father to have 3 occasions for supervised contact prior to the relocation – any contact to be supervised in light of s 61 of the Act criteria, the father's previous convictions and the fact the father had not seen the child since he was 6 weeks old – provisions of the Hague Convention in relation to enforcement were to apply – mother to arrange Skype contact with paternal grandparents and other members of the paternal whanau, send photographs of the child, add the paternal grandparents as Facebook friends, facilitate the child's knowledge of Tikanga Maori and te reo, ensure the child visited NZ before he turned 12 (cost to be borne by the father) – father's consent to relocation was properly given and relocation would have been ordered even without consent – relocation allowed for economic reasons and as the mother's enhanced parenting (functioning better due to increased support and familiarity with her environment) would benefit the child – relocation would enable the child to connect with his German heritage – important the child relocated now rather than later to ensure he was able to adapt – no loss of relationship with the father as there was no relationship at present – consent given for an application for a German passport for the child to be processed as soon as possible.

SLM v BS (FAM-2000-042-000735, Judge RJ Russell) Family Court, Nelson. Domestic violence – successful application to discharge a protection order under s 47(1) Domestic Violence Act 1995 (the Act) – successful application for a protection order under s 14 of the Act – parties had a 2 year relationship – child born Sept 2000 – in 2000 (after separation), each party obtained a protection order against the other – order made for the benefit of the father as the mother repeatedly hit him during an argument just after her mother died – father suffered bruising – 2002, protection order against the father was discharged – parties shared care of the child – mother failed to pay all child support due – father opposed discharge of the protection order arguing failure to pay child support constituted psychological abuse – father's partner posted abusive remarks about the child support issue on the mother's Facebook page – on a number of occasions, the father put signs complaining about child support non-payment in his car outside the mother's business, stood outside the mother's business or across the street with placards regarding child support issues, put tape over his mouth and gave out leaflets explaining his protest to passers-by, sent abusive text messages to the mother regarding child support – 1 staff member left the mother's business as a result of the father's actions – mother contended the father's actions constituted psychological abuse which adversely affected the mother, her relationship with her new partner, customers and her business – mother felt stressed, violated and ashamed as a result of the father's actions – (1) whether to discharge the protection order for the benefit of the father; (2) whether to grant a protection order for the benefit of the mother. HELD: (1) yes – non-payment of child support could not constitute domestic violence under s 3 of the Act – no other actions on the mother's part showed a risk of further domestic violence occurring – were no prosecutions for breach of the order in the 11 years since it was made – no family violence callouts – violence leading to the order appeared to be a one-off incident – mother completed an anger management programme as required by the protection order; (2) yes – father referred to a Stopping Violence programme – a qualifying relationship existed under s 4(1)(d) of the Act – letters sent to the mother and her new partner spelling out child support owed and requesting payment did not constitute psychological abuse – other actions taken by the father taken as a whole over several months constituted harassment under s 3(2)(c)(ii) of the Act – order necessary to put a stop to acts of harassment which occurred as recently as last week.

SRM v CAM (FAM-2010-044-002520, FAM-2009-044-001834, Judge TH Druce) Family Court, North Shore, Aug 16, 2012. Domestic violence – successful applications for discharge of protection order and for contact with grandchildren aged 12 (B), 10 (D) and 9 (L) years old – applicant the father of respondent mother – ongoing conflict between parties in relation to contact with grandchildren – mother concerned about applicant's alcohol consumption – safety issues when children in his care – protection order made in favour of mother late 2009 – psychological abuse – grandfather published account of mother's early history on her Facebook page: (1) whether protection order still necessary – perception of mother – ongoing harassment from father – manipulative behaviour – previous costs order against father remained unpaid – no history of physical violence – severity of domestic violence at lower end of spectrum; (2) whether contact between children and grandfather in their welfare and best interests – all children wanted contact – protection of children's safety – unwillingness of grandfather to acknowledge concerns about drinking – contact with grandfather not a substitute for contact with absent fathers – L's contact with his father prioritised over contact with grandfather. HELD: (1) protection order discharged – conflict between parties focussed on applicant's care of children – matter of safety not abuse – resolution of contact issue likely to reduce conflict; (2) interim order made for contact – regular contact in children's best interests – one day on alternate weekends between 9am and 5pm – overnight care not permitted until grandfather demonstrated more responsibility for drinking behaviour when caring for children.

EDP v RCH (FAM-2011-009-002677, FAM-2011-009-003104, Judge P Von Dadelszen) Family Court, Christchurch, May 10, 2012. Domestic violence – unsuccessful application for final protection order – children 4 and 1 years old – temporary order made in 2011 – history of controlling behaviour with threats of harm – interim parenting order provided for father to have supervised contact – safety inquiry – text messaging and unpleasant Facebook use – 8 domestic incidents reported to police between 2006 and 2012 – paternal grandmother expressed concerns on telephone but not in court – allegations of sexual relationship between father and his half-sister – lingering doubts – complaint made by sister to police – sister did not press charges – no direct evidence – relevancy to contact with sons – contact order – 'lingering doubt' test in Australian case *M v M*. HELD: no longer need for protection order – relationship over – temporary order justified – satisfied children safe in unsupervised care of father – while, in principle, no need for supervision, no contact for over 8 months – given children's ages, contact to be introduced – supervision for short period and frequent – Lawyer for Children to report on progress and proposed contact.

RSH v NH (FAM-2011-063-000426, Judge MA MacKenzie) Family Court, Rotorua, Feb 1, 2012. Unsuccessful application by mother for relocation overseas from New Zealand to South Africa – parents emigrated from South Africa 2001 – 3 children born in New Zealand – separated 2010 – mother wished to relocate to South Africa with children – benefit of extended family – able to work in her professional career – hoped father would also return – father opposed return to South Africa – concerned about children's safety – relocation not feasible financially – children's welfare and best interests paramount – continuity in arrangements – stable ongoing relationships with parents – preservation and maintenance of children's dual heritage – parent wishing to relocate required to show motivation to relocate is not to deny other parent contact or relationship with children – mother's Facebook campaign to support relocation was abusive to children – inappropriate to involve children in adult issues – benefits of relocation to children difficult to establish as proposal lacked sufficient detail. HELD: application to relocate declined – advantages of relocating to South Africa significantly outweighed by advantages of remaining in New Zealand – return to South Africa primarily of benefit to mother – relocation not necessary to foster South African heritage – regular holidays sufficient – interim shared parenting order made on week about basis – children to stay with non-care-giving parent each Thursday night – parenting arrangements to remain in place until further agreement or decision made by court following counsel-led mediation – details of evidence, outcome and decision not to be posted on Facebook.

JMM v ARJ (FAM-2007-009-004557, Judge NA Walsh) Family Court, Christchurch, Apr 29, 2011. Determination of whether wrapping child in clingfilm constituted 'violence' in terms of ss 59 and 60 Care of Children Act 2004 – child aged 4 and a half years old – physically restrained by being bound from below neck to ankles in clingfilm (plastic wrap) – photographs posted on father's Facebook page – existing contact provisions suspended – order made for supervised contact – no face to face contact had occurred since incident – father claimed child not restrained or in danger – wrapped for short period of time – a game – no malicious intent – child said wrapping was father's idea – felt bad – police concluded behaviour was stupid rather than wilful neglect – father's explanation reasonable – mother opposed all contact – feared for child's emotional welfare – police agreed that actions could potentially amount to kidnapping if happened to adult. HELD: wrapping child in clingfilm constituted violence – child incapable of providing consent – father's lack of insight into effects of putting photographs on Facebook was concerning – premature to determine whether any form of contact was safe – expert reports and substantive hearing required.

C21.22   SPORTS PERSONS, SPORTS CLUBS AND SM

There have been no reported cases of which I am aware. The English case of *Cairns v Modi* involved a New Zealand cricketer who was defamed by the use of Twitter as a means of communicating defamatory material.

The following articles may give a flavour,

'Jimmy Spithill tweets "let's beat these f******"', www.3news.co.nz/Top-10-sporting-controversies-of-2013/tabid/415/articleID/325968/Default. aspx#ixzz2x1PjpfLg

'World Cup: Twitter tirade disciplinary hearing delayed', www.nzherald.co.nz/sport/news/article.cfm?c_id=4&objectid=10756753.

'"Top tips" for athletes using social media' (July 2012), www.thomaseggar.com/ebulletins/the-sport-lawyer---sports-disciplinaries-v-criminal-proceedings.

'Employment Today' Issue 180, February 2014, www.employmenttoday.co.nz/full_text/180_last-night.asp.

C21.23   PERSONAL RELATIONS AND RELATIONSHIPS

One aspect is the element of cyberbullying which is being addressed by the Harmful Digital Communications Bill (see C21.2). There have been cases involving the posting of private images where injunctions have issued to prevent publication and, in one case, a civil seizure (Anton Piller) order was granted to enter premises and seize the machines upon which images were stored: *H v McGowan* (High Court Auckland CP147-SW01, 6 April 2001). Further examples are,

AJD v SED [2013] NZHC 3154. Posted threats and accusations on Facebook – S applied to FC for protection order.

Clark v Coles FAM-2007-003-000153, 30 September 2013. Domestic violence – cross-applications for protection order – internet psychological abuse – harassment – Facebook, email, blogs, text messages, phone calls.

Chapman v Hughes FAM-2012-085-000938, 11 September 2013. Allegations of psychological abuse – harassment – intimidation – humiliation – personal information taken from applicant's home – distributed via Internet – persistent stalking – threatening text messages – numerous breaches of previous undertaking by respondent to not contact applicant – contact made with applicant's daughters since temporary protection order made – accessed Facebook account.

R v Hulme [2012] NZHC 1766. Offender threatened to post explicit pictures of victim on Facebook.

Police v Harris-Reardon [2012] DCR 568. Criminal law – defendant charged with harassment, knowing that the harassment was likely to cause that person, given his personal circumstances, to reasonably fear for his safety. Defendant sent the complainant nine requests to be a friend on Facebook in one day and had also created a fictitious Facebook page – defendant stated that his repeated friend requests on Facebook did not qualify as harassment.

R v Pillai HC Auckland CRI-2006-092-002766 Mar 24, 2010. P met 11 of victims on social internet sites and made contact using false identities – P asked victims to send naked photos of themselves.

R v F [2013] NZHC 2498. Later posted some of the photographs on the internet.

MJF v Sperling [2013] NZFLR 715, [2013] DCR 567, Harvey J. Respondent posted messages about the applicant on an online blog – whether the blog posts can fall within the ambit of the Harassment Act.

Brown v Sperling [2012] DCR 753 (extract), Harvey J. Respondent posted messages about the applicant on an online blog and also posted messages on Facebook and Twitter.

R v Milne HC Nelson CRI-2010-042-1429. Criminal offences – threatening victim saying that unless the debt was paid you would reveal the facts of the sexual abuse on Facebook. The texts were threatening and abusive.

R v Patel [2009] NZCA 102. Trying to get the complainant to give him a copy of a photograph that he had seen on the complainant's Bebo website.

C21.24   SM AND PERSONAL DATA OF DECEASED PERSONS

No issues that I am aware of.

C21.25   SM, WEBSITE, SERVICE PROVIDER OR ISP DEFENCE RULES/LAWS

There is a 'safe harbour' provision in the Copyright Act 1994 for ISPs but that is specific to online copyright infringement. The Harmful Digital Communications Bill (see C21.2) contains a 'safe harbour' proposal that has been the subject of submissions by a number of interested content providers and ISPs. The scope of the proposed 'safe harbour' provision is as yet undetermined and will probably involve a number of compromises before it reaches its final form.

C21.26   ECOMMERCE DEFENCE CASES

None.

C21.27   LAWS PROTECTING PERSONAL DATA/ PERSONALLY IDENTIFIABLE INFORMATION

The Privacy Act 1993 is a comprehensive piece of privacy protection legislation. John Edwards, the newly appointed Privacy Commissioner, is very well versed in the technologies of the digital communications paradigm and is already making suggestions for toughening up the remedies for disclosure of private information online.

C21.28   DATA BREACH LAWS AND CUSTOMERS/ USERS/REGULATORS NOTIFIED OF HACKING OR DATA LOSS

No issues that I am aware of.

Chapter C22

Norway

Thomas Olsen PhD
Simonsen Vogt Wiig's Technology, Media and Telecom Department (TMT)

C22.1 INTRODUCTION

Norway is not an EU member state, but it shares some similar and related laws; it is a Civil Law jurisdiction.

C22.2 SPECIFIC SM AND SN LAWS

There are no such laws or regulations.

C22.3 SM CRIMINAL LAW CASES

Rt-2012-1211 (decision by the Norwegian Supreme Court). In this case, a man was taken into custody for aggressive attitude towards the police. The man had inter alia made several posts on his blog where he stated that people should kill police officers or where he glorified that kind of action.

The man appealed for release, and the main question before the court was whether his action was unlawful according to the Penal Code (*Straffeloven*, 1902) section 140 which inter alia prohibits publicly urging or instigating the commission of criminal acts. The key issue was whether the offence had been committed in public, meaning that it had been committed by publication of printed matter (see the Penal Code's definition in section 7).

The court found that a blog post could not be considered publication of printed matter. This interpretation was based on the principle of legality in Article 96 of the Norwegian Constitution and the European Convention on Human Rights (ECHR) Article 7. The rule was not clear enough to be used as a legal basis for the custody.

It should be noted that, as a result of this case, the wording of section 7 has been amended. The new technology-neutral criterion for determining whether an expression is public is whether it is committed in a way which makes it likely to reach a great number of people.

C22.4   SM CIVIL LAW CASES

Rt-2012-901 (decision by the Norwegian Supreme Court). In this case, two Facebook groups wanted to present a written submission to make a certain point in a case. The concrete question was related to insurance for judges pursuant to the Act relating to the courts of justice (*Domstolloven*, 1905) section 60.

The question before the court was whether the Facebook groups were 'organisations or associations' within the meaning of the Norwegian Dispute Act (*Tvisteloven*) section 15-8 (1) litra a.

The Supreme Court found that the term 'organisations' had to be interpreted identically for the entire Dispute Act. In sections 1-4 and 2-1, the term 'organisations' is linked to their right of legal actions. The court stated that the Facebook groups did not have a formal membership arrangement, they did not have any articles of association, nor did they have an administrative board of their own. The court noted that the groups had administrators, but their role was marginal, and the court compared their role to administrators in forums or boards of discussion. The court also stated that the membership of Facebook groups differs from those of formal organisations and associations because the members are not represented by the administrators.

The court therefore found that the Facebook groups were not 'organisations' in the meaning of the Dispute Act section 15-8 (1) litra a.

C22.5   CASES WHERE SM-RELATED EVIDENCE USED OR ADMISSIBLE

See C22.19.

C22.6   SPECIFIC ONLINE ABUSE/ONLINE BULLYING/ CYBERBULLYING LAWS

There are no laws that address online hate speech/abuse or cyberbullying specifically. However, as mentioned above, the legal definition of 'public' in section 7 was amended as a result of the decision in Rt-2012-1211. As a result of this change, hateful expressions towards minority groups that are published in open forums online are considered 'public', and thus are regulated and punishable under section 135a of the Penal Code.

It is important to note that section 135a of the Penal Code only protects certain listed minority groups from online abuse/cyberbullying. Online abuse/cyberbullying in general is not prohibited by this provision. However, cyberbullying or hateful statements made online can in some instances be considered defamatory and thus a breach of section 246 or 247 of the Penal Code.

C22.7 OTHER LAWS APPLIED TO ONLINE ABUSE/ ONLINE BULLYING/CYBERBULLYING

There are few examples of cases concerning online abuse or cyberbullying in the Norwegian court system. However, one example is TOSLO-2013-193789 (decision by the District Court of Oslo). The case was a result of several statements made by the defendant on the Facebook group 'Profetens Ummah'. One of the main questions in this case was whether Norwegian Jews were to be considered a minority group, in which case they would be protected against hateful statements online under section 135a of the Penal Code. The court concluded that Norwegian Jews are a minority group and that the statements made by the defendant in the Facebook group were to be considered hateful. Thus the defendant was convicted under section 135a of the Penal Code.

C22.8 CHILDREN AND SM LAWS OR RULES

There are no such laws or regulations.

C22.9 EMPLOYEES/EMPLOYMENT SM LAWS OR CASES

A police officer was dismissed because of how he used his private Facebook profile. The reason for his dismissal was a combination of his profile photo, where he wore his uniform, and statements made from that same profile. The first statement was about the length of sentence for use of violence, and the second was a very negative description of the Norwegian Prime Minister.

After several rounds in both the local and central board of selection for police officers, the decision was withdrawn and the police officer was reinstated. (See www.nrk.no/ho/_-ytringsfriheten-har-visse-grenser-1.11214506 and www. aftenposten.no/nyheter/iriks/Politimann-mister-likevel-ikke-jobben-7493454. html.)

C22.10 SCHOOL AND UNIVERSITY STUDENT SM CASES

There are no specific laws addressing the issue of the use of SM sites in schools or universities. There are no known cases regarding this topic either.

However, the issue has been raised in the Official Norwegian Report 2009:1 by the Government-appointed Privacy Commission. The Privacy Commission states that

'in the same way adults have a right to privacy at work, students have a right to a private life at school ... Surveillance at school, both in terms

469

of monitoring the use of PCs and other sorts of surveillance, raises questions about the signals that are sent out to young people when it comes to intervening with someone's personal integrity. If children grow up in a society where surveillance is accepted, even when the problem can be effectively addressed by less invasive measures, they will lose perspectives that are fundamental to have when they grow up to play a part in our democracy.' (page 129 in the report, author's translation)

C22.11   RIGHT OR HUMAN RIGHT TO ACCESS THE INTERNET OR SM

There is no such specific right, but such restrictions would in general need to be necessary to safeguard legitimate interests and proportional to avoid being unlawful according to the right to freedom of speech guaranteed in the Norwegian Constitution Article 100 and ECHR Article 10.

C22.12   BANS OR RESTRICTIONS ON INTERNET OR SM

According to the Norwegian Criminal Procedure Act (*Straffeprosessloven*) section 186, when a person is placed in custody, the court can also deny access to the internet and SM (letter ban). Such a restriction can only be imposed if necessary due to further investigations. This authority is quite often used by the courts.

C22.13   IDENTITY THEFT (OR EQUIVALENT)

Identity theft is regulated in the Penal Code (*Straffeloven* 1902), section 190a,

'Any person who unlawfully obtains another person's proof of identity, or uses another person's identity or an identity which may easily be confused with another person's identity, with the intention of

a)   achieving an unjust enrichment for him or herself or another; or

b)   causing another person a loss or disadvantage,

shall be liable to fines or imprisonment for a term not exceeding 2 years.

Any person who aids and abets such an offence shall be liable to the same penalty.' (author's translation)

C22.14   HACKING (OR EQUIVALENT)

This is regulated in the Penal Code section 145,

'Any person who unlawfully opens a letter or other closed document or in a similar manner gains access to its contents, or who breaks into another person's locked repository shall be liable to fines or imprisonment for a term not exceeding six months or to both.

The same penalty shall apply to any person who unlawfully obtains data or software which are stored or transferred by electronic or other technical means.

If damage is caused by the acquisition or use of such unlawful knowledge, or if the felony is committed for the purpose of obtaining for any person an unlawful gain, imprisonment for a term not exceeding two years may be imposed.

Any person who aids and abets such an offence shall be liable to the same penalty.

A public prosecution will only be instituted when it is required in the public interest.'

For an unofficial translation of the Penal Code, see www.ub.uio.no/ujur/ulovdata/lov-19020522-010-eng.pdf.

C22.15   PRIVACY BY DESIGN (PBD) (OR EQUIVALENT)

The Data Protection Act (*Personopplysningsloven*) contains general provisions with regard to adequate technical and organisational security measures, data minimisation and the data subject's right to information and control/involvement with regard to processing of his/her personal data. However, the Act does not contain any specific provisions requiring such measures to be integrated in the systems by design.

On a political level, PbD has been highlighted as an important measure to ensure effective safeguarding of privacy. PbD was an important element in the Official Norwegian Report 2009:1 by the Privacy Commission: see www.regjeringen.no/nb/dep/kmd/dok/nouer/2009/nou-2009-1.html?id=542049.

The importance of PbD was also emphasised in a follow-up Report to the Parliament (Meld St 11 (2012-2013) of the Privacy Commissions report: www.regjeringen.no/nb/dep/kmd/dok/regpubl/stmeld/2012-2013/meld-st-11-20122013.html?id=709739.

The Norwegian Data Protection Authority (*Datatilsynet*) is also concerned with PbD and with providing information to the relevant actors and stakeholders on this topic. More information can be found at www.datatilsynet.no/teknologi/innebygd-personvern/.

C22.16   TWEETING FROM COURTS, AND ANY RULES/LAWS

The general rule is that trials are public – see the Act relating to the court of justice (1915) (*domstolloven*) section 124. It is permissible to report from public trials. To Tweet is a way of reporting, and may therefore be accepted.

There are some exceptions to the general rule that trials are public. Firstly, it is normally not permissible to Tweet in court during proceedings relating to pre-trial detention – see section 129 of the Act relating to the court of justice. Secondly, the court can decide that a trial will be closed, eg on grounds of privacy – see section 125. It is not permissible to Tweet during closed trials.

C22.17   TELEVISION COURTROOM BROADCASTING OR TELEVISION CAMERAS IN COURT, AND RULES OR LAWS

For criminal cases, this is regulated by the Act relating to the court of justice (1915) (*domstolloven*) section 131a. The basic rule is that any broadcasting from the courtroom is prohibited. The court can make an exception when it can be assumed that the broadcasting will not have an unfortunate effect on the case.

The rule in section 131a does not apply to civil cases. Civil cases are regulated by section 133, which is a more general rule about the judge's trial management. This means that it is for each judge to decide, on a case-to-case basis, whether it should be broadcast or not.

There is no tradition in Norway for television broadcasting from the court.

C22.18   SM IN COURTROOMS

During the proceedings relating to pre-trial detention in the criminal case against Anders Behring Breivik (a famous trial in Norwegian history relating to the tragic event at Utøya in July 2012), a 16-year-old boy Tweeted from court. This was unlawful according to the Act relating to the court of justice (1915) (*domstolloven*) section 129. The boy did not know his action was unlawful, but he soon realised as several journalists made him aware on Twitter. The incident had no legal consequences for the boy (see http://e24.no/media/16-aaring-tvitret-fra-rettsmoetet-visste-ikke-at-det-var-ulovlig/20121633).

C22.19   USE OF SM AS EVIDENCE IN COURTS

There are several cases in which SM has been used as evidence in courts in relation to cases concerning sexual activity with minors. In Rt-2013-1211 (decision by the Norwegian Supreme Court) a Norwegian mayor was convicted for sexual activity with a minor. The court partly built the decision on evidence in the form of extracts from Skype conversations between the defendant and the victim, as relied on in case LE-2013-10608-2 (decision by Eidsivating Court of Appeal).

Also in other legal areas, SM has been used as evidence in courts. For instance, in LB-2013-71790 (decision by Borgarting Court of Appeal) the defendant was charged with threatening to kill someone. In a Facebook message to his previous girlfriend, the defendant had threatened to kill her and a number of other people. The court used the Facebook message as evidence of the defendant having committed the crime. The defendant was convicted under section 227 of the Penal Code, which prohibits the issuing of threats to commit crimes that can be penalised with more than six months' imprisonment.

C22.20   PRIVACY, DATA PROTECTION AND SM

In a case regarding a temporary precautionary measure before the Office of the City Recorder (Oslo byfogdembete, TOBYF-2013-39383), the court ordered a Norwegian blogger to delete certain blog posts that contained sensitive private information about two Norwegian public persons. The court found that the posts constituted a breach of the right to privacy under section 390 of the Penal Code. Since the information concerned personal relations between two people who did not have official positions in Norwegian society, the right to privacy prevailed over freedom of speech. The court decided that the blog posts had to be removed immediately in order to prevent any further damage.

C22.21   SM AND FAMILY LAW CASES

LB-2013-31903 (a decision by Eidsivating Court of Appeal) concerned questions of custody, visitation rights and living arrangements for two children. The mother's use of SM sites, in this case Facebook, was used to shed light on her personality. The court viewed the mother's many outbursts on Facebook as evidence of her lacking the ability to control impulsive actions when she got angry. This was one of the court's main arguments for giving the father custody of the children.

C22.22   SPORTS PERSONS, SPORTS CLUBS AND SM

There are no known major scandals involving Norwegian sports persons and the use of SM sites. However, as a result of many minor incidents (see eg www.tv2.no/sport/fotball/tippeligaen/igiebor-det-er-skammelig-3538726.html and www.nrk.no/mr/ville-du-sagt-det-samme-pa-tv_-1.8348769), NISO (the Norwegian sport persons' union) has developed a set of guidelines for the use of SM sites. The guidelines are specifically directed towards sports persons, due to their being in the public eye and thus risking causing major scandals if using SM inappropriately, and are available online at www.vg.no/sport/her-er-nisos-ti-raad-til-utoevere-paa-sosiale-medier/a/10046752/.

C22.23   PERSONAL RELATIONS AND RELATIONSHIPS

There are no known cases that have gone to court. However, the Official Norwegian Report 2009:1 chapter 14.3.4 raises the issue. The Commission on Privacy mentions an example of a false profile being made in the name of a 13-year-old girl on a popular Norwegian webpage. The profile contained substantial amounts of correct personal information about the girl, and the profile stated that the girl wanted sexual contact with older men and that she fantasised about being raped at home. The incident was reported to the police and they discovered that the profile was created by a person in the girl's social circle as revenge because of a disagreement. The issue was presumably resolved between the involved parties without litigation.

C22.24   SM AND PERSONAL DATA OF DECEASED PERSONS

There have been incidents where the police have had trouble cooperating with SM sites in situations where the person is missing but not confirmed deceased. An example of this is the case of the disappearance of Sigrid Schjetnes (see www.vg.no/nyheter/innenriks/sigrid-drapet/facebook-vi-har-gitt-fra-oss-informasjonen-om-sigrid/a/10059575/).

Due to the large need, the Norwegian government has funded the development of a service called slettmeg.no (translated as 'DeleteMe.no'). This service provides information and guidance to people who are experiencing unwanted exposure on the internet. Among the guidelines they have developed is thorough information on how to go about deleting a deceased person's profile on SM sites (see https://slettmeg.no/nyheter/avdode-personer-levende-profiler).

C22.25   SM, WEBSITE, SERVICE PROVIDER OR ISP DEFENCE RULES/LAWS

The Norwegian eCommerce Act (*E-handelsloven*) implements the EU eCommerce Directive. Sections 16 to 18 of the Act provide defences for service providers in this sector and are similar to Articles 12 to 14 of the eCommerce Directive.

C22.26   ECOMMERCE DEFENCE CASES

In 2010 the Norwegian telecom company Telenor was sued by several owners of intellectual property rights. The plaintiffs claimed that Telenor should block the website 'Pirate Bay' and demanded a preliminary injunction. The plaintiffs argued that Telenor contributed to unlawful file-sharing among their end users. The Court of Appeal (LB-2010-6542)/(RG-2010-171) rejected the claim with reference to the Norwegian Act regarding intellectual property rights (Åndsverkloven) which did not make the alleged complicity unlawful. The Court of Appeal commented on the Norwegian Act on e-commerce and said that Telenor's actions – simply transmitting information – most likely was lawful, regardless of the defences in the eCommerce Act.

In 2013 a new provision was added to the Norwegian Act regarding intellectual property rights (section 56 c) where the court may order ISPs to prevent or impede access to websites where content which evidently infringes copyright is made available to a large extent. For an unofficial translation of the Act regarding intellectual property rights, see www.kopinor.no/en/copyright/copyright-act.

The new provision 56 c (author's translation):

'*Section 56c Order to prevent or impede access to websites making available content infringing copyright etc*

Upon a petition from a rights holder the court may order a service provider that offers information society services pursuant to the Electronic Commerce Act section 1 (2) b) to prevent or impede access to websites where content which evidently infringes copyright or other rights pursuant to this Act is made available to a large extent.

In order for the petition to be approved by the court the considerations that favours that an order is given must outweigh the disadvantages that the order will involve. When assessing the court shall balance the interests that calls for the access to the website being prevented or impeded against other interests affected by such order, including the interest of the one that the order is directed at and the owner of the website, and the consideration of freedom of information and freedom of expression. The court shall also take in to consideration the possibility of alternative and less radical measures.

The King may through regulations provide provisions about which orders that can be given to prevent or impede access to a website.'

C22.27 LAWS PROTECTING PERSONAL DATA/ PERSONALLY IDENTIFIABLE INFORMATION

The Norwegian Data Protection Act (*personopplysningsloven*) implements the Data Protection Directive 95/46/EC and provides general rules for the processing of personal data. In addition, Norway has sector-specific privacy and data protection legislation. Important examples are the Personal health data filing system Act (*Helseregisterloven*), with specific requirements regarding the establishment of a health register and the processing of health-related information, and the Act regarding the processing of personal data by the police and prosecuting authority (*Politiregisterloven*).

In addition to the abovementioned Acts, there is legislation dealing with different kinds of matters which also provides data protection in specific situations. An example is the Norwegian Act regarding medical research (*Helseforskningloven*), where it is clearly stated that data protection is an important aspect of safeguarding the integrity of the participants.

C22.28   DATA BREACH LAWS AND CUSTOMERS/ USERS/REGULATORS NOTIFIED OF HACKING OR DATA LOSS

According to section 2-6 of the Data Protection Regulation (*Personopplysningsforskriften*), the data controller must notify the Norwegian Data Protection Authority in case of unauthorized disclosure of confidential information.

Senegal

Boubacar Borgho DIAKITE
Geni & Kebe Law Firm

C23.1   INTRODUCTION

Senegal is a mixed Common Law and Civil Law jurisdiction.

C23.2   SPECIFIC SM AND SN LAWS

There are no specific SM or SN laws. The Government of Senegal has established a new legal framework for information technology and communication through laws passed by the National Assembly, which comprises five laws: the Law on the information society, the Law on electronic transactions, the Law on cybercrime, the Law on the protection of personal data, and the Law on cryptology.

C23.3   SM CRIMINAL LAW CASES

The only criminal cases relating to SM have involved hacking Facebook accounts. Usually, hackers are very rarely found and arrested.

C23.4   SM CIVIL LAW CASES

These types of cases are very rarely mentioned in court.

C23.5   CASES WHERE SM-RELATED EVIDENCE USED OR ADMISSIBLE

No details.

C23.6   SPECIFIC ONLINE ABUSE/ONLINE BULLYING/ CYBERBULLYING LAWS

There are no such laws.

C23.7 OTHER LAWS APPLIED TO ONLINE ABUSE/ ONLINE BULLYING/CYBERBULLYING

The Law on cybercrime has been applied in some cases.

C23.8 CHILDREN AND SM LAWS OR RULES

There are no laws or rules specific to children and SM.

C23.9 EMPLOYEES/EMPLOYMENT SM LAWS OR CASES

Sometimes there are cases where an employer blames his employee's misuse of SM during working hours. Usually these cases can lead to claims of unfair dismissal before the court.

C23.10 SCHOOL AND UNIVERSITY STUDENT SM CASES

There have been cases dealing with the dissemination of images or pornographic videos involving students.

C23.11 RIGHT OR HUMAN RIGHT TO ACCESS THE INTERNET OR SM

There is no specific legislation on this issue, but there are laws that guarantee free access to the new technologies of communication and information.

C23.12 BANS OR RESTRICTIONS ON INTERNET OR SM

There is not any literature, cases, rules or laws in relation to bans or restrictions on the use of or access to the internet or SM. The prosecution of persons for hacking or child pornography has been done under the provisions of the Law on cybercrime.

C23.13 IDENTITY THEFT (OR EQUIVALENT)

Identify theft is dealt with in the Penal Code.

C23.14   HACKING (OR EQUIVALENT)

Hacking is dealt with in the Law on cybercrime.

C23.15   PRIVACY BY DESIGN (PBD) (OR EQUIVALENT)

There are no rules, laws or discussion dealing with this issue.

C23.16   TWEETING FROM COURTS, AND ANY RULES/LAWS

It is not permissible to Tweet from courts during a session.

C23.17   TELEVISION COURTROOM BROADCASTING OR TELEVISION CAMERAS IN COURT, AND RULES OR LAWS

No television courtroom broadcasting or television cameras are permitted in court.

C23.18   SM IN COURTROOMS

No details. Usually before the start of the hearing, the judges invite the public to turn off every electronic device (such as laptop and cell phone).

C23.19   USE OF SM AS EVIDENCE IN COURTS

SM was used as evidence in a case of rape on a minor girl. The Facebook account of the victim had been hacked, but the girl had time to save messages which directly led to the accused being found guilty.

C23.20   PRIVACY, DATA PROTECTION AND SM

There have been cases like this. As regards the protection of personal data, Senegal voted a law to this effect very recently.

C23.21   SM AND FAMILY LAW CASES

No details.

C23.22   SPORTS PERSONS, SPORTS CLUBS AND SM

There have never been any such cases in Senegal.

C23.23 PERSONAL RELATIONS AND RELATIONSHIPS

The courts consider such cases very often in Senegal, where a spouse, for revenge, posts intimate pictures or videos of their partner on SM. .

C23.24 SM AND PERSONAL DATA OF DECEASED PERSONS

There have never been such examples.

C23.25 SM, WEBSITE, SERVICE PROVIDER OR ISP DEFENCE RULES/LAWS

There are regulatory provisions relating to electronic/online trade.

C23.26 ECOMMERCE DEFENCE CASES

No details, because e-commerce is very recent in Senegal.

C23.27 LAWS PROTECTING PERSONAL DATA/ PERSONALLY IDENTIFIABLE INFORMATION

For example,

- Law No 2008-10 of 25 January 2008 on the information society (LOSI);
- Law No 2008-12 of 25 January 2008 on the protection of personal data;
- Law No 2008-08 of 25 January 2008 on electronic transactions;
- Law No 2008-11 of 25 January 2008 on cybercrime.

C23.28 DATA BREACH LAWS AND CUSTOMERS/ USERS/REGULATORS NOTIFIED OF HACKING OR DATA LOSS

No details.

Chapter C24

Serbia

Bojana N Novaković
Baklaja & Igrić

C24.1   INTRODUCTION

The Republic of Serbia is a candidate country for EU membership and is a Civil Law jurisdiction.

C24.2   SPECIFIC SM AND SN LAWS

There are no specific regulations governing SM and SN in the Republic of Serbia.

C24.3   SM CRIMINAL LAW CASES

We do not know of any such cases, but the same may exist for example in connection with certain crimes which may be applicable to SM, and which are prescribed by the Criminal Code of the Republic of Serbia ('Official Gazette of the RS', nos 85/2005, 88/2005, 107/2005, 72/2009, 111/2009, 121/2012 and 104/2013)[1] as follows,

'Ill-treatment and Torture

Article 137

(1)   Whoever ill-treats another or treats such person in humiliating and degrading manner, shall be punished with fine or imprisonment up to one year.

(2)   Whoever causes anguish to another with the aim to obtain from him or another information or confession or to intimidate him or a third party or to exert pressure on such persons, or if done from motives based on any form of discrimination, shall be punished with imprisonment from six months to five years.

---

1   Please note that there is no available version of this law in English.

(3)   If the offence specified in paragraphs 1 and 2 of this Article is committed by an official in discharge of duty,

such person shall be punished for the offence in paragraph 1 by imprisonment from three months to three years, and for the offence specified in paragraph 2 of this Article by imprisonment of one to eight years.

Insult

Article 170

(1)   Whoever insults another person, shall be punished with a fine ranging from twenty to one hundred daily amounts or a fine ranging from forty thousand to two hundred thousand dinars.

(2)   If the offence specified in paragraph 1 of this Article is committed through the press, radio, television or other media or at a public gathering, the offender shall be punished with a fine ranging from eighty to two hundred and forty daily amounts or a fine ranging from one hundred and fifty to four hundred and fifty thousand dinars.

(3)   If the insulted person returns the insult, the court may punish or remit punishment of both parties or one party.

(4)   There shall be no punishment of the perpetrator for offences specified in paragraphs 1 through 3 of this Article if the statement is given within the framework of serious critique in a scientific, literary or art work, in discharge of official duty, journalist tasks, political activity, in defence of a right or defence of justifiable interests, if it is evident from the manner of expression or other circumstances that it was not done with intent to disparage.

Dissemination of Information on Personal and Family Life

Article 172

(1)   Whoever relates or disseminates information of anyone's personal or family life that may harm his honour or reputation, shall be punished with a fine or imprisonment up to six months.

(2)   If the offence specified in paragraph 1 of this Article is committed through press, radio, television or other media or at a public gathering, the offender shall be punished with a fine or imprisonment up to one year.

(3)   If what is related or disseminated resulted or could have resulted in serious consequences for the injured party, the offender shall be punished with imprisonment up to three years.

(4)   The offender shall not be punished for relating or disseminating information on personal or family life in discharge of official duty, journalist profession, defending a right or defending justifiable public interest, if he proves the veracity of his allegations or if he

proves reasonable grounds for belief that the allegations he related or disseminated were true.

(5)   Veracity or falsehood of related or disseminated information from the personal or family life of a person may not be evidenced, except in cases specified in paragraph 4 of this Article.

Ruining the Reputation of Republic of Serbia

Article 173

Whoever publicly ridicules Republic of Serbia, its flag, coat of arms or anthem, shall be punished with a fine or imprisonment up to three months.

Damaging the reputation for racial, religious, ethnic or other affiliations

Article 174

Whoever publicly ridicules a person or group because of a certain race, colour, religion, nationality, ethnic origin, or other personal characteristics, shall be punished by a fine or imprisonment of up to one year.

Violation of reputation of foreign country or an international organization

Article 175

(1)   Whoever publicly ridicules a foreign state, its flag, coat of arms or anthem, shall be punished with a fine or imprisonment up to three months.

(2)   The penalty specified in paragraph 1 of this Article shall be imposed on whoever publicly ridicules the Organization of the United Nations, International Red Cross or other international organization where Serbia is member.

Impunity for Criminal Offences referred in Articles 173 through 175

Article 176

There shall be no punishment of the perpetrator for offences specified in Articles 173 through 175 if the statement is given within the framework of serious critique in a scientific, literary or art work, in discharge of official duty, performing journalist duties, political activity, in defence of a right or defence of justifiable interests, if it is evident from the manner of expression or other circumstances that it was not done with intent to disparage or if he proves the veracity of his allegations or that he had reasonable grounds to believe that what he said or disseminated was true.

Prosecution for Offences against Honour and Reputation

Article 177

(1)   Prosecution for offences specified in Articles 170 through 172 hereof is undertaken by private action.

(2)   If offences specified in Articles 170 through 172 hereof are committed against a deceased person, prosecution is instituted by private action of the spouse of the deceased or person cohabiting with the deceased, lineal descendant, adoptive parent, adopted child, or the deceased person's sibling.

(3)   Prosecution for criminal offence specified in Article 175 hereof is undertaken upon approval of the Republic Public Prosecutor.

Mediation in Prostitution

Article 184

(1)   Whoever causes or induces another person to prostitution or participates in handing over a person to another for the purpose of prostitution, or who by means of media or otherwise promotes or advertises prostitution, shall be punished with imprisonment from six months to five years and fine.

(2)   If the offence specified in paragraph 1 of this Article is committed against a minor, the offender shall be punished with imprisonment from one to ten years and fine.

Showing Pornographic Material and Child Pornography

Article 185

(1)   Whoever sells, shows or publicly displays or otherwise makes available texts, pictures, audio-visual or other items of pornographic content to a child or shows to a child a pornographic performance, shall be punished with a fine or imprisonment up to six months.

(2)   Whoever uses a child to produce photographs, audio-visual or other items of pornographic content or for a pornographic show, shall be punished with imprisonment from six months to five years.

(3)   If the offense referred to in paragraphs. 1 and 2 of this Article is committed against a child, the offender shall be punished for an offense referred to in paragraph 1 by imprisonment of six months to three years, and for the offense referred to in paragraph 2 by imprisonment of one to eight years.

(4)   Whoever obtains for himself or another, possesses, sells, shows, publicly exhibits or in electronic or otherwise makes available pictures, audio-visual or other objects of pornographic content resulting from abuse of a minor, shall be punished with imprisonment of three months to three years.

(5)   Items specified in paragraphs 1 through 4 of this Article shall be confiscated.

The exploitation computer network or other means of communication to commit offenses against sexual freedom of a minor

Article 185b

(1)   Whoever, with intent to commit a criminal offense under Art. 178, paragraph 4, 179 paragraph 3, 180 paragraph 1 and 2, 181 paragraph 2 and 3, 182 paragraph 1, 183 paragraph 2, 184 paragraph 3, 185, and 185a, paragraph 2, of the Code, using a computer network or other means of communication with a minor contracts a meeting and show up at the place of the meeting , shall be punished with imprisonment from six months to five years and fined.

(2)   Whoever commits the offense specified in paragraph 1 of this Article against a child, shall be punished with imprisonment of one to eight years.

Violation of Moral Right of Author and Performer

Article 198

(1)   Whoever under his name or the name of another publishes or puts into circulation copies of another's copyrighted work or performance or otherwise publicly presents another's copyrighted work or performance, in entirety or in part, shall be punished with a fine or imprisonment up to three years.

(2)   Whoever without the author's permission alters or adapts another's copyrighted work or alters another's recorded performance, shall be punished with a fine or imprisonment up to one year.

(3)   Whoever puts into circulation copies of another's copyrighted work or performance in a manner insulting the honour and reputation of the author or performer, shall be punished with a fine or imprisonment up to six months.

(4)   Things referred to under paragraphs 1 through 3 of this Article shall be seized.

(5)   Prosecution for offences specified in paragraph 2 of this Article is initiated by the prosecution, and for offences referred to in paragraph 3 of this Article by private action.

Unauthorised Use of Copyrighted Work or other Work Protected by Similar Right

Article 199

(1)   Whoever without permission publishes, records, copies or otherwise presents in public, in part or entirety, a copyrighted work, performance, phonogram, videogram, show, computer programme or database, shall be punished with a fine or imprisonment up to three years.

(2) The punishment specified in paragraph 1 of this Article shall also be imposed on a person who puts into circulation or with intent to put into circulation keeps illegally multiplied or illegally put into circulation copies of copyrighted work, performance, phonogram, videogram, show, computer program or database.

(3) If the offence referred to in paragraphs 1 and 2 of this Article was committed with intent to acquire material gain for oneself or another, the offender shall be punished with imprisonment from six months to five years.

(4) Whoever produces, imports, puts into circulation, sells, rents, advertises for sale or renting, or keeps for commercial purposes, equipment and devices whose basic or prevailing purpose is to remove, bypass or forestall technological measures intended for prevention of violation of copyright and other similar rights, or who uses such equipment or devices with an aim to violate copyright or other similar right, shall be punished with a fine or imprisonment up to three years.

(5) The things referred to in paragraphs 1 through 4 shall be seized and destroyed.

Unauthorised Removal or Altering of Electronic Information on Copyright and Similar Rights

Article 200

(1) Whoever without authorisation removes or alters electronic information on copyright or other similar right, or puts into circulation, imports, exports, broadcasts or otherwise presents in public a copyrighted work or other work protected by similar right, from which electronic information on rights was removed or altered without authorisation, shall be punished with a fine and imprisonment up to three years.

(2) The things referred to in paragraph 1 shall be seized and destroyed.

Violation of Patent Rights

Article 201

(1) Whoever without permission produces, imports, exports, offers for circulation, puts into circulation, stores or uses for commercial operations a patented product or procedure, shall be punished with a fine or imprisonment up to three years.

(2) If the offence referred to in paragraph 1 results in material gain or damage in an amount exceeding one million dinars, the offender shall be punished with imprisonment from one to eight years.

(3)   Whoever without permission publishes or otherwise presents in public the essence of another's patent that has been applied for, before such patent is published in the manner set out by law, shall be punished with a fine or imprisonment up to two years.

(4)   Whoever without permission applies for a patent or fails to give or gives incorrect name of inventor in the application, shall be punished with imprisonment from six months to five years.

(5)   The things referred to in paragraphs 1 and 2 shall be seized and destroyed.

Unauthorised Use of another's Design

Article 202

(1)   Whoever on his product in circulation uses without authorisation another's design which has been applied for or protected, shall be punished with a fine or imprisonment up to three years.

(2)   Whoever without authorisation publishes or otherwise presents in public the essence of another's design before it has been published in the manner set out by law, shall be punished with a fine or imprisonment up to one year.

(3)   The products referred to in paragraph 1 of this Article shall be seized.

Fraud

Article 208

(1)   Whoever with intent to acquire unlawful material gain for himself or another by false presentation or concealment of facts deceives another or maintains such deception and thus induces such person to act to the prejudice of his or another's property, shall be punished with imprisonment from six months to five years and fine.

(2)   Whoever commits the offence specified in paragraph 1 of this Article only with intent to cause damage to another, shall be punished with imprisonment up to six months and fine.

(3)   If by the offence specified in paragraph 1 and 2 of this Article material gain is acquired or damages caused exceeding four hundred and fifty thousand dinars, the offender shall be punished with imprisonment of one to eight years and fine.

(4)   If by the offence specified in paragraph 1 and 2 of this Article material gain is acquired or damages caused exceeding million five hundred thousand dinars, the offender shall be punished by imprisonment of two to ten years and fined.

CHAPTER TWENTY SEVEN

CRIMINAL OFFENCE AGAINST SECURITY OF COMPUTER DATA

Damaging Computer Data and Programs

Article 298

(1) Whoever without authorisation deletes, alters, damages, conceals or otherwise makes unusable a computer datum or program, shall be punished by fine or imprisonment up to one year.

(2) If the offence specified in paragraph 1 of this Article results in damages exceeding four hundred and fifty thousand dinars, the offender shall be punished by imprisonment of three months to three years.

(3) If the offence specified in paragraph 1 of this Article results in damages exceeding one million five hundred thousand dinars, the offender shall be punished by imprisonment of three months to five years.

(4) Equipment and devices used in perpetration of the offence specified in paragraphs 1 and 2 of this Article shall be seized.

Computer Sabotage

Article 299

Whoever enters, destroys, deletes, alters, damages, conceals or otherwise makes unusable computer data or program or damages or destroys a computer or other equipment for electronic processing and transfer of data, with intent to prevent or considerably disrupt the procedure of electronic processing and transfer of data that are of importance for government authorities, enterprises or other entities, shall be punished by imprisonment of six months to five years.

Creating and Introducing of Computer Viruses

Article 300

(1) Whoever makes a computer virus with intent to introduce it into another's computer or computer network, shall be punished by fine or imprisonment up to six months.

(2) Whoever introduces a computer virus into another's computer or computer network thereby causing damage, shall be punished by fine or imprisonment up to two years.

(3) Equipment and devices used for committing of the offence specified in paragraphs 1 and 2 of this Article shall be seized.

Computer Fraud

Article 301

(1) Whoever enters incorrect data, fails to enter correct data or otherwise conceals or falsely represents data and thereby affects the results of

electronic processing and transfer of data with intent to acquire for himself or another unlawful material gain and thus causes material damage to another person, shall be punished by fine or imprisonment up to three years.

(2)   If the offence specified in paragraph 1 of this Article results in acquiring material gain exceeding four hundred and fifty hundred thousand dinars, the offender shall be punished by imprisonment of one to eight years.

(3)   If the offence specified in paragraph 1 of this Article results in acquiring material gain exceeding one million five hundred thousand dinars, the offender shall be punished by imprisonment of two to ten years.

(4)   Whoever commits the offence specified in paragraph 1 of this Article from malicious mischief, shall be punished by fine or imprisonment up to six months.

Unauthorised Access to Computer, Computer Network or Electronic Data Processing

Article 302

(1)   Whoever, by circumventing protection measures, accesses a computer or computer network without authorisation, or accesses electronic data processing without authorisation, shall be punished by fine or imprisonment up to six months.

(2)   Whoever copies or uses data obtained in manner provided under paragraph 1 of this Article, shall be punished by fine or imprisonment up to two years.

(3)   If the offence specified in paragraph 1 of this Article results in hold-up or serious malfunction in electronic processing and transfer of data or of the network, or other grave consequences have resulted, the offender shall be punished by imprisonment up to three years.

Preventing or Restricting Access to Public Computer Network

Article 303

(1)   Whoever without authorisation prevents or hinders access to a public computer network, shall be punished by fine or imprisonment up to one year.

(2)   If the offence specified in paragraph 1 of this Article is committed by an official in discharge of duty, such official shall be punished by imprisonment up to three years.

Unauthorised Use of Computer of Computer Network

Article 304

(1)   Whoever uses computer services or computer network with intent to acquire unlawful material gain for himself or another, shall be punished by fine or imprisonment up to three months.

(2)   Prosecution for the offence specified in paragraph 1 of this Article shall be instigated by private action.

Making, supply and lend funds to commit offenses against the security of computer data

Article 304a

(1)   Whoever possesses, purchases, sells or gives to another the use of computers, computer systems, computer data and programs to commit a criminal offense under Art. 298 to 303 of this Code, shall be punished with imprisonment from six months to three years.

(2)   The items referred to in paragraph 1 of this Article shall be forfeited.

Impersonation

Article 329

(1)   Whoever with intent to acquire for himself or another any benefit or cause damage to a third person, impersonates an official or member of the military or wears insignia of an official or member of the military without authorisation, shall be punished by fine or imprisonment up to three years.

(2)   The penalty specified in paragraph 1 of this Article shall be imposed also on whoever performs an act that is under exclusive authority of an official or member of the military.

Causing Panic and Disorder

Article 343

(1)   Whoever by disclosing or disseminating untrue information or allegations causes panic, or serious disruption of public peace and order or frustrates or significantly impedes enforcing of decisions of government authorities or organisations exercising administrative authority, shall be punished with imprisonment of three months to three years and fined.

(2)   If the offence specified in paragraph 1 of this Article is committed through media or similar means or at public gathering, the offender shall be punished with imprisonment from six months to five years.'

In addition to the abovementioned, there was a case that was followed by the media and in which a journalist on his Facebook account offered a reward for killing the president of state: http://translate.google.com/translate?prev=_t&i e=UTF8&sl=sr&tl=en&u=http://www.pravda.rs/2014/03/23/pavle-cosic-evo-kako-sam-planirao-atentat-na-vucica/.

Also, there is the current case in which a person opened a Facebook account called 'Najveće drolje osnovnih i srednjih škola' ('The biggest sluts of elementary and secondary schools') which publishes provocative pictures of under-age girls that they themselves posted on their Facebook accounts. Since we do not have particular SM regulations, the professional community is discussing the possible liability of this person, and some of them think that his actions might be associated with a criminal offence related to promoting the publication of pornographic material, insult, torture and similar: www.kurir-info.rs/roditelji-tuzite-pedofile-sa-fejsbuka-oterajte-ih-sve-na-robiju-clanak-1334581.

Finally, regarding the actions of citizens during emergency situations in the country because of flooding, some media reported that several people were arrested for spreading panic through Facebook and other SM, because they claimed that, due to the flooding, there were more victims than the authorities announced: www.kurir-info.rs/privedeno-troje-beogradana-sirili-paniku-na-fejsbuku-preti-im-zatvor-clanak-1386409.

C24.4   SM CIVIL LAW CASES

We do not know of any such cases, but the same may exist for example in connection with compensation of material and non-material damages that occurred due to copyright infringement or the protection of privacy, eg where someone publishes another's photo under his own name, or processes it and publishes such an amended version, or publishes photographs of other persons without their consent, or makes offending comments.

The provisions of the Law on Obligations and Torts ('Official SFRY', nos 29/78, 39/85, 45/89 and 57/89, 'Official Gazette of the FRY', no 31/93 and 'Official Gazette of SMN', no 1/2003)[2] apply to civil law cases as general rules. However, regulations relating to the concrete subject matter (eg provisions of the Law on Copyright and Related Rights or other law) may be applied, which may provide something different from the general rules (according to the rule, *lex specialis derogat legi generali*).

The Law on Obligations and Torts is available online at www.drzavnauprava. gov.rs/files/The%20Law%20of%20Contract%20and%20Torts_180411. pdf; the Law on Copyright and Related Rights ('Official Gazette of the

---

2   Please note that Articles 154–209 of this law regulate the compensation of damage.

RS', nos 104/2009, 99/2011 and 119/2012) is available online at www.zis. gov.rs/upload/THE%20LAW%20ON%20COPYRIGHT%20AND%20 RELATED%20RIGHTS-version%20in%20force%204.1.2013._.pdf; and the Law on Protection of Personal Data ('Official Gazette of the RS', nos 97/2008, 104/2009, 68/2012 and 107/2012) is available online at www.poverenik.rs/en/ legal-framework/laws-zp.html.

Since there is no available version in English of the Law on Public Information ('Official Gazette of the RS', nos 43/2003, 61/2005, 71/2009, 89/2010 and 41/2011), we refer you to some of the relevant provisions of the respective law,

'Concept of a Media Outlet

Article 11

Media outlets are newspapers, radio programmers, television programmers, news agency services, Internet and other electronic editions of the above media outlets and other public information media that use words, images and sound to publish ideas, information and opinions intended for public dissemination and an unspecified number of users.

A media outlet shall not have the status of a legal person.

Protection of Minors

Article 41

To protect the rights of minors, media outlets must take into particular consideration that their content and manner of distribution do not impair the moral, intellectual, emotional and social development of minors.

The content of a media outlet, that might jeopardize the development of minors in terms of Paragraph1 of this Article must be clearly and visibly indicated as such in advance and distributed in a manner making it highly unlikely that a minor will use it.

A minor shall not be made recognizable in the information that is liable to violate his/her rights or interests.

Ban on Public Display of Pornography

Article 42

Printed matter with pornographic content shall not be publicly displayed in a manner making it accessible to minors.

Pornographic printed matter shall not contain pornography on the front or back cover pages and it must include a visible warning that it contains pornography, as well as a warning that it is not intended for minors.

Provisions of a separate Broadcasting Law shall apply to pornographic content in television and radio programs.

VIII

RIGHTS OF THE PERSONS TO WHOM THE INFORMATION REFERS

1. PUBLICATION OF INFORMATION FROM PRIVATE LIFE AND PERSONAL RECORDS

Information from Private Life and Personal Records

Article 43

Information regarding private facts or personal written records (a letter, diary, note, digital record, etc), recordings of images (photographs, drawings, film, video, digital etc) and audio recordings (tape - recordings, gramophone records, digital etc), may not be published without the consent of the person whose private life the information pertains to, or of the person whose words, image or voice it contains, if such publication can lead to the recognition of that person's identity.

Consent shall also be needed for the live transmission of image or voice (via television, radio, etc).

Information and records referred to in Paragraph 1 of this Article may not be published also without the consent of the person they are intended for, or of the person they pertain to, if such publication would infringe on that person's right to privacy or any other right.

Consent granted to one publication, to a specific manner of publication or to publication for a specific purpose, shall not be deemed consent to repeated publication, to publication in a different manner or to publication for a different purpose.

If compensation has been received for the consent to obtain information or to obtain or have insight in a record, it shall be deemed that consent has also been granted to its publication.

Consent of Other Persons

Article 44

If the person referred to in Paragraphs 1 and 2 of Article 43 of this Law is deceased, the consent shall be given by the spouse of the deceased, independently by his/her children having reached sixteen years of age, by his/her parents or brothers or sisters, by the legal person that the deceased participated in (official, member, employee) in the event the information or record refers to his/her activities in the legal person, or by the person authorized therefore by the deceased.

Termination of a legal entity shall not terminate the rights of the person that had participated in the legal entity and that has been personally affected by the information or record.

It shall be deemed that consent has been granted in the event it has been granted by any of the persons listed in Paragraph1 of this Article, notwithstanding the refusal of other persons to grant it.

Exceptional Publication without Consent

Article 45

Exceptionally from Article 43 of this Law, private information or personal records of a person may be published without the consent of the person they refer to if:

- the person had intended the information or the record for the public;

- the information, or record refers to a personality, phenomenon or event of public interest, especially if it applies to a holder of a state or political post and publishing the information is important in view of the fact that the person is discharging those duties;

- the person has given rise to the publication of such information or record by his/her behaviour;

- the information has been disclosed or the record made in a public parliamentary debate or a public debate in a parliamentary body;

- publication is in the interest of judiciary, national security or public security;

- the person did not object to the collection of information or the making of the record, although he/she was aware that this was done for publication purposes;

- publication is in the interest of science or education;

- publication is necessary to alert of a danger (prevention of a contagious disease, search for a missing person, fraud, etc);

- the record includes a multitude of persons or voices (fans, concert audience, protesters, passers-by etc);

- a record of a public gathering is at issue;

- the person is presented as part of the landscape, natural setting, human settlement, square, street or a similar scene.

Protection of the Right to Privacy or of the Right to Personal Records

Article 46

In the event of a breach of the right to privacy or of the right to personal records, the person whose right has been breached may initiate a lawsuit against the responsible editor of the media outlet and demand:

1.   non-publication of the information or record;

2.   the relinquishment of the record, removal or destruction of the published record (erasure of the video or audio recording, destruction of the film negative, removal from a publication, etc);

3.   compensation of material and non-material damages;

4.   publication of the court ruling.

If the published information used a personal record or private life data without authorization, the aggrieved party may demand in his/her charges against the responsible editor part of the profit accrued by publication, commensurate to the degree his/her personal record or private data contributed to the profit.

The lawsuit in Paragraphs 1 and 2 of this Article shall be filed with the district court that is competent for the territory where the seat of the media outlet founder is located.

The right to press charges in Paragraphs 1 and 2 of this Article shall not apply to a person if information about his/her private life or personal record had been published without his/her consent and he/she a posteriori consented to its publication.

Unless otherwise specified by this Law, provisions of a separate law on litigation shall apply to lawsuits concerning breaches of privacy, or the right to private records.'

C24.5   CASES WHERE SM-RELATED EVIDENCE USED OR ADMISSIBLE

We do not know of any such cases but, since legislation does not expressly limits the possibility of using such evidence, SM-related evidence may been used as evidence in court proceedings, but its rating depends on the judge's belief. Also, keeping in mind today's technological possibilities (hacking), such evidence could be challenged in the sense that it does not comes from the person who opened the SM account or to whom the SM account applies (eg false SM account opened in the name of one person by another person).

Since there is no available version of the law in English, we draw your attention to some of the relevant provisions of the Criminal Procedure code ('Official Gazette of the RS', nos 72/2011, 101/2011, 121/2012, 32/2013, 45/2013 and 55/2014),

'Assessing Evidence and Finding of Fact

Article 16

Court decisions may not be based on evidence which is, directly or indirectly, in itself or by the manner in which it was obtained, in contravention of the Constitution, this Code, other statute or universally accepted rules of international law and ratified international treaties, except in court proceedings in connection with the obtaining of such evidence.

The court is required to make an impartial assessment of the evidence examined and based on the evidence to establish with equal care both the facts against the defendant and the facts which are in his favour.

The court assesses the evidence examined which is of importance for rendering a decision at its discretion.

The court may base its judgment, or ruling corresponding to a judgment, only on facts of whose certainty it is convinced.

In case it has any doubts about the facts on which the conduct of criminal proceedings depends, the existence of the elements of a criminal offence, or application of another provision of criminal law, in its judgment, or ruling corresponding to a judgment, the court rules in favour of the defendant.

Unlawful Evidence

Article 84

Evidence collected in contravention of Article 16 paragraph 1 of this Code (unlawful evidence) may not be used in criminal proceedings.

Unlawful evidence is excluded from the case file, placed in a separate sealed cover and kept by the judge for preliminary proceedings until the final conclusion of the criminal proceedings, after which they are destroyed and a record is made about their destruction.

By exception from paragraph 2 of this Article, unlawful evidence is preserved until the final conclusion of court proceedings held in connection with the obtaining of such evidence.

Requirements for Ordering

Article 161

Special evidentiary actions may be ordered against a person for whom there are grounds for suspicion that he has committed a criminal offence referred to in Article 162 of this Code, and evidence for criminal prosecution cannot be acquired in another manner, or their gathering would be significantly hampered.

Special evidentiary actions may also exceptionally be ordered against a person for whom there are grounds for suspicion that he is preparing one of the criminal offences referred to in paragraph 1 of this Article, and the circumstances of the case indicate that the criminal offence could not be detected, prevented or proved in another way, or that it would cause disproportionate difficulties or a substantial danger.

In deciding on ordering and the duration of special evidentiary actions, the authority conducting proceedings will especially consider whether the same result could be achieved in a manner less restrictive to citizens' rights.

Criminal Offences in Respect of Which Special Evidentiary Actions are Applied

Article 162

Under the conditions referred to in Article 161 of this Code, special evidentiary actions may be ordered for the following criminal offences:

1) those which according to separate statute fall within the competence of a prosecutor's office of special jurisdiction;

2) aggravated murder (Article 114 of the Criminal Code), abduction (Article 134 of the Criminal Code), showing, procurement and possession of pornographic materials and exploiting juveniles for pornography (Article 185 paragraphs 2 and 3 of the Criminal Code), robbery (Article 206 para. 2 and 3 of the Criminal Code), extortion (Article 214 paragraph 4 of the Criminal Code), counterfeiting money (Article 223 paragraphs 1 to 3 of the Criminal Code), money laundering (Article 231 paragraphs 1 to 4 of the Criminal Code), abuse of position of the responsible person (Article 234 of the Criminal Code), abuse in connection with public procurement (Article 234a of the Criminal Code), unlawful production and circulation of narcotic drugs (Article 246 paragraphs 1 to 3 of the Criminal Code), threatening independence (Article 305 of the Criminal Code), threatening territorial integrity (Article 307 of the Criminal Code), sedition (Article 308 of the Criminal Code), inciting sedition (Article 309 of the Criminal Code), subversion (Article 313 of the Criminal Code), sabotage (Article 314 of the Criminal Code), espionage (Article 315 of the Criminal Code), divulging state secrets (Article 316 of the Criminal Code), inciting national, racial and religious hatred or intolerance (Article 317 of the Criminal Code), violation of territorial sovereignty (Article 318 of the Criminal Code), conspiring to conduct activities against the Constitution (Article 319 of the Criminal Code), plotting an offences against the constitutional order and security of Serbia (Article 320 of the Criminal Code), serious offences against the constitutional order and security of Serbia (Article 321 of the Criminal Code), illegal manufacture, possession and sale of weapons and explosive materials (Article 348 paragraph 3 of the Criminal Code), illegal crossing of the national boarder and human trafficking (Article 350 paragraphs 2 and 3 of the Criminal Code), abuse of office (Article 359 of the Criminal Code), trading in influences (Article 366 of the Criminal Code), taking bribes (Article 367 of the Criminal Code), offering bribes (Article 368 of the Criminal Code), human trafficking (Article 388 of the Criminal Code), taking hostages (Article 392 of the Criminal

Code) and the criminal offence referred to in Article 98 paragraphs 3 to 5 of the Law on the Secrecy of Data;

3)   obstruction of justice (Article 336 paragraph 1 of the Criminal Code), if committed in connection with the criminal offence referred to in items 1) and 2) of this paragraph.

A special evidentiary action referred to in Article 183 of this Code may be ordered only in connection with a criminal offence referred to in paragraph 1 item 1) of this Article.

Under the conditions referred to in Article 161 of this Code the special evidentiary action referred to in Article 166 of this Code may also be ordered for the following criminal offences:

unauthorised exploitation of copyrighted work or other works protected by similar rights (Article 199 of the Criminal Code), damaging computer data and programmes (Article 298 paragraph 3 of the Criminal Code), computer sabotage (Article 299 of the Criminal Code), computer fraud (Article 301 paragraph 3 of the Criminal Code) and unauthorised access to protected computers, computer networks and electronic data processing (Article 302 of the Criminal Code).

d) Computer Search of Data

Conditions for Ordering

Article 178

If the conditions referred to in Article 161 paragraphs 1 and 2 of this Code are fulfilled, acting on a reasoned motion by the public prosecutor the court may order computer searches of already processed personal data and other data and their comparison with data relating to the suspect and the criminal offence.

Order on a Computer Search of Data

Article 179

The special evidentiary action referred to in Article 178 of this Code is ordered by the judge for preliminary proceedings by a reasoned order.

The order referred to in paragraph 1 of this Article contains data on the suspect, the statutory title of the criminal offence, description of the data it is necessary to search and process by computer, designation of the public authority which is required to conduct the search of the requested data, scope and duration of the special evidentiary action.

A computer search of data may last a maximum of three months, and if it is necessary in order to continue collecting evidence it may be extended two more times at most by three months, respectively. The conduct of a computer search of data is discontinued as soon as the reasons for its application cease to exist.

Conduct of a Computer Search of Data

Article 180

The order referred to in Article 179 paragraph 1 of this Code is executed by the police, Security Information Agency, Military Security Agency, customs service, tax administration or other services or other public authority, or a legal person vested with public authority on the basis of the law.

On concluding a computer search of data the public authority, or the legal person referred to in paragraph 1 of this Article delivers to the judge for preliminary proceedings a report containing: data on the time of commencing and terminating a computer search of data, data searched and processed, data on the official who conducted the special evidentiary action, description of the technical means employed, data on the persons encompassed and results of the implemented computer search of data.

The judge for preliminary proceedings will deliver the report referred to in paragraph 2 of this Article to the public prosecutor.'

Since there is no available version of the law in English, we draw your attention to some of the relevant provisions of the Civil Procedure code ('Official Gazette of the RS', nos 72/2011, 49/2013, 74/2013 and 55/2014),[3]

'Article 7

The parties are required to present all facts on which they base their claims and propose evidence supporting such facts.

The court shall consider and determine only facts presented by the parties and shall exhibit only evidence proposed by the parties, if the law does not stipulated otherwise.

The court is authorized to establish also the facts which the parties have not presented and hear evidence which the parties have not proposed, if based on results of hearing and taking of evidence, it is established that the parties are disposing with claims which they may not dispose of, (Article 3, Paragraph 3).

Article 8

The court shall decide, at its discretion, which facts it will find proved, after conscientious and careful assessment of all evidences presented individually, all evidences taken as a whole as well as taking into consideration the results of the entire proceedings.

---

3   Please note that there is no available version of this law in English.

EVIDENCE PRESENTATION

General provisions

Article 228

Each party is obliged to present facts and propose evidence supporting the claim, or refutation of facts and evidence of the opposing party, in accordance with this law.

Article 229

Evidence presentation includes all facts relevant for taking of decision.

The Court decides which evidence will be presented in order to establish decisive facts.

Article 230

Facts admitted by a party before the court in the course of litigation should not be subject to evidence presentation, nor evidences not contested by the party.

The court may order evidence presentation for such facts as well if it deems that such party is admitting them in order to implement a claim it is not entitled to (Article 3, paragraph 3).

Taking into consideration all the circumstances, court will evaluate, according to its conviction, whether to consider a fact admitted or disputed, when such fact is first admitted by a party, and completely or partially denied afterwards, or when the admission was limited by addition of other facts.

The facts of common knowledge do not have to be proven.

Article 231

If court cannot establish a fact on the grounds of presented evidence (Article 8), existence of such fact will be established by application of the rule about the burden of proof.

The party that claims to have some right carries the burden of proving the fact which is essential for the emergence or exercise of that right, unless otherwise specified by the Law.

A party who disputes the existence of some right carries the burden of proving a fact that has prevented the emergence or exercise of that right or due to which that right ceased to exist, unless otherwise specified by the law.

Article 232

If it has been established that party is entitled to compensation for damages in money or replaceable objects, but the amount, or quantity of such objects cannot be established, or it might be established with inappropriate difficulty, court will decide on amount of money and quantity of such objects at its own discretion.

Article 233

Evidences are presented out at the main hearing, in accordance with the time frame.

The court may decide that evidences should be presented before the requested court. Record of the evidences presented before the requested court shall be read at the main hearing.

The request to present evidence includes information from the case. The court shall specify the circumstances which should be taken into account during presentation of evidences.

Parties involved will be notified about the date for presentation of evidences before the requested court.

The requested court, during the presentation of evidence, has all the authority that has the court when evidences are taken at the main hearing.

Against the decision of the court in which the presentation of evidences is delegated to the requested court no particular appeal is permitted.'

C24.6 SPECIFIC ONLINE ABUSE/ONLINE BULLYING/ CYBERBULLYING LAWS

We do not know of any such laws, but in some cases the relevant provisions of the Criminal Code and Law on Obligations and Torts may be applied as general laws, or some specific laws which among other things may regulate certain issues related to the internet, such as the Law on Electronic Communications ('Official Gazette of the RS', nos 44/2010 and 60/2013).

C24.7 OTHER LAWS APPLIED TO ONLINE ABUSE/ ONLINE BULLYING/CYBERBULLYING

The Criminal Code and Law on Obligations and Torts, as general laws, may be applied, or some specific laws which, among other things, may regulate certain issues related to the internet, such as the Law on Electronic Communications ('Official Gazette of the RS', nos 44/2010 and 60/2013) (see C24.28).

Since there is no available version of the law in English, we draw your attention to some of the relevant provisions of the Criminal Code,

'CHAPTER TWENTY SEVEN

CRIMINAL OFFENCE AGAINST SECURITY OF COMPUTER DATA

Damaging Computer Data and Programs

Article 298

(1) Whoever without authorisation deletes, alters, damages, conceals or otherwise makes unusable a computer datum or program, shall be punished by fine or imprisonment up to one year.

(2) If the offence specified in paragraph 1 of this Article results in damages exceeding four hundred and fifty thousand dinars, the offender shall be punished by imprisonment of three months to three years.

(3) If the offence specified in paragraph 1 of this Article results in damages exceeding one million five hundred thousand dinars, the offender shall be punished by imprisonment of three months to five years.

(4) Equipment and devices used in perpetration of the offence specified in paragraphs 1 and 2 of this Article shall be seized.

Computer Sabotage

Article 299

Whoever enters, destroys, deletes, alters, damages, conceals or otherwise makes unusable computer data or program or damages or destroys a computer or other equipment for electronic processing and transfer of data, with intent to prevent or considerably disrupt the procedure of electronic processing and transfer of data that are of importance for government authorities, enterprises or other entities, shall be punished by imprisonment of six months to five years.

Creating and Introducing of Computer Viruses

Article 300

(1) Whoever makes a computer virus with intent to introduce it into another's computer or computer network, shall be punished by fine or imprisonment up to six months.

(2) Whoever introduces a computer virus into another's computer or computer network thereby causing damage, shall be punished by fine or imprisonment up to two years.

(3) Equipment and devices used for committing of the offence specified in paragraphs 1 and 2 of this Article shall be seized.

Computer Fraud

Article 301

(1) Whoever enters incorrect data, fails to enter correct data or otherwise conceals or falsely represents data and thereby affects the results of

electronic processing and transfer of data with intent to acquire for himself or another unlawful material gain and thus causes material damage to another person, shall be punished by fine or imprisonment up to three years.

(2)   If the offence specified in paragraph 1 of this Article results in acquiring material gain exceeding four hundred and fifty hundred thousand dinars, the offender shall be punished by imprisonment of one to eight years.

(3)   If the offence specified in paragraph 1 of this Article results in acquiring material gain exceeding one million five hundred thousand dinars, the offender shall be punished by imprisonment of two to ten years.

(4)   Whoever commits the offence specified in paragraph 1 of this Article from malicious mischief, shall be punished by fine or imprisonment up to six months.

Unauthorised Access to Computer, Computer Network or Electronic Data Processing

Article 302

(1)   Whoever, by circumventing protection measures, accesses a computer or computer network without authorisation, or accesses electronic data processing without authorisation, shall be punished by fine or imprisonment up to six months.

(2)   Whoever copies or uses data obtained in manner provided under paragraph 1 of this Article, shall be punished by fine or imprisonment up to two years.

(3)   If the offence specified in paragraph 1 of this Article results in hold-up or serious malfunction in electronic processing and transfer of data or of the network, or other grave consequences have resulted, the offender shall be punished by imprisonment up to three years.

Preventing or Restricting Access to Public Computer Network

Article 303

(1)   Whoever without authorisation prevents or hinders access to a public computer network, shall be punished by fine or imprisonment up to one year.

(2)   If the offence specified in paragraph 1 of this Article is committed by an official in discharge of duty, such official shall be punished by imprisonment up to three years.

Unauthorised Use of Computer of Computer Network

Article 304

(1)   Whoever uses computer services or computer network with intent to acquire unlawful material gain for himself or another, shall be punished by fine or imprisonment up to three months.

(2)   Prosecution for the offence specified in paragraph 1 of this Article shall be instigated by private action.

Making, supply and lend funds to commit offenses against the security of computer data

Article 304a

(1)   Whoever possesses, purchases, sells or gives to another the use of computers, computer systems, computer data and programs to commit a criminal offense under Art 298 to 303 of this Code, shall be punished with imprisonment from six months to three years.

(2)   The items referred to in paragraph 1 of this Article shall be forfeited.'

In addition to criminal proceedings, a civil action for compensation of damage resulting from the commission of the aforementioned crimes may be initiated.

C24.8   CHILDREN AND SM LAWS OR RULES

We do not know of any specific laws relating to children and SM, but various laws that contain provisions applicable to minors may apply, eg some crimes prescribed by the Criminal Code in which the minor appears as a victim or offender etc and provisions of the Law on Obligations and Torts, as general law, in respect of compensation of damage, or some specific laws which, among other things, may regulate certain issues related to minors, such as the Family Law ('Official Gazette of the RS', nos 18/2005 and 72/2011),[4] if they are applicable to SM.

C24.9   EMPLOYEES/EMPLOYMENT SM LAWS OR CASES

We do not know of any specific laws involving SM and employees/employment, such as employee use of SM. However, the Labour Law provides for the possibility of employers defining the terms of working obligations, ie duties and discipline, according to their own needs and interests, violation of which may result in termination of employment. Accordingly, an employer may prohibit access to, and use of, SM via a business computer and/or during working hours.

C24.10   SCHOOL AND UNIVERSITY STUDENT SM CASES

We do not know of any specific laws involving students in schools and universities in relation to the use of SM. However, it may be assumed that

---

4   Please note that there is no available version of this law in English.

schools and faculties prescribe rules of discipline, that prohibit the use of cell phones and other electronic devices during classes and exams, or have devices that prevent the use of those electronic devices on school property, or faculty, with the aim of preventing potential abuse, such as cheating.

C24.11   RIGHT OR HUMAN RIGHT TO ACCESS THE INTERNET OR SM

We do not know of any specific literature, cases, rules or laws in relation to a right or human right of access to the internet or SM. In general, human rights and freedoms are regulated by the Constitution of the Republic of Serbia ('Official Gazette of the RS', no 98/2006), which is available online at www. ustavni.sud.rs/page/view/en-GB/235-100028/constitution.

C24.12   BANS OR RESTRICTIONS ON INTERNET OR SM

The Criminal Procedure code, among the measures to secure the presence of the defendant and measures for unobstructed conduct of criminal proceedings, prescribes that the court may decide on ordering the measure of prohibition of approaching, meeting or communicating with a certain person and visiting certain places if there are circumstances which indicate that a defendant could disrupt the proceedings by exerting influence on an injured party, witnesses, accomplices or concealers or could repeat a criminal offence, complete an attempted criminal offence or commit a criminal offence he is threatening to commit.

In addition, there is the measure of prohibition of leaving a dwelling, according to which the court may prohibit the defendant from leaving his dwelling without permission and determine the conditions under which he will stay in the dwelling, such as a prohibition on using the telephone or the internet or receiving other persons into the dwelling.

We do not know of any cases in which court has ordered the aforementioned measures prohibiting communication via the internet and/or SM.

Since there is no available version of the law in English, we draw your attention to some of the relevant provisions of the Criminal Procedure code ('Official Gazette of the RS', nos 72/2011, 101/2011, 121/2012, 32/2013, 45/2013 and 55/2014),

'Types of Measures

Article 188

The measures which may be undertaken against a defendant in order to secure his presence and unobstructed conduct or criminal proceedings are as follows,

1) summonses;

2) bringing [a defendant] in;

3) prohibition of approaching, meeting or communicating with a certain person and visiting certain places;

4) prohibition of leaving a temporary residence;

5) bail;

6) prohibition of leaving a dwelling;

7) detention.

General Conditions for Ordering Measures

Article 189

In ordering measures referred to in Article 188 of this Code, the authority conducting proceedings will take care not to apply a harsher measure if the same purpose can be achieved by a more lenient measure.

If required, the authority conducting proceedings may order two or more of the measures referred to in paragraph 1 of this Article.

The measure referred to in paragraph 1 of this Article will also be repealed *ex officio* when the reasons for ordering it cease to exist, or be replaced with a more lenient measure when the conditions for that arise.

Prohibition of Approaching, Meeting or Communicating with a Certain Person

Conditions for Ordering

Article 197

If there are circumstances which indicate that a defendant could disrupt the proceedings by exerting influence on an injured party, witnesses, accomplices or concealers or could repeat a criminal offence, complete an attempted criminal offence or commit a criminal offence he is threatening to commit, the court may prohibit the defendant from approaching, meeting or communicating with certain persons or visiting certain places.

Together with the measure referred to in paragraph 1 of this Article, the court may order the defendant to periodically report to the police, an officer of the public authority in charge of executing criminal sanctions or other public authority specified by law.

Deciding on the Measure

Article 198

The court decides on ordering the measure referred to in Article 197 of this Code on a motion by the public prosecutor, and after the indictment is confirmed, also *ex officio*.

During the investigation a reasoned ruling ordering, extending or repealing the measure referred to in paragraph 1 of this Article is issued by the judge for preliminary proceedings, and after the indictment is filed by the president of the panel, and at the trial, by the panel. If the measure was not proposed by the public prosecutor, and the proceedings are being conducted in connection with a criminal offence which is prosecutable *ex officio*, the opinion of the public prosecutor will be sought before the decision is rendered.

In the ruling pronouncing the measure referred to in paragraph 1 of this Article the defendant will be cautioned that a harsher measure (Article 188) may be ordered against him if he violates the prohibition ordered against him. The ruling is also delivered to the person in relation to whom the measure against the defendant was ordered.

The measure referred to in paragraph 1 of this Article may last for as long as a need for it exists, but not longer than the time of the final judgment, or the commitment of the defendant to serve a custodial criminal sanction. The court is required to examine once every three months whether the measure is still justified.

The parties and defence counsel may appeal against a ruling ordering, extending or repealing the measure referred to in paragraph 1 of this Article. The public prosecutor may also appeal against a ruling denying a motion for ordering the measure. An appeal does not stay execution of the ruling.

Control of the application of the measure referred to in paragraph 1 of this Article is performed by the police.

d) Prohibition of Leaving a Dwelling

Conditions for Ordering

Article 208

If there exist circumstances indicating that a defendant could abscond, or the circumstances specified in Article 211 paragraph 1 items 1), 3) and 4) of this Code, the court may prohibit the defendant from leaving his dwelling without permission and determine the conditions under which he will stay in the dwelling, such as a prohibition on using the telephone or the internet or receiving other persons into the dwelling.

As an exception from paragraph 1 of this Article, the defendant may leave his dwelling without permission if it is necessary for the purpose of an urgent medical intervention he or another person living with him in the dwelling needs to undertake, or in order to avoid a substantial threat to the life and health of people or property. The defendant is required to notify without delay an officer of the authority in charge of the execution of criminal sanctions about leaving his dwelling, the reasons and the place where he is currently located.'

C24.13 IDENTITY THEFT (OR EQUIVALENT)

We do not know of any specific rules or laws relating to identity theft, but some provisions of the Criminal Code (eg fraud, impersonation etc) may apply, and, from the civil law perspective, some provisions of the Law on Obligations and Torts regarding the compensation of damages.

C24.14 HACKING (OR EQUIVALENT)

We do not know of any specific laws relating to hacking (or equivalent), but some provisions of the Criminal Code (eg see C24.7) may apply, and, from the civil law perspective, some provisions of the Law on Obligations and Torts regarding the compensation of damages.

C24.15 PRIVACY BY DESIGN (PBD) (OR EQUIVALENT)

We do not know of any specific rules, laws or discussion relating to privacy by design (PbD), but there is Law on Legal Protection of Industrial Design ('Official Gazette of the RS', no 104/2009), which is available online at www. zis.gov.rs/intellectual-property-rights/designs/legislative-texts.77.html.

C24.16 TWEETING FROM COURTS, AND ANY RULES/ LAWS

Older versions of the Criminal Code, which were in force until 2012, prescribed the following offence,

'Unauthorized Public Comments on Court Proceedings

Article 336a

Who during the court proceedings and before a final court decision, in order to injure the presumption of innocence and independence of the court, giving public statements in the media, shall be punished with imprisonment up to six months and fined.'

However, the presumption of innocence today remains as a general principle of criminal and constitutional law, which should be respected, as well as the Court Rules ('Official Gazette of the RS', nos 110/2009, 70/2011, 19/2012 and 89/2013)[5] which regulate informing the public about the work of the courts (see C24.17).

---

5   Please note that there is no available version of this law in English.

The Criminal Procedure code ('Official Gazette of the RS', nos 72/2011, 101/2011, 121/2012, 32/2013, 45/2013 and 55/2014) states as follows,

'Presumption of Innocence

Article 3

Everyone is considered innocent until proven guilty by a final decision of the court.

Public and other authorities and organisations, the information media, associations and public figures are required to adhere to the rules referred to in paragraph 1 of this Article, as well as to abstain from violating the rights of the defendant with their public statements on the defendant, the criminal offence and the proceedings.'

C24.17 TELEVISION COURTROOM BROADCASTING OR TELEVISION CAMERAS IN COURT, AND RULES OR LAWS

In general, trials (civil and criminal) are public and anyone older than 16 may attend them, unless it is otherwise provided by law that the public may be excluded (eg in the event that a minor is participating in the procedure, or it relates to family cases, or business or state secrets). According to the Court Rules ('Official Gazette of the RS', nos 110/2009, 70/2011, 19/2012 and 89/2013), photographs, and audio and video recording in the courthouse can be done only with the prior written approval of the President of the court, in accordance with the law.

As far as we are aware, parts of the trials conducted by The Hague tribunal (eg against Slobodan Milošević and Vojislav Šešelj) and parts of the trial for the murder of former Prime Minister Zoran Đinđić have been publicly broadcast.

The Court Rules ('Official Gazette of the RS', nos 110/2009, 70/2011, 19/2012 and 89/2013 – no available version in English) regulate informing the public about the work of the courts as follows,

'Informing the Public on the Courts

Article 57

In order to provide objective, timely and accurate information to the public about the court and the court procedures, the president, judges and court staff are required to provide the necessary conditions, as well as appropriate access to the media regarding the current information and the proceedings of the court, taking into account the interests of process, privacy, and security of the participants in the process.

Time, place and subject of the trial are published daily in a prominent place in front of the room in which the trial held or in any other suitable manner.

In the trial for which there is greater public interest in judicial administration will provide a room that can accommodate larger number of people. The Trial Chamber shall be by order of the president of a trial in a larger room that is provided.

Article 58

Press release about the court and the individual cases by the President, the person responsible for informing public (spokesperson) or a special service for information.

Republican level courts, appellate courts and courts of special classes or more judges determine person responsible for informing the public (spokesperson).

Information on passing the final court proceedings to be published by the law, or by special regulation, as well as in cases where the public is particularly interested.

The information and data provided to the public must be accurate and complete. The data according to specific regulations are confidential and protected information whose disclosure is excluded or restricted by law can not communicated.

When contact with the public and the media will use the resources of modern communications in accordance with the substantive technical possibilities of the court (a press conference - media center, reporting through the web-site and seq).

Equal representation of different media on the trials shall be overseen by the President.

Article 59

Photographs, audio and video recording in the courthouse can be done only with prior written approval of the President, in accordance with the law.

Article 60

Photographs, audio and video recording of the hearing for the purpose of public airing of the video is done with the approval of president, with the prior approval of the presiding judge, judges, and written consent of the parties and Participants recorded action.

In granting permission for taking photos and recording will be based on the interest of the public interest procedure, the privacy and security of participants in the process.

Photographs, audio and video recording in the courtroom, after obtaining the approval shall be carried out under the supervision of judge, in a way that ensures the smooth flow of the trial and order in the courtroom.

Article 61

The court at least once a year, and no later than February 1 of the current year for the previous year makes with the main data on the work, which are prescribed by a special law and the Rules of Procedure, and the importance for the realization of the rights of citizens and the presentation of the work of the court to the public. This Guide contains: name and the seat of the court; annual schedule of work; contact information (phone, fax, web site and e mail), names of managers of judicial administration, data on working hours of the court and its services, names and contacts persons authorized to receive, informing the parties and the handling of complaints, names and contacts of persons authorized for the issuance of certificates and verification of signatures; names and details of persons authorized to allow viewing, copying and copying files.

Informant referred to in paragraph 1 of this Article, a collection of decisions and legal opinions, the court may publish in print or electronic form.'

Since there is no available version of the law in English, we draw your attention to some of the relevant provisions of the Criminal Procedure code ('Official Gazette of the RS', nos 72/2011, 101/2011, 121/2012, 32/2013, 45/2013 and 55/2014),

'Presumption of Innocence

Article 3

Everyone is considered innocent until proven guilty by a final decision of the court.

Public and other authorities and organisations, the information media, associations and public figures are required to adhere to the rules referred to in paragraph 1 of this Article, as well as to abstain from violating the rights of the defendant with their public statements on the defendant, the criminal offence and the proceedings.

a. Publicity of the Trial

General Rule about Publicity

Article 362

The trial is public.

Only persons over 16 years of age may attend a trial.

Excluding the Public

Article 363

From the commencement of the hearing until the conclusion of the trial, the panel may ex officio or upon a motion by a party or the defence counsel, but always after they had stated their positions, exclude the public from the entire trial or a part thereof, if it is necessary for the purpose of protecting,

1)   the interests of national security;

2)   public order and morality;

3)   the interests of minors;

4)   private lives of the participants in the proceedings;

5)   other justified interests in a democratic society.

Exemptions from Excluding the Public

Article 364

The exclusion of the public does not apply to the parties, the defence counsel, the injured party and his representative and the proxy of the prosecutor.

The panel may permit a trial from which the public has been excluded to be attended by certain officials, scientists, scholars and other professionals, and at the request of the defendant also his spouse, close relatives and the person with whom who lives in a common law marriage or other permanent personal association.

The president of the panel will caution persons attending a trial from which the public has been excluded that they are required to maintain the confidentiality of everything they learn at the hearing and indicate to them that disclosure of secret represents a criminal offence.

Decision on Excluding the Public

Article 365

The panel's ruling on excluding the public must be reasoned and made public.

In the ruling referred to in paragraph 1 of this Article the panel also decides which persons are allowed to attend the trial (Article 364 paragraph 2).

The ruling referred to in paragraph 1 of this Article may be challenged only in an appeal against the judgment or ruling which corresponds to a judgment.

Special Case of Excluding the Public

Article 366

The public prosecutor may propose to the court to exclude the public from the trial during the examination of a cooperating defendant or cooperating convicted person.

Before deciding on the motion of the public prosecutor, the president of the panel will defendant and his defence counsel to state their position on the proposal to exclude the public.'

Since there is no available version of the law in English, we draw your attention to some of the relevant provisions of the Civil Procedure code ('Official Gazette of the RS', nos 72/2011, 49/2013, 74/2013 and 55/2014),

'2. Public nature of the trial

Article 321

The trial is public.

Only persons older than 16 years may attend the trial, unless specified otherwise by the law.

Article 322

The court may exclude the public from the whole trial or its part if it is required by reasons of national security, public security, moral, in the interest of public order, privacy of the parties involved or when directed by law. The court may also exclude the public in case when measures for maintaining of order provided under this law would not secure undisturbed proceedings at the trial.

Article 323

Exclusion of the public does not apply to the parties, their legal representatives, attorneys and interveners.

The court may allow certain officials as well as scientists and public workers to attend the trial where the public has been excluded, if in the interest of their official activity, scientific or public work.

The court may allow, upon the motion of a party, presence of two persons at most, designated by such party.

The court will warn persons attending the trial where public is excluded that they are obliged to keep confidential all they learn at the trial, and instruct them about consequences of the breach of such confidentiality.

Article 324

The court shall decide about exclusion of the public by an explained and publicly announced ruling.

No special appeal is allowed against the ruling on exclusion of the public.

Article 325

Provisions about publicity of the trial will accordingly apply to all other hearings.'

C24.18   SM IN COURTROOMS

As already mentioned, trials are public, and any person older than 16 years may attend the same, if not otherwise provided by the law, ie court decision. In this regard, and bearing in mind the provisions of the procedural rules, the public should not misuse the given right by violating the procedural discipline and obstructing the trial, in which case they may be fined. According to the practice of the courts, it is required that cell phones are muted, and some courts (eg for organized crime) require that cell phones are deposited at the entrance of the court.

Since there is no available version of the law in English, we draw your attention to some of the relevant provisions of the Civil Procedure code ('Official Gazette of the RS', nos 72/2011, 49/2013, 74/2013 and 55/2014),

'CONTEMPT OF PROCESS DISCIPLINE

Article 186

The court will, during the proceedings, sanction natural person with a monetary fine from 10,000 up to 150,000 dinars ie legal entity with a monetary fine from 30,000 up to 1,000,000 dinars, which offends in a filing the court, party or other participant in the proceedings.

A fine in accordance with paragraph 1 of this Article shall be imposed to a party and other participants in the proceeding who use their process powers contrary to the objectives for which they were established.

Article 187

If due to the abuse of procedural powers one of the parties suffered damage, the party that sustained damage, on her request, will be awarded compensation for damage by the court.

When a party highlights the claim for compensation of damage from abuse of procedural powers, the court will set aside the procedure for the reason of expediency.

Article 188

The court will sanction with a monetary fine from 10,000 up to 150,000 dinars attorney responsible for receiving of court documents when he/she, contrary to the provisions of the law, does not inform the court regarding address change.

The court shall, upon request of a party, decide that attorney responsible for receiving of court documents must compensate party for costs incurred by unjustified failure to notify changes in address.

Article 189

The court shall impose a fine from 10,000 up to 150,000 dinars to person who obstructs taking of civil actions and service of court documents or court files.

The court shall, upon request of a party, decide that person from paragraph 1 of this Article must compensate costs that were caused by his/her conduct from paragraph 1 this Article.

The court can also define other measures to the person who obstructs taking of civil action.

The sentenced punishment from paragraph 1 of this Article shall not interfere on sentencing of punishment for a criminal offence.

Article 190

The decision related to sanctions from Article 186, 188 and 189 of this law shall define the time period for payment of the fine.

On Enforcement of the fine from paragraph 1 of this Article shall be executed ex officio provisions of the law regulating enforcement of criminal sanctions shall be applied accordingly.

If a punished natural and legal person fails to pay the fine within the period defined in the decision on punishing, the court shall enforce the decision on punishment and the fine ex officio replace it with imprisonment, in accordance with the law that regulates enforcement of criminal sanctions.

If the punished legal person fails to pay the fine within the period defined in the decision on punishment, provisions of the law that regulates liability of legal persons for criminal offence regulating enforcement of fines shall be applied.

Complaint against the decision on punishment from Articles 186, 188 and 189 of this Article shall not postpone enforcement of the decision.

Paragraph 4 of Article 309

The court is in obligation to respect the time frame defined in accordance with Article 308 of this law, as well as to prevent any attempt of ungrounded delay of hearing and to sanction any violation or misuse of the procedural rights and violation of procedural discipline.'

Since there is no available version of the law in English, we draw your attention to some of the relevant provisions of the Criminal Procedure code ('Official Gazette of the RS', nos 72/2011, 101/2011, 121/2012, 32/2013, 45/2013 and 55/2014):

'b. Conducting the Trial

Authority of the President of the Panel

Article 367

The president of the panel conducts the trial.

In session and at the trial, the president of the panel,

1) determines whether the panel is composed in accordance with the provisions of this Code and whether there are any reasons why members of the panel and the record-keeper must be recused (Article 37 paragraph 1);

2) determines whether the preconditions for holding the trial have been fulfilled;

3) is responsible for maintaining order and for applying measures to prevent disturbances of order in the courtroom;

4) is responsible for ensuring that the proceedings run without delays and without examination of questions that do not contribute to a comprehensive consideration of the subject matter to be proved;

5) decides on deviating from the normal course of proceedings stipulated by this Code, owing to special circumstances, in particular the number of defendants and criminal offences and the volume of evidence;

6) gives the floor to the members of the panel, parties, defence counsel, injured party, legal representative and proxy, witness, expert witness and professional consultant;

7) decides on motions made by the parties, unless the panel decides on them;

8) instructs a party to propose additional evidence;

9) conveys into the transcript the contents of the work and the entire course of the trial;

10) undertakes necessary measures to protect witnesses (Articles 102 and 103);

11) rules on other questions, in accordance with this Code.

Authority of the Panel

Article 368

During the trial, the panel decides on,

1) a motion on which there is no agreement between the parties, and on a consensual motion of the parties not accepted by the president of the panel;

2) an objection against a measure of the president of the panel relating to the conduct of the trial;

3) prohibiting, irrespective of permission issued for video recording, video recording of certain parts of the trial on justified grounds;

4) removal from the courtroom, on the exclusion of a defence counsel or proxy, and on continuing, adjourning or deferring the trial for the purpose of maintaining order and conducting the trial;

5) examination of additional evidence, if it deems it necessary for the purpose of eliminating discrepancies or lack of clarity in the evidence examined and that it is necessary in order to discuss the subject-matter of the proving comprehensively;

6) other questions in accordance with this Code.

The panel's rulings are always pronounced and entered in the transcript with brief reasoning.

Protection of the Reputation of the Court and Participants in Proceedings

Article 369

The court is required to protect its reputation and security, the reputation and security of the parties and other participants in proceedings, from an insult, threat and any other assault.

During the entry of a judge or members of a panel into the courtroom and their egress from the courtroom, all those present are required to rise.

The president of the panel will immediately after opening the session, if there are any reasons for it, caution the persons present to behave with decency and to abstain from obstructing the work of the court.

The parties and other participants in the proceedings are required to stand when they are addressing the court, unless justified reasons make this impossible or a questioning or examination is made in another manner.

Persons attending a trial, except for the persons who secure the court and guard the defendant, may not carry firearms or dangerous weapons, and for the purpose of checking whether they are respecting the ban, the president of the panel may order them to be searched.

Measures for Maintaining Order

Article 370

If the defendant, defence counsel, injured party, legal representative, proxy, witness, expert witness, professional consultant, translator, interpreter or other person attending the trial disturbs the order by disregarding orders of the president of the panel to maintain order or by insulting the dignity of the court, the president of the panel will caution him, and if that person continues to disturb the order, will fine him up to 150,000 dinars.

The president of the panel will notify the competent public prosecutor and the State Prosecutors Council about any disturbance of order by the public prosecutor or a person deputising for him, or will adjourn the trial and request that the competent public prosecutor designate another person to represent the prosecution when the trial resumes, with the obligation to notify the court about the undertaken measures.

The president of the panel will notify the competent bar association about a penalty imposed on a lawyer for disturbing the order, with the obligation to notify the court about the undertaken measures.

Removal of the Defendant from the Courtroom

Article 371

If the measures referred to in Article 370 paragraph 1 of this Code are unsuccessful, the panel may order the defendant removed from the courtroom for the duration of a certain evidentiary action, and if after returning to the courtroom the defendant continues to disturb the order, the panel may remove him until the conclusion of the evidentiary proceedings and order, if there exists such a possibility, that the defendant follow the course of the proceedings from a separate room by means of an audio and video link.

Before the conclusion of the evidentiary proceedings the president of the panel will, if the technical link for monitoring the course of the proceedings referred to in paragraph 1 of this Article did not exist, inform the defendant about the course of the evidentiary proceedings for the period during which he was removed from the courtroom, inform him about the testimony given by co-defendants previously questioned, or make it possible for him to read the transcripts of that testimony, if the defendant so requests, and ask him to state his position on the charges, unless he had already done so.

If the defendant in the case referred to in paragraph 2 of this Article continues to disturb the order, the panel may remove him from the courtroom again without a right to attend the trial until its conclusion, in which case the president of the panel or a judge member of the panel will inform the defendant about the judgment in the presence of the record-keeper.

In case a defendant who has no defence counsel is removed from the courtroom in accordance with paragraphs 1 and 3 of this Article, the president of the court will assign a court appointed defence counsel for him (Article 74 item 6 and Article 76).

Excluding Defence Counsel or Proxy

Article 372

The panel will exclude from the further course of the proceedings a defence counsel or proxy who continues to disturb the order after being fined, and ask the party or the person represented to obtain another defence counsel or proxy and notify the competent bar association thereof.

If a defendant or injured party, in the case referred to in paragraph 1 of this Article, cannot immediately obtain another defence counsel or proxy without detriment to their interests, or if in the case of mandatory defence (Article 74) the court is not able to appoint a new defence counsel without harming the defence, the trial will be adjourned or deferred.

If a subsidiary prosecutor or private prosecutor does not obtain another proxy, the panel may decide to resume the trial without a proxy if it finds that his absence would not adversely affect the interests of the person represented.

Removing Other Persons from the Courtroom

Article 373

The panel may remove from the courtroom until the end of the evidentiary procedure the subsidiary prosecutor or private prosecutor or their legal representative who continues to disturb order after the pronouncing of the sentence and will appoint a proxy for him for the rest of the proceedings. If the panel is unable to appoint a proxy immediately without harming the interests of the represented party, the trial will be either adjourned or deferred.

The panel may order that besides the defendant another person referred to in Article 370 paragraph 1 of this Code be removed from the courtroom if he continues to disturb the order even after being cautioned or fined, and may simultaneously remove him and fine him.

The panel may order removed from the courtroom all persons who are attending the trial in accordance with Article 362 of this Code, if unobstructed holding of the trial could not be ensured by the measures to maintain order stipulated by this Code.

Measures to Prevent Delaying Proceedings

Article 374

The panel will caution a defence counsel, injured party, legal representative, proxy, subsidiary prosecutor or private prosecutor undertaking actions obviously aimed at delaying the proceedings.

The president of the panel will notify the competent public prosecutor and the State Prosecutors Council about untimely or inappropriate actions by the public prosecutor or person deputising for him which delay the proceedings, with the obligation to notify the court about the undertaken measures.

The president of the panel will notify the competent bar association about the caution imposed on a lawyer for delaying the proceedings, with the obligation to notify the court about the undertaken measures.

Appeal against Decisions on Maintaining Order at the Trial

Article 375

A ruling on a caution, fine, removal from the courtroom, exclusion of a defence counsel or proxy, and resuming, adjourning or deferring a trial for the purpose of maintaining order and administering the trial is entered in the transcript with reasoning.

A ruling on a fine is appealable. Before it delivers an appeal to a court of second instance, the panel may revoke the ruling on a penalty.

A ruling to remove the defendant from the courtroom until the end of the evidentiary proceedings or until the conclusion of the trial and to exclude a defence counsel may be appealable, but the appeal does not stay the execution of the ruling. No special appeal is allowed against the ruling on the removal from the courtroom or the exclusion of a proxy.

Other decisions on measures to maintain order and administer the trial are not appealable.

Criminal Offence Committed at the Trial

Article 376

If the defendant or another person commits during the trial a criminal offence which is prosecutable *ex officio*, the president of the panel will notify the competent public prosecutor thereof.

If there are grounds for suspicion that a witness, expert witness or professional consultant has perjured himself at the trial, the president of the panel will order taking of a special record made of the testimony given by the witness, expert witness or professional consultant which will be delivered to the competent public prosecutor after being signed by the questioned witness, expert witness or professional consultant, or after the president of the panel notes that they have refused to sign it and lists the reasons for that refusal.'

C24.19   USE OF SM AS EVIDENCE IN COURTS

We do not know of any examples in relation to the use of SM as evidence in the courts (see C24.5).

C24.20   PRIVACY, DATA PROTECTION AND SM

We do not know of any such cases, but it is likely that they may exist (see C24.4).

C24.21   SM AND FAMILY LAW CASES

We do not know of any such cases, but it is likely that they may exist, eg in cases for deciding on child custody (see C24.4).

Unfortunately, there is no English version of the Family Law ('Official Gazette of the RS', nos 18/2005 and 72/2011).

C24.22 SPORTS PERSONS, SPORTS CLUBS AND SM

We do not know of any such cases, but it is likely that they may exist, eg in connection with the execution of an offence or damage in terms of violation of honour and reputation.

C24.23 PERSONAL RELATIONS AND RELATIONSHIPS

We do not know of any such cases, but it is likely that they may exist, eg in connection with the execution of an offence or damage in terms of violation of honour and reputation.

C24.24 SM AND PERSONAL DATA OF DECEASED PERSONS

There are cases in which the Commissioner for Personal Data Protection warns certain health institutions (the clinics – in Serbian: *Dom zdravlja*) to provide technical, personnel, and organizational measures to protect the data in accordance with established standards and procedures. Also, there have been cases of misdemeanour punishment for non-compliance with the provisions of the Law on Protection of Personal Data ('Official Gazette of the RS', nos 97/2008, 104/2009, 68/2012 and 107/2012). For examples (in Serbian only), see www.poverenik.rs/en/cases/2011-05-24-08-14-24/decisions/supervision. html.

In addition, over the past year there has been controversy over Article 5 of the Law on the right to health care of children and pregnant women ('Official Gazette of the RS', no 104/2013) in relation to 'marking' women who have abortions and the potential abuse of such records. According to the Commissioner for Personal Data Protection, the provisions of the Law on the right to health care of children and pregnant women are not contrary to the Constitution and the Law on Protection of Personal Data ('Official Gazette of the RS', nos 97/2008, 104/2009, 68/2012 and 107/2012). However, he warns that it is necessary to prevent potential abuse of the regulations, since the processing of personal data for purposes other than those set out is not permitted.[6]

---

6 Some articles that apply to that case are available at www.rts.rs/page/stories/ci/story/124/%D 0%94%D1%80%D1%83%D1%88%D1%82%D0%B2%D0%BE/1461427/%D0%A8%D0 %B0%D0%B1%D0%B8%D1%9B+%D0%BE+%D0%BF%D1%80%D0%B8%D0%BA% D1%83%D0%BF%D1%99%D0%B0%D1%9A%D1%83+%D0%BF%D0%BE%D0%B4% D0%B0%D1%82%D0%B0%D0%BA%D0%B0+%D0%BE+%D0%B0%D0%B1%D0%B E%D1%80%D1%82%D1%83%D1%81%D0%B8%D0%BC%D0%B0.html; www.telegraf. rs/vesti/892999-ovako-se-borimo-protiv-bele-kuge-drzava-popisuje-zene-koje-su-abortirale; and www.paragraf.rs/dnevne-vesti/101213/101213-vest6.html.

Article 5 of the Law on the right to health care of children and pregnant women ('Official Gazette of the RS', no 104/2013) stipulates,

> *'Article 5*
>
> Specialist doctor in gynaecology and obstetrics is obliged to inform the Republic fund for Health Insurance immediately upon established pregnancy or upon the completion of termination of pregnancy, of pregnant women who are entitled to health care in accordance with this law.
>
> Health institution where the mother gave birth to a stillborn child is obliged to inform the Republic fund immediately upon the birth.
>
> In the case of point 2 of this Article, the mother has the right to health protection in the period of three months after the birth, in accordance with this law.
>
> Specialist doctor of paediatrics is obliged to inform the Republic fund immediately upon finding out about death of a child under the age of one.
>
> On the basis of notification set out in points 1, 2 and 4 of this Article, the Republic fond determines the termination of exercising rights under this law.'

C24.25   SN, WEBSITE, SERVICE PROVIDER OR ISP DEFENCE RULES/LAWS

The legal framework for eCommerce in Serbia primarily consists of the E-Commerce Law, the Electronic Document Law and the Electronic Signature Law.

The E-Commerce Law ('Official Gazette of the RS', nos 41/2009 and 95/2013) regulates the conditions and means of providing services of the information society, the duty to inform service users, commercial messages, rules relating to the contract in electronic form, the liability of providers of information society services, surveillance and misdemeanours.

The Law on Electronic Documents ('Official Gazette of the RS', no 51/2009) regulates the conditions and procedures for handling electronic documents in legal, administrative, judicial and other proceedings, as well as the rights, duties and responsibilities of companies and other legal entities, entrepreneurs and individuals (hereinafter referred to as 'legal and natural persons'), state authorities, territorial autonomy and local government bodies and organs, enterprises, institutions, organizations and individuals entrusted with the affairs of state government, or public authority (hereinafter referred to 'authorities') in connection with this document.

It also defines 'electronic document' as a set of data consisting of letters, numbers, symbols, graphics, audio and video files in the brief, written, decisions, document or any other act which the legal and natural persons or authorities make for use in legal or administrative, judicial or other proceedings before the authorities, if made electronically, digitized, sent, received, stored or archived in electronic, magnetic, optical or other media.

The Law on Electronic Signature ('Official Gazette of the RS', no 135/2004) governs the use of an electronic signature in legal affairs and other legal actions, in operations, as well as the rights, commitments and responsibilities with respect to electronic certificates, unless otherwise specified by separate laws. The provisions of this Law applies to communication among authorities, communication between authorities and interested parties, the submission and development of a decision of an authority in electronic form in administrative, court and other types of proceedings before a state authority, provided the law governing such proceedings provides for the use of an electronic signature.

Unfortunately, there are no available English versions of these Laws, but more details on the legal framework of eCommerce in Serbia and its implementation are available online at www.fic.rs/admin/download/files/cms/attach?id=420 and www.legal500.com/c/serbia/developments/9061.

C24.26   ECOMMERCE DEFENCE CASES

We do not know of any such cases.

C24.27   LAWS PROTECTING PERSONAL DATA/ PERSONALLY IDENTIFIABLE INFORMATION

The Law on Protection of Personal Data ('Official Gazette of the RS', nos 97/2008, 104/2009, 68/2012 and 107/2012) is available online at www. poverenik.rs/en/legal-framework/laws-zp.html.

C24.28   DATA BREACH LAWS AND CUSTOMERS/ USERS/REGULATORS NOTIFIED OF HACKING OR DATA LOSS

The Law on Electronic Communications ('Official Gazette of the RS', nos 44/2010 and 60/2013) governs:

- the terms and manner of performing activities in the electronic communications sector;

- powers of the government authorities in the electronic communications sector;

- the status and operation of the Republic Agency for Electronic Communications;

- fees;

- public consultation procedures in the electronic communications sector;

- performing electronic communications activities according to the general authorization regime;

- design, construction or installation, use and maintenance of electronic communications networks, associated facilities, electronic communications equipment and terminal equipment;

- the official prerogative and common use;

- interconnection and access;

- universal service provision;

- identification of markets susceptible to *ex ante* regulation;

- market analysis;

- designation of operators with significant market power (hereinafter 'operators with SMP') and the Agency's regulatory competencies related to operators with SMP;

- management and use of addresses and numbers (hereinafter 'numbering');

- radio frequency spectrum management, use and monitoring;

- media content distribution and broadcasting;

- protection of rights of users and subscribers;

- security and integrity of electronic communications networks and services;

- protection of privacy within the sector of electronic communications;

- lawful interception and data retention;

- supervision over the enforcement of this Law;

- penalties for actions contrary to the provisions of this Law; and

- other issues of relevance to the functioning and development of electronic communications in the Republic of Serbia.

Unfortunately, there is no complete (with amendments of 2013) version of this law in English (www.ratel.rs/regulations/law.142.html), and we draw your attention to some of the relevant provisions of the respective law,

'Article 124

In order to ensure the security and integrity of public communications networks and services, confidentiality of communications, and protection of personal, traffic and location data, the operator shall take adequate technical and organizational measures, suitable for the existing risks, and in particular measures for the prevention and minimization of the effects of security incidents on users and interconnected networks, as well as measures for ensuring the continuity of operation of public communications networks and services.

If the operator provides the service using some other operator's electronic communications network, associated facilities or services, it shall cooperate with that operator to ensure the security and integrity of public communications networks and services.

In case of a particular risk related to the violation of the security and integrity of public communications networks and services (unauthorised access, significant loss of data, violation of the confidentiality of communications, personal data security, etc), the operator shall inform subscribers of such risk and, in case the risk lies outside the scope of measures to be taken by the operator, of possible means of protection and costs related to the implementation of these measures.

Article 125

The operator is obliged to inform the Republic Agency for Electronic Communications of any violation of the security and integrity of public communications networks and services, which has a significant impact on their work, particularly on injuries that had resulted in violation of the protection of personal data, or privacy of a subscriber or user.

The Republic Agency for Electronic Communications is authorized to inform the public about security breaches and integrity of paragraph 1 of this Article, or ask the operator to do it himself, it assesses that the publication of such information in the public interest.'

Singapore

Sharmini Sharon Selvaratnam
Harry Elias Partnership LLP

Assisted by Mr Lin Chun Long and Ms Jaclyn Leong

C25.1   INTRODUCTION

Singapore is a mixed Common Law and Civil Law jurisdiction.

C25.2   SPECIFIC SM AND SN LAWS

Presently, there are no specific laws dealing with SM and SN. However, there are laws with ambits wide enough to cover conduct/activities over SM and SN sites. For example,

- Copyright Act (Cap 63)

    - One could infringe the Copyright Act by reproducing third party content on SM sites without prior permission of the copyright owners.

    - One could infringe the right of production and right of communication.

- Sedition Act (Cap 290)

    - One could infringe the Sedition Act by posting anything with a seditious tendency online.

    - 'Seditious tendency' is defined by s 3 of the Sedition Act.

    - Definition of 'publication' under s 2 is wide enough to encompass online postings.

- Protection from Harassment Bill

    - On 14 March 2014, the Protection from Harassment Bill 2014 was passed in Parliament. The Bill aims to protect individuals from harassment and related anti-social behaviour. No civil proceedings are to be brought for harassment except under this new legislation.

— The text of the Second Reading Speech by the Minister for Law, K Shanmugam, can be accessed at www.mlaw.gov.sg/news/ parliamentary-speeches-and-responses/2R-by-minister-on-protection-from-harassment-act.html ('Second Reading').

— In his speech, Mr Shanmugam made it clear that the Harassment Bill is also aimed at harassment in the online space, including such acts over SM [websites]. He highlighted that '[c]byer-space makes harassment easier, in some ways, more egregious, because it can be anonymous, borderless, viral and permanent' (Second Reading at [7]).

● Penal Code (Cap 224)

— Offence of Child grooming (s 376E) – One could commit the offence by meeting or travelling to meet a minor under 16 years of age after sexual grooming, having met or communicated with the minor on two or more previous occasions.

— Communication includes online communication, eg internet chat rooms.

— Section 140(1)(b) read with s 140(2) – Procuring of any woman or girl for the purpose of prostitution (the accused in *PP v Malcolm Graham Head* [2014] SGDC 79 procured a minor for prostitution through Facebook).

— Section 267C (the accused in *PP v Yue Mun Yew Gary* [2013] 1 SLR 39 was charged with inciting violence by sharing a video on Facebook).

● Computer Misuse and Cybersecurity Act (Cap 50A)

— An Act to make provision for securing computer material against unauthorised access or modification, to require or authorise the taking of measures to ensure cybersecurity.

● Defamation Act (Cap 75).

C25.3   SM CRIMINAL LAW CASES

For example,

● *Public Prosecutor v Yue Mun Yew Gary* [2012] SGDC 115 / *Public Prosecutor v Yue Mun Yew Gary* [2013] 1 SLR 39 (on appeal)

— The accused shared on a Facebook page a video clip depicting the assassination of the former President of Egypt, Muhammad Anwar al-Sadat, and posted a comment, 'We should re-enact a live version of this on our own grand-stand during our national's parade!!!!!!'. He also stated that, if the ruling government's 'political downfall is not within grasp, we should know what and how next to escalate it'. He also wrote that he was 'sure we all want the physical removal of any influence of the incumbents from the face of the earth';

- He also posted a doctored photograph, depicting General Nguyen Ngoc Loan executing Mr Wong Kan Seng, the former Deputy Prime Minister and Minister of Home Affairs, as his Facebook profile picture;

- At [5]: A police report lodged by an informant stated that he came across postings that advocated the use of violence on public officials on a Facebook page. Also, the accused's picture depicted an act of violence and this made the informant particularly concerned;

- The police commenced investigations against the accused for making postings advocating the use of violence on the SM website Facebook;

- The accused was charged under s 267C of the Penal Code for inciting violence;

- The accused was convicted and sentenced to a fine;

- On appeal, in *PP v Yue Mun Yew Gary* [2013]/[2012] SGHC 188, Quentin Loh J allowed the Prosecution's appeal against sentence. He set aside the fine of $6,000 and enhanced the sentence to two months' imprisonment;

- Considerations of public policy played a part in the enhancing of the sentence;

- Loh J at [51] noted that s 267C was specifically modified to take into account the advent of electronic media;

- Loh J at [52]: while the internet has added completely new paradigms in which we conduct our daily lives and communicate, the downside to this advancement in technology is that some may make use of the seclusion and safety of hiding behind the computer screen to make extreme statements and take extreme views, and that these statements may reach out to a far larger number of people than we realise;

- Loh J at [54] held that the accused's post on Facebook exemplified an abuse of the internet, where the potential impact of any statement was greatly magnified;

- Also, it was important to send a strong signal that the internet was not an entirely unregulated space wherein calls to violence were treated as an acceptable mode of communication.

- *PP v Koh Song Huat Benjamin* [2005] SGDC 272

  – Two accused, Benjamin Koh and Nicholas Lim, were convicted under s 4(1)(a) and punishable under s 4(1) of the Sedition Act for posting racist remarks on their personal blog and an online forum on the internet;

  – Benjamin Koh was sentenced to two months' imprisonment while Nicholas Lim was sentenced to a nominal one day imprisonment;

  – Their remarks or acts warranted invoking s 3(1)(e) of the Sedition Act as it was found that these remarks or acts had the tendency to promote feelings of ill-will and hostility between different races or classes of the population of Singapore;

  – SDJ Richard Magnus at [6]–[7] reiterated the sensitivity of racial and religious issues in Singapore and the fact that these remarks on racial and religious subjects have the potential to cause social disorder, in whatever forum or medium they are expressed;

  – At [8], SDJ Magnus also highlighted the unrefereed domain of cyberspace, and stated that one cannot hide behind the anonymity of cyberspace to pen diatribes against another race or religion. The right to express opinions is not an unfettered right. The freedom of expression must be balanced against the right of another's freedom from offence;

  – At [11] and [15], the highly inflammatory and insulting nature of Benjamin Koh's comments warranted a deterrent custodial sentence.

- *PP v Chong Jasmine* [2014] SGDC 24

  – The accused was charged under the Health Products Act (Cap 122D) and the Optometrists & Opticians Act (Cap 213A) for selling unregistered contact lenses through the use of SM [websites] and carrying out the practice of optometry without a practising certificate;

  – She sold various brands of contact lenses through her Facebook page (at [4] and [10]);

  – The DJ considered community-based sentencing and sentenced the accused to be placed on a 'Day Reporting Order' for a 4-month period and a 'Community Service Order' to serve 150 hours of community service within 12 months.

C25.4   SM CIVIL LAW CASES

For example,

● *Motherhood Pte Ltd v Lau Elaine and others* [2014] 1 SLR 1008

- This was an action by Motherhood Pte Ltd (the Plaintiff) against Lau Elian, Lim Poh Heng, and TNAP Services LLP (the Defendants) for passing off under ss 55(2) and 55(3)(a) of the Trade Marks Act (Cap 332);

- Motherhood Magazine is a monthly print periodical that dealt with parenting issues. The Plaintiff also owned and operated a website and a Facebook page relating to the Plaintiff's magazine;

- The Defendants also had a Magazine named 'Today's Motherhood' (the Disputed Mark) and a Facebook page named 'Today's Motherhood';

- On 28 September 2011, the Plaintiff's solicitors wrote to the Defendants claiming that the Defendants' use of the Disputed Mark constituted an act of passing off and asked that they ceased using any names that were similar to the Motherhood marks;

- In January 2012, the Defendants undertook a rebranding exercising in which they changed the name of their magazine and Facebook page to 'The New Age Parents'. They informed the Plaintiff's solicitors of this on 20 February 2012.

- However, the Plaintiff was not satisfied as the back issues of the Defendants' magazine with the cover page of the Disputed Mark remained available to the public on the Defendants' website. Despite the fact that the back issues were subsequently removed, the Plaintiff still commenced the Suit.

- The Plaintiff's claim was dismissed.

● *AQN v AQO* [2011] SGHC 127

- This is a matrimonial dispute where the wife commenced certain applications in court. In particular, Summons No 5814 of 2010 where the wife applied for orders pertaining to arrangements for counselling for the wife and the third son, access to the third son, the husband's access to the third son etc.

- In support of her application, the wife filed an affidavit where she claimed, inter alia, that the third son had posted on his Facebook page 'that he was forming a club with the clear indication that he was beaten by his brothers' and that the husband had stopped him from joining the drama club, a popular activity of the school. She also claimed that a friend of the third son had posted on Facebook that the third son would not like to spend his birthday with his family.

C25.5 CASES WHERE SM-RELATED EVIDENCE USED OR ADMISSIBLE

For example,

- Used in cases of marital indiscretions in the Family Court;

- *Carolina Herrera Ltd v Lacoste* [2014] SGIPOS 3 – Opponent's evidence include SM posts from Facebook;

- Procuring of a minor through an SM site for the purposes of prostitution and also posting pictures of the minor with injuries on SM after assaulting her,

  - *PP v Malcolm Graham Head* [2014] SGDC 79;

  - The accused, a 33-year-old male, pleaded guilty to 17 out of 41 charges against him;

  - These charges ranged from prostitution-related offences under the Women's Charter, abetting commercial sex with a minor, voluntarily causing hurt/grievous hurt offences under the Penal Code, to driving whilst under a disqualification order and offences under the Misuse of Drugs Act;

  - The accused registered a company for the provision of social escort and paid sexual services and also procured females for the purposes of prostitution;

  - At [18]–[19]: the accused befriended a 16-year-old minor on Facebook (an SM site) and privately messaged her to tell her to leave her contact details if she wanted to earn 'fast cash';

  - The minor agreed to work for the accused and left her particulars with the accused;

  - She then commenced work as a social escort-cum-prostitute and realised at her first booking that she would be required to provide sexual services to her customers;

  - The accused was thus found guilty of procuring a minor for the purposes of prostitution under s 140(1)(b) read with s 140(2) of the Women's Charter;

  - In considering whether to impose caning on the accused, the judge took into account (at [55]) the fact that, after the accused assaulted the minor, he posted photographs of the minor with her injuries on SM;

  - Taking into consideration the accused's lengthy antecedents, the judge sentenced the accused to a total of 7 years' corrective training and 7 strokes of the cane.

C25.6   SPECIFIC ONLINE ABUSE/ONLINE BULLYING/ CYBERBULLYING LAWS

The proposed Protection from Harassment Bill is intended, inter alia, to protect persons against harassment and unlawful stalking and to create offences, and provide civil remedies related thereto.

- Criminal Sanctions/Offences (Part II of the Bill)

  - Harassment will be an offence;

  - It will cover a range of behaviour including cyber-harassment, bullying of children, sexual harassment within and outside the work place and unlawful stalking;

  - The existing penalties for harassment offences will be increased to reflect their seriousness, and enhanced penalties will be provided for repeat offenders;

  - The court will also be empowered to make community orders in appropriate cases.

- Self-help and civil remedies (Part III of the Bill)

  - Victims may apply to the court for Protection Orders requiring harassers to desist from doing anything which may cause further harm to them.

C25.7   OTHER LAWS APPLIED TO ONLINE ABUSE/ ONLINE BULLYING/CYBERBULLYING

- At present, there appears to be no specific legislation to target cyberbullying or abuses occurring online.

- This lacuna has been noted by Parliament, prompting the introduction of the Protection from Harassment Bill.

- Minister for Law, K Shanmugam in his speech to Parliament during the second reading of the Protection from Harassment Bill,

  - Miscellaneous Offences (Public Order and Nuisance) Act (Cap 184) makes harassment a criminal offence. However, from the way the law has been interpreted by the courts, it is not clear if it would apply to harassment online;

  - The Women's Charter and the Moneylenders Act – Covers harassment in the context of family violence or unlicensed moneylending rather than general harassing conduct;

  - While the Penal Code covers offences such as criminal intimidation in both the physical world and online, there are no laws for cyber-harassment, bullying and 'other antisocial acts on the Internet';

    –   The fact is that our existing civil remedies and self-help avenues are also limited;

    –   The High Court's recent decisions in *AXA Insurance (AXA Insurance Singapore Pte Ltd v Chandran s/o Natesan* [2013] 4 SLR 545) and its earlier decision in *Malcomson (Malcomson Nicholas Hugh Betram and another v Mehta Naresh Kumar* [2001] 3 SLR(R) 379) cast doubt as to whether one can even bring a civil action for harassment in Singapore;

    –   Other forms of private action, for example, in nuisance, assault or battery, also have obvious limitations.

- The decision in *Malcomson* appears to imply that legal recourse for victims of such cyberbullying may be available under the tort of harassment. The decision in *Axa Insurance* says otherwise;

- Clause 14 of the Protection from Harassment Bill clarifies the confusion resulting from these two conflicting decisions and abolishes the common law tort of harassment.

C25.8   CHILDREN AND SM LAWS OR RULES

- No specific laws or rules, but there is the offence of child grooming in s 376E of the Penal Code (Cap 224), and the Protection from Harassment Act will cover bullying of children and unlawful stalking.

    –   Parliament has recognised the problem of bullying of children (Second Reading at [25]–[37]).

C25.9   EMPLOYEES/EMPLOYMENT SM LAWS OR CASES

No specific cases, but the Protection from Harassment Act will cover workplace harassment by an employer.

C25.10   SCHOOL AND UNIVERSITY STUDENT SM CASES

No particular cases, but the following incident was reported in the papers (see news.asiaone.com/News/Latest+News/Singapore/Story/A1Story20120814-365300.html),

- Singapore Institute of Management (SIM) student, Justin Wee, 24, was captured on video spewing vulgarities and passing derogatory comments on Malays and Indians;

- Wee appeared to be drunk;

- Video was uploaded on YouTube;

- SIM commenced investigation and convened disciplinary hearing;

- NUS also commenced investigation, as it was apparent from the video that the NUS students instigated Wee to make racist remarks while he was drunk;

- Wee meanwhile sent out an email statement of apology expressing regret for his comments in the video;

- In his email, he said that he realised the video was on YouTube the day after the incident and his requests to make the video private were ignored.

C25.11   RIGHT OR HUMAN RIGHT TO ACCESS THE INTERNET OR SM

No details.

C25.12   BANS OR RESTRICTIONS ON INTERNET OR SM

No details.

C25.13   IDENTITY THEFT (OR EQUIVALENT)

- Section 419 Punishment for cheating by personation

    – Whoever cheats by personation shall be punished with imprisonment for a term which may extend to 5 years, or with fine, or with both.

- *Public Prosecutor v Tan Hock Keong Benjamin* [2014] SGDC 16

    – The accused pleaded guilty to 5 charges that included the following,

        • One charge of possession of someone else's NRIC (ie National Registration Identity Card) without lawful authority under s 13(2)(b) of the National Registration Act (Cap 201);

        • One charge of cheating by personation under s 419 of the Penal Code (Cap 224);

    – In respect of the first charge, the accused was found in possession of a Singapore NRIC belonging to one Liu Weide, who had reported the loss of his NRIC. The accused was unable to give a reasonable excuse for how he came to be in possession of the NRIC.

    – In respect of the second charge stated above, the accused admitted that he had used the NRIC to obtain a Samsung Galaxy S4 mobile phone, by signing up for a mobile phone plan using Liu Weide's name at the mobile phone shop (M1 shop). He had pretended to be the said Liu Weide and showed Liu Weide's NRIC to the staff at the M1 shop. This led the staff to believe that the accused was Liu Weide and he approved the application and the accused was handed the mobile phone. The accused sold the mobile phone subsequently.

- Section 4 of the Computer Misuse and Cybersecurity Act (Cap 50A) may be operative if the information is used to commit or to further the commission of a 'traditional' offence, which is likely to be the case as phishing and related activities are often motivated by illegitimate pecuniary interest and wrongful financial gain.

    – Requires access to computer material as a prerequisite to an offence made out (s 4(1));

    – It is limited to access intended for the commission or the facilitation of the commission of an offence involving property, fraud, dishonesty or the causing of bodily harm and which is punishable on conviction with imprisonment for a term of not less than 2 years (s 4(2)).

C25.14 HACKING (OR EQUIVALENT)

- Computer Misuse and Cybersecurity Act (Cap 50A, Rev Ed Sing 2007)

    – The Computer Misuse and Cybersecurity Act (CMA) makes provision for, inter alia, unauthorised access to computer material, access with intent to commit or facilitate the commission of an offence, unauthorised modification of computer material, unauthorised use or interception of computer service;

    – The interpretation of key phrases such as 'computer', 'data', and 'program or computer program' are liberal to ensure that the ambit and scope of these phrases are sufficiently wide to encompass a wide variety of situations (*Halsbury's Laws of Singapore*, Vol 8(3) at [90.434]);

    – Section 3(1) states that any person who knowingly causes a computer to perform any function for the purpose of securing access without authority to any program or data held in any computer shall be guilty of an offence and shall be liable on conviction to a fine not exceeding $5,000 or to imprisonment for a term not exceeding 2 years or to both;

    – It can potentially be used to restrict some forms of invasive data harvesting conducted by SM applications on their users;

- Section 4(1) states that any person who causes a computer to perform any function for the purpose of securing access to any program or data held in any computer with intent to commit an offence to which this section applies shall be guilty of an offence;

- Section 6(1) states that any person who knowingly secures access to any computer to obtain any computer service without authority; or intercepts any function of a computer; or uses or causes to be used the computer or any other device for the purpose of securing access or intercepting any function shall be guilty of an offence and liable upon conviction to a fine not exceeding $10,000 or to imprisonment for a term not exceeding 3 years or to both. If any damage is caused as a result of an offence under this section, the maximum fine is $50,000 and the maximum term of imprisonment is 5 years;

- Section 15A(1) provides that, where the Minister is satisfied that it is necessary to prevent, detect or counter any threat to national security, essential services or defence or foreign relations of Singapore, the Minister may by a certificate under his hand authorise or direct any person or organisation to take such measures or comply with requirements as may be necessary to prevent, detect or counter any threat to a computer or computer service.

PP v Muhammad Nuzaihan bin Kamal Luddin [1999] 3 SLR(R) 653; [1999] SGHC 275

- Accused was a 17-year-old student;

- During the year end school vacation of 1997, he had become interested in computer security and had discovered certain flaws in Linux operating systems which allowed outside parties to check for vulnerabilities in computer networks;

- Sometime in June 1998, he decided to 'hack' into foreign servers, believing that this would not be easily detected or traced by the relevant system administrators who were mostly located abroad;

- He managed to hack into four foreign sites successfully without being detected by their system administrators;

- He then tested his skills on local servers;

- He 'hacked' into one of the proxy servers of Swiftech Automation Pte Ltd's network and into the File Transfer Protocol server of Singapore Cable Vision Ltd which had earlier rejected his application for an Internet account;

- He was charged under ss 3(1), 5(1) and 6(1)(a) of the CMA;

- He pleaded guilty and was sentenced in the District Court to undergo 30 months' probation;

- The prosecution appealed on the basis that this sentence was manifestly inadequate;

- The judge quashed the probation order and imposed sentences of 2 months' imprisonment for each of the three charges, with the sentence of imprisonment on the first two charges to run consecutively.

Liew Cheong Wee Leslie v PP [2013] 4 SLR 170; [2013] SGHC 141

- The accused, a 35-year-old engineer, was a former employee of Power Automation Pte Ltd;

- During his employment, he worked on a project for the Marina Bay Sands Integrated Resort; his work concerned working with a Power Monitoring Control System (PMCS), a computer system for managing and controlling all digitally controlled equipment in the resort including the casino;

- On 12 May 2010, there was a massive blackout at the casino at around 12.20am which affected all levels from the basement to level 3 of the northern section of the casino;

- After investigations, the accused was charged and convicted on five counts under s 3(1) and one count under s 3(2) of the CMA;

- On the evidence, it was found that the appellant had gone through an elaborate process to give himself remote access through his personal computer and added a personal email which was not known to his employers to the system administrator to gain access to the system;

- Choo J said that the evidence pointed to the inescapable conclusion that the accused deliberately intended to cause the blackout. When there were no instructions or reasons for doing so, the natural inference must be that he did so with mischief in his mind. This was clearly an offence under s 3 of the CMA, and the judge dismissed the accused's appeal against conviction (at [3]);

- Regarding the s 3(2) charge, Choo J held that the Prosecution failed to specify the damage that was caused by the accused's act, thus it was amended to a charge under s 3(1).

C25.15   PRIVACY BY DESIGN (PBD) (OR EQUIVALENT)

The Personal Data Protection Act,

- Establishes a data protection law that comprises various rules governing the collection, disclosure, use and care of personal data;

- recognises both the rights of individuals to protect their personal data, including rights of access and correction, and the needs of organisations to collect, use or disclose personal data for legitimate and reasonable purposes;

- By regulating the flow of personal data among organisations, aims to strengthen and entrench Singapore's competitiveness and position as a trusted, world-class hub for businesses.

C25.16 TWEETING FROM COURTS, AND ANY RULES/LAWS

No details. All pagers, hand phones and beeping devices are to be switched off before entering the courtroom, as these may disrupt the proceedings.

C25.17 TELEVISION COURTROOM BROADCASTING OR TELEVISION CAMERAS IN COURT, AND RULES OR LAWS

No details.

C25.18 SM IN COURTROOMS

No details.

C25.19 USE OF SM AS EVIDENCE IN COURTS

Evidence from SM sites has been used in some cases (see C25.5 and C25.21).

C25.20 PRIVACY, DATA PROTECTION AND SM

The impact of the Personal Data Protection Act (PDPA) in relation to SM sites has yet to be seen. It is stated that 'Provisions relating to the DNC Registry came into effect on 2 January 2014 and the main data protection rules will come into force on 2 July 2014. This allows time for organisations to review and adopt internal personal data protection policies and practices, to help them comply with the PDPA' in the section 'When does the PDPA come into effect?', available online at www.pdpc.gov.sg/personal-data-protection-act/overview.

C25.21 SM AND FAMILY LAW CASES

There are family law cases that rely on evidence or allegations based on information obtained from SM sites,

- *BKU v BKV* [2013] SGDC 287 was a matrimonial dispute.

- – The issues in this case centred on the care and custody of the two children;

- – Pending the settlement of interlocutory matters raised, pursuant to a consent order the husband was given interim care and control of the son while the wife was given interim care and control of the daughter;

- – On appeal, both husband and wife wanted sole custody of both children;

- – Reference was made to the daughter's Facebook page (at [12] and [31]);

- – Status quo was maintained, with the daughter under the care and control of the wife and the son under the care and control of the husband (at [35]).

- *BDJ v BDK* [2012] SGDC 415 was a case concerning a wife appealing against personal protection orders (PPOs) which were granted to her husband, her father-in-law and mother-in-law against her.

  - – In applying for a PPO against his wife, the husband alleged several instances of violence and mistreatment committed by the wife against him;

  - – One of these instances occurred after the wife checked his mobile phone and Facebook account and confronted him over his flirtatious Facebook messages (at [32], [120)) which led her to doubt his fidelity;

  - – The judge held that, while the checking of Facebook and mobile phone messages may not have caused the husband a lack of privacy and led to countless arguments between them, it was likely that the wife did cause harassment to the husband by her actions (at [122]);

  - – The judge found that, based on the cumulative effect of the various allegations of the husband, the wife had, on a balance of probabilities, committed family violence against the husband and that he had good reason to fear her, thus a PPO was granted to the husband against the wife (at [107] to [138]).

- *BDT v BDU* [2012] SGDC 363; [2013] SGHC 106; [2014] SGCA 12

  - – In the landmark case under the International Child Abduction Act (Cap 143C, 2011 Rev Ed) for the return of a 2 plus year-old child to the husband in Germany, brief mention was made of a Facebook message as evidence to question the wife's parent's affidavit ([2012] SGDC 363 at [43]);

  - – The CA affirmed the HC's decision which affirmed the District Court's decision for an order to return the child to Germany.

C25.22 SPORTS PERSONS, SPORTS CLUBS AND SM

No details.

C25.23 PERSONAL RELATIONS AND RELATIONSHIPS

For example,

- *Public Prosecutor v Yeo Jun Hao* [2013] SGDC 96

  − The accused, Yeo Jun Hao (male of 19 years of age) pleaded guilty to one charge of attempted extortion with common intention in that he, together with 2 others (Mah and Syazwan), tried to extort the sum of $2,500 from the victim by threatening to circulate his nude photographs on the internet with the intention of putting the victim in fear of harm to his reputation;

  − Mah created a Facebook account under the name 'Chanel' and befriended the victim on Facebook. They chatted online and began an online relationship;

  − Subsequently, Mah requested that the victim send him his (the victim's) nude photographs. The victim obliged and sent 4 nude photographs to Mah;

  − Mah then devised a plan to extort money from the victim by threatening to post the nude photographs of the victim online. He asked the accused for advice and the accused agreed to assist him on the execution of Mah's plan in return for a share of the money;

  − The accused sent a text message to the victim claiming to be the boyfriend of 'Chanel', forwarded the nude photographs of the victim and demanded $2,500 from him, threatening to circulate the photographs online if the victim failed to pay the money. The victim agreed to hand over the money to the accused;

  − Mah then roped in Shazwan as 'runner' to collect the money in return for $300;

  − The victim, however, reported this to the police and the police successfully laid an ambush and arrested all three accused persons;

  − The accused was sentenced to a period of Reformative Training in the Reformative Training centre.

C25.24 SM AND PERSONAL DATA OF DECEASED PERSONS

No details.

C25.25 SM, WEBSITE, SERVICE PROVIDER OR ISP DEFENCE RULES/LAWS

Citing Warren B Chik, 'Internet Intermediaries and copyright law in Singapore', Law Gazette, April 2010(3):

Immunity for network service providers under the Electronic Transaction Act (Cap 88)

- Section 26 of the Electronic Transaction Act (ETA) provides blanket immunity to network service providers (NSPs) and protects them from any civil or criminal responsibility for third party content;

- However, this immunity does not apply to the copyright regime;

- Section 26(2) of the ETA provides that NSPs are subject to the provisions of the Copyright Act;

- Under s 26(1A) of the ETA, a network service provider shall not be subject to any liability under the Personal Data Protection Act 2012 in respect of third-party material in the form of electronic records to which he merely provides access.

Immunity for network service provides under the Copyright Act (Cap 63)

- Under the Copyright Act (CA), NSPs are granted immunity from copyright infringement for activities that are integral to their functions such as transmission, routing and provision of connections, system caching and storage and information location;

- The Safe Harbour provisions are encapsulated within ss 193B to 193D and ss 252A to 252C of the CA:

  - In short, Safe Harbour provisions are the various requirements that the NSPs have to meet in order to enjoy immunity under the CA;

  - It is important to note that the fact that an NSP elects not to meet the requirements to come under the Safe Harbour provisions does not automatically make it liable to copyright holders for any copyright infringements;

  - Instead, the general provisions of the CA will govern the NSP's liability in relation to copyright infringement, and the complainant will still have to prove primary or secondary infringement on the NSP's part in a court of law;

- The NSPs have to satisfy specific requirements to be eligible for immunity from copyright infringement claims;

- For example, pursuant to s 193D, the court shall not grant any monetary relief or, except as provided for in s 193DB, make any order against an

NSP for any infringement of copyright in any material that occurs by reason of the storage, at the direction of a user of the NSP's primary network, of an electronic copy of the material on the primary network, if the NSP satisfies these conditions:

- NSP does not benefit financially from the copyright infringement;

- NSP expeditiously takes reasonable steps to remove the infringing materials when it becomes aware of such infringement, either on its own accord or via a notice in accordance with s 193D(2)(b)(iii);

- NSP designates a representative to receive notices pursuant to s 193D(2)(b)(iii);

- Section 193A(1) defines NSP:

  - For the purposes of s 193B, as a person who provides services relating to, or provides connections for, the transmission or routing of data; and

  - Other than for the purposes of s 193B, as a person who provides, or operates facilities for, online services or network access and includes a person referred to in paragraph (a).

C25.26 ECOMMERCE DEFENCE CASES

- The case of *RecordTV Pte Ltd v Mediacorp TV Singapore Pte Ltd* [2010] 2 SLR 152 dealt with the safe harbour provisions found within the Copyright Act;

- In this case, the Singapore High Court considered whether an offending online service provider could avail themselves of the safe harbour provisions;

  - The plaintiff was the owner of an internet-based service (RecordTV) which allows the public to request that free-to-air broadcasts be recorded for viewing;

  - Upon receipt of such a request, a copy of that broadcast is made by the plaintiff's servers and users might view the recordings on their home computers at their own convenience;

  - The defendants were the copyright owners of various broadcasts and films which are recordable via RecordTV;

  - After receiving 'cease and desist' letters from the defendants pertaining to the continued operation of RecordTV, the plaintiff commenced an action for groundless threats of copyright infringement. The defendants in turn claimed for copyright infringement;

  - The plaintiff argued that it was a network service provider within the meaning of s 193A of the Copyright Act and therefore entitled

> to rely on any or all of the defences available under Part IXA of the Copyright Act;

> – The High Court rejected the plaintiff's contention;

> – The High Court held that the very nature of the plaintiff's system is such that its purpose is diametrically opposed to the intent of the safe harbour provisions;

> – Furthermore, the operation of the website can hardly be said to be an 'automatic technical process without any selection of the electronic copy of the material by the plaintiff' within the meaning of s 193B.

- The decision went on appeal, but the Court of Appeal held that the plaintiff was not liable for copyright infringement. Hence, it held that it was not necessary to determine whether the plaintiff could rely on any safe harbour provisions: *RecordTV Pte Ltd v MediaCorp TV Singapore Pte Ltd and others* [2011] 1 SLR 830 (Court of Appeal).

C25.27 LAWS PROTECTING PERSONAL DATA/ PERSONALLY IDENTIFIABLE INFORMATION

Personal Data Protection Act 2012 (PDPA) (see C25.15),

- Section 25 – An organisation shall protect personal data in its possession or under its control by making reasonable security arrangements to prevent unauthorised access, collection, use, disclosures, copying, modification, disposal or similar risks;

- Part IX of the PDPA provides for the establishment of a national Do Not Call (DNC) Registry. The DNC Registry allows individuals to register their Singapore telephone numbers to opt out of receiving marketing phone calls, mobile text messages such as SMS or MMS, and faxes from organisations;

- The Act covers personal data stored in electronic and non-electronic forms;

- The Act does not supersede existing statutes, such as the Banking Act and Insurance Act, but will work in conjunction with them and the common law.

C25.28 DATA BREACH LAWS AND CUSTOMERS/ USERS/REGULATORS NOTIFIED OF HACKING OR DATA LOSS

The PDPA does not specifically require customers, users or regulators to be notified if an organisation's data or systems have been hacked or data is otherwise lost, ie there is no breach notification requirement under the PDPA.

Chapter C26

Slovenia

Klara Miletič and Mojca Ilešič
Wolf Theiss

C26.1   INTRODUCTION

Slovenia is an EU member state and is a Civil Law jurisdiction.

C26.2   SPECIFIC SM AND SN LAWS

There are no specific SM and SN laws in Slovenia.

C26.3   SM CRIMINAL LAW CASES

In a criminal law case (Ref no Ips 76261/2010 dated 27 September 2012), the Supreme Court dealt with the question of whether publishing on Facebook an intimate photo of a person which had been taken with the consent of that person is considered unlawful visual recording in the sense of Article 138 of the Criminal Code (Official Gazette of the Republic of Slovenia No 50/12). Article 138 prohibits substantial interference with another person's privacy by taking unauthorised photographs or other visual recordings of that person or his premises without his consent, or transmitting or presenting such photographs or recordings to a third person or otherwise allowing a third person to see such photographs or recordings.

The facts of the case concerned a male who had been in an intimate relationship with the victim for approximately two years, during which time he had taken several naked photographs of the victim with her consent. After their relationship has ended, the victim, who worked as a waitress, refused to serve him a drink on grounds that he was inebriated. Later that day he published a photo of her intimate parts on the 'wall' of his Facebook profile, with comments which clearly indicated the identity of the woman on the photograph. An hour later, the accused removed the photograph. He was convicted at first and second instance, since both courts determined that he acted intentionally and was aware of the fact that he was publishing a photograph which would be seen and recognized by others, and which would clearly infringe the victim's privacy, whereas the victim had given her consent merely for the photographs to remain between her and the accused and not for sharing with others.

The decisions of the courts of first and second instance were based on the teleological interpretation of the law, since the rationale of Article 138 is to protect individuals from considerable interference with their privacy. The Supreme Court, however, has rendered a different judgment justified by the linguistic interpretation of the Article. According thereto, the court has come to a conclusion that the law does not penalise visual recording which interferes with somebody's privacy but is carried out with the consent of that person. The Supreme Court thus acquitted the accused. It nevertheless pointed out that the victim is entitled to legal remedies in civil law to protect her right to privacy. Whether sharing visual content which considerably interferes with another's privacy, albeit taken with their consent, should be penalised, however, is a question for the legislator. The Supreme Court acknowledged that this question is particularly topical, taking into consideration the development of modern technology and the possibilities for publishing content on SM, which often infringe another's right to privacy.

C26.4   SM CIVIL LAW CASES

A judgment of the Higher court in Ljubljana (Ref No II Cp 2066/2012, dated 30 January 2013) also concerns publishing photographs on Facebook. The photographs here at stake revealed internal family occurrences and refer to a family dispute which would otherwise not be known to third parties. The claimant submitted that his right to privacy was infringed as well as his right to one's own image, since others were acquainted with the facts that are not publicly available and belong to his private sphere. The defendant who published the photograph in question defended his acts by pointing out that his Facebook profile was closed and hence accessible only to a narrow group of people. The Higher court decided that the fact that such publication is intended merely for the 'closest circle of friends' does not exclude the illegality of such publication. Namely, even the closest friends represent the public, and a private conversation with one's closest friends may constitute violation of one's right to privacy if thereby a personal matter is revealed which belongs to one's private sphere. The number of people who were familiarized with such a personal matter affects only the intensity of breach, and thus the amount of damages and not the existence of the breach itself.

Another case regarding publishing visual content on Facebook was decided by the Higher court in Maribor (Ref No I Cp 193/2012, dated 8 May 2012), where the claimant sought damages for infringement of her right of honour and her reputation by the publication on the internet of an article which insulted her and her intimate life. The claimant is a school worker and performed a dance act dressed as a cabaret dancer on the occasion of the carnival. One of the students, the first defendant, recorded her performance and published it on Facebook. The fourth defendant wrote a column which considerably defamed the claimant and attached the video recorded by the student. The second and third defendants are the holder of the web page, where the column was published, and the editor-in-chief. The court of first instance rejected the claim against all four defendants, whereas the Higher court upon appeal upheld only the decision regarding the first defendant, ie the student who published the visual content of the dance performance on Facebook. Namely, the conduct of the student who recorded the performance is not illegal, since the performance in question took place within the working hours of the claimant and in the presence of approximately 50 students. The published video thus undoubtedly does not represent an event from the claimant's personal life, but rather depicts an occurrence for which a certain interest of the public to information exists. By performing the act in question, the claimant entered into the public sphere and should take certain possible reactions into account. The court deemed it irrelevant whether the claimant was aware of the fact that she was being recorded. Notwithstanding the principled prohibition of use of personal devices for connection with data and telecommunication network, the claimant, having regard to the circumstances in which she decided to perform the act, should have expected that students would try to record such an event. In the era of today's information technology, she thereby also accepted the risk of transmission of such records to SM. Moreover, the court took into consideration 18 years of experience of the claimant in which she must have been familiar with the use of mobile phones in the school environment. Due to the omnipresence of such technology, the use of mobile devices at least during breaks, at events and on school trips and similar, including the event in question, is normal. On these grounds the Higher court came to the conclusion that the student who merely recorded the performance and published the video on Facebook did not unlawfully infringe the claimant's personal rights.

C26.5   CASES WHERE SM-RELATED EVIDENCE USED OR ADMISSIBLE

Apart from the cases cited above, the courts have also used SM-related evidence in other cases. It derives from the judgment of the Higher Court in Ljubljana dated 9 October 2013 (Ref No II Cp 1172/2013) that the court of first instance used a print-out from a Facebook profile in a case of disturbance of possession. It is not apparent from the judgment of the Higher court what this evidence was supporting, but the Higher court upheld the first instance decision.

Further, the Higher Labour and Social Court admitted a Facebook post as evidence in a case (Ref No Pdp 486/2012). The Higher court admitted the evidence but did not attribute enough weight to the facts that it supported to influence the final decision.

C26.6   SPECIFIC ONLINE ABUSE/ONLINE BULLYING/ CYBERBULLYING LAWS

There are no such specific laws. However, the Information Commissioner has issued Guidelines on protection from online bullying which shed some light on this issue and offer advice on how to tackle potential situations of online abuse or bullying, in particular with regard to children.

C26.7   OTHER LAWS APPLIED TO ONLINE ABUSE/ ONLINE BULLYING/CYBERBULLYING

Currently, the Criminal Code and the Personal Data Protection Act (Official Gazette of the Republic of Slovenia No 94/07) may serve as legal grounds for dealing with cases of online abuse or cyberbullying.

According to the media, there was a case of online bullying in January 2012, where a group of 18 students took intimate photos of their professor, blackmailed her and shared the photos with others. Three of them were supposedly accused of extortion and blackmail (Article 213 of the Criminal Code), while 17 have been accused of unlawful visual recording (Article 138 of the Criminal Code). As mentioned above, decisions of the first instance court are not publicly available, therefore we cannot report on the court epilogue of these accusations. Nevertheless, the mere existence of the accusations shows that certain forms of cyberbullying can be dealt with by criminal law, although the Criminal Code does not provide for specific criminal offences in connection with cyberbullying.

According to the Guidelines on protection from online bullying (see C26.6), online bullying may lead to several criminal offences. Beside those already mentioned, it may also constitute the criminal offence of abuse of personal data (Article 143), such as identity theft, violation of secrecy of means of communication (Article 139) or unlawful publication of private writings (Article 140). What is more, if the bullies insult, circulate anything false, which is capable of damaging his honour or reputation, or if they circulate any matter concerning personal or family affairs, which is capable of injuring that person's honour and reputation, they may be pursued for insult (Article 158), slander (Article 159), defamation (Article 160) or calumny (Article 161).

Apart from the Criminal Code, the Personal Data Protection Act is also relevant, as online abuse or cyberbullying may occur through abuse of personal data which is part of a database. If this is the case, the Information Commissioner is authorised to exercise control and impose fines.

C26.8   CHILDREN AND SM LAWS OR RULES

There are no laws or rules specific to children and SM. The Guidelines of the Information Commissioner (see C26.6) are intended to offer guidance in cases of bullying for victims, parents and teachers.

According to the research of B Lobe and S Muha on the risks of children on the internet (Report for Slovenia (2010)), 19% of children have been bullied online or offline in the year preceding the research. Bullying is recorded to the greatest extent with children aged 15 and 16 and children aged 9 and 10 (approximately 23%).

C26.9   EMPLOYEES/EMPLOYMENT SM LAWS OR CASES

There are no specific laws on the use of SM at work. There is also no case law of the Constitutional Court, Supreme Court or Higher Courts relating specifically to SM and employment, but case law on privacy of communication in the workplace certainly applies to the use of SM as well.

The general legal framework, namely the Constitution of the Republic of Slovenia and the Employment Relationships Act, ensures protection of privacy of employees also at the workplace, including their use of business phones and computers. According to the Administrative Court's judgment (Ref No U-702/99 dated 21 March 2000), the aspect of property over the means of communication is irrelevant for assessing potential breach of privacy. In other words, the employer is not entitled to control means of communication at the workplace simply because he owns the devices.

The extent of the right to privacy depends on the work tasks of the employee and the requirements of the workplace (eg protecting business secrets), whereas control of communications must be transparent and proportional. Control for reasons of snooping, in order to find out whether the employee is wasting the company's time for personal purposes, is neither proportional nor necessary. The employer may terminate the employment if the employee does not fulfil his work tasks, whereby it is irrelevant whether such failure was due to the use of SM, personal email, personal use of phone or other reasons. (See Matej Kovačič, 'Communication privacy at workplace', *Zbornik Kriminaliteta in tehnologija*, Inštitut za kriminologijo pri PF LJ, 2010.)

C26.10   SCHOOL AND UNIVERSITY STUDENT SM CASES

Pursuant to Article 4 of the Rules on the School Order in Secondary schools (Official Gazette of the Republic of Slovenia No 60/10), the use of personal devices for connecting to data and telecommunication networks contrary to school rules is forbidden. As follows from the judgment of the Higher court in Maribor (see C26.4), however, the use of mobile devices at least during breaks, at events and on school trips and similar, is normal and acceptable, due to the omnipresence of this sort of technology.

C26.11 RIGHT OR HUMAN RIGHT TO ACCESS THE INTERNET OR SM

There are no cases, rules or laws in relation to a right or human right of access to the internet or SM. In 2011, an article was published concerning access to the internet as a fundamental right (Matija Damjan, *Pravni Letopis* 2011, p 361), where the author determines the significance of the internet in a democratic society and characterises its relevance from the point of view of not only freedom of expression, but also other constitutionally protected values, such as freedom of work, free choice of employment and free economic initiative.

C26.12 BANS OR RESTRICTIONS ON INTERNET OR SM

We do not know of any cases or laws restricting the use of SM or the internet to persons convicted for particular types of criminal offences. However, according to the Enforcement of Criminal Sanctions Act (Official Gazette of the Republic of Slovenia, No 110/06 as amended), convicted criminals who are serving a sentence may only be allowed to use electronic communications if such use does not put security inside and outside the institution at risk.

C26.13 IDENTITY THEFT (OR EQUIVALENT)

Paragraph 4 of Article 143 of the Criminal Code prohibits assuming the identity of another person and under their name exploiting their rights, gaining property benefits or damaging their personal dignity, under penalty of imprisonment between 3 months and 3 years. There has been no case law on this criminal offence so far.

C26.14 HACKING (OR EQUIVALENT)

Two criminal offences in the Criminal Code concern hacking. Article 221 on attack on information systems penalises breaking into an information system or illegally intercepting data during a non-public transmission into or from the information system. The same Article also prohibits the illegal use of data in an information system or the change, copy, transmission, destruction or illegal import of data in an information system, or obstruction of data transmission or information system operation.

The second criminal offence in the Criminal Code which concerns hacking is breaking into business information systems (Article 237). This offence is committed by anyone who, in the performance of business operations, without authority alters, hides, deletes or destroys any data or computer program or otherwise breaks into a computer system in order either to procure an unlawful property benefit for himself or a third person or to cause damage to the property of another.

C26.15 PRIVACY BY DESIGN (PBD) (OR EQUIVALENT)

There are no rules or laws relating to privacy by design; however, on 6 December 2010 the Information Commissioner issued Guidelines for developing information solutions where the most important requirements to be followed in the development of information solutions encompassing personal data processing are addressed. Therein the concept of PbD is described, promoted and its advantages are pointed out. The target public of the Guidelines are developers of information systems, solutions and applications, and clients commissioning such services.

C26.16 TWEETING FROM COURTS, AND ANY RULES/LAWS

In Slovenian courts, parties and visitors must turn off their mobile devices. Video and audio recordings of courtroom hearings are prohibited by Court Rules (Official Gazette of the Republic of Slovenia, No 17/95 as amended), unless the president of the court approves it in advance. The Criminal Procedure Act (Official Gazette of the Republic of Slovenia, No 32/12, with amendment) stipulates in Article 301 that visual recording is not allowed in the courtroom. On an exceptional basis, the president of the Supreme Court may allow such recording for a particular hearing. In this event, the panel in the hearing may nevertheless decide that certain parts of the hearing are not recorded, if justifiable reasons exist.

In January 2013, an amendment to Criminal Procedure Act was proposed ('Proposal') which touched on this issue. The Government proposed that Article 301 should be changed so as to allow direct transmission of data in the courtroom by way of written messages using means of telecommunication, which refers in particular to Tweeting and sending SMS messages. The Proposal also contains a provision allowing video and audio recording of hearings and direct broadcasting where such recording and broadcasting does not distort the process, does not influence the course and fairness of the process, and does not violate the rights of participants in the hearing. The hearing may by no means be recorded if the accused or his counsel, witnesses or experts explicitly oppose it.

The prohibition of transmission of data in the courtroom, by way of written messages using means of telecommunication, video and audio recording and requests for permission for direct broadcasting, would be decided by the president of the panel if reasons for exclusion of the public are given or if order is distorted.

The Proposal has faced strong opposition from experts, in particular from representatives of the Supreme Court and of the Slovenian Association of Judges, who have argued that the public nature of court proceedings is already sufficiently safeguarded by existing measures, such as the participation of lay judges, and public notice of hearings which may be attended by anyone. In their opinion, the argument for the proposed change of these provisions, namely participation of the public in the judicial function and control thereof, does not carry enough weight to justify such changes.

As a result, the relevant provisions of the Proposal were not included in the Act amending the Criminal Procedure Act (Official Gazette of the Republic of Slovenia, no 47/13), and the issue remains regulated as described above.

C26.17 TELEVISION COURTROOM BROADCASTING OR TELEVISION CAMERAS IN COURT, AND RULES OR LAWS

See above.

C26.18 SM IN COURTROOMS

In a criminal case against former Prime Minister Janez Janša, the judge ordered the journalists to leave the courtroom and return only after they had left their mobile phones and computers outside the courtroom. She also prohibited the accused from using an iPad, despite his assertions that the text of his defence was saved on it.

In a case against some participants in country-wide protests in 2013, the judge, according to the media, used a transmitter to disturb the GSM signal to disable the use of mobile phones in the courtroom. The use of such transmitter was not justified by the judge and caused controversies amongst the public, since the courts are not allowed to do so in the courtroom and could not justify its use on the basis of the court order which prohibits audio and visual recording.

C26.19 USE OF SM AS EVIDENCE IN COURTS

The use of SM as evidence in courts is not problematic in our jurisdiction. According to the Civil Procedure Act (Official Gazette of the Republic of Slovenia, no 73/07 with amendments), parties in the dispute must submit facts that support their claims and propose evidence to support those facts. Evidence is required and allowed for all the facts that are relevant for the judgment. Other than that, there are no limitations as to admissibility of evidence or of SM-related evidence. However, it should be noted that the courts are free in the assessment of evidence, and it is therefore for the court, depending on the circumstances, to decide what weight it will attribute to such evidence.

C26.20 PRIVACY, DATA PROTECTION AND SM

The Information Commissioner has issued several opinions regarding data protection and SM. These principled opinions are not legally binding, and their interpretation of particular provisions is not authentic, since authentic interpretations are only those issued by the Parliament.

In her opinion No 0712-568/2009/2 dated 24 December 2009 regarding false information for registration with an SN, she pointed out that the controller of the SN may require true data for registration, if that is in accordance with their standard terms. The Commissioner is nevertheless striving for SNs to enable anonymized use of their services. She makes it clear that the controller of the SN should inform its users,

- of the name and type of users of their personal data;

- whether obtaining personal data is obligatory or voluntary, including possible consequences, if he does not submit the data voluntarily;

- of details on the right to have access to data, and rights to a transcript, copy, completion, correction, blockage and deletion of his personal data.

Opinion No 0712-2/2009/434 dated 7 April 2009 addresses the question of identity theft in the form of a false profile on Facebook with the data of another person. An email address or SM profile can only be considered personal data if it enables recognition of an individual, which means that an individual must be directly or indirectly identifiable without incurring considerable expense, disproportionate effort or a lot of time. Provided that a Facebook profile is considered personal data, its abuse is a criminal offence in the sense of Article 143 of the Criminal Code (abuse of personal data). Besides criminal sanctions, the Information Commissioner also refers to the 'Report this person' function of Facebook, which enables users to send an anonymous report to the Facebook administrators.

An Opinion dated 12 December 2012 was issued as a response to a query regarding the use of data obtained through Facebook by a Social Work Centre in the process of deciding on the right of parents to a reduction of kindergarten costs. The applicant contended that she lives alone with her children and the Centre required this fact to be confirmed by two witnesses. In turn, the Centre obtained photos from Facebook of the applicant proving that the applicant is living with a partner, and not as a single parent as she claimed. The applicant considered such manner of obtaining evidence disputable and turned to the Information Commissioner. The latter explained that the Social Work Centre is entitled to process those personal data that are relevant for the decision. They must determine factual circumstances and thus also verify whether the applicant lives in a non-marital partnership or is considered single. Relevant data may be obtained from the applicant herself or from databases of authorised bodies and organisations, as well as from visiting publicly available websites. If the Facebook profile is set so as to enable free accessibility of one's photos, the holder of the profile is considered to have given consent to everyone, including public authorities, to access such photos. The Social Work Centre is bound by the principle of substantive truth and is therefore not only allowed, but also required, to ascertain true facts of the matter relevant for the decision. Obtaining photographs from a publicly available Facebook profile is therefore within their competence and authorisation. Had the profile of the applicant been closed to the public, obtaining such data and processing it for the purposes of the process would not be permissible.

C26.21 SM AND FAMILY LAW CASES

See the final paragraph in C26.20.

C26.22 SPORTS PERSONS, SPORTS CLUBS AND SM

We do not know of any such case.

C26.23 PERSONAL RELATIONS AND RELATIONSHIPS

See C26.3.

C26.24 SM AND PERSONAL DATA OF DECEASED PERSONS

We do not know of any such case.

C26.25 SM, WEBSITE, SERVICE PROVIDER OR ISP DEFENCE RULES/LAWS

The eCommerce Directive has been implemented into Slovenian law by the Electronic Commerce Market Act (Official Gazette of the Republic of Slovenia, no 96/09). Articles 12 to 15 of the Directive regarding defences have been transposed almost verbatim in Articles 8 to 11 of the Electronic Commerce Market Act.

C26.26 ECOMMERCE DEFENCE CASES

The Higher Court in Ljubljana has dealt with the defence regarding hosting in a judgment (Ref No I Cp 3037/2011 dated 9 May 2012). The court acknowledged the legal capacity, as defendant, of a service provider who stored the information in a claim for damages incurred by insult in an online blog on the basis of

Article 11 of the Electronic Commerce Market Act. A service provider is not liable if he is not aware of the illegal activity or information. However, in the case at hand, the defendant was informed of the illegality by a letter from the claimant. The court held that, from the date of receipt of the letter onwards, the service provider was obliged to remove the blog in question or, if he failed to remove it, he becomes jointly and severally liable for its content.

C26.27 LAWS PROTECTING PERSONAL DATA/ PERSONALLY IDENTIFIABLE INFORMATION

Data protection in Slovenia is regulated by the Personal Data Protection Act (Official Gazette of the Republic of Slovenia, No 86/2004 with amendments), which applies to the processing of personal data if: (i) the data controller is established, has its seat or is registered in Slovenia, or if its branch is registered in Slovenia; or (ii) the data controller is not established, seated or registered in a member state of the EU and uses automated or other equipment located in Slovenia for the processing of personal data, except where such equipment is used solely for the transfer of personal data across the territory of Slovenia.

'Personal data' is defined as any information whereby an individual can be identified, directly or indirectly, in particular by reference to an identification number or to one or more factors specific to his physical, physiological, mental, economic, cultural or social identity, where the method of identification does not incur large costs or disproportionate effort or require a large amount of time.

Personal data of the data subject may only be processed if it is prescribed by statute or if the data subject has given his consent. In the latter case, the data subject must be informed, prior to the processing, in written or other appropriate form, of the purpose for which the data is being processed. Without explicit consent, personal data in the private sector may be processed also if: (i) that is essential for the fulfilment of lawful interests of the private sector which outweigh the interests of the data subject; or (ii) the data subject has a contractual relation with the private sector or such contract is being negotiated, provided that data processing is necessary and appropriate for conducting the negotiations, concluding the contract or fulfilling the contract. The data processor may only process the data for the purpose for which the data was obtained.

If the data processor is a private entity with more than 50 employees, further statutory requirements apply. The data processor must: (i) in its internal acts, prescribe the procedure and measures for the protection of personal data, as well as determine the person liable for a particular filing system and persons who may process the data due to the nature of their work; and (ii) establish a catalogue for each filing system and notify the filing system to the Information Commissioner within 15 days before establishing a filing system.

If the data controller in Slovenia transmits the data to the parent company or a third party, who acts as a data processor, he may only do so by a contract of data processing, if the third party is registered for such activity and ensures the measures that are required. The contract must be concluded in writing and must determine safety and technical measures taken for the protection of personal data. The contractual data processor may only process the data for the purpose and in a manner that the contract of data processing allows him to.

The data processor is also required to enable data subjects to exercise their right with regard to data protection and ensures organisational and technical measures for the protection of the processed data in order to prevent unauthorised access to, or modification, destruction and loss of, the data.

C26.28 DATA BREACH LAWS AND CUSTOMERS/ USERS/REGULATORS NOTIFIED OF HACKING OR DATA LOSS

Article 146 of the Electronic Communications Act (Official Gazette of the Republic of Slovenia, No 109/2012 with amendments) stipulates that, in case of special risk to the security of the network, the public communication services provider must immediately inform its customers of such risk by announcements on its website and other appropriate measures. If the risk exceeds the scope of available measures, it must also inform its customers of all possible measures to eliminate the risk, including the probable costs of such measures. Prompt and effective access to such protective measures should be available to customers.

Chapter C27

South Africa

Rosalind Davey and Rovina Asray, assisted by Sthembile Shamase
Bowman Gilfillan

C27.1   INTRODUCTION

South Africa is a Common Law jurisdiction.

C27.2   SPECIFIC SM AND SN LAWS

There are no specific laws that regulate SM and SN in South Africa. However, the laws of general application apply.

In considering the applicable laws, we are of the view that the starting point is the Constitution of the Republic of South Africa, Act 108 of 1996 (the Constitution), more specifically, the Bill of Rights which establishes and entrenches a natural person's rights to privacy, dignity and freedom of expression, among others.

Although our Constitutional dispensation provides for the right to freedom of expression which encapsulates the right to freedom of speech (which is the right that most people seem to use when defending themselves against claims of 'social media misuse'), it is important to understand that this right may be limited. The right to dignity on the other hand is a non-derogable right. Thus, where statements on SM impact negatively on another person's dignity, the defence that the author of such statements was exercising his/her right to freedom of speech is unlikely to succeed.

C27.3   SM CRIMINAL LAW CASES

In the case of the *State versus Thabo Bester*, which is unreported at this stage, the accused was dubbed the 'Facebook Rapist'.

The accused earned this name because he used the SM site to lure women. He claimed that he was a modelling scout. He would make claims to the women that international modelling scouts were interested in signing them. He would then arrange to meet them.

He was initially convicted of the rapes of two women in Durban. He was sentenced to 50 years' imprisonment for the two counts of rape, as well as for charges of armed robbery, by the Magistrate of the Durban Regional Court. He was then found guilty of the murder of another victim and sentenced to life (25 years) by the then Western Cape High Court, Cape Town.

On appeal, the High Court of KwaZulu Natal, Pietermaritzburg has subsequently reduced the sentence handed down by the Durban Regional Court from 50 years to 30 years.

C27.4   SM CIVIL LAW CASES

SM law is, as yet, an underdeveloped area of law. However, there are emerging, precedent-setting cases on SM.

In this regard, see *H v W*(12/10142) [2013] ZAGPJHC 1 which was delivered by the South Gauteng High Court in early 2013. In this case the court determined an application for an interdict where a defamatory comment had been posted on Facebook by a former 'friend' of the applicant. The court did not hesitate to grant the interdict and to order that the author of the post should remove it.

That defamatory content on SM is unlikely to be tolerated by the South African courts was further highlighted in the case of *Isparta v Richter and another* [2013] JOL 30782 (GNP) /2013 (6) SA 529 (GNP). This case dealt with an action for damages as a result of certain defamatory comments being posted on Facebook by the first defendant (who was married to the second defendant). The plaintiff sued the defendants for defamation, claiming that one of the comments had disparaged and belittled her, whilst a second had been malicious and was aimed at damaging her reputation by implying that she allowed inappropriate interaction between her teenage stepson and minor daughter, and was a bad mother. In issue was whether the posted comments had referred to the plaintiff and, if so, whether they were individually, or collectively and individually, defamatory.

The court held that, although the first message did not constitute serious defamation, its publication on the plaintiff's Facebook wall was gratuitous and was done with the intention to place the plaintiff in a bad light. The second impugned posting was scandalous to the extreme. It suggested that the plaintiff encouraged and tolerated sexual deviation, even paedophilia. The court found that both statements were defamatory, individually and collectively, and considered the combined effect of the comments on the reputation of the plaintiff and awarded damages to the tune of ZAR40,000.

Another case which illustrates that South African courts are taking the use of SM seriously was the case of *CMC Woodworking Machinery (Pty) Ltd v Pieter Odendaal Kitchens* 2012 (5) SA 604 (KZD). In this case the Kwazulu-Natal High Court authorised substituted service of a Notice of Set Down and pre-trial directions on the defendant via a private Facebook message. While the court stressed that each case should be considered in its own context, it confirmed that 'even courts need to take cognisance of social media [websites], albeit to a limited extent, for understanding and considering applications such as the present'.

C27.5   CASES WHERE SM-RELATED EVIDENCE USED OR ADMISSIBLE

The cases mentioned in C27.3 and C27.7 are the main cases in South Africa that we are currently aware of.

C27.6   SPECIFIC ONLINE ABUSE/ONLINE BULLYING/ CYBERBULLYING LAWS

The Protection from Harassment Act 17 of 2011 (Harassment Act) provides for the issuing of protection orders against harassment. Harassment is defined as,

> 'directly or indirectly engaging in conduct that the respondent knows or ought to know a) causes harm or inspires the reasonable belief that harm may be caused to the complainant or a related person by unreasonably ... ii) engaging in verbal, electronic or any other communication aimed at the complainant or a related person, by any means, whether or not conversation ensues; iii) sending, delivering or causing the delivery of ... electronic mail or other objects to the complainant or a related person or leaving them where they will be found by, given to, or brought to the attention of, the complaint or a related person.'

In terms of the Harassment Act, electronic service providers can be forced to hand over the name, surname, identity number and address of the offender to whom the IP address, email or cell phone number belongs. In addition, if electronic communications service providers, or their staff, fail to hand over information, they can be fined R10,000, while staff can be jailed for six months.

There is also the Electronic Communications and Transactions Amendment Bill 2012, which was published for comment under Government Gazette Number 35821 on 26 October 2012. The Bill proposes to insert a new definition of cyber-crimes into the Electronic Communications and Transactions Act 25 of 2002 (ECTA). In terms of the ECTA, 'cyber-crime' is defined as 'any criminal or other offence that is facilitated by or involves the use of electronic communications or information systems, including any device or the internet or any one or more of them'. (Please note that the Bill is presently in a draft form and is still under consideration).

C27.7 OTHER LAWS APPLIED TO ONLINE ABUSE/ ONLINE BULLYING/CYBERBULLYING

Although we do not know of any cases where it has been applied, we are of the view that the Employment Equity Act 55 of 1998 (EEA) may be relevant.

In terms of section 6(3) of the EEA, the harassment of an employee is a form of unfair discrimination and is prohibited on any one or a combination of grounds of unfair discrimination listed in subsection (1).

Section 6(1) lists the grounds on which discrimination is prohibited. These are: race, gender, sex, pregnancy, marital status, family responsibility, ethnic or social origin, colour, sexual orientation, age, disability, religion, HIV status, conscience, belief, political opinion, culture, language and birth.

Therefore, it is likely that, in the workplace, if an instance of online abuse or cyber-bullying is based on one of the listed grounds, the provisions of the EEA would apply.

C27.8 CHILDREN AND SM LAWS OR RULES

Section 2 of the Harassment Act provides for the application for a protection order and states 'Notwithstanding the provisions of any other law any child or person on behalf of a child may apply to the court for a protection order without the assistance of a parent, guardian or any other person'.

The Children's Act 38 of 2005 defines 'abuse' as including any form of harm or ill-treatment deliberately inflicted on a child, and includes bullying by another, or exposing or subjecting a child to behaviour that may harm the child psychologically or emotionally. The objects of the Act include protecting children from abuse or degradation and generally promoting the protection, development and well-being of children. We are of the view that this Act is broad enough to apply to SM abuse/bullying and harassment.

C27.9 EMPLOYEES/EMPLOYMENT SM LAWS OR CASES

The following reported cases involved dismissals for SM misconduct,

Sedick & another v Krisray (Pty) Ltd (2011) 32 ILJ 752 (CCMA)

The Operations Manager and a Bookkeeper posted derogatory comments on their respective Facebook walls pertaining to the director and management. The employees were charged with misconduct for, among others, bringing the name of the company into disrepute in the public domain. A disciplinary hearing was held and the employees were dismissed. Considering the employees' positions within the company, what they had written, where they had posted the comments, to whom these comments were directed and to whom they were accessible, the Commissioner confirmed that the posts were capable of bringing the company's good name and reputation into disrepute. The employees' dismissals were therefore upheld.

Fredericks v Jo Barkett Fashions [2011] JOL 27923 (CCMA)

An employee posted derogatory comments about her employer on her unprotected Facebook profile. The employee was charged with misconduct by the company and, following a disciplinary hearing, she was dismissed. In the CCMA arbitration that followed, the employee alleged that her right to privacy had been infringed. The Commissioner referred to and confirmed the reasoning in the *Sedick* case and the employee's dismissal was upheld.

Media Workers' Association of SA on behalf of Mvemve and Kathorus Community Radio (2010) 31 ILJ 2217 (CCMA)

The employee posted comments on his Facebook profile which were critical of the organisation's Board and of its station manager, whom he alleged was engaged in criminal activity. The employee was requested to issue a public apology on Facebook, which he refused to do. The employee was subjected to a disciplinary hearing and dismissed. The Commissioner based his decision on the fact that the employee had tarnished the image of his employer by posting unfounded allegations on Facebook without addressing his grievances internally. The employee's dismissal was upheld.

As stated above, of possible relevance is the EEA which prohibits unfair discrimination. Section 6(3) of the EEA provides that 'Harassment of an employee is a form of unfair discrimination and is prohibited on anyone, or a combination of grounds of unfair discrimination listed in subsection (1)'. We are of the view that this section will apply to cyber-bullying or harassment of employees/colleagues using SM websites.

C27.10   SCHOOL AND UNIVERSITY STUDENT SM CASES

At present, there are no cases involving students in relation to the above.

C27.11   RIGHT OR HUMAN RIGHT TO ACCESS THE INTERNET OR SM

No such right exists in terms of South African law. This notwithstanding, perhaps an argument could be made for the existence of such a right as an extension of the right to basic education contained in section 29(1)(a) of the Constitution which provides that 'Everyone has a right to basic education'.

C27.12 BANS OR RESTRICTIONS ON INTERNET OR SM

There are no such cases that have been reported at this stage.

C27.13 IDENTITY THEFT (OR EQUIVALENT)

At present, South African law does not provide for a specific crime of identity theft. That notwithstanding, the perpetrator of such a crime will not necessarily escape civil or criminal liability. The crime of identity theft is usually committed simultaneously with other crimes. A person who assumes the identity of another will therefore most likely be charged with the common law crime of fraud or for a statutory offence under the ECTA (see C27.4).

In addition, it is likely that identity theft will fall into the ambit of the definition of 'cyber crimes', as contemplated in the Electronic Communications and Transactions Amendment Bill B-2012 (discussed in C27.4).

C27.14 HACKING (OR EQUIVALENT)

The ECTA at section 86 provides,

'86. Unauthorised access to, interception of or interference with data

(1)   Subject to the Interception and Monitoring Prohibition Act, 1992 (Act No. 127 of 1992), a person who intentionally accesses or intercepts any data without authority or permission to do so, is guilty of an offence.

(2)   A person who intentionally and without authority to do so, interferes with data in a way which causes such data to be modified, destroyed or otherwise rendered ineffective, is guilty of an offence.

(3)   A person who unlawfully produces, sells, offers to sell, procures for use, designs, adapts for use, distributes or possesses any device, including a computer program or a component, which is designed primarily to overcome security measures for the protection of data, or performs any of those acts with regard to a password, access code or any other similar kind of data with the intent to unlawfully utilise such item to contravene this section, is guilty of an offence.

(4)   A person who utilises any device or computer program mentioned in subsection (3) in order to unlawfully overcome security measures designed to protect such data of access thereto, is guilty of an offence.

(5)   A person who commits any act described in this section with the intent to interfere with access to an information system so as to constitute a denial, including a partial denial, of service to legitimate users is guilty of an offence.

The Interception and Monitoring Prohibition Act, 1992 (Act No. 127 of 1992) referred to above was overturned by the Regulation of Interception of Communications and Provision of Communication-Related Information Act 70 of 2002 (RICA). Section 2 of RICA provides:

"2. Prohibition of interception of communication

Subject to this Act, no person may intentionally intercept or attempt to intercept, or authorise or procure any other person to intercept or attempt to intercept, at any place in the Republic, any communication in the course of its occurrence or transmission.'"

C27.15   PRIVACY BY DESIGN (PBD) (OR EQUIVALENT)

No details.

C27.16   TWEETING FROM COURTS, AND ANY RULES/ LAWS

It is permissible to Tweet from the courts, but there have been instances where the court has prohibited Tweeting during certain witness testimony. For example, the judge in the Oscar Pistorius trial banned live Tweeting during the testimony of the state witness and pathologist, but subsequently reversed this decision. In another case, the judge banned the use of SM during the testimony of a rape victim (see www.iol.co.za/news/crime-courts/modimolle-social-media-ruling-analysed-1.1428972).

C27.17   TELEVISION COURTROOM BROADCASTING OR TELEVISION CAMERAS IN COURT, AND RULES OR LAWS

It is permissible for television courtroom broadcasting in certain cases, as has been highlighted in the criminal trial of Oscar Pistorius.

In *Multichoice (Proprietary) Limited v National Prosecuting Authority* 2014 JDR 0330 (GNP) (*Multichoice* case), the court ruled that broadcasting and media houses could broadcast the criminal trial of Oscar Pistorius. In reaching this verdict, the court had regard to a series of other cases that had been heard before in relation to the broadcasting of criminal trials.

In *SA Broadcasting Corporation Ltd v Thatcher and others* 2005 (4) All SA 353 (C) the court was directly confronted with a request to broadcast criminal court proceedings. The court, after conducting an authoritative analysis of the legal landscape regarding this issue, locally and internationally, granted limited coverage, stating that it had to 'exercise its discretion to issue a just and equitable order while taking cognisance of its inherent power to regulate its own proceedings'. This involved balancing the right to privacy against the right of freedom of expression which, in the case of the media, translates into freedom of the press.

In *Dotcom Trading 121 (Pty) Limited v King NO and others* 2000 (4) SA 973 (C) the issue was whether to allow the audio broadcasting of the proceedings of the King Commission that was established to investigate match fixing in the sport of cricket in this country. That court expressed itself on this issue as follows,

> 'It is almost self-evident in my view that the prohibition of the direct radio transmission of proceedings by a radio broadcaster constitutes a limitation on what is essential to the activities of the medium of communication. I have heard no argument and I can see no reason in logic why a limitation on what constitutes the very essence and distinguishing feature of the radio broadcasters' medium of communication does not constitute an infringement of the radio broadcasters' freedom which is enshrined in section 16(1)(a). It is not without reason, so it appears to me, that section 16(1)(a) of the Constitution does not limit its guarantee to the freedom of the press, but specifically extends this freedom to other media of communication and expression as well. Each of these media of communication and expression has its own distinguishing features and each of them can be limited in a different way. The video camera most probably provides the ultimate means of communication. But radio also has its advantages over the print media. Not only the words spoken, but the emphasis, the tone of voice, the hesitations, etcetera can be recorded and communicated. To prevent the radio broadcaster from recording the evidence is to deprive him of that advantage over the print media.'

In *South African Broadcasting Corporation Limited v Downer SC NO and others* 2007 (1) All SA 384 (SCA), the Supreme Court of Appeal considered and refused an application by the SABC to televise and sound record the appeal proceedings that it was due to hear. This decision was taken on appeal to the Constitutional Court, whose judgment is reported as *South African Broadcasting Corporation Ltd v National Director of Public Prosecutions* 2007 (1) SA 534 (CC). The Constitutional Court, whilst confirming the SCA decision, explored the appropriate approaches to be followed by courts when considering applications of this nature. At paragraph 68, that court said,

> 'the time has come for courts to embrace the principle of open justice and all it implies. However, in our view, it should be borne in mind that the electronic media create some special difficulties for the principle of open justice. Broadcasting, whether by television or radio, has the potential to distort the character of the proceedings. This can happen in two ways: first, by the intense impact that television, in particular, has on the viewer in comparison to the print media; and second, the potential for the editing

of court proceedings to convey an inaccurate reflection of what actually happened. This is particularly dangerous given that visual and audio recordings can be edited in a manner that does not disclose the fact of editing. This distorting effect needs to be guarded against. It arises not so much from the presence of cameras and microphones interfering with the court proceedings themselves. But more dangerously, it may arise from the manner in which coverage can be manipulated, often unwittingly, to produce communications which may undermine rather than support public education on the workings of the court and may also undermine the fairness of the trial. Such distortions are much more likely to arise from edited highlights packages than from full live broadcasts.'

In *Midi Television (Pty) Ltd v Director of Public Prosecutions (Western Cape)* 2007, ZASCA 56; 2007 (5) SA 540 (SCA), at paragraph 9, the court stated,

'Where constitutional rights themselves have the potential to be mutually limiting – in that the full enjoyment of one necessarily curtails the full enjoyment of another and vice versa – a court must necessarily reconcile them. They cannot be reconciled by purporting to weigh the value of one right against the value of the other and then preferring the right that is considered to be more valued, and jettisoning the other, because all protected rights have equal value. They are rather to be reconciled by recognising a limitation upon the exercise of one right to the extent that it is necessary to do so in order to accommodate the exercise of the other (or in some cases, by recognising an appropriate limitation upon the exercise of both rights) according to what is required by the particular circumstances and within the constraints that are imposed by s 36.'

In the *Multichoice* case the court granted the order permitting televised broadcasting of the proceedings, subject to certain conditions. These included *inter alia* that the equipment to be used for the filming of the trial needed to comply with technical specifications, in that: the three cameras to be used needed to be installed in as unobtrusive a location as possible; the cameras had to be remotely controlled and pre-set to ensure that no extreme close-ups of any person in attendance were taken; the equipment had to be deactivated so that no recording could take place when the court was not in session; the use of movie lights, flash attachments or artificial lighting devices was prohibited; and no visible or audible light or signal was allowed.

There were also conditions for the broadcasting of the audio-visual recordings of certain portions of the proceedings. In this regard, the broadcasting was permitted only in respect of: the opening argument of the state and accused; any interlocutory applications during the trial; the evidence of all experts called to give evidence for the state, excluding evidence of the accused and his witnesses; the evidence of any police officer or former police officer in relation to the crime scene; the evidence of all other witnesses for the state, unless such a witness does not consent to such recording and broadcasting and the presiding judge rules that no such recording and broadcasting can take place;

closing argument of the state and the accused; delivery of the judgment on the merits; and delivery of the judgment on sentence, if applicable.

The court further specified conditions for the use of still photography during the trial, which were similar to the conditions for the use of audio-visual recording.

The court also stated that any witness whose testimony is to be broadcast in audio-visual form may subject his or her consent to such broadcast to reasonable conditions which include the broadcasting of the evidence: a) from behind, with the face of the witness obscured from public view; b) from the front, but with the face of the witness obscured from public view; c) only by way of a 'wide shot', and the Presiding Judge may on good cause withdraw the permission and/or change the conditions set out above.

Notwithstanding the above, the Presiding Judge retains the discretion to refuse live broadcasting in the event that it becomes apparent that the witness's right to privacy or dignity and/or the accused's right to a fair trial is being impeded by the presence of the cameras or the recording, transmitting and/or broadcasting.

C27.18   SM IN COURTROOMS

During the Oscar Pistorius trial, the judge originally banned Tweeting during the testimony of the forensic pathologists. However, the judge subsequently overturned this decision (see the cases mentioned in C27.15).

C27.19   USE OF SM AS EVIDENCE IN COURTS

No details, although there have been claims that posts on Facebook were unlawfully intercepted and breached both privacy rights and RICA. In the case of *Sedick v Krisray* (referred to in C27.7), one of the employees claimed an infringement of her privacy. However, the Commissioner did not entertain this argument. He was of the view that, as the employees had not set the privacy settings, the posts fell wholly in the public domain and therefore the provisions of RICA did not apply. A similar claim was made in the case of *Fredericks v Jo Barkett Fashions* (also referred to in C27.7), but this claim was also unsuccessful and the Commissioner confirmed the decision in *Sedick v Krisray*.

Although not an SM case, *Smith v Partners in Sexual Health (Non-Profit)* (2011) 32 ILJ 1470 (CCMA) is interesting. This case concerned an employer who had obtained access to an employee's private internet-based Gmail account. The employee was employed as an administrator by the company. The company set up a business Gmail account in order to correspond with donors and sponsors, and to attend to general administrative matters. The employee was responsible for coordinating the company's correspondence on the Gmail account. The employee also had a private Gmail account which she accessed intermittently from the company's computer. The employee used the automatic sign-in feature for her account.

While the employee was on leave, the CEO accessed the employee's work computer and logged into what was ostensibly the company's Gmail account. Upon accessing the account, the manager was inadvertently taken into the employee's personal account. Here the CEO discovered correspondence between the employee, third parties and former employees of the company, pertaining to the company's confidential internal affairs. These communications also referred to the CEO in derogatory terms.

The employee was charged with material breach of contract, insubordination (insolence) and insulting behaviour, and bringing the name of the company into disrepute. The company alleged that the employee's comments were so severe that the trust relationship had been irreparably damaged. A disciplinary hearing was held and the employee was dismissed.

In the ensuing CCMA arbitration, the employee alleged that her emails had been obtained in violation of her right to privacy and in contravention of the Interception Act. The Commissioner considered whether the employee had waived her expectation to privacy when she elected to use the automatic sign-in feature. This possibility was dismissed by the Commissioner, who noted that the contents of a private internet-based email account differed materially from the content on SM sites, where access to the public was generally unrestricted by default and readily accessible.

The Commissioner drew a distinction between the Gmail account and an email account which is established on a personal or work computer. The Commissioner confirmed that, notwithstanding that an employee may use an employer's property to access a Gmail account, the messages would nonetheless be stored on a server which was owned and administered by Google. In such cases, an employer cannot claim ownership of or access the content in the Gmail account, since the service contract for the account is concluded between Google and the individual. In contrast, the Commissioner observed that, when an email account is established and located on a personal or work computer, the message will be downloaded from the main server and stored on the user's hard drive or a local server. In such an instance, the email would have a physical presence on the computer and would thus arguably entitle the employer to access it. The Commissioner conceded that, had the employee downloaded her Gmail emails onto the employer's computer, the employer may have had a claim to such emails.

The Commissioner considered the date stamps on the email printouts provided by the employer and found that only one of the emails produced as evidence at the arbitration had been printed on the day that the CEO accidentally accessed the employee's account. The rest of the emails had been printed on different dates and, as such, the Commissioner concluded that the company must have accessed the employee's account subsequently in a deliberate attempt to obtain printouts of the emails. In doing so, the employer had breached the provisions of the Interception Act and the employee's right to privacy.[1]

The Commissioner confirmed that any evidence which is based on a breach of a constitutional right will only be admissible if it is justified by the provisions of section 36(1) of the Constitution.[2] The Commissioner held that, in this instance, there was nothing to justify a limitation of the employee's right to privacy through the employer's interception of her communications. As such, all but one of the emails were inadmissible. The Commissioner concluded that, on the substance of the one email which was lawfully before the CCMA, the employee's dismissal was substantively unfair.

C27.20   PRIVACY, DATA PROTECTION AND SM

In the case of *Sedick v Krisray* (see C27.7), two employees had been making derogatory remarks about their employer and about the management staff. These comments had been posted on Facebook. Following a disciplinary hearing, the employees were dismissed for 'bringing the company name, director, management and staff into serious disrepute in the public domain'.

Following their dismissal, the employees referred an unfair dismissal dispute to the CCMA. At the arbitration proceedings to settle the dispute, one of the employees argued that her privacy had been invaded and that her employer did not have a right to investigate the Facebook posts that she made. The Commissioner held that the employee had waived her right to privacy. In reaching this conclusion, the court had regard to the fact that she had not used the privacy options available on Facebook to restrict who had access to her Facebook page; as such, the posts on her wall were available to the public in the same way that blogs and public comments on news media sites, or letters published in newspapers, are available.

C27.21   SM AND FAMILY LAW CASES

No details.

---

1   Another issue which companies need to be aware of is that such conduct constitutes a criminal offence in terms of sections 86, 88 and 89 of the Electronic Communications and Transactions Act 25 of 2002 (ECTA) relating to unauthorised access to, interception of or interference with data; attempts, and aiding and abetting of the interception of data; and penalties, respectively.

2   Section 36(1) of the Constitution provides that 'the rights in the Bill of Rights may be limited only in terms of law of general application to the extent that the limitation is reasonable and justifiable in an open and democratic society based on human dignity, equality and freedom, taking into account all relevant factors, including (a) the nature of the right; (b) the importance of the purpose of the limitation; (c) the nature and extent of the limitation; (d) the relation between the limitation and its purpose; and (e) less restrictive means to achieve the purpose'.

C27.22 SPORTS PERSONS, SPORTS CLUBS AND SM

There are no such controversies or cases that have been reported at this stage.

C27.23 PERSONAL RELATIONS AND RELATIONSHIPS

The closest case that there is in this regard is the case of *H v W* (12/10142) [2013] ZAGPJHC 1 (discussed in C27.3).

The applicant ('H') and respondent ('W') were described by the court as close friends. This friendship lasted for many years. The parties in the proceedings were so close, that the applicant and his wife had appointed the respondent as guardian of their three minor children in the event that both the applicant and his wife died or became incapacitated.

The respondent made the following post on Facebook about the applicant,

> 'I wonder too what happened to the person who I counted as a best friend for 15 years, and how this behaviour is justified. Remember I see the broken hearted faces of your girls every day. Should we blame the alcohol, the drugs, the church, or are they more reasons to not have to take responsibility for the consequences of your own behaviour? But mostly I wonder whether, when you look in the mirror in your drunken testosterone haze, you still see a man?'

The applicant complained that the above post published information which portrayed him as,

(i)   a father who did not provide financially for his family;

(ii)   a father who would rather go out drinking than care for his family; and

(iii) a person who had a problem with drugs and alcohol.

The court ordered that the offensive post be removed.

C27.24 SM AND PERSONAL DATA OF DECEASED PERSONS

At this stage, no such case has come before our courts.

C27.25 SM, WEBSITE, SERVICE PROVIDER OR ISP DEFENCE RULES/LAWS

Sections 74 and 75 of the ECTA provide,

'74. Caching

(1)   A service provider that transmits data provided by a recipient of the service via an information system under its control is not liable for

the automatic, intermediate and temporary storage of that data, where the purpose of storing such data is to make the onward transmission of the data more efficient to other recipients of the service upon their request, as long as the service provider—

(a)   does not modify the data;

(b)   complies with conditions on access to the data;

(c)   complies with rules regarding the updating of the data, specified in a manner widely and used by industry;

(d)   does not interfere with the lawful use of technology, widely recognised and used by industry, to obtain information on the use of the data; and

(e)   removes or disables access to the data it has stored upon receiving a take-down notice referred to in section 77.

(2)   Notwithstanding this section, a competent court may order a service provider to terminate or prevent unlawful activity in terms of any other law.

75. Hosting

(1)   A service provider that provides a service that consists of the storage of data provided by a recipient of the service, is not liable for damages arising from data stored at the request of the recipient of the service, as long as the service provider—

(a)   does not have actual knowledge that the data message or an activity relating to the data message is infringing the rights of a third party; or

(b)   is not aware of facts or circumstances from which the infringing activity or the infringing nature of the data message is apparent; and

(c)   upon receipt of a take-down notification referred to in section 77, acts expeditiously to remove or to disable access to the data.

(2)   The limitations on liability established by this section do not apply to a service provider unless it has designated an agent to receive notifications of infringement and has provided through its services, including on its web sites in locations accessible to the public, the name, address, phone number and email address of the agent.

(3)   Notwithstanding this section, a competent court may order a service provider to terminate or prevent unlawful activity in terms of any other law.

(4)   Subsection (1) does not apply when the recipient of the service is acting under the authority or the control of the service provider.'

C27.26 ECOMMERCE DEFENCE CASES

No details.

C27.27 LAWS PROTECTING PERSONAL DATA/ PERSONALLY IDENTIFIABLE INFORMATION

The purpose of the Protection of Personal Information Act No 4 of 2013 (POPI), set out in section 2, is to,

'(a) give effect to the constitutional right to privacy, by safeguarding personal information when processed by a responsible party, subject to justifiable limitations that are aimed at—

   (i) balancing the right to privacy against other rights, particularly the right of access to information; and

   (ii) protecting important interests, including the free flow of information within the Republic and across international borders;

(b) regulate the manner in which personal information may be processed, by establishing conditions, in harmony with international standards, that prescribe the minimum threshold requirements for the lawful processing of personal information;

(c) provide persons with rights and remedies to protect their personal information from processing that is not in accordance with this Act; and

(d) establish voluntary and compulsory measures, including the establishment of an Information Regulator, to ensure respect for and to promote, enforce and fulfil the rights protected by this Act.'

Also, Chapter VIII of the ECTA sets out the universally accepted data protection principles describing how personal data, as defined in the ECTA, may be collected and used. This chapter of the ECTA applies only to [personal] information that has been obtained through electronic transactions.

The ECTA definition for 'personal information' includes information relating to race, gender, pregnancy, marital status, national, ethnic or social origin, colour, sexual orientation, age, physical or mental health, well-being, disability, religion, conscience, belief, culture, language and birth. Section 51 furthermore determines that a data controller must have written permission of the data subject for the collection, processing or disclosure of any personal information on that data; a data controller may not electronically request, collect, collate, process or store personal information which is not necessary for the lawful purpose for which the personal information is required; and a data controller may not disclose any of the personal information to a third party unless required or permitted by law or specifically authorised by the data subject.

C27.28 DATA BREACH LAWS AND CUSTOMERS/ USERS/REGULATORS NOTIFIED OF HACKING OR DATA LOSS

In terms of section 22(1) of POPI, where there are reasonable grounds to believe that the personal information of a data subject has been accessed or acquired by any unauthorised person, the responsible party must notify (a) the Information Regulator and (b) the data subject, unless the identity of the data subject cannot be ascertained. The notification of the data subject may be delayed if a public body responsible for the prevention, detection or investigation of offences or the Regulator determines that notification will impede a criminal investigation by the public body concerned.

Chapter C28

Spain

José M Baño Fos
Baño Leon Abogados

C28.1 INTRODUCTION

Spain is an EU member state and is a Civil Law jurisdiction.

C28.2 SPECIFIC SM AND SN LAWS

None. SM and SN issues are regulated by the joint application of the Law
on Data Protection (Ley Orgánica de Protección de Datos), the Decree on
Data Protection (Reglamento de Protección de Datos) and the general laws on
criminal, civil or employment law.

C28.3 SM CRIMINAL LAW CASES

There have been cases of libel or slander for the content published on SM in the
criminal courts but they apply the general principles of the Spanish Criminal
Code for this type of conduct. The most interesting aspect of the debate is the
liability of the webmaster for information posted by the SM users. A recent
case has concluded that the webmaster is liable for the information if he knew,
or ought to know, the illegality of its content (see County Court of Toledo
Judgment 41/2012 of 1 June, JUR\2012\253135). There have been cases, as
well, of sexual crimes committed through the internet.

C28.4 SM CIVIL LAW CASES

Similarly to the situation explained above, there have cases under the Act for
the Protection of Honour (Ley de Derecho al Honor) that took place in the
context of the internet. In this regard, the Spanish Supreme Court has recently
ruled on the liability of the webmaster. Supreme Court Judgment 128/2013 of
26 February RJ\2013\2580.

C28.5   CASES WHERE SM-RELATED EVIDENCE USED OR ADMISSIBLE

The issue of SM is most recurrent in administrative law cases where a party sues another one for posting personal data on SM without his/her consent, as well as in employment cases as a valid reason for dismissing an employee.

C28.6   SPECIFIC ONLINE ABUSE/ONLINE BULLYING/ CYBERBULLYING LAWS

Not yet. The Spanish Congress has set up a special commission to study the possibility of such laws.

C28.7   OTHER LAWS APPLIED TO ONLINE ABUSE/ ONLINE BULLYING/CYBERBULLYING

The Spanish Penal Code.

C28.8   CHILDREN AND SM LAWS OR RULES

Only at the regional level, the region of Andalucía has issued such a norm (Decreto 25/2007, de 6 de febrero. Establece medidas para el fomento, la prevención de riesgos y la seguridad en el uso de Internet y las tecnologías de la información y la comunicación (TIC) por parte de las personas menores de edad).

C28.9   EMPLOYEES/EMPLOYMENT SM LAWS OR CASES

There are no specific rules covering SM and employment law. There have been cases dealing with the issue of the use of SM at work and the possibility of dismissing an employee for such use, as well as the possibility of dismissing an employee for posting information harming the company on SM.

C28.10   SCHOOL AND UNIVERSITY STUDENT SM CASES

No details.

C28.11   RIGHT OR HUMAN RIGHT TO ACCESS THE INTERNET OR SM

The most recent case and the most relevant has been the Mario Costeja case relating to the right to be forgotten, which was considered by the European

Court of Justice. One of the allegations by Google to oppose the cancellation of certain information relating to this person was precisely the right of every citizen to access the internet and be adequately informed. The application of the ECJ ruling to the particular case by the Spanish courts is still pending.

C28.12 BANS OR RESTRICTIONS ON INTERNET OR SM

There have been some papers discussing the issue.[1]

So far, these restrictions have only been imposed indirectly through more general restrictions – for example, the prohibition to reach or contact a victim by the offender (Article 48.2 of the Spanish Criminal Code) or to undertake the same business activity as the one where the crime was committed (Article 129 of the Spanish Criminal Code).

C28.13 IDENTITY THEFT (OR EQUIVALENT)

Under Article 401 of the Spanish Penal Code, identity theft, irrespective of the context (real or virtual), constitutes a crime.

C28.14 HACKING (OR EQUIVALENT)

Under Article 278 *et seq* of the Spanish Penal Code.

C28.15 PRIVACY BY DESIGN (PBD) (OR EQUIVALENT)

There have been some conferences on the matter, but it has not progressed significantly.

C28.16 TWEETING FROM COURTS, AND ANY RULES/LAWS

The issue does not yet appear to have been dealt with by the courts, and should be assessed under the general norms on whether the hearing is public or not. In a recent case concerning embezzlement by the treasurer of a political party, the court opened proceedings for Tweets that occurred during the testimony of the treasurer. The deposition was held in camera, though. The decision is pending.

---

1   See eg David Felip i Saborit, '"Poner Puertas Al Campo", Sobre la Posibilidad de Prohibir Penalmente el Uso de las Tecnologías de la Información y la Comunicación,' *Revista Catalana de Dret Públic*, Núm 35, 2007, available at www10.gencat.net/eapc_revistadret/ revistes/revista/article.2007-10-30.0222883972/es.

C28.17 TELEVISION COURTROOM BROADCASTING OR TELEVISION CAMERAS IN COURT, AND RULES OR LAWS

It is a decision of the court to allow the presence of cameras. The Spanish Constitutional Court ruled that it is for each magistrate to decide. However, the cameras have been used only to record for later broadcast; the issue of live broadcasting has not been raised yet.

C28.18 SM IN COURTROOMS

This could generally include SN use in courtrooms by the public, journalists, broadcasters, bloggers, jurors, lawyers, witnesses or Judges.

In the recent case concerning the treasurer of a political party, apparently one of the lawyers present Tweeted some of the responses of the treasurer to the questions asked by the judge. The controversy arose not because of the use of Twitter but because the deposition took place in camera (ie it was not a public hearing), and so was without access to the press. The judge opened an investigation which, to our knowledge, has not been closed at the time of writing.

C28.19 USE OF SM AS EVIDENCE IN COURTS

As explained above, the most frequent use of SM is as a valid reason to dismiss employees.

C28.20 PRIVACY, DATA PROTECTION AND SM

See answer below.

C28.21 SM AND FAMILY LAW CASES

The issues regarding family law and SN are mostly related to three questions:

(1) Parental agreement for handling of personal information of minors younger than 14. There is a consensus that both parents have to provide their consent.

(2) Use of personal information within the family context. That is up to what percent of people the use is still considered personal and beyond the reach of the data protection laws.

(3) The use of personal information by amateur sports clubs and associations. In this regard, see the opinion published by the Spanish Data Protection Agency that focused on the audience that could access the information.

See www.agpd.es/portalwebAGPD/canaldocumentacion/informes_juridicos/
common/pdf_destacados/2013-0197_Red-social-deportiva.-Publicaci-oo-n-
de-v-ii-deos-de-menores..pdf.

C28.22 SPORTS PERSONS, SPORTS CLUBS AND SM

There has been some controversy regarding comments by José Luis Saéz
(Spanish Basketball Association) on the role of the Spanish Olympic
Committee on Twitter that was later decided by the Court of Arbitration for
Sport, arguing that no sanction should be imposed as the comments fell within
the freedom of expression of Mr Saéz.

C28.23 PERSONAL RELATIONS AND RELATIONSHIPS

There are starting to be more cases of complaints to the police for blackmailing
using this type of confidential information. See the following press clip:
www.lasprovincias.es/sociedad/201407/16/detenida-publicar-anuncios-
ofreciendo-20140716161454.html.

C28.24 SM AND PERSONAL DATA OF DECEASED PERSONS

More information can be found in the following report by the Spanish Data
Protection   Agency: www.agpd.es/portalwebAGPD/canaldocumentacion/
informes_juridicos/cesion_datos/common/pdfs/2009-0278_Cesi-oo-n-de-datos-
de-personas-fallecidas-c--exclusi-oo-n-de-la-aplicaci-oo-n-de-la-LOPD.pdf.

In principle, the laws on data protection do not apply to deceased persons.

C28.25 SM, WEBSITE, SERVICE PROVIDER OR ISP DEFENCE RULES/LAWS

See C28.3 and C28.4.

C28.26 ECOMMERCE DEFENCE CASES

See C28.3 and C28.4.

C28.27 LAWS PROTECTING PERSONAL DATA/ PERSONALLY IDENTIFIABLE INFORMATION

The two key norms are the Law on Data Protection and the Decree on Data
Protection (see C28.2).

C28.28 DATA BREACH LAWS AND CUSTOMERS/ USERS/REGULATORS NOTIFIED OF HACKING OR DATA LOSS

The decision of the Spanish High Court of 25 February 2010 (ROJ: SAN 843/2010) has concluded that there is not an infringement of the duty of secrecy by reason of the attack, but that the holder of the information might infringe its obligations if he does not act diligently afterwards in avoiding the dissemination of the information. For more information, see www.poderjudicial.es/search/indexAN.jsp?org=an&comunidad=13#.

Chapter C29

Sweden

Erica Wiking Häger and Sara Backman
Mannheimer Swartling Advokatbyrå AB

C29.1 INTRODUCTION

Sweden is an EU member state and is a Civil Law jurisdiction.

C29.2 SPECIFIC SM AND SN LAWS

The Act on Electronic Bulletin Boards applies to anyone who provides or administers a place for electronic messages. This includes interactive websites such as websites with chat functions, sites that have the option to leave comments and other communication services where a visitor can publish information or pictures. What is decisive for the applicability of the Act is whether the user of the electronic service can both send own messages and read messages from others. The Act does not include email services as such, or providing storage space. Further, the Act does not apply to non-interactive websites or a company's/company group's or authority's intranet.

The provider or administrator of the service has an obligation under the Act to monitor the messages provided through the electronic message board. The scope of the required monitoring depends on the size of the service, ie the practical possibility of monitoring all messages. The monitoring should be combined with a so-called 'abuse button', ie a possibility for the users to inform the provider/administrator in a simple way of illegal messages or messages that violate the site's general terms and conditions. As regards the frequency of the monitoring, the preparatory works to the Act set out that monitoring once per week should be sufficient.

Certain messages must be removed: messages whose content obviously entails instigation, incitement to racial hatred, child pornography crimes or illegal violence depictions, and messages where it is clear that the user has infringed a copyright or related right protected by the Copyright Act.

The provider/administrator of an electronic message board can be held criminally liable (fines or imprisonment for up to two years) if he/she fails to monitor the site and remove the types of messages described above. Liability under the Act was tried by the Helsingborg District Court, case no FT 7487-09. In that case the Court considered that postings made on a private person's blog could be tried under the Act, but that the postings had the character of slander which is not a crime covered by the liability to remove the message.

C29.3 SM CRIMINAL LAW CASES

There are several SM-related criminal cases. For example, it is not uncommon that a child molester or other sex perpetrator contacts his/her victims through SM sites. It is also fairly common that persons can be reported for slander or defamation for postings on SM sites or be held liable for messages on a person's blog (see eg Göta Court of Appeal, case no FT 2010-10, in which a blog owner was convicted of slander for postings made on the blog). Messages posted on SM sites can also be used as evidence in criminal law cases, eg to support a claim that a person in fact has committed a specific crime or, on the other hand, to provide a person with an alibi for an alleged crime.

One example is a woman who claimed insurance money for an alleged break-in where goods, including valuable jewellery, worth around SEK 300,000 had been stolen. The insurance company noted several pictures on the woman's Facebook site where the woman, after the reported incident, carried the jewellery in question. The woman has now been prosecuted for attempted fraud (www.dagensjuridik.se/2013/11/bestulen-kvinna-fick-sitt-facebook-konto-granskat-av-trygg-hansa-atalas-bedrageriforsok).

C29.4 SM CIVIL LAW CASES

There are several SM-related civil law cases. For example, employees have been fired for using SM sites for private purposes during work (see eg AD 1999 no 49 and Luleå District Court, case no T 2270-10). Further, marketing law cases as well as intellectual property disputes between companies or individuals can involve marketing made through SM, and private persons can claim compensation for improper use of their personal data over SM. The aforesaid only includes a few examples of SM civil law cases which we believe to be fairly common in Sweden.

C29.5 CASES WHERE SM-RELATED EVIDENCE USED OR ADMISSIBLE

Sweden applies the rule of free production of evidence, ie there are no evidence admissibility rules limiting SM-related evidence. Thus, SM-related evidence is admissible and is commonly used.

C29.6 SPECIFIC ONLINE ABUSE/ONLINE BULLYING/ CYBERBULLYING LAWS

No details.

C29.7 OTHER LAWS APPLIED TO ONLINE ABUSE/ ONLINE BULLYING/CYBERBULLYING

The Penal Code applies to crimes committed online. The most common crimes related to online abuse, online bullying or cyberbullying would be unlawful threat (Penal Code, Chapter 4, para 5), molestation (Penal Code, Chapter 4, para 7), incitement to racial hatred (Penal Code, Chapter 16, para 8) and slander (Penal Code, Chapter 5, para 1–2).

Unlawful threat is defined as: 'A person who raises a weapon against another or otherwise threatens to commit a criminal act, in such a manner that the nature thereof evokes in the threatened person a serious fear for the safety of his own or someone else's person or property'.

Molestation is defined as: 'A person who physically molests or by discharging a firearm, throwing stones, making loud noise or other reckless conduct molests another'.

Incitement to racial hatred is defined as: 'A person who, in a disseminated statement or communication, threatens or expresses contempt for a national, ethnic or other such group of persons with allusion to race, colour, national or ethnic origin or religious belief'.

Slander is defined as: 'A person who points out someone as being a criminal or as having a reprehensible way of living or otherwise furnishes information intended to cause exposure to the disrespect of others'.

The penalty for unlawful threat and molestation is fines or imprisonment up to one year; for incitement to racial hatred, the penalty is fines or imprisonment up to two years; and, for slander, the penalty is fines or imprisonment up to two years. Slander can normally only be prosecuted by the plaintiff, ie not by a public prosecutor.

C29.8 CHILDREN AND SM LAWS OR RULES

No details.

C29.9 EMPLOYEES/EMPLOYMENT SM LAWS OR CASES

There is no law regulating SM and employees/employment.

However, there have been cases where an employee has been dismissed for using SM for private purposes during working hours (see eg AD 1999 no 49 and Luleå District Court, case no T 2270-10). In this regard, it should be noted that the employer usually owns the computer equipment and has the right to decide how the equipment shall be used.

Further, an employee is bound by a general duty of loyalty towards his/her employer. When an employee chooses to criticise his/her employer through SM, this duty of loyalty can cause a conflict with the fundamental right to free speech safeguarded by the Swedish constitution. As a general principle, an employee may not criticise his/her employer so that the business is seriously damaged or otherwise hinder the employer's business, and it is considered that the employee should first try to raise the question directly with the employer. However, the employee's right to free speech is often given much weight, which is why only more serious public criticism, threats or serious claims of disloyal behaviour entitle the employer to dismiss the employee. It should be noted that employees within the public sector are often given much more freedom to criticise their employers compared to employees within the private sector. An example is AD 2011:74, in which case a police officer was dismissed for writing about his work on SM. The court held that this was within his right, ie that his right to freedom of speech weighed heavier than the police authority's interests.

C29.10   SCHOOL AND UNIVERSITY STUDENT SM CASES

There do not appear to be any such laws or cases.

C29.11   RIGHT OR HUMAN RIGHT TO ACCESS THE INTERNET OR SM

There does not appear to be any such right. However, Sweden is a member of both the UN and the EU. Within the UN, the special investigator Frank LaRue presented a report in 2011 setting out that access to the internet is a human right. Within the EU, there are rights in EU legislation granting the right to access the internet. Thus, Sweden is bound to respect these frameworks.

In Sweden, it is not possible to completely stop internet access for a certain person, only to block specific websites.

C29.12   BANS OR RESTRICTIONS ON INTERNET OR SM

Normally, imprisoned persons are not given access to the internet. Exceptions apply for education and in certain other special situations but, in such case, access is given under the supervision of personnel. Persons charged with a crime may be subject to restrictions on the use of the internet or certain SM sites. After a person has served his/her sentence, he/she is, however, free to use the internet without any restrictions.

C29.13   IDENTITY THEFT (OR EQUIVALENT)

This is covered by the Penal Code's provisions on fraud and fraudulent behaviour (Penal Code, Chapter 9, para 1–3).

Fraud is defined as: 'If a person by deception induces someone to commit or omit to commit some act which involves gain for the accused and loss for the deceived or someone represented by the latter'.

C29.14   HACKING (OR EQUIVALENT)

The Penal Code's provision on illegal use of computer information (Penal Code, Chapter 4, para 9c) applies in case someone gains access to data intended for automatic processing or, without proper authorisation, changes, deletes or blocks or adds data to a register. The penalty is fines or imprisonment for up to two years. Hacking can also constitute professional misconduct, eg where an employee gains improper access to certain data belonging to the employer. Other crimes may also become relevant, depending on what the hacker does (eg theft, fraud and copyright infringement).

C29.15   PRIVACY BY DESIGN (PBD)
(OR EQUIVALENT)

Under the Personal Data Act, the personal data controller is obliged to undertake appropriate technical and security measures to protect the personal data. The Data Inspection Board (the supervisory authority for personal data processing) promotes the principles of PbD in these measures. Further, the Act on Electronic Communication (which applies to electronic communication networks and communication services) requires that certain appropriate technical and organisational measures are undertaken to ensure that the data being processed or stored are protected. However, the aforesaid does not entail any absolute requirement to implement a PbD or otherwise to consider the entire life cycle.

The EU Commission, in its proposal for a new Data Protection Regulation, has proposed a requirement on PbD. It remains to be seen when, if and how the proposed Regulation will look in its final form and whether this will include the PbD requirement.

C29.16   TWEETING FROM COURTS, AND ANY RULES/ LAWS

Hearings and meetings in Swedish courts are, as a general rule, open to the general public (there are exceptions for the court to have the hearing behind closed doors). Parties and visitors participating are, however, obliged to comply with regulations regarding, inter alia, sound and visual recordings and transmissions. Visual recordings and transmissions are prohibited under the Swedish code of judicial procedure (Chapter 5, Section 9). Hence, Tweets including pictures or a video recorded in the court room are not allowed under Swedish law. There is no such direct prohibition regarding typing or transferring text messages from a court room.

C29.17   TELEVISION COURTROOM BROADCASTING OR TELEVISION CAMERAS IN COURT, AND RULES OR LAWS

Visual recording or picture transmission in court is prohibited under the Swedish code of judicial procedure (Chapter 5, Section 9). Hence, it is not permitted to broadcast television from court. It is, however, possible for the court to allow the general public to take part in, for instance, a hearing in court through sound and/or visual transmission on premises other than the court room. It is unusual that courts use this possibility and, to our knowledge, it has only happened in a few exceptional cases. The prohibition against visual recordings or transmissions applies also to the display on other premises.

C29.18   SM IN COURTROOMS

The Parliamentary Ombudsmen (a government agency appointed to ensure that government agencies treat citizens in accordance with the law) recently gave a statement regarding a case where a judge had used his mobile phone to type a text message during a hearing. The Parliamentary Ombudsmen stated, inter alia, that a judge must pay full attention to the hearing and concluded that it is not in line with the judicial task to pursue other irrelevant tasks, such as typing text messages, during a hearing. Hence, one can assume that the same would apply to (lay and ordinary) judges' use of Tweets or other SM in courtrooms during a hearing.

C29.19   USE OF SM AS EVIDENCE IN COURTS

SM material is fully admissible as evidence in Swedish courts. Thus, prosecutors as well as parties in civil cases are free to refer to SM material.

C29.20   PRIVACY, DATA PROTECTION AND SM

There have been many such controversies and cases, varying from an authority's processing of personal data through SM to personal attacks from private individuals through SM. As the question is quite wide, we do not provide further details in this regard.

C29.21   SM AND FAMILY LAW CASES

There do not appear to be any such cases.

C29.22   SPORTS PERSONS, SPORTS CLUBS AND SM

It is becoming more and more common for athletes to use SM. However, according to an article in the newspaper *Göteborgsposten* ('Policy för sociala medier saknas', dated 15 April 2013, by Petter Nilsson), it is rare that the major soccer teams in Sweden – that may have the most to lose from the athletes' use of SM – have a policy for the use of SM.

There have been a couple of instances where the use of SM has caused debate, of which we mention four of them below (information on the cases is taken from the said article in *Göteborgsposten*),

1.   The coach and the captain of a bandy team forwarded a death threat against the referee. The club stopped both of them from participating in the next match. The bandy association also suspended them for a certain period of time. After the end of the season, the coach had to leave his position;

2.   Two players in one of the bigger soccer clubs took a photograph of a cake decorated with a naked woman and published it on Instagram. The picture, that was taken during a celebration with the entire team, caused some controversy. The club dissociated itself from the picture but did not punish the players;

3.   One man was dismissed from the national snowboard team after having published photographs of himself at a strip club. The national team had earlier requested him to change his behaviour on SM;

4.   The floorball association suspended one of the players for a month and a half after the player called one referee a 'baboon judge' on his Twitter account.

C29.23   PERSONAL RELATIONS AND RELATIONSHIPS

There are a number of such cases. According to an article by Professor Mårten Schultz in the legal online newspaper, *Dagensjuridik* ('Hovrättens domskäl om hur synen på sexlivet har förändrats borde inte få skrivas utan robust stöd', 22 October 2013), sex tapes and sexual pictures distributed online are almost becoming a new type of criminal case. Thus, we believe that cases involving SM and personal relationships are fairly common.

The said article discusses a recent case where the Court of Appeal reduced the amount of damages awarded by the District Court from SEK 130,000 to SEK 25,000, which several online blogs and articles have – together with Professor Mårten Schultz – considered too low to compensate for the integrity violation. In the relevant case, a video tape showed a girl having sex together with her then current boyfriend. The boyfriend did later, without her approval or knowledge, publish the tape on a number of pornographic internet sites. Another recent case (see the article '16-årig flicka åtalas för ha spridit nakenbild på skolkamrat – "jag ville hämnas"', 22 August 2013, *Dagens Juridik*) concerns a 16-year-old girl being accused of slander, after having published a picture of another young girl when she was naked. The picture was published through SM. The girl accused of slander has stated to the police that her motive for publishing the picture was revenge for postings made on other SM.

C29.24   SM AND PERSONAL DATA OF DECEASED PERSONS

The Personal Data Act only applies to living persons. We are not aware of any controversies or cases in relation to the SM and personal data of deceased persons. However, we are aware that the handling of deceased persons' SN accounts has been discussed in the media and that companies offering services to handle SM accounts after a person's death have been established (eg Aftercloud). Further, by contacting the SM provider it may be possible for the relatives to close down or change an SM account into a memory account for the deceased.

C29.25   SM, WEBSITE, SERVICE PROVIDER OR ISP DEFENCE RULES/LAWS

Sweden is a member state of the EU and, as such, is bound by the EU eCommerce Directive, which has been implemented in Sweden primarily through the so-called eCommerce Act.

C29.26   ECOMMERCE DEFENCE CASES

One example is the fairly well-known Pirate Bay case (see Svea Court of Appeal, B 4041-09), where the providers of the Pirate Bay site (used for file sharing) claimed that they could not be held liable for copyright infringement with reference to the E-commerce Act. According to the defendants, they were to be considered as service providers under the E-commerce Act that could not be held responsible for the actions of the users of the service. The Court held that the E-commerce Act was relevant to the case, but that the liability exceptions in the said Act did not apply to the defendants considering that the Pirate Bay service is not a pure transfer or caching service and as the functions provided through Pirate Bay were deemed to have promoted the users' copyright infringement. Thus, the exceptions from liability set out in the E-commerce Directive and the E-commerce Act – for service providers maintaining a business of a purely technical, automatic and passive nature, with no knowledge or control over the transferred or stored information – did not apply to the defendants in the Pirate Bay case.

C29.27 LAWS PROTECTING PERSONAL DATA/ PERSONALLY IDENTIFIABLE INFORMATION

The Personal Data Act is based on Directive 95/46/EC which aims to prevent the violation of personal integrity in the processing of personal data. There are also separate personal data laws, such as the Patient Data Act and special provisions in other Acts, but the main legislation in this area is the Personal Data Act.

Under the Personal Data Act, the controller of personal data is responsible for ensuring compliance with the Act. This entails, amongst other things, that: personal data shall only be processed if it is lawful, in a proper manner and in accordance with good practice; it shall only be gathered for specific, explicitly stated and legitimate purposes; it shall not be processed for any purpose that is incompatible with that for which the data was gathered; the processing shall be adequate and relevant to the purpose of the processing; the processing shall be necessary having regard to the purpose of the processing; the data which is processed is correct and, if it is necessary, up-to-date; the data shall be rectified, blocked or erased, if it is incorrect or incomplete, having regard to the purpose of the processing; and the data shall not be kept for a longer period than is necessary.

The Act is fairly lengthy and complex, which is why we do not provide a full summary in this regard. The full text of the Act can be found on the Data Inspection Board's website at www.datainspektionen.se/in-english/legislation/the-personal-data-act/.

Under the Act, a company or organisation has a responsibility to ensure that personal data handled through SM sites follow the provisions of the Act. Thus, there is an obligation not to publish sensitive personal data, to delete personal data and monitor visitors' comments to detect sensitive data, and to take appropriate security measures to protect the data.

Failure to comply with the Act can entail an obligation for the company or organisation to pay damages to the person whose personal data has been violated. Further, an individual person who intentionally or negligently violates the Act can be sentenced to fines or imprisonment of up to two years.

C29.28 DATA BREACH LAWS AND CUSTOMERS/ USERS/REGULATORS NOTIFIED OF HACKING OR DATA LOSS

Under the current Personal Data Act, there is no specific obligation to report personal data breaches. However, there is a general notification requirement to notify the Data Inspection Board of each processing of personal data. This general notification requirement is, however, subject to a number of exceptions. The more important exceptions include if a company has obtained the data subject's consent to the processing, processing made by a non-profit organisation, processing in running text, and if a company has appointed (and notified the Data Inspection Board of) a personal data representative.

In addition thereto, there is a general obligation on the data controller to inform the personal data subject of the processing of his/her data. The information shall include the name of the data controller, information on the purpose(s) for which the data will be processed, and 'all other information necessary in order for the data subject to be able to exercise his/her rights in connection with the processing, such as information about the recipients of the information, the obligation to provide information and the right to apply for information and obtain rectification'. According to the Data Inspection Board, information on a person's data being hacked or deleted may also be covered by this information requirement, although this is not clear from the Act or from case law.

Under the proposed new Data Protection Regulation on an EU level, there will be a requirement to report personal data breaches to the supervisory authority. 'Personal data breach' means a breach of security leading to the accidental or unlawful destruction, loss, alteration, unauthorised disclosure of, or access to, personal data transmitted, stored or otherwise processed. The proposal also includes a notification requirement to the personal data subject if the personal data breach is likely to adversely affect the protection of the personal data or privacy of the data subject. However, notification to the data subject will not be required if the controller demonstrates to the satisfaction of the supervisory authority that it has implemented appropriate technological protection measures, and that those measures render the data unintelligible to any person who is not authorised to access it. If the proposal for a new Data Protection Regulation is approved, there will be fairly strict requirements on what information the notification shall include and short deadlines for when the notification is to be provided.

Further, within the telecommunication area, there is currently an obligation under the Act on Electronic Communication, on those providing generally availably electronic communication services, to report integrity breaches to the supervisory authority (the Swedish Post and Telecom Authority). Integrity breaches mean circumstances leading to the unintentional or unauthorised deletion, loss or change or unauthorised disclosure of or unauthorised access to data processed in connection with the services. According to this Act, there is also an obligation to notify the individual concerned in case the integrity incident can be assumed to negatively affect his/her personal integrity. Such notification is not required, however, if the service provider can demonstrate that adequate security measures, ie measures that make the data impossible to read for the recipient, were applied at the time of the integrity incident.

Chapter C30

Switzerland

PD Dr Simon Schlauri
Ronzani Schlauri Attorneys, Zurich

C30.1   INTRODUCTION

Switzerland is not an EU member state (but some of its laws bear similarities) and is a Civil Law jurisdiction.

C30.2   SPECIFIC SM AND SN LAWS

There are no specific SM and SN laws.

C30.3   SM CRIMINAL LAW CASES

In a decision of the Cantonal Court of Zurich of November 25, 2013 (SB130371; not yet legally effective) a 23-year-old unemployed man was convicted of 'Causing fear and alarm among the general public' according to Article 258 of the Swiss Criminal Code. After having received only a few birthday greetings on Facebook, he had released the following posting: 'Is nobody happy about me having been born? I swear I will take revenge … I will destroy all of you … Nobody will be able to protect you now. Pow! Pow! Pow!'.

In a Federal Court Decision of February 21, 2014 (1B_52/2014), a husband was forbidden to contact his wife, inter alia, via Facebook or Twitter.

In a case of May 5, 2014 the District Court of Horgen condemned a 22-year-old man for indecent assault, rape, sexual acts with children and pornography in an exemplary case of 'sexting'. The offender had contacted the victim over a social network and first forced her to send him nude images. Over time, the victim had sent the offender over 700 pictures and finally agreed to sexual intercourse due to the psychological pressure (citation not yet available).

In a case before the District Court of Uster, a man who had attacked Muslim inhabitants of Switzerland by Twitter ('Kristallnacht') was condemned for racial discrimination according to Article 261bis of the Swiss Criminal Code on May 19, 2014 (citation not yet available).

C30.4   SM CIVIL LAW CASES

A Federal Court decision of 4 November 2013 (5A_309/2013; Medialex 2014 p 41) dealt with a complaint against a prominent person who had posted texts which violated the personality of his ex-lover on Facebook.

C30.5   CASES WHERE SM-RELATED EVIDENCE USED OR ADMISSIBLE

In a Federal Court decision BGE 134 IV 266 the court defined the area of application of the Federal Law on Undercover Investigation (BVE). Every approach of a suspected person with the aim of criminal investigation, by a police officer who cannot be identified as such, has to be seen as undercover investigation (also undercover participation in chat rooms, etc). Therefore the prerequisites of an undercover investigation have to be met before the investigation starts (a judicial review is needed). In case the prerequisites are not met, the evidence is not admissible.

C30.6   SPECIFIC ONLINE ABUSE/ONLINE BULLYING/ CYBERBULLYING LAWS

There are no such laws.

C30.7   OTHER LAWS APPLIED TO ONLINE ABUSE/ ONLINE BULLYING/CYBERBULLYING

The general provisions about the protection of personality (Article 28 ss Civil Code) may be applicable, as well as some provisions of the Criminal Code (eg threatening behaviour, coercion or extortion according to Articles 180 and 181 or 156 Criminal Code).

C30.8   CHILDREN AND SM LAWS OR RULES

There are no laws or rules specific to children and SM. The general laws apply, eg Article 301 Civil Code (parental care), which gives parents the right to prohibit their children from using SM.

C30.9   EMPLOYEES/EMPLOYMENT SM LAWS OR CASES

Federal Court Decision 4A_22/2014 of April 23, 2014: Setting up an SM profile may be considered as a breach of a non-competition clause in labour law.

The Swiss Federal Court (BGE 139 II 7) ruled in early 2013 that the clandestine surveillance of an employee with spyware is illegal: an employer who suspects an employee to be misusing the company's IT infrastructure, eg chatting traffic, emails exchanged, web traffic, SM activities, may not deploy clandestine surveillance software to monitor the employee's computer activity.

The use of SM by employees may be prohibited or restricted by an employer. To enforce such a rule, he may supervise internet traffic anonymously (ie not broken down to traffic of individual employees). If an employer identifies abuse of the internet access, he may, after a written announcement, also perform controls on individual employees. In cases of abuse, dismissal may be reasonable, in serious cases even without notice. Key loggers or similar software to control employees are not allowed in any case.

Offensive postings on SM against an employer may lead to dismissal due to breach of loyalty or to sexual harassment.

C30.10   SCHOOL AND UNIVERSITY STUDENT SM CASES

There are no such laws or cases.

C30.11   RIGHT OR HUMAN RIGHT TO ACCESS THE INTERNET OR SM

According to Article 92 para 2 of the Swiss Constitution and Article 16 of the Federal Telecommunications Act (FMG), a basic telecommunications services offer has to be made available to all sections of the population and in all the regions of the country by the incumbent telecom firm (Swisscom). This basic service must comprise a basic internet service (ie two megabits per second).

According to the rules of the Swiss Conference on Social Welfare (Skos), internet access and a computer are considered basic needs and may therefore be paid by social aid.

C30.12   BANS OR RESTRICTIONS ON INTERNET OR SM

There have been no cases, rules or laws, nor literature, which would ban or restrict the use of or access to the internet and/or SM.

C30.13   IDENTITY THEFT (OR EQUIVALENT)

There are no specific rules or laws relating to identity theft; general laws are applicable (eg fraud).

C30.14   HACKING (OR EQUIVALENT)

Article 143 Criminal Code covers unauthorized obtaining of data: any person who, for his own or for another's unlawful gain, obtains for himself or another person data that is stored or transmitted electronically or in some similar manner and which is not intended for him and has been specially secured to prevent his access is liable to a custodial sentence not exceeding five years or to a monetary penalty.

Article 143bis covers hacking (unauthorized access to a data processing system): any person who obtains unauthorised access by means of data transmission equipment to a data processing system that has been specially secured to prevent his access is liable on complaint to a custodial sentence not exceeding three years or to a monetary penalty.

Article 144bis covers damage to data: any person who without authority alters, deletes or renders unusable data that is stored or transmitted electronically or in some other similar way is liable on complaint to a custodial sentence not exceeding three years or to a monetary penalty.

C30.15   PRIVACY BY DESIGN (PBD) (OR EQUIVALENT)

There are rudimentary rules in the Federal Act on Data Protection (FADP) which may form the basis of a privacy by design approach. Article 4 para 2 states that data processing must respect proportionality, ie if data is not needed for a certain aim, it must not be processed. Article 7 FADP and the corresponding articles in the Federal Ordinance on Data Protection state rules about data security. Swiss data protection authorities take a pragmatic approach.

C30.16   TWEETING FROM COURTS, AND ANY RULES/LAWS

Court proceedings are governed by cantonal laws, and so there may be several different regimes. In the canton of Zurich, the court itself decides if the use of certain means of communication by the audience is restricted. There are no written rules for the use of Twitter in courtrooms, though.

C30.17   TELEVISION COURTROOM BROADCASTING OR TELEVISION CAMERAS IN COURT, AND RULES OR LAWS

Court proceedings are governed by cantonal laws, and so there may be several different regimes. Nevertheless, television cameras are usually banned from courtrooms.

C30.18   SM IN COURTROOMS

A newspaper article (Markus Hofmann, NZZ August 9, 2013) mentions a political discussion about the use of SM in courtrooms. The article cites a politician who asks for a ban of Twitter in courtrooms and a lawyer who doubts the proportionality of such a ban.

C30.19   USE OF SM AS EVIDENCE IN COURTS

According to Article 157 of the Swiss Civil Procedure Code (CPC), the court forms its opinion based on its free assessment of the evidence taken. Electronic files are permitted as means of evidence according to Article 168 in conjunction with Article 177 of CPC. In Federal Court Decision 5A_822/2013 of November 28, 2013, Facebook postings were considered valid evidence for a clear manifestation of will. In Federal Court decision 6B_1061/2013 of April 7, 2013, the court held that Facebook postings were not the only deciding elements of proof, but were admissible as indicative evidence that the appellant was guilty of sexual acts with a minor.

C30.20   PRIVACY, DATA PROTECTION AND SM

There have not been any such court decisions in Switzerland yet, but, as all over Europe, the Swiss public follows the developments closely.

C30.21   SM AND FAMILY LAW CASES

Except for the cases already mentioned, there do not appear to be any other cases in relation to family law.

C30.22   SPORTS PERSONS, SPORTS CLUBS AND SM

No details.

C30.23   PERSONAL RELATIONS AND RELATIONSHIPS

No details.

C30.24   SM AND PERSONAL DATA OF DECEASED PERSONS

There have not been any such court cases. An article by Matthias Schweizer and Elke Brucker-Kley, TREX 2014, 36 ss, deals with digital legacy.

C30.25 SM, WEBSITE, SERVICE PROVIDER OR ISP DEFENCE RULES/LAWS

There are no such rules. In particular, Switzerland did not implement the privileges for access and hosting providers of the eCommerce Directive. Switzerland is not legally obligated to do so, because it is not a member state of the EU.

C30.26 ECOMMERCE DEFENCE CASES

In a Federal Court decision 5A_792/2011 of January 14, 2013, the Swiss newspaper *Tribune de Genève* was required to remove a blog post which violated personality rights from its blog hosting websites and to pay legal costs. The court held that there were no eCommerce defences as in the EU, and so the standard rules had to be applied. There have not been any decisions about liability for damages of providers in Switzerland, though.

C30.27 LAWS PROTECTING PERSONAL DATA/ PERSONALLY IDENTIFIABLE INFORMATION

The Federal Act on Data Protection aims to protect the privacy and the fundamental rights of persons when their data is processed (Article 1 FADP). Unlike the corresponding EU law, the FADP covers personal data of natural persons *and legal entities*. In addition, Article 43 of the Federal Act on Telecommunications states that no person who is or has been responsible for providing a telecommunications service may disclose to a third party information relating to subscribers' communications or give anyone else an opportunity to do so (secrecy of communication). Article 321ter Criminal Code threatens such behaviour by public officials, employees or auxiliaries of an organisation providing postal or telecommunications services with a custodial sentence not exceeding three years or a monetary penalty. The secrecy of communication not only covers personal data, but all content and metadata of telecommunication and postal services.

C30.28 DATA BREACH LAWS AND CUSTOMERS/ USERS/REGULATORS NOTIFIED OF HACKING OR DATA LOSS

There are no such laws.

Chapter C31

Taiwan

CF Tsai Sr and Lu-Fa Tsai
Deep & Far Attorneys-at-Law

C31.1 INTRODUCTION

Taiwan is a mixed Common Law and Civil Law jurisdiction.

C31.2 SPECIFIC SM AND SN LAWS

Although there are no specific SM and SN laws, there is a first law named the Social Order Maintenance Law and a second law named the Meeting And Processions Act. Nevertheless, the former will not be a concern if an SN activity does not interrupt or disturb others. As to the latter, the same applies since it basically governs political activity. Generally, an SN activity of a commercial nature or for social purposes will not violate the laws in any way. An SN activity of religious character or for the public interest can even ask for free help from the government or police bureau. Apart from that, an SN activity having criminal attributes or intentions will violate the relevant laws, eg the Criminal Code or criminal provisions embedded in various laws.

C31.3 SM CRIMINAL LAW CASES

There have been many types of SM criminal law cases. In the absence of an SM law, an SM activity cannot be determined to be lawful or not, only until when judged case by case as to its content. As a famous case, a male, Yu-Ling Tsai, invited one female and 18 males through the internet to have a sex party in a private chartered train coach. The male was sentenced to six months' imprisonment because of sex intermediary due to intent to profit.

C31.4 SM CIVIL LAW CASES

In the above case, the Taiwan Railroad Administration (TRA) accused Mr Yu-Ling Tsai of causing reputational damage, and he was asked to place apology advertisements in the nation's top four newspapers. Yu-Ling Tsai's attorney argued against this claim, asserting that the TRA was a beneficiary rather than a victim of the sex party, citing that rent revenue derived from private chartered coaches significantly increased after the sex party. Indeed, the number of rentals rose from 11 a year before the sex party to at least 41 a year after the sex party.

C31.5 CASES WHERE SM-RELATED EVIDENCE USED OR ADMISSIBLE

It is believed that SM-related evidence has been used in the daily practice of the court or administration. As long as the evidence is proven to be true (that is, true in the original appearance as it appears in the SM medium, rather than as to its substantive contents), it is admissible before the court or the administration for the apparent purpose. Given that users of SM websites may be anonymous or post nonsensical or non-factual content, further evidence is required if one desires to prove the truthfulness of the substantive content.

C31.6 SPECIFIC ONLINE ABUSE/ONLINE BULLYING/ CYBERBULLYING LAWS

There are no such laws, but this does not mean such action is not punishable or criminal. If such an action can be proven to be criminal or defamatory in nature, the punishment may be substantially harsher than an action taken outside the computer medium.

C31.7 OTHER LAWS APPLIED TO ONLINE ABUSE/ ONLINE BULLYING/CYBERBULLYING

In addition to the Criminal Code governing most instances of computer crimes, there are other laws that address computer crimes, eg the Child and Youth Sexual Transaction Prevention Act, the Copyright Act, the Computer-Processed Personal Data Protection Act, the Communications Security and Surveillance Act, and the Telecommunication Act.

C31.8 CHILDREN AND SM LAWS OR RULES

As mentioned above, the Child and Youth Sexual Transaction Prevention Act was specifically enacted to protect children, but it is related to only sexual transactions.

C31.9 EMPLOYEES/EMPLOYMENT SM LAWS OR CASES

There are no such laws or cases, but discussions are ongoing. The government has made it clear that public servants can use Facebook during working hours if it is necessary for performing her/his duty. In private enterprises, it is hard to prohibit employees from accessing SM websites, although it is theoretically possible to monitor such access by the employee.

C31.10   SCHOOL AND UNIVERSITY STUDENT SM CASES

Schools or universities usually build facilities ensuring that students have free access to the internet.

C31.11   RIGHT OR HUMAN RIGHT TO ACCESS THE INTERNET OR SM

Taiwan is a country with widespread free rights, including access to the internet or any SM activity. Because such access is regarded as an automatically existing right, there is no notable literature, case, rule or law to this effect.

C31.12   BANS OR RESTRICTIONS ON INTERNET OR SM

Although there is the Child and Youth Sexual Transaction Prevention Act, the bans or restrictions are limited to the shutdown of the illegal website or the cessation of the hacking action. The court order will not and cannot ban or restrict a prosecuted person from use of, or free access to. the internet or any legal website.

C31.13   IDENTITY THEFT (OR EQUIVALENT)

The Computer-Processed Personal Data Protection Act (see C31.7) prohibits or punishes an entity from the illegal use or collection of personal data.

C31.14   HACKING (OR EQUIVALENT)

There is no specific law directed to hacking. It is punishable, however, under the Criminal Code, eg provisions of forgery or obstruction of computer use.

C31.15   PRIVACY BY DESIGN (PBD) (OR EQUIVALENT)

Although the Computer-Processed Personal Data Protection Act makes no mention of PbD, the personal data user will never violate the Computer-Processed Personal Data Protection Act when its use of the personal data is based on the concept of PbD. Having said that, this does not mean this country has well-established PbD laws or practices, but that there must be various discussions or rules or even law through the introduction or development of the PbD concept.

C31.16 TWEETING FROM COURTS, AND ANY RULES/LAWS

As is known, in a free country, any action can be done if not prohibited. Since there is no law or rule prohibiting the use of Twitter in court at present, one can Tweet from the court as long as there is no resulting outcome violating an applicable law.

C31.17 TELEVISION COURTROOM BROADCASTING OR TELEVISION CAMERAS IN COURT, AND RULES OR LAWS

There is a Court Observation Rule (COR) stipulating that people may observe a court hearing upon permission. Nevertheless, since, in general, no or very few people are interested in observing a case or trial, people normally can freely observe or attend a court hearing even without permission from the court as stipulated in the COR. For a case drawing public attention, the court will arrange a televised courtroom. In this situation, the COR will function and only those who are permitted through a public drawing of lots can attend the televised courtroom. No video recording is permissible, and video records can only be made following permission from the presiding judge.

C31.18 SM IN COURTROOMS

As mentioned, in a free country, any action can be done if not prohibited. Accordingly, for a case of public attention where the COR is applicable, as long as the COR provision – that no video recording is permissible while a video record can only be made following permission from the presiding judge – is not violated, any person can freely use SM in the courtroom. Certainly, for a general case where the COR is not really applicable, its inherent rule that no video recording is permissible, while a video record can only be made following permission from the presiding judge, cannot be violated.

C31.19 USE OF SM AS EVIDENCE IN COURTS

As mentioned, SM-related evidence has been used in the daily practice of the court or administration. Specifically, the evidence is naturally admissible before the court or the administration for its apparent truthfulness, subject to further evidence if one desires to prove the truthfulness of the substantive content behind the superficial SM records.

C31.20 PRIVACY, DATA PROTECTION AND SM

There have been many cases dealing with the disclosure or leakage of personal data for commercial or illegal use. The protection of privacy or personal data is referred to in the Computer-Processed Personal Data Protection Act. While there are discussions or studies whether or when the government can expropriate SM records, there is not much controversy to this effect.

C31.21 SM AND FAMILY LAW CASES

Since building an SM website or society per se does not violate any law, eg the Computer-Processed Personal Data Protection Act, there is no controversy to this effect. As to the family law, there have been many debates or controversies regarding same-sex marriage or multiple families, which, it is believed, are not likely to be legalized in the near future.

C31.22 SPORTS PERSONS, SPORTS CLUBS AND SM

There are such cases. Nevertheless, there are no controversies that the club or society can exercise its discipline on its members as long as the discipline is proportional in measure and is not related to corporal punishment. Only when the discipline becomes physical abuse of a person and/or torture will it raise controversy.

C31.23 PERSONAL RELATIONS AND RELATIONSHIPS

There is no controversy about the protection or protectability of personal relations or relationships, eg private images. Such protection, however, is not tradable, exchangeable or reciprocal if it involves a criminal element. For example, a wife-exchange club will not violate any law if the spouses know the content or give their consent in advance.

C31.24 SM AND PERSONAL DATA OF DECEASED PERSONS

There have been cases related to the personal data of deceased persons. Nevertheless, there are few controversies about the protection or protectability of such personal data, because such data normally can be categorized as either personal interest permanently existent under the Civil Code or property interest under the Copyright Act, which are inheritable by an immediate relative or spouse. Nevertheless, there was one small dispute as to whether a reporter is free to take a photo of a photo of a deceased person where the photo was selected by his/her own family members to serve as an identifier of the deceased person for a funeral farewell ceremony. Specifically, as long as such photo-taking action is fair or reasonable, there is no violation of the applicable law.

C31.25   SM, WEBSITE, SERVICE PROVIDER OR ISP DEFENCE RULES/LAWS

There are rules named the Taiwan Personal Information Protection and Administration System Maintaining and Operating Norms and the Taiwan Personal Information Protection and Administration System Regulations. Any business authenticated by the Taiwan Personal Information Protection and Administration System (TPIPAS) agency can own a renewable Data Privacy Protection Mark (DP.mark) for two years. The government advocates the establishment of a website CIS (Corporate Identification System) in order to reduce phishing threats. The government also built an information security report service website to formulate an 'information security joint defence' mechanism, in order to enhance the information security ability of eCommerce businesses through transaction security norms in regard to the network websites, suppliers and logistics providers. Also, there is the establishment of an EC-Cert information security event report website to report information security events, and joint defence and information-sharing regarding the newest trends in information security attacks.

C31.26   ECOMMERCE DEFENCE CASES

In March 2004, money in the network bank accounts of two commercial banks was stolen. The two banks confirmed that their firewalls were intact and the account users did not use lazy passwords or leak their passwords, where some account owners had even changed their passwords two times. After looking into the matter, the police eventually found that the money was stolen by an invader using more than ten different IP addresses primarily located in the US and India to transfer the money to dummy accounts. After the bank screened all bank accounts that were logged on by the IP addresses provided by the police, they then detected whether the computers of the bank account owners had viruses or Trojan Horses (Backdoor. Powerspider. B), and it was confirmed that all the computers were infected with viruses (Beagle, MyDoom, Bugbear). In order to curb the expansion of the fraud, the Financial Bureau of the Ministry of Finance required on March 26, 2004 that all banks temporarily shut down the function of transferring money to a non-designated bank account unless there was a phone call confirmation in advance, and instructed that the ceiling sum of NT$100,000 for transferring money to a non-designated bank account would be changed from per transaction to per day from July 1, 2004. After all of the banks adopted measures to deter such fraud, the function of transferring money to a non-designated bank account resumed in May 2004.

C31.27 LAWS PROTECTING PERSONAL DATA/ PERSONALLY IDENTIFIABLE INFORMATION

The Computer-Processed Personal Data Protection Act (see C31.7) prohibits or punishes an entity from illegal use or collection of personal data.

C31.28 DATA BREACH LAWS AND CUSTOMERS/ USERS/REGULATORS NOTIFIED OF HACKING OR DATA LOSS

As mentioned in C31.25, there are rules set out in the Taiwan Personal Information Protection and Administration System Maintaining and Operating Norms and the Taiwan Personal Information Protection and Administration System Regulations, under which the government built an information security report service website to formulate an 'information security joint defence' mechanism, in order to enhance the information security ability of eCommerce businesses through transaction security norms in regard to the network websites, suppliers and logistics providers. Also, there is the establishment of an EC-Cert information security event report website to report information security events, and joint defence and information-sharing regarding the newest trends in information security attacks.

Chapter C32

United Kingdom

Jonathan McDonald
Travers Smith LLP

C32.1 INTRODUCTION

The United Kingdom is an EU member state and is a Common Law jurisdiction.

C32.2 SPECIFIC SM AND SN LAWS

The UK government is monitoring whether new legislation is required related specifically to addressing abusive behaviour on SM and SN. In July 2014 the European heads of policy for Twitter and Facebook were called before a specialist parliamentary committee (the House of Lords Communications Committee) to answer questions about SM offences. Whilst the businesses' representatives acknowledged that they could not monitor their networks for abusive content, they argued that no new legislation was needed and pointed to software developments (similar to a spam filter) that were currently in development to try and provide a technical solution to this problem. The committee will deliver its report in late 2014.

For other laws that have been applied in cases involving SM and SN, see C32.7.

C32.3 SM CRIMINAL LAW CASES

Since at least 2011, there have been a very large number of SM criminal law cases each year. A response to a Freedom of Information request (a request for the release of data held by public bodies in the UK) made by Sky News in 2014 revealed that, across 34 police forces, since 2011, 19,279 adults had been investigated for SM-related offences (predominantly abusive behaviour). Of these, 11,292 were subject to police action (either charged with a criminal offence, fined, cautioned or warned verbally), including 1,203 children. The majority of such cases, however, do not reach the higher courts that have power to create precedents (ie the courts whose judgments are binding on lower or equivalent courts) and whose judgments are usually reported in the law reports, but instead take place in the magistrates' courts (the lowest criminal court in

England, where all criminal cases start) and are therefore rarely reported in the law reports.

With respect to those SM-related cases that have been reported, in *Paul Chambers v Director of Public Prosecutions* [2012] EWHC 2157 the English High Court confirmed that the offence of 'improper use of a public electronic communications network' under section 127(1)(a) of the Communications Act 2003 could apply to a message posted on Twitter. Section 127(1)(a) provides that a person is guilty of an offence if he sends by means of a public electronic communications network a message or other matter that is grossly offensive or of an indecent, obscene or of menacing character. It did not matter that Twitter was a private company as it operated via a public electronic communications network. It equally did not matter that the message was viewed as content on the internet, it still constituted a message. The court, however, overturned a criminal conviction ruling that a Tweet saying 'Crap! Robin Hood Airport is closed. You've got a week and a bit to get your shit together otherwise I am blowing the airport sky high!!' was not a menacing message as it did not create fear or apprehension in those to whom it was communicated or who might reasonably be expected to see it.

The offence of improper use of a public electronic communications network is the most common criminal offence that directly relates to SM. *Paul Chambers v Director of Public Prosecutions* is the only case to be heard by the English High Court involving SM and the offence of improper use of a public electronic communications network. There have, however, been a number of other cases that have not been reported but have gained notoriety through the press involving this offence or the closely related offence of 'sending letters etc with intent to cause distress or anxiety' under section 1 of the Malicious Communications Act 1998.

R v Azhar Ahmed (9 October 2012) – an individual was convicted under section 127 of the Communications Act 2003 of sending a grossly offensive message via Facebook after posting messages following the deaths of six British soldiers in Afghanistan including the comment 'all soldiers should die and go to hell'.

R v Duffy (13 September 2011) – an individual was convicted under section 1 of the Malicious Communications Act 1998 of sending grossly offensive messages after writing abusive messages on Facebook tribute pages for teenagers who had died.

There are also numerous examples of criminal cases in which SM played a part, although the offences may have been committed even if SM was unavailable, albeit in a different way (ie naming a rape victim, breaching an injunction etc).

It has also been announced by Justice Secretary Chris Grayling that the sentence for those convicted of online trolling will be increased under the Criminal Justice and Courts Bill to up to two years in prison. Already, there are a growing number of examples of convictions, most recently a conviction involving 18 weeks' imprisonment for trolling Stella Creasy MP on Twitter. Current prosecutions occur under the Malicious Communications Act 1998, for which the sentence is capped at six months' imprisonment.

C32.4   SM CIVIL LAW CASES

Chris Lance Cairns v Lalit Modi [2012] EWHC 756 (QB). In this case the High Court awarded £90,000 in damages to the New Zealand cricketer, Chris Cairns, in a successful libel claim against Lalit Modi, the former chairman and commissioner of the Indian Premier League, following a Tweet by Modi that accused Cairns of matchfixing. The court found that, although the Tweet was only sent to Modi's 65 followers, Modi was considered an expert in his field and he was likely to have a specialist cricket-loving audience, increasing the likelihood that his message would go viral. Since then, the Court of Appeal has upheld the judgment and the size of the award.

Lord McAlpine of West Green v Bercow (21 October 2013) (unreported). This was a common law libel action brought by Lord McAlpine, a former politician, against the defendant (who had 56,000 followers on Twitter and held what could be described as minor celebrity status in the UK). The defendant had issued a Tweet saying 'Why is Lord McAlpine trending? *Innocent face*'. This was in the wake of a BBC current affairs programme that reported on the abuse of boys at children's homes and included an interview in which two victims said that they suffered sexual abuse at the hands of a 'leading Conservative politician from the Thatcher years', a description which could apply to Lord McAlpine. The defendant said in a statement, the making of which was part of a settlement agreed between the parties, that her allegation was completely without foundation. Her allegation caused the claimant great distress and embarrassment and her irresponsible use of Twitter contributed substantially to the claimant's eventual decision to issue a public statement denying the allegations. The defendant also apologised to the claimant and agreed to pay him damages and his costs.

C32.5   CASES WHERE SM-RELATED EVIDENCE USED OR ADMISSIBLE

Examples are limited. In *R v Wright (Jackson), R v Cameron (Daniel), R v Martin (Craig)* [2013] EWCA Crim 1217 the Court of Appeal ruled in relation to three convictions of inflicting grievous bodily harm that the first defendant's (Cameron) appeal against a sentence of eight years' detention should be dismissed, noting that '[the defendant] had made entries on the social media site "Facebook" after the event [at which the attack was committed]. Those entries were a disgrace and showed no appreciation of the seriousness of the attack.'

C32.6   SPECIFIC ONLINE ABUSE/ONLINE BULLYING/ CYBERBULLYING LAWS

There are no such laws, but see C32.2 in relation to possible changes to legislation in the future.

C32.7   OTHER LAWS APPLIED TO ONLINE ABUSE/ ONLINE BULLYING/CYBERBULLYING

Online abuse/online bullying/cyberbullying can be considered a criminal offence under the Protection from Harassment Act 1997 (which is, on the whole, relevant for incidents that have happened repeatedly), which prohibits behaviour amounting to harassment of another (section 1), provides a criminal offence for such behaviour (section 2), and provides a more serious criminal offence of someone causing another person to fear, on at least two occasions, that violence will be used against them.

Also see C32.3 for details of the offence under section 127 of the Communications Act 2003 (and the proposed increase in sentence for online trolling), and C32.23 regarding a proposed new criminal offence of revenge porn in the UK.

C32.8   CHILDREN AND SM LAWS OR RULES

No details.

C32.9   EMPLOYEES/EMPLOYMENT SM LAWS OR CASES

There are no specific laws; however, there are a number of reported SM cases, and the use of SM is not infrequently raised as an issue in employment disputes, to the extent that ACAS (the Advisory, Conciliation and Arbitration Service – a non-departmental public body of the Government, that promotes industrial relations practice) has published a social media 'good practice' guide (www. acas.org.uk/index.aspx?articleid=3375).

Some specific reported cases include,

Whitham v Club 24 Ltd (t/a Ventura) ET/1810462/10. The employment tribunal ruled that a dismissal of an employee for posting mildly derogatory comments on Facebook that were viewable by a 'closed' group of friends (which in this case numbered around 50 although included two colleagues) was unfair. The employer had failed to produce evidence to show that the comments had put its reputation at risk and harmed its client relationships, and therefore dismissing the employee fell outside the band of reasonable responses open to the employer in the circumstances.

Gill v SAS Ground Services UK Limited ET/2705021/09. The employment tribunal held that employers may use entries on SM as evidence in disciplinary proceedings.

Smith v Trafford Housing Association [2012] EWHC 3221 (Ch) HC. The High Court upheld a breach of contract claim against an organisation that demoted a Christian manager for using SM to say that holding civil partnership ceremonies in churches was 'an equality too far'.

Weeks v Everything Everywhere Ltd ET/2503016/2012. The employment tribunal held that an employee was fairly dismissed for making threats on SM to a colleague who had reported him to the employer for repeatedly referring to his workplace as 'Dante's Inferno'.

C32.10   SCHOOL AND UNIVERSITY STUDENT SM CASES

There are no particular laws and no cases reported in the law reports involving students in schools and universities in relation to the use of SM. However, the General Teaching Council (the professional body for teachers and university lecturers in the UK) published figures in 2011 (the latest figures available), revealing that over 40 teachers had been referred to it for unprofessional conduct related to the inappropriate use of SM.

C32.11   RIGHT OR HUMAN RIGHT TO ACCESS THE INTERNET OR SM

There are no cases, rules or laws in relation to a right of access to SM. There is, however, case law guidance in relation to a right of access to the internet. The leading case is the Court of Appeal hearing of *R v Smith* [2012] 1 WLR 1316.

R v Smith involved an examination of the terms of a Sexual Offences Prevention Order under the Sexual Offences Act 2003 where the defendant had committed offences on the internet, and as such the court was required to examine whether it was necessary to prevent him from doing so again by imposing restrictions on his computer use or internet access. The court said that access to the internet was a qualified right. That is, it could be restricted but only if the restriction was provided for by law and was necessary/proportionate. It was inappropriate to attempt to lay down a rule that one particular provision be adopted in all cases but, in the circumstances of the instant case, in which it was necessary/proportionate to restrict access to the internet, the court's preferred method was to require the preservation of a readable internet history coupled with the defendant's submission to inspection on request.

Other restrictions have also been imposed in the past, including the complete barring of a defendant from possession of a computer or access to the internet.

More recently, however, terms of that kind (in relation to sexual offences at least) have been quashed as unnecessary and disproportionate.

It may therefore be said that the current position under UK law is that internet access is a qualified right (akin to Article 10 of the ECHR, although it has not expressly been discussed in terms of 'human rights'), and it is difficult to see how a complete ban on a person's use of the internet under UK law could currently be justified.

C32.12 BANS OR RESTRICTIONS ON INTERNET OR SM

There are no rules specifically relating to SM, although there are more general rules in relation to access to the internet.

In relation to sexual offences, where a defendant has committed such offences by use of the internet, a Sexual Offences Prevention Order under the Sexual Offences Act 2003 may be issued restricting access to the internet (see C32.11 for further details).

In relation to hacking, in the case of *R v Mangham (Glen Steven)* [2012] EWCA Crim 973, the defendant had committed offences contrary to the Computer Misuse Act 1990 namely by securing unauthorised access to computer material with intent, contrary to section 1 and committing unauthorised modification of computer material contrary to section 3. As these had constituted 'serious crimes' under the Serious Crime Act 2007, the lower court had imposed a serious crime prevention order (SCPO, a type of injunction), restricting the defendant to owning and using only one personal computer with internet access. He had to notify the authorities of any employment use and was forbidden to use encryption or data-wiping software on his personal computer. He was also forbidden from deleting any user log or history or from having more than two email accounts. His email accounts also had to be with UK-based service providers. Whilst the Court of Appeal quashed the serious crime prevention order on the grounds that the defendant did not pose a future risk (an SCPO is designed not to punish but is preventive in character), it is possible that an SCPO remains a restriction that may be imposed for computer hacking in the future.

C32.13 IDENTITY THEFT (OR EQUIVALENT)

No laws specifically relate to identity theft, rather this offence is covered under various pieces of legislation, comprising the Theft Act 1968, the Data Protection Act 1998, the Identity Cards Act 2006, and the Fraud Act 2006.

C32.14 HACKING (OR EQUIVALENT)

The Computer Misuse Act 1990 criminalises unauthorised access to computer material (s 1), and unauthorised impairment of the reliability of computer systems or data (s 3) may also apply. The Police and Justice Act 2006, section 37, also created new offences relating to the making, supplying and obtaining of tools used in the existing Computer Misuse Act 1990 offences.

C32.15   PRIVACY BY DESIGN (PBD) (OR EQUIVALENT)

There are no specific laws dealing with PbD.

The Information Commissioners Office (the UK's privacy regulator) has published brief guidelines on privacy by design: http://ico.org.uk/for_organisations/data_protection/topic_guides/privacy_by_design. The general status of ICO guidance is that, whilst it does not have the force of law, it does in effect provide a benchmark against which an organisation's compliance with the Data Protection Act 1998 (DPA) may be evaluated. However, the ICO PbD guidance does not actually contain any obligations and it is therefore difficult to see how it could be used as an effective benchmark.

C32.16   TWEETING FROM COURTS, AND ANY RULES/ LAWS

It is permissible for the press, although rules for the general public are more restricted.

For the press, the use of Twitter has been permitted since 2011, when the Lord Chief Justice (head of the judiciary and President of the Courts of England and Wales) issued new Practice Guidance on 'The Use of Live Text-Based Forms of Communications (including Twitter) from Court for the Purposes of Fair and Accurate Reporting'.

Under the guidance, it is presumed that representatives of the media and legal commentators using live text-based communications from any courts sitting in public session in England and Wales do not threaten the administration of justice and, accordingly, Tweeting is permitted. Permission can be withdrawn by the court, however, at any time.

Ordinary members of the public do not have an automatic right to use Twitter (etc) and must apply to the judge for permission, although this can be done informally.

C32.17   TELEVISION COURTROOM BROADCASTING OR TELEVISION CAMERAS IN COURT, AND RULES OR LAWS

Since 2013 the Crime and Courts Act 2013 has allowed legal arguments and the final judgment for criminal and civil cases in the Court of Appeal and Supreme Court to be broadcast. Filming is subject to a 70-second delay, allowing offensive language to be screened out.

The Government also intends to extend filming to allow the broadcast of sentencing remarks in the Crown Court. However, victims, witnesses, offenders and jurors will continue to be protected, and will not be part of broadcasts.

C32.18   SM IN COURTROOMS

In *Attorney General v Fraill*; *R v Knox (Gary)* (Divisional Court, 16 June 2011), a juror in a drugs trial who contacted an acquitted defendant via Facebook, whilst the jury was still deliberating its verdicts in relation to the other defendants, was guilty of contempt of court and was sentenced to eight months' imprisonment.

In *Attorney General v Davey* [2013] EWHC 2317 (Admin), the defendant had been acting as a juror when he posted a message on the internet which set out his view about the case he was trying. Using his Facebook account, he stated that he was a juror in a child sex offence case and thus had the opportunity to lawfully cause problems for a paedophile. He was committed for contempt of court for using the internet to post an opinion regarding a defendant and to research a case.

C32.19   USE OF SM AS EVIDENCE IN COURTS

See C32.5.

C32.20   PRIVACY, DATA PROTECTION AND SM

There have been numerous incidents of controversy with respect to data protection and SM in the UK; however, there have been no cases in which a breach of the law has been cited. In 2014, it was reported that the ICO was going to investigate Facebook for a possible breach of the UK Data Protection Act 1998 for conducting a psychology study on up to 700,000 of its users, during which their news feeds were manipulated without their knowledge.

C32.21   SM AND FAMILY LAW CASES

In the case of *Re J (A Child)* [2013] EWHC 2694 (Fam) the High Court granted a contra mundum (against the world) injunction preventing the naming of a baby whose father had posted information about the child on Facebook in breach of an undertaking to the court. The judge said that, in principle, an English court can grant a contra mundum injunction against the world including a foreign-based internet website provider, ie Facebook. Among other things, it had to be shown that the person being injuncted could be properly served and that there was a real possibility that the order would be enforceable. Whilst the case involved family law, a key principle discussed was the right to privacy, namely the child's privacy. The court said that the injunction would only be justified if it was necessary to protect the child's right to privacy under Article 8 of the European Convention on Human Rights (the right to privacy) which had to be balanced against the public interest in discussing the workings of the family justice system. The court then granted the injunction more narrowly than was requested. The party requesting the injunction had also asked the court to prevent publication of images of the baby, but the court declined to grant this.

There is also anecdotal evidence to suggest that SM material is increasingly being cited in divorce proceedings (ie with flirtatious messages sent on SM cited as evidence of unreasonable behaviour); however, such cases rarely reach the higher courts and so there have been no examples reported in the law reports.

C32.22   SPORTS PERSONS, SPORTS CLUBS AND SM

There have been plenty of controversies involving sports persons and clubs that have made the national newspapers. This is unsurprising, given that the mature UK sports markets encourage sports persons to use SM, especially Twitter, as a means of generating publicity for their clubs. The most common story involves a sportsperson Tweeting something controversial or offensive. Where this is found to be the case, action is usually taken at club level, with disciplinary proceedings being a private contractual issue between the sportsperson and their club.

Those examples that do stand out are where a sport's governing body has taken disciplinary action against a sportsperson for misconduct involving SM. For example, the Football Association (the governing body of English football) fined a Hull City player, Yannick Sagbo, in 2014 for using SM to support a player's hand gesture that the FA considered to have anti-Semitic undertones. This was considered a breach of FA rules prohibiting 'abusive and/or indecent and/or insulting and/or improper' conduct and Sagbo was fined £15,000. In 2012 a Manchester United player, Rio Ferdinand, was fined £45,000 for a breach of the same rule after making comments on Twitter about the then Chelsea player Ashley Cole, and more recently in 2014.

Also see discussion of *Chris Lance Cairns v Lalit Modi* [2012] EWHC 756 (QB) in C32.4.

C32.23   PERSONAL RELATIONS AND RELATIONSHIPS

SM 'revenge porn' has been a topical issue in the last year. Numerous groups, including National Stalking Helpline, Women's Aid and Safer Internet Centre UK, have campaigned against the lack of law allowing the exposure of explicit images posted by ex-partners or friends.

There have been calls for new legislation, as this controversial issue has steered debates over who is to blame. Some commentators contend that victims' protection should be limited on the grounds that they should not have sent (where so applicable) the images in the first place. However, the counterargument is made that these images are only shared within the confines of a trusting relationship and that judging victims' actions in this way is unhelpful. (Of course, not all images on revenge porn-type websites are created by the victims.)

There are some protections under the current UK law; for instance, victims may be able to bring a claim if the image is of a person under the age of 18 or breach of copyright or harassment can be proved. But UK law has been criticised for offering inadequate protection, and being inconsistent and hard to use. This is an area, however, where we may see continued political attention in the future.

A Twitter troll, Peter Nunn, was also jailed for 18 weeks for online abuse threats against Stella Creasy MP and others, and banned from contacting his victims.

New legislation is expected which will expressly outlaw revenge porn, including a custodial sentence of up to two years.[1] Other laws may also continue to apply, such as the Communications Act 2003 and the Malicious Communications Act 1988.

C32.24 SM AND PERSONAL DATA OF DECEASED PERSONS

Unlike other jurisdictions, there have not been any specific cases presented to the UK courts. However, there is anecdotal evidence to suggest that more people are choosing to include internet passwords in their wills, to maintain a digital legacy. Google's 'Inactive Account Manager' (available in the UK) allows its users to control relatives' and friends' access to their online accounts after they die. A range of websites, such as Pass My Will, Legacy Locker and Deathswitch, have also emerged in recent years, helping people to administer post-mortem access to their digital estates with 'e-wills'.

The more surprising issue arises with mobile applications that allow users to post posthumous SM updates (such as LivesOn and DeadSocial). LivesOn does this by using Twitter bots powered by algorithms to analyse online behaviour and learn where and what a subscriber normally posts, so it can keep on scouring the internet, favouring Tweets and posting links. DeadSocial allows

---

1   See O Bowcott, 'Revenge porn to be criminal offence with two years in jail, New legislation will punish practice of sharing sexually explicit media on internet without consent, says justice secretary,' Guardian, 12 October 2014.

a user to set up a series of messages to be sent out posthumously, via Facebook and Twitter.

C32.25 SM, WEBSITE, SERVICE PROVIDER OR ISP DEFENCE RULES/LAWS

Under the Electronic Commerce (EC Directive) Regulations 2002, a service provider (which may include a website and, by extension, an SN provider) is generally not liable for any material where it: (a) acts as a mere conduit; (b) caches the material; or (c) hosts the material. The most relevant of these for SNs is the hosting defence, which has been interpreted broadly by the courts. The defence may be lost, however, where the service provider has performed an 'active role' in an unlawful activity or has gained an awareness of the unlawful activity or content (*L'Oreal v eBay* Case C-324/09).

C32.26 ECOMMERCE DEFENCE CASES

See C32.25.

C32.27 LAWS PROTECTING PERSONAL DATA/ PERSONALLY IDENTIFIABLE INFORMATION

The Data Protection Act 1998 is the main piece of legislation that governs the protection of personal data in the UK.

C32.28 DATA BREACH LAWS AND CUSTOMERS/ USERS/REGULATORS NOTIFIED OF HACKING OR DATA LOSS

There is no general requirement to report data breaches to a regulator or to an affected customer or user.

There are some industry-specific exceptions to this rule; for example, in the telecommunications sector, service providers are required to report serious incidents (and other sectors also have some measures in place requiring the reporting of disruptive incidents), but none of these are applicable to SM.

Chapter C33

United States

Eric P Robinson, Esq.

C33.1 INTRODUCTION

Government in the United States is based on: separation of powers amongst the legislative, executive and judicial branches; checks and balances between the three branches; and a federal system of power distributed between national and state government (and local governments, which are creations of state governments).

The First Amendment to the federal US Constitution, added to the document as part of the Bill of Rights in 1791, provides that 'Congress shall make no law ... abridging the freedom of speech, or of the press ...'. This admonition has been applied to all branches of the federal government, not just Congress. See eg *NY Times Co v United States* 403 US 713, 718-19 (1971) (applying First Amendment to executive branch actions). It also applies to the states and their subsidiary local governments by virtue of the Fourteenth Amendment, which provides that states may not deprive 'any person of life, liberty, or property, without due process of law,' which includes free speech rights under the First Amendment. See *Gitlow v New York* 268 US 652 (1925) (applying free speech provisions of the First Amendment to state governments).

Every state constitution includes an equivalent provision, applicable to state and local governments in that state. For simplicity, in this chapter both the federal and states provisions will be referred to under the general rubric of 'the First Amendment'.

While the level of First Amendment protection for certain forms of speech, such as political speech or commercial speech, may vary, speech on the internet does not receive any diminished protection because of the medium used. See *Reno v ACLU* 521 US 844 (1997) (finding federal law barring constitutionally protected indecent material from the internet unconstitutional) and *American Civil Liberties Union v Ashcroft* 535 US 564 (2002) (same for subsequently enacted provisions). Thus, for example, a federal appeals has held that a Facebook 'like' is speech protected by the First Amendment. *Bland v Roberts* 730 F3d 368 (4th Cir 2013).

C33.2 SPECIFIC SM AND SN LAWS

The federal and state governments have adopted few, if any, laws that specifically apply to SM and SN. An important federal law regarding the internet generally is section 230 of the Communications Decency Act, 47 USC § 230, discussed in C33.25.

While there are few statutes directly addressing SM, in recent years individual federal and state agencies have adopted new regulations or modified existing rules to continue disclosure and other existing requirements to new forms of media. Examples include the Securities and Exchange Commission allowing disclosure of corporate financial information via SM, see Report of Investigation Pursuant to Section 21(a) of the Securities Exchange Act of 1934: Netflix, Inc, and Reed Hastings (SEC April 2, 2013), and Food and Drug Administration extending required disclosures of drug restrictions and complications to SM advertising. See Food and Drug Administration Safety and Innovation Act, Pub L No 112-144, 126 Stat. 993 (2012), § 1121 (requiring FDA to issue guidance on internet and SM promotion of regulated medical products). Government-sanctioned industry self-regulation groups have also similarly updated their rules. See eg Guidance on Social Media and Web Sites, Reg Notice 10-06 (FINRA Jan 2010) (discussing applicability of FINRA R. 2210 regarding public communications by broker dealers to SM).

C33.3 SM CRIMINAL LAW CASES

In addition to the criminal provisions discussed in the specific sections below, there have been several criminal cases that have involved use of SM.

In its 2014–15 term the US Supreme Court will hear an appeal from a man who was convicted of communicating threats against his wife in postings to SM. The Third Circuit Court of Appeals upheld the conviction on the grounds that a reasonable person would understand the posts to be threatening; the defendant argues that the conviction should be reversed because he did not intent to actually carry out the threats. *Elonis v United States* No 13-983 (US cert granted June 16, 2014) (appeal of *United States v Elonis* 730 F3d 321 (3d Cir 2013)).

While most 'flash mobs' – large groups of people organized via SM which suddenly appear at a specific location, perform some action, then disperse – are benign and even amusing, there have been some instances where flash mobs have resulted in violence and criminal activity. Concerns over such instances led the city of Cleveland, Ohio to amend its anti-rioting ordinance in 2011 to specifically address use of electronic devices to organize violent 'flash mobs'. Ord No 1393-11 (Cleveland, Ohio 2011) (amending Cleveland City Code § 625.08(a)(6)).

The same year the Los Angeles County Sheriff's Department did not pursue a threatened prosecution of rapper The Game after he Tweeted a sheriff's department phone number to his followers, saying they should call the number to apply for an internship with him.

SM material has also been used as evidence. In one such case, an Iowa man pleaded guilty to a federal gun charge after his probation officer saw a picture of him on MySpace holding a rifle and a handgun. *US v Figueroa* No 1:09-cr-00033-LRR (ND Iowa 2009).

C33.4   SM CIVIL LAW CASES

Defamation

There have now been several trials and verdicts in defamation lawsuits stemming from SM. In two highly publicized cases, singer Courtney Love settled one case stemming from her Twitter posts, and won a jury verdict in her favour in another. See *Simorangkir v Love* No BC410593 (Cal Super LA County) (settled Feb 2011); *Gordon & Holmes v Love* No BC462438 (Cal Super LA County) (jury verdict Jan 24, 2014). Several federal and state courts have held that SM defendants enjoy the same First Amendment protections in libel suits as traditional journalists, including the same standards of proof for plaintiffs, see eg *Obsidian Finance Group LLC v Cox* 740 F3d 1284 (9th Cir 2014), cert denied, 134 SCt 2680, 189 L Ed 2d 223 (US May 27, 2014), and protection under state reporters' shield laws from being forced to reveal confidential sources. See *O'Grady v Superior Court* 139 Cal App 4th 1423, 44 Cal Rptr 3d 72 (Cal App, 6th Dist 2006); *Mortgage Specialists, Inc v Implode-Explode Heavy Indus, Inc* 160 NH 227, 999 A2d 184 (NH 2010). But a few courts have reached the contrary conclusion when they have deemed that the SM material was not journalistic in nature. *Obsidian Fin Group, LLC v Cox* No CV-11-57-HZ, 2011 US Dist LEXIS 120542 (D Or Oct 18, 2011), clarified by No CV-11-57-HZ, 2011 US Dist LEXIS 137548, 40 Media L Rep 1084 (D Or Nov 30, 2011), rev'd on other grounds, 740 F3d 1284 (9th Cir 2014), cert denied, 134 SCt 2680, 189 L Ed 2d 223 (US May 27, 2014).

Service of process

Several courts have approved service of process via email in appropriate circumstances, see Comment (Svetlana Gitman), (Dis)service of Process: The Need to Amend Rule 4 to Comply With Modern Usage of Technology, 45 J Marshall L Rev 459 (2012) (collecting cases), and Florida requires service via email in most cases. Florida Rule of Judicial Administration 2.516(a). A few courts have explicitly allowed service by SM: see *Marriage of Jessica Mpafe v Clarence Mdjounwou Mpafe* Court File No 27-FA-11 (Minn Dist Ct, Fam Div, Hennepin County) (May 10, 2011) (allowing service via email, Facebook, MySpace or other SM sites); *FTC v PCCare247 Inc* 2013 US Dist LEXIS 31969, 2013-1 Trade Cas (CCH) P78294 (SDNY Mar 7, 2013) (allowing service via email and Facebook); *FTC v Pecon Software LTD* 2013 US Dist LEXIS 134205 (SDNY Sept 18, 2013) (same). But see *FTC v Pecon*

Software Ltd 2013 US Dist LEXIS 111375, 2013-2 Trade Cas P78475 (SDNY Aug 7, 2013) (rejecting proposed service via Facebook when FTC had not conclusively shown court that the named defendants were 'highly likely' to be reached by such service). A New York family court judge recently allowed service in a child support case via Facebook after other, more conventional means of service proved impossible. *Noel B v Anna Maria A*, Docket No F-00787-13/14B (NY Fam Ct Sept 12, 2014). Other court rulings that have considered such service and have rejected it include *Fortunato v Chase Bank USA*, NA, 2012 WL 2086950 (SDNY June 7, 2012); and *Joe Hand Promotions, Inc v Carrette* 12-2633-CM (D Kan July 9, 2013).

C33.5 CASES WHERE SM-RELATED EVIDENCE USED OR ADMISSIBLE

This section focuses on Fourth Amendment search and seizure issues related to SM. For a discussion of discovery of SM content and admissibility of such content as evidence, see C33.19.

In two cases with implications for government acquisition and use of SM content in criminal prosecutions, the US Supreme Court has distinguished between government's role as an employer and its police function.

In *City of Ontario v Quon* 560 US 746 (2010), the court held that a public employer may review the text messages sent from and received to a government-owned pager used by a police sergeant as part of his employment. The review, done because of overage charges, showed that most of the sergeant's messages were not work related, and included several sexually oriented messages. 'Because the search was motivated by a legitimate work-related purpose, and because it was not excessive in scope,' the court held, the search was reasonable under the Fourth Amendment. Id at 764.

But in *US v Jones* 132 SCt 945, 181 LEd2d 911 (US 2012), the court unanimously held that the police must obtain a warrant before attaching a GPS tracker to a suspect's car, even though the police would not need a warrant to physically follow the car to determine its location.

The US Supreme Court recently held that a warrant is required for a police search without consent of the data contained in a cell phone in the possession of someone who has been arrested, except under 'exigent circumstances,' such as imminent erasure of the data. *Riley v California*, ___ US ___, 134 SCt 2473, 189 LEd2d 430 (June 25, 2014). The law regarding use of cell phones as tracking devices may be affected by the *Riley* decision, but currently remains unclear. Prior to the ruling in *Riley*, the 5th Circuit held that a warrant is not required to access cell phone tower records that can be used to track an individual phone. *In re Application of the United States for Historical Cell Site Data*, 724 F 3d 600 (5th Cir Tex 2013). But the 11th Circuit recently reached the opposite conclusion, ruling that a warrant *is* required. *US v Davis* 754 F3d

1205 (11th Cir June 11, 2014), reh'g en banc granted by 573 Fed Appx 925 (11th Cir Fla Sept 4, 2014) (vacating prior decision).

Most courts that have considered police searches of SM have held that a warrant is not required because users should not have a reasonable expectation of privacy in their SM posts. See eg *Guest v Leis* 255 F3d 325 (6th Cir 2001) (internet bulletin board); *US v Meregildo* 883 FSupp2d 523 (SDNY 2012) (Facebook); *US v Lustig* 3 F Supp 3d 808 (SD Cal 2014) (Craigslist).

C33.6 SPECIFIC ONLINE ABUSE/ONLINE BULLYING/ CYBERBULLYING LAWS

In studies, between 18.8 and 34.6 percent of students report that they have experienced bullying or abuse online at some point. Meanwhile, between 11.5 and 19.4 percent say they have behaved in ways that meet the definition of cyberbullying. Citing these statistics, the Cyberbullying Resource Center concludes that '[c]yberbullying is neither an epidemic nor a rarity. But is it something that everyone has a responsibility to work toward ending.' Justin W Patchin, *Cyberbullying: Neither an Epidemic nor a Rarity*, March 21, 2013, http://cyberbullying.us/cyberbullying-neither-an-epidemic-nor-a-rarity/.

Every state and the District of Columbia have laws addressing online stalking and harassment. According to the Cyberbullying Research Center, all states except Montana address bullying, which generally occurs within schools and other youth communities. Many of these laws require schools to adopt policies to prevent cyberbullying. Forty-seven states – all but Alaska, Montana and Wisconsin – have laws addressing electronic harassment, with 20 states having provisions specifically addressing cyberbullying and harassment online. Municipalities have also attempted to adopt their own laws on the subject. See eg Local Law F for 2010, Prohibiting Cyberbullying in Albany County, § 2 (Albany County, NY adopted Nov 8, 2010) (held unconstitutional in *People v Marquan* M, 2014 NY Slip Op 04881, 2014 NY LEXIS 1527, 2014 WL 2931482, 42 Media L Rep 2005 (NY 2014)).

There is no specific federal statute addressing cyberbullying, although 47 USC § 223 makes it a federal crime to knowingly use a telecommunications device to make, create, solicit, or initiate transmission of a comment, request, suggestion, proposal, or image which is obscene or is child pornography with intent to harass another person; or with knowledge that the recipient is under 18 years of age.

A Congressional bill proposed in 2009 would have imposed a fine and up to two years' imprisonment for anyone who 'transmits in interstate or foreign commerce any communication, with the intent to coerce, intimidate, harass, or cause substantial emotional distress to a person, using electronic means to support severe, repeated, and hostile behavior.' Megan Meier Cyberbullying Prevention Act, HR 1966, 111th Cong (2009). Another bill would have required schools receiving federal funding to initiate internet safety programs, including cyberbullying prevention. Student Internet Safety Act of 2009, HR 780, 111th Cong (2009).

C33.7 OTHER LAWS APPLIED TO ONLINE ABUSE/ ONLINE BULLYING/CYBERBULLYING

In 2006, 13-year-old Megan Taylor Meier committed suicide after a boy she had been communicating with through MySpace began to taunt and ridicule her, and sent her messages sayingthat the world would be better off without her. It turned out that the boy's account was fake, and had been created by 47-year-old Lori Drew, along with Drew's daughter and an 18-year-old employee of Drew. Although Drew's daughter had been friends with Megan, their relationship was rocky and Drew created the fake MySpace account in order to determine whether Megan was spreading malicious rumours about her daughter.

After local prosecutors declined to prosecute on the grounds that Drew's intent did not meet the standard of Missouri's harassment law, federal prosecutors in California – where MySpace's servers were located – charged Drew under the Computer Fraud and Abuse Act, 18 USC § 1030, on the theory that Drew's creation of a fake MySpace profile, which was contrary to MySpace's terms of service, constituted unauthorized access and use of the MySpace computer system. A federal jury in California acquitted Drew of most charges and deadlocked on one charge, but convicted her of a misdemeanour charge under the Act. The trial judge issued a judgment of acquittal, overruling the jury's verdict on the grounds that applying the statute to violation of a site's terms of service made it unconstitutionally vague. *United States v Drew* 259 FRD 449 (CD Cal 2009).

Courts have also confronted online harassment by creditors. The Fair Debt Collection Practices Act, 15 USC § 1601, *et seq*, prohibits debt collectors from using abusive, unfair, or deceptive practices to collect payments. Although the Act does not address use of SM, courts have applied its provisions to collection agents who used SM and other methods to intimidate debtors. See eg *Sohns v Bramacint*, Civil No 09-1225, 2010 WL 3926264 (D Minn October 1 2010) (granting summary judgment to plaintiff debtor against collection agent who mentioned debtor's daughter's MySpace photo); *Beacham v MarkOne Financial LLC*, No 10-12883CI-15 (Fla Pinellas Cnty Ct 2011) (ordering debt collector to stop contacting debtor and her friends on Facebook).

C33.8 CHILDREN AND SM LAWS OR RULES

The Child Online Privacy Protection Act (COPPA 15 USC § 6501, *et seq*) and Federal Trade Commission rules adopted under the Act require websites and online services that knowingly collect information from children younger than 13 to follow parental notice and consent requirements. These rules apply not only to sites and services that collect such information but also to those that integrate services provided by others that collect personal information.

The FTC has hinted that these rules should also apply to mobile apps directed at children. See Federal Trade Comm'n, Mobile Apps for Kids: Current Privacy Disclosures Are Disappointing (2012 report). Meanwhile, a federal bill to extend these provisions to children up to age 15 was introduced in 2013. See S 1700 / HR 3481 (113th Cong 2013).

California has adopted its own statute, 'Privacy Rights for California Minors in the Digital World,' 2013 Cal Laws chap 336 (2013), which goes into effect Jan 1, 2015. This law requires websites to provide a method for minors to remove their prior postings, Cal Bus & Prof Code § 22581, and prohibits online advertising to minors for products that cannot be sold to children, such as tobacco and alcohol. Cal Bus & Prof Code § 22580.

In the early 2000s, the federal government and many states passed statutes extending to electronic communication their existing laws outlawing distribution of content that is 'harmful to minors'. Courts held several of these statutes unconstitutional on the grounds that they unconstitutionally limited adult speech. See eg *Ashcroft v Free Speech Coalition* 535 US 234 (2002) (affirming injunction against enforcement the Communications Decency Act, part of the Telecommunications Act of 1996, Pub L 104-104 (1996)) and *Ashcroft v ACLU* 542 US 656 (2004) (affirming injunction against enforcement of Child Online Protection Act, Pub L 106-554 (1998)). Other courts limited enforcement of these provisions to communications directed specifically to children, not to general web postings. See eg *Florence v Shurtleff Civil No* 2:05CV000485 (D Utah declaratory judgment May 15, 2012).

C33.9   EMPLOYEES/EMPLOYMENT SM LAWS OR CASES

Many states have enacted statutes barring employers from requesting that employees and job applicants provide access to their SM accounts to facilitate monitoring and background checks, and several other states have considered such laws. Maryland was the first state to adopt such a law, 2012 Md Laws chap 233 (2012); in Maine, the legislature overrode a gubernatorial veto of a bill to study the issue. 2014 Me Laws chap 112 (2014). Congress has also proposed bills on the issue. See SN Online Protection Act, HR 537, 113th Cong (2013); Password Protection Act of 2013, HR 2077, 113th Cong. (2013).

In 2011, the Federal Trade Commission sent a letter to a company that provided internet-based background investigations of potential employees stating that, to the extent that the information it provided to employers included credit information, the company may be subject to the Fair Credit Reporting

Act. Letter to Renee Jackson, Counsel for Social Intelligence Corporation, Matter No 112 3014 (FTC May 9, 2011). Online background checks may also be actionable if they result in statutorily prohibited discrimination. See eg EEOC Enforcement Guidance No 915.002 (April 25, 2012) (holding that an employer's use of an individual's criminal history in making employment decisions may, in some instances, violate the prohibition against employment discrimination under Title VII of the Civil Rights Act of 1964).

When statutes have not banned the practice, courts have issued mixed opinions on the propriety of employers searching employees' electronic messages. In *City of Ontario v Quon* 560 US 746 (2010), the Supreme Court unanimously held that a public employer's search of an employee's text messages on an employer-issued pager did not violate the Fourth Amendment's prohibition of unreasonable searches. But the courts in *Konop v Hawaiian Airlines, Inc* 302 F3d 868 (9th Cir 2002), cert denied, 537 US 1193 (2003) and *Pietrylo v Hillstone Restaurant Group*, Civil No 06-5754, 2009 US Dist LEXIS 88702 (D NJ 2009) (unpublished) reached contrary results and found privacy violations when employers obtained passwords to access websites that employees used to gripe about their employers.

Employee use of SM to discuss working conditions may also be protected by federal labour law. Thus the National Labor Relations Board has ruled against an SM policy that barred employees from disparaging the company, *Costco Wholesale Corp*, 358 NLRB 106 (Sept 7, 2012); and that a non-profit social services provider unlawfully discharged five employees who had posted comments on Facebook relating to allegations of poor job performance previously expressed by one of their co-workers. *Hispanics United of Buffalo, Inc*, 359 NLRB No 37 (Dec 14, 2012). But it also held that an auto dealership was justified in firing an employee of an auto dealership who disparaged a sales event on Facebook. *Karl Knauz Motors, Inc*, 358 NLRB No 164 (Sept 28, 2012).

The NLRB has issued three memoranda in recent years that review cases regarding employee use of SM. See *Operations Memorandum: Report of the Acting General Counsel Concerning Social Media Cases*, OM 12-59 (NLRB May 30, 2012); *Operations Memorandum: Report of the Acting General Counsel Concerning Social Media Cases*, OM 12-21 (NLRB Jan 24, 2012); and *Operations Memorandum: Report of the Acting General Counsel Concerning Social Media Cases*, OM 11-74 (NLRB Aug 18, 2011). By reviewing these cases, the goal of the memoranda is to establish guidelines for employers.

Employers are also increasingly using publicly available SM evidence in workers' compensation litigation. See eg *Clement v Johnson's Warehouse Showroom, Inc* 2012 Ark App 17, 388 SW3d 469 (2012) (affirming use of Facebook and MySpace photos as evidence in workers' compensation hearing). See also *Romano v Steelcase Inc* 30 Misc 3d 426, 907 NYS2d 650 (2010) (granting access to plaintiff's private postings on SM sites in personal injury suit).

Another emerging issue concerning SM in an employment context regards ownership of SM accounts created during employment. In *Eagle v Morgan*, 2013 US Dist LEXIS 34220, 37 IER Cas (BNA) 395 (ED Pa Mar 12, 2013), the court held that a company's continued use of a former employee's LinkedIn account after she left the company constituted misappropriation of her identity, but that the former employee was not entitled to damages.

C33.10   SCHOOL AND UNIVERSITY STUDENT SM LAWS OR CASES

Public school action in response to students' postings online would seemingly create problems with the US Supreme Court's admonition in *Tinker v Des Moines Independent School District*, 393 US 503, 506-07 (1969) that neither 'students [n]or teachers shed their constitutional rights to freedom of speech or expression at the schoolhouse gate.' Yet in subsequent cases the Court has held that public schools may control speech and discipline students for speech that disrupts school-sponsored activities. See *Bethel School District v Fraser*, 78 US 675 (1986) (obscenity-laden student speech to high school assembly); *Hazelwood School District v Kuhlmeier*, 84 US 260 (1988) (high school newspaper article on teen pregnancy); and *Morse v Frederick*, 551 US 393 (2007) ('Bong hits for Jesus' banner at Olympic torch relay during school day, which high school permitted students to attend).

In the context of the internet and SM, lower courts have ruled for both students and schools. In *Layshock v Hermitage School District*, 650 F3d 205 (3d Cir 2011) (en banc) a federal appeals court affirmed a grant of summary judgment to a student in his civil rights lawsuit against a school that disciplined him for using a non-school computer to create a MySpace page mocking the principal. But in another case the same appeals court reversed summary judgment for a different school district that was sued by another student who had created a sexually explicit MySpace profile that used the principal's photograph, but not his name. *JS v Blue Mountain. School Dist*, 650 F3d 915 (3d Cir Pa. 2011) (en banc). Another federal appeals court upheld a school's discipline against a student who created a MySpace page mocking another student. *Kowalski v Berkeley County Sch*, 652 F3d 565 (4th Cir 2011). The US Supreme Court declined to review these decisions. 132 SCt 1097, 181 Led 2d 978 (US 2012) (denying certiorari in *Layshock* and *JS*) and 132 SCt 1095, 181 L Ed 2d 1009 (US 2012) (denying certiorari in *Kowalski*).

North Carolina was the first state to enact a statute barring students from creating fake SM profiles of school employees. 2012 NC Laws chap 149 (2012). Indiana proposed a similar law in 2013. HB 1364 (Ind Legis 2013). In other states, prosecutors have used laws such as archaic criminal defamation statutes in such cases. See eg *Mink v Knox* 613 F3d 995 (10th Cir 2010) (reviving student's civil rights lawsuit over criminal libel prosecution over website marketing professor). Some school employees have filed civil suits on their own. See eg *Draker v Schreiber* 271 SW3d 318 (Tex App San Antonio 2008) (civil suit by principal over fake MySpace profile).

Most of the state statutes that bar employers from requiring their employees and potential employees to reveal their SM accounts include similar provisions that apply to post-secondary educational institutions as to enrolled and potential students. Several states have also barred schools from using contractors to monitor their students' SM postings, including those of student athletes.

Missouri repealed a law which would have banned teachers from having personal SM websites which allow exclusive interaction with current or former students after a state court judge enjoined enforcement of the statute on the grounds that it would have a chilling effect on speech. SB 1 (Mo Legis Special Session 2011) (repealing SB 54, § 162069 (Mo Legis 2011) after it was enjoined by *Missouri State Teachers v Missouri*, Case No 11AC-CC00553 (Mo Cir Ct, Cole County order Aug 26, 2011)). A provision of the Missouri law requiring school districts to have a written policy on SM and other electronic communications between school employees and students remains. SB 54, § 162.068 (Mo Legis 2011). New Jersey has a similar statute. 2014 NJ Laws chap 2.

Aside from these statutes, a federal court in Minnesota held that a public school's requirement that students allow access to their SM content violated the students' rights of privacy and free speech, leading the school district to settle the case with a $70,000 payment to a student who was forced to reveal her Facebook account. *RS ex rel SS v Minnewaska Area Dist No 2149*, 894 FSupp 2d 1128 (D Minn 2012).

C33.11 RIGHT OR HUMAN RIGHT TO ACCESS THE INTERNET OR SM

The concept that there is a human right to internet access or SM has not gotten much traction in the United States.

The Federal Communications Commission (FCC) does, however, oversee a Universal Service Fund, financed by taxes on communications services, that pays for advanced telecommunications services – including high-speed internet connections – for schools, classrooms, health care providers, and libraries. The constitutionality of the Universal Service Fund was upheld in *Texas Office of Public Utility Counsel, et al v FCC* 265 F3d 313 (5th Cir 2001), cert denied, *Nat'l Ass'n of State Util. Consumer Advocates v FCC* 535 US 986 (2002). This funding includes the requirement that recipients install software to filter access to obscene, pornographic and other offensive websites. This mandate was upheld in *United States v American Library Association* 539 US 194 (2003).

By 2018, the fund will be replaced with the Connect America Fund, focused on expansion of broadband internet to underserved areas. The planned conversion was upheld in In re: FCC 11-161, 753 F3d 1015 (10th Cir 2014).

Some municipalities have created, often through public-private partnerships, local networks offering broadband internet connections at no or low cost. Private telecommunications providers have generally opposed creation of these networks, and in some cases have sued to stop them. Several state legislatures have also banned local governments from creating such networks. The FCC chairman said in 2014 that the agency was prepared to act to override such bans, but this proposal has encountered Congressional opposition.

Private providers – notably Google – have implemented programs to offer basic levels of internet service in selected municipalities for free, with enhanced services available at additional cost.

Another concept related to universal internet access that the FCC has tried to adopt is 'net neutrality,' the idea that providers of internet access should treat all online information providers equally by providing online material from all sources to all and end users at the same speed, rather than offering faster connections to providers who pay for the privilege. The FCC's efforts have been stymied by the agency's decision in 1976 distinguishing between basic voice and data communication and enhanced services which involved processing of voice and data. The basic service, basically limited to telephone voice and fax services and the infrastructure that they used (wires, switching stations, etc), was and remains subject to detailed FCC regulations. But the enhanced services, including most modern broadband internet services, are not. This distinction was codified in the Telecommunications Act of 1996, Pub L 104-104, 110 Stat 56 (1996), and ratified by US Supreme Court in *National Cable & Telecommunications Assn v Brand X Internet Services* 545 US 967 (2005).

With this distinction in place, the FCC has had a difficult time issuing regulations regarding internet service, including net neutrality. Two efforts by the FCC to enforce net neutrality have been struck down by the courts because of the Commission's limited role in regulating broadband connections enacted in 1976. See *Comcast Corp v FCC* 600 F3d 642 (DC Cir 2010) and *Verizon v FCC* 740 F3d 623 (DC Cir 2014). The FCC considered various alternatives in the wake of the *Verizon* decision.

C33.12   BANS OR RESTRICTIONS ON INTERNET OR SM

Generally, restrictions on speech are suspect under the First Amendment. *Near v Minnesota* 283 US 204 (1919); *New York Times v United States*, 403 US 713 (1971); *Nebraska Press Association v Stewart*, 437 US 539 (1976). But statutes, regulations, and court orders limiting or restricting speech online have been upheld in certain circumstances.

For example, several states have passed laws barring registered sex offenders from accessing SM sites. See eg 730 Ill Comp Stat 5/3-3-7(a)(7.12); Ky Rev

Stat Ann § 17.546; Minn Stat Ann § 244.05(6)(c); NY Penal Law § 65.10(4-a) (b); Tex Gov't Code Ann. § 508.1861. Several of these statutes have been found unconstitutional. See eg *Doe v Jindal* 853 F Supp 2d 596 (MD La 2012); *Doe v Neb* 898 F Supp 2d 1086 (D Neb 2012); *Doe v Prosecutor*, 705 F3d 694, 89 ALR 6th 771 (7th Cir 2013) (Indiana statute); *State v Packingham*, 748 SE2d 146 (NC Ct App 2013), appeal granted, 749 SE2d 842 (No 366PA13) (NC Nov 7, 2013) (Argued Sept 8, 2014). After its statute barring sex offenders from SM was struck down, Louisiana adopted a new law requiring them to identify themselves as offenders on SM. La Rev Stat § 15:542.1(D) (added by 2012 La Acts chap 385 § 1), while also enacting a modified version of the prior statute. Many SM sites also have their own policies barring registered sex offenders.

But not all courts have ruled against restrictions on use of SM. A New Jersey appeals court upheld restrictions placed on a woman's blogging about her family as a condition of her parole in a criminal case stemming from a custody dispute, because of the limited nature of the restriction. See *State v HLM* No A1257-12, 2014 NJ Super Unpub LEXIS 1079 (NJ AppDiv May 13, 2014) (unpublished).

Limitations on attorney speech and advertising can also cover SM. The California Bar recently concluded, for example, that any SM discussion of an attorney's professional qualifications or availability for employment is subject to ethical rules regarding attorney communications. Cal Bar Formal Op 2012-186 (Dec 12, 2012). See also ABA Formal Opinion 10-457 (Aug 5, 2010) (applying advertising rules to attorney websites). Attorney communication via SM also presents issues regarding the formation of an attorney-client relationship and, if such a relationship exists, client confidentiality. The ABA has proposed a new comment to Model Rule of Ethics 1.18 which would outline the factors in determining whether if she an attorney-client relationship is created via online communication.

Other SM limitations have emerged in the form of contractual provisions restricting customers' online reviews and comments. A new California law prohibits such provisions (Cal Civil Code § 1670.8, added by 2014 Cal Laws chap 308).

Courts now routinely issue protection orders that include SM, and any contact – including an online 'like' or 'poke' – can lead to an arrest for violating such an order.

C33.13 IDENTITY THEFT (OR EQUIVALENT)

Some states, including California and New York, have passed laws specifically criminalizing identity theft online. See Cal Penal Code § 528.5; Miss Code § 97-45-33; NY Penal Law § 190.25(4); and Tex Penal Code § 33.07. Others have laws barring online impersonation to commit financial fraud. Ariz Rev Stat § 13-2008(A); Cal Penal Code § 530.5(a); and NY Penal Law § 190.25(1).

States without such laws have used general identity theft statutes to prosecute defendants who have created SM profiles in the guise of someone else. See eg *In re Rolando S* 197 Cal App 4th 936, 129 Cal Rptr 3d 49 (Cal App 2011), modified by 2011 Cal App LEXIS 1051 (Cal App Aug 10, 2011) (deleting one non-substantive sentence), rev denied, 2011 Cal LEXIS 10793 (Cal Oct 19, 2011). Prosecutors in other states have used cyber-harassment and cyberstalking statutes. Fake SM profiles have also led to civil actions for claims such as defamation and invasion of privacy. See eg *Draker v Schreiber*, 271 SW3d 318 (Tex App San Antonio 2008); *La Russa v Twitter Inc* No CGC-09-488101 (Cal Super 2009) (trademark claim; settled). Impersonation online is also frequently a violation of the contractual terms of service of most SM websites.

C33.14 HACKING (OR EQUIVALENT)

The primary criminal federal statute against computer hacking is the Computer Fraud and Abuse Act 18 USC § 1030 (CFAA), which makes it a crime to obtain information from a computer after accessing it without authorization. The statute also creates a civil action if the unauthorized access causes damage or financial loss. See 18 USC § 1030(g).

California and other states have their own versions of this statute. See eg Cal Penal Code § 484-502.9.

Courts disagree on whether use of a computer system or website in violation of the service's terms of use constitutes exceeding authorized access under the statute. Compare *EF Cultural Travel BV v Explorica Inc* 274 F3d 577 (1st Cir 2001) and *United States v Nosal* 676 F3d 854 (9th Cir 2012) (en banc). Congressional efforts to clarify the statute have not succeeded. Unauthorized use of material to which the user legitimately had authorized access is not a violation of the Act. *WEC Caroline Energy Solutions LLC v Miller* 687 F3d 199 (4th Cir 2012) cert denied 133 S Ct 831, 184 L Ed 2d 645 (US 2013); *LVRC Holdings v Brekka* 581 F 3d 1127 (9th Cir 2009).

Aside from the unsuccessful prosecution of Lori Drew for creating a fake MySpace profile that led to a teenage girl's suicide (see C33.7), the most prominent prosecution under CFAA was of Aaron Schwartz, a hacker and activist who downloaded a large portion of the JSTOR database of academic articles. Schwartz committed suicide in 2013, before the case went to trial.

C33.15 PRIVACY BY DESIGN (PBD) (OR EQUIVALENT)

The Federal Trade Commission endorsed privacy by design concepts in a 2012 report, *Protecting Consumer Privacy in an Era of Rapid Change*, and called for corporations to incorporate privacy protections and data protection into their operations. The report states that companies should collect and retain only the information required to conduct normal business with their customers, and specifically flag collection of additional data. The report also recommends the adoption of comprehensive data management programs to protect and maintain consumer information. The commission also noted that these principles were consistent with its settlements regarding user privacy with Google and Facebook. See *In the Matter of Google Inc* FTC Docket No C-4336 (Oct 13 2011) (consent order).

C33.16 TWEETING FROM COURTS, AND ANY RULES/LAWS

Historically, American courts were reluctant to allow still and audio-video photography and recording equipment (see below). While much of this opposition has waned, it continues regarding newer devices such as smartphones, tablets, and laptops.

Policies vary widely: sometimes from building to building, and sometimes from courtroom to courtroom. Some courts ban the devices from the courthouse entirely, while others allow only selected individuals – usually judges, court personnel, police, and sometimes journalists – to possess and use these devices. Many courts that do allow the devices limit use to the hallways and other areas outside of courtrooms.

An informal survey of federal district courts in 2010 found that 41 of the 92 federal district courts (44 percent) allowed electronic devices into their courthouses, while the other 48 districts (51 percent) banned the devices except for court personnel and probation and pre-trial officers. Among the district courts that allowed the devices in the building, one-third prohibited the public from bringing the devices into courtrooms, while two-thirds allowed the devices in courtrooms but required that they be turned off or silenced.

The best practical advice for those who wish to use new media tools in court is to check local court rules and practice by checking with the court's public information officer, the court's clerk, or (as a last resort) the judge's staff for the procedure in an individual judge's courtroom.

Individuals who use electronic devices, despite court policies against their use, can be held in contempt and jailed. In 2010 a blogger was banned from a Colorado courtroom for using a cell phone in violation of the court's policy, but was permitted to observe the trial in an overflow video room.

Individual state court judges in several states, including California, Colorado, Kansas, Michigan and Ohio, have allowed live Tweeting of proceedings from their courtrooms in recent years. In 2012, the Kansas Supreme Court amended the state's courts rules to explicitly permit Tweeting and texting from courtrooms. 2012 SC 87 (Kan Oct 18, 2012) (order amending Kan Sup Ct R

1001); Iowa did the same in 2014. In the matter of Chapter 25 of the Iowa Court Rules and Amendments to Expanded News Media Coverage Rules (Iowa order Apr 29, 2014) (amending Iowa Ct R 25.1–25.10). Federal judges in Florida, Iowa, Kansas, Massachusetts, Pennsylvania, South Dakota, and Washington DC have also allowed live Tweeting, but in *United States v Shelnutt*, 2009 US Dist LEXIS 101427, 37 Media L Rep 2594 (MD Ga Nov 2, 2009) a federal court denied a media request to send Tweets from the courtroom during trial on the grounds that Federal Rule of Criminal Procedure 53 bars broadcasting of judicial proceedings (see C33.17).

Even judges who allow electronic devices in their courtrooms may place restrictions on their use, such as prohibiting photography of the jurors or sensitive witnesses. A Kansas state judge declared a mistrial in a 2012 murder case after a reporter Tweeted a photo which inadvertently showed a juror.

C33.17   TELEVISION COURTROOM BROADCASTING OR TELEVISION CAMERAS IN COURT, AND RULES OR LAWS

Most state trial and appellate courts now allow at least some still and video camera coverage of their proceedings. Most federal trial and appeals courts, and the US Supreme Court, generally do not allow such coverage. These policies have also been applied to newer forms of technology, such as smartphones (see C33.16).

The twentieth century saw a long fight over still and video camera access to court proceedings. This fight still continues to some extent today, and the history explains some of the restrictions that still exist on usage of still and video cameras in court.

There were generally no official rules on use of cameras to record court proceedings until the 1930s. In 1934, however, the trial of Bruno Hauptmann in New Jersey state court for the kidnapping and murder of the baby of aviator Charles A Lindbergh attracted extensive media attention, including disruptive flash photography and a snuck-in movie camera. The debacle led the American Bar Association in 1937 to adopt Judicial Canon 35, which recommended that both still and movie cameras be banned from courtrooms. In 1962, the ABA amended Canon 35 to also ban television cameras.

All but two states – Texas and Colorado – adopted bans in their courts. At the same time, Congress banned cameras in federal court. The US Supreme Court endorsed these bans in *Estes v Texas* 381 US 532 (1965), in which it reversed a conviction for swindling because of the disruptions caused by cameras in the Texas courtroom. The following year, in *Sheppard v Maxwell* 384 US 333 (1966), the Court reversed a murder conviction because of extensive coverage and disruptive behaviour of print, radio and television reporters, even though most of the disruption occurred outside the courtroom.

But even in *Estes* the Court was open to the possibility of allowing cameras if the technology became less obtrusive. 'When the advances in these arts permit reporting by printing press or by television without their present hazards to a fair trial,' the Court wrote, 'we will have another case.' *Estes* 381 US at 540.

These changes in technology came in the 1970s, with smaller, less intrusive cameras. In 1978, the ABA considered changing its rule to allow each court to decide for itself, but ultimately decided not to change the 1937 canon. But the same year, the Conference of State Chief Justices voted that each state should create its own policy towards cameras in courts. This led several states to begin experiments allowing such coverage, which the US Supreme Court endorsed in *Chandler v Florida*, 449 US 560 (1981), refusing to reverse a murder conviction and holding that *Estes* did not entirely prohibit camera use in courtrooms, as long as they were unobtrusive.

Now, most states allow for some form of cameras in the courtroom. Most states allow camera coverage of trials, but place restrictions on their use. Many states still bar their use in family court and other specialized courts. A few states prohibit camera coverage of trials, and allow coverage in appellate courts only. The Georgia Court of Appeals recently held that the ability to use cameras in trials is not exclusively for the established media, and that individual citizens can use cameras on the same terms. *McLaurin v Ott* 327 GaApp 488, 759 SE2d 567 (Ga App 2014).

The District of Columbia bans cameras entirely from all local court proceedings, although the DC Court of Appeals offers streaming audio and video of its arguments online.

Appellate courts in several states now offer their own live video streams of their proceedings online. In 2011 and 2012, proceedings from a Massachusetts district court were streamed live and archived online through a project coordinated by Boston public radio station WBUR. The project survived legal challenges, see *Commonwealth v Barnes* 461 Mass 644, 963 NE2d 1156 (2012); and *District Attorney for the Norfolk District v Justices of the Quincy District Court*, No SJ-201-0306 (Mass Aug. 14, 2012) (single justice order by Botsford, J), but stopped streaming when the project's funding ran out.

Camera access to the federal courts is more patchy. The federal courts conducted a limited test of camera coverage of civil trials in several federal district courts from 1991 through 1994. At the conclusion of the test, the committee examining the issue unambiguously recommended that federal courts allow televised proceedings. But the federal Judicial Conference as a whole rejected this recommendation, and concluded in 1994 that 'the intimidating effect of cameras on some witnesses and jurors was "a cause for serious concern".'

Despite this conclusion, in 1996 some judges of the Southern and Eastern districts of New York allowed camera coverage of particular cases. See *Marisol A v Giuliani*, 929 F Supp 660 (SDNY 1996); *Katzman v Victoria's Secret Catalogue*, 923 F Supp 580 (SDNY 1996); *Sigmon v Parker Chapin Flanau &*

Kimpl, 937 F Supp 335 (SDNY 1996); *Hamilton v Accu-Tek*, 942 F Supp 136 (EDNY 1996).

In reaction to the *Marisol* decision, in March 1996 the Judicial Conference passed a resolution allowing each federal circuit to decide the issue for itself, while strongly urging the circuits to follow the Conference's 1994 policy and to 'abrogate any local rules of court that conflict with this decision.'

Currently, camera coverage of federal criminal trials is still generally prohibited, except to allow remote viewing by victims under 42 USC § 10608. See Fed R Crim Pro 53; see also *United States v Hastings*, 695 F2d 1278, 1279, n 5 (11th Cir 1983), reh'g denied, 704 F2d 559 (11th Cir 1983). The situation regarding civil trials depends on whether the federal appeals court to which a particular district court is assigned has taken action under the Judicial Conference policy to invalidate any district court rules allowing such coverage. If the applicable appeals court has not taken such action, the district court's rule on the issue, if any, applies. The Second and Ninth circuits have not acted to ban cameras in their district courts, so that district courts within these circuits can have their own policies.

In 2011, the federal courts began a second three-year experiment which allowed cameras in 14 federal trial courts to video record civil trials with consent of the judge and both parties, and post the video online. Meanwhile, in a separate program, a total of 32 federal trial and bankruptcy courts offer audio recordings of their proceedings through their websites.

There has been growing pressure for the US Supreme Court to allow still and video cameras to cover its proceedings. The court already posts transcripts of arguments daily, and audio of arguments each week. In February 2014, a video posted to YouTube showed both a portion of the oral argument in the US Supreme Court in a campaign finance case in October 2013 and an activist's interruption of argument before the court in another case a few days before the video was posted. Both portions of the video were apparently shot with hidden cameras in violation of the court's prohibition of cameras.

Several bills have been introduced in Congress in the past several years to require or urge federal courts, including the Supreme Court, to allow cameras. In addition, in 2014 several media organizations began an advertising campaign advocating that cameras be allowed in the Supreme Court.

C33.18   SM IN COURTROOMS

With the high usage of SM in American society, it is inevitable that Facebook, Twitter and other SM sites and services will increasingly become a factor in legal proceedings. SM can become a problem when used by trial participants in ways that endanger fundamental principles of fairness and impartiality of the courts.

Many of the issues that have arisen from SM have involved jurors using SM to conduct research or communicate with others about a case.

For several years now, courts have been giving jurors more detailed admonitions and jury instructions against educating themselves about cases online. While most courts now have modern jury instructions which tell jurors not to use the internet or SM during trial, it is increasingly apparent that these instructions must specifically mention particular websites and services, and should also include a rationale and explanation for the restrictions that will counteract the habit of 'digital natives' to constantly communicate, research and 'share' online.

There are numerous instances in which jurors have been found to be using the internet or SM during trial. Several of these have resulted in mistrials or reversals of jury verdicts.

In *Wardlaw v State* 185 Md App 440, 971 A2d 331 (Md Ct Special App 2009), a juror used the internet to research the definition of 'oppositional defiant disorder,' a disorder that a therapist testified that she had diagnosed a key witness as having. The appellate court, in a unanimous, three-judge decision, concluded that the trial court's failure to question the jurors about the influence of the internet research required a reversal.

In another Maryland case – the high-profile prosecution of Baltimore Mayor Sheila Dixon for political corruption charges – the court discovered that five of the jurors had become Facebook friends and communicated during the trial. The issue became moot after Dixon pleaded guilty. *State v Dixon*, Case Nos 109009009, 109210015 and 109210016 (Md Cir Ct, Baltimore County indictments filed Jan 9, 2009).

In *People v Wadle* 77 P3d 764 (Colo App 2003) aff'd, 97 P3d 932 (Colo 2004), the appeals court granted a new trial in a case where a juror did research online about the drug Paxil, which the criminal defendant accused of murdering her step-grandson had taken, and shared that research with other jurors. The Arkansas Supreme Court reversed a murder conviction in a case where one juror Tweeted during the trial, while another fell asleep. *Erickson Dimas-Martinez v State*, 2011 Ark 515, 385 S W 3d 238 (Ark 2011). In 2014 a Pennsylvania judge reversed a murder conviction after discovering that a juror had conducted online research and discovered the history of the case and the defendant's criminal record. A federal judge who found out that a juror had 'friended' the plaintiffs in a personal injury and wrongful death case after the trial held that the timing of the online connection meant that the jury verdict for the defence need not be vacated. *Wilgus v F/V Sirius Inc* 665 F Supp 2d 23 (D Me 2009) (denying new trial motion).

A few courts have found jurors in contempt for using SM during trials. A Texas judge sentenced a juror who sent a 'friend' request to the defendant in a personal injury case to two days of community service. A Florida court imposed a three-day jail sentence for criminal contempt on a juror who sent a friend request to the defendant in an auto negligence case. After the friend request was discovered and the juror was dismissed, the juror wrote on Facebook, 'Score ... I got dismissed!! apparently they frown upon sending a friend request to the defendant ... haha.' A New York woman pleaded guilty in 2009 to a misdemeanour charge of attempted unlawful grand jury disclosure after she posted comments to a newspaper website about her experience several months earlier serving on a grand jury that refused to issue an indictment in the 2007 death of a man in police custody.

But courts have not found all juror use of SM to be problematic. In 2006, the New Hampshire Supreme Court rejected a murder convict's effort to overturn a guilty verdict based on a juror's pre-trial blogging, in which the juror said he was going on jury duty and, 'now I get to listen to the local riff-raff try and convince me of their innocence.' *State v Goupil* 154 NH 208, 908 A2d 1256 (NH 2006). A federal court later rejected the defendant's habeas corpus petition based on a similar argument regarding the juror's blog postings. See *Goupil v Cattell* 2008 DNH 46, 2008 WL 544863, 2008 US Dist LEXIS 14774 (D NH Feb 26, 2008) (unpublished).

In August 2011, California adopted a statute making it a crime for jurors to use SM and the internet to do research or disseminate information about cases. 2011 Cal Laws chap 181 (codified at Cal. Penal Code section 166(a)(6)). But two years after the law went into effect the state's Judicial Council recommended that the statute be repealed, saying that the possibility of criminal sanctions actually impeded courts' inquiries into improper online activity by jurors. The criminal provisions were repealed in 2014, 2014 Cal Laws chap 99, although civil penalties remain.

SM use affecting trials is not limited to jurors: other trial participants, including judges, have been found to be using the internet and SM.

An Ohio trial judge was removed from a murder case after comments on the case on a local newspaper's website were traced to her office computer. (Her daughter claimed to have made the posts.) *State v Sowell (Saffold)*, 134 Ohio St 3d 1204, 2010-Ohio-6723, 981 NE 2d 869 (Ohio 2010) (Pfeifer, Acting CJ). The Second Circuit Court of Appeals upheld a decision by District Judge Denny Chin that relied on internet research in deciding whether a convicted bank robber had violated his terms of supervised release. *US v Bari*, 599 F3d 176 (2d Cir 2010). But see *Ibey v Taco Bell Corp* 2012 WL 2401972, 2012 US Dist LEXIS 91030 (June 18, 2012) (court may not take judicial notice of information on LinkedIn profile because its reliability can be questioned).

An ABA ethics opinion concluded that judges may participate in electronic SM, but must avoid any conduct that would undermine the judge's independence, integrity, or impartiality, or create an appearance of impropriety. ABA Formal Op 462 (Feb 21 2013). The Florida Supreme Court's Judicial Ethics Advisory Committee went even further, declaring that judges may not ethically be SM 'friends' with lawyers who may appear before the judge in court. Fla Sup Ct

Jud Ethics Op 2009-20 (Nov 17 2009). The Massachusetts Judicial Ethics Committee agreed, adding that a judge must recuse him or herself when an SM 'friend' appears before the judge. Mass Jud Ethics Comm. Opinion 2011-6 (Dec 28 2011). The Oklahoma Judicial Ethics Advisory Panel concluded that judges may be 'friends' with attorneys who do not appear before them. Oklahoma Judicial Ethics Opinion 2011-3 (July 6 2011).

California forged a middle course, concluding that the propriety of judges' online friendships depended on a number of factors. Cal Jud Ethics Comm. Op 66 (Nov 23 2010). Maryland urged judges to 'proceed cautiously' in their use of SM. Md Jud Ethics Comm Op 2012-07 (June 12 2012). Other states, while also urging caution, concluded that judges could participate in SM. See NY Jud Ethics Comm. Op 08-176 (Jan 29 2009); Ky Jud Ethics Comm. Op JE-119 (Jan 20 2010); Ohio Jud Ethics Comm. Op 2010-7 (Dec 3 2010); and SC Advisory Comm on Stds of Jud Conduct Op No 17-2009 (Oct 2009).

The Florida District Court of Appeal followed that state's ethics ruling in disqualifying a judge who was Facebook friends with the prosecutor. *Domville v Florida*, 103 So 3d 184 (Fla App 4 Dist Sept 5 2012), rev denied 110 So 3d 441 (Fla 2013). A North Carolina judge was publicly reprimanded for posting comments on Facebook regarding a pending support and custody hearing, which were visible to the judge's 'friends,' including one of the lawyers involved in the hearing. B Carlton Terry Jr, Inquiry No 08-234 (NC Jud Stds Comm'n. April 1 2009).

SM usage by trial attendees has also led to problems. In 2010 an Ohio judge found two trial attendees, who separately pointed a Flip camera and a cell phone towards the jury during trial testimony in a murder case, guilty of contempt of court and sentenced them to 30 and 60 days in jail. The judge also declared a mistrial in the murder case. In a New York sex-abuse case, four trial observers were arrested after they used a cell phone to take pictures of the alleged victim as she testified and posted one of the pictures on Twitter.

Another trial participant whose SM use raises questions is counsel. Most of the discussion of attorneys' use of SM has focused on conducting research of trial participants, particularly researching potential jurors during 'voir dire'.

A 2014 ABA ethics opinion concluded that 'a lawyer may review a juror's or potential juror's Internet presence, which may include postings by the juror or potential juror in advance of and during a trial, but a lawyer may not communicate directly or through another with a juror or potential juror.' ABA Formal Op Formal Opinion 466 (April 24 2014). This was in accord with earlier opinions of the New York City Bar Association and the New York County Lawyers' Association. NY Cnty Law Ass'n. Formal Op 743 (May 18 2011); NYC. Bar Ass'n Formal Op 2012-02 (2012). The city bar's opinion expanded on what constitutes a 'communication,' and concluded that 'it is an attorney's duty to research and understand the properties of the service or website she wishes to use for jury research in order to avoid inadvertent communications.'

Other ethics opinions have considered attorneys' online research about other trial participants. The New York State Bar found it ethical for an attorney to obtain information from an adverse, unrepresented party's public SM page, as long as the attorney does not request access beyond that available to all web users. NYS Bar Ass'n Ethics Op 843 (Sept 10, 2010). But the San Diego County Bar found that sending a 'friend' request to an adverse represented party is improper. San Diego County Bar Legal Ethics Opinion 2011-2 (May 24 2011). Similarly, the Philadelphia Bar Association found that it is unethical for an attorney to 'friend' a witness with an eye towards impeachment of that witness during trial because such communication is deceptive. Phila. Bar Ass'n Ethics Opinion No 2009-02 (Mar 2009).

This does not mean that all courts will allow online research of jurors. A New Jersey trial court barred the plaintiff's attorney in a medical malpractice case from using a laptop to look up potential jurors via the courthouse's open WiFi, saying that allowing it without advance notice would be unfair to opposing counsel. An appeals court rejected the trial court's reasoning, saying that no court rule required such notice. *Carino v Muenzen*, A-5491-08T1, 2010 WL 3448071, 2010 NJ Super. Unpub. LEXIS 2154 (NJ Sup Ct App Div Aug 30 2010) (unpublished), certif denied, 13 A3d 363 (NJ, Feb 1 2011).

C33.19   USE OF SM AS EVIDENCE IN COURTS

This section focuses on discovery of SM content and admissibility of such content as evidence. For a discussion of Fourth Amendment search and seizure issues related to SM, see C33.5.

As more information is posted on SM sites, it is inevitable that lawyers would seek to introduce such material as evidence in both civil and criminal litigation. Yet a 2013 survey by lawyers.com found that a majority of SM users in the US do not know that their posts, Tweets, check-ins, and other SM material can be used as evidence in court.

The Federal Rules of Civil Procedure were amended in 2006 to allow for discovery of electronically stored information, see FRCP R 33(d) and 34(a) (1)(A), and courts have generally allowed use of such evidence as long as it is relevant and can be properly authenticated.

For a court to allow discovery of such information, the party seeking it must show that the material sought is relevant to the case and not just a 'fishing expedition.' Compare eg *Moore v Miller* 2013 US Dist LEXIS 79568 (D Colo June 6, 2013) (allowing such discovery) with *Salvato v Miley* 2013 US Dist LEXIS 81784 (MD Fla June 11, 2013) (disallowing it) and *Tompkins v Detroit Metro*. Airport, 278 FRD 387 (ED Mich 2012) (disallowing).

Discovery of SM postings may include both material that is publicly available and material that is available only to 'friends' or other users of a particular site. Thus courts have ordered disclosure of user names and passwords when the party seeking discovery can show that relevant information may be available in the non-public material, based on the publicly available information on the site. See eg *Zimmerman v Weis Markets Inc* 2011 Pa Dist & Cnty Dec LEXIS 187 (Pa County Ct May 19, 2011) (allowing discovery of non-public sections of SM profiles); *Thompson v Autoliv ASP Inc* 2012 US Dist LEXIS 85143, 2012 WL 2342928 *4 (D Nev June 20, 2012) (allowing discovery); *Tompkins v Detroit Metropolitan Airport* 278 FRD 387, 388-89 (ED Mich 2012) (denying discovery); *McMillen v Hummingbird Speedway Inc* 2010 Pa Dist & Cnty. Dec LEXIS 270, 2010 WL 4403285 (Pa Com Pl Sept 9, 2010) (allowing discovery); *Keller v Nat'l Farmers Union Prop & Cas* 2013 US Dist LEXIS 452 (D Mont Jan 2, 2013) (denying discovery).

In *Griffin v State*, 419 Md 343, 19 A3d 415 (Md Apr 28, 2011), the Maryland Court of Appeals – the state's highest court – outlined the requirements for authentication of SM evidence.

'The first, and perhaps most obvious method would be to ask the purported creator if she indeed created the profile and also if she added the posting in question ... The second option may be to search the computer of the person who allegedly created the profile and posting and examine the computer's internet history and hard drive to determine whether that computer was used to originate the SN profile and posting in question ... A third method may be to obtain information directly from the SN website that links the establishment of the profile to the person who allegedly created it and also links the posting sought to be introduced to the person who initiated it.' Id at 363, 19 A3d at 427.

In some cases, courts have narrowed broad SM discovery requests in order to limit them to relevant information. See eg *Wilkinson v Greater Dayton Reg'l Transit Auth* 2014 US Dist LEXIS 64522 (SD Ohio May 9, 2014).

Because it may be called upon as evidence, it is good practice for businesses to record and retain their SM activities. Failure to do so, as well as destruction of such material by a party (by 'deleting' the posts) may be considered destruction of evidence. See eg *Painter v Atwood* 2014 WL 1089694, 2014 US Dist LEXIS 35060 (D Nev Mar 18, 2014) reconsid denied 2014 US Dist LEXIS 98669 (D Nev July 21, 2014) (imposing sanctions for deletion of text messages and Facebook posts relevant to the issues in the case).

C33.20   PRIVACY, DATA PROTECTION AND SM

In order to be legally cognizable, privacy claims must be based on a reasonable expectation that information is not public, based on both an individual's perception of privacy and society's standards. See *Katz v United States* 389 US 347 (1967) (because of reasonable expectation of privacy in a closed telephone booth, government must obtain a subpoena to record the phone conversation).

The US Supreme Court recently applied this standard to electronic surveillance by attaching a GPS tracker to a car. *US v Jones* 132 SCt 945, 181 L Ed 2d 911 (US 2012) (warrant required for police to attach GPS tracker). While concurring in this result, Justice Sonya Sotomayor stated that '... it may be necessary to reconsider the premise that an individual has no reasonable expectation of privacy in information voluntarily disclosed to third parties. This approach is ill suited to the digital age, in which people reveal a great deal of information about themselves to third parties in the course of carrying out mundane tasks.' Id at 957, 181 L Ed 2d at 926.

Lower courts have applied this 'reasonable expectation of privacy' standard in Fourth Amendment contexts involving government access and private claims over unauthorized access and/or disclosure of material from SM. See eg *Guest v Leis* 255 F 3d 325 (6th Cir 2001) (government access to posts on internet bulletin board); *Moreno v Hanford Sentinel Inc* 172 Cal App 4th 1125; 91 Cal Rptr 3d 858 (Cal App 2009) (dismissing privacy suit against newspaper that published plaintiff's MySpace post about her hometown); *US v Meregildo* 883 F Supp 2d 523 (SDNY 2012) (government access to Facebook posts); *People v Harris*, 36 Misc 3d 613, 945 NYS 2d 50, 2012 NY Slip Op 22109 (NYC Crim Ct 2012) (government access to Twitter posts), aff'd, 43 Misc 3d 136(A), 2014 NY Slip Op 507670(U) (NY App Term, Apr 24, 2014); *Ehling v Monmouth-Ocean Hospital Service Corp* 872 F Supp 2d 369 (2012) (declining to dismiss privacy claim against employer who accessed employee's Facebook posts); *US v Lustig* 3 F Supp 3d 808 (SD Cal Mar 11, 2014) (government access to Craigslist post).

Traditional privacy claims, such as intrusion or public disclosure of private facts, can also be asserted against someone who posts the information to SM, just as if the information was disclosed on any other medium. See eg *Zimmerman v Barr* Case No 2014CA000613 (Fla Cir Ct Seminole County filed Mar 10, 2014) (privacy suit over Tweeting of plaintiff's home address).

Users of SM sites and services may also assert privacy expectations based on the sites' stated privacy policies. The Federal Trade Commission recommends that all SM sites and services have a privacy policy, and will initiate proceedings against sites and services without such policies as well as those that do not act in accordance with such policies. The FTC reached settlements with Google in 2011 and Facebook in 2012 over allegations that the sites made users' information available in ways that were contrary to the assurances of the sites' own privacy policies. See eg *In re Google*, FTC No 102-3136 (2011); *In re Facebook*, FTC No 092-3184 (2012). Google also reached settlements with the FTC and 37 states and the District of Columbia over its circumvention of users' 'do not track' settings. *US v Google* No CV 12-04177 SI (ND Cal dismissed pursuant to settlement Nov 16, 2012); *In re Google Cookie Placement Consumer Privacy Litigation*, Case No 1:12-md-02358-SLR (D Del settled 2013).

The FTC has also taken action against entities whose databases of users' and customers' personal and financial information have been stolen because of inadequate security, on the grounds that weak protection of such databases is an unfair trade practice and violates the Fair Credit Reporting Act, if applicable to the organization. The first of these cases involved an email sent to customers which included all customers' email addresses, visible to all recipients, in the To: field. The case was settled with an agreement that the company would change and report to the FTC on its data practices for 20 years. See *In the Matter of Eli Lilly and Company*, Docket No C-4047 (FTC 2002).

Private parties have also filed lawsuits making privacy claims over SM. A suit over privacy issues on Google Buzz ended with the company paying $8.5 million to cover attorney fees and costs and to create a fund dedicated to internet privacy policy or privacy education. *In re Google Buzz User Privacy Litigation*, Case No 5:10-cv-00672-JW (ND Cal June 2, 2011) (approving settlement). A class action suit over Facebook's 'sponsored stories' program, which placed users' photographs and information in advertisements directed at their friends, ended with a settlement in which Facebook agreed to change its terms of service and pay $10 million in *cy pres* restitution. *Fraley v Facebook*, Case No CV 11-01726 RS (ND Cal final judgment Sept 19, 2013) (approving settlement).

Among the revelations by former National Security Administration (NSA) contractor Edward Snowden was the PRISM program, which was reported to have directly tapped into the servers of major American internet companies to collect information, including SM data, of non-Americans flowing through the US-based systems. The program, which was reportedly approved by the classified Foreign Intelligence Surveillance Court (known as the FISA Court), was reported to also collaterally collect and store information about United States citizens. In response, US-based technology companies were reportedly taking steps to make their systems inaccessible to government surveillance.

C33.21   SM AND FAMILY LAW CASES

As in other types of cases, SM postings can be used as evidence in family law cases, particularly those involving child custody or distribution of assets. In a 2010 survey of members of the American Academy of Matrimonial Lawyers, 81 percent said that they had seen an increase in use of SM evidence in divorce cases since 2005.

In *Caples v Caples* No 2002-1758 (La Dist Ct 2011), aff'd, 103 So 3d 437 (La App 2012) a father unsuccessfully tried to use the fact that the grandmother allowed a 10-year-old to have a Facebook profile as grounds for taking custody of the child. While the court rejected this argument, it did order that the Facebook profile be deactivated.

In *New Jersey v HLM* No A-1257-12T3 (NJ App Div May 13 2014) (unpublished), the appeals court affirmed a lower court order barring a mentally disturbed woman from blogging about her ex-husband and children.

C33.22 SPORTS PERSONS, SPORTS CLUBS AND SM

The legality of controls on SM usage in a sports context depends on the nature of the restriction and the nature of the authority imposing it.

Private entities – that is, corporations and individuals not acting on behalf of a government entity – can generally restrict speech as they wish. So private sports leagues, and their constituent teams, can place restrictions on the SM usage of their employees and participants. As employers, however, they would be limited in accessing employees' SM accounts under the laws discussed in C33.9.

Private sports entities' efforts to control others' use of information about their events, including scores, photographs and video, have yielded mixed results. In *NBA v Motorola*, 105 F3d 841 (2d Cir 1997), the appeals court held that Motorola's transmission to its pagers of 'real-time' NBA basketball game scores and information from observers monitoring live television and radio broadcasts of the games did not violate the league's rights. But in *Morris Communications Inc v PGA Tour*, 364 F3d 1288 (11th Cir 2004) *reh'g denied*, 107 Fed Appx 890 (11th Cir May 28, 2004) *cert denied*, 543 US 919 (2004), the 11th Circuit Court of Appeals held that the PGA had a legitimate business reason for requiring media entities to license – for a fee – information from its real-time scoring system, and thus did not violate antitrust law. In 2007 the National Collegiate Athletic Association (NCAA) got into a spat with a *Louisville (Ky) Courier-Journal* reporter who was blogging from games; the NCAA then clarified that live updates could include only scores and time remaining. The International Olympic Committee has had similar dust-ups over blogging by athletes and others.

The situation is more complicated when the league involves government entities such as an athletic association of public schools. But in *Wis Interscholastic Ath Ass'n v Gannett Co* 658 F3d 614 (7th Cir 2011), the court held that such an association could sell the exclusive rights to stream video of high school football games.

Athletic departments at public schools, particularly colleges, have less ability to limit SM activities of their participants under the recently passed statutes barring them from demanding access to SM accounts. These statutes are discussed in C33.10. More generally, public schools can limit students' speech only if the limitations are content-neutral, further an important government interest, and are 'narrowly tailored' to further that interest. *US v O'Brien* 391 US 367 (1968). See C33.10.

C33.23 PERSONAL RELATIONS AND RELATIONSHIPS

One of the primary uses of SM is to connect with and remain in contact with friends and family. Two-thirds of SM users surveyed in a 2011 study by the Pew Research Internet Project said that staying in touch with current friends and family was a major reason why they used the sites and services; half of the users said that they used SM sites to reconnect with old friends.

While SM offers the opportunity for closer relationships with a larger number of people than otherwise possible, it can also play a role in friction and dissolution of personal relationships. Some of these conflicts have resulted in lawsuits.

In *Bonhomme v St James*, a woman sued another woman who posed as a man and pursued an online romantic relationship with the plaintiff, including exchanging photographs, hand-written letters, phone calls (with the poser's voice disguised) and real-world gifts. The imposter then faked the man's death, including condolence letters to his 'girlfriend.' The Illinois Supreme Court affirmed dismissal of the victim's case, holding that she could not recover for fraudulent misrepresentation, which the court said is limited to business or personal transactions. 2012 IL 112393, 970 NE2d 1 (2012).

A lawsuit by a woman who was sexually assaulted by a man she met through the site led Match.com to initiate a policy of checking members against sex offender registries. See *Doe v Match.com* No CV11-03795 SVM (CD Cal settled Aug 22 2011). But most lawsuits of this type have been dismissed under the terms of section 230 of the Communications Decency Act. See *Doe v SexSearch.Com* 551 F3d 412 (6th Cir 2008); *Doe v MySpace Inc* 528 F3d 413 (5th Cir 2008), cert denied, 555 US 1031 (2008); *Beckman v Match.com* 2013 WL 2355512, 2013 US Dist LEXIS 78339 (D Nev May 29 2013). Section 230 is discussed in C33.25.

C33.24   SM AND PERSONAL DATA OF DECEASED PERSONS

Only about one-third of Americans have wills, and less have given any thought to the fate of their SM profiles and activities after their death. Meanwhile, SM sites have various policies regarding profiles of deceased users.

In one highly publicized case, Yahoo! refused to give the parents of a marine killed in Iraq in 2004 their son's password, although the company did provide some of the emails in the account after it was ordered to by a Michigan probate court judge. A Wisconsin couple whose son committed suicide in 2010 obtained court orders to access his Google and Facebook accounts, although it still took several months to access the Facebook account. Another prominent case involved web pioneer Leslie Harpold, who died suddenly in 2006 at age 40. While her friends asked that her websites be preserved, her family decided to remove the sites.

A handful of companies have emerged to manage SM users' desires for their SM accounts after death. Google provides its own 'Inactive Account Manager' for this purpose.

A handful of states have passed statutes addressing this issue, including Connecticut (2005 Conn Act No 136); Idaho (Idaho Code § 15-5-424(z)); Indiana (Ind Code § 29-1-13-1.1); Nevada (Nev Rev Stat § 143(1); Oklahoma (Ok Stat Tit 58 § 269); Rhode Island (RI Probate Prac & Proc Law § 33-27-1, *et seq*); and Virginia (Va Code §§ 64.2-109 and 64.2-110). These laws vary in coverage and in their terms. A committee of the Uniform Law Commission has drafted a Uniform Fiduciary Access to Digital Assets Act addressing posthumous treatment of SM and other electronic accounts and has promoted its adoption by individual states.

C33.25 SM, WEBSITE, SERVICE PROVIDER OR ISP DEFENCE RULES/LAWS

An important federal law regarding the internet generally is section 230 of the Communications Decency Act, 47 USC § 230. This statute provides that 'interactive computer services,' including SM websites and services, are generally immune from civil or criminal liability – except for federal criminal and intellectual property laws – for material posted by users of the site or service. Courts have interpreted this statute broadly, dismissing virtually all types of claims against websites and services for content posted by individuals and entities other than the operator of the site or service.

While general screening and minor editing of material posted by users is permitted, a website or service operator editing the material to add a basis for liability – for example, adding a defamatory statement – can waive the immunity by making the operator the provider of the content. Courts have also held that immunity may be waived if a website or service is structured in such a way that users are compelled to post material that violates the law. See eg *Fair Housing Council of San Fernando Valley v Roommates.com*, LLC 521 F3d 1157 (9th Cir 2008) (no immunity for roommate site that included illegal housing restrictions amongst listing choices), *MCW Inc v badbusinessbureau. com*, 2004 WL 833595, 2004 US Dist LEXIS 6678, Civ No 3:02-CV-2727-G (ND Tex April 19 2004). But when such information is posted by users with no prompting from the site operator, section 230 immunity applies. *Chicago Lawyers' Committee for Civil Rights Under Law Inc v Craigslist Inc* 519 F3d 666 (7th Cir 2008).

While promoters of the internet and SM defend section 230 immunity as important protection that supports the creation and adoption of new websites and technologies, the provision has also been criticized for being too broad. In 2013 the attorneys general of 47 states sent a letter to the leaders of the Congressional commerce committees urging that the statute be amended to specifically exempt obscenity, sexual exploitation of children, and state criminal laws from the immunity.

Another statute, the Digital Millennium Copyright Act, Pub L 105–304, 112 Stat. 2860 (1998), includes numerous provisions regarding copyright in the digital era. Title II of the Act, separately known as the Online Copyright Infringement Liability Limitation Act, 17 USC § 512, provides that online service providers (OSPs) are protected under a 'safe harbour' for copyright infringement claims over infringing material posted by users, as long as the OSP implements prescribed 'notice and takedown' procedures to block or remove infringing material upon notification by a copyright owner. The statute also allows copyright owners to subpoena records in order to determine the identity of infringers who post such material.

C33.26 ECOMMERCE DEFENCE CASES

Forty-seven states and the District of Columbia have adopted the Uniform Electronic Transactions Act (UETA), which provides a set of standard state laws for e-commerce transactions, including use of electronic signatures and records. The three remaining states – Illinois, New York and Washington – each have their own statutes regarding these issues. See 5 Ill Comp Stat § 175/1-101; NY State Tech Law § 301, *et seq*; and Wash Rev Code § 19.34.300, *et seq*.

In addition, Congress has enacted the Electronic Signatures in Global and National Commerce Act (E-SIGN), which establishes the validity of electronic records and signatures, although it does not mandate their use. Pub L No 106-229, 114 Stat 464 (2000), 15 USC §§ 7001–7006. The Act also applies when states have either not adopted a law on the subject or have enacted provisions that are inconsistent with the E-SIGN Act. The statute's requirements must be met for an electronic signature to be valid; the mere fact that a document is electronic is not in and of itself sufficient. *Campbell v Gen Dynamics Gov't Sys Corp* 407 F3d 546 (1st Cir 2005).

C33.27 LAWS PROTECTING PERSONAL DATA/ PERSONALLY IDENTIFIABLE INFORMATION

Unlike Europe, the United States has adopted only a few laws placing limits on disclosure of personal data and personally identifiable information. Examples of such laws include the Fair Credit Reporting Act, Pub L 91–508, 84 Stat 1114 (1970), codified at 15 USC § 1681 *et seq*, the Right to Financial Privacy Act, Pub L 95–630, 92 Stat 3641 (1978), codified at 12 USC §§ 3401-3402, and the Fair and Accurate Credit Transactions Act, Pub L 108–159, 117 Stat 1952 (2003) (amending 15 USC § 1681 *et seq*), which place limitations of disclosure and use of personal financial information. The Health Insurance Portability and Accountability Act (HIPAA) includes provisions that restrict disclosure of personal health information. See 42 USC § 1320d, *et seq*; see also 45 CFR § 160 101, *et seq* (implementing regulations). And the Family Educational Rights and Privacy Act of 1974 (FERPA, also known as the Buckley Amendment), Pub L No 93-380, 88 Stat 484 (1974), codified at 20 USC § 1232, restricts disclosure of educational records.

Several states have adopted their own laws regarding online privacy. California's Online Privacy Protection Act of 2003, codified at Cal Bus & Prof Code §§ 22575–22579, requires entities such as websites and SM services that collect information to have and conspicuously display a privacy policy disclosing how they use the information that they collect, including whether the information is sold to other entities or used for web tracking. Utah requires disclosure if personal information will be sold. Connecticut requires disclosure regarding the use of Social Security numbers. Conn Stat § 42-470. Massachusetts, Minnesota, and Nevada have laws that require collectors of personal information to safeguard that information. See Mass Gen'l L chap 93H; Minn Stat chap 325M; Nev Rev Stat chap. 603A.

C33.28 DATA BREACH LAWS AND CUSTOMERS/ USERS/REGULATORS NOTIFIED OF HACKING OR DATA LOSS

All but three states – Alabama, New Mexico, and South Dakota – have adopted statutes creating a duty to disclose breaches of personal financial information. Many of these statutes follow the model set by California's law, 2002 Cal Laws chap 915. In 2008, California expanded this law to cover medical information. 2007 Cal Laws chap 699. But these laws still vary somewhat on what entities and what personal information are covered, what constitutes a breach, and form and recipients of the notice.

While there is no federal statute regarding disclosure of data breaches, several federal government entities have adopted regulations on the subject. The Federal Reserve has adopted guidelines for banks, thrifts and other financial entities to follow regarding disclosure of breaches of financial data. See Interagency Guidance on Response Programs for Unauthorized Access to Customer Information and Customer Notice, 12 CFR Part 30, app B (Office of the Comptroller of the Currency); 12 CFR Part 208, app D-2 and Part 225, app F (Federal Reserve Board); 12 CFR Part 364, app B (FDIC); and 12 CFR Part 570, app B (Office of Thrift Supervision). The Federal Department of Health and Human Services (HHS) and Federal Trade Commission have adopted similar rules regarding breaches of health information. 45 CFR §§ 164.400-414 (HHS); 16 CFR Part 318 (FTC). The FTC also acts against data breaches that occur because of lapses in companies' privacy policies.

Some data breaches have resulted in litigation. A study of such federal cases from 2005 to 2011 found suits including 86 causes of action, most commonly unfair business practices claims, claims under the Fair Credit Reporting Act, and breach of contract claims. About half of these cases settled, with slightly less ended by the courts' grant of either a motion to dismiss or a motion for summary judgment. S Romanosky, D Hoffman, and A Acquisti, 'Empirical Analysis of Data Breach Litigation', 11 *J Empirical L Studies* 74 (2014).

Chapter C34

Uruguay

Federico Florin
Guyer & Regules

C34.1 INTRODUCTION

Uruguay is a Civil Law jurisdiction.

C34.2 SPECIFIC SM AND SN LAWS

None.

C34.3 SM CRIMINAL LAW CASES

No details.

C34.4 SM CIVIL LAW CASES

No details.

C34.5 CASES WHERE SM-RELATED EVIDENCE USED OR ADMISSIBLE

SM-related evidence, as a private document, is on par with other information from the web, photographs, etc.

C34.6 SPECIFIC ONLINE ABUSE/ONLINE BULLYING/ CYBERBULLYING LAWS

No details.

C34.7 OTHER LAWS APPLIED TO ONLINE ABUSE/ ONLINE BULLYING/CYBERBULLYING

Criminal libel laws have been applied to online content.

C34.8 CHILDREN AND SM LAWS OR RULES

While there are no specific laws for children and SM, Uruguay is party to the NY Convention on the Rights of the Child and the Optional Protocol on the Sale of Children, Child Prostitution and Child Pornography and has passed laws regarding child pornography and the distribution of the same, including uploading to the internet.

C34.9 EMPLOYEES/EMPLOYMENT SM LAWS OR CASES

In some cases, SM material has been used as evidence in labour claims.

C34.10 SCHOOL AND UNIVERSITY STUDENT SM CASES

No details.

C34.11 RIGHT OR HUMAN RIGHT TO ACCESS THE INTERNET OR SM

No details.

C34.12 BANS OR RESTRICTIONS ON INTERNET OR SM

There have been several criminal prosecutions for child pornography, and there is at least one ongoing case of libel for uploading personal photographs and videos to the web.

C34.13 IDENTITY THEFT (OR EQUIVALENT)

No specific details, but it can be punished if it is used as a means to commit another crime.

C34.14   HACKING (OR EQUIVALENT)

No specific regulations, but there are penal regulations on the privacy of public confidential documents that could be applicable.

C34.15   PRIVACY BY DESIGN (PBD) (OR EQUIVALENT)

No details.

C34.16   TWEETING FROM COURTS, AND ANY RULES/LAWS

In court during hearings, it is prohibited to use mobile phones.

C34.17   TELEVISION COURTROOM BROADCASTING OR TELEVISION CAMERAS IN COURT, AND RULES OR LAWS

No details.

C34.18   SM IN COURTROOMS

No details.

C34.19   USE OF SM AS EVIDENCE IN COURTS

SM material has been used as evidence in labour cases (see C34.9). It is treated as any other private document.

C34.20   PRIVACY, DATA PROTECTION AND SM

There has been at least one criminal libel case for the uploading of personal data to the web (see C34.12).

C34.21   SM AND FAMILY LAW CASES

No details.

C34.22   SPORTS PERSONS, SPORTS CLUBS AND SM

No details.

C34.23 PERSONAL RELATIONS AND RELATIONSHIPS

There are ongoing criminal actions for the uploading of private images (see C34.12).

C34.24 SM AND PERSONAL DATA OF DECEASED PERSONS

No details.

C34.25 SM, WEBSITE, SERVICE PROVIDER OR ISP DEFENCE RULES/LAWS

No details.

C34.26 ECOMMERCE DEFENCE CASES

No details.

C34.27 LAWS PROTECTING PERSONAL DATA/ PERSONALLY IDENTIFIABLE INFORMATION

Law N. 18.331 governs the protection of private data and the action of 'Habeas Data'. It contains provisions related to general data protection principles, the rights of data owners, the obligations of data controllers and data users, the supervising authority, sanctions, and rules of procedure to judicially recover personal data or 'Habeas Data'.

C34.28 DATA BREACH LAWS AND CUSTOMERS/ USERS/REGULATORS NOTIFIED OF HACKING OR DATA LOSS

No details.

Index

[All references are to paragraph number]